READER'S DIGEST

YOUR
COOKERY
QUESTIONS
ANSWERED

PUBLISHED BY THE READER'S DIGEST ASSOCIATION LIMITED
LONDON • NEW YORK • SYDNEY • CAPE TOWN • MONTREAL

EDITOR
Brenda Houghton

ART EDITOR
Louise Bruce

———— ◆ ————

CONTRIBUTORS

The publishers would like to thank the following people
for their contributions to this book

CONSULTANT
Peter Taylor Cert.Ed., Académie Culinaire de France

WRITERS
Pat Alburey · Val Barrett · Arabella Boxer · Jackie Burrow · Maxine Clark
Shirley Gill · Patricia Lousada · Caroline Marsh · Sonya Mills · Jenni Muir · Ann Nicol
Janey Orr · Louise Pickford · Brenda Ratcliffe · Anne Sheasby · Rosemary Stark
Terry Tan · Jane Thomas · Caroline Waldegrave · Hilaire Walden · Jeni Wright

PHOTOGRAPHERS
Karl Adamson · Gus Filgate · Vernon Morgan

HOME ECONOMISTS
Pat Alburey · Maxine Clark · Louise Pickford · Bridget Sargeson

STYLISTS
Penny Markham · Fanny Ward

ILLUSTRATOR
Christine Pilsworth

———— ◆ ————

DESIGNERS
Kate Harris · Megan Huston · Keith Miller · Claire Sadler

ASSISTANT EDITORS
Claire Clifton · Nance Fyson · Marion Moisy · Jenni Muir

RESEARCHER
Lucy Berridge

PROJECT SECRETARY
Lou Algar

———— ◆ ————

READER'S DIGEST GENERAL BOOKS

EDITORIAL DIRECTOR
Robin Hosie

ART DIRECTOR
Bob Hook

EXECUTIVE EDITOR
Michael Davison

MANAGING EDITOR
Paul Middleton

EDITORIAL GROUP HEADS
Julian Browne · Noel Buchanan · Cortina Butler

RESEARCH EDITOR
Prue Grice

PICTURE RESEARCH EDITOR
Martin Smith

CONTENTS

---◆---

$\mathcal{T}$ABLE OF RECIPES

HOW TO USE THE RECIPES

All the recipes are given in both metric and Imperial measures, but they are not interchangeable. The two sets are not precise equivalents, as that would involve unwieldy decimal points or fractions. Use either all metric or all Imperial measures in any given recipe.

All spoon measures given, for both wet and dry ingredients, are for a level spoon. If you are using a set of cook's measuring spoons, the 5 ml spoon equals 1 level teaspoon, the 15 ml spoon equals 1 level tablespoon.

All the microwave recipes in this book were tested in an 800 Watt microwave oven. If you are using a less powerful one, increase the cooking time by 10 seconds for every minute given in the recipe and then check. If you are using a more powerful model, reduce the cooking time by 10 seconds for every minute given in the recipe and then check. If a dish appears to need further cooking, cook it in bursts of 10 seconds or so only, and keep checking for when it is ready.

*M*EAT

Navarin of lamb with haricot beans 368

*P*OULTRY AND GAME

*S*EAFOOD

Lobster thermidor 224

*V*EGETARIAN

$\mathcal{V}$EGETABLES AND ACCOMPANIMENTS

$\mathcal{D}$ESSERTS

Boozy pears 284

Hot buttered cucumber with dill 128

SAUCES, STOCKS AND STUFFINGS

JAMS, PICKLES AND PRESERVES

BREADS, BISCUITS AND CAKES

DRINKS

MISCELLANEOUS

Classic white loaf 51

ABALONE

SINGULAR SHELLFISH

I have eaten abalone in Chinese restaurants but never seen it on sale in Britain. What is it?

Sometimes known as ormer, this is a large shellfish which was once prolific around the Channel Islands but is now quite scarce in Europe. It is found mainly in the South Pacific and on both coasts of North and South America.

The edible part of the shellfish is the muscle with which it clings to the rocks, concealed beneath its single pearly shell. It must be beaten to tenderise it, yet has a delicate flavour that is much prized in Oriental cooking. Once tenderised, it can then be eaten raw or very quickly seared in butter or oil.

Fresh abalone is difficult to find in Britain but you can buy canned abalone in Chinese shops. This is sliced thinly and then poached briefly in chicken stock, stir-fried or simply served with a squeeze of lemon. However, in many Chinese recipes calling for abalone, scallops are an acceptable substitute.

Fresh abalone needs to be tenderised before it can be eaten.

ADDITIVES

THE 'E' LIST

Are some 'E' numbers listed in food contents safer or more natural than others?

A wide variety of substances are added to foods during processing, including preservatives, antioxidants, emulsifiers and stabilisers, colourings and sweeteners. While some enhance the taste of food, others improve its keeping quality or increase the nutritional value. In each category, both natural and synthetic substances have been recognised as safe for use in food by the European Community and included in the EC's permitted list, identified by an 'E' number.

The list of permitted additives includes naturally occurring substances such as pectin (E440a), obtained from apples and used as a gelling agent, and lecithin (E322), obtained primarily from soya beans and widely used as an emulsifier or stabiliser. Other permitted additives are manufactured copies of natural substances, such as ascorbic acid (E300), the chemical name for vitamin C and identical to naturally occurring vitamin C.

In addition to these natural or nature-identical compounds, there are a substantial number of listed additives which are synthetic. But although additives with an E number vary in the extent to which they can be called natural, they have all been recognised as safe.

COCHINEAL COPIES

Is red cochineal still available? If not, what alternative could I use for a strong red colouring?

Although genuine cochineal (E120) is still available, it is rarely used because of its high cost: this colouring is extracted from the female cochineal insect and it takes more than 70 000 insects to produce just 500 g (1 lb 2 oz) of red colour. However, it does provide a strong

colour which is hard to match. Another group of red food colourings, anthocyanins (E163), derived from vegetables, fruit and berries, tends to have a bluish tinge.

Artificial cochineal is usually coloured with carmoisine (E122), a synthetic azo dye. People who suffer from asthma and eczema may be sensitive to azo dyes, and react by wheezing or with a rash to this and other red colourings based on them, such as amaranth (E123) and ponceau 4R (E124).

Such dyes are listed as safe because they are safe for most people and it is believed that the benefits for the many outweigh the risks for the few. There is no absolute guarantee of safety in foods: some people are allergic to particular additives, just as some people are allergic to shellfish or berries.

ORGANIC STANDARDS

Does buying food labelled organic always mean the product will be free of additives and pesticides, or does it mean different things in different shops?

People who buy organic vegetables and fruit expect them to have been grown using only organic fertilisers (compost or animal manure) without the use of chemical pesticides and herbicides. They also expect that no synthetic additives have been used in their preservation after harvesting. If an additive has been used, such as pectin in an organic jam, it will have derived from an organic source.

Organic meat is taken to mean that the animal has been raised without any antibiotics or growth-promoting substances, and that it has been allowed space to roam in free-range or pasture conditions, eating natural food, not concentrates. After slaughter, organically reared meat is not treated with polyphosphates, as may be the case with non-organic meat, fish and particularly poultry.

However, in some cases food advertised as organic has not lived up to customers' expectations, as periodic checks by the Ministry of Agriculture, Fisheries and Food have shown. The higher prices that people are willing to pay for organic foods may tempt unscrupulous traders to pass off non-organic produce as the real thing.

To combat confusion about the meaning of 'organic', the United Kingdom Register of Organic Food Standards (UKROFS) has been set up to lay down legal standards and coordinate the labelling of organic foods. Farmers who want their produce labelled as organic must subscribe to one of the six organisations registered with UKROFS.

These organisations are: the Biodynamic Agricultural Association; Organic Farmers and Growers; the Organic Food Federation; the Soil Association; the Irish Organic Farmers and Growers; and the Scottish Organic Producers Association.

Each organisation has its own symbol which can be used in labelling by manufacturers and these guarantee the produce is organic. Look out particularly for food that carries the approval of the Soil Association and UKROFS, both of which have high standards and inspect farms annually.

SPREADS OR BUTTER?

Low-fat spreads seem to list many chemicals in their ingredients. Are these spreads really healthier than butter or margarine?

There is general agreement among health experts that in Western countries we tend to eat too much fat, particularly saturated fat, and that reducing the overall amount of fat in their diet can help people to be healthier. Food manufacturers now produce a wide range of low-fat products, including low-fat and reduced-fat spreads based on butter or margarine. These spreads contain considerably more water than is permitted in margarine or butter and, as a result, a number of emulsifying agents are added to them to prevent the fats and water from separating. Labelling regulations require that these additives

are declared. However, remember that all foodstuffs are ultimately made of chemicals, there is just no legal requirement to declare the chemical composition of butter.

On balance, if using a low-fat spread helps to reduce someone's intake of fat, it is generally a healthier choice than butter or ordinary margarine. (See also NUTRITION.)

ALMONDS

BITTER AND SWEET

How many different types of almond are there?

There are two types, bitter and sweet, but bitter almonds are only used commercially. The almonds we buy are sweet ones, mainly from California and Spain, but those from Jordan, which are long and thin, have the best flavour.

If possible, buy whole almonds with their skins on and blanch them yourself (see NUTS) for recipes such as the one overleaf, as they have more flavour than ready-skinned ones and are not so dry. Nuts lose their flavour quickly, so buy them in small quantities.

EXPENSIVE EXTRACTS

What is the difference between almond extract and essence?

Almond extract is a pure, natural product made from oil of bitter almonds and has a good flavour, but the quality is reflected in the high price. Almond essence is made using artificial flavourings and is therefore much cheaper.

It is worth the effort of seeking out almond extract in good delicatessens, health food shops and the larger branches of supermarkets. Whichever you use, for the best results always add cautiously.

PRALINE CRUNCH

What is praline and what would you use it for?

Almond praline is a mixture of caramelised sugar and almonds, ground up by hand or in a food processor after cooking. It is used as a crunchy flavouring for ice cream, creamy desserts, pastry and cakes, or sprinkled over puddings and gâteaux. Mixed with cream, chocolate and rum, praline makes wonderful truffles. Once made, it will keep in an airtight container for one to two weeks.

MAKING PRALINE FLAVOURING

Sweet, nutty praline is made by caramelising almonds in sugar and then crushing the mixture to make a delicious, crispy flavouring for desserts.

1 Put 75 g (2¾ oz) of caster sugar and 75 g (2¾ oz) of unskinned almonds into a heavy saucepan. Stir continuously over a moderate heat until the sugar dissolves completely and turns golden caramel. Pour onto a baking tray lined with baking paper and leave in a cool place to set.

2 Peel the baking paper off the back of the set praline. Put the praline into a strong polythene bag and crush it with a rolling pin, coarsely or finely, as the recipe dictates. The praline may also be ground in a food processor, but process it for only a few seconds at a time, or it will turn to dust.

Almond and pear flan

Serves: 8
Preparation time: 2 hours plus 3 - 4 hours or overnight chilling
Cooking time: 40 minutes

For the filling
300 ml (10 fl oz) milk
150 ml (5 fl oz) double cream
1 vanilla pod, halved lengthways
100 g (3 ½ oz) almonds, blanched
2 eggs, size 2
2 egg yolks, size 2
75 g (2 ¾ oz) caster sugar
100 g (3 ½ oz) plain flour
75 g (2 ¾ oz) unsalted butter, diced and chilled
90 ml (3 ¼ fl oz) amaretto, kirsch or brandy

For the pears
225 g (8 oz) granulated sugar
Finely pared zest and strained juice of 1 lemon
1 kg (2 lb 4 oz) small firm, ripe pears

For the flan case
100 g (3 ½ oz) plain flour
25 g (1 oz) icing sugar
50 g (1 ¾ oz) ground almonds
75 g (2 ¾ oz) unsalted butter
2 egg yolks, size 2
175 g (6 oz) apricot jam

This glistening fruit and nut flan uses ground almonds in the pastry and in the filling to add both delicate flavour and a crunchy texture.

1 To make the filling, pour the milk and cream into a saucepan, add the vanilla pod and bring to the boil. Remove at once from the heat, cover and leave to infuse for 30 minutes.
2 Toast the almonds under a grill until they are pale golden all over. Grind finely and set aside.
3 Put the eggs, egg yolks and caster sugar into a bowl and whisk until thick and creamy. Fold in the flour.
4 Remove the vanilla pod from the milk, rinse and set aside. Gradually whisk the milk and cream into the egg and flour. Sieve into a saucepan and cook over a low heat, stirring, until the custard is extremely thick.
5 Remove from the heat, turn the mixture into a bowl and gradually beat in the butter, then the ground almonds and alcohol. Cover with cling film to stop a skin forming and chill for 3 - 4 hours or overnight.

6 To cook the pears, pour 500 ml (18 fl oz) of water into a stainless steel, enamel or nonstick saucepan, add the vanilla pod, sugar, lemon zest and lemon juice. Bring to the boil, stirring, until the sugar has dissolved, then reduce the heat.
7 Peel, halve and core the pears. Add the pear halves to the sugar syrup, cover and cook gently for 10 - 15 minutes until only just tender. Let the pears cool in the syrup, then chill until needed.
8 To make the flan case, sift the flour and icing sugar into a mixing bowl, then mix in the ground almonds. Rub in the butter with your fingertips until the mixture resembles fine breadcrumbs. Add the egg yolks and mix with a fork to form a soft, but not sticky dough.
9 Turn out onto a lightly floured surface and knead for a few seconds until smooth. Roll out the dough to a neat circle, large enough to line a

25 cm (10 in) fluted flan tin. Fit the dough into the tin, pressing it well into the flutes using a little ball of dough so there is less risk of tearing a hole in it. Trim the edge and prick the base and sides lightly all over with a fork, then chill for 30 minutes. While it is chiling, preheat the oven to 220°C (425°F, gas mark 7).
10 Bake the flan case in the centre of the oven for 15 - 20 minutes, until crisp and golden. Remove from the oven and allow to cool in the tin.
11 To assemble the flan, first drain the pears on kitchen paper. Heat the apricot jam, sieve it, return it to the pan and bring to the boil.
12 Turn out the flan case onto a flat serving plate and brush the inside with some hot jam. Spoon in the filling, spread it evenly, then arrange the pears on top.
13 Boil up the remaining jam. Brush it evenly over the pears and chill the flan until ready to serve.

NUTTY THICKENER

Is it true that ground almonds can be used as a thickener in soups or stews?

Yes, they can: almonds were often used to add texture and flavour to a 'white' soup and are still used for this purpose in some traditional Spanish dishes. The delicate flavour of almonds blends particularly well with fish and chicken.

But ground almonds do not thicken soups in the same way as starchy ingredients such as flour, which blend into the liquid to make a thick, smooth sauce. Instead, ground almonds add body, texture, flavour and richness.

Rough guidelines on amounts to use are as follows: to a thin broth, add 50 g (1¾ oz) of ground almonds to each 500 ml (18 fl oz) of liquid. To thicken about 1.25 litres (2 pints 2 fl oz) of puréed fish or vegetable soup, add 25 g (1 oz) of ground almonds; or add 25 g (1 oz) of whole blanched almonds when you are puréeing the soup. It is best to start off with a small amount of almond and add more, a little at a time, if necessary.

ANCHOVIES

MILKY SOLUTION

I love the flavour of anchovies, but they can be extremely salty. How can I reduce the saltiness?

You can rinse them in cold water then pat them dry. Alternatively, if you have the time, soak them in milk for 20 minutes or so, then rinse and dry. Jars of anchovies in olive oil from Italian delicatessens are less salty than canned brands, but they cost more. Some fishmongers and delicatessens sell anchovy fillets marinated in olive oil loose by weight. These are sweet and delicious, and can be used in any recipe calling for anchovy fillets.

If you have visited Portugal or Spain, you may have seen pressed salted anchovies for sale loose, and these can now sometimes be found in Britain. They are very salty and bony and should be rinsed, scaled, boned, and then soaked in milk before use.

This Italian recipe (below) mixes milk-soaked anchovies with other simple yet flavour-intensive Mediterranean ingredients to make crisp Anchovy Crostini, ideal for handing round with pre-dinner drinks when a hint of salt whets the appetite.

Anchovy crostini

SERVES: 4 - 6
PREPARATION TIME: 30 minutes
COOKING TIME: 5 minutes

100 g (3½ oz) canned anchovies in olive oil
125 ml (4 fl oz) milk
12 black olives
250 g (9 oz) mozzarella cheese
1 French baguette or Italian ciabatta bread
2 cloves garlic, halved
3 tablespoons virgin olive oil
125 ml (4 fl oz) sun-dried tomato paste or pesto
2 teaspoons dried mixed herbs
Black pepper

1 Drain the anchovies and soak them in the milk for 20 minutes. Meanwhile, cut the olives in half and stone them, and slice the mozzarella cheese into 24 thin portions.
2 Rinse and pat dry the anchovies, then cut each one in half.
3 Cut 24 slices of baguette, each about 1 cm (½ in) thick. If using ciabatta bread, cut 12 slices, then cut each slice in half.
4 Toast the bread lightly, then immediately rub one side of each slice with the cut side of the garlic and brush with olive oil.
5 Spread each crostini with tomato paste or pesto and cover with a slice of mozzarella. Sprinkle with herbs, and top each with two pieces of anchovy, crisscrossed.
6 Put the crostini under a hot grill for 2 - 3 minutes until the mozzarella melts. Put half a black olive in the centre of each crostini, sprinkle on some pepper and serve hot, or at warm room temperature.

ANISEED

SMALL BUT STRONG

What is aniseed?

Aniseed is the seed of the Mediterranean anise. This annual plant, a member of the parsley family, grows to about 45 cm (18 in) high, with sharply indented leaves and tiny white flowers, and resembles both dill and fennel in appearance although its flavour is quite distinct. Despite its name, it is not related to the star anise tree, which is an Eastern flavouring.

The liquorice flavour is found in the seed, which looks much like a caraway seed: small, oval, grey and ribbed. It is best bought already ground as it should be finely and evenly ground before use and it is difficult to grind evenly at home. You will most often find it in Eastern shops, and because it soon loses its flavour it is best to buy a small amount and replace it often.

VERSATILE FLAVOURING

How is aniseed used?

Aniseed can be substituted for caraway seeds in seed cake, added to rye or wholemeal bread, used in plain or spiced biscuits and included in a Mediterranean fish soup. Or, as is done in the Middle East, it can be used to make an infusion, with or without tea leaves.

Aniseed was much used in medieval Britain, both as a medicament and as a flavouring, but its taste fell out of fashion and today aniseed balls are almost the only reminder of its past popularity.

It is still popular elsewhere, however. In central Europe aniseed is widely used for flavouring sweet dishes, cakes and biscuits. In many Mediterranean countries it is used to flavour absinthe-related drinks, called variously anisette, arak, ouzo, Pernod and raki. In India and South-east Asia the seeds are used in curries, and are also chewed whole, after a meal, as a digestive.

APPLES

WHICH TYPE TO USE?

Why do some recipes specify using dessert apples and others cooking apples - does it matter which ones are used?

Cooking and dessert apples react differently when cooked. If you want the apples to be soft and fluffy when they are cooked, a Bramley or similar cooking apple would work best. If it is important for the apples to retain their shape – on top of a flan, for example – a dessert apple such as russet, Cox or Golden Delicious would be ideal.

MICROWAVE BAKING

Can I cook baked apples in the microwave? I have heard that they could explode.

Apples will not explode in the microwave as long as you score through the skin so that the steam can escape as they cook.

Cut deeply into the skin around the centre of some medium cooking apples, then core and place in a deep, microwave-safe dish, in batches of up to four. Fill the centres with sugar or fruit filling then add a few tablespoons of water or apple juice to the dish.

Cover with microwave-safe cling film, making sure it does not touch the apples, and pull back one edge to vent. Cook the apples on High for 4–6 minutes or until they are tender but retain their shape. Stand for 2–3 minutes before serving.

Keep the colour

To prevent apples discolouring after they have been peeled, put them, either whole or in slices, in water containing the juice of one or two lemons. Plain effervescent vitamin C tablets can be used instead of lemon juice and will not affect the apples' flavour.

PLUGGING THE LEAK

How can I stop the juices leaking out of my apple pies as they cook?

Many fruits, not just apples, make too much juice as they cook in a pie, and this can make the pastry soggy or make it stick to the tin on cooling. The answer is to toss the fruit in a little flour, as this will soak up the juices and help to thicken them as they cook. Flavour the flour with spices if you like.

Toss apples in flour to absorb the juices when making a pie. Mix with your hands to avoid damaging the fruit.

PERFECT PIE

Is one way of making apple pie better than all the others?

Most cooks develop their own method; personal preference dictates whether to use shortcrust pastry, flaky pastry or puff pastry, and whether the pie is filled with uncooked apple slices for a firm texture or precooked apples for a softer, fluffier filling.

The recipe for Perfect Apple Pie (right) is made with buttery pastry and a spicy apple filling which retains the shape and texture of the apples. If you choose the smaller amount of sugar specified in the ingredients list, it has a refreshing tangy flavour, but if you have a sweet tooth, use the larger amount.

Bake the pie in an enamel pie plate on a preheated baking tray. This ensures that the pastry at the bottom of the pie will be brown and cooked, and not soggy. And use a baking tray with a small edge to catch any juices which might overflow as the pie cooks.

Perfect apple pie

SERVES: 6
PREPARATION TIME: 45 minutes
COOKING TIME: 1 hour

FOR THE PASTRY
225 g (8 oz) plain flour
50 g (1 ¾ oz) self-raising flour
A pinch of salt
25 g (1 oz) caster sugar
175 g (6 oz) chilled butter, diced
1 egg, size 2, beaten with
    2 tablespoons cold water
Caster sugar for dredging

FOR THE FILLING
25 g (1 oz) plain flour
175 - 225 g (6 - 8 oz) caster sugar
1 teaspoon ground mixed spice
Finely grated rind of 1 lemon
1 kg (2 lb 4 oz) Bramley apples
25 g (1 oz) ground almonds
25 g (1 oz) butter, diced
6 - 8 cloves
1 tablespoon lemon juice

---

1 To make the pastry, sift the flours, salt and caster sugar into a large mixing bowl then rub in the butter until the mixture resembles fine breadcrumbs. Make a well in the centre, pour in the beaten egg and water and mix with a rounded knife to form a soft, but not sticky dough.
2 Knead the dough on a lightly floured surface for a few seconds until smooth, then wrap and chill while preparing the filling. Put an ungreased baking tray on the centre shelf of the oven and preheat the oven to 220°C (425°F, gas mark 7).
3 Put the flour, caster sugar, mixed spice and lemon rind into a mixing bowl and stir together.
4 Core, peel and slice the apples, add them to the bowl and mix.
5 To assemble the pie, roll out half the chilled dough into a neat round, about 28 cm (11 in) in diameter. Line a 25 cm (10 in) enamel pie plate with the dough. Roll out the remaining dough into a neat round just a little larger than the first.
6 Sprinkle the ground almonds over the dough on the dish and spread half the spiced apple mix on top. Dot half the butter over the apples and add half the cloves. Cover with

Tart Bramley apples are flavoured with tangy lemon, warm spice and ground almonds to give a refreshing twist to every family's all-time favourite pie.

APRICOTS

MAKING JAM

Can I make a successful jam using fresh apricots?

Yes, this is a good way of using imperfect or slightly unripe fruit. Apricots contain only a moderate amount of pectin, so the best way to ensure a good set, good flavour and attractive colour is to use jam sugar with added pectin and follow the manufacturers' instructions.

If you do not have any jam sugar, it might be necessary to add some lemon juice and to give the apricots a fairly lengthy boil in order to obtain a good set. However, this can darken the colour of the jam and also affect the flavour.

CHOOSING CAREFULLY

Which apricots are best for eating and which should I cook?

The apricots sold in Britain are sweet dessert apricots, meant for eating. In other parts of Europe, cooking varieties known in French as *abricots à confiture* (jam apricots) are more readily available. Their sharp flavour makes them more suitable for cooking.

For eating fresh, choose apricots that have a healthy blush to them, with no brown markings, or broken or dented skin. Avoid any that have a greenish tinge as these are unlikely to ripen once bought. Most dessert apricots can be poached for adding to fruit salads, but avoid the larger, more exotic varieties as these disintegrate when cooked.

For any other cooking purposes, choose less perfect, firmer fruit and poach them in syrup to serve with cream, to purée into a sauce or to use in pies, tarts and flans – or the Apricot Pudding with Angostura Cream (overleaf). For this hot, light and spicy soufflé pudding, the apricots can be cooked a few hours ahead, or even the day before.

See also: **DRIED FRUIT**

the rest of the apple slices and add the remaining cloves. Dot with the remaining butter and sprinkle over the lemon juice. Add any juices left in the apple bowl.

7 Brush the edge of the dough on the plate with cold water then cover the pie with the second round of dough. Squeeze the edges firmly together to seal then trim off the excess dough with a knife, holding the knife angled outwards to help to prevent the edge shrinking inwards as the pie bakes.

8 Using the back of the knife blade, tap all round the edge of the dough to give it a flaky appearance. With the tip of the knife, make shallow indents around the edge of the pie at 2.5 cm (1 in) intervals to make an attractive fluted pattern.

9 Roll out the dough trimmings and use them to make apple shapes and leaves to decorate the pie. Brush the shapes with cold water and arrange them on top of the pie. With a small, sharp knife, make a small hole in the top of the pastry lid to allow the steam to escape during cooking.

10 Put the pie on the heated baking tray and bake on the centre shelf of the oven for 30 minutes.

11 Lower the temperature to 190°C (375°F, gas mark 5), cover the pie loosely with foil to prevent it over-browning, and continue cooking for another 25 - 30 minutes, or until the apples are tender. Check that the filling is fully cooked by pushing a skewer through the hole in the top: it should meet no resistance.

12 When cooked, remove the pie from the oven and dredge it with caster sugar while it is hot so the sugar melts slightly and sticks to the pie. For the best flavour, allow the pie to cool for an hour or so to room temperature before serving.

13 Serve with vanilla-flavoured whipped cream, or with ice cream.

Apricot pudding with Angostura cream

SERVES: 4
PREPARATION TIME: 30 minutes
COOKING TIME: 50 minutes

FOR THE PUDDING
115 g (4 oz) granulated sugar
Finely pared zest and strained juice
     of 1 lemon
7.5 cm (3 in) cinnamon stick
4 cloves
8 allspice berries
1 kg (2 lb 4 oz) fresh apricots,
     halved and stoned

FOR THE TOPPING
3 egg yolks, size 2
Finely grated zest and strained
     juice of 1 lemon
25 g (1 oz) plain flour
4 egg whites, size 2
50 g (1 ¾ oz) caster sugar
1 tablespoon icing sugar for sifting

FOR THE ANGOSTURA CREAM
225 ml (8 fl oz) double cream
1 teaspoon ground cinnamon
1 tablespoon Angostura bitters
1 tablespoon caster sugar

1 To make the pudding, first pour 250 ml (9 fl oz) of water into a wide flameproof casserole, or a stainless-steel, enamel or nonstick saucepan. Add the sugar, lemon zest and juice and all the spices and bring to the boil, stirring often until the sugar dissolves. Add the apricots, cover and cook gently for 5 minutes.
2 Using a slotted spoon, remove the apricots and place them in a buttered, shallow 1.25 litre (2 pint 2 fl oz) ovenproof dish. Strain the syrup then boil it until reduced by about half. Pour the hot syrup over the apricots and set aside. Preheat the oven to 190°C (375°F, gas mark 5).
3 To make the topping, whisk the egg yolks and lemon rind together in a large bowl until the mixture is pale and slightly thickened. Whisk in the lemon juice, then gently fold in the flour. If necessary, whisk briefly until smooth.
4 Whisk the egg whites until stiff but not dry, then gradually add the caster sugar, whisking each addition in well, until the meringue is stiff and shiny. Fold a quarter of the meringue into the egg yolk, lemon and flour mixture until smoothly blended, then fold in the rest.
5 Spoon this soufflé mixture in mounds over the apricots and bake on the centre shelf of the oven for 25 - 30 minutes, or until it is set and golden. If the pudding appears to be browning too much as it cooks, cover it loosely with a sheet of foil.
6 To make the Angostura cream, whisk the double cream with the other ingredients until thickened, pour into a serving bowl and chill.
7 Remove the apricot pudding from the oven and, while it is hot, sift the icing sugar over the top. Serve with the Angostura cream.

ARROWROOT

CLEAREST OF ALL

What is the advantage of using arrowroot rather than cornflour to thicken dishes?

Arrowroot is a pure starch and has tiny grains, which makes it more easily digested than other thickening agents, and particularly good for invalid diets.

Arrowroot is also valuable for thickening liquids such as fruit and vegetable juices and to use as a glaze, as it remains transparent with a gelatinous texture, unlike cornflour which goes cloudy.

Arrowroot and cornflour are used in the same quantities to thicken liquids and in the same way: to thicken 300 ml (10 fl oz) of sauce, such as a gravy or a custard, mix 2 tablespoons of arrowroot with the same quantity of cold liquid.

Heat the rest of the liquid to boiling point, then pour it into the blended mix and stir well. Return the sauce to the heat and bring to the boil, stirring continuously until it is thickened and smooth, then simmer gently for a minute.

If you are making a glaze, use only 1 tablespoon of arrowroot for each 300 ml (10 fl oz) of liquid.

ARTICHOKE

DISPOSABLE FEAST

Globe artichokes look rather spiky and daunting. Is there an easy way to deal with them?

Globe artichokes, also known as French artichokes, are members of the thistle family, as their hairy central 'choke' suggests. They are usually eaten as a starter.

The easiest way to cook artichokes is to boil them until soft and serve them whole. At the table, you pull off each leaf, dip the plump base end in sauce and then pull the flesh off with your teeth, discarding the rest of the leaf.

When you get to the papery purple leaves at the centre, pull them off and discard them, then cut away the choke and eat the delicious artichoke heart with a knife and fork.

Another way to prepare them is to trim the top third off each raw artichoke, then quarter them and cut out the chokes. To prevent discoloration, drop each piece as it is ready into a bowl of water acidulated with lemon juice. Then cook them as they are or add them to vegetable stews or other dishes.

MINIATURE DELIGHTS

I have occasionally seen what looks like tiny artichokes in the shops. How are they prepared?

In recent years, 'baby' artichokes have become available in early spring. These have an appealing delicate flavour and require almost no preparation as the leaves are young and tender and the choke is unformed. They cook in minutes: cut them in half or into quarters and fry in olive oil with some sliced garlic for 3–4 minutes. Serve with a sprinkling of sea salt, a squeeze of lemon juice and fresh crusty bread.

Alternatively, braise them gently with other vegetables such as aubergines, courgettes and tomatoes, with a generous amount of onion and garlic and some mixed herbs. In Italy, they are sometimes cut in half, dipped in a lightly spiced coating batter and deep-fried to make an unusual fritter.

ARTICHOKES AND WINE

I have read that artichokes are incompatible with any wine. Is this true, and if so why?

Not exactly. Globe artichokes contain an acid named cynarin which affects our tastebuds, so that food and wine consumed with them, or soon after, taste sweeter than they normally would. French baby-food manufacturers have used this to advantage, mashing soft artichoke bases into vegetable purées to appeal to the sweet infant palate. Grown-ups have found that a young white Muscadet or a spicy red wine from Côtes-du-Rhône are good with an artichoke dish.

See also: JERUSALEM ARTICHOKE

Fresh summer artichokes, served hot or cold with herb-flavoured butter or a salad dressing, are an easy and elegant way to start a meal.

COOKING AND SERVING ARTICHOKES

An artichoke is usually boiled or steamed whole until it is tender, and then the leaves are pulled off and eaten one by one.

1 Wash the artichokes and remove discoloured leaves from the base.

2 Break off the stalks close to the base, pulling away any strings. Pack the artichokes in one layer in a stainless-steel or enamel saucepan. Sprinkle on some salt and lemon juice, then add enough water to come halfway up the artichokes.

3 Bring to the boil, cover tightly and simmer for 40 - 45 minutes until a leaf from the middle of an artichoke pulls out easily. Tip the artichokes into a colander and leave upside-down to drain for 5 minutes.

4 For a dinner party presentation, peel back the outer leaves, pull out the purple central cluster of leaves and scoop out the inedible choke beneath with a spoon.

ASPARAGUS

A TASTE OF EARLY SUMMER

Asparagus seems to be available all year round in some shops. Is there an optimum time to eat it?

British-grown asparagus is in season for only about six weeks in May and June, and this is the time to serve it at its best, as a course in its own right. Imported asparagus is fine (if usually rather expensive) for garnishes and in crispy stir-fries throughout the year.

HEADS ABOVE WATER

What is the best way to cook asparagus without spoiling the shape of the tips?

The trick is to keep the delicate heads above the cooking water (see box, right). The stems should be cut off to a level that leaves them all the same size. Perfectionists also peel the lower stems with a small sharp knife or vegetable peeler, and this is certainly necessary with older asparagus, especially Argenteuil (white) asparagus which has a thick woody skin. Before cooking, wash the tips gently in cold water to rid them of any grit.

ECONOMICAL SPRUE

I have occasionally seen bunches of fine asparagus labelled 'sprue'. What does this mean?

Sprue is the name for the thinnings or first pickings of the asparagus bed. The flavour is good, and they should be cheaper than asparagus proper. There is no need to scrape them before cooking.

Cook them fully immersed in water in a saucepan, and eat them hot or cold, on their own or as an accompanying vegetable. Use them in stir-fries or tarts, or with potatoes and peas or broad beans in an early summer vegetable stew. They can also be processed with some onion and potato to make a cream soup, as in the following recipe.

Sprue soup

SERVES: 4 - 6
PREPARATION TIME: 15 minutes
COOKING TIME: 15 - 20 minutes

50 g (1 ¾ oz) butter
1 medium onion, finely chopped
500 g (1 lb 2 oz) sprue
150 g (5 ½ oz) potato, diced
Salt and black pepper
100 ml (3 ½ fl oz) whipping cream

1 Heat the butter in a large pan, add the onion and fry gently until soft but still white, for about 7 minutes.
2 Add the sprue, potato and 750 ml (1 pint 7 fl oz) of water, bring to the boil and cook for 5 minutes.
3 Remove 12 stems of sprue, cut off and reserve the top 5 cm (2 in) of each one, then return the stems to the water and continue to cook the vegetables for a further 5 - 8 minutes until they are all very soft.
4 Drain the vegetables but retain the cooking liquid. Then liquidise the vegetables in a blender or processor and push the purée through a sieve, loosening it with a tablespoon or so of the cooking liquor if necessary.
5 Return the cooking liquid and the vegetable purée to the pan, stir well and bring to the boil. Turn off the heat, season to taste and add half the cream. Ladle the soup into four soup plates, then trickle in the remaining cream and arrange three sprue tips in the centre of each plate.

FINGER FOOD

How should I serve asparagus?

Asparagus is traditionally served hot with butter or a butter sauce such as hollandaise, or cold with a vinaigrette dressing or mayonnaise. With your fingers, pick up the stem by its base, dip it in the sauce and eat from the tip downwards.

For a substantial starter or a light supper dish, serve it with a softly boiled or fried egg: dip the tips into the yolk, then eat with white bread or toast. Egg and butter can be incorporated in a dressing that provides contrasting crispness. In the recipe opposite, warm asparagus is topped with a crispy egg crumble.

COOKING ASPARAGUS

Asparagus takes 10 – 15 minutes to cook, depending on how thick the stalks are. These need longer cooking than the tips, and determining cooking time can be tricky. Here are three solutions to the problem:

IN AN ASPARAGUS STEAMER

To cook in a specially designed asparagus steamer, stand the stems upright in the wire basket and add water to about halfway up their length. Simmer until tender when pierced just above the water level with the tip of a knife.

IN A WOK

Shorter stems of asparagus can be cooked in a wok. Arrange them like the spokes of a wheel, so that only their bases are immersed in the cooking water. Cover with the lid and simmer until tender.

IN A PAN

Tied bundles of asparagus can be cooked in a deep saucepan, held up by new potatoes. Cover with a dome of foil tucked in tightly around the outer rim of the pan and cook until tender. The asparagus-flavoured potatoes can be eaten hot or cold.

Warm asparagus with egg crumble

SERVES: 6
PREPARATION TIME: 15 minutes
COOKING TIME: 10 – 15 minutes

1 kg (2 lb 4 oz) asparagus, prepared
100 g (3 ½ oz) soft white bread,
   crusts removed
150 g (5 ½ oz) butter
2 eggs, hard-boiled
Salt and black pepper

A simple topping of fried breadcrumbs and hard-boiled egg adds crunch to tender green stems of fresh asparagus.

1 Cook the asparagus until tender, in an asparagus steamer, a wok, or a deep saucepan (see box, opposite).
2 Meanwhile, put some plates to warm. Make the breadcrumbs in a food processor or with a grater.
3 Heat the butter in a heavy-based pan, add the breadcrumbs and fry them until golden brown. Mash the eggs with a fork, mix them into the crumbs and season to taste.
4 When the asparagus is cooked, drain the stems well and arrange them on the warmed plates. Scatter the egg crumble mixture over each helping and serve immediately.

ASPIC

COOL AND CLEAR

What is aspic?

Aspic is the transparent, lightly coloured savoury jelly in which cold fish, poultry and meat are sometimes served. It is used as a garnish, when it is often chopped; to glaze and protect fish and other foods from drying out (the clear aspic allows any garnish to be seen); and to set savoury foods in a mould. It can also be mixed with béchamel, cream or mayonnaise to make a chaud-froid sauce to coat cold pieces of chicken, fish and so on, as in the recipe for Chicken with Orange and Tarragon Chaud-froid on the next page.

A SUCCESSFUL SET

How do I make aspic?

The traditional method is time consuming but still produces the best flavour: a good, concentrated stock is clarified by whisking egg whites and shells into it then straining it well to give a clear consommé, and this sets to a jelly on cooling.

For a quicker alternative, a thinner homemade stock can be jellied by adding a little gelatine which sets on cooling; a can of jellied consommé can be used in meat dishes.

Simplest of all is to buy a packet of aspic jelly powder and follow the instructions by adding boiling water (or substitute sherry, wine, lemon juice, or vinegar for some of the water to boost the flavour).

Aspic garnish

To make a garnish of chopped aspic, dissolve aspic jelly powder in boiling water following the packet instructions and pour a 1 cm (½ in) layer into a shallow baking tin. Leave until cold and chill until firm. Turn the aspic onto greaseproof paper and chop it with a wet knife.

Chicken with orange and tarragon chaud-froid

SERVES: 8
*PREPARATION TIME: 40 minutes plus
a few hours cooling and setting*
COOKING TIME: 30 minutes

FOR THE CHICKEN
*8 skinless chicken breast fillets,
   weighing about 1.5 kg (3 lb 5 oz)*
A pinch of salt
4 peppercorns
1 shallot, peeled and sliced
1 bay leaf
4 sprigs tarragon
2 large strips orange peel

FOR THE SAUCE AND GLAZE
25 g (1 oz) butter
20 g (³/₄ oz) plain flour
2 tablespoons double cream
2 tablespoons orange juice
*24 g (0.85 oz) packet aspic
   jelly powder*
250 ml (9 fl oz) boiling water
*To garnish: tarragon leaves; bed of
   chopped aspic; orange wedges*

Cold chicken breast, coated in a refreshing chaud-froid sauce and a cool aspic glaze, makes a perfect summer dish for formal and informal occasions alike.

1 Put the chicken breasts into a wide saucepan or deep frying pan. Pour in 500 ml (18 fl oz) of water and add the flavourings. Cover and bring to the boil, then reduce the heat and simmer for 30 minutes.
2 Leave the chicken to cool in the cooking liquor if time allows. Strain the liquor and set aside to use later.
3 To make the chaud-froid sauce, heat the butter in a saucepan, stir in the flour and cook the roux over a moderate heat to a sandy texture.
4 Reduce the heat and gradually add 300 ml (10 fl oz) of the reserved cooking liquor, stirring continuously until thickened and smooth. Simmer for 20 minutes, stirring occasionally. Stir in the cream and orange juice and leave until cool.
5 Meanwhile, in a small bowl, pour the boiling water over the aspic jelly powder to make a jelly of double the normal strength. Stir well to dissolve, then set aside until it has cooled and almost reached setting point.
6 Measure out 150 ml (5 fl oz) of this concentrated aspic jelly and stir it into the cooled sauce, then set aside until the sauce thickens to the

consistency of thick cream, but is not set. To the remaining 100 ml (3½ fl oz) of concentrated jelly add another 100 ml (3½ fl oz) of cold water to make a thinner, clear jelly for the final glaze.
7 Wipe the cooked and cooled chicken breasts with kitchen paper and place them on a wire rack over a large plate or a tray to catch the drips. Carefully spoon the thick chaud-froid sauce over the chicken to cover the breasts completely (any sauce that drips onto the plate or tray can be reheated and used again). Set the chicken aside and leave the sauce to set completely.
8 When the reserved aspic glaze is beginning to thicken, carefully spoon it over the coated chicken breasts and leave to set.

9 When the glaze is nearly set, decorate the chicken with tarragon leaves, pressing them onto the glaze.
10 Arrange the chicken on a bed of chopped aspic (see previous page), garnished with orange wedges.

To the rescue!

If the chaud-froid sauce or the aspic jelly sets before you are ready for it, soften it by reheating it briefly in the microwave oven. Heat it on Low, in bursts of 10 - 15 seconds only, until it reaches the required consistency.

AUBERGINE

OIL CONSUMPTION

Aubergines seem to absorb an enormous quantity of oil. Is there any way of reducing this?

Instead of frying slices of aubergine, as many traditional recipes recommend, brush the slices with oil and then either grill them, turning to cook both sides (as in the recipe for Aubergine with Garlic Yoghurt below), or bake on a non-stick oven sheet in a hot oven.

Vegetarian turkey

Grilled aubergine makes a good meat substitute for vegetarians, especially at the Christmas table, when chunky slices marry well with the traditional vegetables.

Aubergine with garlic yoghurt

SERVES: 2
PREPARATION TIME: 40 minutes
COOKING TIME: 8 - 10 minutes

1 large aubergine
Salt
1 clove garlic, crushed
150 ml (5 fl oz) yoghurt
Black pepper
2 tablespoons olive oil
Mint, shredded, optional

1 Cut the aubergine lengthways in pencil-thick slices, sprinkle each lightly with salt and stack them in a colander. Stand in the sink to drain for 30 minutes. Meanwhile, mix the garlic into the yoghurt and season with salt and black pepper to taste.
2 Preheat the grill to medium hot. Rinse the aubergine slices and pat dry with kitchen paper. Brush one side with oil and grill until lightly browned, then brush the other side with oil and grill that. Serve hot or at room temperature, topped with the garlic yoghurt dressing. Garnish, if you like, with fresh mint.

JUST ADD SALT

Why do most recipes recommend salting aubergine slices for half an hour before cooking them? Is this always necessary?

Aubergines grown outdoors in the Mediterranean region and similar warm climates develop bitter juices, which are drawn out by the salting process. This is sometimes referred to as disgorging. Many year-round aubergines sold in Britain are grown in greenhouses, and these probably won't be bitter, but the disgorging process does improve the texture of the cooked vegetable. However, it can leave them rather salty, so rinsing is advisable.

DISPOSABLE SKIN

My children find the tough skin of aubergine indigestible. Can I peel them before cooking?

Aubergines sliced for grilling tend to fall apart without their skins, but they can be peeled for cutting into cubes and adding to stews. Peeled slices make excellent fritters, the flesh soft within a crisp batter coating. For a Mediterranean dip, grill or roast the vegetable until the skin blisters and can be peeled off, then mash the flesh to a cream with plenty of olive oil, lemon juice and crushed garlic, and season to taste.

LARGE FAMILY

I have sometimes seen rather pale and elongated aubergines. Can these be used in the same way as the dark purple ones?

Yes, they can. Outdoor-grown aubergines, from the Mediterranean, Asia or the United States (where the vegetable is known as eggplant) come in a wide range of sizes and colours. They include tiny white 'pea aubergines', larger round ones in green, yellow, white or mauve, and slender, elongated shapes in shades of violet, often streaked with cream or pale green. Whatever their shape and colour, look for unblemished skin, firm texture and a fresh green calix at the stem.

AVOCADO

TENDER FLESH

Is there a way of speeding up the ripening of an avocado?

It is sensible to buy avocados still on the firm side, since once ripe the flesh bruises very easily.

Avocados will ripen in a few days at room temperature in the fruit bowl, but the process can be speeded up by putting them in a roomy paper bag and placing them in a warm place such as the airing cupboard. They are ripe when they 'give' all over to slight pressure and feel especially yielding at the stem end. If you want to keep ripe avocados for a few days, store them in the salad drawer of the refrigerator.

KEEPING UP APPEARANCES

Does rubbing an avocado with lemon stop it from discolouring, and if so, for how long?

Rubbing the cut surfaces of an avocado with citrus juice or vinegar is the only known method of conserving the pale green of avocado flesh (do not believe old wives' tales about replacing the stone to keep the colour). But the effect is not long-term: you cannot expect it to last for much more than a few hours, after which the flesh will darken. Guacamole, the spicy avocado dip, can be kept fresh-looking for about a day by laying cling film directly onto its surface.

SIMPLE PLEASURES

I am tired of plain avocado vinaigrette. Can you suggest other ways of serving avocado?

Avocados are best eaten very ripe and uncooked, and are at their simplest halved and stoned, served with an olive oil vinaigrette dressing. But they can also be puréed raw, with chicken stock and cream, into a chilled summer soup. And their buttery richness (at one time avocado was called 'poor man's butter' and 'midshipman's butter') works extremely well in partnership with sharp fruits.

Three simple, fruity treatments for avocados:

• For a rich yet healthy starter, try a dressing thickened with lightly sweetened rhubarb. For four people, cook four thick sticks of rhubarb, purée and mix it with 2 tablespoons of walnut oil and a splash of lemon juice. Season and spoon the dressing into the halved avocados.

• Avocado makes a good side salad, sliced and combined with chunks of pineapple (excellent with cold ham or grilled gammon) or mixed with segments of sweet pink grapefruit and garnished with coriander leaves to serve with roast chicken.

• You can also fill the cavity of two halved avocados with a homemade Waldorf-salad mix: stir together a diced apple, 2 celery stalks and a little chopped walnut in a dressing made with 3 tablespoons of walnut oil and 1 tablespoon of lemon juice.

Fruity accompaniments such as a rhubarb dressing (top) or chunks of pineapple (bottom), suit rich avocado.

BABIES' DIETS

SPECIAL NEEDS

Should babies and toddlers be kept on a low-fat diet like adults?

The short answer is, no. A baby or toddler needs to get about 50 per cent of its calories from fat. This concentrated source of energy is essential because of the small size of an infant's stomach and the enormous requirement of energy for development. To provide the necessary amount of energy from carbohydrate foods would require a bulky diet, which a baby's tiny stomach could not cope with. Without adequate amounts of fat, it is hard for a baby to grow properly.

Breast, bottle or 'follow-on' milk should be used up to the age of one year. Even full-fat cow's milk does not provide enough vitamins and minerals, and should be used as the main milk drink only after the age of one. Semi-skimmed milk is not suitable before the age of two, and skimmed milk not before five, and then only if the child is eating a varied diet and growing well.

However, it has become generally accepted that atherosclerosis (the process which leads to heart disease and which is related to high consumption of saturated fats) can start in early life, and it has been suggested that by about five years of age, children should be getting close to 35 per cent of their energy from fat, rather than 50 per cent.

Fatty foods should be supplied as part of a varied diet with plenty of fruit and vegetables, starchy foods such as bread, potato and pasta, and good sources of protein such as fish, poultry and lean meat. Dairy products are important as a source of calcium as well as protein to a growing child, but by the age of five you could start shifting over to semi-skimmed milk and low-fat yoghurts.

A MENU FOR BABIES

How can I start my baby off on a truly varied and balanced diet? Is there anything babies will not or should not eat?

Try a variety of foods, starting with baby rice or a rice-based cereal mixed with breast milk or formula, followed by puréed unsweetened fruit, unsalted vegetables and meat.

Start your baby from four months of age on 1 teaspoon of different single, smooth foods at one meal and gradually increase to 2 teaspoons. At five months gradually increase the amount and variety of the foods offered, and at six to eight months offer minced or mashed foods and finger foods as well. For a balanced meal, the best sequence is fruit and vegetable purée, rice-based cereal then meat. By about one year of age, the child can be offered chopped-up family meals, plus 600 ml (1 pint) of milk a day.

Some egg yolk can be introduced from six months, and well-cooked whites at eight months.

Avoid adding sugar to the baby's food, as well as salt (including salty stock cubes), which a baby's kidneys cannot cope with, and delay using spices until six months.

Babies do not mind runny food, but they can find dry food difficult. As a guide, allow 100 ml (3 ½ fl oz) of liquid to each 100 g (3 ½ oz) of dry food. Babies have more adventurous palates than you might think, so consider feeding them purées of more interesting vegetables, such as sweet potatoes and courgettes as well as carrots and peas. Bananas are usually a favourite fruit, as they are sweet and strongly flavoured; they are also nutritionally valuable, and their bulkiness makes them a good 'filler' throughout childhood.

PUT IT ON ICE

I want to make all my baby's food but am going back to work. How can I cope?

Freeze your own baby food. This is cheaper than buying it ready-made and the meals will contain fewer artificial colours and additives. At first, freeze the purée in ice-cube trays, transfer the cubes to freezer bags and thaw one or two at a time. As your baby's appetite increases, freeze the food in larger containers. The following baby meals can be prepared alongside family meals and will each make four servings.

Fish in cheese sauce

75 g (2 ¾ oz) white fish, cooked, boned and skinned
75 g (2 ¾ oz) potato, boiled
25 g (1 oz) cheese, grated
200 ml (7 fl oz) hot water

Mash the ingredients together with a fork, or purée in a food processor, then divide into portions and freeze.

Cauliflower and lentils

3 tablespoons red lentils
3 - 4 cauliflower sprigs

Cook the lentils and the cauliflower together in 300 ml (10 fl oz) of water for 15 minutes or until soft. Mash with a fork, then divide and freeze.

Chicken dinner

75 g (2 ¾ oz) chicken, cooked
50 g (1 ¾ oz) potato, boiled, or sweet potato, cooked
50 g (1 ¾ oz) carrots, cooked
200 ml (7 fl oz) hot water

Purée all the ingredients in a food processor, then divide and freeze.

Fruity rice

2 tablespoons rice pudding, canned or homemade
2 tablespoons fruit purée, or two pieces canned fruit in natural juice (apricot, pineapple or peach), or half a banana

Mash the ingredients together with a fork, then divide and freeze.

BACON AND GAMMON

KNOW THE DIFFERENCE

What is the difference between a bacon and a gammon joint?

A bacon joint is cut from the body of a pig that has been cured whole; a gammon joint is cut from the hind leg. However, they can be used interchangeably in recipes.

TOO SALTY

How can I reduce the saltiness in joints such as gammon?

If you think the joint may be too salty, soak it in cold water overnight. To test if this has removed enough salt, cut off a small piece and eat it as it is or fry it gently first. If the meat is still very salty, put the joint into a saucepan, cover with cold water and bring to the boil. Drain off the water; the joint is now ready for cooking.

However, modern curing techniques mean that salted meats such as gammon are not as salty as they used to be, and they often do not need to be soaked at all.

TENDER AND MOIST

I recently boiled a gammon joint but the meat was tough and dry. What went wrong?

Toughness and dryness are the result of cooking the meat at too high a temperature for a long time. If you cook a joint in water, adjust the heat so that the water bubbles only very gently throughout. Joints weighing less than 4.5 kg (10 lb) should be simmered for 20 minutes per 500 g (1 lb 2 oz) plus an extra 20 minutes, larger joints for 15 minutes per 500 g (1 lb 2 oz) plus an extra 15 minutes; the cooking time should be calculated from when the water reaches simmering point.

Gammon and bacon can also be successfully baked, wrapped in foil so they retain their moisture, in an oven preheated to 180°C (350°F, gas mark 4). Cooking times are the same as those for cooking in water.

Another way of cooking a moist gammon joint is to braise it on a bed of beans and other vegetables, as in the recipe below.

Gammon and beans

SERVES: 4
PREPARATION TIME: 10 - 15 minutes plus 30 minutes - overnight soaking
COOKING TIME: 3 hours

---

225 g (8 oz) haricot beans, soaked for 30 minutes in boiling water
1 sprig rosemary
1 carrot, chopped
1 onion, finely chopped
2 cloves garlic, chopped
2 sticks celery, chopped
125 g (4 ½ oz) large mushrooms, chopped, optional
400 g (14 oz) canned tomatoes, chopped
1 ½ tablespoons tomato purée
1 ½ tablespoons Dijon mustard
2 tablespoons molasses sugar or dark brown sugar
Black pepper
750 g (1 lb 10 oz) gammon joint, soaked overnight if necessary

---

1 Drain the soaked beans and put them into a large saucepan. Add the rosemary and pour in enough water to cover by 5 cm (2 in). Bring to the boil without covering the pan, boil for 10 minutes then drain.
2 Pour on some fresh water to cover the beans by 5 cm (2 in), bring to the boil then cover the pan and cook at a low boil for at least 50 minutes or until the beans are tender.
3 When the beans are almost ready, add the chopped carrot and cook for a further 10 minutes. Preheat the oven to 160°C (325°F, gas mark 3).
4 Drain the water from the pan and tip the vegetables into a casserole. Stir in all the other vegetables and flavourings. (Because of the salt in the gammon, you should not need extra salt.) Nestle the gammon joint into the beans. Cover the casserole and cook in the oven for 1 ½ hours.
5 Remove the lid and braise for a further 30 minutes.

'USE BY' DATES

How long can bacon be kept, and can it be frozen?

In the past it was possible to keep bacon for several weeks, but nowadays, because of changes in curing techniques, it should not be kept for more than one to two weeks (smoked bacon can be kept for two days longer than unsmoked). The 'use by' date on prepacked bacon may state a longer period than this, but once the packet has been opened the meat should be used quite quickly. Put loose bacon in a plastic bag and keep it securely wrapped in the refrigerator.

Bacon can be frozen, though it loses some of its flavour. Vacuum-packed joints can be kept in the freezer for three months; home-wrapped uncooked joints for two months; vacuum-packed rashers for

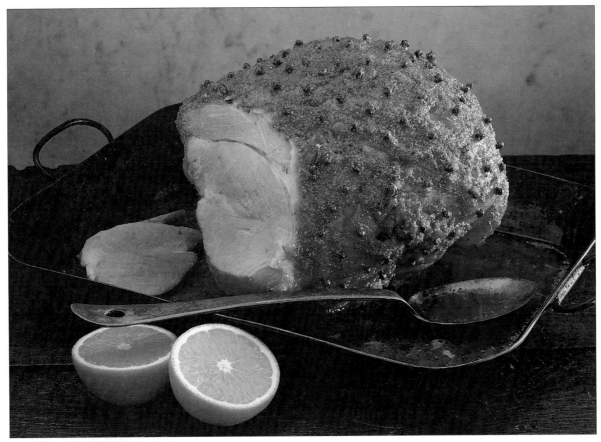

A hearty roast gammon joint, studded with cloves and covered with an aromatic glaze, is transformed into a party piece.

four to six weeks; home-packed rashers for four weeks (interleave them with cling film so you can separate them easily, then store them in a plastic bag). Rashers can be grilled or fried from frozen, but joints should be thawed overnight in the refrigerator.

GLAZING OVER

I have enjoyed glazed ham joints at large parties. Could I cook a gammon joint and glaze it in the same manner myself?

Yes, you can. It is not difficult to make a glaze, and is a good way of making a gammon joint look special. The glaze in the recipe (right) uses a mixture of sweet and strong flavours to add a rich, distinctive coating to a baked gammon. The joint can be eaten hot as soon as it is cooked, or cold for a buffet dinner or as leftovers – the flavour develops over a day or two.

Glazed gammon joint

SERVES: 8
PREPARATION TIME: 20 minutes
COOKING TIME: 1 1/4 hours for a 1.5 kg (3 lb 5 oz) joint

FOR THE GAMMON
1.5 kg (3 lb 5 oz) gammon joint
4 - 6 tablespoons dry white wine or water
About 10 cloves

FOR THE GLAZE
1 tablespoon clear honey
40 g (1 1/2 oz) dark soft brown sugar
1 tablespoon whole-grain mustard
1 teaspoon freshly grated ginger
2 tablespoons orange juice
Black pepper

1 Preheat the oven to 180°C (350°F, gas mark 4). Lay a piece of foil large enough to enclose the gammon on a large baking tray, put the gammon onto it and lift up the sides of the foil. Pour the wine or water gently over the joint and then fold the foil loosely over it, sealing the edges tightly so moisture does not escape. Bake the meat for 40 minutes per kg (18 minutes per lb) - about an hour for a joint weighing 1.5 kg (3 lb 5 oz).
2 While the joint is cooking, stir all the glaze ingredients together.
3 When the gammon has cooked, remove it from the oven and unwrap it. Turn up the oven heat to 200°C (400°F, gas mark 6). Using a sharp knife, slice between the skin and fat of the gammon, pulling the skin back as you move across the joint, until the skin comes away. Score the layer of fat in crisscross parallel lines spaced about 2 cm (3/4 in) apart to form diamond patterns, taking care not to pierce the meat. Then place the joint on a rack in a roasting tin.
4 Stud the gammon with cloves and brush with the glaze. Return to the oven and bake for 15 minutes. Serve immediately or leave until cold.

BAKING

DRY HEAT

What is the difference between baking and the other methods of cooking in the oven?

The chief difference between them is that baked foods, such as bread, biscuits, cakes, pastries, baked potatoes and soufflés, are cooked by dry heat. There is no surrounding bath of fat or liquid as there is with roasted or casseroled dishes.

Baking is one of the very oldest cooking techniques. Early ovens made of stone or brick were filled with wood, which was set alight. After burning, the ashes were raked out and bread or other dishes put in to cook in the residual heat. Today's baked dishes are cooked on the same principle, with heat coming from every side.

ACCURATE HEAT

Is it absolutely essential to have the right temperature for baking?

Because baked dishes do not have the protection of fat or liquid, they can burn easily and need to have fairly precise cooking temperatures. Unfortunately, the thermostats on many domestic ovens are not all that accurate. For best results, it is worth buying an oven thermometer and using it with your baking over a few weeks (see OVENS AND HOBS). This will give you the chance to adjust the oven settings.

PAPER PREFERENCES

What is the difference between greaseproof paper and baking paper with silicon?

Greaseproof paper is a type of non-absorbent paper which can be used for various purposes in the kitchen: layering fragile foods such as pancakes, wrapping food for storage, and lining cake tins. Baking paper (which is sometimes also called baking parchment) contains heat-resistant silicon that gives excellent anti-sticking properties. Although it costs more than greaseproof paper, baking paper is especially good for lining oven trays when you make meringues and other dishes with a high sugar content. These foods are liable to stick to greaseproof paper.

BAKING IN PARCELS

How can I tell when food being baked in individual paper or foil parcels has been fully cooked?

The whole point of cooking in a parcel, or *en papillote*, is for the diner to open it at the table and experience the sudden escape of aromas. Therefore, you should not open a parcel to check whether the food has been cooked. Choose food which cooks quickly at a high heat, such as filleted fish and finely chopped vegetables and fruit, and stay faithful to the times that are suggested in the recipe.

A small amount of liquid in the parcel creates a steamy atmosphere which helps to cook the food more quickly. The puffed parcels release an explosion of appetising smells as they are opened on the plate.

BANANAS

GREEN OR YELLOW

Is it better to buy bananas while they are still green or when they have turned yellow?

That depends on what you intend doing with them. Bananas are fully ripe when they turn deep yellow and brown speckles appear on the skin. The flesh becomes sweeter and fuller in flavour as they mature, so buy ripe ones if you want to eat them the same day. If you are buying bananas to eat later in the week, choose those that are still green or just beginning to turn yellow as they will ripen quite quickly once you get them home.

For cooking purposes, especially for savoury dishes, use fruit that is not completely ripe and still has partly green or pale yellow skin, as

Healthy option

Bananas are handy to carry, easy to peel and highly nutritious. They are a very good source of potassium, iron and many key vitamins except B_{12} and D. Look for small bananas, which are often the sweetest and most delicious.

they are much easier to slice and the flavour is not so dominating. However, for the moist, high-fibre Banana Tea Bread recipe (right), it is best to use fruit that is ripe.

KEEPING A DISTANCE

Is it correct that bananas should not be kept in a bowl alongside other sorts of fruit?

Bananas give off a gas called ethylene which makes any surrounding fruit ripen faster and possibly spoil. Keeping bananas separate from other fruit lets them all ripen naturally. However, if you want to ripen fruit quickly, such as peaches that are hard, put a ripe banana in with them. Bananas dislike the cold and it is best to store them at room temperature, not in the refrigerator.

STOP THE BROWNING

When I include sliced bananas in desserts they tend to turn brown very quickly. Is there any way I can prevent this from happening?

The riper the banana, the more quickly it seems to turn brown. If you need attractive slices, choose bananas that are not too ripe and use a stainless-steel knife to cut them. To decorate a gâteau or a dessert, just brush the slices with freshly squeezed lemon juice. Do not turn them in a bowl of lemon juice as this can make them slimy.

When mashing bananas, however, turning the slices in a bowl of lemon juice first not only keeps the flesh white but also encourages the slices to soften into a creamy paste.

Banana tea bread

MAKES: 12 slices
PREPARATION TIME: 40 minutes
COOKING TIME: 1 ¼ - 1 ½ hours

500 g (1 lb 2 oz) ripe bananas
Finely grated zest of 1 lemon, and
2 tablespoons lemon juice
115 g (4 oz) unsalted butter
115 g (4 oz) soft light-brown sugar
1 teaspoon vanilla extract/essence
1 egg, size 2
115 g (4 oz) self-raising flour
115 g (4 oz) plain wholemeal flour
1 teaspoon baking powder
A pinch of salt
1 teaspoon ground cinnamon
115 g (4 oz) seedless raisins
175 g (6 oz) fresh dates, stoned
and roughly chopped
25 g (1 oz) slivered or flaked
almonds
1 tablespoon icing sugar

1 Preheat the oven to 180°C (350°F, gas mark 4). Line a 21.5 × 11.5 × 6 cm (8½ × 4½ × 2½ in) loaf tin with nonstick baking paper, allowing the paper to stand a full 2.5 cm (1 in) above the edges of the tin.

2 Peel the bananas, cut them into slices and put them into a bowl. Add the lemon juice and mash well with a fork or potato masher.

3 Put the butter, sugar and lemon zest into a large bowl and beat well together with a wooden spoon or an electric hand-held mixer until light and fluffy, then beat in the vanilla.

4 Add the egg and beat well, then work in the mashed bananas.

5 Sift the flours, baking powder, salt and cinnamon into the banana mixture, tipping the bran left in the sieve into the bowl. Then gently mix together with a large spoon and stir in the raisins and dates.

6 Spoon the mixture into the tin, level the surface and sprinkle on the almonds. Bake for 1 ¼ - 1 ½ hours, or until the loaf is well risen and golden brown. The tea bread is ready when a skewer or knife inserted in the centre comes out clean.

7 Let the loaf rest for 30 minutes before removing it from the tin, then put it on a wire rack to cool. When it is completely cold, gently remove the baking paper. Store the loaf in an airtight tin for up to a week.

8 When you are ready to serve the tea bread, sift the icing sugar over the top. Slice the loaf and eat either plain or spread with butter.

STRONG INGREDIENT

Are bananas a good addition to a mixed fruit salad?

Bananas have a strong flavour and are probably best left out of any fruit salads containing delicately flavoured fruits such as melons, peaches or grapes. They can work well in a highly spiced sugar syrup, perhaps with rum and one or two other fruits that are also strong in flavour, like orange or pineapple. Some red fruits, such as raspberries and plums, will turn bananas pink.

Almond flakes add a crisp decorative touch to this moist Banana Tea Bread, made with added dates and raisins.

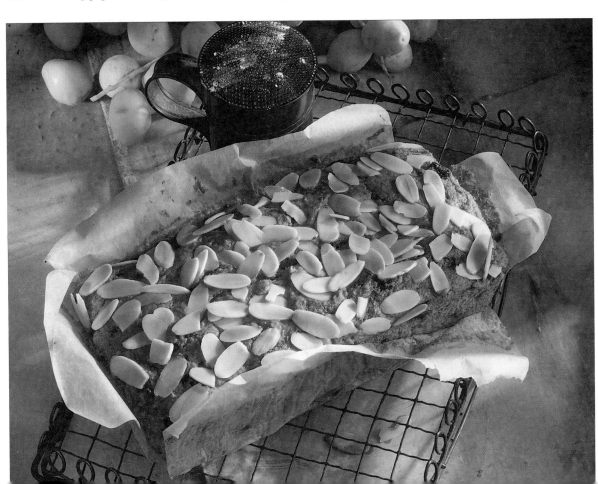

BARBECUES

CHOOSING EQUIPMENT

I am planning to buy a barbecue but am unsure about which type to choose. Can you advise me?

There are many types of barbecue available. The most basic is one you make yourself from bricks and an iron grill. Although this can be an attractive feature in the garden, it is permanently installed and the grill is usually fixed so it is difficult to control the temperature.

Portable barbecues, which fold into a suitcase, are easy to carry around and ideal for picnics and holidays. The most popular model, known as hibachi or firebowl in Japanese, has a grate to hold the charcoal, adjustable grills and vents to control the air flow. As portable barbecues are usually quite small, the amount you can cook at one time is limited. Flimsier disposable models come with enough charcoal for about one (small) barbecue.

Standard barbecues are usually about 60 cm (2 ft) across and have a built-in windbreak. They generally have more than one grill, which makes it easier to cook different types of food at the same time, such as sausages that need quick cooking and chicken joints that need much slower cooking.

Covered, kettle barbecues are the most efficient. Charcoal burns in baskets on either side and the food is put on a rack in the centre so that it cooks using the indirect heat reflected off the lid.

The most expensive barbecues are covered models where blocks of lava rocks are heated by gas or electricity. This takes less time and is less messy than using charcoal, but the food is cooked in the same manner as in a conventional covered barbecue. It will have the smoky flavour, but this is from fat and juices spitting onto the lava rocks, not from the charcoal.

COOKING GUIDELINES

What are the cooking times for different foods on the barbecue?

Timings depend very much on the individual barbecue being used. As you gain more experience, you will be able to judge the cooking times very accurately. The key point to remember is that the coals ought to be ash-grey and radiating heat, but no flames, before you begin to cook. This can take anything from 40 minutes to as much as an hour, so you must plan ahead. Follow the guidelines shown below and you will avoid having meat or fish which becomes charcoal on the outside but stays raw in the centre.

Some foods can be precooked in the oven or on the hob to help to ensure they are well cooked. Thick chicken joints, large sausages and pork chops can all be cooked for half of their total time and then completed on the barbecue.

Below are some rough guidelines on how long to allow. The figures are total cooking times and you should turn the meat or fish over halfway through:

- CHICKEN: joints 40 minutes, drumsticks 20–30 minutes.
- LAMB CHOPS: 10–20 minutes, depending on thickness.
- LEG OF LAMB: (on the bone) allow 35 minutes per kg (15 minutes per lb) for well done.
- PORK CHOPS: 30–40 minutes, depending on size.
- RIB OF BEEF: 25 minutes per kg (10 minutes per lb), rare.
- SAUSAGES: 10–16 minutes.
- STEAK: 6–10 minutes for rare, 10–16 minutes for medium and 16–20 minutes for well done.
- WHOLE SMALL FISH: 12–16 minutes.
- WHOLE LARGE FISH: 20–30 minutes.

CHOOSING CONVENIENT FISH RACKS

Barbecuing fish is easier if you use a special fish rack. To prevent the fish sticking to the metal, brush the rack inside and out with oil – but do not preheat it. Before starting, you can stuff a whole fish with fresh herbs or wrap it in vine leaves. Oil the fish or fish steaks, place in the rack, close it tightly and place the rack on the barbecue grill. Turn the rack over once during cooking and baste the fish often through the metal bars, so that the flesh will stay moist.

A large, fish-shaped rack is the ideal container for a good-sized whole fish such as grey mullet or sea bass. These are otherwise hard to turn on the grill.

A square or rectangular fish rack allows you to line up wide and narrow fish fillets or steaks side-by-side so that they all cook together in an even way.

Small whole fish such as sardines are best cooked in a rack with individual compartments. These will hold the fish firmly and stop them slipping around.

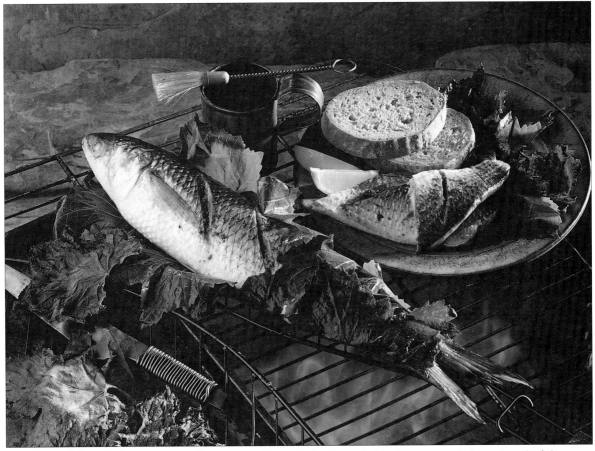

Vine leaves make a good protective coat for a grey mullet on the barbecue, but peel them away before eating the fish.

EXPERIMENT WITH FISH

This summer I should like to try cooking fish on the barbecue. As I am a complete novice, can you suggest the best fish to choose?

Fish is excellent to barbecue: the intense heat and quick cooking sear the outside while keeping the flesh moist and full of flavour. Oily fish cooked whole in their skins are ideal. The skins release their oils into the flesh while providing a protection against the heat, so the firm flesh does not fall apart.

The very best fish to cook whole are bass, herring, mackerel, red or grey mullet, salmon, sardines and trout. The recipe, right, for grey mullet is easy and a good one for beginners. Sea bass are dearer but can also be cooked in this way. For easy handling and turning, use a special fish rack to barbecue fish (see box, opposite page).

Grey mullet in vine leaves

SERVES: 4
PREPARATION TIME: 20 minutes plus 1 hour marinating
COOKING TIME: 20 minutes

1 packet vine leaves preserved in brine
1 grey mullet, weighing about 2 kg (4 lb 8 oz), gutted with head and tail left on
Salt and black pepper
4 cloves garlic, sliced lengthways
1 large bunch fresh herbs such as chervil, dill, marjoram, oregano, parsley or rosemary, according to taste
90 ml (3 1/4 fl oz) virgin olive oil
2 tablespoons balsamic vinegar
To serve: lemon or lime wedges

1 Drain the vine leaves and place them in a bowl. Pour on enough boiling water to cover, soak them for about 5 minutes and drain again.

2 Slash the skin of the fish quite deeply in several places on each side. Sprinkle the cavities with salt and pepper, and then push the garlic and fresh herbs very deep inside.

3 Put the fish in a nonmetallic dish. Whisk together the oil and vinegar with salt and pepper to taste, then pour over the fish.

4 Cover and marinate the fish in the refrigerator for at least an hour. Meanwhile, preheat the barbecue.

5 Brush a fish rack liberally inside and out with vegetable oil, but do not preheat the metal bars. Wrap the fish in the vine leaves, then place the parcel carefully in the rack.

6 Close the metal rack and put it on the oiled barbecue grid. If you do not have a fish rack, you can also just secure the leaves with string.

7 Cook the fish for 20 minutes, turning once. Unwrap and serve the grey mullet immediately, garnished with lemon or lime wedges.

BARBECUING LARGE CUTS

How can I barbecue a large piece of meat, such as a leg of lamb?

It is possible to cook a large piece of meat successfully on a barbecue, and in the United States Thanksgiving turkey is often cooked in this way. The technique works best with a covered barbecue which gives an indirect, reflected heat and greater temperature control.

Put the joint on the grill, with a drip pan underneath to catch the juices, and adjust the air vents to ensure very slow, even cooking. Check the coals from time to time and add more charcoal gradually if it seems necessary. The cooking times are approximately the same as when you are using an oven, although they can be quicker. This is because temperatures fluctuate in a barbecue and may become a good deal higher than you would have in an oven. If you are in any doubt, especially with poultry, use a meat thermometer to check the joint's inner temperature.

An excellent method of cooking a whole leg of lamb is to butterfly bone it. The joint is opened out like a book and the meat takes less time to cook (see BONING).

TENDERISING MARINADES

Why are meat and fish so often marinated before barbecuing?

Marinades are helpful to tenderise meat and enhance the flavour – and they are particularly useful for barbecuing, where the intense heat can result in dry food. Barbecue marinades are usually based on tomato, onion and garlic, which suit the smoky flavours particularly well. Tomato is often included for its tenderising effect, but any other acid ingredients, such as vinegar or lemon juice, can be used.

A marinade may include garlic, fresh ginger, lemon juice, olive oil, sherry and brown sugar, as well as soy sauce to provide a tangy flavour. The following recipe for Barbecued Lamb offers another suggestion (see also MARINADE).

Barbecued lamb

SERVES 4
PREPARATION TIME: 5 - 15 minutes, plus 2 - 4 hours marinating
COOKING TIME: 8 - 10 minutes

FOR THE MEAT
650 g (1 lb 7 oz) lamb leg steak, cut into 2.5 cm (1 in) cubes

FOR THE MARINADE
4 tablespoons olive oil
2 tablespoons lemon juice
1 tablespoon each chopped fresh flat-leaf parsley and chopped fresh thyme
A pinch of dried oregano
Black pepper and salt
To serve: lemon wedges

1 If the butcher has not prepared the lamb steak, trim it and cut it into cubes. Put these chunks of meat in a shallow, nonmetallic dish.
2 Mix together the olive oil, lemon juice, herbs and pepper. Pour the marinade over the lamb, turn the meat in it and leave in a cool place for 2 - 4 hours, turning occasionally.
3 If you leave the meat to marinate in the refrigerator, be sure to remove it 30 minutes before cooking.
4 Meanwhile, preheat the barbecue until it is white hot. Oil the metal rack and put it 7.5 - 10 cm (3 - 4 in) above the glowing coals.
5 Lift the lamb from the dish and reserve the marinade. Lightly oil four skewers and thread the cubed lamb onto them, keeping the meat towards the pointed skewer ends.
6 Put the kebabs on the grill rack and cook for 8 - 10 minutes, turning the skewers frequently and basting with the reserved marinade.
7 Sprinkle the cooked lamb cubes with salt, and serve them with lemon wedges and a mixed salad.

Turning sausages

If you are cooking lots of sausages over the barbecue, thread them onto skewers first to make turning them easier. The sausages will then brown more evenly as they grill.

PLAN TO DEFROST

Could I barbecue meat and fish directly from frozen?

Cooking frozen food on a barbecue is not recommended. Poultry, large cuts of meat and large whole fish that are frozen would be cooked, and even charred, on the outside by the fierce heat well before the centre had become sufficiently hot.

Small cuts of meat such as minute steaks and small fish could be cooked from frozen if you add extra time, but the texture of the rapidly defrosted meat will be impaired.

PREPARING KEBABS

What is the best way to cut up meat for a barbecued kebab?

Trim the fat and connective tissue from the meat, then cut across the grain into fairly even-sized cubes that are no larger than 5 cm (2 in) thick. You should skewer the cubes closely together if you prefer rarer meat with pink centres. Make a point of separating the cubes more if you want to cook the meat so that it is much better done.

Any lean cut of meat can be used to make kebabs. For example, you can try using cubes of either pork tenderloin or fillet, or the fillet end of leg of pork. Other good choices for making skewered kebabs are lamb tenderloin or fillet end of leg of lamb, fillet of beef and chunks of either turkey or chicken breast.

PROTECTING FISH

Does fish need to be wrapped in foil before going on the barbecue?

Fish steaks or whole fish do not need to be wrapped in foil to be cooked on the barbecue, but it is generally better to choose a meatier fish such as a monkfish, shark, swordfish or tuna rather than a white fish, which may fall apart.

The fish can be wrapped up in bacon to provide protection, or it can be marinated to lubricate the flesh – but if the marinade has lime or lemon juice, do not leave it too long (see box on opposite page).

Care with fish marinades

Do not marinate fish for longer than an hour in any solution which contains either lime or lemon juice, as the acid in the citrus fruit will start to 'cook' the fish.

BARBECUING VEGETABLES

Should vegetables be marinated before they are barbecued?

Vegetables cannot be made tender by marinating, but using marinades also enhances the flavour of food. The results on vegetables can be surprising and delicious.

For instance, try marinating thick slices of aubergines, courgettes and red and yellow peppers, plus halved plum tomatoes, in olive oil with some crushed garlic, sprigs of thyme and a squeeze of lemon.

Then cook the vegetables on a grid placed directly over the hot coals, starting with the aubergines which need 6 minutes on each side, add the courgettes for 4–5 minutes on each side, followed by the peppers for about 2–3 minutes on each side and then the tomatoes, skin side down only, for 2–3 minutes.

Grilled asparagus is wonderful with a mixture of hazelnut oil and red wine vinegar. Use three parts of oil to one part of vinegar, whisk the two together and pour the marinade over the asparagus spears.

You can cook the spears straightaway, or leave them soaking in the marinade for about an hour. Put the asparagus spears on a grill which is directly over the hot coals, and rotate them to allow quick cooking for 2–3 minutes on each side.

A popular choice to barbecue is corn-on-the-cob. Pull the corn husk back, without taking it off the stalk, and then remove the silky threads. Coat the corn cob with a barbecue sauce and cover it again with the husk. Wrap each cob in foil and leave to marinate for 30 minutes. Cook the prepared corn parcels on the cooler part of the grill for about 15–20 minutes, turning frequently.

BARBECUED FRUIT

Do you have any suggestions for barbecued puddings?

Your guests may have had enough of barbecued food after eating the main course, and a fresh fruit salad or some homemade ice cream to follow is often the most refreshing choice. However, fruit does lend itself to being barbecued and the soft flesh of bananas is especially delicious when grilled.

Split the whole banana lengthways through the skin, without removing the flesh, and sprinkle orange juice, rum, brown sugar and cinnamon down the middle.

Dot the banana flesh with butter, sandwich the fruit back together and wrap it in foil. Grill the banana slowly for about 5–10 minutes, turning the parcel over carefully about halfway through cooking. A variety of other fleshy fruits, such as nectarines and peaches, can be cooked in the same way, but they will need to have their hard stones removed beforehand.

Fruit kebabs are very attractive and cook quickly. Cut a mixture of firm-fleshed fruit into chunks and thread them onto a kebab skewer. Choose fruits with a harmonious mix of colours and flavours. Sprinkle with caster sugar and a liqueur of your choice, or the juice and zest of one orange, and leave them to soak for at least 2 hours. Then drain the kebabs, save the marinade, and grill the fruit for 5–10 minutes. Turn them often while they cook, basting with a little marinade.

To serve, arrange the mixed fruit kebabs decoratively onto a platter and pour over the remaining juice.

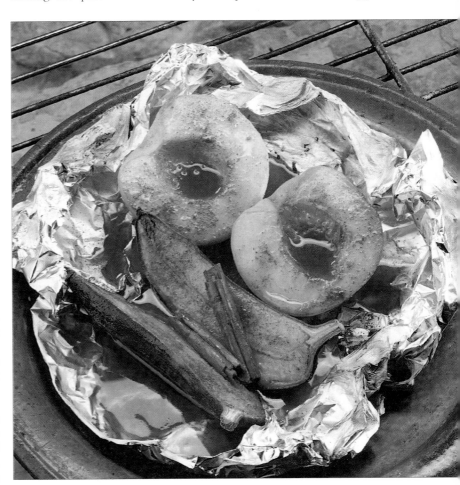

Barbecued peaches and bananas sprinkled with sugar, cinnamon and rum are wonderful. Serve in their warm juices with the aromas wafting from the parcel.

BARLEY

LOW-GLUTEN FLOUR

What is barley flour, and how does it differ from other flours?

This is flour produced by milling the whole grain. Barley is notably low in gluten, the protein that gives bread dough its elasticity. For this reason, it needs to be used with other, higher-gluten flours to make successful yeasted bread.

While barley flour or meal does not make good leavened bread when used on its own, it adds considerable flavour to tea breads and scones and can be used to thicken soups and milk-based sauces.

As one of the earliest cereals farmed, barley grains were used for making bread before wheat. While much barley is now used for animal feed, it is still malted for brewing and remains an important grain for human food in the Near East.

REFINED GRAINS

What is the difference between whole grains and pearl barley?

Whole grains are the grains as they are harvested, while pearl barley has had the outer layer removed to reveal a polished white kernel. Whole grains must be softened before being cooked in order to be edible. Soak them in plenty of cold water for at least 2 hours or even overnight. The whole grains are then often combined with meat, and lamb in particular, as in the classic recipe for Scotch broth. The barley thickens this wholesome soup as well as adding flavour and a pleasing nutty texture.

As pearl barley has been well polished to remove the outer husk, the grain cooks more quickly and no prior soaking is necessary. Pearl barley is also used to thicken and enhance the flavour and texture of soups and is the key ingredient in Lemon Barley Water (following the step-by-step instructions below).

MAKING LEMON BARLEY WATER

This traditional summer drink is extremely easy to make. Allow plenty of time for cooling, as it is most appealing served chilled with ice and lemon slices.

1 Wash three large lemons, dry them and pare the zest using a potato peeler. Place the pieces of peel in a bowl and add 75 - 125 g (2¾ - 4½ oz) of caster sugar, according to taste.

Put 3 tablespoons of pearl barley in a large saucepan, pour in 1.25 litres (2 pints) of water and bring to the boil. Cover and let the grains simmer for 10 minutes, until they are soft.

2 Pour the water and barley over the sugar and peel and leave to cool.

3 Squeeze the lemons and strain the juice into a jug to discard the pips. Strain the barley liquid into the juice.

BATTER

RESTING BATTER

Should I let pancake batter stand for an hour or two before using?

While it is not strictly necessary, taking the time to cover and rest the pancake batter in a cool place for 15–30 minutes allows the starch in the flour to swell, giving a lighter result. If the batter is cooked just after being made, the pancakes will tend to have a bubbly surface rather than appearing flat. A short time resting is useful, but do not leave the batter to stand for more than 12 hours or it may begin to ferment.

Batter left to stand for an hour or more may separate out. If so, just stir to remix. If it thickens slightly, thin it with some extra liquid.

VARYING THE MIX

Can I use the same batter for different dishes, such as waffles, fritters and pancakes?

The batters that are used to make pancakes, waffles and such dishes are much the same. It is the exact proportions of all the ingredients that vary slightly.

Pancakes, crêpes, baked batter puddings, Yorkshire pudding and toad-in-the-hole are made with a basic pouring batter (see the box opposite). To make crêpes, which are slightly lighter than pancakes, the batter is thinned with a few tablespoons of extra liquid.

Fritters and battered foods such as fish, shellfish and vegetables are made with coating batter. This uses the same amount of flour, salt and egg as pouring batter, but only half of the liquid. Whisked egg whites may be folded into a coating batter and sugar added for sweet fritters.

The type of liquid used in batters (whether milk, a mix of milk and water, or beer) will influence the result. Water makes a light batter, milk helps to make it smoother and causes it to brown faster, while beer adds lightness and flavour.

EASY ON WHISKING

How long should you beat batter to achieve a good texture?

Basic batter needs only fairly brief stirring or whisking in order to combine the ingredients. If you beat the mixture too much, this tends to develop the gluten in the flour and results in the batter becoming tough when it is cooked. The exception is any yeast-raised batter, which does need to be beaten heartily to develop gluten.

MAKING BASIC BATTER

This basic batter will make 8 – 10 pancakes. Include 3 tablespoons of extra milk if making lighter crêpes, and halve the liquid for making a thicker, coating batter.

1 Sift 100 g (3½ oz) of plain flour and a pinch of salt into a bowl and make a well in the centre, then break in one egg and beat with a balloon whisk or wooden spoon. (You can also use a food processor for a few seconds or a hand-held electric mixer for slightly longer.)

2 Beat in 300 ml (10 fl oz) of milk, little by little, incorporating the surrounding flour gradually so the batter becomes very smooth.

3 The batter may be used at once, but it is much better if it is left in a cool place for some 30 minutes, allowing the starch grains to soften.

SUCCESSFUL DROP SCONES

My drop scones tend to be stodgy, although I leave the batter to rise. What am I doing wrong?

Drop scones, like waffles, need a raising agent to help to make them light and bubbly – which is why self-raising flour is used with these. A disadvantage is that self-raising flour starts into action as soon as it becomes wet, so the batter must be used straightaway.

If self-raising flour batter is left to stand, the bubbles escape and the results will be heavier instead of lighter pancakes. Try this speedy idea for light-as-air Drop Scones (below). The secret is that batter for this delicious recipe must be made just before you make the scones.

Drop scones

MAKES: 12 – 15 scones
PREPARATION TIME: 15 minutes
COOKING TIME: 10 – 15 minutes

100 g (3½ oz) self-raising flour
1 – 2 tablespoons caster sugar
1 egg, size 3, beaten
150 ml (5 fl oz) milk

1 Mix the flour and sugar in a bowl and make a well in the centre. Stir in the egg and add enough milk to make a thick batter, stirring gently.
2 Lightly grease a large griddle or heavy frying pan with vegetable oil and preheat it. Gently drop individual tablespoons of the mixture onto the griddle or pan and cook them over a moderate heat until bubbles show.
3 Flip the scones over with a palette knife and continue cooking them for a further 2 - 3 minutes, until golden. Repeat with the remaining batter.
4 Keep the cooked scones warm by wrapping them in a folded tea towel. Serve either warm or cold with jam, butter, cream or honey.
VARIATION
Add 50 - 75 g (1¾ - 2¾ oz) of raisins, sultanas, or chopped dried apricots, a teaspoon of ground mixed spice or the finely grated zest of an orange to the batter before cooking. Reduce the calories and fat by using semi-skimmed instead of whole milk.

Staying unstuck

To give a richer flavour to pancakes and crêpes, and to help to prevent them sticking to the pan, stir in 1 – 2 tablespoons of melted butter or oil to the batter before cooking.

YEASTY FISH BATTER

What sort of batter do I use for coating fish before deep-frying?

Batter helps to protect delicate foods such as fish from the intense heat of deep fat. A crisp coating forms which stops fat penetrating the food, so it stays soft and tender inside. The batter used for fish is usually a savoury coating batter, using beer instead of milk to add flavour as well as air, or a more robust yeast-raised batter.

Yeast batter is preferred for the coating of fish because although it is strong enough to protect the fish, it has a particularly light texture. To make a yeast batter that will coat 350 g (12 oz) of fish, you need a teaspoon of dried yeast, 150 ml (5 fl oz) of milk or water, 100 g (3½ oz) of plain flour and a pinch of salt. The yeast is dissolved in the liquid and then added to the flour and salt.

Unlike an ordinary batter, yeast-raised batter is beaten vigorously to develop gluten in the flour. Leave it to stand in a cool place for up to an hour, until risen and bubbly.

Save it!

Cooked pancakes may be refrigerated for up to two days. They also freeze well for up to three months, if separated with pieces of greaseproof paper. Thaw the pancakes overnight in the refrigerator. To reheat, warm them in the oven or heat gently on both sides in melted butter in a frying pan.

BAVAROIS

ADDED EGG

What is the difference between a blancmange and a bavarois?

Blancmange is made from milk set with either cornflour or gelatine. Bavarois is a milk and egg custard, enriched with whipped cream and often egg whites, and set with gelatine. Also known as Bavarian cream or crème bavaroise, bavarois is lighter than blancmange and has generally replaced it as a popular dessert. Both are usually flavoured and sometimes coloured, poured into a mould to set and then chilled.

RICH OR LIGHT

Can I use cream instead of milk to make a richer bavarois?

Yes, and if you prefer to go the other way and reduce the calorie and fat content, you can elect instead to use semi-skimmed milk and half-fat cream or fromage frais. This enticing recipe for Raspberry Bavarois lets you choose.

Raspberry bavarois

SERVES: 6
PREPARATION TIME: 1 hour, plus
3 - 4 hours chilling time
COOKING TIME: none

225 g (8 oz) raspberries, fresh or
    frozen, defrosted
500 ml (18 fl oz) single or
    double cream
3 eggs, size 3, separated
100 g (3 ½ oz) caster sugar
15 g (½ oz) powdered gelatine
150 ml (5 fl oz) double cream
Sunflower, grapeseed or vegetable
    oil, for greasing
To decorate: icing sugar, fresh
    raspberries and mint sprigs

1 Purée the raspberries in a blender or food processor then set aside.
2 Put the 500 ml (18 fl oz) of cream in a pan and bring it to the boil.
3 In a bowl, whisk together the egg yolks and sugar until pale and fluffy.

This luscious, creamy bavarois is flavoured and decorated with fresh raspberries topped with icing sugar and mint. It can be low-fat if you choose the variation.

Pour the hot cream onto the whisked egg mixture, then strain the custard into a heavy-based saucepan. Cook over a gentle heat, stirring until it is thick enough to coat the back of a spoon. Do not boil.
4 Sprinkle the gelatine powder over 3 tablespoons of water in a small bowl and leave to soak for about 2 minutes until spongy.
5 Place the bowl over a small pan of simmering water and stir until the gelatine has dissolved.
6 Stir the gelatine and the raspberry purée into the custard. Then stand the mixture in a bowl filled with ice and stir gently until thickened.
7 Lightly whip the 150 ml (5 fl oz) of double cream and fold it into the fruity custard. Whisk the egg whites until stiff and fold them in carefully.
8 Lightly oil a mould, pour in the bavarois and chill 3 - 4 hours to set.
9 When the bavarois has become firm, stand the mould in hot water for a few seconds. This will make the dessert much easier to unmould.

Turn it out onto a serving dish, dust it with icing sugar and decorate with fresh raspberries and sprigs of mint.
VARIATION
For a less fattening version, use semi-skimmed milk instead of cream in the custard, and plain fromage frais or half-fat cream after the fruit and gelatine have been incorporated.

OCCASIONALLY SAVOURY

I saw bavarois included on a savoury menu. Does a bavarois not have to be a sweet dish?

Bavarois usually refers to a sweet dessert. However, you can make savoury bavarois using a custard base without sugar, combined with savoury ingredients. These may be asparagus, smoked fish or cheese and onion, usually in the form of a purée, and then set with gelatine. Use either just cream, or a mixture of cream and yoghurt or fromage frais, and fold this into the cooled custard before it becomes fully set.

BEANS

A QUESTION OF SEASON

French beans seem to be available all year, but when is the best time for broad and runner beans?

Early summer is the time for home-grown broad beans, which are traditionally dressed with butter and summer savory. Dill also goes particularly well with these. When the pods become very large, the beans inside are best blanched and skinned. This treatment works all year round for frozen broad beans, and the bright green kernels add freshness to mixed-bean salads.

Runner beans come into season in the late summer. String and slice them, then cook quickly in boiling salted water. You can serve them hot, dressed with butter or olive oil, or in a sauce. French beans are also delicious eaten cold as a salad. Try mixing the beans with omelette strips, as in the following recipe. Serve as a starter with warm bread.

French bean and omelette ribbon salad

SERVES: 4
PREPARATION TIME: 15 minutes
COOKING TIME: 8 - 9 minutes

2 eggs
Salt and black pepper
3 tablespoons olive oil
350 g (12 oz) french beans
1 large clove garlic, thinly sliced
1 teaspoon red wine vinegar
1 teaspoon chilli vinegar
2 sun-dried tomatoes in oil, chopped
2 teaspoons capers

1 Beat the eggs lightly with a fork, add salt and pepper, then make two thin omelettes and turn onto plates.
2 Top and tail the beans and cook for 3 - 4 minutes in boiling, salted water. Drain and transfer to a dish.
3 Fry the garlic for 30 seconds in a tablespoon of oil; remove from the heat. Add the remaining oil, vinegars and sun-dried tomatoes, mix together and toss into the beans.
4 Roll each omelette and slice into thin ribbons. Curl the slices loosely over the salad; scatter with capers.

French beans are threaded with omelette ribbons for this piquant salad. The strips of egg and sun-dried tomatoes add good contrasts in colour and texture.

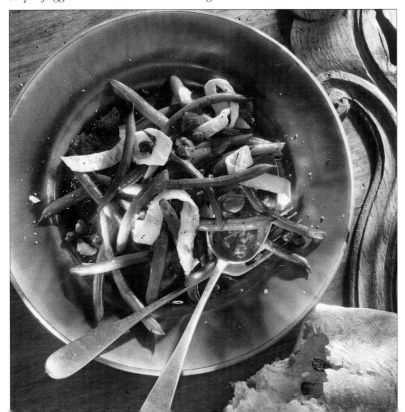

STRINGING BEANS

Many green beans are sold when they are small and do not need to have their strings removed. Older french beans and runner beans (pictured below) need stringing.

1 With a small, sharp knife, cut each bean from the outer side across the stalk end towards the deeply grooved inner side. Stop just short of the edge and pull the string along the length of each bean.

2 If a string breaks short, cut away a thin strip along the edge to remove it. Nick the top of the outer edge. If a string has been formed there, pull it out as well.

SLICING BEANS

Slicing larger green beans thinly and not too long ensures that they cook through more quickly and also retain their best flavour.

With long diagonal cuts, slice across and down the pod right through the beans inside. Aim to produce slices measuring about 5 mm (¼ in) wide and 7.5 - 10 cm (3 - 4 in) long.

Warm salad of tangled runner beans

SERVES: 4
PREPARATION TIME: 15 minutes
COOKING TIME: 4 - 5 minutes

500 g (1 lb 2 oz) runner beans
½ red onion
Salt and black pepper
4 tablespoons olive oil
1 tablespoon red wine vinegar
150 g (5½ oz) cherry tomatoes, some halved
50 g (1¾ oz) small black olives
To garnish: basil leaves

1 String and thinly slice the beans diagonally. Peel the onion, cut it in half and then slice downwards into thin crescents. Put these slices into an attractive serving bowl.
2 Cook the beans in boiling salted water until just tender; this should take about 4 minutes after the water returns to the boil. Drain and put the beans immediately over the onion slices so the heat slightly wilts them.
3 In a small bowl, stir the oil and vinegar briskly together and toss into the beans, along with the cherry tomatoes, olives and black pepper.
4 Tear leaves of basil over the salad just before serving. The dish is best still warm or at room temperature.

BEAN SPROUTS

SPROUTING SEEDS

Can I sprout any dried bean?

Beans, peas and lentils are all seeds that can be used for sprouting. As long as they are not too old or have not been damaged or deliberately split in processing, they should sprout. You can also use grains such as barley, whole oats, wheat and millet. These can then be used singly or in mixtures in salads and sandwiches, very lightly cooked in stir-fries, or as a crunchy garnish for cooked food. Bean sprouts that are surplus to your immediate needs can be loosely wrapped in cling film and stored in the salad drawer of the refrigerator.

GROWING BEAN SPROUTS

Sprouting beans is very easy and is a good way to have a fresh, crunchy, high-protein salad filling on hand. The sprouts can also be added to stir-fries as well as pasta dishes.

Soak a handful of beans (mung beans are shown here) overnight in cold water and they will double their bulk. Rinse in a sieve under the cold tap and transfer to a jar. They should fill the jar about one-quarter full.

1 Cover the jar with a square of loose-woven cloth held in place with an elastic band. Leave the jar on its side.

2 Place in a warm, well-ventilated place out of direct sunlight. Twice each day, uncover the jar. Fill it with cold water, swirl, replace the cover and drain water through the cloth.

3 The seeds should start to sprout on the second day. After a few days, the sprouts will have grown to about 1 - 2 cm (½ - ¾ in) long, which is when they are at their most nutritious.

BEEF

BREAKING DOWN FIBRES

Why should you beat steak?

Steak is beaten to break down the fibres a little, making the meat more tender. Nowadays, cattle are killed while still young and tender so beating steaks is less necessary, but you can do so if you want to shorten their cooking time. Lay the uncooked meat between two sheets of cling film or greaseproof paper, and then pound it firmly with a meat mallet, the flat of a heavy knife, or a rolling pin. A gentler technique for tenderising steak is to marinate it for a few hours.

TOUGH STEAKS

Sometimes when I cook steak, it is very chewy. Is the problem with the meat I buy or the method I use for cooking?

The tenderness is affected by the choice of meat. Look for flesh with a little fine marbling of fat as this dissolves in cooking and helps to tenderise the steak. Animals that have been carefully reared to conservation grade (see MEAT) and Scotch beef are apt to be most tender. It is also important that the meat should have been well hung in a cool place for about 14 days. During hanging, flavour develops and the natural enzymes in the meat break down the tough tissues, making it firmer, drier and more tender. The meat will also look much darker in colour. Bright red steak is more likely to be tough.

If you buy from a good butcher, these points will be covered. But how you cook steak, and for how long, also affects how easy it is to chew. Good-quality raw steak is already tender and overcooking it does not tenderise it but makes it tough. This recipe for Perfect Steak (right) gives the optimum cooking times. Always bring the steak to room temperature for an hour or so before you start cooking.

KNOW YOUR STEAK

Steaks come in many forms, from dainty tournedos to chateaubriand that will feed two or more hungry people.

Choose fillet and sirloin steaks for real tenderness, but more robust cuts such as rump for their succulent flavour.

1 FILLET STEAK is cut from the thick centre section of the fillet, just below the sirloin. It is small in diameter, weighs about 175 g (6 oz), is tender and very lean. Fillet steaks are extremely good but they are expensive.

2 PORTERHOUSE STEAK can serve two people. It is usually a double thickness of sirloin steak with two separate 'eyes' of meat. (American porterhouse steak also includes some fillet.)

3 T-BONE steak is a thick cut that includes the rib bone with the sirloin on one side of the 'T' and the fillet on the other. It serves one person generously.

4 SIRLOIN STEAK is cut from the top part of the sirloin, above the ribs. It is not as fine-textured or tender as fillet, but is less coarse than rump. Entrecôte is the French word for sirloin steak.

5 RUMP STEAK is cut across the grain of the rump. It is marbled with a little fat, has a border of fat and is coarser and tougher than fillet or sirloin. It has a good flavour and many people consider it the best for grilling and frying.

6 CHATEAUBRIAND is a joint cut from the thickest end of the fillet and can serve two to four people. After an initial grilling, the steak is usually put in the oven to finish cooking.

7 MINUTE STEAK is cut thinly from the upper part of the sirloin and is beaten so that it cooks quickly to be tender.

8 TOURNEDOS are small round steaks cut from the centre or thin end of the fillet, weighing about 115 g (4 oz). They are wrapped in pork fat or bacon and tied into shape before cooking.

Perfect steak

SERVES: 4
PREPARATION TIME: 5 minutes
COOKING TIME: 3 – 10 minutes

1 tablespoon mild olive oil
4 rump, sirloin or fillet steaks
Salt and black pepper

TO FRY

1 Brush a large, heavy, nonstick frying pan with oil and place it over a high heat until very hot.
2 Sprinkle the steaks with black pepper, add them to the pan and brown for 1 - 1½ minutes each side then cook for these times, turning the meat over halfway through:
• BLUE: 2 minutes (the meat offers little resistance when pressed).
• RARE: 3 minutes (the meat feels spongy when pressed).
• MEDIUM: 4½ minutes (the meat resists when pressed).
• WELL DONE: 5 - 7 minutes (the meat feels firm when pressed).
3 For blue or rare steak, keep the heat high. For longer cooking, lower the heat after the initial browning.

TO GRILL

1 Preheat the grill for 10 minutes until it is very hot. Make vertical cuts through any fat around the edge of the steak at 2.5 cm (1 in) intervals.
2 Brush both sides with oil. Season with black pepper, put on the grill rack and cook 7.5 cm (3 in) from the grill for a minute each side.
3 Reduce the heat to medium and grill for these times, turning the meat over halfway through:
• BLUE: 2½ minutes.
• RARE: 3½ minutes.
• MEDIUM: 5½ minutes.
• WELL DONE: 6 - 8 minutes.
4 Transfer the steaks to warm plates, sprinkle with salt and serve with mustard or béarnaise sauce.

DRAMATIC TOP RIB

I usually cook rolled topside or sirloin, but would like to try top rib of beef. How is it cooked?

Because top rib is cooked on the bone, it has more flavour than boned and rolled joints and looks more dramatic. Top rib is not difficult to prepare, as the following recipe for Roast Rib of Beef shows.

Roast rib of beef

SERVES: *6 - 8; allow about 350 g (12 oz) per person*
PREPARATION TIME: *5 minutes*
COOKING TIME: *1 ¼ - 2 hours*

Rib of beef on the bone weighing about 2.25 kg (5 lb)
Salt and black pepper
Plain flour, optional
Powdered mustard, optional

1 Preheat the oven to 230°C (450°F, gas mark 8). Weigh the beef and calculate the cooking time. For rare meat, cook for 35 minutes per kg (15 minutes per lb); for medium cook for 45 minutes per kg (20 minutes per lb); if you prefer your beef well done, cook for 55 minutes per kg (25 minutes per lb).
2 Sprinkle black pepper over the beef. If you would like a dry crust on the surface, rub a little seasoned flour, perhaps also flavoured with dry mustard, over the fat; some people like to do this to the meat as well.
3 Place the beef with the rib bones pointing upwards, or balanced on the two ends of the bones with the fat uppermost, in a roasting tin that will hold it comfortably. (If the tin is too small, the joint will steam and if it is too large, the juices will burn.)
4 To begin with, roast the joint for about 15 minutes until it is well browned on the outside. Then lower the temperature to 180°C (350°F, gas mark 4) and continue the roasting for the time you have calculated it needs. Baste the roast frequently with the meat juices during cooking so it does not become too dry. Meanwhile, put a carving dish to warm.
5 Transfer the beef to the warmed carving dish, cover loosely with a

Perfect roast beef is rosy in the centre and splendid served with béarnaise sauce. Offer horseradish as well, along with roast potatoes and Yorkshire pudding.

dome of foil and leave to rest in a warm place for at least 15 minutes.
6 Carve the rib (see CARVING) and serve with gravy, Yorkshire pudding and horseradish or béarnaise sauce.

RAISED WITH KINDNESS

How can I tell if the meat I buy comes from an animal that has been raised kindly?

Apart from the humane aspect, it is generally believed that happier animals produce more tender meat. In fact, all animals should be reared and slaughtered according to basic legal welfare standards.

If you are concerned that even greater care and attention have been paid, find a sympathetic butcher who knows about the origins of the meat being sold and how the animals have been treated. You could also look for ranges of meat that have special accredited labels, such

as the RSPCA's Freedom Food or one guaranteeing organic rearing (see MEAT and ADDITIVES).

DISEASE-FREE

How can I be sure that the beef I buy is free from the disease BSE?

All British beef on sale should be clear of BSE (bovine spongiform encephalopathy). Parts of dead animals that could carry disease (the head, brain, intestines, spinal cord and offal from cattle aged over six months old, and the intestines and thymus gland from calves) may not be sold. Cattle over 30 months old may not be sold for beef, and the carcasses of younger cattle must be boned in licensed plants and the possibly infected trimmings destroyed. If an animal is thought to be infected with BSE, the whole body is destroyed. Precautions are being taken, but no guarantee is total.

BEER

COOKING WITH BEER

Which beer is best for cooking?

Any type of beer can be used for cooking. Strong, full-bodied ales and stout are the best for braising, stewing, casseroling or marinating dark meats and game; dark beer, particularly stout, will add a rich colour. The slight bitterness of strong ales and some stouts is used to counteract the richness of strongly flavoured meats such as venison, and also the sweetness imparted by some vegetables, such as carrots, onions and parsnips. Strong ale or stout can also be used to enrich sweet puddings, such as Christmas pudding. The very slight bitterness is the perfect foil for the sweetness of the fruit.

Light ales and lager go well with chicken, fish, pork or rabbit. They can also be used in desserts, for poaching fruits and for making cakes and puddings.

BEER FOR CARBONADE

Which beer should be used to cook the Flemish version of beef carbonade? When I made the dish recently it tasted very bitter. Was the beer responsible and, if so, how could I have corrected it?

The traditional Flemish version uses a light beer, but a darker beer such as stout will give carbonade a richer colour and flavour. The degree of bitterness varies from one brand of stout to another, and will be reflected in the dish. The bitterness in your beef carbonade could have been due to burning the onions slightly when frying, but it is more likely that you chose a beer that was too bitter. Next time, try using a light Belgian beer.

Adding a bit more brown sugar, which is traditionally part of the recipe anyway, would have helped to counteract the bitterness. You could also have added extra gently fried onions for sweetness.

CRISPY BATTER

I have heard that beer can be used to make a tasty batter. How is such a coating made?

Light ale or lager can be mixed into a crisp batter for coating meat and fish as well as fruit and vegetables. Guinness can also be used to make a batter for oysters. The following recipe uses a light ale batter to coat a mixture of ready-prepared frozen seafood. You can also use whatever other combination of seafood you prefer, such as prawns, squid and strips of sole or plaice.

Seafood in light ale batter

SERVES: 4
PREPARATION TIME: 20 minutes plus
1 hour standing time
COOKING TIME: about 25 minutes

FOR THE BATTER
150 g (5 ½ oz) plain flour
A pinch of salt
225 ml (8 fl oz) light ale or lager
25 g (1 oz) butter, melted

FOR THE SEAFOOD
800 g (1 lb 12 oz) frozen fruits de
    mer (an equally divided mixture
    of mussels, tiger prawns, scallops
    and squid rings), thawed
50 g (1 ¾ oz) plain flour
Salt and black pepper
3 tablespoons chopped fresh dill
2 tablespoons chopped fresh parsley
About 1.5 litres (2 pints 15 fl oz)
    corn or vegetable oil for
    deep-frying
1 egg white, size 2
To garnish: 3 tablespoons chopped
    fresh dill or parsley, and some
    lemon wedges

1 To make the batter, sift the flour and salt into a large mixing bowl and make a well in the centre. Pour in the beer and whisk to a thick batter.
2 Whisk in the melted butter then cover and leave to stand for an hour.
3 Drain the thawed seafood and dry it well with kitchen paper. Divide the various different types of seafood into separate groups.
4 Put the 50 g (1 ¾ oz) of flour into a large bowl and season it well with

salt and pepper, then add the herbs and mix well together so that all the flavours are blended.
5 Half fill a deep-frying pan with oil and heat it until it reaches 190°C (375°F) on a frying thermometer. If you do not have a thermometer, drop a cube of dry bread into the oil; it should brown in about 30 seconds.
6 Meanwhile, preheat the oven to 150°C (300°F, gas mark 2) and line two large baking trays with pieces of kitchen paper.
7 To complete the batter, whisk the egg white until stiff but not dry, then gently fold it into the batter mixture.
8 Add the mussels to the seasoned flour and toss them until lightly coated. Remove them from the flour, shaking off the excess, and put them into the batter. With your fingers, gently turn the mussels in the batter until evenly coated. Lift them out carefully one at a time, allowing the excess batter to run into the bowl.
9 Carefully drop the coated mussels into the hot oil and then cook for about 2 - 3 minutes until the batter is crisp and golden brown, turning to ensure an even browning. Remove the mussels with a slotted spoon and drain them well on one of the baking trays, then transfer to the second tray and keep warm in the oven.
10 Flour and batter the prawns as you did the mussels, then cook them in two batches. Coat and cook the scallops in the same way, also in two batches, and repeat with the squid.
11 Arrange the seafood pieces on a heated serving dish and garnish with chopped dill or parsley.
12 Serve with lemon wedges, crusty bread and add a bit of colour with a tossed mixed-leaf salad.

Deep-frying in batches

Do not be tempted to deep-fry too many pieces of food at any one time as this causes the oil temperature to drop and the food then becomes soggy. Cook only six to eight pieces at a time, and give the oil an opportunity to come back to temperature in between.

BEETROOT

HOT AND COLD

Why is beetroot almost always sold cooked? Is it edible raw?

You can grate raw beetroot into a salad or add it to the Russian soup borscht, but this rather misses the soft, voluptuous sweetness that is a main feature of this tasty vegetable. Cooking is quite a lengthy process and must be done while the beetroot is unpeeled. Any break that is made in the skin will allow the crimson juices to leak into the cooking water, leaving a vegetable that is pale and less flavoursome. There is no advantage in cooking beetroot yourself, although this is necessary if you grow your own.

The cooked and peeled beetroot can be reheated in a sauce or dressed cold as a salad, but be aware that it is likely to stain everything it touches (including your clothes). This colouring can be used to good effect in a white sauce, but it is prudent to partner beetroot with other red vegetables in a mixed salad – for example, sliced onto a bed of radicchio and garnished with red onion rings.

Beetroot goes well with sharp fruits, beetroot and orange being a popular mix, served hot or cold. Arrange an appealing salad with alternating slices of orange and beetroot garnished with chives, coriander leaves or parsley. Or try this unusual blend of beetroot and rhubarb (above right). The timbales are an excellent partner to spring lamb, duck breast, venison or saddle of hare. Bake them on the bottom shelf, below the meat.

Stylish dressing

A simple dressing for sliced hot beetroot is a spoonful of good marmalade thinned lightly with fresh orange juice. Garnish with coriander leaves or ground seeds.

Beetroot and rhubarb timbales

SERVES: 4
PREPARATION TIME: 20 minutes
COOKING TIME: 45 minutes

---

150 g (5 ½ oz) trimmed rhubarb, cut into 2.5 cm (1 in) pieces
4 tablespoons ruby port
75 ml (2 ½ fl oz) crème fraîche
175 g (6 oz) beetroot, cooked, peeled and sliced
½ teaspoon ground cumin
2 eggs, size 2
Salt and black pepper
Cayenne pepper
½ - 1 teaspoon sugar
To garnish: sprigs of fresh dill

---

1 Preheat the oven to 200°C (400°F, gas mark 6). Generously butter four cocotte pots or heatproof teacups.

2 Put the rhubarb and the port into a pan, cover and cook for 10 minutes or until the rhubarb collapses.
3 Put all but a tablespoon of the crème fraîche into a food processor. Add the beetroot and the cumin, break in the eggs and process.
4 Add the cooked rhubarb to the mixture and process briefly again to a chunky purée. Season with salt, plenty of black pepper, a pinch or two of cayenne and sugar to taste.
5 Spoon into pots, banging them down lightly to settle. Stand the pots in a roasting tin and pour in boiling water to halfway up the sides of the pots. Bake for 45 minutes.
6 Remove the pots from the water and allow to cool before turning out.
7 Add a swirl of the reserved crème fraîche to each timbale if you like, along with a sprig of dill.

Timbales of beetroot and rhubarb, enriched with crème fraîche, are an unusual accompaniment to strong-tasting meats such as duck breast. Use dill to garnish.

BISCUITS

AVOIDING BURNT EDGES

Why do my biscuits always burn?

Oven temperatures do vary. If you think your oven may be slightly too hot, check the heat by using an oven thermometer (see OVENS AND HOBS). An extra minute or two can be crucial when you are baking thin biscuits, and you may find you need to use a slightly lower setting than the one indicated. Avoid the temptation to overcook. Cooked biscuits may seem soft when they have just come out of the oven, but they will be firm and crisp when cool. These sturdy biscuits (below) are less likely to burn than more fragile recipes, and they make good healthy treats for lunch boxes.

Raisin and hazelnut oat cookies

MAKES: about 30
PREPARATION TIME: 20 minutes
COOKING TIME: 12 - 15 minutes per batch (or 35 - 45 minutes for the full three batches)

125 g (4 1/2 oz) butter plus extra for greasing
125 g (4 1/2 oz) light, soft-brown muscovado sugar
175 g (6 oz) self-raising wholemeal flour
A pinch of salt
50 g (1 3/4 oz) rolled porridge oats
25 g (1 oz) hazelnuts, shelled and chopped
50 g (1 3/4 oz) seedless raisins
1 1/2 tablespoons black treacle
1 egg, size 3, beaten

1 Preheat the oven to 180°C (350°F, gas mark 4) and then grease three baking sheets with butter.
2 Melt the rest of the butter gently in a pan. Remove it from the heat and stir in the remaining ingredients until they are well mixed.
3 Scoop rounded teaspoons from the mixture and roll into balls the size of a walnut, then place the balls on the baking sheets.

4 Bake for 12 - 15 minutes or until set. Cool for 1 - 2 minutes on baking sheets, then transfer the cookies to a wire rack until cold. Store them in an airtight tin for up to a week.

DIFFICULT DIGESTIVES

Is there an easy recipe for good digestive biscuits?

Home-cooked food often tastes the best but digestive biscuits are an exception to the rule. There is no easy way to match the texture and flavour of those that are produced by commercial companies, and the special recipes they use are a very closely guarded secret.

KEEPING IN SHAPE

Why do my biscuits spread all over the tray, even though I am careful to spoon out only very small quantities of the mixture?

While some types of biscuits, such as brandy snaps, are meant to spread, others should hold their shape during cooking. Be sure to measure the ingredients accurately. Fat and sugar melt during cooking, and using too much of either will cause the biscuits to spread and merge into one another. Leave a space between each portion, about 7.5 cm (3 in), to allow room for some widening. This allows each biscuit to keep its shape.

Check that you are using the type of fat that is recommended. If a recipe uses butter and you want to use margarine, choose a type that is suitable for cooking. Firm packet or block margarine is better for biscuit mixtures than a softer margarine meant for spreading.

The recipe given for Refrigerator Biscuits (right) avoids the problem of spreading by including a large amount of flour to fat. This helps the biscuits to retain their shape well. The dough will keep in the refrigerator for up to a week (so you can slice and cook fresh biscuits when needed), or it can be frozen for up to two months. Defrost it at room temperature for 15 minutes, then slice and bake.

Lemon or orange refrigerator biscuits

MAKES: about 55 - 60
PREPARATION TIME: 25 minutes plus 1 hour chilling
COOKING TIME: 10 - 12 minutes per batch (or 30 - 35 minutes for the full three batches)

125 g (4 1/2 oz) butter, softened, plus extra for greasing
125 g (4 1/2 oz) caster sugar
1 egg, size 3
Grated rind of 1 large lemon or 1 medium orange
225 g (8 oz) plain flour
1 teaspoon baking powder
To decorate: flaked almonds

1 Butter two or three baking sheets. Cream the butter and sugar until light. Beat in the egg and the rind. Sift the flour and baking powder together, then add them to the butter mixture and mix well to make a dough. Alternatively, you can make the dough in a food processor. Put the ingredients into the bowl and then process for 30 seconds.
2 Knead the dough lightly on a floured surface until smooth, then return it to the bowl, cover and chill for about 30 minutes.
3 Divide the dough in half and form each portion into a roll about 20 cm (8 in) long. Wrap each roll separately in foil or cling film. Return to the refrigerator for a further 30 minutes.
4 Preheat the oven to 180°C (350°F, gas mark 4).
5 Cut the roll into 5 mm (1/4 in) thick slices and place them on the baking sheets, putting a few almond flakes on top of each biscuit.
6 Bake for 10 - 12 minutes or until the biscuits are pale golden. Leave them to cool slightly, then transfer to a wire rack and leave until cold.
7 Store the biscuits in an airtight tin for up to a week.

Sweet solution

Putting a few sugar cubes in your biscuit tins helps to keep biscuits crisp and fresh for much longer.

Gingerbread men

MAKES: 10 - 12, using a
13 cm (5 in) cutter
PREPARATION TIME:
30 minutes
COOKING TIME: 15 - 20
minutes per batch

250 g (9 oz) plain flour
A pinch of salt
1 teaspoon ground ginger
1 teaspoon bicarbonate of
  soda
60 g (2 1/4 oz) butter, plus
  extra for greasing
60 g (2 1/4 oz) caster sugar
1 1/2 tablespoons golden
  syrup
3 tablespoons black treacle
1/2 egg, size 3, beaten
To decorate: 2 tablespoons
  currants, a 5 cm (2 in)
  piece of glacé angelica,
  washed, dried and sliced,
  or 12 small orange and
  lemon jelly slices plus
  1 tablespoon icing

1 Preheat the oven to 180°C
(350°F, gas mark 4). Butter
and lightly flour two large
baking sheets.
2 Sift the flour, salt, ginger
and bicarbonate of soda into
a mixing bowl and make a
well in the centre.
3 Put the butter, sugar, syrup
and treacle into a heavy pan
and stir them over a low heat
until all are melted. Pour the
mixture into the flour.
4 Add the egg and, using a
wooden spoon, mix to a firm
dough. The dough may be
sticky when warm, but it gets
firmer as it cools so do not
knead in extra flour as it may
become too dry.
5 Roll out the dough on a
lightly floured surface to
3 mm (1/8 in) thick. Using a
gingerbread man cutter, cut
out as many shapes as you
can. With a palette knife,
carefully lift the gingerbread
men onto the baking sheets.
6 Form the leftover dough
into a ball, roll again and cut
out more shapes. Repeat the

FANCY BISCUITS

◆

*Festive biscuits are fun to make for all
manner of parties and celebrations. Small
children will enjoy helping you to decorate the
gingerbread men and iced biscuits, or tying
sparkling biscuits onto the Christmas tree.
Gift-wrapped florentines make a personal
present for grown-up friends.*

*Hot from the oven and awaiting their colourful decorations are
homemade party biscuits, florentines and gingerbread men.*

rolling and cutting until all
the dough has been used.
7 Press two currants onto
each head to make the eyes
and place more down the
front for the buttons.
8 If you want to make green
bow ties, cut the angelica
into strips and shape them
into two small triangles. Put
them in place and press down
slightly. (Jelly or iced bow
ties are added after cooking.)
9 Bake for 15 - 20 minutes
until the biscuits are cooked.
Do not overcook them. The
biscuits may still be soft
when you take them out
of the oven, but they
will turn crisp as
they cool
down.

Leave them to cool on the
tray for 5 minutes then leave
on wire racks until cold.
10 Wash the baking sheets,
butter them again and bake
the next batch of biscuits.
11 To make bow ties from
the jelly slices, cut each slice
almost in half and open it out
to form a bow tie. Stick them
on with a dab of icing. Iced
bow ties are added using a
piping bag fitted with a fine
writing pipe, and royal icing.
12 Store the biscuits in an
airtight tin for up to a week.

Christmas tree biscuits

MAKES: 16
PREPARATION TIME:
50 minutes
COOKING TIME: 20 - 25
minutes for 2 batches

150 g (5 1/2 oz) plain flour
25 g (1 oz) cornflour
1/2 teaspoon baking powder
85 g (3 oz) caster sugar
85 g (3 oz) butter, diced
1 egg white, size 3
16 small fruit-flavoured
  clear boiled sweets, in
  assorted colours
Thin coloured ribbon

1 Preheat the oven to 180°C
(350°F, gas mark 4), and line
two large baking trays with
baking paper.
2 Put the flour, cornflour,
baking powder and sugar
into a bowl. Add the butter
and rub in until the mixture
resembles fine breadcrumbs.
3 Stir in the egg white and
mix to a fairly soft dough.
4 Knead the dough lightly
until smooth and free from
cracks, then roll it out 5 mm
(1/4 in) thick. Cut out shapes
using a 9 cm (3 1/2 in) round
cutter or star cutter.
5 With biscuit cutters 2.5 cm
(1 in) in diameter, cut a circle
or heart out of the centre of
each biscuit. Then spread out
the biscuits on one of the
prepared baking trays.
6 Place one boiled sweet in
each biscuit 'window'. Push a
skewer through the biscuit to

make a hole large enough for a ribbon to pass through.

7 Bake for 10 - 12 minutes, until the sweets have melted and filled the centres and the biscuits are pale gold. Leave to cool on the trays, then re-mark holes with a skewer.

8 Meanwhile, roll out the rest of the dough, cut out the next batch of biscuits, place on the second tray and bake.

9 When all the biscuits have cooled, peel off the baking paper. Pass a ribbon through each hole and tie the biscuits onto the tree. They will keep for two to three days.

Iced party biscuits

MAKES: 20 - 24
PREPARATION TIME:
55 minutes
COOKING TIME: 8 - 10 minutes
per batch of 2 sheets

Use the Christmas Tree Biscuit dough (left) to make these biscuits, plus
To decorate: 175 g (6 oz) icing sugar, sifted; 2 edible food colourings; desiccated coconut, silver balls and hundreds and thousands

1 Preheat the oven to 180°C (350°F, gas mark 4). Line two baking sheets with baking paper. Roll out the dough to 5 mm (¼ in) thick and cut it into fancy shapes. Lay them out on the baking sheets and cook for 8 - 10 minutes until golden. Cool on a wire rack.

2 To decorate, mix the icing sugar with a tablespoon or two of warm water to make a paste dense enough to coat a spoon thickly.

3 Divide the icing between three cups. Leave one white

then add a little colouring, drop by drop from a skewer, to each of the other two cups and mix it in well.

4 Quickly spoon a little icing over each biscuit, spreading it to the edges. Before it sets, sprinkle on some desiccated coconut, silver balls and hundreds and thousands.

5 The biscuits may be stored without icing in an airtight tin for about a week. Icing tends to soften them, so once they are decorated, it is best to eat them the same day.

Florentines

MAKES: 20 - 24
PREPARATION TIME:
30 minutes, plus 15 minutes for chocolate decoration
COOKING TIME: 10 minutes per batch of 4

60 g (2¼ oz) unsalted butter
60 g (2¼ oz) demerara sugar
1 tablespoon golden syrup
25 g (1 oz) plain flour, sifted
60 g (2¼ oz) flaked almonds
60 g (2¼ oz) glacé cherries, roughly chopped
25 g (1 oz) glacé angelica, finely chopped
60 g (2¼ oz) chopped mixed peel
175 g (6 oz) dark chocolate

1 Preheat the oven to 180°C (350°F, gas mark 4), and line two large baking trays with baking paper.

2 Melt the butter, sugar and syrup in a small saucepan over a low heat, then remove the pan from the heat. Add the flour, flaked almonds, glacé cherries, angelica and mixed peel. Stir the mixture gently until blended.

3 Dot the baking sheets with small heaped teaspoons of the mixture, leaving 7.5 cm (3 in) between each biscuit. Flatten slightly into a circular shape.

4 Bake for 10 minutes or until just set and golden. Cool for 1 - 2 minutes until beginning to firm, then lift with a palette knife and put on a rack to cool. Leave until cold and crisp.

5 Line the baking sheets with fresh paper and bake the next batch.

6 Meanwhile, break the chocolate into a basin, set it over a pan of simmering water and leave it until it is melted and smooth.

7 Take the pan off the heat. Using a small palette knife, spread the smooth side of each biscuit with a thin layer of chocolate and draw a wavy line with a fork. Place on a wire rack and leave for the chocolate to harden.

8 Store the biscuits in an airtight tin, layered between baking paper to protect them, for three to four days.

CHRISTMAS TREE BISCUIT

ICED PARTY BISCUITS

FLORENTINES

GINGERBREAD MEN

BISQUE

RICH SHELLFISH SOUP

I see bisque on restaurant menus, but am never sure what it is...

Bisque is a thick shellfish soup, most commonly made with lobster or prawn. (The term was once also applied to a purée of game or poultry.) The soups are well flavoured and often slightly spicy, getting their distinctive coral colour from the shells which are boiled up with the fish stock: the recipe was originally invented as a way of using up damaged shellfish. Bisques are often flambéed with brandy and wine, as in the recipe below.

Lobster bisque

SERVES: 4
PREPARATION TIME: 1 hour
COOKING TIME: 45 minutes

500 g (1 lb 2 oz) cooked lobster
25 g (1 oz) butter
1 small onion, sliced
1 small carrot, sliced
1 stick celery, sliced
1 tablespoon brandy
60 g (2¼ oz) rice
150 ml (5 fl oz) dry white wine
Flavourings: 1 bay leaf,
*   2 – 3 parsley stalks, 1 blade of*
*   mace and 1 strip of lemon peel*
2 teaspoons lemon juice
½ teaspoon salt
A pinch of cayenne pepper
150 ml (5 fl oz) single cream,
*   optional*

FOR THE LOBSTER BUTTER
25 g (1 oz) softened butter
Reserved lobster coral, tomalley
*   and flaked claw meat*
½ teaspoon tomato purée, optional

1 With a large, sharp cook's knife, cut the lobster in half lengthways. Remove and discard the stomach sac from the head and the thread-like intestine running along the tail meat. Also remove but reserve the coral (roe) if there is any, and creamy green liver, known as tomalley.

2 Crack open all the shells and remove the meat, but do not throw the shells away. Cut the body meat into chunks, flake the rest of the meat, and reserve the lot.
3 Put the shells in a plastic bag and crush coarsely with a rolling pin, or cut up with kitchen scissors.
4 Melt the butter in a large pan and add the vegetables and the shells. Fry over a medium heat for 5 minutes, stirring occasionally.
5 Remove from the heat, pour in the brandy and carefully ignite.
6 When the flames are out, add the rice, wine and flavourings, and pour on 1.5 litres (2 pints 15 fl oz) of cold water. Bring to the boil and simmer, uncovered, for 30 minutes.
7 Liquidise all the contents of the pan. Rub the purée through a sieve to remove any bits of shell, ensuring all the rice is pushed through.
8 Return to a clean pan and bring gently to the boil, stirring from time to time. Season with lemon juice, salt and cayenne pepper to taste.
9 To make the lobster butter, blend the softened butter with the reserved coral and tomalley with a fork, then work in the reserved flaked claw meat. If you like, stir in the tomato purée to deepen the colour.
10 Gradually whisk the lobster butter into the soup then add the pieces of body meat. You can add the cream at this stage if you wish. Simmer for 2 minutes and serve.
VARIATION
Fresh lobster may be substituted for the cooked lobster (see LOBSTER for preparation), but the bisque will take longer to prepare.

Subtly spicy lobster bisque is even more luxurious when enriched with lobster butter, made by blending the reserved roe and tomalley with softened butter.

BLACK PUDDING

READY-TO-EAT SAUSAGE

Do I have to cook black pudding before eating it?

This black-skinned sausage is usually sliced and fried, traditionally for breakfast, but it is sold already cooked so it can also be eaten cold straight from the packet, in sandwiches and salads. The taste and texture could be described as similar to that of liver sausage.

Also known as blood sausage, because it is made mainly from pig's blood, black pudding originates from the Midlands and the north of England. The Irish version, drisheen, is made from either pig's or sheep's blood.

Apart from blood, which gives it the dark colour, black pudding contains oatmeal, groats (crushed grains of oat or wheat), onion, fat, herbs (traditionally pennyroyal, a type of mint) and spices. It will keep for only a few days in the refrigerator but can be frozen.

Continental versions of black pudding include French *boudin noir* and German *blutwurst*, which are both often served as a main meal with mashed potato and cooked apple. The Spanish version, *morcilla*, is one of the ingredients of *fabada*, a rich stew.

BLANCHING

RETAINING THE COLOUR

What is the point of going to the trouble of blanching vegetables?

Blanching and refreshing is a method of cooking vegetables for 1 – 2 minutes in boiling water and then cooling them rapidly in iced water. It is chiefly done to set the colour before they are added to another dish such as a stew, stir-fry, terrine or salad. This method of cooking is particularly suitable for green vegetables such as french beans as their colour becomes very intense and, as long as you reheat them rapidly, the colour remains.

Blanching is also a useful method of precooking a large quantity of vegetables, as they can be boiled in advance until nearly tender, refreshed and chilled and then swiftly reheated to final readiness when they are wanted.

The term comes from the French word for whiten and the technique was originally used to remove traces of blood from sweetbreads or brains, leaving them pale, or to boil off the brown skin of almonds, revealing the white kernels.

VITAMIN LOSS

Do you lose many vitamins by blanching vegetables and then reheating them?

If you blanch and refresh the vegetables rapidly, and also reheat them very quickly, the vitamin loss will only be slight. However, certain vitamins, such as vitamin C, are water-soluble and will leach out during any water-based cooking process, so it is wise practice to eat raw vegetables on a regular basis, as well as cooked ones.

BLACKBERRY, BLACKCURRANT, BLUEBERRY: see SOFT FRUIT

BOILING

SLOW TO FAST BOIL

What is the difference between boiling, poaching and simmering?

The three words all refer to cooking in liquid on top of the stove, but the temperatures are different. Many dishes described as boiled are in fact poached or simmered.

When water is heated up just enough to 'shiver' at about 82°C (180°F), it is perfect for poaching fish and other delicate foods which would otherwise break up.

A gentle simmer at 85–93°C (185–200°F) produces liquid that hardly moves except for occasional

bubbles in the same place in the pan (ideal for cooking joints of meat and whole birds).

A true boil is used for the quick cooking of vegetables, rice and pasta, and for boiling puddings, some cereals and dumplings. A gentle boil is used to reduce liquids when making jams and sauces.

BOILING MEAT OR FISH

Are boiled beef and other similar dishes really boiled?

When a recipe refers to boiled beef, fish or chicken, it really means it should be simmered as any meat or fish subjected to fast boiling throughout cooking would become tough and flavourless.

Unlike braising and stewing, the cooking liquid used in boiled meats is not generally part of the finished dish, but it is often used to make the sauce (this is especially common with chicken) or kept to use as a stock (boiled beef or ham). Bacon stock can be used as the basis for a delicious pea soup.

PRESERVING NUTRIENTS

I have read that boiling is not the best way to cook vegetables. If this is true, what are the alternatives?

Boiling often results in a considerable loss of nutritional value, as many vitamins are lost if the cooking water is discarded. Vegetables cooked for only a few minutes will retain more vitamins than vegetables boiled for longer. It takes no more time to steam vegetables (cooking them above boiling water rather than in it), and this method retains more of their nutritional goodness and flavour.

The best equipment for steaming is a bamboo or metal steamer, or a collapsible steamer that can be put inside a saucepan. Bring the water to a rolling boil (with bubbles all over) and add the vegetables spread out in a single layer. The rack should be about 2.5 cm (1 in) above the boiling water and the steamer should be covered with a tightly fitting lid to retain the heat.

Skimming the surface

When simmering meat, add a spoonful of cold water to the pan every now and then to encourage the impurities to rise. When the liquid comes to a boil again, take the pan off the heat and skim off any scum with a metal spoon.

COOKING ROOTS

Should root vegetables be boiled more fiercely than leaf vegetables?

No, root vegetables such as potatoes should be covered with cold unsalted water and simmered to cook them through. Green leaf vegetables should be plunged into a large quantity of salted boiling water and cooked quickly to keep their colour, taste and nutrients.

PARBOILING METHOD

What is parboiling and what are the advantages of this?

Parboiling means partly boiling vegetables so that further cooking produces the right finished result. It is similar to blanching, but the vegetables are cooked longer (for 10 minutes rather than one or two).

For example, vegetables that will be roasted or deep-fried are often parboiled first to ensure they are fully cooked inside when golden and crisp outside. Parboiling may be done ahead of time and the partly cooked vegetables kept in the refrigerator for up to 24 hours.

ADDING SALT

When boiling vegetables, should salt be added before or after the water comes to the boil?

Salt water boils at a lower temperature than plain water so the water will come to the boil faster if you add the salt at the start. But remember that you do not have to add salt at all. Try reducing the amount you use, or leaving it out altogether and see if you can acquire a taste for healthier vegetables.

BONING

ADVANTAGES OF BONING

I sometimes see recipes that call for boned poultry or joints. As it seems to take a great deal of time and effort, is it really worth it?

The great advantage of serving boned meat or poultry is first that it is much easier to carve and second that it goes much farther. For example, a 1.5 kg (3 lb 5 oz) chicken with stuffing will serve eight to ten people. When you are catering for large numbers, boned poultry is particularly useful.

Although boning poultry for the first time can be daunting, it becomes much easier with practice (see the box on the opposite page). And you don't have to do it all at once: if you like, do the boning in stages – just cover the bird loosely with cling film and refrigerate it each time you have a break. People with little experience of boning will probably find it easier and quicker to deal with a leg of lamb, as there are only three large bones to remove (see box, below).

Boning meat or poultry enables you to use plenty of delicious stuffing, which will keep the meat very moist during cooking. For chicken, try a stuffing made with ricotta and Parmesan cheeses, black olives, basil and pine nuts – all bound together with egg. Or try mixing pistachio nuts and chopped dried apricots with chicken livers and some fresh white breadcrumbs, also bound together with egg.

Turkey takes particularly well to a sausage-meat stuffing. For a traditional stuffing, add chopped mint, parsley, sage and thyme to the sausage meat. For a spicier version, add caramelised onion, sultanas, a pinch of cayenne pepper and some ground cumin. Duck and goose harmonise well with fruit, and citrus fruit in particular cuts through the fattiness. A small grain such as bulgur wheat or couscous makes a good stuffing base to which you can add a little orange juice, a few sliced kumquats, ginger and some chopped red onion.

And a boned leg of lamb can be enriched by an Arabian stuffing of apricots, bulgur wheat, nuts and oranges (see LAMB).

BUTCHERS' SERVICE

Can I ask a butcher to do the boning for me?

Yes, if you are a regular customer and are able to give a few days' notice. But do not expect a stranger to be willing to do this for you as there is little profit in it.

BONING A LEG OF LAMB

Boning a leg of lamb enables you to add a stuffing, which will give the meat extra flavour and succulence, and makes it very easy to carve. Or you can lay it flat under the grill or on a barbecue, skin side nearest the heat, where it will cook in just 15 minutes, being turned once. To ensure a neat, easy job, use a narrow, rigid boning knife.

1 There are three bones to remove: the shank bone, which juts out of the meat at the narrow end; the middle bone, which is attached to the shank bone by a ball and socket joint; and the V-shaped pelvic bone, which turns across the thick end of the joint.

2 Lay the leg fleshy side down. Start at the shank end and, holding the knife like a dagger, cut through the flesh down to the shank bone beneath. Change your grip to the normal one and cut along the bone, keeping the knife as close to the bone as possible, so as not to waste any of the meat.

3 Scrape round the ball and socket joint then cut along the middle and pelvic bones. Use your fingers to locate each bone in turn and work from both ends of the leg if you find it easier. Gradually ease the bones out, one by one. The boned meat is now ready to be stuffed, rolled and tied up for roasting.

4 To open the boned meat out flat for grilling (known as butterfly boning), make two further parallel cuts through the thick pieces of meat on either side of the space left by the middle bone. Beat the meat once or twice with a wooden mallet to even out the thickness, then grill or barbecue.

BONING CHICKEN

You can bone all poultry by the same method, bearing in mind that the carcass of goose or turkey is very much larger than that of a chicken. Essential tools for the job are a sharp kitchen knife and kitchen scissors.

1 Put the chicken breast side down and cut through to the backbone. Feel for the fleshy 'oyster' at the top of each thigh and cut round it to remove it from its pocket, then gently scrape the flesh away from the carcass.

2 Continue cutting away from the backbone until the whole rib cage is exposed. Where the thigh meets the pelvis, cut through the sockets so that the legs stay attached to the body flesh and skin, not to the carcass.

3 Keep working right round the bird, then use scissors to cut off most of the rib cage, leaving only the breastbone in the centre. With a heavy knife, cut through the foot joints to remove the knuckle end of the legs.

4 Working from inside the top of the thigh, scrape the leg bone clean, pushing the flesh down until you can free the bone. Remove the tendons, then bone the other leg.

5 Now for the wings. Cut off the pinions (the last small bone on the wing which has no real meat) with a heavy knife and scrape the wing bones clean as you did the leg bones.

6 Carefully lift up and scrape the breastbone free, working from the middle of the bird towards the tail. Take care not to puncture the skin, as there is no flesh under it at this point.

7 Keep the neck flap of skin intact, and fold it over once the chicken has been stuffed. Seal as much of the stuffing as possible, then sew up the bird or wrap it in a roasting net.

TRUSSING AND TYING

How do I tie up a boned bird?

There are two ways. You can either sew up a stuffed and rolled bird using a trussing needle and string, sewing across one end first, down the length of the roll and then across the other end.

Alternatively, you can fold the bird into shape around the stuffing then wrap it in a piece of muslin or a roasting net. Dip the cloth in melted butter or oil and wring out lightly. Put the stuffed bird in the centre of the cloth, flap side uppermost, then wrap the cloth around it tightly, securing it at both ends with string like a Christmas cracker.

The cooking time should be calculated according to the bird's weight after it has been stuffed, using the table in ROASTING. Be sure it is fully cooked through, particularly if you have used a sausage-meat stuffing. Check by inserting a skewer into the centre of the joint – the juices should run clear.

If you have wrapped the bird in muslin there is no need to baste it during cooking – but remove the cloth before the bird is completely cold or it will stick.

BRAINS: see OFFAL

BRAISING

GENTLE COOKING

What is the difference between braising and stewing?

Braising is a method of cooking meat and poultry slowly in a covered pan, using a bed of chopped vegetables which can also include diced ham or bacon for flavour. Water or stock should be added to come halfway up the joint.

Braising tends to use a slightly better cut of meat than stewing and a whole cut is generally chosen. The meat is usually fried briefly to brown it first, then placed in a pan or casserole with a tight-fitting lid and cooked either on the hob or in the oven. It cooks gently in its own juices and the steam from the vegetables, which impart their flavour.

The term 'braising' is also used sometimes to mean cooking vegetables in the oven in a covered dish with a little liquid. For example, heads of celery are braised in vegetable or meat stock.

Stewing is a method in which the added liquid (beer, cider, stock, water or wine) covers the meat and is heated to just under boiling point. This technique is reserved for the toughest cuts of meat which need long, slow cooking, and the meat is generally cut into chunks to aid the tenderising process.

Leftovers

When braising meat, chop any leftover bones, such as those from a chicken carcass, and add them to the bed of chopped vegetables. The bones and vegetables are discarded after cooking, but they add extra flavour to the braising liquid and to the cut of meat.

RICH STOCK

Does braising meat create its own stock, or should I add some stock or alcohol for richness?

Braising meat produces a delicious, full-flavoured stock whether you use just water or add stock or alcohol. For a simple family supper, water flavoured with vegetables, herbs and black peppercorns produces a sufficiently well-flavoured dish. However, the addition of stock and/or wine enriches the taste and gives added flavour.

For a really elegant braised dish, set aside the cooked meat and keep it warm, then strain the stock, discarding the vegetables, and reduce it by rapid boiling to a syrupy consistency. Glaze the meat with the reduced sauce and garnish with other freshly cooked vegetables.

BEST FOR BRAISING

Which are the best ingredients to use for braising?

Tougher cuts of meat such as beef flank and older game birds are ideal candidates. They are often marinated in the braising liquid first to start the tenderising process and then cooked in a slow oven at 140°C (275°F, gas mark 1) with vegetables and herbs to add flavour. The traditional vegetables are leek or onion, carrot and celery.

Some other wonderful combinations are shin of beef with Spanish onions and thyme, or with onions, paprika and tomato purée. Venison is a very low-fat meat and is often braised to keep it moist. It is very tasty marinated and braised in red wine flavoured with garlic, juniper berries and orange peel. Pheasant is excellent braised in a mixture of chicken stock and white wine, with Cox's apples and celery.

Braising is also useful for vegetables with tough membranes which are then broken down by slow, moist cooking. Celery, for instance, is transformed into a mild aromatic dish when braised in stock and butter. Other vegetables that benefit from braising are fennel (delicious with olive oil and vermouth); artichoke hearts in beef stock with butter, thyme and a splash of red wine; leeks with butter and lemon juice; and chicory with chicken stock, butter and lemon juice.

BRAN

RICH IN FIBRE

What exactly is bran?

Bran is the husk, or outer layer, of all cereals, although wheat bran is the most common bran sold commercially. Bran is usually separated from the grain during the milling process of flour production. It is a valuable source of fibre and is an added ingredient in many breakfast cereals. It is also sold simply as bran, which can be used to enrich

breads, crispbreads and tea breads, or it can be toasted and used in muesli. In the recipe below, bran and seeds are toasted and mixed with dried fruits and oats to produce a muesli that is less sweet than most commercial brands.

Homemade muesli

MAKES: 8 – 10 breakfast portions
PREPARATION TIME: 5 minutes
COOKING TIME: 10 – 12 minutes

50 g (1 ³⁄₄ oz) wheat bran
50 g (1 ³⁄₄ oz) sunflower seeds
25 g (1 oz) poppy seeds
125 g (4 ¹⁄₂ oz) hazelnuts, finely chopped
225 g (8 oz) mixed dried fruits, such as apricots, cherries, figs, raisins and sultanas
125 g (4 ¹⁄₂ oz) dried banana chips
225 g (8 oz) jumbo oats
125 g (4 ¹⁄₂ oz) barley flakes
2 teaspoons ground cinnamon
To serve: milk, fresh fruits and brown sugar, optional

1 Dry-fry the bran, sunflower seeds and poppy seeds together in a large nonstick frying pan for 3 - 4 minutes or until they become golden and start to release their aroma. Transfer them to a large bowl.
2 Dry-fry the chopped hazelnuts for 5 - 6 minutes until browned. Add to the bran and leave to cool.
3 Cut the larger of the dried fruits into small chunks and stir them into the toasted mixture along with the oats, barley flakes and cinnamon. Transfer to an airtight container.
4 Serve the muesli as you wish with milk, chopped fresh fruits of your choice and a sprinkling of brown sugar if you fancy.

OFF THE SHELF

Where can I buy bran?

Nowadays, many of the large supermarkets sell packets of bran, and they are normally found near the breakfast cereals. You can also buy bran in most good health food stores. It keeps well in its sealed packet or an airtight container, in a cool place, for up to three months.

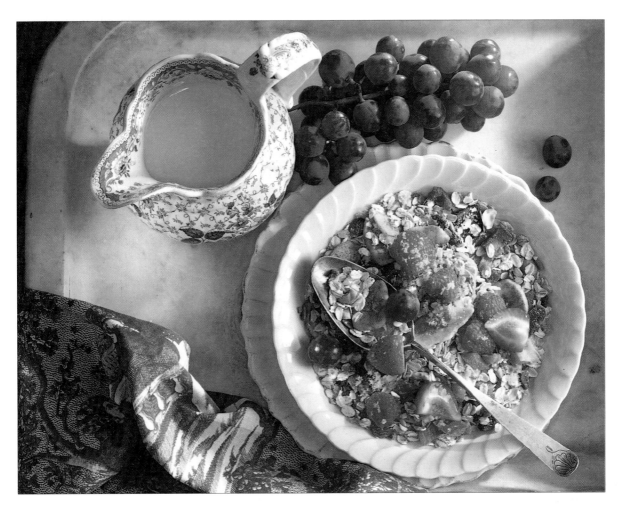

A dash of cinnamon, a scattering of seeds and nuts, and fresh and dried fruit add life to a homemade muesli.

BRANDY BUTTER

COUNTING CALORIES

Which is more fattening with my Christmas pudding, brandy butter or double cream?

It is hard to say which is the more fattening of the two, since a typical recipe for brandy butter contains less fat than full-fat double cream but more calories, because of its high sugar content.

In a recipe such as the one to the right, a tablespoon of brandy butter contains 6.1 g (about ⅛ oz) of fat and 91 Calories, whereas a table-spoon of full-fat double cream contains marginally more fat but only 67 Calories. Technically, you could substitute low or reduced-fat spreads for butter when making brandy butter, but that would be defeating the purpose of this rich indulgence. If you enjoy such luxuries only on special occasions, you should let your tastebuds decide which is best.

Brandy butter

SERVES: 6 - 8 (makes about 10 tablespoons)
PREPARATION TIME: 20 minutes
COOKING TIME: none

75 g (2 ¾ oz) unsalted butter, softened
75 g (2 ¾ oz) caster sugar
1 - 2 tablespoons brandy

1 Using a wooden spoon, beat the butter until it is white and creamy.

2 Add the sugar a little at a time, beating well after each addition, until it has all been incorporated.
3 Gradually beat in the brandy, adding a few drops at a time only and being careful not to allow the mixture to curdle.
4 Put the brandy butter in a suitable dish, cover with cling film and chill for 2 - 3 hours before serving.

VARIATIONS

If you prefer a smoother texture, use sifted icing sugar or a mix of half icing sugar, half caster sugar instead of caster sugar only.

For a change of flavour, add 50 g (1 ¾ oz) of ground almonds to the brandy butter before chilling, or a tablespoon of very finely chopped preserved stem ginger.

Or use a different alcohol, such as rum (perhaps with a dash of lemon juice) or whisky, with soft brown sugar instead of caster sugar.

BRANDY SNAPS

BE PREPARED

I love brandy snaps but they look very complicated and I have never summoned up the courage to make them. Is it difficult?

You don't need to be brave, but you do need to concentrate and be well prepared. Measure the ingredients accurately and, when melting the mixture, take care that it does not become too hot.

Line the metal baking trays with baking paper and leave plenty of space around each spoonful of the mixture on the sheet to allow for spreading. The biscuits should be about 7.5 cm (3 in) apart.

Cook no more than two trays at a time, or some biscuits may become too firm before you are ready to roll them into shape. If this should happen, simply return the tray to the oven for a few seconds to let them soften, then roll up.

Be sure to have several wooden spoons and a few wire racks to hand so that you can cope very quickly with rolling and cooling.

The recipe (right) makes crisp and delicate biscuits which go well with creamy desserts like syllabub or ice cream. Alternatively, simply fill them with cream or fruit.

Brandy snaps

MAKES: about 20
PREPARATION TIME: 35 - 40 minutes
COOKING TIME: 8 - 10 minutes for each batch

60 g (2 ¼ oz) unsalted butter, plus
    extra for greasing
60 g (2 ¼ oz) plain flour, sifted
1 teaspoon ground ginger
60 g (2 ¼ oz) caster sugar
3 tablespoons golden syrup
1 tablespoon brandy or lemon juice
150 ml (5 fl oz) double cream,
    whipped, optional

1 Lightly butter two baking sheets and line them with baking paper.
2 Preheat the oven to 180°C (350°F, gas mark 4) and be sure you have at least four wooden spoons to hand for rolling the biscuits round later.
3 Sift the flour and ground ginger into a small bowl.
4 Gently warm the butter, sugar and syrup in a small pan until the butter has melted. Remove from the heat and add the spiced flour and brandy or lemon juice. Stir until smooth.
5 Spoon level teaspoons of dough onto the baking sheets, spaced well apart as the mixture will spread. (Try about 4 teaspoons per baking sheet for the first batch and see how much room is needed.)
6 Bake for 8 - 10 minutes until the brandy snaps have spread and are golden brown. Remove the trays

from the oven. Leave the biscuits to cool for a minute or two, then gently loosen them with a palette knife. They should be firm but pliable.
7 Using both hands, roll the biscuits neatly but not too tightly around the handles of the wooden spoons. Place them on a wire rack and leave them to set for 1 - 2 minutes.
8 As soon as one has set, slide it off the spoon and leave it until cold and crisp. Store the brandy snaps in an airtight tin, layered between sheets of baking paper, for up to four days.
9 Before serving, put whipped cream into a piping bag fitted with a 1 cm (½ in) star nozzle. Pipe whirls of soft cream into the ends.

BREAD

FRESH OR NOT?

Why should bread a few days old be used for summer pudding and bread-and-butter pudding?

Fresh bread loses both shape and texture when it is moistened by a sauce, while bread that is a day or two old will absorb moisture and still retain its shape. Stale bread is also preferable for french toast since its firm shape makes it easier to crisp the outside when it is fried.

USE YOUR FIST

What does the term 'knocking back' bread dough mean?

It is the term used for punching the dough with the fist when it has risen to twice its original size. The punch helps to disperse the air bubbles that are produced by the yeast throughout the dough.

PROVING IN A MICROWAVE

When making bread, is it possible to speed up the proving/rising by using a microwave oven?

Yes, dough can be risen in a micro-wave oven. Once the dough is kneaded, place it in an ungreased bowl and cover it with lightly oiled cling film. Put the bowl in the oven

---

ROLLING BRANDY SNAPS

Use a palette knife to separate the baked brandy snaps from the metal sheets. With careful handling, the biscuits should shape easily around the handles of wooden spoons. Gently slide them off the handles when they are formed.

1 Loosen the brandy snaps from the baking sheet and roll them around the wooden spoon handles.

2 Remove the handles after a few minutes, when the biscuits are firm. Put the biscuits on a wire rack.

and heat on High for 10 seconds, then leave the bowl to stand for 20 minutes in the microwave or in a warm place, by which time the dough should have doubled in size. If it has not risen sufficiently, heat it on High for another 10 seconds, then stand for a further 10 minutes.

For the second rise, remember you cannot use a metal loaf tin in the microwave. If you have a nonmetallic tin, place the dough in it, microwave on High for 10 seconds, then let it stand for just 5 minutes. Continue with the recipe as usual after proving.

A CHOICE OF YEASTS

Does it make any difference whether you use fresh yeast or dried yeast in breadmaking?

There is little difference between the results achieved by using dried or fresh yeast. However, dried yeast is almost twice as concentrated as fresh, so in a recipe calling for 25 g (1 oz) of fresh yeast, use no more than 15 g (½ oz) dried. Easy-blend yeast is even more concentrated (see box, overleaf).

You will find that using a bit less yeast and leaving dough to prove longer produces a better-tasting and longer-lasting loaf. Any yeast can be used for this Classic White Loaf.

Freshly baked bread smells and tastes wonderful, and it need not take too much time or forward planning. You can use any type of yeast to make this white loaf.

Classic white loaf

MAKES: 2 small loaves
PREPARATION TIME: 25 minutes, plus 2 – 4 hours rising time
COOKING TIME: 40 minutes

---

15 g (½ oz) fresh yeast; or
  2 teaspoons dried yeast plus
  1 teaspoon sugar; or 1 sachet
  easy-blend yeast
300 ml (10 fl oz) lukewarm water
500 g (1 lb 2 oz) strong plain flour
2 teaspoons salt
15 g (½ oz) butter or lard
To glaze: a pinch of salt mixed with a little water

---

1 Blend the fresh yeast in the warm water. If using dried yeast, dissolve the sugar in the warm water first, then sprinkle in the dried yeast and set aside for 15 minutes until it is frothy. If using easy-blend yeast, add it directly to the flour.
2 Sieve the flour and salt into a large mixing bowl and rub in the fat. Pour the yeast mixture, or the lukewarm water if using easy-blend yeast, into the centre. Stir to form a dough, then knead with your hands until the dough gathers and leaves the side of the basin.
3 Turn it out onto a floured surface and knead for 10 minutes or until the dough is firm, not sticky.
4 Put the dough back into the bowl, cover with a polythene bag and leave in a warm place for 1 - 2 hours until doubled in volume.
5 Punch the raised dough down and knead well again. Grease two 450 g (1 lb) loaf tins. Divide the dough in

two and roll each portion lightly into a loaf shape to fit in the tin.
6 Place the dough, seam side down, in the prepared tins. Cover the tins loosely with polythene bags, and leave for about 40 minutes at room temperature for the bread to rise.
7 Preheat the oven to 230°C (450°F, gas mark 8). When the bread has risen, brush the top with some salted water, then bake for 35 minutes.
8 The loaves should have shrunk from the sides of the tins and if you remove them carefully, they should sound hollow when tapped on the base. If they do not sound hollow, return them to the tins and cook for just a few minutes more.
9 When the loaves are done, take them out of their tins and place on a wire rack to cool completely.

USING YEAST

Bread needs yeast to make it rise. While fresh yeast is both quick and easy to use, it may be difficult to find (try either health food shops or bakers' supplies stores).

Either plain dried yeast or easy-blend dried yeast can be bought in most supermarkets, and these can be used instead of the fresh variety. The quantities given below raise 500 g (1 lb 2 oz) of flour, which is enough to make two small loaves.

FRESH YEAST

To cream fresh yeast, combine 15 g (½ oz) of the yeast with the recipe's tepid (not hot) water in a bowl. Mash well with a fork until a very smooth paste is formed.

DRIED YEAST

To reactivate dried yeast, dissolve a teaspoon of sugar in the recipe's lukewarm water, then sprinkle over 2 teaspoons of the yeast and let it stand for 10 - 15 minutes until it is frothy. Stir the mixture well so it becomes a smooth paste.

EASY-BLEND YEAST

Easy-blend dried yeast is quick to use because it is added straight into the flour, and there is no need to mix it first with water. The easy-blend variety comes in small sachets of 6 or 7 g and one is equivalent to 15 - 25 g (½ - 1 oz) of fresh yeast or 2 teaspoons of dried yeast. Check the instructions before you mix.

STORING YEAST

How long does yeast keep?

Fresh yeast will keep for up to two weeks in a plastic storage box in the refrigerator. This box should have a tight lid in which you have made a few small air holes. There should be enough holes to prevent any condensation but not so many as to overexpose the yeast to air.

The yeast should be a creamy beige, smooth and in one piece. Yeast that is dry, crumbled and grey is stale and will not work.

Dried yeast should be stored in a cool, dry place. It will keep almost indefinitely, but try to observe the 'use-by' date on the packet. If you use it after the expiry date, always check that the yeast foams after it has dissolved. If it does not, the bread will not rise properly.

EASY MIXING

Is there a labour-saving way of making bread if you do not have a mixer with a dough hook?

A food processor will mix the bread ingredients together and will also form them into a ball so that considerably less kneading will be required. Bread that is made with wholemeal flour is much less work to produce because it has a low gluten content. It needs only a little kneading and then just one rising in the tin before being baked.

FRENCH COPY

Could I make French bread?

It is very difficult to make a good homemade baguette as it needs a special steam oven and French flour. Even the French sticks you see being made in supermarkets usually employ bread dough that has been imported from France.

KEEPING MELBA TOAST

How long can I keep Melba toast in a tin before it goes soft?

If the tin is airtight, crispy Melba toast can be kept for a few weeks before it will taste stale. If it goes

soft, it can be made crisp again by heating it briefly in a hot oven.

You can make Melba toast using ordinary sliced white bread. Toast the slices, cut off the crusts, and use a very sharp thin knife to cut each slice open and separate it into two thinner slices. Toast the inner slices under a grill, and then leave the bread to cool. Store the Melba toasts in an airtight container.

REACTIVE BUTTERMILK

Why is buttermilk an essential ingredient of soda bread?

Buttermilk is high in lactic acid, and when mixed with baking soda, which is an alkali, the chemical reaction that results produces a gas called carbonic acid. This has the effect of aerating the dough and making it much lighter. Soured cream can be substituted for buttermilk, as it is also acid.

SOURDOUGH STARTER

What is fermented dough starter?

It is a thick mixture of 15 g (½ oz) of dried yeast, 600 ml (1 pint) of water and 250 g (9 oz) of flour which is covered tightly and left at room temperature for about three days to develop sourdough flavour. The blend is used to leaven bread.

This initial dough starter can be replenished by adding equal parts of flour and water, and used again after 24 hours when it has risen and become bubbly. Using dough starter gives bread more flavour.

CRISPY SNACKS

What is the difference between brushetta and crostini?

Brushetta is the Italian version of garlic bread. Slices are grilled, then rubbed with garlic, dribbled with olive oil and sprinkled with salt. These slices are often topped with roasted peppers, cheese or cold meats (see page 263).

Crostini are simply small rounds of grilled bread, used as a base for spreads made with chicken livers or other ingredients (see page 13).

USING BREADCRUMBS

When should you use different types of breadcrumbs?

Dried white breadcrumbs are used for coating foods such as rissoles, veal or fish before frying. Use day-old bread from a farmhouse-type loaf, remove the crusts and place slices in one layer on a baking tray. Bake at 120°C (250°F, gas mark ½) for 15–20 minutes until the bread is dry, but do not allow it to colour.

Alternatively, you can leave the slices in a warm place for one to two days, covered with kitchen paper, until they are dry. Crush the dried crumbs with a rolling pin, or in a food processor.

Browned, dried breadcrumbs are used for covering ham and for gratins. Use crusts from farmhouse-type bread and dry at 120°C (250°F, gas mark ½) for about 30 minutes until they just begin to take on colour, then crush with a rolling pin or in a food processor. White crumbs fried in butter until golden are used for serving with game.

Fresh, white breadcrumbs are preferred for thickening sauces, for stuffings and bread sauce – and for adding to desserts such as treacle tart. Use day-old, rather than just-baked bread, and cut the crusts off. Either rub the pieces through a sieve with your palm, or make crumbs in a food processor.

TASTY WHOLEMEAL

I find wholemeal bread is often rather dry and unappetising. Is there a way of giving it a more interesting taste?

Wholemeal flour tends to make heavier bread than white, so if you mix a little white flour into a wholemeal loaf recipe, the bread will be lighter. Nuts also lighten the texture and add moisture.

The recipe for Walnut Bread (right) uses plenty of water and honey, which produces a very rich, moist appetising loaf that makes a great partner for cheese. For the maximum flavour, use the freshest walnuts that you can find.

Roughly chopped fresh walnuts add a crunchier texture to a simple wholemeal loaf, while a tablespoon of honey keeps the consistency light and moist.

Walnut bread

MAKES: 2 small loaves
PREPARATION TIME: 20–30 minutes, plus 2–3 hours rising time
COOKING TIME: 45 minutes

---

15 g (½ oz) fresh yeast; or
  2 teaspoons dried yeast plus
  1 teaspoon sugar; or 1 sachet
  easy-blend dried yeast
500 ml (18 fl oz) lukewarm water
1 tablespoon honey
375 g (13 oz) wholemeal flour
175 g (6 oz) strong white flour
2 teaspoons salt
Butter for greasing
125 g (4½ oz) walnuts, chopped
To glaze: 1 egg, size 2, beaten with
  ½ teaspoon salt

---

1 Dissolve the fresh or dried yeast in the water and honey. Add easy-blend dried yeast directly to the flour.
2 Sieve the flours and salt into a bowl. Make a well in the centre and add the yeasty water or plain water if using easy-blend yeast.
3 Stir with a wooden spoon to form a dough, adding a little more flour if the dough seems too moist, but keep it all as loose as you can possibly handle. This will make the final loaf that much lighter.
4 Turn out onto a floured board and knead for 10 minutes, flouring your hands if necessary, until the dough is smooth and elastic.
5 Lightly grease a bowl, put in the dough and cover with a polythene bag. Leave to rise in a warm place for about 1½–2 hours.
6 Grease two 18 cm (7 in) round cake tins. Punch the dough down and knead in the walnuts. Divide the dough in two and place each portion in a tin. Cover with polythene bags, allowing space for the bread to rise, and leave for about an hour until the dough has doubled in size.
7 Preheat the oven to 220°C (425°F, gas mark 7).
8 Slash the top of each loaf a few times with a sharp knife and brush with the egg glaze.
9 Bake for 15 minutes, then lower the heat to 190°C (375°F, gas mark 5) and bake for a further 30 minutes. Turn out onto a rack to cool.

HOMEMADE FOCACCIA

My family have grown to like the Italian breads ciabatta and focaccia but they are expensive. Could I make them myself?

Ciabatta is hard to reproduce at home as the dough has to be very soft, and it requires a special steam oven to achieve its airy texture. Focaccia bread, which is also made with olive oil, has a denser texture and is easier to bake at home – as in the following recipe.

Virgin olive oil gives focaccia its rich flavour. The taste is sharpened and enhanced by the aroma of fresh sage.

Focaccia

MAKES: *1 loaf*
PREPARATION TIME: *25 - 35 minutes, plus 2 - 2 ½ hours proving time*
COOKING TIME: *35 minutes*

*15 g (½ oz) fresh yeast; or
    2 teaspoons dried yeast plus
    1 teaspoon sugar; or 1 sachet
    easy-blend dried yeast
300 ml (10 fl oz) lukewarm water
500 g (1 lb 2 oz) plain or strong
    flour, or half of each
2 level teaspoons salt
75 ml (2 ½ fl oz) virgin olive oil
12 fresh sage leaves, chopped*

1 Dissolve the yeast in the warm water, adding the sugar if using dried yeast. If using easy-blend dried yeast, add it directly to the flour.
2 Sift the flour and salt into a bowl, make a well and add the yeast water, or the plain water if using easy-blend yeast, and 4 tablespoons of the olive oil. Stir from the centre, gathering up some flour as you stir, until you have a rough dough.

3 Turn the dough out onto a floured surface and knead for 10 minutes until it is smooth and elastic.
4 Place the dough in a lightly oiled bowl, cover with a polythene bag and leave it to rise in a warm place for 1 ½ - 2 hours until doubled.
5 Place a heavy baking sheet in the centre of the oven and preheat it to 200°C (400°F, gas mark 6).
6 Punch the dough down and knead it again, this time sprinkling the sage on top and folding it in evenly.
7 On a lightly floured surface, roll the dough out into a circle 30 cm (12 in) in diameter. Allow it to rise slightly for about 30 minutes. Make dimples in the surface and dribble over the remaining oil.
8 Either slide a floured board under the bread and then quickly slide it off onto the hot baking sheet, or pick up the dough with your hands and toss it onto the baking sheet. Do not worry if the shape is irregular.
9 Bake for about 35 minutes or until the bread has become a deep golden colour, then cool on a rack.

BROCCOLI

CRISP AND COLOURFUL

How can I cook broccoli so that the florets have not become soggy by the time the stem is tender?

Divide a fresh head of broccoli into biggish florets, and cut each stem into a long, tapering wedge. Cook all the parts by either steaming or boiling briefly. You can also keep broccoli florets firm and crisp by putting them into a stir-fry after brief blanching in boiling water.

VARIATIONS ON A THEME

What is the difference between purple and green broccoli?

There are two sorts of broccoli, sprouting broccoli with purple or white heads, and calabrese which has blue-green heads.

Sprouting broccoli is leafier than calabrese and can be served as a starter vegetable in its own right,

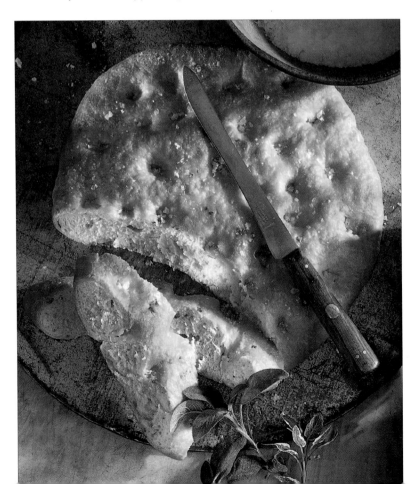

with mayonnaise. Green broccoli, called calabrese, reflects the vegetable's Italian origins. The cooks of Calabria chop the florets into a pasta mix (see below) made salty-sweet with anchovy sauce or paste and some sultanas. This is topped with crisply fried crumbs.

Calabrian pasta

Serves: 5 - 6 as a starter,
3 - 4 as a main course
Preparation time: 15 minutes
Cooking time: 12 - 15 minutes

50 g (1 ¾ oz) sultanas
200 g (7 oz) green broccoli
350 g (12 oz) dried tagliatelle or
  spaghetti
100 ml (3 ½ fl oz) olive oil
75 g (2 ¾ oz) fresh white
  breadcrumbs
2 cloves garlic, finely chopped
25 g (1 oz) pine nuts
2 teaspoons anchovy sauce or
  anchovy paste
Black pepper
3 tablespoons fresh parsley, chopped
Cayenne pepper

1 Leave the sultanas to soak in a cup of boiling water.
2 Slice the thick stem bases of the broccoli diagonally and divide the heads into small florets, each with a wedge of stem attached. Then blanch them in boiling water, cooking for just 30 seconds after the water has come back to the boil. Drain, refresh under the cold tap and leave to drain.
3 Cook the pasta in a large pan of boiling, salted water until al dente (cooked but firm), for about 12 - 15 minutes. While it is cooking, put a serving bowl in a low oven to warm.
4 Heat the oil in a frying pan and fry the breadcrumbs on medium heat for about 5 minutes until they start to become crispy, then add the garlic and pine nuts. After a minute or two, when the pine nuts begin to colour, add the broccoli and stir over the heat until everything is hot.
5 Drain the pasta, and then set the colander quickly back on top of the saucepan. This will catch the last tablespoon of water and help to keep the pasta warm and moist.

Dark-green calabrese makes a fine contrast to pale spaghetti, and goes well with other Italian ingredients such as anchovies, garlic, pine nuts and sultanas.

6 Return the pasta to the pan, stir in the anchovy sauce or paste and mix in the drained sultanas.
7 Add black pepper to taste and half of the chopped parsley, then tip the pasta into the heated serving bowl.
8 Mix the remaining parsley into the fried breadcrumb and broccoli mixture and scatter over the pasta.
9 Sprinkle with cayenne pepper and toss the mixture at the dining table.
Variation
Vegetarians can omit the anchovy sauce or paste and use chopped black olives to make a salty contrast.

No Wastage

Is there anything I can do with large broccoli stalks? It seems wasteful to throw them away.

Cutting chunky stalks into diagonal slices produces attractive shapes which can be cooked separately. They can also be added to the florets, or chilled and used later in a stir-fry or served with a vinaigrette dressing. Even thick base stems can be used if they are first sliced into very thin discs. Cook these for the same time as the rest.

BRUSSELS SPROUTS

IN THE RAW

I always try to eat as many raw vegetables as possible – but what can I do to make raw Brussels sprouts more appetising?

Raw Brussels sprouts are surprisingly good finely shredded in a slaw-type winter salad with carrots, celery and spring onion plus plenty of chopped parsley, watercress or mustard and cress. The salad below is good with baked potatoes and cold meat or hot sausages for a family supper; it is also appropriate for an autumn or winter buffet as it will stand for an hour or two without wilting and is easy to multiply for larger numbers.

Winter salad of shredded Brussels sprouts

SERVES: *4*
PREPARATION TIME: *20 minutes*
COOKING TIME: *10 minutes*

---

8 - 10 fresh chestnuts
225 g (8 oz) Brussels sprouts
2 medium carrots, cut into ribbons
   with a potato peeler
2 medium leeks, thinly sliced
1 bunch watercress, trimmed
A small bunch of parsley, finely
   chopped
Salt and black pepper
1 rounded teaspoon Dijon mustard
1 teaspoon runny honey
1 tablespoon cider vinegar
4 tablespoons olive oil
1 tablespoon walnut oil

---

1 Roast the chestnuts on a baking tray for 5 - 10 minutes until the skins crack. Peel them while they are still warm then break into rough pieces.
2 Trim the sprouts and shred thinly across. Mix the prepared vegetables, watercress, parsley and the broken chestnuts in a wide salad bowl. Add salt and black pepper to taste.
3 In a small bowl, mix together the mustard, honey and cider vinegar then beat in both of the oils. Toss the dressing into the salad and serve.

Chestnuts and sprouts are a popular combination used here in a new way. This crunchy raw vegetable salad has a delicious honey and mustard dressing.

CROSS CUT

Why do some recipes tell you to make a crisscross in the stalk of a Brussels sprout?

The only time you need to cut a cross in the bottom of a sprout's stem is when you are cooking a batch of various sizes. On these occasions, cut a cross in the larger sprouts. This allows heat to penetrate more easily to the middle so that the larger sprouts cook in the same time as the smaller ones.

Brussels sprouts are at their best when they are very tight, small buds and, since most supermarkets now sell them in a fairly regular and quite small size, crosscutting the stalks is rarely necessary.

WIDE APPEAL

My children declare they hate Brussels sprouts. Is there any way of converting them?

Brussels sprouts are traditionally served with chestnuts, especially for Christmas dinner, but they are good with other nuts too. Try them sliced and stir-fried, then finished with hazelnut oil and a scattering of toasted hazelnuts or pine kernels, or with some walnut oil and a dressing of walnuts ground to a paste with anchovies. Or you could try the recipe for Stir-fried Hot Slaw (right), where the grated apple adds a sweetness that appeals to children, and the hazelnuts provide a crunchy, contrasting texture.

Stir-fried hot slaw of Brussels sprouts

SERVES: 4
PREPARATION TIME: 15 minutes
COOKING TIME: 4 – 6 minutes

---

400 g (14 oz) Brussels sprouts
50 g (1 ³⁄₄ oz) hazelnuts
3 tablespoons olive oil
2 sticks celery, destrung and finely sliced
2 cloves garlic, crushed or finely chopped
4 fat or 6 slender spring onions, sliced
2 tablespoons lemon juice
1 eating apple
2 tablespoons hazelnut or walnut oil
Salt and black pepper

---

1 Trim the sprouts and slice them thinly across their girth. Toast the hazelnuts on a baking tray under a hot grill, shaking regularly until the skins are flaky. Rub the skins off the nuts when they are cool enough to handle, then leave them to cool.
2 Heat the olive oil in a wok or wide pan and stir-fry the celery for a minute. Add the garlic then, after just 30 seconds, the spring onions, sprouts and lemon juice. Stir-cook until they are all hot through.
3 Grate the unpeeled apple straight into the pan, leaving only the core. Stir to heat through, then stir in the hazelnuts and the hazelnut or walnut oil. Season thoroughly, adding more lemon if desired (it depends on the apple's sweetness), and serve hot.

BUCKWHEAT

GOLDEN TRIANGLE

What is buckwheat, and is it a healthy addition to the diet?

Buckwheat, although classified as a grain, is actually the triangular seed of a member of the rhubarb family and no relation to wheat. It contains beta carotene, most of the B group vitamins and is a nutritious source of complex carbohydrates. Buckwheat is also gluten-free. Both the grain and its flour are used in cooking. Buckwheat is sold both plain and roasted. Roasted buckwheat is slightly darker and has a richer, more intense flavour than plain. The recipe for Buttered Buckwheat below is a wholesome and tasty substitute for rice to accompany curries and stews.

Buttered buckwheat

SERVES: 2 – 4
PREPARATION TIME: 15 minutes, plus 30 minutes infusing
COOKING TIME: 20 minutes, plus 5 minutes resting

---

50 g (1 ³⁄₄ oz) unsalted butter, softened
Grated zest and juice of 1 lime
1 clove garlic, crushed
1 tablespoon freshly chopped coriander
¹⁄₄ teaspoon ground mixed spice
Salt and black pepper
A pinch of cayenne pepper
225 g (8 oz) roasted buckwheat
500 ml (18 fl oz) boiling water or vegetable stock

---

1 In a small bowl, beat together the softened butter, lime zest and juice, garlic, coriander, mixed spice, salt and black pepper and cayenne. Cover and set aside to infuse for at least 30 minutes. Meanwhile, preheat the oven to 200°C (400°F, gas mark 6).
2 Lightly grease a roasting dish, sprinkle the buckwheat into it and pour over the boiling water or stock. Cover the dish with foil and a tight-fitting lid if possible, and bake for 20 minutes. Remove from the oven and leave to rest for 5 minutes.
3 Remove the lid and foil and stir in the spiced butter, forking it gently through the buckwheat. Serve the buckwheat at once to accompany a spicy meat or vegetable stew.

DO IT YOURSELF

I prefer roasted buckwheat but sometimes it is difficult to buy. Can I roast it myself?

Yes. Simply dry-fry ordinary buckwheat, or stir it with a little oil, in a heavy frying pan over a moderate heat for 4 – 5 minutes until lightly browned. Allow to cool, place in a dry, airtight container and store for a maximum of two weeks.

The exotic flavours of coriander and lime add tang to buckwheat and its traditional accompaniment of butter.

BULGUR WHEAT

CRACKED GRAIN

What is bulgur wheat, and why does it cook so quickly?

Bulgur wheat, or cracked wheat, is wheat which has been boiled until it cracks, which enables it to readily absorb moisture. Therefore bulgur wheat is ready to use in recipes far more quickly than the whole grain.

If bulgur wheat is to be served in a salad, such as the Middle Eastern salad tabbouleh, it is usual to soak the grains for 30 minutes and then use them without further cooking. In the following recipe, however, the bulgur wheat is first soaked then baked in vine leaves.

Bulgur-stuffed vine leaves

MAKES: 16 parcels
PREPARATION TIME: 30 minutes plus 30 minutes soaking
COOKING TIME: 30 - 40 minutes

125 g (4 1/2 oz) bulgur wheat
25 g (1 oz) butter
1 medium onion, finely chopped
2 cloves garlic, crushed
1 teaspoon each ground coriander, ground cumin and ground cinnamon
25 g (1 oz) currants
25 g (1 oz) pine nuts, toasted
Salt and black pepper
1 tablespoon each freshly chopped coriander and mint
16 large vine leaves in brine
300 ml (10 fl oz) vegetable stock

1 Place the bulgur wheat in a bowl and cover with plenty of cold water. Soak for 30 minutes, then strain.
2 Preheat the oven to 190°C (375°F, gas mark 5).
3 Heat the butter in a frying pan and cook the onion and garlic with the ground spices for 5 minutes. Add the strained bulgur wheat and fry for a minute. Remove the pan from the heat and add the currants, pine nuts, seasoning, coriander and mint.
4 Drain the brine from the vine leaves, then rinse well and pat dry.

5 Place a tablespoon of bulgur mixture in the centre of each leaf and roll it up, folding in the sides to form neat rolls. If you like, secure each one with a cocktail stick.
6 Place the stuffed rolls in a small shallow baking dish to fit closely together. Pour over the stock, cover with foil and bake for 30 - 40 minutes until all the liquid has been absorbed. Remove from the oven, allow to cool slightly and serve the stuffed vine leaves warm with Greek yoghurt or a fresh tomato sauce.

The vine leaves are wrapped around a spicy bulgur wheat mixture featuring currants, pine nuts and fresh herbs.

BUNS

ROLL WITH IT

What is the difference between a bun and a roll?

Buns are made from sweetened, yeasted dough enriched with fat whereas rolls are less sweet, or unsweetened, and are not enriched. Buns tend to be flavoured with raisins or spices and glazed or decorated before baking. Chelsea, Bath, currant and hot cross buns are popular examples.

DON'T RUSH BUNS

I recently made hot cross buns but they were leaden. Do you have any foolproof advice?

The most common mistake is not allowing enough time for the dough to rise. It can take much longer than some recipes indicate because of variations in room temperature, yeasts and even flour. The flavour and the texture of any yeast-baked product improves with slow rising so do not try to rush the process. The recipe below produces a batch of lovely, moist buns.

Hot cross buns

MAKES: 18 buns
PREPARATION TIME: 25 - 40 minutes, plus 2 - 3 hours rising time
COOKING TIME: 15 - 20 minutes

500 g (1 lb 2 oz) strong white flour
50 g (1 3/4 oz) soft light brown sugar
2 teaspoons mixed spice
1/2 teaspoon salt
25 g (1 oz) fresh yeast, or 15 g (1/2 oz) dried yeast plus 1 teaspoon sugar, or 1 sachet easy-blend yeast
300 ml (10 fl oz) lukewarm milk
2 eggs, size 2, lightly beaten
50 g (1 3/4 oz) butter, softened, plus extra for greasing
125 g (4 1/2 oz) currants
25 g (1 oz) chopped mixed peel
To glaze: 4 tablespoons milk mixed with 2 tablespoons sugar

1 Put the flour, sugar, mixed spice and salt in a bowl and mix well.
2 Dissolve the fresh or dried yeast in 4 tablespoons of the milk, adding the sugar if using dried yeast. Blend the yeast mixture into the remaining milk. If using easy-blend yeast, add it directly to the flour.
3 Make a well in the spiced flour and add the milk, eggs and butter. Stir until a soft dough is formed.
4 Turn out onto a floured board and knead for 5 - 10 minutes until the dough is smooth and elastic. Knead in the currants and mixed peel.
5 Place the dough in a greased bowl, then cover and leave it for 1 1/2 - 2 hours until it has doubled in size.
6 Grease a baking sheet. Knock the dough back then divide into 18 small buns. Mark each one with a cross. Arrange on the baking sheet and leave to prove until doubled in size, about 30 - 45 minutes. Preheat the oven to 190°C (375°F, gas mark 5).
7 Brush the bun tops with a little sweetened milk and bake for 15 - 20 minutes or until risen and browned.

BUTTER

SWEET AND MILD

What is the difference between English and Continental butter?

There are two main varieties of butter, sweet cream and lactic. Both may be salted, slightly salted or unsalted and, confusingly, unsalted butter is sometimes referred to as 'sweet butter' on the Continent.

The butter most commonly made in England is the bright yellow sweet cream variety, made from fresh pasteurised or soured cream, and usually with a salt content of between 1.5 per cent and 3 per cent. The salt acts as a preservative and flavouring and although English unsalted butter is available, it is less common than salted butter.

Continental lactic butter is typically made from pasteurised fresh cream ripened with a culture of lactic acid and is usually, though not always, unsalted. It has a mild and delicate tang and tends to come from Denmark, Holland or France.

Whey butter, typically sold in farm shops and cheesemongers, is made from the whey left over after cheesemaking and boasts a highly salted, strong and cheesy flavour.

The term 'farmhouse butter' indicates that the butter has been made on a farm using milk from that farm. Organic butter is also available, made from the milk of cows fed on organic pastures.

BEST BUTTER

Which is the best or most versatile butter to use for cooking?

A lightly salted butter is fine for general cooking purposes except where the recipe specifically calls for unsalted butter. Using butter in cooking adds substance, flavour and a certain richness to foods, as well as improving the taste and appearance. In particular, butter is the ideal fat for many cakes, pastries and biscuits such as these Butter Whirl Biscuits (above right).

Butter whirl biscuits

MAKES: 14 – 16
PREPARATION TIME: 25 minutes
COOKING TIME: 15 – 20 minutes

175 g (6 oz) salted butter, softened, plus extra for greasing
50 g (1 ¾ oz) icing sugar, sifted
A few drops of vanilla essence
175 g (6 oz) plain flour, sifted
7 - 8 glacé cherries, halved

1 Preheat the oven to 180°C (350°F, gas mark 4) and lightly grease two baking sheets.
2 Cream the butter and icing sugar together until light and fluffy. Add the vanilla essence, then stir in the flour and mix well.
3 Spoon the mixture into a piping bag fitted with a 1 cm (½ in) star nozzle. Pipe 14 - 16 flat whirls onto the baking sheets and place a cherry half in the centre of each one.
4 Bake for 15 - 20 minutes until pale golden. Cool on the sheets for a few minutes, then transfer to a wire rack to cool completely. Store them in an airtight container for up to a week.
VARIATIONS
To make chocolate butter whirls, melt 25 - 50 g (1 - 1 ¾ oz) of plain chocolate and beat into the creamed butter and sugar before adding the flour. For lemon or orange butter whirls, add the finely grated zest of a lemon or small orange to the creamed butter and sugar mixture.

FRYING WITH BUTTER

Why do recipes tell you to add oil to butter for frying?

Butter is not easy to use for frying. In addition to butterfat, it contains water, milk solids and other impurities that make it burn at lower temperatures than most vegetable oils. By putting a little oil in the pan, then adding the butter and cooking the food over a low heat, you can help to prevent the butter burning and spoiling the dish.

You can also minimise the problem by using clarified butter (see box, overleaf) or concentrated butter. Developed for use in cooking, concentrated butter has the milk

solids, salt and impurities removed during the manufacturing process and therefore can be heated to higher temperatures than regular butter. You use less of it than you would regular butter – 75 g (2 ¾ oz) of concentrated for every 100 g (3 ½ oz) of ordinary butter – but when using concentrated butter in dough or pastry mixtures, extra liquid should be added to compensate for the lower moisture content.

BUTTER CLARIFIED

When and why would you need clarified butter?

Clarified butter is melted butter from which the salt, water, milk solids and other impurities have been removed, leaving pure butter-fat (see box, below). It will not burn when heated and so is good for sautéing and shallow-frying.

STRONG, SWEET GHEE

Are ghee and clarified butter the same thing?

No, they are not. Ghee is an Indian version of clarified butter which is made by simmering butter until all the moisture has evaporated and the butter caramelises. This results in a stronger, sweeter and rather nutty flavour. Ghee is often made from buffalo's milk or cow's milk, although ghee made from vegetable oils is also widely available.

SAFE STORAGE

Will homemade herb butter keep as long as ordinary butter?

No, it will not. Unsalted butter may be kept in a refrigerator for up to two weeks; salted butter for three weeks and concentrated butter will keep for at least three months. But herb butter will keep for two days only as the oil in the herbs will turn the butter rancid. However, herb and other flavoured butters may be frozen for up to a month.

QUICK DEFROST

Can I freeze butter and then defrost it in the microwave?

To freeze butter, place freshly purchased, unopened packs in airtight freezer bags or wrap them with foil. Salted butter may be frozen for three months and unsalted butter for six months. To defrost, unwrap the butter, place it on an ovenproof dish and thaw it on the Defrost setting. A 250 g (9 oz) pack of butter will thaw in a microwave in around 6–8 minutes and will begin to soften after 10 minutes.

ADDING VALUE

What can I do with herb and garlic butters besides use them to top steaks? And can you suggest some other flavourings for butter?

Herb and other savoury flavoured butters are excellent tossed with pasta, spread on hot breads, added to soups and sauces or used as a topping for jacket potatoes. Grilled chicken or fish and steamed vegetables are also good matches.

Anchovies, curry powder, lemon zest, mustard, onion, paprika and tomato purée can all add an interesting savoury flavour to butter.

Sweet butters for pancakes can be made with sugar plus ground almonds, brandy, lemon or orange zest, mixed spices, rum or walnuts. (See also recipe in GINGER.)

HOW TO CLARIFY BUTTER

By melting and straining (or 'clarifying') butter, you separate the butterfat from the water, milk proteins, salt and carbohydrates which make it splutter and burn when used for cooking. Clarified butter will keep for up to two months in the refrigerator or up to three months in the freezer.

IN THE MICROWAVE

1 To make about 100 g (3½ oz) of clarified butter you will need to start with 175 g (6 oz) of ordinary butter. Cube the butter and place it in a 500 ml (18 fl oz) ovenproof jug. Heat it on High for 1–2 minutes, or until the butter is melted and foaming.

2 Using a metal spoon, skim off and discard the foam from the surface of the melted butter.

3 Carefully pour off and reserve the clear yellow liquid, which is the clarified butter, leaving any milky residue behind in the jug.

ON THE HOB

1 Gently heat 175 g (6 oz) of butter in a small, heavy-based saucepan over a low heat until the butter has melted and started to foam.

2 Remove from the heat and stand a few minutes, until the sediment has settled on the base of the pan.

3 Line a sieve with some fine muslin or a J-cloth then pour the butter through into a clean bowl. Discard any milky sediment that is left in the pan.

NOT EVEN A PINCH

If a recipe calls for unsalted butter, can I use salted butter instead if I do not have any, or will it spoil the finished recipe?

If a recipe states unsalted butter it is always best to use it. Unsalted butter is often specified for delicate pastries such as croissants, and for cakes, icings, confectionery such as butterscotch, and other sweet foods. In those cases, even a pinch of salt would be obvious and would change the flavour of the finished dish. It is also better to use unsalted butter for delicate sauces such as hollandaise, and then to add salt to the sauce to taste.

Sometimes, however, salted butter is a crucial part of the dish because the salt highlights the flavours of the other ingredients, as in this quick, easy recipe for Smoked Mackerel Pâté with Garden Herbs.

Smoked mackerel pâté with garden herbs

SERVES: 6 as a starter
PREPARATION TIME: 15 minutes
COOKING TIME: none

---

350 g (12 oz) smoked mackerel
70 g (2 ½ oz) salted butter, softened
Finely grated zest and juice of
*   1 small lemon*
3 tablespoons creamed horseradish
*   sauce*
2 - 3 tablespoons chopped fresh
*   mixed herbs, parsley or tarragon*
Black pepper
To garnish: lemon slices and
*   watercress*

---

1 Skin the mackerel and discard any bones. Flake the flesh of the fish into a bowl and mash it with a fork.
2 Mix the butter with the fish, then add all the other ingredients and mix thoroughly. (If a smoother texture is preferred, mix in a blender or food processor; you can add a tablespoon of cream if you like.)
3 Spoon the mixture into a serving dish and level the surface. Garnish the pâté with the lemon slices and watercress and serve it with warm crusty bread or Melba toast.

This fish pâté with green herbs makes a hearty lunch when served with bread and a mug of cider, but you could also offer it as an elegant dinner party starter.

THEME AND VARIATIONS

Can you tell me the difference between beurre blanc, beurre monté and beurre noir?

They are all sauces based on butter but quite different in flavour.

• BEURRE BLANC is a pale, creamy sauce similar to hollandaise. To make beurre blanc, dice 75 g (2 ¾ oz) of cold unsalted butter. Simmer 3 tablespoons of white wine vinegar with 75 ml (2 ½ fl oz) of white wine or water in a small saucepan with a chopped shallot until the mixture has reduced to about 2 tablespoons of liquid. Add a tablespoon of double cream if you like and bring to the boil. Reduce the heat and whisk in the butter pieces, one by one, until the sauce is thick, pale and creamy. The sauce may be served as it is or strained to remove the shallots. Beurre blanc marries well with chicken, egg, fish and vegetables.

• BEURRE MONTE is similar to beurre blanc but the base may be any slightly thickened liquid such as a sauce made by reduction, a sauce thickened with flour, or some stock. Cold butter is whisked into the sauce in the same way as when making beurre blanc.

• BEURRE NOIR or 'black butter', is a sauce made by cooking butter until it turns dark brown. A little vinegar or lemon juice is added to the butter, then flavourings such as capers or parsley. Beurre noir is best served with grilled or fried fish, eggs and vegetable dishes. Beurre noisette is similar to beurre noir, however, the butter is cooked only until it is medium-brown, then the seasonings are added.

CABBAGE

A QUESTION OF TIMING

I enjoy eating cabbage, but find the smell that is produced during cooking unpleasant. Is there any way of avoiding it?

There are dozens of varieties of cabbage – including red, green, white, savoy, pointed and drumhead, as well as closely related curly kale and spring greens – but they all release smelly hydrogen sulphide gas in cooking.

The amount of gas they produce doubles between the fifth and seventh minutes of boiling, so to cut down on the smell, you must either keep the cooking time to under 5 minutes, which suits the looser-headed varieties best, or opt for much longer cooking in a closed oven to cook off this effect and achieve a mellowness of flavour.

Green and savoy cabbages are best cooked fast by adding the leaves to boiling water. Red and white cabbage, having greatest resilience in the leaves, respond well to slow cooking.

Alternatively, all cabbages can be sliced into thin shreds and quickly stir-fried, perhaps with the addition of caraway seeds, lemon juice, soy sauce or chopped chilli, and eaten while still a little crisp.

Ruffled leaves and deep colour make savoy the distinctive aristocrat of the winter cabbage patch. Cooked fast with juniper berries and gin, as in the following recipe, it is a fitting partner for dark game dishes and pork and will not cause smells in your kitchen.

Savoy in gin

SERVES: *4 as an accompaniment*
PREPARATION TIME: *15 minutes*
COOKING TIME: *5 minutes*

---

1 savoy cabbage weighing
  500 - 700 g (1 lb 2 oz - 1 lb 9 oz)
6 juniper berries
2 cloves garlic
Salt
50 g (1 ¾ oz) butter, softened
3 tablespoons gin
Black pepper

---

1 Trim away any tired or damaged leaves from the cabbage, cut it into quarters and shred it finely, cutting out and discarding the stem. Wash thoroughly and drain well.

2 With a pestle and mortar, crush the juniper berries, garlic and salt together to produce a rough paste. Alternatively, if you have no pestle and mortar, chop the berries and garlic finely, sprinkle on the salt and mix thoroughly. Mix the paste into the softened butter.

3 Cook this flavoured butter in a large saucepan over a low heat until it starts to sizzle, but do not let it begin to brown. In the meantime, put a serving dish to warm.

4 Toss the drained cabbage in the flavoured butter, turn up the heat to medium and stir the cabbage well to coat it in the butter. Stir in the gin, cover the pan tightly and cook on a medium heat for 4 minutes, shaking the pan vigorously once or twice.

5 Remove from the heat, grind on black pepper to taste, stir and serve immediately in the warmed dish.

VARIATION

Baby cabbages can now be found in many shops, and they can be used in this dish instead of larger specimens. Cut them into quarters and blanch in boiling water for a minute. Drain well and add to the flavoured butter then continue with the recipe above.

A splash of gin and some chopped juniper berries and garlic turn baby savoy cabbage into an aromatic dish that goes well with strong-flavoured meat.

RETAINING COLOUR

How can I prevent red cabbage losing its colour during cooking?

Red cabbage is inclined to turn a dingy purple in the long cooking required to soften it. You can avoid this by cooking it in a microwave oven. Finally shredded, it will be cooked in 6 minutes on High.

If using a conventional oven, a good splash of red wine or red wine vinegar in the latter stages of cooking, as in the recipe below, goes some way to restoring its vibrant ruby colour. Because of the long cooking time of this dish, it makes sense to make it in a large quantity; the red cabbage keeps well in the refrigerator and some say it is even better reheated. Bake some potatoes or a potato gratin while it is cooking to utilise the oven heat, and serve with pork chops or good-quality sausages.

Baked red cabbage with apple and spice

SERVES: 6 - 8 as an accompaniment
PREPARATION TIME: 35 minutes
COOKING TIME: 2 hours

---

1 kg (2 lb 4 oz) red cabbage
2 - 3 bay leaves
1 medium onion
4 cloves
Salt
3 eating apples, such as Cox's
    Orange Pippin
75 g (2 ¾ oz) lard
1 tablespoon soft brown sugar
2 tablespoons red wine vinegar
300 ml (10 fl oz) beef stock
100 ml (3 ½ fl oz) red wine

---

1 Preheat the oven to 160°C (325°F, gas mark 3). Cut the cabbage into quarters and chop it into shreds, cutting out the stalk. Put the bay leaves into a large, heavy casserole and pack the cabbage on top.
2 Peel the onion, stud it with the cloves and bury it in the middle of the cabbage. Sprinkle on some salt.
3 Peel the apples, cut them into quarters and discard the cores. Cut the apples into slices. Heat the fat in a large frying pan and fry the apple slices, tossing until they just begin to turn golden, then tip them with their fat over the cabbage, spreading the apple in a layer.
4 Dissolve the sugar in the vinegar and add the stock. Pour it over the apples and cabbage, then cover the casserole and bake for 1 ½ hours.
5 Uncover, pour in the red wine, stir and return to the oven for a further 30 minutes.
6 Remove and discard the studded onion, sprinkle on some salt and a good dash of pepper, and serve.

VARIATION
Vegetarians can replace the lard with 4 tablespoons of cooking oil, and use strong, good quality vegetable stock instead of beef stock.

EXOTIC CABBAGE

I have heard of a cabbage called pak choi. Where can I get it, and how is it prepared?

Pak choi is a cabbage without a heart, with deep green and fleshy leaves clustered on thick, juicy, white stems. A native of China and Hong Kong, pak choi used to be available only in Chinese food shops in Britain, but it is now grown in Holland and has become widely available in supermarkets.

Brief steaming or stir-frying is recommended to retain flavour and juiciness. It takes happily to the garlic, ginger and soy treatment of Chinese cooking, but also adapts well to being served as an accompanying vegetable without any herbs or spices, Western-style.

TENDER SLAW

I know that coleslaw is supposed to be good for you, but I find it boringly chewy to eat and rather indigestible. How can I make it more appealing?

It does seem perverse that slaws are usually made with white cabbage, whose raw leaves are almost as tough as those of red cabbage. Choose, instead, Chinese leaves, a much more tender member of the cabbage family, as in the following recipe. Heads can weigh up to 700 g (1 lb 9 oz), so one head will make enough for a small buffet party. Indeed because the cabbages in slaws remain crisp and sit well in their dressing even if made some hours before, they are always a practical choice for a buffet table. However, because they require so little time to prepare, they are also good as part of an informal family lunch or cold supper.

Chinese leaf slaw

SERVES: 4
PREPARATION TIME: 15 minutes
COOKING TIME: none

---

250 g (9 oz) Chinese leaves
2 medium carrots
3 tablespoons mayonnaise
1 teaspoon Dijon mustard
3 tablespoons olive oil
2 teaspoons cider vinegar
Celery salt and black pepper
1 tablespoon coarsely chopped
    walnut kernels, optional

---

1 Rinse the Chinese leaves, shake dry and shred them, cutting across the head and discarding the stem.
2 Peel and coarsely grate the carrots and mix them with the shredded leaves in a salad bowl.
3 Mix the mayonnaise and mustard together then stir in the olive oil and vinegar. Season with celery salt and plenty of black pepper and toss into the salad. Scatter it, if you like, with chopped walnuts.
4 Serve the salad immediately, or cover it and store in the refrigerator for up to 6 hours before serving.

Save it!

If you have some Chinese leaves left over after making the Chinese Leaf Slaw above, keep them in the salad drawer of the refrigerator and use them as part of a stir-fry later in the week. Try them cooked with garlic, ginger, or a Chinese black bean sauce.

CAKES

STEPS TO SUCCESS

Why do my cakes sometimes have airholes, or crack and peak?

Holes can be caused by overmixing, or unevenly or insufficiently folding in the flour. The mixture should be soft and dropping at this stage and if it is too dry, pockets of air can get trapped. This will also happen if the flour and raising agent are not sifted together thoroughly to mix them.

To prevent cracking, make sure you use the right sized tin and that the oven is not too hot. Place cakes in the centre of the oven, not too high up where it will be hotter and the cake will peak and crack.

AVOIDING CURDLING

How do you prevent a cake mixture from curdling, and can you save it if it does?

Curdling occurs when cold eggs are added to the mixture too quickly, separating the fat from the sugar and eggs. A curdled mixture holds far less air, so the cake will be flat. Mixtures containing fat and sugar need to be soft and light to absorb the eggs easily. Eggs should be at room temperature and added gradually. Adding a teaspoon of flour with each addition of egg can also help to prevent curdling.

If the mixture starts to curdle, dip the base of the bowl into warm water briefly, and whisk to restore the light consistency.

THAT SINKING FEELING

Why does my cake come out of the oven looking perfect and then sink dramatically?

Cakes will sink if they have not been baked for long enough, so follow the time stated in the recipe, use a timer, and don't be tempted to open the oven door during cooking. Using too cool an oven or opening and shutting the oven door during baking will cause sinking, as will too much raising agent in the cake mixture.

Cakes are ready when they are firm in the centre and have slightly shrunken away from the sides of the tin; sponges should spring back when touched with your finger.

RESCUE REMEDIES

Is there any way to save a cake that has turned out badly?

If things go wrong during baking, disguise the damage as follows:
• For a burnt cake, slice off the top and shave the sides with a potato peeler. Paint the surface with some warmed sieved jam and cover with a thin layer of bought marzipan or ready-to-roll icing.
• If a cake breaks, stick the pieces back together with jam, then cover with frosting or jam sprinkled with desiccated coconut.
• If the middle sinks, cut it out and turn the cake into a ring cake. Spread whipped cream over the cake, and fill the cavity with fresh fruit such as raspberries.
• If a sponge comes out flat, cut it into fancy shapes, sandwich them together with cream and jam and dust them with icing sugar.

LIGHT AS A FEATHER

How can I make a really feather-light sponge cake?

To produce light sponge cakes, it is vital to measure out the ingredients accurately and stick to the recipe. If you add too much egg, fat, flour or baking powder it will make the cake heavy and doughy.

It is air that makes cakes light, so beat the sugar and butter until pale, soft and fluffy, and fold in the flour gradually, being careful not to knock out any air. And be sure to use an appropriate fat – if you use soft tub margarine instead of butter or block margarine in a creamed recipe, the mixture will be too wet and the cake will be flat.

The following recipe for creamed sponge produces a light, airy cake, and is always a favourite.

Classic Victoria sponge

SERVES: 8
PREPARATION TIME: 20 minutes
COOKING TIME: 30 minutes

175 g (6 oz) butter or block
  margarine
175 g (6 oz) caster sugar
3 eggs, size 3, beaten
175 g (6 oz) self-raising flour, sifted
A few drops vanilla essence
75 ml (2 ½ fl oz) raspberry jam
150 ml (5 fl oz) whipping cream,
  whipped
2 tablespoons icing sugar

1 Preheat the oven to 180°C (350°F, gas mark 4). Grease two 20 cm (8 in) round sandwich tins, and line their bases with greaseproof paper.
2 Beat the butter or margarine until very soft, using a mixer if possible, then add the sugar and beat until the mixture is light, pale and fluffy.
3 Beat in the egg gradually, adding a teaspoon of flour with each addition to prevent curdling. Fold in the rest of the flour then add the vanilla essence and a teaspoon of water.
4 Divide the mixture between the tins and smooth the surfaces level. Bake for 30 minutes or until risen and light golden. The cakes should spring back when lightly pressed in the centre with your fingers.
5 Leave to cool in the cake tins for a couple of minutes, then turn out onto wire racks to cool thoroughly.
6 Spread the jam over the top of one cake and the whipped cream on the underside of the other. Sandwich the two layers together and lightly dust over the icing sugar.

Save it!

This Victoria sponge will keep, undecorated, in a cake tin or large airtight container for up to three days; once decorated, use within one day. Freeze undecorated layers, tightly wrapped in foil, for up to two months.

FAT-FREE SPONGE

Is it possible to make a sponge cake without using fat?

The lightest sponge cakes are made without any fat at all, by the whisking method. To replace the bulk of the missing fat, the sugar and eggs are whisked together over hot water until the mixture becomes so thick that a trail is left when the beaters are lifted away.

Alternatively, you can replace some of the flour with lighter cornflour, as in the following recipe for Angel Food Cake. This is usually served as a cake, perhaps accompanied with some whipped cream, but you can also serve it as a pudding, each slice accompanied by fresh fruit and a raspberry coulis.

Whisked egg whites give a melt-in-the-mouth lift to delicate Angel Food Cake, a fat-free version of the classic sponge.

Angel food cake

SERVES: 12
PREPARATION TIME: 30 minutes
COOKING TIME: 35 minutes

50 g (1 ¾ oz) plain flour
25 g (1 oz) cornflour
75 g (2 ¾ oz) icing sugar
1 teaspoon cream of tartar
A few drops vanilla essence
A few drops almond essence
6 egg whites, size 3
A pinch of salt
175 g (6 oz) caster sugar
To garnish: whipped cream and a
*   selection of soft fruit such as*
*   raspberries and whitecurrants*

1 Preheat the oven to 190°C (375°F, gas mark 5). Have ready to hand an ungreased 23 cm (9 in) ring-shaped or tubular cake tin. If you do not have one, use a round cake tin and put an empty can upside-down in the centre to make the hole.

2 Sift the flour, cornflour and icing sugar together in a small bowl.
3 Put the cream of tartar, essences, egg whites and salt in a bowl. Whisk until the egg whites form soft peaks, then gradually whisk in the caster sugar and continue whisking until the mixture forms stiff peaks.
4 Fold in the flour mixture a little at a time, being very careful not to overmix so you don't lose the air, then spoon it into the tin.
5 Bake for 35 minutes or until the cake springs back when touched with a finger and a skewer inserted into the mixture comes out clean.
6 To cool, invert the cake upside-down in the tin on a wire rack: the steam from the cake will help to release it from the tin.
7 When cool, gently run a palette knife round the sides of the tin, then turn out. Decorate the top and fill the hole with soft fruit, and serve with whipped cream.

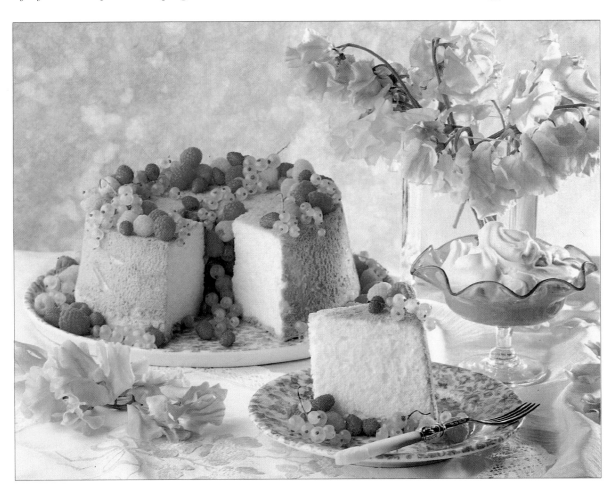

BUTTER OR OIL?

Can cakes be made with oil instead of butter or margarine? And if so, would it be healthier?

Fruit cakes and sponges made with lightly flavoured oils such as corn or sunflower oil are very easy to mix (though they need extra raising agent to stop them becoming heavy), and they stay moist longer. But it is debatable whether they are healthier: although oil contains less saturated fats than butter or margarine, it has just as many calories.

The following rich and filling Carrot Cake is made using oil, is easy to make and will keep for up to five days in a cake tin.

Carrot cake

SERVES: 8
PREPARATION TIME: 30 minutes
COOKING TIME: 50 minutes

FOR THE CAKE
1 large ripe banana
85 ml (3 fl oz) sunflower or
*   corn oil*
75 g (2 ¾ oz) soft dark brown
*   sugar*
2 eggs, size 3, beaten
50 g (1 ¾ oz) carrots, finely
*   grated*
100 g (3 ½ oz) sultanas
50 g (1 ¾ oz) walnuts, chopped
Finely grated zest of 1 orange
½ teaspoon ground cinnamon
150 g (5 ½ oz) plain flour
1 teaspoon baking powder
1 teaspoon bicarbonate of soda

FOR THE ICING
75 g (2 ¾ oz) soft cream cheese
50 g (1 ¾ oz) icing sugar
Finely grated zest of 1 lemon
1 tablespoon lemon juice

1 Preheat the oven to 180°C (350°F, gas mark 4). Grease a 900 g (2 lb) loaf tin and line it with baking paper.
2 With a fork, mash the banana in a large mixing bowl, then mix in all the remaining ingredients briefly, sifting in the flour, baking powder and bicarbonate of soda last.
3 Beat to a smooth batter, then pour into the tin and bake for 30 minutes.

4 Turn the heat down to 160°C (325°F, gas mark 3) and bake for a further 20 minutes until the cake is firm to the touch and a warmed skewer comes out cleanly.
5 When cooked, leave the cake to cool in the tin for 5 minutes until it is firm enough to handle, then turn it out and peel away the paper. Leave to cool completely on a wire rack.
6 When the cake is thoroughly cool, beat all the ingredients for the icing together with a wooden spoon, then swirl the mixture over the cake.

Is it done?

To test if a cake is cooked, warm a skewer or knitting needle and insert it into the centre; it should come out cleanly, with no cake mixture sticking to it.

RIGHT-SIZED TINS

Does it matter if a cake mixture is baked in a slightly different tin to the one specified in the recipe?

Yes, very much. If the tin is too large, the cake will be flat and shrunken. If it is too small, the cake will bubble or bulge up and over the sides of the tin.

However, the mixture for a round tin will fit a square tin that is about 2.5 cm (1 in) smaller; for instance, a mixture designed to fill a 20 cm (8 in) round tin can be used to fill a 18 cm (7 in) square tin.

To adapt a recipe to fill a shaped tin, for example the number '9' for a birthday cake, fill your usual tin with water to the level the mixture normally reaches. Then pour the water into the new tin to the level required and estimate the quantity of mixture needed, doubling or halving the recipe as required.

TURNING OUT

Should I turn cakes out of their tin as soon as they are cooked?

Most light cakes, such as a Victoria sponge, should be turned out of their tins while they are still warm,

or else the underside may go soggy with condensation or form a thick, dark outer crust. However, they will break up if they are turned out immediately they are out of the oven, so leave them in the tin for 3–5 minutes to firm up.

Heavy cakes, such as fruit cakes, are best left in the tin until they are completely cold to allow them to solidify, especially if they are going to be stored and matured.

GIVING FLOUR A LIFT

Why do some recipes use plain flour and baking powder, and others self-raising flour?

Self-raising flour has more lifting power than a blend of plain flour and baking powder, so this is the best flour to use for heavy mixtures. Plain flours can raise a light mixture with the aid of baking powder, especially if the recipe also contains eggs or egg whites which will help to aerate the mix.

To make your own self-raising flour, simply sift 500 g (1 lb 2 oz) of plain flour with 4 level teaspoons of baking powder.

RAISING AGENTS

What exactly is baking powder?

Baking powder is a mixture of bicarbonate of soda, which is an alkali, and cream of tartar, which is an acid. When liquid is added, the two react to produce carbon dioxide, and the heat of the oven expands these gas bubbles to raise the mixture. You can make your own baking powder from one part bicarbonate of soda to two parts cream of tartar. Bicarbonate of soda can be used as a raising agent on its own, but has an unpleasant aftertaste, so it is best used for strongly flavoured, spicy cakes.

When using soft margarine in place of hard butter in a cake, as in the recipe for Frosted Walnut Cake opposite, it is advisable to add additional baking powder to the self-raising flour to provide an extra lift, and thus give an even surface to the cooked cake.

Rich and creamy frosting turns a crunchy triple-decker walnut cake into a luscious teatime treat.

Frosted walnut cake

SERVES: 12
PREPARATION TIME: 40 minutes
COOKING TIME: 30 minutes

FOR THE CAKE
225 g (8 oz) self-raising flour
1 teaspoon baking powder
225 g (8 oz) soft margarine
225 g (8 oz) soft light brown sugar
4 eggs, size 2, beaten
75 g (2 3/4 oz) walnuts, chopped
1 tablespoon black treacle

FOR THE FROSTING
1 egg white, size 2
175 g (6 oz) caster sugar
A pinch of salt
A pinch of cream of tartar
To garnish: walnut halves and
  demerara sugar

1 To make the cake, preheat the oven to 160°C (325°F, gas mark 3). Grease three 20 cm (8 in) sandwich tins and line their bases with a layer of nonstick baking paper.
2 Sift the flour and baking powder together into a large bowl. Add the remaining cake ingredients and beat lightly until the mixture develops a soft dropping consistency.
3 Spoon the mixture equally into the tins, level the surface and bake them for about 30 minutes or until springy to the touch in the centre.
4 Leave in the tins for 5 minutes then turn out to cool on wire racks.
5 To make the frosting, place all the frosting ingredients in a large, clean, heatproof bowl, add 2 tablespoons of water and whisk, with an electric whisk if possible, until foaming.
6 Set the bowl over a pan of boiling water and whisk until the mixture forms soft peaks - about 7 minutes with an electric whisk.
7 Working quickly, as the frosting will set as it cools, sandwich the cakes together with one-third of the frosting to form a triple-layered cake, then swirl the remainder over the top and sides. Decorate with a few walnut halves scattered on top of the cake and sprinkle with demerara sugar if you like.

STORING CAKES

What is the best way to store cakes, and how do I keep a cake moist once it has been cut?

Store them in airtight tins rather than plastic boxes, as plastic can encourage mould and also taints cakes with lingering smells. Do not store cakes and biscuits in the same tin, as the moisture from the cake will make the biscuits soggy.

Once a cake has been cut, you can keep it moist for a few days by wrapping it in foil before storing it, or inverting a mixing bowl over it.

See also: TRAYBAKES

All-in-one Sponge Cake

MAKES: *1 × 20 cm (8 in)*
round cake, to serve 10
PREPARATION TIME:
15 minutes
COOKING TIME:
50 – 60 minutes

225 g (8 oz) soft margarine
225 g (8 oz) caster sugar
4 eggs, size 3
225 g (8 oz) self-raising flour
1 teaspoon baking powder
A few drops vanilla essence

1 Preheat the oven to 180°C (350°F, gas mark 4). Grease a 20 cm (8 in) round cake tin and line the base of it with greaseproof paper.
2 Put the margarine, sugar and eggs in a mixing bowl, then sift in the flour, baking powder and vanilla essence. Beat the mixture lightly until it is thoroughly blended but be careful not to overmix.
3 Spoon the mixture into the tin and spread it level. Bake for 50 – 60 minutes or until the cake is golden and firm to the touch in the centre.
4 Leave the cake to cool in the tin for 3 minutes then turn it out onto a wire rack and leave to cool further; peel away the greaseproof paper while the cake is still slightly warm. It will keep for three to four days in an airtight tin.

CELEBRATION CAKES

◆

Even if you rarely bake cakes, there is no problem with this easy sponge – simply beat all the ingredients together and you have the base for the splendid cakes shown here. Icing is simple too: use ready-made sugarpaste icing to cover the cakes, and ready-made royal icing for all the pretty decorations.

The easy basic sponge cake, cooked in a heart shape, just needs to be iced and decorated to make the elegant, quilted cake below.

Golden Wedding Cake

PREPARATION TIME: *4 hours, plus 24 hours drying time, plus time to make the All-in-one Sponge Cake*

1 heart-shaped Sponge Cake (see method below)
4 tablespoons apricot jam, sieved
675 g (1 lb 8 oz) ready-to-roll sugarpaste icing
Yellow paste food colouring
50 g (1 ¾ oz) royal icing
Roses, dried gypsophila and gift-wrapping ribbon

1 You need a 20 cm (8 in) heart-shaped cake tin for this cake. You might be able to borrow one from your local cake shop. Otherwise you can make the cake in a square tin and then cut it into a heart shape: trim away the sides to a slope and trim the offcuts to make the round shapes to put at the top. Stick them to the cake with a little jam.
2 Brush the cake all over with apricot jam. Add yellow colouring to 450 g (1 lb) of the ready-to-roll icing and mix well. Roll out the icing and drape it over the cake. Smooth it down over the top and sides of the cake, then trim the edges. Smooth down with your palms to make a completely flat surface.

GOLDEN WEDDING CAKE

3 To give a quilted effect to the top of the cake, use the edge of a ruler to mark on crisscross lines.
4 With the royal icing, pipe small dots round the top edge and base of the cake.
5 To make the roses, divide up the remaining sugarpaste icing into two or three parts. Before rolling them out, add different amounts of colour to each to make two or three shades of yellow.
6 Roll each portion of icing into a number of pea-sized balls. Make a teardrop-shaped petal from one of these balls then make five or six more and roll each petal round the first one, overlapping. Pull away the bulky base part and open out the petals.
7 Place the rose in an egg carton or bun tin lined with crumpled foil. Make the rest of the roses, harmonising the various shades of petal. Leave them all to dry for 24 hours.
8 To serve the cake, decorate it with the roses, gypsophila and strips of gift-wrapping ribbon pulled into curls.

VARIATION
If you are short of time, use bought silk flowers instead of making icing roses.

TEDDY BEAR CAKE

Teddy Bear Cake

PREPARATION TIME: 2 hours, plus time to make the All-in-one Sponge Cake

1 round chocolate sponge cake flavoured with 2 tablespoons of cocoa powder dissolved in 3 tablespoons of boiling water added to the basic recipe with the vanilla
1 chocolate swiss roll
6 tablespoons sieved marmalade
550 g (1 lb 4 oz) ready-to-roll sugarpaste icing
Brown, red and black paste food colouring
Bootlace liquorice and liquorice allsort sweets

1 Start by making the ears. Cut out two crescent-shaped indents from either side of the cake where the ears will be. Cut two pieces from the swiss roll, each of the same height as the cake, and place one in each indent: these are the bear's ears.
2 Brush the top and sides of the cake with marmalade. Place the two cut-out pieces of sponge cake in the centre of the face to form the snout.
3 Colour 300 g (10½ oz) of the icing dark brown and roll it out thinly to a circle large enough to cover the cake.
4 Drape the icing over the top and sides, smooth down and trim the edges, setting the trimmings aside.
5 Roll out two circles from the reserved white icing to make up the eyes and place a liquorice allsort on each.
6 Colour all but a teaspoon of the remaining icing a lighter brown and divide it into three balls. Flatten one ball into an oval to cover the raised snout, place it over the top and smooth down. Roll out the remaining balls, cut them into two semicircular shapes and stick them on top of the ears. Prick them and the snout all over with a fork.
7 With the remaining icing, make a black nose and red tongue and stick them on.
8 Cut thin strips of liquorice for the eyelashes and mouth shape and press into place.

DAISY CHRISTENING CAKE

Daisy Christening Cake

PREPARATION TIME: 1 hour 20 minutes, plus 2 – 3 hours drying time, plus time to make the All-in-one Sponge Cake

1 round sponge cake
6 tablespoons seedless raspberry jam
4 tablespoons apricot jam
750 g (1 lb 10 oz) ready-to-roll sugarpaste icing
50 g (1¾ oz) royal icing
Pink, yellow and blue paste food colouring
Narrow pink or blue ribbon

1 Divide the cake in two horizontally, spread raspberry jam on the bottom layer, then press the cake back together.
2 Brush the top and sides of the cake with sieved apricot jam. Roll out three-quarters of the sugarpaste icing to a circle large enough to cover the top and sides. Lay it on the cake, trim the edges and smooth flat using your palms.
3 To make the daisies, roll half the remaining sugarpaste icing into 18 pea-sized balls, then shape each ball into a teardrop. Pinch the thin end to make a stalk, then flatten out the rounded end so it looks like a large thumb tack.
4 Using small scissors, snip tiny 'petals' all around the edge, then use the tips of the scissors to prick small dots over the centre.
5 Leave to dry out for a few hours on foil, crumpled to stop the icing sticking to it.
6 With an artist's small paint-brush, colour the outer tips pink and the centre yellow using food colouring.
7 Roll out the remaining sugarpaste icing thinly and cut it into six 1 cm (½ in) wide strips. Dab the end of each strip with a little royal icing, then twist them and hang them in a garland round the top of the cake.
8 Using a dab of royal icing, stick on two or three daisies where the loops join.
9 Colour the remaining royal icing pink or blue. Pipe the child's name on the top of the cake, then pipe a simple border round the base.
10 When the icing is dry, tie pink or blue ribbon round the side of the cake.

CANAPES

TASTY NIBBLES

I have eaten delicious canapés at parties, but never tried to make them at home. Can you suggest some quick and colourful ideas?

It is very easy to make your own canapés by simply using triangles of rye bread or shapes of toasted bread as the bases. Or you can try making attractive little croustade cases (see box, right).

The toppings and fillings used for canapés can be simple as well. Spread triangles of rye bread or toast with slivers of smoked salmon sprinkled with black pepper and lemon juice, or spread them with dill mayonnaise and top with some gravad lax. Try also caper and olive tapenade (see page 72) with slices

of soft mozzarella cheese and some halved cherry tomatoes, seasoned with olive oil, salt, pepper and basil.

For a tasty tuna pâté filling for croustades, blend 200 g (7 oz) of canned tuna, 75 g (2¾ oz) of salted butter and the juice of a lemon with 3 tablespoons of mayonnaise. This will make enough to fill about ten croustade cases. Even simpler, fill the bases with either whipped Mascarpone cheese or soured cream before adding a topping.

Choosing an attractive garnish with the right complementary taste is extremely important when you are making canapés. The garnish must be both delicate and small. Any of the following would make a good finishing touch: a slice of olive, a half teaspoon of caviar or salmon roe, a sprig of some fresh herb, a dusting of paprika or a tiny rosette of piped cream or mayonnaise. See below for more ideas.

Pink gin tastes great with filled croustade canapés: try soured cream topped with smoked salmon; quail's eggs, salmon roe and dill; tapenade with mozzarella, cherry tomatoes and basil; or lumpfish roe and chives on soured cream.

MAKING CROUSTADE BASES FOR CANAPES

These baked bread shapes are easy and quick to make. Fill them with savoury mixtures and serve with drinks either before a meal or as part of a buffet dinner.

1 Preheat the oven to 180°C (350°F, gas mark 4). Gently melt some butter - you need 150 g (5½ oz) for every 12 croustades you are making.

2 Use a fluted pastry cutter with a diameter of about 6 - 7.5 cm (2½ - 3 in). Cut rounds of thinly sliced white bread and dip these in melted butter. Press the rounds firmly into the wells of a bun tin.

3 Place the tin in the oven, with a second bun tin nested on top of the first to keep the bread in shape. Bake for 15 - 20 minutes, until the croustades are firm.

4 Lift the croustades from the tin with a palette knife and place them on a wire rack to cool. Fill imaginatively and serve.

WORKING AHEAD

Do canapés have to be made immediately before serving?

No, the various spreads for fillings can be made in advance and kept refrigerated (although the colour of some foods, such as avocado, might spoil). The croustade or toast bases can also be made 24 hours ahead if they are kept stored in an airtight container. However, it is best to assemble the canapés as near to the serving time as possible so the toast or croustade bases stay crisp.

HOW MUCH IS ENOUGH?

Are there any guidelines about how many canapés I should make for a drinks party?

The amount of food guests will consume depends on the occasion, as well as on their appetites. Here are some very rough guidelines for the number of canapés you should produce for various get-togethers:
- COCKTAIL PARTY: Allow around ten canapés for each person.
- LUNCHTIME DRINKS: Allow up to 15 canapés per person if guests are unlikely to go on to a meal.
- PRE-LUNCH OR PRE-DINNER DRINKS: Allow four to five canapés for each person before the meal.
- WEDDING RECEPTION: Allow about eight cocktail canapés, plus four miniature sweet cakes or tiny pastries, for each person.

See also: CHEESE BISCUITS

CANNELLONI

CHEESY FILLING

I am tired of cannelloni stuffed with spinach. Could you suggest a more interesting filling?

Spinach or meat are the most usual stuffings for the rolled pancakes of pasta called cannelloni, but this tasty recipe for Ricotta Cannelloni (right) shows a clever alternative. Three different cheeses are combined with a fresh vegetable sauce.

Ricotta cannelloni

SERVES: 4 - 6
PREPARATION TIME: 30 minutes
COOKING TIME: 50 minutes

FOR THE SAUCE
2 tablespoons light olive oil
1 medium onion, chopped
1 carrot, finely chopped
1 stalk celery, chopped
400 g (14 oz) canned chopped
   tomatoes
A pinch of dried thyme
A pinch of sugar
Salt and black pepper
40 g (1 1/2 oz) Parmesan cheese,
   freshly grated

FOR THE CANNELLONI
250 g (9 oz) mozzarella cheese,
   chopped
175 g (6 oz) cooked ham, chopped
250 g (9 oz) ricotta cheese
2 tablespoons parsley, chopped
2 eggs, size 2
Several gratings of fresh nutmeg
Salt and black pepper
12 sheets of fresh or dried lasagne
   pasta, 10 x 8 cm (4 x 3 1/4 in)
Butter for baking

1 To make the sauce, gently heat the oil and sauté the onion, carrot and celery until they soften. Add the chopped tomatoes, thyme and sugar and season to taste. Simmer, partially covered, for at least 30 minutes.
2 Prepare the filling by mixing the mozzarella, ham, ricotta, parsley and eggs together very well. Season the mixture generously with gratings of nutmeg, salt and pepper.
3 Preheat the oven to 190°C (375°F, gas mark 5).
4 Bring a large pan of water to the boil. Add 2 tablespoons of salt and a little oil and poach the fresh pasta, three sheets at a time, for a minute or two. Dried pasta needs 4 minutes.
5 Dip the cooked pasta in a bowl of cold water, then spread on tea cloths to dry. Butter an ovenproof dish.
6 When the sheets are cool enough to handle, lay them out on a work surface and divide the ricotta filling equally among them, placing the mixture on the shorter end of each sheet. Roll up and enclose.
7 Put a little sauce in the bottom of the dish, arrange the pasta seam side down in it and spread the rest of the sauce on top. Dot with butter and sprinkle with the Parmesan cheese.
8 Bake for 20 minutes, then serve.

Controlling your pasta

Lasagne sheets for cannelloni and other pasta will not boil over if you rub oil inside the pan. Also, pour a little more oil in the cooking water to stop the pasta sticking together.

CAPERS

FLAVOURSOME BUDS

What are capers?

They are the small, unopened buds of a thorny plant that grows wild all around the Mediterranean. Capers are picked and then pickled in salty vinegar. They should be kept swimming in this liquid after the jar has been opened.

SAUCES AND SPREADS

How are capers used?

Some sauces, such as the one for English leg of mutton, use capers – and the buds are also good served with chicken, veal and salmon.

In southern Europe, the caper is more likely to be included in salty spreads, such as the recipe for Provençal Tapenade (see overleaf). This highly flavoured purée from Provence is often served with raw vegetables or pasta.

You can also spread tapenade on thin slices of dried French bread and eat it as a canapé with drinks – perhaps while waiting for meat to cook on the barbecue.

Tapenade can be a very tasty addition to cut hard-boiled eggs as a first course. Either mash the yolks with tapenade and pile them back into the whites, or place the halves on lettuce and put a teaspoon of the spread over each half of egg.

Capers have been used since Roman times and are essential to the tangy flavour of tapenade. This versatile spread tastes best on French bread, topped with olives.

Provençal tapenade

MAKES: *350 g (12 oz), or about 30 smallish canapés*
PREPARATION TIME: *30 minutes*
COOKING TIME: *none*

35 g (1 ¼ oz) canned anchovy fillets, drained
2 tablespoons milk
85 g (3 oz) capers, drained
175 g (6 oz) black olives, drained and stoned
75 g (2 ¾ oz) canned tuna, drained and flaked
1 tablespoon mustard powder
150 ml (5 fl oz) olive oil
1 - 2 tablespoons brandy
½ teaspoon mixed spice, or a mix of black pepper, ground cloves and grated nutmeg

1 Put the drained anchovy fillets in a shallow dish, cover with milk and leave to soak for 10 minutes.
2 Put the capers and stoned olives in a processor and blend to a purée. Drain the anchovies and add them to the caper and olive mixture, along with the tuna and mustard powder. Process until smooth.
3 Add the olive oil a little at a time, processing all the while. When it is properly amalgamated, stir in the brandy and spices.
4 This is best served immediately, spread on thin slices of French bread which have been dried in the oven.

CARROTS

ADDING HERBS

Are there any herbs that would add a bit of excitement to a plain vegetable like carrots?

Carrots are simple and marry well with almost any herb. In winter, dried thyme, rosemary or even lavender bring a fragrance to the sweet, maincrop vegetable. Dill is the gentle, classic herb used with all types of carrots, while mint is a spring and early summer favourite. Parsley is a good addition any time, as is coriander, particularly if you like your carrots cooked in a blend of orange juice and butter.

CUTTING MATTERS

Does the way I cut carrots affect how the vegetable cooks?

The way a carrot is chopped does affect its finished texture (see box, opposite). Carrots that are sliced into discs cook soft and are ideal for simple boiled carrots or to be made into purées. Batons, which are cut lengthways, can be cooked fast and stay crisp for stir-fries or to toss into pasta. You can also 'roll-cut' a carrot for maximum surface and angles so that it will caramelise, as in the recipe below.

Roll-cut carrots in butter and Marsala

SERVES: *4*
PREPARATION TIME: *10 minutes*
COOKING TIME: *15 - 18 minutes*

500 g (1 lb 2 oz) medium carrots
Salt
25 g (1 oz) butter
90 ml (3 ¼ fl oz) Marsala
Black pepper

1 Peel and roll-cut the carrots, then spread them in a wide, heavy-based pan. Sprinkle with salt, dot with the butter and add the Marsala. Cover and cook over a medium heat for about 15 minutes until they are soft.
2 Leave a serving dish to warm. Uncover the carrots and continue cooking, shaking the pan constantly over the heat until the carrots begin to look roasted around the edges and the liquor is reduced to a glaze.
3 Transfer the carrots to the warmed serving dish, grind black pepper over them and serve immediately.
VARIATION
To make a refreshing cooked carrot salad, substitute 2 tablespoons of olive oil for the butter, and use water with the juice of half a lime and a teaspoon of sugar in place of the Marsala. Allow the carrots to cool, then shred mint leaves over them.

You can choose different styles of cutting carrots and these will suit varied occasions and dishes. Note that the variation in appearance also leads to some differences in how the carrots will cook. Here are some of the most common shapes and how to make them:

TO SLICE

Hold the peeled carrot firmly and cut in either diagonal or straight slices which are as thick as a pound coin. These coin-sized slices will soften well during cooking.

TO MAKE BATONS

Halve the peeled carrot lengthways, and across if it is very long. You can then slice the chopped carrot into short batons which are about the thickness of a thin pencil.

TO 'ROLL-CUT'

Cut a wedge at an angle across the thick end of a peeled carrot, then continue making diagonal cuts, turning the carrot about one-third around between each cut.

CARVING

BOARDS OR PLATES

Is it better to carve meat on a board or on a plate?

You can use either a board or a plate as long as it is large enough and sits firmly on a surface that is nonslip. The platter or board used should be almost flat, as carving in a deep dish is virtually impossible.

If the table is slippery and the serving plate is china, put a cloth mat or folded napkin underneath to keep the dish from moving. And while it may look attractive to put the potatoes and other vegetables around the joint, this can make carving awkward and messy.

Another essential requirement for carving is a razor-sharp knife and a carving fork with a guard to prevent the knife slipping.

RULES FOR CARVING

Are there some general rules for effective carving?

For regular, attractive slices, make sure that the cuts go across the grain of the meat. Cutting with the grain tends to result in slices that are shredded and stringy. However, when carving undersides of joints like sirloin of beef or leg of lamb, it is easier to cut more thickly and with the grain of the meat.

Cold meat is generally sliced thinner than hot meat. If you are going to serve the meat cold, wait until the joint cools before carving or the slices will lose their juices, colour and texture. It is also much easier to carve a cold joint.

NO WISHBONE

What is the best technique for carving poultry?

When carving small poultry, use a short, flexible carving knife and a table fork or small carving fork (see box, page 75). It is much easier to carve chicken at the table if the wishbone is removed before the

bird has been cooked. The method is quite simple: pull back the skin at the neck end to expose the breastbone, then cut and scrape with a short, sharp knife to extract the wishbone. Do not cut too deeply into the meat as you work. After the bone has been removed, tuck the skin back under the bird.

RELAXED MEAT

I often read that you should let meat rest before carving. Why is this so important?

Whatever meat you have roasted, you should always take it out of the oven and leave it to stand for about 15 – 30 minutes, depending on size, before it is carved.

Cover the joint with aluminium foil and put it in a warm place. Resting allows the juices to sink back from the surface and they can then be reabsorbed to tenderise the meat. It also makes meat easier to carve, as juices will not spurt out.

POWER CARVING

Are electric carving knives worth buying and using?

Electric carving knives are labour-saving if you have large amounts of meat to carve. However, they can be unwieldy and noisy and are not very suitable for use at the table.

Also, it can be difficult to achieve very thin slices with an electric knife, especially when carving hot meat. Great care must be taken as electric knives are very sharp and can be dangerous to use.

To the rescue!

If you want to avoid unattractive holes in your poultry when carving, turn the fork over. With practice, you will find that you can hold the bird securely with the back of the prongs without making marks in the meat.

SPECIAL TIPS

Are there different methods of carving various kinds of joints?

If the meat has been boned first, carving is easy, whatever the joint. You can simply cut the slices in the thickness you prefer, moving across the grain of the meat.

If the meat is on the bone, you will need to adjust your carving techniques accordingly. Always use a carving fork with a thumbguard, for safety. Here are a variety of common carving tasks with details about how best to proceed.

CARVING LOINS

Loins and best end of lamb, pork, veal and venison are roasted on the bone to prevent shrinkage and preserve the flavour. But when you are ready to carve, it is easier to remove the meat from the rib cage and then slice it to the desired thickness. Pork is shown below.

1 Cut down between the chine bone and the meat and then angle the knife between the meat and the ribs, cutting the meat free of the bones. Remove the crackling from the joint in one piece.

2 The meat can now be sliced, and the crackling can be cut with scissors into the same number of pieces as there are slices of meat.

CARVING LEGS

Legs of lamb, pork, veal and venison should all be carved in the same manner. The pictures below show the method used on a leg of lamb.

1 Put the leg meaty side up and cut a shallow 'V' from the middle. Carve slices downwards from both sides of the 'V', then turn the leg over and slice the rest of the meat horizontally.

2 Legs can also be cut in diagonal slices starting from the knuckle end. While this is most common with hams, the technique is an alternative you can try with all legs of meat.

CARVING A LARGE RIB OF BEEF

Cooking a rib of beef on the bone helps to conduct heat to the centre of a joint and gives a rich flavour. You can remove all the meat from the bone in one chunk and then carve it, but this rather spoils the effect. Try this way instead.

1 Place the rib of beef on its side and start by making a 5 cm (2 in) deep cut along the ribs. Be sure to go the full length of the ribs with your cutting.

2 Stand the meat up, rib side down. Carve several slices, lift these off and place them on a warm dish.

3 Turn the rib back on its side and make a second 5 cm (2 in) cut. Stand the joint up and carve more.

CARVING POULTRY

A chicken, duck, goose and small turkey are all carved in the same manner. As it can be quite tricky to carve slices from the breast of a small bird, it is sometimes easier to remove the breast in one piece. See the pictures below and right for illustrations of this technique on a small chicken.

1 Lay the bird on its side and cut under the thigh, lifting the whole leg up with a fork. To halve the leg and make two portions, cut through the joint at the top of the drumstick.

2 Cut down the breast, halfway across and through the shoulder, then cut all around to remove the shoulder, wing and a long strip of breast all in one piece. Lift this piece with the fork, holding the body down with the knife, and cut away.

3 If the chicken is only a small one, simply cut away the remaining breast in one piece. Alternatively, if the chicken is large enough, you can carve the breast into slices by starting at the wing end. Work your way systematically towards the back.

CARVING TURKEY

A small turkey can be carved like a chicken (see above) – but one that weighs more than 4.5 kg (10 lb) is not easy to move from side to side. For a bigger turkey, it can be much better to put it on a board and carve it while it is firmly in place, as shown in the pictures below and right.

1 Remove the trussing string then cut between the body and the thigh all around. When these cuts are made, cut through the connecting sinews.

2 Pull the leg away from the body and you can then carve the flesh into very small slices that are slanted parallel to the bone.

3 Cut down through the shoulder joint, removing a small piece of breast meat attached to the shoulder and wing. Turn the bird and cut away the shoulder and wing on the other side in the same manner. This now clears the way for slicing the breast.

4 A turkey breast is large enough to carve into thin slices on the bone. Turn the fork over so that the prongs do not puncture the meat and stay out of the way of the knife. Alternatively, you can remove the whole breast, lay it flat and carve it across the grain.

SHOULDER OF LAMB

A shoulder can be quite tricky to carve because of the arched bone that runs through it. The secret is to carve it with the bone away from you, so you can get at the meat.

Put the shoulder skin side up and cut a long slice from the centre, on the side opposite the bone. Carve out more thick slices on either side, then horizontal slices from the top over the central bone. Turn the joint over and carve horizontally.

SADDLE OF LAMB

You can carve saddle of lamb by removing the loins from either side of the backbone and cutting across the grain. Alternatively, carve it on the bone as shown here.

1 The chump end of the saddle should be carved into thin slices across the grain of the meat, and at right angles to the backbone.

2 The main part of the saddle, lying each side of the backbone, is cut into thin strips or narrow slices down its full length.

CASSEROLE

HEARTY MIXTURES

What is the difference between a casserole, stew and daube?

All use long, slow, moist cooking in a covered container to tenderise tough meats and vegetables, but they differ in the ingredients and type of pot used.

A casserole uses small pieces of meat and vegetables and is usually cooked in the oven. A stew is often made on the hob (and originally would have been cooked slowly over an open fire). A daube makes use of a large cut of meat, often beef, braised in wine. Traditionally, it was cooked over a fire in a tall casserole with an indented lid full of hot charcoal, so it had heat from both the top and bottom.

FLOURING AND FRYING

Why do recipes tell you to flour and fry the meat first when it is going to be casseroled for hours?

The meat is fried partly to seal in the juices, and also to give it a rich brown colour. Flour protects meat, and helps to thicken the gravy.

Fry the meat in small batches, for only a minute or two each batch. It is not necessary to move the meat around in the pan. Simply turn each piece so it browns all over.

To flour meat, place the cubes into a paper or polythene bag and add the flour and seasoning. Hold the bag closed and shake until all the meat has been coated.

Using a polythene bag to toss meat in flour helps to ensure an even coating.

MAKING AND USING BEURRE MANIÉ

If your finished casserole is too thin, you can thicken the sauce by adding beurre manié – a simple paste made with equal quantities of flour and butter.

1 Soften the butter and place it in a small bowl along with the flour. Stir and mash with a fork until a thick paste has been formed.

2 Gradually add small pieces of the beurre manié paste to the sauce of the cooked casserole. Stir in the paste until the sauce thickens and is smooth.

LENGTHY COOKING

Recipes often suggest cooking casseroles for 2 - 3 hours to make them tender, but I find that it can take about 4 hours. Am I doing something wrong?

The cooking time for a casserole depends largely on the cut of meat that is used. Nowadays, relatively tender cuts of meat are included which can be cooked successfully in as little as 2–3 hours.

In previous times, traditional casseroles were made with the tougher cuts from the leg, neck and shoulder of older animals. The well-developed muscle fibre and connective tissue could be broken down only by slow, moist cooking. Casserole meat is usually cut into pieces to accelerate this process.

These tough cuts of meat usually have an excellent flavour, with the connective tissue dissolving to a gelatine during slow cooking. This gives a very soft texture and an excellent rich, velvety sauce, but the process may take 4 hours.

To make a casserole that cooks in a shorter amount of time but still has plenty of flavour, try the meat from a shoulder of venison. It is too dry to roast but is excellent when used in a fruity recipe such as Venison Casserole with Cranberries and Orange (right).

Venison casserole with cranberries and orange

SERVES: 4 - 6
PREPARATION TIME: 25 minutes plus marinating time
COOKING TIME: 1 ¾ hours

FOR THE MARINADE
250 ml (9 fl oz) red wine
2 tablespoons olive oil
A sprig of fresh thyme
2 bay leaves
2 strips of orange rind

FOR THE CASSEROLE
1 kg (2 lb 4 oz) venison stewing steak, diced
2 tablespoons oil
150 g (5 ½ oz) streaky bacon, rind off and chopped
250 g (9 oz) onions, peeled, sliced
1 stick celery, sliced
50 g (1 ¾ oz) flour
250 ml (9 fl oz) stock or water
Juice of 1 orange
Salt and pepper
150 g (5 ½ oz) cranberries

---

1 Mix the marinade in a large bowl and add the venison. Cover and leave at room temperature for 2 - 3 hours, or overnight in a refrigerator.
2 Preheat the oven to 160°C (325°F, gas mark 3).
3 Drain the venison, reserving the marinade but discarding the orange peel, and pat dry with kitchen paper.

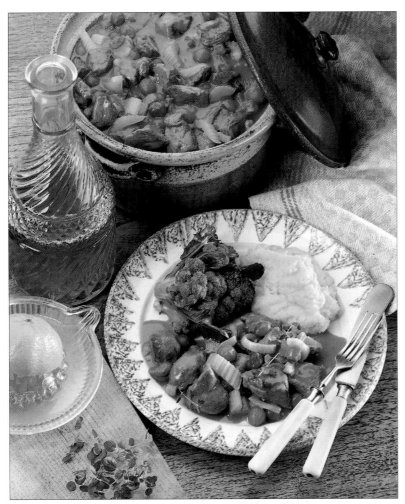

Red cranberries add a bright touch to the rich, dark colour of this venison casserole. Using a marinade adds flavour and helps to speed the cooking time.

WHITE CASSEROLES

Are a fricassée and a blanquette the same dish?

No, although both are white stews. A fricassée is made from poultry and other white meat, and the meat is just turned in fat but not browned before cooking in a white sauce.

For a blanquette, the meat or seafood is poached in stock and a sauce is made with the liquor after cooking, to pour over the meat.

Fricassée really should be made with fresh meat but the modified Turkey Fricassée below is an excellent way of using leftovers.

Turkey fricassée

SERVES: *4*
PREPARATION TIME: *20 minutes*
COOKING TIME: *20 minutes*

---

50 g (1 ¾ oz) butter
1 medium onion, chopped
1 stick celery, sliced
500 g (1 lb 2 oz) cooked turkey, boned, skinned and in pieces
50 g (1 ¾ oz) flour
500 ml (18 fl oz) turkey, chicken or ham stock
150 ml (5 fl oz) cream or milk
A pinch of ground nutmeg
1 teaspoon lemon juice
Salt and black pepper
150 g (5 ½ oz) mushrooms, sliced
1 tablespoon chopped parsley, tarragon or thyme

---

1 Heat the butter in a medium or large saucepan or flameproof casserole, then add the chopped onion and celery and sauté them over a medium heat for 5 minutes.
2 Add the turkey pieces and sauté for 5 minutes. Stir in the flour and cook gently for a minute. Gradually add the stock and stir until the sauce is thickened and smooth.
3 Add the cream, nutmeg and lemon juice, add salt and pepper to taste and bring to the boil slowly, stirring.
4 Add the mushrooms, cover and simmer gently for 10 - 15 minutes, stirring occasionally until heated.
5 Stir in the parsley, tarragon or thyme. Serve hot with rice and a green vegetable or salad.

4 Heat the oil in a large saucepan or flameproof casserole dish and fry the venison until slightly browned, then remove from the pan. Add the bacon, onion and celery and sauté for 5 minutes. Stir in the flour and cook gently for a further minute.
5 Add the stock, reserved marinade and orange juice and bring to the boil, stirring until thickened. Add the venison, salt and pepper and return to the boil. Then simmer for just 2 minutes, stirring occasionally.
6 Transfer the casserole to the oven and cook, covered, for an hour.
7 Add the cranberries and return to the oven, covered, for 30 minutes until the cranberries are cooked.
8 Remove the herbs from the liquid and garnish with fresh thyme. Serve with mashed potatoes or noodles.

STOCK QUESTION

Why do recipes require the use of stock for casseroles - don't the ingredients give enough flavour?

A well-flavoured stock will give a better taste than plain water. However, it is quite acceptable to use plain water with the tougher cuts of meat. These are anyway best left to cook for a long time along with other flavourings such as herbs, vegetables, spices and wine.

Adding some bones is another way in which you can help to improve the taste of a casserole. Shank bones have a hollow centre which contains a soft material called marrow. Putting these bones in enhances the stock flavour as well as providing good nutrients.

CAULIFLOWER

PICK AND CHOOSE

How should I go about selecting a cauliflower? Some I have had have been disappointing when cooked.

Look for firm, creamy-white florets that are tight and without brown speckles. Check also the condition of the base of the stem. If it is dry and discoloured, the cauliflower is certainly past its best.

The outer leaves of a cauliflower are usually cut away before they are sold. This helps you to see the head but removes what would be a clue to a limp, older cauliflower that is definitely best avoided.

SOAKING UP FLAVOURS

Why is cauliflower so often served with a sauce?

Cauliflower is a particularly bland vegetable served on its own. The absorbent heads are much better soaking up a cheese sauce to make a tasty lunch or family supper dish, as in the recipe shown on the right.

The ability to soak up flavours also makes cauliflower an excellent ingredient to add to stir-fries, or to include in vegetable curries.

Cauliflower cheese and bacon gratin

SERVES: 4
PREPARATION TIME: 20 minutes
COOKING TIME: 35 minutes

500 g (1 lb 2 oz) cauliflower
250 ml (9 fl oz) milk
Salt
25 g (1 oz) butter, plus extra for
    greasing dish
1 clove garlic, finely chopped
75 g (2 ¾ oz) rindless bacon, diced
25 g (1 oz) plain flour
100 ml (3 ½ fl oz) double cream
50 g (1 ¾ oz) Gruyère cheese,
    grated
Pepper and grated nutmeg
2 tablespoons finely grated
    Parmesan cheese

1 Break up the cauliflower into florets and cut the stalk diagonally into 5 mm (¼ in) slices.
2 Bring a large pan of salted water to the boil and cook both the florets and sliced stem for 7 - 8 minutes.

Take 75 ml (2 ½ fl oz) of the cooking liquid and mix it with the milk and then drain the florets thoroughly.
3 Preheat the oven to 200°C (400°F, gas mark 6). Butter a gratin dish and scatter chopped garlic over the base.
4 Melt the butter in a frying pan and fry the bacon for 5 minutes or until it releases its fat. While it is cooking, heat the milk mixture.
5 Sprinkle the flour into the bacon pan and stir over a gentle heat for about 2 - 3 minutes without letting it brown. Remove the pan from the heat and gradually stir in enough milk mixture to make a thick sauce.
6 Add more milk mixture and as the sauce thins, return it to the heat and add the rest of the milk mixture; stir constantly until the sauce begins to bubble. Reduce the heat and simmer for about 5 minutes. Stir in the cream slowly and return to boiling point.
7 Remove from the heat and add half the Gruyère cheese. Stir until the cheese has melted, then season with salt, pepper and grated nutmeg.
8 Spread the cauliflower florets in the prepared gratin dish and slowly pour the sauce over, allowing it to permeate the florets.
9 Mix the remaining Gruyère cheese and the Parmesan and scatter over the sauce. Bake for about 20 minutes, until the top is bubbling nicely and has become well browned.

CAVIAR

TYPES OF CAVIAR

What is the difference between the various types of caviar and why are some so expensive?

Caviar is the roe (or eggs) of the sturgeon. These are very lightly salted, which helps to preserve and flavour them. The three main types of caviar – beluga, oscietra and sevruga – come from different varieties of sturgeon. These originate mainly from fish in the Caspian Sea that are over 15 years old.

The most expensive caviar is from the beluga, as only about a hundred fish are caught each year.

Bacon adds a scrumptious extra flavour to the traditional combination of cauliflower in a cheese sauce. Let the dish brown handsomely for best appeal.

The eggs are fragile and vary in colour from light to dark grey with a white spot. Sevruga is small and dark grey, with a light, sweet taste.

Nutty-flavoured eggs from the oscietra are small and black when the fish are young – but become larger and golden as the fish ages.

CAVIAR SUBSTITUTES

Are there any inexpensive versions of caviar available?

Pressed caviar, a favourite with the Russians, is a mixture of damaged or fragile eggs pressed through muslin after salting and costs less than real caviar. Other less dear varieties include salmon caviar, also known as red caviar or keta, which is shiny and orange-red in colour, and lumpfish caviar, which is very small and black. Although these are not really 'true' caviars, they have a similar, highly salted taste.

SERVING SUGGESTIONS

If I were lucky enough to be given caviar, how should I serve it?

Set the can in a bowl filled with ice. Open the chilled can just before serving, as air causes caviar to oxidise, affecting the flavour. Serve it simply, with triangles of hot toast and unsalted butter.

Blini (buckwheat pancakes) and soured cream are also good with caviar, as are smoked salmon and new potatoes with crème fraîche. Avoid sharp accompaniments such as egg, lemon, onion and parsley which only detract from the flavour. Serve champagne and iced vodka as the traditional drinks.

CELERIAC

RICH MASH

How is the vegetable celeriac prepared and cooked?

As one of our knobblier home-grown roots, celeriac needs to be thickly peeled and cut straight into water acidulated with lemon juice

to prevent discoloration. It cooks to a good purée, which is often mixed with mashed potato to soften its flavour and make the texture drier, as in the recipe below. Chopped celery adds a crunchy contrast. The purée goes well with game, and is very good with fish, particularly as the topping to a fish pie.

Celeriac and potato purée with celery

SERVES: 4
PREPARATION TIME: 10 minutes
COOKING TIME: 30 minutes

400 g (14 oz) celeriac
Juice of 1 lemon
400 g (14 oz) even-sized floury potatoes, suitable for mashing
50 g (1 ¾ oz) butter
2 tablespoons milk
Salt, black pepper and a pinch of nutmeg
1 large stalk celery, destrung and finely diced

1 Peel the celeriac thickly and cut it into even chunks. Drop the pieces straight into a bowl of water mixed with half of the lemon juice.
2 Drain the celeriac and put it into a pan of boiling water containing the rest of the lemon juice.
3 Bring the water back to the boil, then reduce the heat to simmering point and cook the celeriac until soft. Cooking time varies, but should be about the same as for potatoes.
4 Drain the celeriac well, returning it to the pan and shaking over the heat to dry the pieces thoroughly. Then purée the celeriac in a food processor or by thorough mashing.
5 Scrub the potatoes and cook them whole for 15 - 25 minutes until soft. Drain and skin when cool enough to handle, then mash with a potato masher. (Never use an electric tool on potatoes as it turns them gluey.)
6 Mix the two purées together. Warm the butter in the milk until it melts, swirl in salt and pepper and a good grating of nutmeg, and then beat it into the mash.
7 Mix in the celery, spread in an oven dish and keep warm until ready to eat, or reheat in the oven.

SALAD DAYS

Can celeriac be used in salads?

Yes. In France, celeriac is popular either sliced or grated as a crunchy hors d'oeuvre, celeriac rémoulade, served tossed in mayonnaise spiked with capers (see recipe page 234).

BLANCHING CELERIAC

Celeriac is blanched before being used in a salad both to set the colour and to soften the flavour.

1 Cut away the knobbly base using a strong, sharp knife. Peel the celeriac thickly and cut into slices. (If you were going to mash it, you could cut it into chunks.)

2 Cut the slices by hand into thin strips, or shred on the julienne-cutting disc of a food processor, and put them into cold water acidulated with the juice of half a lemon.

3 Boil water with juice from the other half lemon. Drain the celeriac and drop it in. When the water returns to the boil, take out the vegetable and run under a cold tap. Drain it and dress the salad.

CELERY

KEEPING IT CRISP

Celery seems to wilt and go soft quite quickly in the fridge, even when left in its polythene sleeve. Is there a way of keeping it crisp?

A whole head of celery will keep fresh for up to a week standing upright in a jug or wide mug with its base in water. You can break off individual stems for use and the remainder will keep, so long as it is still attached to its root base, through which it can absorb water.

To prepare celery, cut the strings from coarser outer stems, trim them and wash all the celery carefully to remove trapped earth. The celery can then be served standing upright in glasses of water as a crisp partner to cheese. For best effect, leave some of the leaves attached.

CHARD

DOUBLE THE USE

There seems to be almost as much stem as leaf on chard. How much of the stem should I discard?

The whole of chard's white stem, which looks a bit like a celery stalk, is wonderfully juicy and some people consider it to be the best bit of the vegetable. It should be cooked separately from the leaf. Cut away the leaf with scissors, peel and destring the fat white stems, cut into 10 cm (4 in) batons and steam or poach them until just tender. Serve hot as a starter with a creamy sauce or cold with vinaigrette.

The leafy part is rather coarser than spinach but can substitute for it. French cooks often use it to give a green marbled effect to a pork pie or terrine, as in the following recipe. The Chard and Pork Terrine is useful as part of a buffet or big picnic spread, and leftovers can be served sliced with French bread or in sandwiches.

Chard and pork terrine

SERVES: 12
PREPARATION TIME: 20 minutes
COOKING TIME: about 1¼ hours

1.5 kg (3 lb 5 oz) belly pork (rind removed and reserved), minced
150 g (5½ oz) streaky bacon in a piece, diced
1 teaspoon each ground mace and celery salt
½ teaspoon each salt and black pepper
Green leaf from 500 g (1 lb 2 oz) chard
To garnish: fresh bay leaves or sprigs of rosemary

1 Ask the butcher to derind and mince the pork and to give you the rind. (If doing it yourself, cut off the rind and set it aside.) Dice the meat and process it to a coarse mince.
2 Mix the pork with the streaky bacon, sprinkle on the mace, celery salt, salt and pepper and work in by hand. To check the seasoning of the meat, fry a teaspoon of the mixture on both sides, then taste it and adjust the seasoning as necessary.
3 Wash the chard and pack it into a pan with no added water. Cover it tightly and simmer for 5 minutes, until the chard is wilted, then drain.
4 Preheat the oven to 160°C (325°F, gas mark 3) and grease a terrine tin of 2 litre (3½ pint) capacity.
5 When the chard is cool enough to handle, press it into a ball and squeeze out the liquid with your hands. Put the ball on a board and slice across at 1 cm (½ in) intervals. Turn and cut again at right angles.
6 Using your hands, mix the chard into the meat mixture then pack it into the tin. Cut the reserved pork rind into rectangles and press it, fat side down, on top of the terrine.
7 Cover the tin with foil, stand it in a roasting tin in the middle of the oven, then pour in boiling water to come halfway up the terrine. Bake

The attractive green marbling in this go-anywhere terrine is formed by chard leaves. You can save the stems of the vegetable to serve another time.

for about 1¼ hours – the exact time will depend on the shape of the tin.
8 Lift a section of rind and insert a skewer into the terrine, then press to squeeze out some juice; it is ready when the juice runs clear.
9 Remove from the oven and leave to stand for 5 - 10 minutes. Uncover, then remove the covering rind. If there is a lot of liquid, pour off a little and set aside, leaving the rest in the terrine to keep it moist.
10 Cool the terrine completely in the tin. Turn out onto a serving plate, cover with cling film and store it in the refrigerator. The liquid you have reserved will set to a jelly which can be warmed to brush onto the chilled terrine as a glaze. Serve garnished with bay leaves or rosemary sprigs.

CHEESE

LOCAL FLAVOUR

What is 'farmhouse cheese'? Does this mean the cheese is of better quality than cheese which is not labelled 'farmhouse'?

The term 'farmhouse' is not legally regulated, so its use is no guarantee that the cheese has been made, as one might expect, on a small scale using traditional equipment. Generally, the term indicates that the cheese has been made on a farm, using the milk of that farm and, frequently, its neighbours. However, this can include a wide area and a large number of animals. Similarly, creameries (cheese producers not based on farms) may be very large or quite small operations, and may take milk from fewer animals than large farmhouse producers.

There is no reason why farmhouse cheeses should necessarily be better than creamery cheeses. Whether Cheddar tastes mild or strong, for instance, will depend primarily on its age. But it is true to say that fine or specialist cheeses are most often made on a small scale, by cheesemakers who use traditional methods, and these are often called 'artisan cheeses'.

RENNET FROM PLANTS

What is vegetarian cheese?

Often cheeses are made using rennet to curdle the milk. Rennet is a preparation made from rennin, an enzyme that acts as a coagulant and is usually taken from the stomachs of calves or sheep. Vegetarian cheeses contain rennet from plant sources, or chemically or genetically engineered rennet that does not require the death of an animal. The cheese will taste the same whatever rennet it is made from. Vegetarian cheeses are made from the same milk as non-vegetarian cheeses and are therefore unsuitable for consumption by vegans.

SAFE TO EAT

Is unpasteurised cheese safe?

Yes. Most Swiss cheeses are made with unpasteurised milk and, by law, some French cheeses, such as Brie de Meaux and Roquefort, can be made authentically only with unpasteurised milk. Pasteurisation, or heat treatment, destroys potentially harmful bacteria and thus enables large industrialised cheesemakers to mix milk from different herds to give a uniform flavour to the finished product.

Unpasteurised cheeses, which are also called 'raw milk' cheeses, are made from milk that has not been heat-treated and the variable flavour of the milk, and therefore the unique taste of the cheese made from it, is part of the appeal these cheeses have for connoisseurs. In any case, most of the pathogens that may be present in the milk are destroyed during cheese making.

However, Britain's Department of Health has warned that even though all milk, whether it is pasteurised or not, comes from dairy herds that are regularly inspected for disease, the very elderly, the very young, pregnant women and people who suffer from immune deficiencies should avoid all soft cheeses, both pasteurised and unpasteurised, because they are more susceptible to the risk of listeria.

SHEEP AND GOATS

How do goat's milk and other animals' cheeses differ from cheeses made with cow's milk?

When they are young, mild and creamy, fresh goat's milk cheeses taste quite similar to cheeses made from cow's milk. Their characteristic tang develops with age and very mature goat's milk cheeses have a strong 'farmyard' flavour though they should always taste clean. Unlike most cow's milk cheeses, the paste is usually bright white in colour, except for hard goat's milk cheese, which is pale yellow.

Goat's milk cheeses are just as high in fat as cow's milk cheeses, but both goat's and ewe's milk cheeses are easier to digest than cow's milk cheeses because their fat particles are smaller; some people who are intolerant of cow's milk can tolerate goat's milk.

With their high flavour, goat's cheeses cannot easily be substituted for cow's milk cheeses in cooking, but if you like the taste, they are good in soufflés, or grilled and served with salads.

Ewe's milk is very high in fat and therefore tends to be made into hard cheeses such as pecorino. However, some soft ewe's cheeses are available; though sharp, they are milder than goat's cheeses and should have a pleasing mellow nuttiness and a firm, creamy texture.

Buffalo milk, used for mozzarella in southern Italy, has a distinctive high aroma and stronger flavour.

Save it!

If you have a glut of cheese, you can freeze some of it for use in cooking. Stilton freezes well, as do semi-hard cheeses and ricotta. But fresh cheeses can go off while defrosting, or become bitter within a day if frozen near the end of their shelf life.

FRESH CHEESES AND PASTA FILATA CHEESES

Fresh cheeses, such as cream and curd cheeses, are less than three weeks old and mild in flavour. They have a soft, moist, creamy texture, bright white colour and no rinds.

Pasta filata cheeses, where the curd is soaked in warm whey to give a putty-like texture, are shaped by hand and have no rinds. They are sometimes aged and/or smoked.

1 RICOTTA, a fresh Italian cheese made with whey and naturally low in fat, has a light milky flavour good for cooking.
2 GOAT'S CHEESE BUTTONS are young, fresh cheeses, sometimes flavoured with herbs, and will develop a rind with age.
3 BOURSIN, from France, is a fresh cream cheese flavoured with garlic and herbs.

4 MOZZARELLA DI BUFALA is a young pasta filata cheese made with buffalo's milk and is good for salads or melting.
5 FETA, which tastes very salty, hails from Greece and may be made with either ewe's milk or cow's milk.
6 CREAM CHEESE is made from single or double cream and has a velvety texture.

7 PROVOLONE, a pasta filata cheese, ranges from mild in flavour when young to strong and spicy when matured.
8 CURD CHEESE is a fresh cow's milk cheese with a light, creamy taste.
9 COTTAGE CHEESE, mild in flavour and low in fat, is made by draining cheese curds and coating them with cream.

KEEPING CHEESE FRESH

Where is the best place to store cheese and how should I wrap it?

Ideally, cheese should be stored in a cool, well-ventilated place, at a temperature of 8–10°C (45–50°F).

However, most people now store cheese in the refrigerator, and this is adequate providing it is kept in the warmer areas, such as the vegetable compartments or the door. To avoid cheese being tainted by the aromas from other foods, keep it in its own plastic box or compartment in the refrigerator.

Wrap individual pieces of cheese in waxed paper or foil. Grease-proof paper draws the fat from the cheese and encourages mould; cling film can induce sweating, although it may be used to cover just the cut surfaces of hard and blue cheeses. Whatever the material used, do not wrap cheese tightly; allow it to breathe. The harder the cheese, the longer it will keep. Cheeses such as Cheddar and other British regional cheeses, and Continental hard cheeses such as Emmental, Gouda, Gruyère, Manchego, Parmesan and Sbrinz, can be kept for months if they are properly wrapped and stored. A little mould or cut surfaces which have become slightly dried and cracked can simply be trimmed away as the quality of the remaining cheese will not have been affected.

RIPENED, UNPRESSED CHEESES

Ripened, unpressed cheeses are over three weeks old and have a bloomy white rind, as in Camembert or Brie, or boast the natural blue-grey surface mould of St Marcellin *and goat's cheeses such as St Maure. Most blue cheeses are also unpressed: it is the spaces between the curds that create the environment in which the blue veining can develop.*

1 EPOISSES is spicy and tangy and washed in white wine or eau-de-vie-de-marc.
2 SHROPSHIRE BLUE, with deep blue veins and orange paste, is strong and piquant.
3 CAMEMBERT should taste creamy and fruity and have a flecked white rind.
4 CHAUMES is a mild cheese with a nutty flavour and thin orange rind.

5 BLUE STILTON becomes creamier and bluer as it matures, developing a deeper, more mellow flavour and succulence.
6 TALEGGIO, from Italy, has a washed rind, a creamy paste and a mild, fruity flavour.
7 CAMBAZOLA is a German combination of mild, creamy white rinded cheese and lightly spicy blue mould.

8 BRIE, with its pleasant mushroomy aroma and a fruity flavour, should not be too runny or chalky in the middle.
9 ASH-COVERED GOAT'S CHEESE should have a clean white paste and a flavour that becomes more distinctive with age.
10 ROQUEFORT, made from ewe's milk, is typically strong and salty in flavour.

COOK'S CHOICE

Which cheeses are best to have on hand in the kitchen for cooking?

Strong, mature cheeses are generally better for cooking than mild cheeses as you can use less of them to achieve the same degree of flavour. Cheddar is the most widely used cheese for cooking in Britain, but other British regional cheeses are equally versatile and delicious. In Continental Europe, Gruyère is very popular for cooking because of its excellent flavour and good melting qualities. The Dutch cheese Gouda is a good alternative.

Emmental and Italy's *pasta filata* cheeses such as mozzarella and Provolone make excellent melting cheeses and are popular because although they become stringy, they maintain their creamy qualities during cooking longer than other cheeses. Emmental is classically used with Gruyère in fondues, and mozzarella and Provolone are good for topping pizzas. Greece's Halloumi, which is similar to *pasta filata* cheeses and is soaked in brine, can be dry-fried like a steak.

Blue cheeses melt well and retain their piquancy, making them useful for sauces, pasta, grilled dishes, soufflés, soups, salad dressings, pâtés and for topping red meats.

Very hard, grainy cheeses such as Parmesan and the Swiss cheese Sbrinz are useful sprinkled over foods, but they also melt well in sauces, soufflés and risottos. Their lengthy maturation and subsequent high cost means they are often combined with other cheeses such as Swiss Gruyère, but even a small quantity will add a lot of flavour.

Smooth, fresh cheeses such as curd cheese, cream cheeses and Italian ricotta have a mild, milky flavour that is excellent in desserts, cheesecakes for example, and can be used in savoury fillings for pastries or pasta. Soft, fresh, flavoured cheeses, such as those with garlic and herbs, salmon or ham, can be melted to make sauces or used in savoury fillings. Keep the cooking time for these fresh cheeses brief, otherwise they will separate.

Goat's milk cheeses are slightly less versatile than most but can be used for pizzas and crostini. They combine particularly well with nuts. Rinded goat's cheeses are best when peeled before being cooked in case the rind imparts too much of a farmyard flavour. Very fresh goat's cheeses are mild enough to be used in sweet cheesecakes.

HARD PRESSED CHEESES

Hard cheeses are pressed during maturation to expel the whey from the curds. They may be crumbly or smooth-textured, and become drier and less rubbery with age. Very hard pressed cheeses have a grainy texture that becomes more pronounced as the cheese matures. Semi-hard cheeses are pressed lightly to give the finished cheese a firm but slightly yielding or crumbly texture.

1 EMMENTAL has a winy, fruity flavour, many holes and good melting qualities.
2 DOUBLE GLOUCESTER has a mellow flavour and a slightly waxy texture.
3 PARMIGIANO REGGIANO, a Parmesan cheese, is excellent to use for grating.
4 SAGE DERBY is made by adding the juice from sage leaves to cheese curds, giving a subtle herb flavour.

5 EDAM, when young, is smooth, supple and mild in flavour.
6 MANCHEGO is a ewe's milk cheese with a strong flavour and dry texture.
7 CAERPHILLY, here smoked, has a crumbly texture and a lightly sour flavour similar to buttermilk.
8 CHEDDAR has a close texture and a nutty bite when well matured.

MELTING CHEESE TOPPING

When I sprinkle cheese on top of a dish to be grilled or baked, it exudes oil and looks unpleasant. What am I doing wrong?

Providing that you have chosen a cheese appropriate for grilling or baking, it is most likely that the cheese has been overcooked. In fact, cheese really does not need to be cooked at all, only melted. Do not put it too close to a fierce grill. Once cheese reaches temperatures above 75°C (167°F) it is likely to become hard, stringy or unpleasantly chewy, because the heat encourages the proteins, fat and water in the cheese to separate.

WHEN TO SERVE

At a dinner party, should I serve the cheese before or after dessert?

The French and other Continental Europeans offer the cheese board before dessert to accompany the last of the red wine that has been served with the main course. This completes the savoury part of the meal before guests move on to the sweet course, a logical progression for the palate and the one generally preferred by cheese enthusiasts.

In Britain, there is a tradition of ending the meal with a savoury to accompany the port, and cheese is often served after dessert. With today's lighter meals, cheese is frequently offered as an alternative to dessert. Do whichever you prefer.

EFFECTIVE WAYS TO CUT DIFFERENT TYPES OF CHEESE

Different cheeses are cut in different ways because of their varying shapes, but in all cases, the most polite way to cut a piece of cheese is to ensure that each person has an equal ratio of paste to rind. Use a long-bladed, sharp knife to cut cheese. When serving a variety of cheeses to guests, try to provide a separate knife for each cheese so that the moulds and flavours of the cheeses do not mix. Choose a cheese board made from wood, marble or glass. Avoid storing or serving cheese under a glass dome because it creates a humid atmosphere in which the cheeses will deteriorate.

STILLTON AND OTHER BARREL-SHAPED CHEESES

1 Remove the top from the Stilton truckle, or other cheese barrel, with a cheese wire or a warm and wet, long-bladed serrated knife.

2 Cut into the top of the cheese a wedge large enough to place on the cheese board for guests to cut from, as for Cheddar (see below).

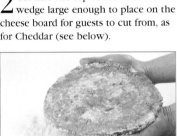

3 Remove the portion by carefully cutting through underneath it, from the side of the cheese cylinder. Lift the wedge out with an ordinary knife or a Stilton serving knife, which is very similar to a cake slice.

4 Place a clean, damp cloth over the cut surface of the Stilton truckle to prevent the paste of the cheese from drying out. Cover this with the top of the truckle before storing the cheese in a cool, well-ventilated place.

BRIE AND OTHER LARGE, THIN WEDGES

1 Do not cut across the soft paste centre of the cheese. Cut a triangle down one side, narrow at the outside edge and wider at the centre.

2 Repeat, cutting from alternate sides of the wedge each time. Do not cut too close to the outside rind towards the end – this ensures that the last piece of the cheese will still contain a generous portion of the creamy paste.

PONT L'EVEQUE AND OTHER SQUARE CHEESES

1 Cut the cheese diagonally into two equal right-angled triangles. (If there are only two or three people having a cheese course, wrap one of the cheese triangles for use another time.)

2 Cut each right-angled triangle of the whole Pont l'Evêque or other square cheese into halves. Then cut each piece into quarters, as and when required by your guests.

CHEDDAR AND OTHER HARD WEDGES

Lay the wedge of Cheddar on its side and cut thin, triangular slices across the wedge moving from top to bottom, so that each piece of cheese forms an equal-sized portion.

Save it!

Hard cheese seems to go farther when grated finely. This is particularly useful for topping baked dishes, grilling, and people who are watching their weight. Dried-up pieces of cheese can be grated and frozen for adding later to sauces and cooked dishes.

IDEAL SELECTION

How do I put together a good, interesting cheese board?

The key is to maintain balance by choosing both mild and strong cheeses, so that even a fussy dinner guest can find something to enjoy. Choose cheeses of contrasting textures and flavours, for example one hard, flavoursome cheese (such as Cheddar), one soft, milder cheese (Brie), and a piquant blue (Stilton).

Using this basic format, it is possible to substitute a number of cheeses to create variety and interest. For instance, the hard cheese could be smoked, the softer cheese flavoured with garlic and herbs, and the piquant blue switched for an ash-covered goat's cheese. Do not overload the cheese board with too many cheeses but do provide more than one knife.

For a dinner party of up to eight people, three or four cheeses is enough. Even buffet parties require no more than five. Each guest is likely to eat only 50 g (1¾ oz) of cheese in total, so it is best to opt for large, inviting pieces of a limited number of cheeses rather than meagre portions of several. Alternatively, try offering one cheese only, particularly at a small dinner party. A single large portion or whole perfect cheese looks inviting and keeps cost and wastage low.

Irrespective of which style of cheese board you offer your guests, try to keep the accompaniments to a minimum. Cheese connoisseurs will appreciate eating the cheese on its own with a knife and fork, perhaps with plain, good bread or crackers. Lightly dressed leafy salads, celery and radishes are good vegetable alternatives, and apples, fresh or dried apricots, figs, grapes and walnuts match many cheeses. However, it is not necessary to offer all these on a cheese board, or any accompaniments at all.

CHEESE BISCUITS

STRONG AND HARD

What is the best cheese to use when making cheese biscuits?

Choose a firm, hard cheese which will grate finely; ordinary Cheddar may be too soft and could produce a sticky dough that is difficult to roll. For a good strong flavour use a mature Cheddar or Gruyère, perhaps combined with some freshly grated Parmesan. To achieve a crisp, short texture, the pastry should be bound with a little egg, as in the following recipe for rich Cheese Biscuits and Straws.

Cheese biscuits and straws

MAKES: *20 biscuits or 40 - 60 straws*
PREPARATION TIME: *25 minutes for biscuits; 40 minutes for straws, plus 30 minutes chilling time for both*
COOKING TIME: *10 - 15 minutes for biscuits; 5 - 8 minutes for straws, per batch*

---

125 g (4½ oz) plain flour
A pinch each of salt, dry mustard powder and cayenne pepper
75 g (2¾ oz) butter, diced
25 g (1 oz) mature Cheddar, finely grated
25 g (1 oz) Parmesan, finely grated
1 egg, size 3, beaten
For the biscuits: 20 flaked almonds or walnut pieces, or poppy or sesame seeds
For the straws: mild paprika

---

1 Sift the flour, salt, dry mustard powder and cayenne pepper into a bowl. Add the butter and rub it in with your fingers until the mixture resembles fine breadcrumbs. Using a fork, stir in the grated cheeses and gradually add half the beaten egg until the mixture clings together.
2 Draw the flour, cheese and egg mixture together with the tips of your fingers, then remove from the bowl and knead the dough gently for a few minutes on a lightly floured board until it is smooth.
3 Place the dough in a polythene bag and chill in the refrigerator for about 30 minutes until the dough is firm enough to roll out.
4 When ready to bake the pastry, preheat the oven to 200°C (400°F, gas mark 6) and line two baking sheets with baking paper.

TO MAKE BISCUITS
1 Roll out the prepared cheese pastry to 5 mm (¼ in) thick. Using plain or fluted cutters, cut out some rounds about 5 cm (2 in) in diameter.
2 Place the cut rounds of pastry on the baking sheets, then brush them lightly with the rest of the beaten egg. Place a piece of almond or a nut on each biscuit, or sprinkle each of them lightly with a pinch of poppy seeds or sesame seeds.
3 Bake the biscuits 8 - 10 minutes or until golden. Remove from the oven and leave on the baking tray for 1 - 2 minutes, then place them on a wire rack to cool. Repeat with the pastry trimmings to make more biscuits.

TO MAKE STRAWS
1 Roll out the prepared pastry into a strip 5 mm (¼ in) thick and 20 cm (8 in) wide. Using a sharp knife, trim the sides neatly then cut the pastry in half lengthways. Cut each strip across into straws 5 mm (¼ in) wide.
2 Arrange them in neat lines, but not touching, on baking sheets (they do not need to be glazed). Bake for 5 - 8 minutes until pale in colour. Remove from the oven and leave on the tray for 1 - 2 minutes, then carefully place them on a wire rack to cool.
3 To decorate, dip the ends of each cheese straw into mild paprika.
4 Reroll the pastry trimmings, cut out more cheese straws and bake.

Both these types of biscuit will keep well for a week providing they are stored in an airtight container and kept in a cool place.

CHEESECAKE

SUITABLE CHOICE

Many cheesecake recipes specify the use of full-fat soft cheese. What would happen if I used low-fat soft cheese in them instead?

Many soft, fresh low-fat cheeses are suitable for making uncooked, chilled cheesecakes. You can substitute or combine cream cheese, medium-fat soft cheese, skimmed milk soft cheese, cottage cheese, curd cheese, ricotta, mascarpone, quark or, as in the recipe on the right for Muesli Cheesecake, you can use fromage frais.

However, for a richer cooked cheesecake it is safer to use the cheese that is recommended in the recipe, or one very similar. Low-fat cheeses curdle more easily when heated and they may separate when used in a cooked cheesecake.

Fresh lemon and muesli cheesecake

SERVES: 6 - 8
PREPARATION TIME: 45 minutes, plus 4 hours chilling time
COOKING TIME: 5 minutes

---

75 g (2 ¾ oz) salted butter or margarine
175 g (6 oz) muesli with no added sugar
1 tablespoon powdered gelatine
300 g (10 ½ oz) plain fromage frais, 8 per cent fat
75 g (2 ¾ oz) caster sugar
150 ml (5 fl oz) reduced-fat double cream
2 eggs, size 3, separated
Finely grated rind and juice of 1 lemon
To decorate: fresh fruit such as cherries or strawberries

---

1 Melt the butter or margarine in a small saucepan then stir in the muesli. Press the muesli mixture over the base of a 20 cm (8 in) flan dish or loose-bottomed cake tin to make a crust. Chill the crust in the refrigerator for around 30 minutes.
2 Put 3 tablespoons of cold water in a bowl and sprinkle the gelatine over it. Leave to soak for 2 minutes until it turns spongy. Place the bowl over a pan of simmering water and heat until the gelatine has dissolved to a liquid. Set aside to cool slightly.
3 Place the fromage frais, sugar, cream, egg yolks, lemon rind and juice in a large bowl and stir well. Add the gelatine and mix again.
4 In a separate bowl, whisk the egg whites until stiff, then carefully fold them into the cheese mixture.
5 Pour the mixture into the tin and chill for 4 hours or until firm.
6 Carefully remove the cheesecake from the tin and place it on a serving plate. Decorate it with cherries or strawberries just before serving.

Sumptuous but low in fat, this tangy cheesecake is made with muesli, fresh lemon and reduced-fat double cream.

CHERRIES

RAPID STONE REMOVAL

What is the quickest way to remove stones from cherries?

Use a cherry stoner, available from most kitchen shops. First, remove the stems from the cherries. Place them one at a time and with the stalk end uppermost on the base of the cherry stoner, then close the plunger to push out the cherry stone. Alternatively, you can use the point of a knife to split the fruit and carefully prise out the stones.

Stoning cherries inside a polythene bag prevents the cherry juice splashing over the work surface or your clothes.

KNOW YOUR CHERRIES

Which are the best cherries to eat fresh and which should I choose for use in cooking?

There are three basic types of cherry: sweet, semi-sweet and sour. The cherries that you generally find in shops are sweet or semi-sweet dessert cherries and they can be red, black or pale-skinned (sometimes referred to as white cherries). Some are plump and tender, others have a firmer flesh.

Sour cherries are red and the best known is the morello cherry, which has a strong acidic flavour. Morello cherries are suitable only for cooking and can be poached, used for sweet and savoury pies, added to desserts, savoury dishes, or made into preserves. Dessert cherries can also be used for cooking but will not have the same deep cherry flavour as morello cherries.

CHESTNUTS

SOFT OPTIONS

How do you cook fresh chestnuts once they have been peeled?

For stuffings or to serve with vegetables, gently boil fresh chestnuts in salted water or stock for about 30 minutes until just tender – they should feel soft when pierced with a fine skewer but not break up.

For purées, fresh chestnuts will need to be cooked a little longer so that the nuts will be soft enough to pass easily through a sieve or vegetable mill, or be processed in a blender or food processor.

For stews and casseroles, add the chestnuts raw and allow them to soften in the cooking liquid along with the recipe's other ingredients.

When using chestnuts in cakes and desserts, cook them barely covered with some sugar syrup or sweetened milk in a lidded, heavy-based saucepan, stirring often.

CHESTNUT CHOICES

Is there an alternative to using fresh chestnuts in recipes?

There are several. Dried chestnuts are available throughout the year from health food shops and when

Healthy option

Chestnuts are the ideal nut for dieters as 100 g (3½ oz) contains only 170 Calories and 2.7 g fat, with merely a trace of saturated fat. The same quantity of hazelnuts, by comparison, has 650 Calories and 63.5 g fat, with 4.7 g saturated fat.

reconstituted, by soaking in water, they can be cooked and used in the same way as fresh chestnuts.

Frozen peeled chestnuts, available from around September until early spring, taste identical to the fresh variety and are worth buying in bulk and storing in the freezer.

Vacuum-packed raw chestnuts are easy to use, have a long shelf life and are a good alternative.

Canned whole and puréed chestnuts have been processed so do not have as good a flavour as fresh. Be sure when using canned chestnut purée in recipes that you have not purchased the sweetened version.

Fresh, dried or frozen chestnuts can be used for the Chestnut and Chickpea Soup (right) which is filling enough to serve as a main course with bread and salad.

PEELING CHESTNUTS

It is easier to peel off the thick outer skin and thin brown inner skin of fresh chestnuts after you have gently boiled them for around 5 minutes. Do this while they are still warm and have cooled only just enough to be handled.

1 Cut a deep cross through the tough skin on the rounded side of each chestnut. Cover with cold water in a large saucepan and boil for 5 minutes.

2 Remove the nuts from the water with a slotted spoon and peel. If they become harder to peel as they cool, bring them to the boil again.

Velvety chestnut and chickpea soup

SERVES: 6

PREPARATION TIME: 40 minutes, plus 30 minutes soaking if using dried chickpeas

COOKING TIME: 2¾ hours when made with dried chickpeas, 1¼ hours if using canned chickpeas

---

125 g (4½ oz) dried chickpeas, soaked 30 minutes in boiling water, or 400 g (14 oz) canned chickpeas, drained and rinsed

60 g (2¼ oz) butter

1 large onion, finely chopped

225 g (8 oz) leeks, sliced and washed

500 g (1 lb 2 oz) frozen peeled chestnuts, thawed, or 600 g (1 lb 5 oz) fresh chestnuts, peeled, or 225 g (8 oz) dried chestnuts soaked overnight in cold water and drained

1.5 litres (2 pints 15 fl oz) chicken or vegetable stock

Salt and black pepper

Strained juice of 1 lemon

4 tablespoons single cream

To serve: grated mature Cheddar, finely sliced spring onions and ciabatta bread

---

1 If using dried chickpeas, drain off the soaking water and rinse them thoroughly. Put them into a saucepan and cover with at least 10 cm (4 in) of cold water. Bring to the boil and then boil the chickpeas hard for 15 minutes. Drain and rinse well.

2 Return the chickpeas to the pan, cover them with fresh cold water and bring to the boil. Lower the heat, partially cover the pan and simmer for 1¼ hours or until the chickpeas are just tender, then drain.

3 Melt the butter in a large saucepan, then add the onion and drained leeks and cook them over a moderate heat for 5 – 10 minutes, or until they are softened but not browned.

4 Add the cooked chickpeas (if you are using canned chickpeas, drain and add them now) to the pan with the chestnuts and stock. Bring to the boil, then reduce the heat, cover the pan and simmer for an hour, or until the chestnuts are very soft.

The floury texture of chestnuts is used to velvety effect in this warming soup. A garnish of sliced spring onions and mature Cheddar adds bite.

5 Remove the saucepan from the heat, cool the soup for 10 minutes then purée it in batches in a food processor or a blender, or pass it through a vegetable mill.

6 Return the soup to the saucepan, season well and reheat. Stir in the lemon juice and cream, then pour into individual bowls and sprinkle with the grated cheese and spring onion. Serve with warm ciabatta.

FIRE DRILL

Can I roast fresh chestnuts on an open fire at home?

Yes, but split the skins first to prevent them exploding. Shake the chestnuts over the fire in a long-handled frying pan, turning them occasionally, until the skins are blackened. The chestnuts will peel easily when cooled slightly.

CHICKEN

FREEDOM SHOWS

If I want to eat delicious chicken produced in a healthy way, what should I look for when shopping?

Look for fresh chickens labelled either free-range, traditional free-range or free-range total freedom, all of which conform to standards set by the European Commission. They will have had access to open-air vegetation and are about twice as old as battery-housed chickens.

Although corn-fed chickens are widely thought to be free-range, they usually are not and often have dye added to the feed to tint the flesh a bright yellow colour.

By comparison with intensively reared chickens, the dark meat of a free-range chicken is darker and softer, the white meat is drier and a little firmer and the skin is thicker. Free-range chickens are particularly good for roasting and boiling as well as for making stock.

The French free-range chicken known as poulet de Bresse has a particularly good flavour. It needs only very simple cooking, as in the following recipe for the classic French dish Poule au Pot accompanied by stuffed cabbage parcels.

Poule au pot

SERVES: 8
PREPARATION TIME: 25 minutes
COOKING TIME: 1 hour 40 minutes

1.8 - 2.25 kg (4 - 5 lb) roasting
   or boiling fowl with giblets
2 onions, quartered
225 g (8 oz) carrots, quartered
225 g (8 oz) turnips, halved or
   quartered
1 bouquet garni

FOR THE STUFFING
6 eggs, size 3
350 g (12 oz) fresh breadcrumbs
6 tablespoons chopped parsley
350 g (12 oz) gammon, diced
8 shallots, chopped
Finely grated zest of 2 lemons
Salt and black pepper
8 large Savoy cabbage leaves
To serve: toasted French bread

1 Remove the giblets from the bird, then chop up the liver and set it aside to add to the stuffing later.
2 Truss the chicken and place it in a large pot or casserole. Cover it with water then add the vegetables and the bouquet garni. Season, bring it to the boil, then cover and simmer the chicken for 1 hour 20 minutes.
3 Meanwhile, make the stuffing: beat the eggs and stir in the breadcrumbs, parsley, gammon, shallots, lemon zest, chicken liver, salt and pepper.
4 Blanch the cabbage leaves, then refresh under cold water and pat dry. Spread the leaves flat, in four groups of two, and place a quarter of the stuffing onto each centre. Wrap up each pair of leaves into a parcel and tie with string to hold together.
5 When the chicken has been cooking for 1 hour 20 minutes, add the cabbage parcels to the pot. Cook for a further 20 minutes or until the chicken is tender and the juices that flow when a skewer is inserted into the bird are not pink.
6 When the chicken is cooked, drain off the stock and reserve it. Put the chicken and vegetables in a warm place and leave the cabbage parcels to drain in a colander.
7 To serve, season the stock to taste and serve most of it as soup for the first course, poured over toasted French bread. Reserve some of the stock to serve with the bird.
8 Set the chicken on a large serving dish. Surround the chicken with the vegetables and cabbage parcels and moisten with the reserved stock.
9 Carve the chicken at the table. Snip the string that surrounds the stuffed cabbage parcels and add half a parcel to each serving of meat, along with a selection of the stock-moistened vegetables.

Much of the stock used to cook Poule au Pot is served first as a soup. The stuffed cabbage leaf parcels provide extra colour, as do onion wedges and herbs.

PERFECT ROASTING

When roasting a bird, how do I achieve moist flesh as well as a crisp, brown skin?

Be sure the skin is dry by patting it with kitchen paper before roasting. Smear it with butter, season with a little salt and pepper and squeeze some lemon juice all over.

For even cooking, lay the bird in the roasting tin on its side for the first third of the time, turn on the other side for the next third and finish with the breast uppermost. This ensures the bird is evenly cooked and makes it less likely the breast will scorch. Roast at 200°C (400°F, gas mark 6) for 35–45 minutes per kg (15–20 minutes per lb), plus 15–20 minutes. Baste often to keep the flesh moist and to colour the skin golden brown.

When the bird is cooked, turn off the heat and rest it for 15 minutes with the oven door ajar so the skin does not go soggy, then carve.

SUCCULENT MEAT

What is the best way to keep a skinless breast succulent?

If you are on a low-fat diet, you can lightly poach the breast in stock, or cook it in a foil parcel with some sliced vegetables and seasonings so that all the moisture is retained. If you do not mind using a little oil, marinate the chicken in a mixture of olive oil, orange juice, honey and some mustard, then grill. Baste the chicken breast with the marinade during cooking to keep it moist.

FROZEN FLAVOUR

Can frozen chicken taste as good as the fresh variety?

While frozen chicken is inferior in taste to fresh, free-range frozen birds have more flavour than fresh battery chickens. Remember that frozen poultry has added water, which drains out when the bird is defrosted, so weigh the bird after it has thawed to calculate the cooking time. Defrost the chicken in the refrigerator, away from cooked

JOINTING A CHICKEN INTO EIGHT PIECES

When cooking a dish which requires joints of chicken, such as a casserole, it is considerably cheaper to buy a whole chicken and joint it yourself than to buy the ready-prepared smaller cuts. Follow the simple process below:

1 Place the chicken breast side up on a board. Pull a leg gently away from the body and use a heavy cook's knife to cut through the skin between the body and leg. Bend the leg outwards until the ball pops out of the socket joint, then cut through the flesh under the joint. Repeat with the other leg.

2 To separate the thigh from the drumstick, stand one leg on the board so that it forms a natural 'V' shape. Hold the end of the drumstick in one hand and cut firmly through the joint where the two bones meet at the centre of the 'V'. Repeat the process with the other leg.

3 To separate the wings from the body of the chicken, make a deep cut into the breast meat near to the inside of each wing, angling the knife diagonally towards the neck end of the bird so that the uncut breast forms a diamond shape. Cut down into the meat far enough to expose the bones.

4 To free the wings completely from the rest of the body, use a pair of poultry shears or ordinary kitchen scissors to cut carefully between the ball and socket joints and through the remaining flesh and bone. Make sure there are no sharp splinters of bone embedded in the cut portions.

5 To remove the breast meat, lay the carcass of the bird on its side, and, using poultry shears or kitchen scissors, cut through the thin rib cage on either side of the backbone. Do not throw the backbone away as it can be frozen and used for stock.

6 Divide the breast into two, cutting crossways or lengthways through the bird's flesh using a knife and then through the bones and cartilage with the shears or scissors. On large birds, each portion can be further divided into two to give four pieces of breast.

foods, allowing 2 hours per 500 g (1 lb 2 oz). When buying packs of frozen poultry, avoid any with pink ice crystals as these show signs of thawing and refreezing.

SELF-BASTING BRICKS

What is the reason for cooking chicken in a brick?

Cooking chicken in a clay brick is healthy, because you don't need to use fat. The method is also very easy, because there is no basting.

The 'brick' is a hollow, unglazed container which is put into a cold oven. As the oven heats, steam from the food condenses on the lid of the brick and bastes the food. The bird will be tender, flavoursome and moist – lightly browned and sitting in delicious juices.

Chicken in a brick

SERVES: *4 - 6*
PREPARATION TIME: *15 minutes plus 10 - 30 minutes soaking*
COOKING TIME: *about 1¾ hours*

1.5 kg (3 lb 5 oz) fresh roasting or boiling chicken
1 lemon
Salt and black pepper
1 onion, sliced
2 carrots, diced
2 celery sticks, sliced
Sprigs of fresh herbs
10 large cloves garlic, unpeeled

1 Soak the chicken brick in cold water for 10 - 30 minutes before use. Halve the lemon and place one half inside the cavity of the bird.
2 Season the bird inside and out with the salt and pepper. Slice the remaining half of the lemon and place it in the bottom of the brick.
3 Mix the vegetables together then spread evenly over the sliced lemon. Place the chicken on the vegetables, tuck in the herbs and scatter the garlic cloves over the bird.
4 Cover the brick and place it in a cold oven. Set the oven to 230°C (450°F, gas mark 8) and cook for 55 minutes per kg (25 minutes per lb) plus an extra 25 minutes. Serve the bird with the vegetables and garlic.

CHICKPEAS

VERSATILE PULSE

Are there other uses for chickpeas besides hummous?

Chickpeas are versatile, nourishing and useful in soups and stews, cooked with or without meat. You can also incorporate them in bean salads and vegetable dishes and use them to make a type of Middle Eastern patty called falafel.

Dried chickpeas need overnight soaking and long cooking to make them tender. For this reason, it is much easier to buy canned chickpeas, which are already cooked, to make hummous. Traditionally, a fluid, oily paste of sesame seeds called tahina is added to the chickpea mixture, but in the recipe for a Cheat's Hummous below, sesame seed oil is used instead.

Cheat's hummous

SERVES: *2 as starter, 4 with other salads and dips*
PREPARATION TIME: *5 minutes*
COOKING TIME: *none*

400 g (14 oz) canned chickpeas
1 - 2 cloves garlic, crushed
Juice of ½ lemon
75 ml (2½ fl oz) olive oil
1 tablespoon sesame oil
Salt and black pepper
A pinch of cayenne pepper
To garnish: black olives
To serve: hot pitta bread

1 Drain and thoroughly rinse the chickpeas, then purée them in a food processor with the garlic and lemon juice until smooth, or mash them vigorously in a large bowl.
2 Add 4 tablespoons of the olive oil, the sesame oil, salt and pepper to taste and process or mash again.
3 Spread the hummous in a saucer or flat dish and trickle the remaining olive oil in a zigzag over the top.
4 Sprinkle the hummous lightly with cayenne pepper and garnish with the black olives. Serve at room temperature with hot pitta bread.

CHILLI

SHAPELY CUES

Is the colour of a fresh chilli any indication of how hot the flavour will be?

No. Most chillies are green when they are unripe and then ripen to yellow, orange, reddish-brown and purple or near-black. The fruity flavour increases with maturity but not the intrinsic heat. As a rough guide, smaller and slimmer chillies are the hottest, but there are exceptions. The only safe course is to become familiar with the common varieties (see chart, opposite).

CAYENNE SUBSTITUTES

If a recipe calls for cayenne and I have only chilli powder or hot sauce, could I use that instead?

Yes, chilli powder is very similar to cayenne pepper. Both are made from dried capsicums that have been finely ground, but cayenne is a little bit hotter. Hot pepper sauce may also be used as a substitute in liquid dishes, but it should not be used in dry mixtures.

THE CHILLI FAMILY

I am confused by the wide variety of chillies. How should all these different types be used?

Chilli is one of the world's favourite seasonings and there are hundreds of types. The capsicum family of pepper-producing plants first came to Europe in the 16th century from South America. Chillies were then taken to India and the Far East where they became very popular.

Some chillies are used fresh and the type of fresh chilli you choose for cooking will have a considerable effect on how hot the finished dish will be (see chart, opposite). Others are dried and ground and used to make such ingredients as chilli powder, cayenne pepper and red pepper flakes. Chillies are also used in fiery sauces like Tabasco.

IDENTIFYING FRESH CHILLIES

These are the most common fresh chillies, with their heat indicated on a scale of 1 – 10 (10 being the hottest). Removing the internal pith and seeds reduces the heat, but remember not to touch your face while cutting chillies and always wash your hands afterwards. Wear rubber gloves if you have any cuts.

TYPE	DESCRIPTION AND USES	HOTNESS
Anaheim	Red or green, up to 15 cm (6 in) long, tapering and with thickish flesh. Stuff and roast them, or shred into sauces and salads.	2 – 3
Dutch	Bright green or red and shiny, 10 cm (4 in) long, sweet, hot and intense. Use them in salsas or add to any other dish that needs a heat boost.	5 – 6
Fresco	Red or green, 5 cm (2 in) long and quite stubby, smooth and waxy skin, thick flesh. These are good used raw in sauces and ceviches, or they can be roasted and then chopped into a sauce.	6 – 7
Thai	Skinny and curving, red or green, about 4 cm (1½ in) long, thin-fleshed and packed with red-hot seeds. These peppers add considerable fire to the cooking of South-east Asia.	7 – 8
Habanero, Jamaican hot bonnet and Scotch bonnet	Habaneros can be red, yellow, green or brown in colour. Jamaican hot bonnets are red while Scotch bonnets are yellow. All are recognisable by their squat shape, 4–5 cm (1½–2 in) long. Use them in curries, tropical fruit sauces and chutneys, Caribbean fish dishes and marinades.	9 – 10

CHINESE COOKING

GETTING STARTED

Can you suggest a starter pack of ingredients that I could use to make most Chinese dishes?

The following ingredients are the foundation of common dishes:
• SAUCES: Have on hand a bottle each of chilli sauce, hoisin sauce, oyster sauce, dark soy sauce, light soy sauce, yellow or black bean sauce and some sesame oil.
• CANNED VEGETABLES: Plan to stock a can each of bamboo shoots, black mushrooms, straw mushrooms and some water chestnuts.
• SEASONINGS: Keep a jar of 5-spice powder, garlic (fresh or puréed), root ginger (fresh or puréed) and some sesame seeds.

• NOODLES AND RICE: Stock packs of dry egg noodles, dry rice noodles and dry rice vermicelli, plus bags of fragrant Thai or basmati rice, and perhaps a bag of glutinous or sticky rice as well.

BE PREPARED

Does it always take a long time to prepare the varied ingredients for an everyday Chinese dish?

It is a fallacy that Chinese cooking needs considerable work ahead of time, even if the cooking process is very quick. Really long preparation is required only for the grand, imperial dishes that few people bother to cook at home anyway.

However, organising even a very simple meal, such as a stir-fry, is easier if some of the work is done beforehand. Slicing the meats in advance allows you to marinate

them, giving a delicious flavour to the finished dish. Vegetables can be washed, dried, sliced and kept in a plastic bag (not soaking in water) until they are needed. Then you can relax, knowing the meal can be cooked in just a few minutes.

PERFECT RICE

How much rice is required for a Chinese meal, and is it best to have a special rice cooker?

In Asia, rice is regarded as a bland base and contrast for richly sauced dishes and it is usually eaten in the ratio of seven parts rice to three parts other food. A typical Asian serving would be 100 g (3½ oz) of rice per head. Western diners like a higher ratio of main dish food to their rice, and the usual serving is 55–85 g (2–3 oz) per person.

In some parts of the Far East, electric rice cookers have become very popular. These are worth the expense only if you frequently cook large quantities of rice. The simple and effective way to cook perfect, fluffy rice (below) is to use what many British homes already have: a microwave oven. (See also RICE.)

Microwave rice

SERVES: 4
PREPARATION TIME: 5 minutes
COOKING TIME: 11 - 12 minutes

250 g (9 oz) basmati or easy-cook rice, yielding about 400 g (14 oz) of cooked rice

1 Wash the rice, drain and place in a microwave container large enough to hold the cooked grains when they have expanded. Add enough fresh cold water to rise 2.5 cm (1 in) above the surface of the rice.
2 Place in the microwave and cook on High, uncovered, for 12 minutes without stirring, until the water has been absorbed. Rake the cooked rice with a fork to fluff up the grains before serving and season to taste.
VARIATION
For brown or glutinous rice, add water to a level 3 cm (1¼ in) above the rice and cook for 15 minutes.

ROUNDED MEAL

What dishes should I include in a Chinese meal for my family?

Traditionally, most Chinese family meals feature four dishes and a soup, which is drunk throughout the meal and between mouthfuls of the other dishes.

Flavours should be based on the yin and yang concept of contrasts. For example, a typical meal might include deep-fried chicken (which is succulent), steamed fish (light), sweet-and-sour pork (rich and soft) and some water chestnuts (crisp). Dishes are shared, and the ideal menu would feature one dish per person, normally of chicken, fish, pork and a vegetable, generally accompanied by rice or noodles.

Starters are not usually a part of the traditional Chinese meal. If you do want a starter, select something light such as the Hot-and-Sour Soup (right). It lends itself to considerable variations, although the basic seasoning remains much the same. It can be left as a light, spicy vegetable-based soup, or you can add some pieces of chicken, pork or seafood to make it heartier.

Hot-and-sour soup

SERVES: 4 as a starter
PREPARATION TIME: 10 minutes
COOKING TIME: 15 minutes

---

225 g (8 oz) chicken, pork or prawns, diced (if using prawns, reserve 12 to use as a garnish)
1 litre (1 pint 15 fl oz) chicken stock or water
75 g (2 ¾ oz) can Sichuan preserved vegetables
1 egg white, size 3, lightly beaten
1 teaspoon cornflour, dissolved in 3 tablespoons water
1 - 2 red chillies, deseeded and finely chopped
1 teaspoon black pepper
2 tablespoons sesame oil
To garnish: chopped spring onions or crisply fried shallots

---

1 In a large saucepan, bring the first three ingredients to the boil; simmer for 10 minutes if using chicken or pork, 5 minutes if using prawns.
2 Add the remaining ingredients and stir gently over a low heat.
3 After 5 minutes or so, when the soup has thickened slightly, remove it from the heat, sprinkle with the garnishes and serve in warm bowls.

HEIGHTENING FLAVOUR

Why do so many Chinese dishes contain monosodium glutamate?

Monosodium glutamate, or MSG, is glutamic acid, or concentrated salt, used by Chinese cooks to boost the flavour of a dish rather as we use ordinary salt. It is not expensive and keeps indefinitely.

If used well, MSG can do much to improve the flavour of a dish, but it is true that some chefs add too much. In quantity, MSG can cause extreme thirst and other reactions like swollen neck glands, flushes and throbbing headaches. Using salt instead, along with sugar or vinegar, is enough to bring out most flavours in food.

Alternatively, use a tablespoon or two of sesame oil or oyster sauce. These are complete seasonings in that they combine salt and flavouring with the richness of the base product. If you add one or both of these, there is no need to use salt, stock cubes or, indeed, MSG.

CHINESE BREAKFAST

What is dim sum?

Dim sum, also known as *yum cha* and *tien sin*, is a collection of little snacks served to accompany tea. It is a tradition that began in Chinese tea houses around 500 years ago.

Many dishes, primarily breakfast fare but now also lunch and dinner, are served, usually from trolleys piled high with steaming baskets. Popular dim sum dishes include custard tarts, dumplings such as *siew mai* (filled with prawns and pork) and steamed won tons.

EASY DUMPLINGS

Can I make won tons at home?

Stuffed won tons are simple to make at home. The only special ingredients you need are the won ton skins, which are now widely available either frozen or fresh in Chinese supermarkets.

Minced pork and fresh prawns are the essential ingredients for the stuffing. In the following recipe,

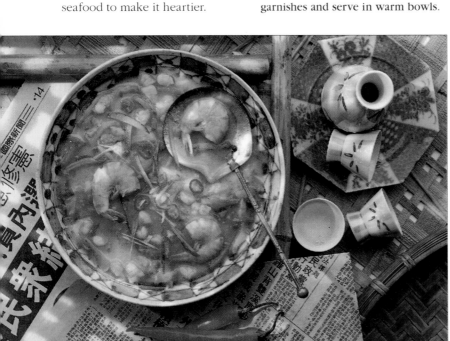

Hot-and-Sour Soup, here made with prawns, takes its fiery flavour from the spicy preserved vegetables of Sichuan and finely chopped red chillies.

the use of crunchy water chestnuts and the firm white tops of spring onions in the stuffing mixture provides the right contrast to the soft texture of the won ton skins.

Won ton dumplings

MAKES: 30
PREPARATION TIME: 20 - 30 minutes
COOKING TIME: 10 minutes to steam, or 15 - 20 minutes to deep-fry

1 spring onion, green and
*   white parts, finely chopped*
5 water chestnuts, finely chopped
115 g (4 oz) prawns, shelled,
*   deveined and minced*
225 g (8 oz) minced pork
1 egg, lightly beaten
A pinch of black pepper
1 tablespoon light soy sauce
1 tablespoon sesame oil
2 teaspoons cornflour
30 won ton skins, each 5 cm
*   (2 in) square*

1 Combine all of the ingredients except the won ton skins in a bowl.
2 Test the seasoning of the stuffing mixture by bringing a pan of water to the boil, dropping a teaspoon of the mixture into it and cooking it for just a minute. Taste the stuffing and adjust the seasoning as necessary.
3 Take one won ton skin at a time and place a heaped teaspoon of the mixture in the centre of each. Then moisten the four edges of the won ton skin, gather up the corners and twist lightly to form a little pouch.
4 Place the won tons on a slightly oiled plate, twisted side up but not touching each other, and steam them in a wok for 10 minutes. Or, deep-fry them for 15 - 20 minutes until crisp.

Dampening the edges of each won ton skin helps to hold the pouches together.

KNOW YOUR CHINESE SAUCES

Tasty sauces are added to most Chinese dishes to enhance their flavour. Matching the right sauce to the ingredients can make a simple dish special.

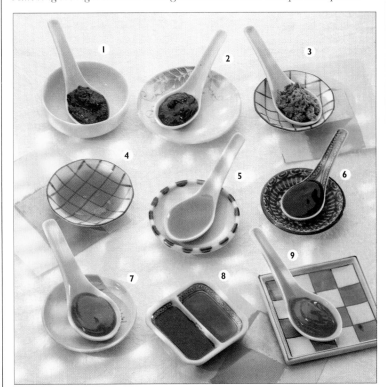

1 BEAN SAUCE, sometimes known as crushed bean sauce, is made from black or yellow soya beans that have been fermented and blended with flour and salt. Black bean sauce is the saltier of the two and much darker.
2 HOISIN SAUCE is made from soya bean purée, sugar, flour, maltose, salt and spices. This is also known as barbecue sauce because it is used to marinate Chinese roast or barbecued pork. It has a sweet flavour rather than the more pungent taste of Western barbecue sauce. Hoisin sauce is good as a rub for meats and poultry before grilling or barbecuing, and for use in marinades. It also accompanies Peking or aromatic roast duck and mandarin pancakes.
3 CHILLI PASTE is prepared from chillies, soya bean extract, salt, sugar and flour.
4 SESAME OIL is the pure, thick extract of roasted sesame seeds and used as a seasoning or condiment rather than as a cooking oil. It is typically added to soups and stir-fried dishes at the last minute to give a nutty fragrance.
5 LEMON SAUCE includes lemon extract, corn syrup, sugar, rice vinegar, spices and corn starch, and is very good for use in chicken and seafood dishes.
6 OYSTER SAUCE is thick, aromatic and salty. Made from oyster extract and soy sauce, it is used both as a complete seasoning and a stir-fry ingredient.
7 PLUM SAUCE is made from Chinese plums, corn syrup, sugar, rice vinegar, ginger, chillies, spices and corn starch. It is useful for sweet-and-sour dishes, and as a table sauce for barbecued meat or poultry and cold appetisers.
8 SOY SAUCE is a salting agent made from fermented soya beans and comes in a range of colours including light, dark, very dark and thick. The saltier light soy sauces are used to season almost every Chinese dish. Dark soy sauces are caramelised and sweeter in flavour so tend to be used more as dips and rich colouring for soups and stews.
9 BEAN CURD SAUCE is a thick sauce made from fermented bean curd and salt that is used in rich Chinese stews. It comes in two varieties, white or red. There is no difference in flavour between the two, but the red bean curd sauce will make some dishes look much richer.

CHIPS

HEALTHIER CHIPS

Is there any way of reducing the amount of fat in chips?

Deep-frying by traditional methods trebles the calorie content of the potatoes, but there are several ways to control this. Traditional chips are made with floury potatoes that soak up fat; use waxy varieties instead – Maris Piper or Maris Peers are the best varieties for chips. Do not peel them as the skin helps to reduce the fat and is a good source of fibre. And cut chips in thick wedges rather than thin fries so that there is less surface area and the chips will therefore absorb less fat.

Dripping, lard or other meat fat is the traditional cooking medium; for healthier chips, switch to vegetable oils, such as sunflower, peanut or corn, which are high in polyunsaturated fats. Be sure the oil is hot enough: when the temperature is too low, the chips will absorb more fat. You can use the recipe below to oven-roast chips and avoid deep-frying completely to use far less fat.

Oven chips

SERVES: 4
PREPARATION TIME: 20 minutes
COOKING TIME: 40 - 45 minutes

500 g (1 lb 2 oz) large, waxy
  potatoes
3 tablespoons corn or sunflower oil
Sea salt to taste

1 Preheat the oven to 220°C (425°F, gas mark 7). Scrub the potatoes and pat dry but do not peel. Cut them lengthways into thick chips.
2 Put the chips in a bowl and toss by hand with the oil and sea salt.
3 Spread the chips on two baking sheets and bake for 40 - 45 minutes, turning them three or four times. Swap over the baking sheets halfway through cooking for even browning.
4 Remove the chips from the oven, then drain them on kitchen paper to remove surplus oil before serving.

Lightly sprinkling thick-cut potatoes with oil and salt before cooking them in the oven produces chips that not only taste great but are healthier too.

CHOCOLATE

CHOOSING THE BEST

What makes a good chocolate?

The key things to look for are cocoa solids and cocoa butter. The more cocoa solids a chocolate contains, the deeper and more intense the chocolate flavour will be. The wrapping must list the quantity of cocoa solids: any containing less than 50 per cent has little real chocolate taste: one with 70 per cent or more will have a much stronger, finer chocolate flavour.

The amount of cocoa butter listed on the packet will also help you to determine the quality of the chocolate. The more cocoa butter the chocolate contains, the softer it is, melting more easily and having a unique, mouth-filling quality.

But there is a huge demand for cocoa butter for use in cosmetics, which makes it very expensive, and so in cheaper chocolate vegetable oils are substituted for the real thing, reducing the flavour. Cocoa butter does not have to be listed on the packet by percentage, but you can work out how much is present by its position in the ingredients list, since these are shown in order of volume. If vegetable oil comes higher on the list than cocoa butter, it is an inferior chocolate.

As a general rule, the thinner and smaller the pieces of chocolate, the finer the chocolate will be. Another way of identifying good chocolate is how smooth it feels on the tongue. This is because high quality chocolate undergoes a longer period of conching, or stirring, while it is being made. Very fine chocolate with a superior flavour is expensive, but you do not have to use as much to get an intense chocolate taste, so it is a good idea to pay a little more for the best.

GENTLY MELT IT

When I melt chocolate, it occasionally becomes grainy or seizes up. Why is this, and how can I prevent it happening?

When melting chocolate, remember that you are not heating or cooking it. Chocolate will melt in the heat of your hand, and that is how gentle the melting process should be. Chocolate that is grainy, or turns thick and seizes up in a solid mass, has been overheated.

It is also important that the chocolate be kept dry, as even one drop of water will cause it to seize. When you are melting chocolate in a bowl over a saucepan of water, take the pan off the heat before putting the bowl on top as boiling water creates droplets of steam that may fall on the chocolate. And do not add any other liquids to the chocolate until it has melted.

When you are melting chocolate in a microwave, check its progress every 5 - 10 seconds: the chocolate will retain its shape even though it has softened (see box, right).

Save it!

If chocolate seizes, it can be rescued by adding a teaspoon of solid vegetable fat or a pale vegetable oil for each 25 g (1 oz) of chocolate. The resulting chocolate can be used in cakes and desserts, but will not be so good for making decorations.

CHILL WHITE FIRST

Whenever I have tried to melt white chocolate it has just turned crumbly. What do I do wrong?

Some types of white chocolate have had some, or all of the cocoa butter replaced with vegetable oil and these are extremely difficult to melt. White chocolate should never be directly substituted for dark or milk chocolate. Technically, white chocolate is not chocolate at all as it does not contain any cocoa solids. Should a particular recipe require white chocolate and it has to be melted, check that the type you buy contains a high level of cocoa butter and always chill and then finely grate before very gently melting it. If it seizes, white chocolate is impossible to rescue.

EXTRA SMOOTH

What is 'couverture' chocolate, and what does 'tempering' mean?

Couverture chocolate is a type of chocolate used by professional confectioners. It contains more cocoa butter than ordinary chocolate and so melts and spreads easily. But cocoa butter is composed of fat crystals, and after melting some of these may recrystallise and form grey streaks in the chocolate called bloom which, though harmless, looks unattractive. So couverture chocolate has to be tempered: that is, heated and cooled to precise temperatures to prevent bloom and then spread and worked on a marble slab as it cools to produce a chocolate with a very smooth and shiny texture. All chocolate ideally needs tempering, but for most everyday cooking it is satisfactory to just use good plain chocolate.

CAROB STAND-IN

Can carob be used as a substitute for chocolate in recipes?

Not really. Carob is the dried pod of the carob tree and has a sweet taste vaguely like that of the cocoa bean. Chocolate contains caffeine, but carob does not, so some people

MELTING AND DIPPING CHOCOLATE

Great care must be taken when melting chocolate, but it is worth the effort. Melted chocolate can be used in a variety of chocolate desserts, cakes and ice cream as well as in sweetmeats such as truffles. Firm, fresh fruits and whole nuts become doubly tempting when dipped in high-quality melted chocolate.

MELTING ON THE STOVE

1 Chop the chocolate into very fine pieces with a sharp knife. Fill a saucepan one-third full of water and bring it to the boil, then take it off the heat. Put the chocolate in a heatproof bowl and place it over the hot water in the saucepan to melt it slowly.

2 The base of the bowl must not touch the water because even one drop splashing accidently into it will make the chocolate seize and ruin it. Leave it standing and stir the mixture occasionally until it is very smooth.

MELTING IN THE MICROWAVE

1 Break the chocolate into small pieces, then cook them uncovered in a bowl. Use High for small amounts of dark chocolate, Medium for more than 250 g (9 oz), and Low or Medium for melting white or milk chocolate.

2 Heat for 30 seconds, stir and cook again in 5 or 10 second bursts, checking and stirring, until melted.

DIPPING IN CHOCOLATE

1 Choose large, perfect nuts, such as almonds, brazils, hazelnuts, macadamias, unsalted peanuts or walnuts, and dip them one at a time.

2 Place the nut on a small fork then lower it into the cooled, melted chocolate. Lift it straight out again and gently tap the fork on the side of the bowl to remove excess chocolate. Using a toothpick, push the nut gently off the fork and onto a tray lined with baking paper. Apples, bananas and other fruit can be dipped in the same way, after first being peeled, cut, then patted dry with kitchen paper.

3 For half-dipped fruits choose those fruits with stems or stalks such as cherries, physalis and strawberries, or dried or glacé fruits such as apricots and prunes, or candied stem ginger.

4 Holding the stem or the top of the fruit, lower it halfway into the melted chocolate. Lift it straight out, shake off the excess chocolate then place it on trays lined with baking paper to set. When the fruits are set, store them in a cool, dry place until you are ready to serve.

prefer to use it for health reasons. Carob can be bought as a powder to use in place of cocoa, and in chips and bars, but it should not be thought of as a substitute for good quality chocolate. Both the flavour and texture of carob are very different from the real thing.

CHOCOLATE SAUCE

What is the best way to make a smooth chocolate sauce?

Use roughly equal amounts of double cream and finely grated plain chocolate. For example put 100 ml (3½ fl oz) of double cream into a saucepan and bring it to the boil. Remove it from the heat immediately and leave for 30 seconds to cool. Add 100 g (3½ oz) of chocolate and stir well until the sauce is smooth and glossy. You could then add a flavouring such as cherry, coffee or orange brandy if you wish, and use it at once if the sauce is to be served warm. To serve the sauce cold, stir in 2–3 tablespoons of milk and leave it to cool at room temperature, stirring occasionally.

MESSY GRATER

My recipe for chocolate truffles involves grating lots of chocolate, but the chocolate always melts in my hand. I've tried using a food processor but it reduces chocolate bars to a sticky mess. Is there any way to get around this?

The process of grating chocolate generates friction heat which can melt it and make it sticky. The solution is to use chocolate that has been well chilled. Break off small pieces at a time, leaving the rest in the refrigerator, and grate or chop it finely in a food processor with the grating disc. Brush the grater with a dry pastry brush at intervals.

In the following recipe, grated chocolate is blended with cream, butter and liqueur to make wickedly rich truffles. If you feel particularly extravagant, decorate them with some 24 carat gold leaf, available from art shops. When consumed in tiny quantities, it is edible.

Chocolate dipped truffles

MAKES: *about 35 truffles*
PREPARATION TIME: *45 minutes, plus chilling and freezing time*
COOKING TIME: *5 minutes*

FOR THE FILLING
150 ml (5 fl oz) double cream
350 g (12 oz) plain dark chocolate, chilled then finely grated
50 g (1 ¾ oz) unsalted butter, diced
1 - 2 tablespoons liqueur, optional

FOR THE COATING AND DECORATION
350 g (12 oz) plain dark chocolate, cocoa powder, white chocolate, thin sheets of gold leaf

1 Put the double cream into a small saucepan and bring it to the boil. Remove it from the heat then add the grated chocolate and the butter, stirring constantly until the mixture is thick, dark and smooth. Add some liqueur if desired, then transfer the mixture to a small bowl and chill it until it is quite firm.

2 Using a melon baller or teaspoon, shape balls 2.5 cm (1 in) in diameter. Put them on a tray lined with baking paper and freeze until solid.
3 Melt the dipping chocolate, then remove half the truffles from the freezer and dip them one by one into the chocolate. Shake off the excess and place the truffles on a tray lined with baking paper. Dip the remaining truffles the same way.
4 If you want a contrast of smooth and soft surfaces, roll some of the truffles in cocoa powder straight away, before the coating has fully set. Leave the rest to set completely. Then pipe a little melted white chocolate decoratively onto some of them and, using your fingertip, press a little of the gold leaf onto others. Stored in an airtight container in the refrigerator, the truffles will keep for two weeks, or they can be frozen for a month.

Made from the finest chocolate and decorated with real gold, truffles are the ultimate after-dinner luxury.

CHOICE FOR COOKING

What is the best chocolate for cooking? And when a recipe says dark chocolate what should I use?

The best chocolate for cooking is plain, dark chocolate containing a high percentage of cocoa solids. This type is often labelled 'Continental' chocolate. Plain chocolate chips can also be used, but because they have a lower cocoa butter content, they melt less easily.

Milk chocolate is rarely used in cooking as it does not have the depth of flavour of plain chocolate, but it can be used if it is chilled and then finely grated before melting. These steps are necessary because milk chocolate can easily seize up.

'Chocolate flavour' cake coverings or coatings are not chocolate at all. They contain no cocoa solids and most or all of the cocoa butter has been replaced with coconut or palm oil. Although they are very easy to melt and handle, these coatings do not have the flavour or texture of real chocolate. It is a false economy to cook with very inexpensive chocolate or substitutes as the results are never quite right.

SAVOURY CHOCOLATE

Why do some Mexican recipes add chocolate to meat dishes?

For the native Central and South American civilisations, chocolate was not the sweet confection we know today with its added sugar and vanilla. They used it as a strong, bitter flavouring to deepen the flavour of spicy casseroles.

The Mexican speciality, *Mole Poblano de Guajolote* (turkey in a ground chilli sauce), is said to have been invented in the 16th century and uses chocolate to add a subtle flavour and colour. However, there are variations on the original *mole* (pronounced 'molay') that include chicken or pork. The following recipe uses the traditional turkey, but chocolate can also be used to enrich and intensify the flavours of game dishes made with duck, hare, pigeon and venison.

Mexican turkey mole

SERVES: 4 - 6
PREPARATION TIME: 30 minutes
COOKING TIME: about 1 hour

1 clove garlic, finely chopped
2 - 4 fresh green chillies, deseeded and finely chopped
1 small onion, chopped
60 g (2¼ oz) ground almonds
150 - 300 ml (5 - 10 fl oz) well-flavoured chicken stock
1 wheatflour tortilla, torn into small pieces
400 g (14 oz) canned tomatoes, chopped or whole
1 tablespoon tomato purée
2 tablespoons sesame seeds
A pinch of ground cloves
A pinch of ground cinnamon
A pinch of aniseed, optional
60 g (2¼ oz) raisins
Salt and black pepper
2 tablespoons olive oil
60 g (2¼ oz) butter
1 kg (2 lb 4 oz) boned turkey, cut in 2.5 cm (1 in) cubes
25 g (1 oz) plain dark chocolate, roughly chopped

1 Preheat the oven to 180°C (350°F, gas mark 4). Put the garlic, chillies, onion and almonds into a blender or food processor. Add a little of the stock and blend until smooth.
2 Add the tortilla with a little more stock and blend until smooth, then add the tomatoes and their juice, the tomato purée, half the sesame seeds, the cloves, cinnamon, aniseed and raisins and blend. When the mixture is smooth, add enough stock to make it the consistency of thick cream and season to taste with salt and pepper.
3 Pour the sauce into a saucepan and cook gently for about 5 minutes.
4 Heat the oil and half the butter in a frying pan. Sauté the turkey until golden, drain, then put in a casserole.
5 Add the chocolate to the sauce and stir until it has melted. Pour the sauce over the turkey, then cover it and cook it in the oven for about an hour or until the turkey is tender.
6 Heat the remaining butter in a pan and fry the remaining sesame seeds for a minute or two. Sprinkle them over the mole before serving.

CHOCOLATE CAKE

BEST FOR A CAKE

What sort of chocolate is best for making a chocolate cake?

The quality of chocolate varies, but generally, the more cocoa solids it contains, the better the chocolate (see CHOCOLATE). Most large supermarkets now stock good quality dark chocolate for cooking. Use the best you can find for the following recipe, such as a plain chocolate with 70 per cent or more cocoa solids. This rich and elaborate cake includes layers of meringue and sponge that can be made the day before, leaving only the mousse and ganache to prepare on the day you want to serve it.

This decadent extravaganza combines rum, cream and chocolate in layers of mousse, meringue and buttery sponge.

Death by chocolate

SERVES: 12
PREPARATION TIME: 1 ½ - 2 hours plus about 2 hours chilling
TOTAL COOKING TIME: 2 hours

FOR THE MERINGUE
2 egg whites, size 3
50 g (1 ¾ oz) caster sugar
50 g (1 ¾ oz) icing sugar
15 g (½ oz) cocoa powder

FOR THE SPONGE
6 eggs, size 2
175 g (6 oz) caster sugar
100 g (3 ½ oz) self-raising flour
25 g (1 oz) cocoa
2 tablespoons cornflour
75 g (2 ¾ oz) unsalted butter, melted gently

FOR THE GANACHE TOPPING
50 g (1 ¾ oz) caster sugar
50 g (1 ¾ oz) unsalted butter
425 ml (15 fl oz) double cream
2 tablespoons dark rum
450 g (1 lb) dark chocolate, melted

FOR THE MOUSSE FILLING
115 g (4 oz) unsalted butter
225 g (8 oz) dark chocolate
3 tablespoons dark rum
2 eggs, size 3, separated
300 ml (10 fl oz) whipping cream
To garnish: chocolate leaves (see page 99) and icing sugar

1 To make the chocolate meringue, preheat the oven to 120°C (250°F, gas mark ½) and line a 23 cm (9 in) spring-clip tin with baking paper.
2 Whisk the whites until stiff, then gradually whisk in the caster sugar.
3 Sift the icing sugar and the cocoa powder together and then gently fold them into the meringue.
4 Spread the mixture into the cake tin and bake for 1 - 1 ½ hours, or until the meringue is crisp and dry.
5 To make the sponge, preheat the oven to 180°C (350°F, gas mark 4). Grease a 23 cm (9 in) spring-clip tin and line its base with baking paper.
6 Put the eggs and sugar together in a bowl, stand it over a pan of hot

water and whisk the mixture until it is creamy and thick enough to leave a ribbon-like trail when the beaters are lifted from the mixture.

7 Sift the flour, cocoa and cornflour together then gently fold them into the egg mixture a little at a time, alternating with the melted butter.

8 Spread the mixture into the cake tin and bake for about 30 minutes until the cake is quite firm to the touch in the centre.

9 Turn the cake out of the tin to cool for about 30 minutes and, when it is completely cold, carefully slice the cake in half horizontally.

10 To make the ganache, heat the sugar with the butter, cream and rum until the sugar has dissolved. Stir in the melted chocolate, then chill the mixture for 30 minutes until set.

11 To make the mousse, melt the butter, chocolate and rum in a bowl over a pan of warm water. Let it cool slightly, then beat in the egg yolks and fold in the cream.

12 Whisk the egg whites until they form stiff peaks, then fold them into the chocolate mixture. Leave it to set for 30 minutes – 1 hour.

13 To assemble the cake, when the mousse has set, put a sponge layer on a serving plate, spread half the mousse on it, then put the meringue layer on top. Spread the remaining mousse on top of the meringue, then top with the other sponge.

14 Spread the ganache over the cake, garnish with chocolate leaves and dust with icing sugar. Serve immediately or chill for a few hours.

CHOPPING

EVEN-SIZED PIECES

Is there a way of chopping onions that is superior to the others?

The most important thing is to ensure the pieces are an even size so that they all cook at the same rate (see box, above right). If some of the pieces are very small, they may catch and burn before the larger ones are cooked, resulting in a dish that tastes bitter and scorched.

CHOPPING VEGETABLES

When chopping vegetables use a very sharp cook's knife with a secure handle which is easy to grip and will not slip. To lessen tears when chopping onions, try peeling and chopping them sitting down so your face is not directly over the onions, or run the peeled onions under cold water before you chop them.

ROOT VEGETABLES

1 To chop large root vegetables, here a potato, take a slice off one edge, put it cut side down, hold it and slice down firmly using your knuckles as a guide, against the blade of the knife.

2 Stack the slices and slice across them to cut them into sticks. Then pile up these sticks and slice them at right angles to the previous cuts to make chunks. Keep slicing the chunks until they are as thin as you need them for your dish. Keep your fingertips tucked well under all the time that you are cutting the vegetables.

ONIONS

1 Leave the root on to help hold the onion together. Slice it lengthways through the core, then peel it. For finely diced onion, slice once or twice more lengthways, then lay it flat.

2 Make a series of parallel cuts across the onion, down to the chopping board, avoiding the root end.

3 Make a second series of parallel cuts at right angles to the first while holding the onion firmly in your hand, keeping your fingers well away from the sharp knife.

CHOPPING BOARDS

What is the best material for a chopping board?

Wood is generally preferred for chopping boards as a thick board made of seasoned wood will last forever and the food does not slide over the surface. Wood also has the advantage of not blunting knives as quickly as other materials.

Doubts have been raised about the hygiene of wood, but in 1993 research at the University of Wisconsin found that wooden boards may be better than plastic for keeping bacteria at bay. A variety of boards were deliberately contaminated and left overnight. Levels of bacteria on the wooden boards were virtually undetectable while bacteria levels had actually risen on some of the plastic boards. The researchers surmised that bacteria may be sucked in by the porous structure of wood and destroyed by the antimicrobial chemicals that protect trees from infection.

Other materials used for chopping boards are polypropylene and toughened glass, both of which can be sterilised easily. In a restaurant or other professional kitchen, these polypropylene boards are often colour coded so that different ones are used for raw meat, cooked meat, fish, fruit and vegetables to avoid cross-contamination.

Whatever material you choose, be sure to scrub your board thoroughly in hot fresh water and soap or an antibacterial cleaner after every use. If the board is washed properly and stored on its edge and not in contact with other surfaces, contamination will be minimal.

USING A MEZZALUNA

What is the best way to chop fresh green herbs?

The easiest way to chop most herbs is with a large, sharp knife. You have much more control and it is quicker than using scissors (except in the case of chives). If you are chopping herbs in bulk, an Italian mezzaluna is a handy tool. This is a double-handed chopper with a semicircular blade which you use with a rocking motion. While these are usually single bladed, they may have up to four parallel blades which can make fast work of large piles of herbs. (See also HERBS.)

CHOPSTICKS

CHOPSTICK VARIETIES

There are many types of chopstick available. Which should I buy?

It is best to use bamboo chopsticks, as plastic and lacquered ones are slippery and morsels tend to slide off them. Japanese chopsticks have a pointed end as this makes it easier to pick up pieces of marinated fish, for example. Chinese chopsticks are blunt because in China it is thought unlucky to bring sharp implements to the table.

SUPER STICKS

How are chopsticks used? And are they any better than a fork?

Chopsticks are used mainly to scoop up noodles and to shovel rice from bowl to mouth, holding

---

HOW TO USE CHOPSTICKS

Using chopsticks may seem complicated, but by following these simple steps showing the basic technique, you will find them quite easy to manage.

1 The first chopstick rests between the base of your thumb and the tip of your third finger, near the top third of the chopstick. This chopstick should remain stationary while the second chopstick moves up and down.

2 Rest the second chopstick above the first one, holding it between the base of your first finger and the tip of your second finger. Use this finger and the tips of the others to raise and lower the top chopstick to grasp food.

---

the bowl close to the lips. Chinese people never use chopsticks to pick up rice by the grain to convey to the mouth, as falling grains symbolise bad luck. Except for noodles, most Chinese food is cooked in bite-size pieces in a sauce, and using chopsticks gives the perfect ratio of morsel to sauce.

Chopsticks have the advantage over forks in that you do not spear pieces of food but slide the chopsticks under and lift them up. This is especially important with deep-fried foods, as piercing the crispy batter before the morsel reaches the mouth will release air and moisture, which causes the coating to deflate and spoils the effect. Turning food with chopsticks when shallow frying also avoids piercing the flesh, which would allow the juices inside the food to escape.

When preparing food such as Japanese tempura, the use of chopsticks to dip the ingredients in batter helps to give a nice, thin coating and the end result is much lighter than would be the case if using a perforated spoon.

Although chopsticks are used exclusively in China and Japan, and among Chinese and Indo-Chinese communities in South-east Asia, they are not a part of Thai culinary culture unless noodles are being

served. In Thailand, food is always eaten with a fork and spoon, but not as we would use them in Britain – the spoon is used as a scoop and the fork is employed to push the food onto the spoon.

CHOUX PASTRY

LAST-MINUTE FILLING

How far ahead can I put cream into éclairs or profiteroles without making them soggy?

Once the éclairs have been filled with cream the pastry starts to soften, so ideally they should be eaten within a couple of hours or they will become soggy.

Choux pastry also tastes best on the day it is made but this is not always practical. Instead, the paste can be made the day before, left in a covered bowl and refrigerated overnight. Shape and bake the pastry the following day. Alternatively, unfilled cooked éclairs and profiteroles can be frozen in plastic containers. To thaw, either place the frozen pastries on baking trays and put them into a hot oven for 5 minutes, or leave them out in their containers to thaw at room temperature for an hour or so.

SOGGY RESULTS

My éclairs looked cooked when I took them out of the oven, but on cooling, they were wet inside. What should I do next time?

Choux pastry needs a hot oven, so preheat the oven and make sure it has come up to temperature before putting the éclairs inside. To ascertain whether the éclairs are cooked, check the sides and any cracks in the baked pastry; they should look brown, not pale in colour.

When the éclairs are cooked, transfer them immediately to a cooling rack, but do not turn the oven off. They are usually slit so that the steam can escape from inside, as in the recipe below. After the initial cooking, dry them out a little in the oven before filling.

Coffee éclairs

MAKES: about 30 small éclairs
PREPARATION TIME: 50 minutes plus a few hours cooling and setting
COOKING TIME: 25 – 30 minutes

FOR THE CHOUX PASTRY
75 g (2 ¾ oz) plain flour
A pinch of salt
50 g (1 ¾ oz) butter, diced, plus extra for greasing
2 eggs, size 3, beaten

FOR THE FILLING
300 ml (10 fl oz) double cream
1 tablespoon caster sugar, optional

FOR THE GLACE ICING
2 teaspoons instant coffee granules
2 tablespoons boiling water
175 g (6 oz) icing sugar, sifted

---

1 Preheat the oven to 220°C (425°F, gas mark 7), then line two baking sheets with prepared baking paper (see box, right).
2 Sift the flour and the salt onto a large sheet of greaseproof paper.
3 Put the butter in a heavy-based saucepan. Add 150 ml (5 fl oz) of water and bring slowly to a rolling boil over a low heat.
4 As soon as the liquid is boiling, take it off the heat, tip in the flour and beat well with a wooden spoon

until it thickens to a paste around the spoon and leaves the sides of the pan clean. Cook the pastry 2 - 3 minutes more then leave to cool for a few minutes until you can touch it.
5 Add the egg a little at a time, beating well between each addition, until the paste is as glossy as before and reaches dropping consistency.
6 Spoon the paste into a piping bag fitted with a 1 cm (½ in) nozzle and pipe out equal lengths of pastry on the prepared baking sheets.
7 Bake for about 20 - 25 minutes until the éclairs are well risen, crisp and golden. Remove the éclairs but leave the oven on. Make a small slit along one side to let the steam escape and then return the éclairs to the oven for a few minutes to dry out. Remove and cool on wire racks.
8 To make the filling, whisk the cream and caster sugar until thick. Spoon into a piping bag fitted with a 1 cm (½ in) nozzle. Split open the éclairs and pipe in a little cream.
9 To make the icing, dissolve the coffee in a tablespoon of boiling water. Sift the icing sugar into a bowl, then stir in the dissolved coffee with another tablespoon of hot water until the icing will coat the back of a spoon thickly.
10 Dip the top of each éclair into the icing and leave to set. Keep in a cool place and eat within 2 hours.

When making choux pastry, beating the mixture thoroughly as you add each egg will help to keep it glossy.

SAVOURY TREATS

Can I use a savoury filling for choux pastry instead of a sweet one for a change?

Crisp choux pastry is very versatile and delicious in savoury recipes. To boost the flavour when making savoury dishes, add a little salt and pepper or some grated cheese to the choux paste before baking it.

Savoury choux buns make good buffet party food, served hot and filled with cheese, ham or mushrooms in a well-flavoured white sauce. Cold éclairs can be filled with chicken, crab, egg or prawn bound with a herb-flavoured mayonnaise. Or make a gougère by piping savoury choux pastry into a circle, baking it, then filling the ring with a flavoursome sauce.

PIPING ECLAIRS

To help you to pipe éclairs of equal length, take a sheet of baking paper and draw rows of evenly spaced lines, 5 - 7 cm (2 - 2 ¾ in) long and 2 cm (¾ in) apart, on one side. Then turn it over and use it to line your baking sheet.

1 Stand the piping bag in a large jar or jug and turn back the top to form a cuff. Spoon the choux paste into the bag. Do not overfill the piping bag, but allow some room at the end.

2 On the prepared baking sheets, pipe out small éclair shapes tracing over the guide lines you have drawn. Cut the piped paste neatly from the end of the nozzle with a dampened knife.

CHRISTMAS PUDDING

PRESERVING SPIRIT

I once made a Christmas pudding months ahead to give it time to mature. But when I unwrapped it, the pudding had turned mouldy. What did I do wrong?

A good Christmas pudding will keep for up to a year, so long as it is properly wrapped, is kept in a cool, dark, dry place and is well laced with brandy or some other spirit before storing. The alcohol acts as a preservative, as does the large quantity of dried fruit and sugar.

Once the pudding has been steamed, allow it to cool completely in its covering. When cold, take off the cover, pierce the pudding in several places with a fork or skewer, and trickle over 1–2 tablespoons of brandy, whisky or rum. Wrap the pudding in greaseproof paper, then overwrap it in foil or seal it in a polythene bag. Store in a cool, dark, dry place.

Check the pudding occasionally and moisten it with a little more spirit if it looks as if it is starting to dry out, but don't overdo it or it will eventually become too moist. Wrap the pudding securely back in its covers each time you check it.

LOW-CALORIE SWEETNESS

Is there any way of cutting down on the calories and the fat in Christmas pudding yet retaining its traditional taste?

You can considerably reduce both the calorie and fat content without greatly affecting the flavour.

The following recipe omits the usual sugar and suet, and adds instead grated apple and carrot to a mixture of dried fruit and spices. When serving six people, each portion of this pudding contains about 360 Calories and just under 8 g (¼ oz) of fat; in a 'conventional' Christmas pudding of the same size, each portion would contain upwards of 450 Calories and more than 15 g (½ oz) of fat.

The combination of dried fruit and carrot in this pudding is sweet, but it is not sweet enough to act as a long-term preservative, and the pudding should not be matured for more than two weeks.

Low-calorie Christmas pudding

SERVES: 6 - 8
PREPARATION TIME: 30 minutes, plus overnight soaking of fruit
COOKING TIME: 5 hours initially, plus 2 hours before serving

100 g (3 ½ oz) each raisins, sultanas and currants
100 g (3 ½ oz) ready-to-eat dried apricots, chopped
90 ml (3 ¼ fl oz) brandy
Juice of 1 orange and 1 lemon
1 teaspoon each finely grated lemon and orange rind
75 g (2 ¾ oz) wholemeal flour
75 g (2 ¾ oz) fresh wholemeal breadcrumbs
50 g (1 ¾ oz) blanched almonds, chopped
150 g (5 ½ oz) carrot, coarsely grated
1 eating apple, peeled and coarsely grated
2 teaspoons ground mixed spice
2 eggs, size 3, beaten

1 Put all the dried fruit, brandy, orange and lemon juice and rind in a bowl and mix well. Cover and leave them to soak overnight.
2 Put the fruit mixture and all the remaining ingredients into a bowl and stir until evenly mixed. Spoon the mixture into a greased 1.4 litre (2 pint 10 fl oz) basin, pressing it down, and level the surface.
3 Cover with a double layer of greased, pleated greaseproof paper and foil. Secure them with string and make a string handle to make it easy to lift the basin in and out of a pan.
4 Put the pudding in a steamer set over boiling water and cover. Steam the pudding over rapidly boiling water for 5 hours - topping up the boiling water when necessary.

5 Let the pudding cool completely. Remove the wrapping and cover with a clean layer of greaseproof paper, then a layer of foil. Store in a cool, dark, dry place for two weeks.
6 To finish cooking the pudding, leave it wrapped in its basin and steam as before for 2 hours.
7 Unwrap and turn out onto a serving plate. Serve with Greek yoghurt or fromage frais.

Flambéed pudding

A pudding is twice as impressive if you flambé it. Pour some rum, brandy or whisky into a small pan and warm it over a gas flame or electric hob – do not let it get too hot or the spirit will evaporate. Take the pudding and heated spirit to the table, pour the spirit over the pudding and set fire to it.

MICROWAVE PUDDING

Can I make Christmas pudding in a microwave oven?

Yes. Follow your favourite recipe, replacing all but 2 tablespoons of the spirit with orange juice or apple juice. Press the mixture into a greased basin. Cover with a suitable plate and cook on Medium for 20–30 minutes until the top of the pudding is just slightly moist. Leave the pudding to stand, covered, for 5 minutes before turning out, or store for up to two weeks.

FIRE RISK

Is it safe to reheat Christmas pudding in a microwave oven?

Never reheat in a microwave oven a Christmas pudding which contains coins or medallions, nor one which has just been laced with alcohol as then it could catch fire.

You can, however, reheat one in a microwave if the alcohol has been incorporated into the pudding mixture. Heat single portions on Medium for 1–1½ minutes; whole puddings on Medium for 3–5 minutes depending on size.

CHUTNEY

PREPARING THE JARS

How do you sterilise jars?

Wash them in warm soapy water, then put them in a pan of boiling water for 10 minutes. You can also sterilise jars in the microwave: half-fill them with cold water, then heat them on High for about 3 minutes or until the water boils. Whichever method you use, then put the jars upside-down in an oven preheated to 140°C (275°F, gas mark 1) and leave them to dry for 10 minutes.

The jars must be clean, dry and warm when the hot chutney is added. As soon as you have filled the jar, cover the chutney with a waxed disc and seal with a glass, plastic or plastic-coated lid. Do not use bare metal as the vinegar in chutney would corrode it.

MOULDY CHUTNEY

The last batch of chutney I made developed mould. What could have gone wrong?

The most likely explanation is that you did not use enough vinegar, as this is the ingredient that preserves the chutney against spoilage.

There needs to be at least 1 litre (1 pint 15 fl oz) of vinegar to every 3 kg (6 lb 8 oz) of fruit and vegetables, as in the following recipe for Tomato and Red Pepper Chutney.

Other possible causes of mould are under-cooking the mixture, so it retains too much moisture, or the use of unsterilised jars.

Chutney with mould growing on its surface should not be eaten, as the mould may have produced toxins within the entire jar.

A chunky tomato and red pepper chutney adds bittersweet 'bite' to cheese sandwiches and cold meats.

Tomato and red pepper chutney

MAKES: *about 1 kg (2 lb 4 oz)*
PREPARATION TIME: *30 minutes*
COOKING TIME: *1 3/4 - 2 1/4 hours*

1 tablespoon yellow mustard seeds
1 tablespoon black peppercorns
1 teaspoon cumin seeds
1 bay leaf
1 kg (2 lb 4 oz) ripe tomatoes, skinned and roughly chopped
4 shallots, chopped
3 red peppers, seeded and roughly chopped
4 cloves garlic, crushed
600 ml (1 pint) white wine vinegar
175 g (6 oz) light muscovado sugar
Grated rind and juice of 1 lemon
1 tablespoon salt

1 Put the flavourings in a piece of muslin and tie up to make a parcel.
2 Put the tomatoes, shallots, red peppers and garlic into a stainless-steel preserving pan and add the vinegar, sugar, lemon rind and juice, and the salt. Push in the muslin bag containing the flavourings and cook gently, stirring all the while, until the sugar has dissolved.
3 Bring the mixture to the boil, then simmer gently, uncovered, for 1 3/4 - 2 1/4 hours or until the chutney has reduced and thickened, stirring occasionally. The chutney is ready when a wooden spoon run along the bottom of the pan leaves a line that remains clear for a few seconds.
4 Remove the muslin bag from the pan. While the chutney is still very hot, spoon it into warm, sterilised jars. Cover each jar of chutney with a waxed disc, then seal it at once with a nonmetallic or plastic-coated lid. When the chutney has cooled, label the jars and store them for a month in a cool, dark, dry place to allow the flavours to mature. Once opened, consume within a month.

PAN CHOICES

Can I use any sort of preserving pan for making chutney?

Only stainless-steel or aluminium pans should be used for chutney. Copper pans, which transmit heat

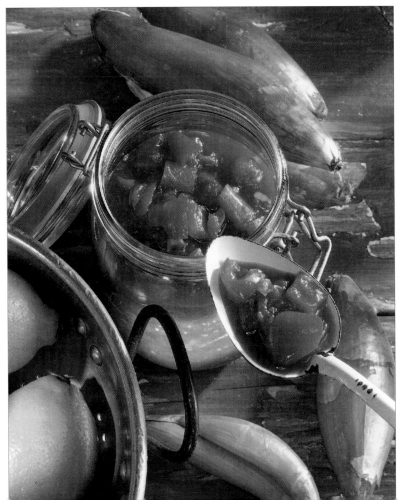

quickly, are good for making sweet jam but not for soaking fruit or making preserves such as chutney that contain vinegar, as the acids react with the metal.

ONION JAM

I have often seen 'onion confit' on restaurant menus. What is it?

Onion confit is a popular garnish in many restaurants, and is easy to make at home. Basically, it consists of either whole button onions or sliced onions, cooked very slowly in oil with spices, vinegar and sugar until they are reduced to a jam-like consistency. Herbs can be added to enhance the flavour.

Its full, rich flavour is especially good served hot with roast meats and game, or served at room temperature with pâtés and terrines.

TEST WHEN READY

How can I tell when a chutney has cooked enough to be bottled?

Chutney is ready when it has reduced and thickened to a jam-like consistency and no excess liquid remains. Long, slow cooking is best for chutneys, so that the ingredients can break down and all the flavour is extracted.

Once cooked and bottled, store chutney in a cool, dry, dark place for at least a month before eating, to allow the flavours to develop and mellow. If kept in the correct conditions, unopened jars keep for up to a year; once opened, consume within a month.

To test whether chutney is ready to be taken off the heat, run a wooden spoon across the bottom of the pan: it should leave a dry channel for a few seconds.

CITRUS FRUIT

PROTECTIVE COATING

I have been told that all citrus fruits are waxed. Why is this done, and is it unhealthy?

After harvesting, most citrus fruits are washed before being packed and transported. As the washing process removes some of the fruits' natural protective coating, they are given a thin coating of wax to help prevent dehydration, extend their storage life and generally improve their appearance. The waxes used for coating fruits are made from natural products and they must conform to EC regulations on food additives.

The washed fruit is also treated with preservatives and pesticides to prevent the fruit decaying and protect it against insect damage. These substances are controlled by British and EC legislation and safety assessments, taking account of the fact that the peel may be used for cooking (see also ZEST).

If these additives make you uneasy, buy organic fruit, which is neither waxed nor treated with fungicides. Seville oranges, used for marmalade, are free of wax and fungicide, but unwaxed lemons (unless they are organic) will have

---

PEELING AND SEGMENTING CITRUS FRUIT

The thin skin that separates the segments in oranges and grapefruit can be a little tough. When dividing oranges for inclusion in fruit salad, and when preparing grapefruit, it is best to remove these membranes, as shown below.

PREPARING AN ORANGE

1 With a very sharp knife, cut a thin slice from the top and bottom of the orange, then cut the peel and pith away from the side of the orange, cutting from top to bottom.

2 Hold the orange over a bowl to catch the juice and cut down each side of each segment, as close to the white membrane as you can, then ease it out. Squeeze the leftover membrane to extract the juice, which can then be sweetened and used for syrup.

PREPARING A GRAPEFRUIT

1 Cut the grapefruit in half across its width, then run a curved-blade grapefruit knife with a serrated edge around the flesh of the fruit, ensuring that all is loosened from the skin.

2 Using the tip of a small sharp knife, cut along either side of the grapefruit segments to separate them from the tough white membrane that divides them. Then carefully lift out the membrane by pulling the central stem, leaving the segments in place.

been treated with fungicides. It is best to wash citrus fruit before use, even if you are discarding the rind, as the various substances can come off on your fingers and be eaten with the fruit. Scrubbing the fruit under a warm tap with a clean nail-brush will help to remove them.

RELEASING THE JUICE

How can I tell which oranges or lemons contain the most juice?

It is difficult to tell, but as a general rule, choose smooth, thin-skinned fruit that feel heavy as these are usually juicier than those with a knobbly rind. To get more juice out of a lemon or orange, roll it backwards and forwards under your hand on the work surface a few times before you squeeze it.

If the fruit has gone hard, pop it into the microwave on High for 30 seconds before squeezing.

THE CITRUS FAMILY

The large family of citrus fruits are all widely available. The fruits are invaluable for their juice, in cooking and for healthy snacks. Here is a guide to those you are most likely to find, with some tips on how to use them.

1 *Satsuma;* 2 *Lemon;* 3 *Pomelo;* 4 *Grapefruit;* 5 *Pink grapefruit;* 6 *Lime;* 7 *Minneola;* 8 *Navel orange;* 9 *Kumquat*

• ORANGES Sweet oranges, available all year round, include thick-skinned Jaffa oranges and smaller, tight-skinned juicy varieties such as Valencia and navel. Bitter Seville oranges, available only in January and February, are mainly used for making marmalade. Bittersweet blood oranges, with red-streaked skin and flesh, are also used in cooking.

• SOFT CITRUS FRUIT These small, soft-skinned fruits are all hybrids of the Chinese mandarin orange. The range includes tangerines and the virtually seedless clementines and satsumas. Other recent introductions include clauselinas, ellendales and topaz.

• LEMONS AND LIMES The versatility of lemons makes them invaluable to the cook. Their juice can counterbalance oily fish, or sharpen up a cream sauce for fish, meat or poultry. Lemon is also the main flavouring in many desserts. Limes are the tropical equivalent of the subtropical lemon. They are smaller but stronger and 'drier' in flavour and should be used with caution when added as a flavouring, especially the rind.

• GRAPEFRUIT The two main varieties are white grapefruit, which has a thick skin and pale yellow, sharp-tasting flesh which can be sprinkled with sugar before eating, and thinner-skinned pink grapefruit with sweeter pink to deep ruby-coloured flesh. The pomelo is the much larger ancestor of the grapefruit, occasionally seen in the shops; it too is quite sweet. All can be used in salads, savoury dishes and desserts.

• MINNEOLA A cross between a mandarin orange and a grapefruit, minneolas have a distinctive bell shape with a bump like a lemon, and a sharp flavour.

• UGLI FRUIT A hybrid of grapefruit and tangerine with knobbly skin and sweet, pink-tinged flesh. It can be eaten in the same way as pink grapefruit.

• KUMQUATS have tender, sweet, thin skin and tart flesh. Can be eaten whole.

CLAMS

AUTHENTIC CHOWDER

Can I get the right clams in this country to make an American clam chowder?

Quahogs or hard-shell clams are named in the United States according to size, starting with little necks and cherrystones and going up to the largest sharps or chowder clams, which can measure up to 13 cm (5 in). It is these large ones that are minced up for chowders, as they have a strong flavour and will withstand long cooking, but you can use any clams and simply add them later in the cooking.

New England clam chowder is rich and creamy; the Manhattan version below is tomato based and almost Italian in flavour.

Manhattan clam chowder

SERVES: 4
PREPARATION TIME: 20 minutes
COOKING TIME: 25 minutes

1 kg (2 lb 4 oz) Venus or other
    clams
50 g (1 3/4 oz) salt pork or
    unsmoked fat bacon in a piece,
    or ready-made lardons
25 g (1 oz) lard
1 onion, finely chopped
1/2 teaspoon dried thyme
1 medium potato, diced
400 g (14 oz) canned chopped
    tomatoes
Salt and black pepper
3 tablespoons chopped parsley
To serve: cream crackers or
    French bread

1 Wash the clams in several changes of cold water, scrubbing if necessary, and discard any that are chipped, broken or already open.
2 Put the clams into a deep pan, add 600 ml (1 pint) of water, cover tightly and cook over a high heat for about 10 minutes until they open.
3 Tip the clams into a colander set over a large bowl to catch the liquor, then strain this juice through a sieve lined with muslin to remove any sand. Retain the liquor.
4 Shell the clams, discarding any that are closed and the empty shells. Chop the clam meat and set aside.
5 Dice the pork or bacon. Heat the lard in a pan then add the meat and fry gently until the fat is released and the cubes are crisp. Lift out the meat with a slotted spoon and set aside.
6 Fry the onion and thyme in the lard and meat fat over a very gentle heat for 5 minutes until the onion is soft and transparent.
7 Add the diced meat, along with the potato, strained clam liquor and tomatoes in their juice. Bring to the boil then simmer for 10-15 minutes until the potatoes are cooked.
8 Add the chopped clams and season to taste, then bring back to the boil. Transfer the soup to a heated tureen and sprinkle with parsley. Serve with cream crackers or French bread.

NATURAL CLAMS

Can I get clams to open without cooking them in liquid, which seems to reduce their flavour?

Yes. Large clams can be prised open and eaten raw like oysters, but it is easier after a quick blast of heat in a hot oven or over a barbecue. Place small clams in a dry, covered pan and heat them briskly till they open, shaking them about briefly. Keep the juices for adding to sauces and soups or to mix with tomato juice and vodka in a very superior Bloody Mary.

CLING FILM

PLASTIC SAFETY

Is cling film safe for all kitchen use, or does it affect some foods?

Cling film is indispensable in the modern kitchen, but there have been fears in recent years that some of the substances used in its manufacture could migrate into foods, particularly those with a high fat content such as fried meats, pastries and some cheeses. The Ministry of Agriculture, Fisheries and Food and cling film manufacturers have carried out research into the matter and now give consumers the following advice:

All cling films, as well as food wraps that contain PVC (polyvinyl chloride) or PE (polyethylene), are suitable for use in contact with all foods, except almost pure fat, such as lard, oil or foods in an oily medium (for example tuna fish or meat that is being marinated). If cling film is in direct contact with these, a small migration of substances will occur.

Never use cling film on warm food, or where it may melt into it, such as in a conventional oven. When reheating or cooking food in a microwave oven, do not let the cling film touch the food.

COCONUT

WEALTH OF CHOICE

What is the difference between desiccated, flaked, shredded and creamed coconut?

They are all derived from fresh coconuts, but differ in how they are processed. Desiccated coconut is the shredded white flesh of the coconut from which all the moisture has been extracted. It can be bought either flaked or in shredded strands graded fine or medium.

Desiccated coconut in all its forms is suitable for both sweet and savoury dishes, but is used mainly in cakes and biscuits. The longer strands and flakes are usually used for garnishing and decorating.

Creamed coconut, sold as a solid block, is formed from desiccated coconut that has been ground to an oily paste which sets when chilled. The block is sealed in polythene, and once opened, can be stored in the refrigerator for many weeks. Simply cut off pieces and add them to traditional South-east Asian and Indian curries, or to stews, casseroles and soups to enrich them and give them added flavour.

FRESHEN UP

If I want to use fresh coconut instead of desiccated, should I use the same amount?

The flavour of desiccated coconut is more intense than that of fresh, so replace desiccated with at least twice the amount of fresh coconut, be it flaked, grated or shredded. Either grated fresh coconut or desiccated coconut can be used for this Goan-style chicken dish.

Chicken with coconut, Goan-style

SERVES: 4
PREPARATION TIME: 40 minutes; allow extra time if preparing a fresh coconut
COOKING TIME: 1 hour

2 teaspoons ground coriander
1 teaspoon each ground cumin, cumin seeds, ground cinnamon, freshly grated nutmeg, paprika and mustard seeds
1/2 teaspoon black pepper
A pinch of cayenne pepper
200 g (7 oz) finely grated fresh coconut, or 85 g (3 oz) desiccated coconut
4 tablespoons olive oil
2.25 kg (5 lb) chicken, cut into 8 pieces and skinned
225 g (8 oz) onions, finely sliced
350 g (12 oz) red peppers, thickly sliced
6 cloves garlic, crushed
2 small fresh green chillies, seeds removed and chopped
1 tablespoon grated ginger
1 tablespoon plain flour
400 ml (14 fl oz) chicken stock
1 - 2 teaspoons salt
150 g (5 1/2 oz) natural yoghurt
4 tablespoons chopped fresh coriander
To serve: lemon and lime wedges

1 Put all the spices, the pepper and cayenne pepper into a small bowl, mix well together and set aside.
2 Heat a heavy-based frying pan over a moderate heat until it has become quite hot. Sprinkle the fresh or desiccated coconut into the pan and stir gently with a fork to keep

The flavours of Europe and Asia come together in a mild chicken curry, in which coconut and a wealth of herbs and spices are wrapped in creamy yoghurt.

the strands separate. Heat until it becomes golden brown, taking care not to let it catch and burn. Remove from the heat and set aside.
3 Heat the oil in a large flameproof casserole or saucepan, then add the chicken pieces, a few at a time, and fry until they are golden brown all over. As the pieces brown, remove them from the pan, put them on a plate and set aside.
4 Add the onion and red pepper to the fat remaining in the pan and cook them gently until they become softened, but not browned. Stir in the garlic, chillies and ginger and cook for a minute, then add the flour and the spice mixture, stir well and cook for a further minute.
5 Stir in the toasted coconut, pour in the stock and bring to the boil. Return the browned chicken pieces to the pan, season well with salt and

stir until all the pieces are coated with the curry mixture. Reduce the heat, cover the pan and cook gently for an hour, stirring from time to time. Leave a serving dish to warm.
6 Stir the yoghurt and coriander into the dish and remove it from the heat. If you have used a saucepan to cook the chicken, transfer the meat and curry mixture to the warmed serving dish. Serve with basmati rice, and with wedges of lemon and lime to squeeze over.

ALL CUT UP

How do you cut up the meat from a fresh coconut?

After cracking open a coconut and cutting the meat from the shell (see panel, overleaf), remove the paper-like brown skin with a small paring knife and shred the flesh in

CRACKING OPEN A COCONUT

The hard shell of a coconut may seem a formidable obstacle, but it will in fact crack open naturally if tapped in the correct places.

1 With a corkscrew, make a hole in each of the coconut's three 'eyes' (the small bare patches at the pointed end). Pour out the white liquid from inside the coconut.

2 There is no need to use drastic measures to open a coconut. Coconuts have an invisible natural fault line which runs right around the circumference, just above the centre towards the pointed end. With a small hammer or a heavy kitchen steel, tap the coconut firmly all around the centre and the fruit will split open naturally into two halves, revealing the white flesh.

3 With a small sharp knife, make a series of cuts through the flesh then lever out the portions. Peel off any outer skin which remains attached to portions of flesh.

---

a food processor or grate it by hand. If you need thin flakes, use the wide cutting blade on a grater or a mandolin cutter.

MILKING A COCONUT

Is coconut milk the liquid in the middle of the fruit? And what is the difference between canned coconut milk, creamed coconut milk and coconut milk powder?

The liquid in the middle of a coconut is not coconut milk but coconut water, a delicately flavoured liquid which can be drunk straight out of the shell or added to fruit juices. Coconut milk comes from the flesh of the coconut, shredded or otherwise processed to extract a thick, white liquid. It can be used in both savoury and sweet dishes.

Coconut milk is sold in cans, in which form it is very easy to use, or in blocks, in which case it has to be reconstituted with hot water. Coconut milk powder is coconut milk that has been dehydrated, and it too needs to be reconstituted with warm water. Also available is UHT coconut cream, which is slightly thicker and richer than coconut milk but used in the same way.

You can get a little thin milk from desiccated coconut by soaking it in hot water and squeezing it through a muslin cloth.

HEAT WITH CARE

Is there any danger of coconut milk curdling when you cook it?

Yes, it will curdle if cooked on a high heat or if it is too thick. Never place a block of creamed coconut directly onto a heated surface as it will burn: always melt it down with enough water to cover, either on the stove or in a microwave oven.

When a recipe calls for coconut milk to be added at the end, it is to prevent it rendering down to oil during prolonged boiling. If a dish does not require more than 30 minutes of simmering, it doesn't matter when you add the milk. But once you have added it, do not stir the dish again until ready to serve.

COFFEE

CHOOSING COFFEE

I am confused by all the different types of coffee I see in the shops. Can you offer some guidance?

The best coffees are made purely from beans of the arabica strain, or contain a high proportion of them. The shrubs which produce arabica beans are slow to grow and mature, producing a fine flavour. Some coffee blends, particularly espresso blends, and poor quality instant coffees are made with a high proportion of robusta beans. These have a bold, coarse flavour, a very high proportion of caffeine and are much cheaper to produce.

The quality of a particular coffee is assessed by its body, acidity and aroma, each of which will have been affected by the degree of roasting the bean has undergone.

If you enjoy mellow coffee, try Colombian, which is sweet and smooth, or Mysore, which has a light body. Mild coffees include Costa Rican, which has a sweet and tangy acidity, and Brazilian, which is typically described as elegant. Kenyan coffee has high acidity and a full flavour, while Java is rich, heavy and spicy. Jamaican Blue Mountain has a flavour that is rich, sweet and mellow.

GROUND RULES

How do I make a decent cup of coffee? Mine often turns out too weak or too bitter.

There are many ways of brewing coffee: in filter pots, plunger pots (cafetières), and electric drip coffee makers to name but a few. You can make consistently good coffee whichever method you choose if you observe the following rules.

Coffee should be stored in an airtight container in the freezer: any contact with air causes loss of flavour. Experiment until you find a blend you like then buy whole beans and delay grinding until the last moment. The finer the beans are ground, the more rapidly the flavour becomes stale and bitter.

Heat water to just under boiling point, about 95°C (200°F), or bring the water to the boil and then allow it to cool for 2–3 minutes before pouring it over the coffee. A higher temperature will extract too much of the coffee solids, giving a bitter taste; a lower temperature will not extract enough flavour, resulting in a weak coffee. The coffee should be in contact with the water for about 2 minutes only. Strong coffee is achieved not by allowing the coffee to brew longer, but by using more ground coffee per cup.

To make medium-strong coffee, allow 2 heaped tablespoons of ground coffee per 175 ml (6 fl oz) of water. If you want weaker coffee, use the same measure of coffee but more hot water.

STRONG AND THICK

How can I make cups of espresso or Turkish coffee at home?

Espresso (Italian for 'pressed out') is a very strong coffee made by forcing a mixture of steam and water through twice the normal amount of finely ground coffee.

At one time, espresso was available only in cafés and restaurants with enough space to hold professional espresso machines, but there are now many smaller machines designed for home use. In addition, some coffee is labelled espresso for filters and cafetières; this kind will have the strength of an espresso, but without the steam treatment it is not likely to taste the same.

Turkish or Greek coffee is made with finely ground coffee in a long-handled open pot (*ibrik*), or an ordinary small saucepan. Water and sugar are put in the pot and are brought to the boil, the coffee is added and the pot returned to the heat. When the mixture is brought to frothing point the pot is removed until the froth settles. It is frothed and removed twice more, and then this strong, sweet brew is poured into tiny cups to serve.

IRISH ESSENTIAL

Can I make a successful Irish coffee without using sugar?

In a word, no. The combination of sugar and alcohol in the coffee makes the coffee more dense, which in turn allows the cream to float over the surface. If sugar is not used, the cream will mix in with the coffee as soon as it is added.

For each serving, put 1 teaspoon of sugar and 3 tablespoons of Irish whiskey into a warm, tall-stemmed glass and fill two-thirds full with strong black coffee. Stir briefly, then pour double cream gently over the back of a teaspoon placed close to the surface, so that the cream does not sink. Serve immediately, drinking the coffee through the layer of cream. The cream often works best when used at room temperature.

RICH FLAVOUR OF MOCHA

What is mocha?

Mocha is a strong-flavoured coffee bean which came originally from Mocha, a port on the Red Sea. The term is now applied to any beverage or confection flavoured with coffee, and is mostly used to denote a mixture of coffee and chocolate flavours used in such foods as cakes, icings and ice creams.

ROASTED ROOTS

What are dandelion coffee and chicory coffee?

Dandelion coffee is made from the dried and roasted roots of dandelions. It is served black, with or without sugar, and has a slightly bitter and nutty flavour.

Chicory coffee is mostly found in France, where most coffee is made from rough-tasting robusta beans. Roasted and ground chicory root is added to mellow the taste of the bean and bulk up the coffee.

REMOVING THE CAFFEINE

How is coffee decaffeinated, and is the process safe?

Caffeine is removed from unroasted coffee beans, either by water or solvent. In the water method, the beans are soaked to bring the caffeine to the surface; the caffeine is then filtered out, removing about 97 per cent of it.

In the solvent method, the beans are soaked in chemicals until most of the caffeine has been leached out. The beans are then washed before drying and roasting. Many people are concerned about solvent residues, but there is no legal requirement for manufacturers to state which method has been used.

IMPROVISING A CAPPUCCINO

In cafés and restaurants, cappuccino is usually made in a special machine, but the milk can also be made frothy with a whisk or in a blender.

1 For two cappuccinos, make 175 ml (6 fl oz) of very strong coffee, using 3 tablespoons of ground beans. Heat 150 ml (5 fl oz) of milk until it almost reaches boiling point. Take off the heat and whisk until all the milk is frothy.

2 Divide the coffee between two large cups, top up with whisked milk and spoon some froth onto each one. Sprinkle with powdered drinking chocolate or some finely grated dark chocolate and serve immediately.

CORN (MAIZE)

A QUESTION OF LANGUAGE

I always thought that the word corn referred to wheat, but have recently discovered there is a difference. Could you explain?

In Britain, corn is often used to describe all cereals, especially wheat, but the term used in the United States – maize – is becoming widespread. There are two basic types: sweetcorn, which is eaten as a vegetable or dried to form the kernels that become popcorn; and field corn, used as animal feed or processed to make cornmeal, cornflour, hominy and oil. Blue cornmeal takes its name from the black and blue kernels of a particular American variety of sweetcorn and is used in tortilla chips and pancakes.

CORN KERNELS

Are hominy and grits the same, and where do they come from?

Hominy is made from corn kernels in a process whereby the outer hull is removed and the remaining kernel left to dry. The dried kernel is then soaked overnight, or cooked for several hours, before it can be added to slow-cooking meat stews.

Grits are made by grinding dried hominy to provide a finer cereal that then needs no presoaking. They require a shorter cooking time than cornmeal, which is made from the whole grain of corn, but grits have less fibre, flavour and texture. The cereal is used throughout the south of the United States, usually cooked to a mush and served with bacon and eggs for breakfast.

MAKE A MEAL OF IT

Polenta appears on many menus nowadays, but seems different in each restaurant. Are there several ways of preparing it?

In northern Italy wet polenta, a savoury corn porridge, is served like mashed potato to soak up the

A comforting alternative to mashed potatoes, polenta's velvety texture is enhanced with butter and Parmesan.

juices from a stew, as in the recipe to the right. Polenta takes a long time to cook, and needs stirring throughout, but instant polenta, taking about 5 minutes to make, is now widely available.

Wet polenta can be a meal in its own right, flavoured with cheese, pepper and a little virgin olive oil. Chopped vegetables, herbs and olives are other good additions.

Polenta is also frequently served in 'cakes', made by allowing wet polenta to cool and set. This is then cut into squares, slices or triangles and grilled or fried (see box, opposite). These cakes, while also served with stews, can make delicious snacks topped with grilled red peppers, rocket and tomatoes.

For a substantial snack, cut the set polenta into small circles, take two and sandwich with a slice of mozzarella. Coat in egg and breadcrumbs and fry on both sides until the outside is crispy and the cheese is melted in the centre.

Creamy polenta

SERVES: 4 - 6
PREPARATION TIME: 5 minutes
COOKING TIME: 40 - 45 minutes

---

*175 g (6 oz) polenta or coarse
  cornmeal*
A pinch of sea salt
50 g (1 3/4 oz) butter
*75 g (2 3/4 oz) Parmesan cheese,
  freshly grated*
Black pepper

---

1 Measure out the polenta and put it in a bowl. Bring 1.2 litres (2 pints) of salted water to a rolling boil in a large, heavy-based saucepan.
2 To avoid lumps forming, sprinkle in the polenta with one hand while beating continually with a wooden spoon with the other, until all the polenta is incorporated in the pan.
3 Cook, uncovered, over as low a heat as possible for 40 - 45 minutes, stirring frequently. The polenta is cooked when it comes away cleanly from the sides of the pan.
4 Remove from the heat and stir in the butter, Parmesan and pepper. Season with extra salt if necessary and serve with a rich meat stew.

POLENTA TRIANGLES

This recipe requires 175 g (6 oz) of instant polenta, which serves 4 – 6 people as a meal accompaniment.

1 Bring 1.2 litres (2 pints) of salted water to a rolling boil.

2 Sprinkle the instant polenta into the boiling water while stirring constantly with a wooden spoon.

3 Stir for 3 - 4 minutes. Remove from the heat, season and beat in 25 g (1 oz) of butter and 50 g (1¾ oz) of freshly grated Parmesan cheese.

4 Pour into a greased tin, smooth with a palette knife and leave to set. Turn out and cut into triangles.

5 Brush a heavy-based frying pan with oil. Fry the triangles for 3 minutes on each side until golden.

CORN-ON-THE-COB

SIMPLE IS BEST

What is the best way to cook and serve corn-on-the-cob?

In late summer, the whole cobs make a splendid if rather messy starter to an informal meal.

Strip off the outer husk, pull away the silky hairs and trim the stems. Cook them for 15 minutes at a rolling boil without salt, which makes the skins of the kernels tough and spoils the sweet flavour. You can add a pinch of sugar for extra sweetness. Serve them with butter or olive oil, salt and pepper or cayenne pepper. Baby corn cobs can be eaten whole but they lack the sweetness of fully grown corn cobs.

STRIPPING GRAINS FROM THE COB

Raw kernels may be cut from the cob and then simmered. They can also be cut after the cob has been cooked whole, but they may lose their shape in the process.

1 Strip off the outer leaves of the corn ear and pull away the silky hairs around the cob's kernels.

2 Hold cob stem-down. With firm, downward strokes, cut away the kernels using a heavy, sharp knife.

CREAMY COMFORT

I have used frozen corn kernels in rice salads and thick soups. Are there any other uses for them, and could I use canned instead?

When fresh sweetcorn is out of season, frozen corn makes a fair substitute and is better than the canned variety, which tends to lack that special juicy texture.

Frozen corn can be stirred into a thick pancake batter to make corn-cakes (about the size of a Scotch pancake), which are a very good accompaniment to fried chicken and great with a breakfast fry-up. They can also be served hot as a starter: place two or three pancakes in the cupped leaf of a crisp iceberg lettuce and accompany with a spicy salsa sauce.

Alternatively, this soft Corn Pudding (below) can be served as a sauce or a starchy accompaniment to roast chicken, baked gammon, or smoked haddock fillets.

Corn pudding

SERVES: 4 – 6
PREPARATION TIME: 20 minutes
COOKING TIME: about 45 minutes

50 g (1¾ oz) butter
400 g (14 oz) fresh or thawed
  frozen corn kernels
200 ml (7 fl oz) double cream
250 g (9 oz) plum tomatoes,
  skinned and chopped
Salt and black pepper
A pinch of cayenne pepper

1 Preheat the oven to 180°C (350°F, gas mark 4). Using half the butter, liberally grease an ovenproof dish.
2 Put the corn and cream into a food processor and process them to a chunky, porridge-like consistency.
3 Stir the chopped tomatoes into the corn mixture. Add salt and pepper.
4 Pour the corn mixture into the prepared dish, dot the remaining butter over the top and sprinkle the dish lightly with cayenne pepper.
5 Bake until the top is browned and crusty (about 45 minutes) then stand the dish in a warm place for 5 - 10 minutes before serving.

CORNED BEEF

UNITED STATES CONFUSION

What is corned beef and how did it get its name?

In Britain the term refers to beef that has been cured, boiled, heavily pressed and put into cans.

The name, however, comes from an American joint which is known in Britain as salt beef – brisket or silverside cured in brine. The early United States colonial settlers preserved joints of beef by coating them with grains (or corns) of salt, a process known as corning, hence the term corned beef.

The recipe for Red Flannel Hash (right) blends the British version of corned beef in a fry-up with beetroot to turn it an attractive red.

Beetroot adds sweetness and colour to this corned beef hash, a handy combination of store cupboard items and leftovers for brunch or supper.

Red flannel hash

SERVES: 2
PREPARATION TIME: 10 minutes
COOKING TIME: 20 - 30 minutes

---

2 - 3 tablespoons corn oil
1 onion, finely chopped
200 g (7 oz) corned beef, diced
350 g (12 oz) cooked potato,
   roughly mashed
1 small cooked beetroot, diced
1 tablespoon Worcestershire sauce

---

1 Heat the corn oil in a large heavy frying pan, add the onion and fry until lightly browned.
2 Mix the corned beef, potato and beetroot together, then add to the cooked onions in the pan. Sprinkle with Worcestershire sauce and stir thoroughly to combine.
3 Flatten the mixture into a cake and leave over a low heat until crisp and brown underneath. (Do not cook it too quickly or the crust will stick irrevocably to the pan.)
4 Turn the hash out onto a plate, brown side uppermost, and serve with a green vegetable or salad.

GOOD IN SMALL AMOUNTS

Corned beef looks very fatty - is it a healthy meat to eat?

There is a fairly high proportion of fat in corned beef, about 12 g per 100 g (just under ½ oz per 3½ oz) of meat, but because it is a pressed product, it is so dense and rich you will not want to eat very much of it. The calorie content is 217 per 100 g (3½ oz). Buy corned beef thinly sliced for making sandwiches, and in cans as a store cupboard standby for salads or corned beef hash.

CORNFLOUR

KNOW THE DIFFERENCE

What is the difference between cornflour and cornmeal, and can they be used in the same way?

The two differ considerably. Cornflour, ground to a fine chalky white powder, has a high proportion of starch and is a valuable thickening agent in sauces. It is also added to some cakes and biscuits.

Cornmeal, or polenta, is a much coarser flour, used in making polenta, muffins and some breads, in particular the corn bread of the United States, which can be sweet or savoury. See also CORN (MAIZE).

LUMPY SAUCES

I often have trouble when I use cornflour as it makes my sauces lumpy. What can I do?

When used properly, cornflour is an excellent thickener. Place the required amount of cornflour in a small bowl and stir in a little cold water (1 - 2 tablespoons) until it is completely blended. Add a little of the hot sauce to the cornflour mixture, blend well and then whisk this back into your main sauce, which should be just below boiling point. Stir the sauce continually until it reaches a steady simmer, then cook it gently for 2 minutes and serve.

See also: ARROWROOT

COURGETTES

EDIBLE SKIN

Is it necessary to peel courgettes?

The skin of young courgettes is thin and need not be removed for most purposes, but the dark green skin of older courgettes can be bitter and should be removed.

One garnishing treatment calls for just some of the skin to be discarded: using a potato peeler, shave the vegetable thinly lengthways to produce very thin slices. Throw away the first slice and the last, which consist mostly of green skin, and drop the remaining, green-edged slices into a pan of boiling water. Drain and refresh them under the cold tap as soon as the water returns to the boil.

YOUNG AND FRESH

I have read recommendations to salt courgette slices before cooking. Is it necessary and why?

Salt draws out water from moist vegetables, a process known as disgorging. Left to grow, courgettes would become marrows, and therefore be very wet indeed, but picked young they are merely juicy.

The best courgettes are those up to 10 cm (4 in) long, which do not need disgorging. There is no point in salting courgettes if you are then going to cook them using a moist method such as steaming, poaching, braising or stir-frying.

Rather than salting larger courgettes, you can reduce the moisture content by choosing a dry cooking method: split them in half lengthways and grill them; cut them in long diagonal slices and cook on an oiled, ridged griddle pan; or halve them lengthways, scoop out the seed column, then stuff and bake.

A classic Italian cooking method is to batter batons of courgettes and fry them crisp, as in the following recipe, to serve with grilled fish or as part of the collection of battered fried fish called *fritto misto*.

Battered and fried courgettes

SERVES: 4 as a starter or accompaniment
PREPARATION TIME: 10 minutes
COOKING TIME: 6 - 10 minutes

400 g (14 oz) courgettes
75 g (2¾ oz) plain flour
Oil for deep-frying
Salt

1 Top and tail the courgettes and cut them lengthways into batons about 6 mm (¼ in) wide.
2 Put the flour into a large bowl and gradually beat in 150 ml (5 fl oz) of cold water with a fork, then continue beating to make a smooth batter that coats the back of a spoon, adding an extra 1 - 2 tablespoons of water if necessary. (If the batter is too runny, beat in some flour, a tablespoon at a time, until the mixture reaches the required consistency.)
3 Heat the oil to 190°C (375°F), at which point a small cube of bread will brown in 40 seconds.
4 Pour the batter into a shallow dish or soup plate. Add a tablespoon of flour to the courgettes and turn them in it to make a dry surface to which the batter can cling.
5 Turn batches of courgette batons in the batter, picking them out with a fork to drop straight into the hot oil. They should sizzle immediately.
6 Fry the courgettes in batches until crisp and golden, about 3 - 5 minutes, drain on kitchen paper and serve immediately, sprinkled with salt.

COUSCOUS

NORTH AFRICAN PASTA

What is couscous, and how should I use it?

Strictly speaking, couscous is a pasta made from grains of semolina given a coating of extra fine flour so that they absorb moisture more easily, but it looks and is cooked like a grain. For a salad dish, simply soak the couscous in cold water for 20 minutes; no cooking is required.

QUICK COUSCOUS

The following method is a quick way of preparing couscous. Allow 55 - 85 g (2 - 3 oz) of the raw pasta grains for each person.

1 Place the couscous in a sieve and run it under cold water until all of the grains are moistened.

2 Place the couscous in a muslin-lined steamer, cover and steam over simmering water or stock for 8 - 10 minutes or until all the grains are fluffed up and tender. Serve the couscous immediately.

Drain the couscous and then toss with salad vegetables, fruit, nuts, spices and a dressing. The mixture goes well with grilled meats and fish, or plain grilled vegetables.

Couscous was invented in North Africa, where the most common method of cooking it is to steam it over a stew, allowing the grains to swell and soften as they absorb the steam and the flavour of the stew.

The North African chicken recipe overleaf is cooked this way. It is named after the tagine, the conical dish in which it is traditionally cooked, but you can use a double boiler, a steamer, a saucepan with a bamboo steamer on top, or put the couscous in a sieve over the stew. The sauce from the stew is usually served separately, to pour over the meat and vegetables, with extra chilli sauce on the side.

Chicken tagine with couscous

SERVES: 4 - 6
PREPARATION TIME: 30 minutes, plus at least 1 hour marinating
COOKING TIME: 40 minutes

4 tablespoons olive oil
2 cloves garlic, crushed
½ teaspoon chilli flakes
2 teaspoons each ground coriander and paprika
1 teaspoon each ground cumin, turmeric and cinnamon
700 g (1 lb 9 oz) skinless chicken breast fillet, cut in 2.5 cm (1 in) slices
1 onion, chopped
2 medium potatoes, cubed
2 large carrots, thickly sliced
300 ml (10 fl oz) chicken stock
300 ml (10 fl oz) tomato juice
2 tablespoons tomato purée
1 tablespoon chilli sauce
125 g (4½ oz) sultanas
2 tablespoons chopped fresh coriander
Salt and black pepper
350 g (12 oz) couscous
To garnish: lemon wedges and sprigs of fresh coriander

A combination of sweet spices, dried fruit and chilli adds an intriguing complexity to the flavour of this North African stew of couscous and chicken.

1 Put 2 tablespoons of the olive oil in a bowl and stir in the garlic, chilli flakes and all of the spices. Add the sliced chicken to the oil mixture, toss well, then cover and marinate it for at least an hour.
2 Heat the remaining oil in a frying pan, add the onion and fry it for 5 minutes, then add the potatoes and carrots and fry for another 5 minutes. Transfer to a large saucepan.
3 Remove the chicken slices from the marinade and pat them dry. Put them in the frying pan and stir-fry for 3 - 4 minutes or until golden.
4 Add the chicken to the vegetables and pour over the stock, tomato juice, tomato purée and chilli sauce. Bring to the boil, cover and simmer for 15 minutes, then stir in the sultanas, coriander, salt and pepper.
5 Place the couscous in a sieve and wash it under cold running water. Put the couscous in a muslin-lined steamer (the holes of a steamer are too big for the grain without a cloth)

and set it over the stew. Cover and simmer for 8 - 10 minutes until the couscous is cooked.
6 Serve the couscous on individual plates, topped with the chicken and vegetable tagine. Pour the excess cooking juices into a serving jug to offer alongside the couscous with some wedges of lemon and extra chilli sauce. Garnish the tagine with sprigs of fresh coriander.

SWEET THOUGHTS

Can I use couscous in desserts?

Yes. Steam the couscous over boiling water then top with a generous pat of butter, a few raisins and sprinkle sugar over to taste. Stir in some milk if you like. Alternatively, flavour the cooked couscous with the juice of an orange, chopped dates, and nuts such as pistachios.

CRAB

SOME LIKE IT HOT

Is there a way of eating crab hot?

If you are prepared to kill and cook it yourself, you can have hot fresh crab. If you do not want to do this, you will have to buy your crab ready-cooked and therefore cold.

You can, however, use the cooked white crab meat (which you can sometimes buy ready-flaked) in hot recipes. Add it, with a dash of brandy, to cream sauces to top poached fish or use it in Maryland Crab Cakes (right). Another idea from the United States, Eggs New Orleans, features crabmeat sautéed in butter and a little brandy, with poached eggs and paprika on top.

Maryland crab cakes

SERVES: 4 as a starter
PREPARATION TIME: 15 minutes (with ready-flaked crab), plus 1 hour optional chilling time
COOKING TIME: 5 minutes

350 g (12 oz) flaked white crabmeat
50 g (1¾ oz) soft white breadcrumbs
2 tablespoons finely chopped spring onions
2 tablespoons chopped parsley
1 teaspoon mustard powder
1 egg, size 3
3 tablespoons mayonnaise
1 teaspoon Worcestershire sauce
Salt, black pepper and a pinch of cayenne pepper
Flour, for coating
Butter or oil, for shallow frying
To serve: salad leaves, lemon wedges and salsa

1 Mix the crabmeat, breadcrumbs, spring onions, parsley and mustard powder together in a large bowl.
2 In a separate bowl, beat the egg lightly with a fork, then mix in the mayonnaise and Worcestershire sauce. Mix this thoroughly into the dry ingredients and season to taste with salt, black pepper and cayenne.
3 Shape the crab mixture into four even cakes and flour them lightly. The crab cakes will be firmer and easier to handle if you chill them for up to an hour in the refrigerator before cooking.
4 Fry them on both sides in butter or oil, or a mixture of both, until hot and lightly browned. Drain them on kitchen paper and serve hot with salad leaves, lemon wedges and salsa, such as Sweet Tomato Salsa (see FISH) or Coriander Salsa (see HERBS).

DRESSING A COOKED CRAB

Large-bodied crabs have plenty of body meat, while long-legged crabs have their meat mostly in the legs and claws. The larger the crab, the easier it is to extract the meat. Break open the shell or get the fishmonger to open a cooked crab for you, and then simply pick out as much meat as you can from the crevices and rearrange it in the shell as shown. The brown meat can be mashed and mixed with breadcrumbs to lighten its flavour. Serve dressed cooked crab with mayonnaise, lemon wedges and brown bread and butter.

1 Pull off the claws and legs. Crack open the claws with a small hammer and scoop the white meat into a bowl with a lobster pick, skewer or the tip of a small, sharp knife. Keep the legs for a decorative garnish.

2 Twist off the tail flap and discard then stand the crab on its edge and push out the central body chamber from the upper shell using your thumbs. Or crack the body with a knife and pull apart with your hands.

3 Remove the greyish 'dead men's fingers' (lungs or gills) from around the body and discard. Pick up the back shell and remove the stomach sac from just below the head. Check the shell just in case any bits of the grey matter have fallen in and remove if necessary.

4 Use a sharp knife or your hands to split the crab's body into halves or quarters, then carefully remove the white crab meat using a pick or skewer and a teaspoon. Fork it through and discard any small pieces of membrane. Reserve the flesh in a bowl.

5 Spoon the brown meat from the back shell into a separate bowl with any coral meat. Tap the underside of the shell with a small hammer to break back to the natural inner rim. Wash, dry and rub the shell with oil.

6 Season both meats with some salt, pepper and a squeeze of lemon juice. Spoon them back into the shell, placing the white meat on each side and the brown meat down the middle, then garnish with parsley.

CRANBERRIES

AUTUMN PLEASURES

Are cranberries available all year round or just at Christmas?

Fresh cranberries are in season and at their peak between October and December, but they usually remain available to the end of January. You can also get them frozen all year round for both sweet and savoury cooking, making them into jelly, tarts or piquant sauces to serve with game and other meat.

SCARLET SAUCE

Can I use frozen cranberries to make cranberry sauce?

Yes, you can, and they should be cooked while they are still frozen. Cranberry sauce is most often served with roast turkey, but the recipe below can also be used as a topping for ice cream or cheesecake, as a filling for sponge cakes or meringue nests, combined or topped with whipped cream.

Cranberry sauce

SERVES: 6 - 8
PREPARATION TIME: 10 minutes
COOKING TIME: 10 minutes, plus
2 - 3 hours chilling time

350 g (12 oz) cranberries, fresh
   or frozen
1 orange
1 lemon
125 g (4½ oz) caster sugar
2 tablespoons arrowroot

1 Rinse fresh berries under a cold tap, remove the stalks and any berries that are bruised or shrivelled.
2 Peel the rind from the orange and lemon, avoiding the white pith, then cut it into fine shreds. Squeeze the orange and lemon and strain the juice into a stainless-steel, nonstick or enamel saucepan.
3 Add the rind, the caster sugar and the fresh or frozen cranberries. Cook over a moderate heat for 5 minutes or until the cranberries start to pop.

4 Drain the berries through a nylon sieve into a bowl to catch the juice, and set the berries aside. Blend the arrowroot with 3 tablespoons of cold water and stir it into the juice.
5 Return the juice to the saucepan and bring to the boil, stirring, until the sauce thickens. Continue stirring for a minute to cook the arrowroot. Remove from the heat and cool.
6 Put the cranberries into a bowl, stir in the sauce and mix it in well. Allow it to cool completely before covering the bowl with cling film. Chill for 2 - 3 hours or overnight.

CRAWFISH

CRUSTACEAN CONFUSION

Is crawfish another name for crayfish or are they different?

They are different. Crawfish (also known as *langouste* and rock or spiny lobster) are what are often served as lobster around the Mediterranean. Although they have only small claws with not much meat, the fine white body meat is excellent and there is a good proportion of it in comparison to total weight. They are commonly sold at about 2 kg (4 lb 8 oz) weight; you should allow 600 - 700 g (1 lb 5 oz - 1 lb 9 oz) shell-on weight per person.

Crayfish, on the other hand, are small freshwater crustaceans found in Britain, Scandinavia and in the bayous of Louisiana, where they feature in Cajun cooking. They can be difficult to find in British shops; for recipes that call for crayfish, you can use large prawns instead.

CREAM

LOW-FAT DRAWBACK

I've tried to whip single cream but it is always a failure. Why?

It does not contain enough butterfat to thicken when beaten. Fat globules trap whisked air, forming the characteristic foam and texture

of whipped cream. A minimum of 35 per cent fat is necessary for whipping, and single cream contains just over half that amount.

OVERWHIPPED CREAM

How can I rescue my cream if I have whipped it too much?

It is quite easy to overwhip cream, particularly double cream. When this happens the cream develops a grainy appearance with a yellowish tinge, and the flavour is affected. There is no remedy, though if you carry on whisking, you should end up with some usable butter. Always chill the cream before you start whisking and beat it firmly but carefully and not too fiercely.

WHIPPING CREAM

For best results, before whipping chill both the mixing bowl and the hand whisk or the blade attachments of the electric whisk, as well as the double or whipping cream.

1 Whisk the cream in the bowl until it starts to thicken.

2 Continue to whisk more slowly until the cream stands in soft peaks. If you want stiffly whipped cream, continue whisking slowly until firmer peaks form. The higher the fat content of the cream, the more quickly it will thicken. Do not whip any longer than is necessary, or the cream will become grainy.

Save it!

If you want to freeze a dish such as a casserole or soup that will require the addition of cream at the end, it is best to freeze the dish without adding the cream. Reheat the dish to boiling point to kill any bacteria, then lower the heat and mix in the cream. Do not add the cream before the dish has been reheated.

ADDING EGG WHITE

Is it possible to make a lighter type of whipped cream?

You can lighten whipped cream by folding in one whisked egg white to every 300 ml (10 fl oz) of whipping cream. This lightened cream must be used within 2 hours as it is less stable than standard whipped cream. Whipped UHT cream which is sold in aerosols is also unstable. This 'cream' has added sugar, a propellant and stabilisers. It is not really whipped cream but a foam which will collapse very quickly.

GENTLE WARMING

How can I be sure that cream won't curdle if I add it to hot dishes such as casseroles?

Cream is usually added just before serving and warmed gently. For example, when adding cream to a fricassée, or mushroom soup, to thicken, enrich and give them a smooth texture, it should be added at the last minute and warmed just enough to heat it through.

Single cream is more likely to curdle when heated than double cream, which does not curdle when boiled on its own and which can be safely added to most hot dishes. However, double cream may curdle if added to a dish that contains a lot of acid, such as lemon juice, or a much-reduced white wine sauce. To prevent this happening, after adding the cream, reheat it slowly.

FRESH CREAMS

TYPE OF CREAM	CHARACTERISTICS	FAT CONTENT
Half cream	Thin and light, suitable for pouring. Use in coffee, on cereals, in sauces and for dressings. Not suitable for whipping.	13% butterfat; 148 Calories per 100 g (3½ oz)
Single cream	Versatile cream that is thick enough for pouring. Extra-thick single cream has been homogenised to produce a spoonable cream that can be used as a topping for puddings and desserts. It is not suitable for whipping because of the fat content.	19% butterfat; 198 Calories per 100 g (3½ oz)
Soured cream	Made by adding lactic acid to pasteurised cream. This process results in a cream that is slightly thicker than single cream, with a refreshing but acidic flavour. Used in many dishes including dips, cheesecakes and baked potato toppings, and also for enriching soups, sauces and casseroles. Not suitable for whipping.	20% butterfat; 205 Calories per 100 g (3½ oz)
Whipping cream	Will double in volume if it is whipped correctly; also suitable for pouring. Use for piped decorations, or for folding into cold desserts to give a light texture; will not hold its shape on hot foods. Ready-whipped cream has added stabilisers to maintain the texture and often contains sugar, which raises the calorie count.	40% butterfat; 373 Calories per 100 g (3½ oz)
Crème fraîche	A cultured thick cream with a delicate trace of sourness. In France crème fraîche is the standard cream, used extensively in cooking. It keeps better than fresh cream: about 10–14 days in a refrigerator. Not suitable for whipping.	15–40% butterfat; 170–380 Calories per 100 g (3½ oz)
Double cream	Versatile cream which adds richness and texture to many dishes. Can be poured or whipped. It will turn to butter if it is overwhipped. Extra-thick double cream has been homogenised to make it thick for putting on puddings and desserts, but it is not suitable for whipping.	48% butterfat; 449 Calories per 100 g (3½ oz)
Clotted cream	Very rich, thick yellow cream traditionally associated with the West Country, made by gently heating thick cream. It spreads easily on scones, and is often served with puddings and desserts.	63% butterfat; 586 Calories per 100 g (3½ oz)

Lower or reduced-fat creams
These low-fat creams are now available in single, double or whipping varieties. They are made from a varying blend of buttermilk, vegetable oils and butter and each type contains about half the fat of its full-cream equivalent. Low-fat creams keep well in the refrigerator because of their lower fat content. They are good for cooking and can be used in any recipe that requires cream.

EASY ADDITIONS

Will cream separate if I add another flavouring to it?

No, you can add flavourings such as rose and orange-flower waters, fruit brandy, dark rum, Cointreau or any other cordial or liqueur. Just pour the flavouring ingredient into the cream and stir quickly and continuously until it is well mixed then chill until needed. The syllabub recipe below shows how wine and double cream are whisked together for a stylish refreshing dessert.

Lemon syllabub

SERVES: 6 - 8
PREPARATION TIME: 25 minutes, plus 6 hours standing and chilling time
COOKING TIME: none

150 ml (5 fl oz) dry white wine
75 g (2 ¾ oz) caster sugar
Finely grated rind and juice of 1 lemon
300 ml (10 fl oz) double cream
To decorate: pared lemon rind and sprigs of mint

1 Put the wine, sugar, lemon rind and juice in a large bowl, stir to mix, then cover and set aside in a cool place for 4 hours.
2 Add the double cream and whip the mixture until softly stiff, being careful not to overwhip it. Spoon the syllabub into glasses and chill for about 2 hours before serving.
3 Just before you are ready to serve, garnish with the thinly pared lemon rind and sprigs of fresh mint.
VARIATIONS
For a milder flavour, use sweet cider instead of white wine. For added volume and lightness, fold in two whisked egg whites after whipping.

SMETANA OR SMITANE

What is smetana, and what is it used for? Can you cook it?

Smetana (also called smitane or smatana) is made from skimmed milk which has been enriched with cream and treated with a souring culture. It contains only about 10 per cent butterfat, so it is a good low-fat substitute for cream. It is used in both sweet and savoury dishes, particularly in Eastern Europe, but must be watched when it is being heated as it curdles easily.

FREEZING CREAM

Can cream be frozen?

Yes, as long as it has a butterfat content of 35 per cent or more. You can freeze double and whipping cream but not single cream, as it separates on thawing. However, single cream can be frozen if it is incorporated into a dish.

The best results are achieved by half-whipping the cream before freezing. The cream should then be placed in a suitable freezer container, leaving room for expansion. Home-frozen cream will keep in the freezer for up to three months and should be defrosted in the refrigerator overnight or at a cool room temperature for a few hours.

Whipped cream may be piped into rosettes straight onto waxed paper before open freezing. Once frozen, the rosettes can be packed in layers in a rigid container and used as required. They should be put into their final position before they are thawed, which will take about 30 – 45 minutes at room temperature, double that time in the middle of the refrigerator.

TANGY FRENCH CREAM

Can I substitute crème fraîche for cream and use it the same way?

Yes, the French do, although it is not suitable for whipping. The high fat content of crème fraîche means it does not curdle when heated, and it is therefore suitable for many hot dishes such as soups, where it acts as an excellent thickener, and casseroles. It combines the qualities of sweet thick cream and soured cream, and is often used in place of soured cream to give a slight tang.

You can also eat crème fraîche with jam, conserves, fruit purées or aromatic honey. Or serve it with cakes, tarts or any dessert you would usually garnish with cream.

Save it!

Don't waste leftover cream. Small amounts can be frozen in an ice-cube tray, a tablespoon per cube. Defrost them and use as required, or add the cubes of frozen cream directly from the freezer to the dish on the heat.

FRESH FROMAGE FRAIS

Should I use fromage frais like a cream or like a cheese?

Fromage frais, which means 'fresh cheese' in French, is made from skimmed cow's milk and may have been enriched with cream. It can be either soft and floppy or quite firm as the fat content varies from zero to 8 per cent, and the flavour ranges from mild, clean and slightly acidic to rich and creamy. It is also available in sweetened versions.

Fromage frais can be used like cream in both sweet and savoury dishes, but it cannot be whipped, and as it curdles easily on heating it may separate. So if it is to be added to a hot dish, add it off the heat, stir it in well and then reheat it gently for a few seconds only.

As a dessert, fromage frais can be served fresh with fruit or sugar, or substituted for cream or cheese in cheesecakes and various other chilled desserts. You can also use fromage frais instead of cream for filling a pavlova, a gâteau or any other cream-filled dessert.

Fromage frais will keep for up to two months in the freezer; stir it well once it has been thawed.

SIMPLY SOURED

Can I turn ordinary cream into soured cream easily?

Yes, you can. Simply stir 1 – 2 teaspoons of lemon juice into 150 ml (5 fl oz) of single or double cream, depending on how thick you like it. Left to stand, the cream will thicken in 30 minutes. The taste and texture will be only slightly different and it is a good substitute for commercially cultured soured cream. To make a lighter version, without the need to add lemon juice, blend equal quantities of single or double cream and yoghurt.

Creams, fresh and soured, are an ideal base for quick and easy party dips, as the following recipes show. They are best eaten on the day they are made. They may be kept in the refrigerator for up to 24 hours but will not keep well for any longer.

Serve them with raw vegetables (tiny vegetables are perfect), corn chips, bread sticks, crisps, or pitta bread warmed in the oven, or use them to fill baked potatoes.

Soured cream and fresh chive dip

SERVES: 4 - 6
PREPARATION TIME: 10 minutes
COOKING TIME: none

100 g (3 1/2 oz) cream cheese
150 ml (5 fl oz) soured cream
3 tablespoons chopped fresh chives
Salt and black pepper
To garnish: cayenne pepper

Put all the ingredients in a bowl and mix until well blended. Transfer to a serving bowl, then sprinkle the top of the mixture with cayenne pepper. Serve immediately or cover and keep it chilled until it is needed.

Avocado dip

SERVES: 6 - 8
PREPARATION TIME: 20 minutes
COOKING TIME: none

2 ripe avocados, roughly chopped
2 tablespoons lemon juice
1 small onion, roughly chopped
2 cloves garlic
150 ml (5 fl oz) soured cream
Salt and black pepper
A few drops of Tabasco sauce, optional

Put all the ingredients in a blender or food processor and blend until smooth. This dip should be made at the last minute because the avocado will darken if it is left too long.

Blue cheese dip

SERVES: 6 - 8
PREPARATION TIME: 20 minutes
COOKING TIME: none

175 g (6 oz) Stilton cheese, crumbled
1 shallot, finely chopped
150 ml (5 fl oz) soured cream
Salt and black pepper
2 teaspoons lemon juice

1 Put the cheese, shallot and soured cream in a bowl and mash them until they are soft. Keep on mashing until well mixed and very smooth.
2 Taste for seasoning; it should be quite sharp. Add the lemon juice drop by drop until the dip tastes sharp but not too acidic. Do not let the lemon become overpowering.

For this dip use a well-flavoured cheese: it is an excellent way of using up slightly overripe Stilton which is past its prime; too far gone for serving on the cheese board but too good to let go to waste.

Tomato and basil dip

SERVES: 6 - 8
PREPARATION TIME: 25 minutes
COOKING TIME: none

100 g (3 1/2 oz) medium or low-fat soft cheese
2 shallots, finely chopped
350 g (12 oz) tomatoes, skinned, deseeded and finely chopped
150 ml (5 fl oz) double cream or thick Greek yoghurt
2 - 3 tablespoons fresh basil, torn with your fingers
Salt and black pepper

1 Cream the cheese with a fork until it is soft and smooth, then stir in the shallots and tomatoes (and the yoghurt if using) and mix them all together very well.
2 If using cream, whisk it until it stands in soft peaks. Fold it into the cheese and tomato mixture, add the basil and season to taste. Transfer to a serving dish, cover and chill.

Creamy dips with hearty flavours are unbeatable for parties, and are extremely simple to make. Clockwise from the top: tomato and fresh basil; blue cheese with shallots; soured cream and chives; and avocado with a dash of tangy lemon.

CREME BRULEE

SKIP THE GRILLING

Can I make crème brûlée if I do not have a proper grill?

Yes. This classic French dessert is made from a thick, baked vanilla custard and sprinkled with caster sugar which is melted to caramel. This is usually done under a grill (as in the recipe, right) but the dish can also be browned in the oven at 200°C (400°F, gas mark 6) for about 15 minutes, until the sugar bubbles.

Alternatively, you can make a caramel topping separately by gently heating 75 g (2¾ oz) of sugar in 75 ml (2½ fl oz) of water until it dissolves, then boil until it changes to a rich caramel colour and pour it over the custards. Leave for a few minutes to harden, then serve.

Or pour the caramel thinly onto a greased baking sheet, allow it to set, then break it into small pieces and sprinkle over each custard.

Banana and ginger crème brûlée

SERVES: 6
PREPARATION TIME: 45 minutes, plus several hours chilling time
COOKING TIME: 1 hour

---

600 ml (1 pint) double cream
1 vanilla pod, split lengthways
4 egg yolks, size 3
100 g (3½ oz) caster sugar
2 teaspoons ground ginger
2 bananas, sliced and tossed in lemon juice

---

1 Preheat the oven to 150°C (300°F, gas mark 2). Put the cream and the vanilla pod into the top of a double saucepan, or into a bowl placed over a pan of simmering water, and heat gently until almost boiling. Remove from the heat and remove the vanilla pod (store it in sugar for use later).

2 Beat the egg yolks with half the sugar until the mixture is light and creamy, then stir in the cream.

3 Sprinkle the ginger over the sliced bananas, then divide them equally between six individual ramekins.

Pour the custard carefully over the bananas, dividing it equally.

4 Put the ramekins in a roasting tin and pour in sufficient hot water to come halfway up the sides of the dishes. Bake for an hour or until set.

5 Remove the banana creams from the roasting tin and leave to cool, then refrigerate them for several hours, preferably overnight.

6 Preheat the grill to a high heat. Sprinkle the remaining sugar over the desserts to form a thin, even layer. Grill for 2 - 3 minutes until the sugar turns to caramel. Allow it to cool, then chill for 2 - 3 hours. The creams should not be served until the caramel layer is crisp.

VARIATIONS
You can use other fruits, such as apricots, blackberries or raspberries, as an alternative to the bananas, and other spices in place of the ground ginger – try cardamom, cinnamon, mixed spice or nutmeg.

Underneath the 'burned cream' crust of this extravagant dessert is a surprise filling of banana and spicy ginger.

SLIMLINE BRULEE

I love crème brûlée, but worry about it being too rich. Could I make a lighter version?

Yes, by adding thick yoghurt or fromage frais to a custard made from skimmed milk and using gelatine to set it, as in the recipe below.

Light crème brûlée

SERVES: *4*
PREPARATION TIME: *15 minutes, plus 1 - 1½ hours chilling time*
COOKING TIME: *10 minutes*

200 ml (7 fl oz) skimmed milk
2 - 3 drops vanilla essence
3 egg yolks, size 3
40 g (1½ oz) caster sugar
1 tablespoon powdered gelatine or 4 sheets gelatine
200 ml (7 fl oz) Greek yoghurt or fromage frais
20 g (¾ oz) demerara sugar

1 Bring the milk and vanilla essence to the boil and take off the heat.
2 Whisk the egg yolks and caster sugar together until light. Stir them into the hot milk and return to a low heat, stirring continuously, until the custard coats the back of a spoon.
3 Remove from the heat, add the gelatine, stir until it has dissolved and strain the custard into a bowl. Cool it over iced water until it has set.
4 Whisk in the yoghurt or fromage frais, pour into four ramekins and chill until completely set.
5 Preheat the grill to a high heat. Sprinkle the sugar over the creams and grill until it turns to caramel. Chill for 30 - 45 minutes.

CREME CARAMEL

SLOW AND STEADY

Why does my crème caramel contain so many air bubbles?

Crème caramel is cooked in a bain-marie in order to achieve a slow and gentle transmission of heat to the egg mixture. If the egg custard is not cooked in a bain-marie, the oven heat will go directly into the mixture and cook it too quickly, resulting in a custard that contains air bubbles and a grainy or curdled texture. If this does happen there is no remedy. Immersing the dish in cold water will help to stop the cooking process quickly, but it may already be too late for rescue.

Small air bubbles, giving the custard a pitted appearance, can also be created if cold milk was used to make the custard instead of milk that was heated first. You should have no problems with air bubbles if you follow the recipe for crème caramel below, which has a hint of spice from cinnamon and luxurious warmth from the vanilla.

Orange crème caramel

SERVES: *4 - 6*
PREPARATION TIME: *45 minutes, plus 3 - 4 hours cooling and chilling time*
COOKING TIME: *1 hour 10 minutes*

125 g (4½ oz) caster sugar
2 oranges and their thin rind (remove all the white pith)
1 stick cinnamon
600 ml (1 pint) milk
4 eggs, size 3
A few drops of vanilla essence

1 Put 100 g (3½ oz) of sugar in a heavy saucepan with 150 ml (5 fl oz) of water and heat gently, stirring from time to time until all the sugar has dissolved. Then bring to the boil and bubble rapidly without stirring until the caramel is golden in colour.
2 Pour it into a 15 cm (6 in) soufflé dish and set aside to cool.
3 Put the orange rind, cinnamon stick and milk in a saucepan and heat gently until almost boiling. Remove the pan from the heat and set aside to infuse for 10 minutes.
4 Preheat the oven to 160°C (325°F, gas mark 3). Whisk the eggs and remaining sugar together. Strain the milk, discarding the orange rind and the cinnamon, and pour it onto the egg mixture, whisking well. Whisk in the vanilla essence, then strain the custard over the cooled caramel.
5 Stand the dish in a roasting tin filled with enough hot water to come three-quarters of the way up the sides of the dish. Bake for an hour until well set. Meanwhile, peel and divide the oranges into segments, picking off all the pith. Put them in a serving dish, cover and chill.
6 Remove the cooked custard from the bain-marie and set it aside to cool completely. When cold, cover and chill for several hours.
7 Before serving the custard, loosen it around the edges then carefully invert it onto a plate, allowing the caramel to drain out over the baked custard. Stand the baking dish in hot water to soften any caramel that has stuck to the dish, then pour it over the crème caramel on the plate.
8 Serve garnished with the well-trimmed orange segments and, if you wish, a delicate dusting of ground cinnamon and a veil of icing sugar, preferably vanilla flavoured.

CROUTONS

FAR LESS FAT

How can I make croutons that are healthy but still tasty?

Croutons are usually made by frying 5 mm (¼ in) cubes of bread in oil or butter, which is delicious but rather high in fat. They can also be toasted, which cuts out the fat, but this tends to reduce the flavour. For a reasonable compromise, toss the cubes in a little olive oil, salt and pepper, then spread them on a baking sheet and bake them in an oven preheated to 190°C (375°F, gas mark 5) for about 10 minutes or until they are completely crisp.

CRUMBLE

TIPS ON TOPS

I hate crumble topping that is too thick and chewy. Is there any way to determine how much to add?

The shape and size of the dish you use will determine how much topping you should add. Choose a wide shallow dish rather than a narrow, deep one for a crumble; in a deep dish there will be a little less crunchy crumble showing on top, but plenty underneath which will not become crisp. Using a shallow dish with more surface area will result in a thinner, crispy topping.

Don't worry if some of the juice from the fruit seeps through the crumble. These sticky parts taste sweet and delicious – they are one of the best bits and every crumble should have some. The recipe on the right should provide plenty of crunchy topping and 'gooey bits'.

Add mango for sweetness

If you want to cut down on the sugar in your crumble, add two large sweet ripe mangoes, cut into chunks and cooked in very little water, then mix with the other fruit.

EXTRA CRUNCH

Are there any variations on the traditional flour, butter and sugar crumble? Sometimes I would like my crumbles to have something more in the way of crunch.

You can add texture in several ways. Sprinkle the crumble topping with 25 g (1 oz) of coarsely chopped hazelnuts or walnuts, or flaked almonds as in the recipe on the right, before baking. Or use a coarser sugar such as demerara instead of caster sugar, and replace 25 g (1 oz) of the flour with the same weight of rolled oats or crushed amaretti biscuits. Add these at the same time as the sugar.

Apricot, orange and almond crumble

SERVES: 5 - 6
PREPARATION TIME: 30 - 35 minutes
COOKING TIME: 40 - 45 minutes

FOR THE FRUIT MIXTURE
1 kg (2 lb 4 oz) fresh ripe apricots, stoned and cut into quarters
50 g (1 ¾ oz) granulated sugar
Finely grated zest of half an orange
2 - 3 tablespoons orange juice

FOR THE CRUMBLE TOPPING
175 g (6 oz) plain flour
125 g (4 ½ oz) butter, diced, plus extra for greasing
50 g (1 ¾ oz) caster sugar
25 g (1 oz) flaked almonds, optional
To serve: single cream or mascarpone cheese

---

1 Preheat the oven to 200°C (400°F, gas mark 6). Butter a shallow 1.7 litre (3 pint) ovenproof dish.
2 Arrange the apricots in the dish and sprinkle each layer with sugar. Add the orange zest and juice.
3 To make the crumble topping, sift the flour into a bowl and rub in the butter until the mixture resembles breadcrumbs. Stir in the sugar and continue to rub in until the mixture begins to cling together in crumbs.
4 Spread the crumble evenly over the fruit and press down lightly. Sprinkle with flaked almonds.
5 Bake for 25 - 30 minutes, then reduce the temperature to 180°C (350°F, gas mark 4) and continue cooking for a further 15 minutes until the top is well browned and the fruit is tender.
6 Serve the crumble warm, with single cream or spoonfuls of thick mascarpone cheese.

VARIATIONS
Blackberries, blueberries, tayberries and other soft fruit can also be very successfully cooked in a crumble. Put them into the prepared dish and sprinkle 50 g (1 ¾ oz) of soft brown sugar and 2 tablespoons of water over them instead of the orange zest and juice. Then cover with crumble topping and cook as in the recipe. You can also add a tablespoon of liqueur or fruit brandy to the filling.

CRYSTALLISED FLOWERS

SWEET BLOOMS

Which flowers are suitable for crystallising? Are some of them better than others?

Many highly scented flowers are edible: acacias, fruit blossom, jasmine, lilac, mimosa, clove-scented pinks, primroses, roses and violets. Never eat flowers that have been treated with pesticides or any that are grown from bulbs as they are toxic. The flowers must be perfect, very fresh and completely dry. Use them as quickly as possible as they will begin to fade and wilt rapidly.

MAKING SUGAR-FROSTED FLOWERS

For elegant decorations use these easy-to-make sugar-coated flowers.

1 Using an artist's soft paintbrush, gently coat a flower all over with a little lightly beaten egg white.

2 Dust the flower all over with caster sugar, using a sieve, and shake off any excess. The flower should have a thin dusting of sugar which should not stick in lumps. Put the flowers on a wire rack and leave in a warm place to dry for several hours or overnight.

DELICATE DUSTING

Is there an uncomplicated way of making decorative sugar flowers?

There are two methods. In the simplest, known as sugar-frosting, the flowers are brushed with egg white and then dusted with caster sugar (see box, below left) and this will preserve them for up to two days.

If you want them to last longer you need to use gum arabic (available from cake decorating shops and some chemists) dissolved in rose or orange-flower water. To use gum arabic as a covering, melt 15 g (½ oz) of gum arabic in 2 tablespoons of flower water. The gum must be thoroughly dissolved so follow the packet instructions.

Using an artist's paintbrush, coat the flowers, petals or leaves on all sides with the gum arabic mixture, then dust them all over with caster sugar. Place the flowers on a baking tray lined with baking paper and leave them in a warm place for one to two days until they are dry and hard. Stored in a glass jar with a tight-fitting lid, they will keep for up to a year.

As this method takes quite some time and the flowers tend to lose their shape, it is best-suited for petals and flowers that are strongly scented and flavoured and have a good colour, such as mimosa, rose petals or violets. They can be used whole as decorations, or can be crushed and stirred into meringues or whipped cream for a delicate flavouring. Frosted flowers are a pretty touch on a cake or trifle.

The following recipe uses simple frosted rose petals as a decorative and edible touch of colour. For a violet soufflé use candied violets.

The appeal of a creamy rose-flavoured confection is doubled when decorated with powerfully fragrant sugar-frosted rose petals of deep red and vivid pink.

Rose-petal soufflé

SERVES: 4 - 6
PREPARATION TIME: 30 minutes, plus 2 hours setting time
COOKING TIME: none

1 tablespoon powdered gelatine
3 eggs, size 2, separated
125 g (4½ oz) caster sugar or rose-petal sugar (see SUGAR)
1 tablespoon rosewater
1 - 2 drops pink food colouring, optional
300 ml (10 fl oz) double cream
To decorate: 12 sugar-frosted rose petals or tiny rose buds

1 Put 3 tablespoons of water into a small bowl standing in a pan of hot water. Sprinkle on the gelatine and stir until it is completely dissolved.
2 Whisk together the egg yolks and sugar until thick and creamy. Stir in the gelatine, rosewater and pink food colouring, if you are using it.
3 Whip the cream until soft peaks form and fold it carefully into the creamed egg yolks and sugar.
4 Whisk the egg whites until stiff and fold them into the mixture.
5 Pour the soufflé into a serving dish or stemmed glasses and leave it to set in the refrigerator for 2 hours. To serve, arrange a few frosted rose petals on the surface of the soufflé or around the individual portions.

CRYSTALLISED FRUIT

TIME AND SUGAR

I would like to offer crystallised fruits as Christmas presents. Can you tell me how to make some?

Crystallised fruits, though expensive to buy, can be made quite cheaply at home and make lovely presents. The fruit is simply saturated in a sugar syrup then left to dry, and although the process takes more than a week, it requires only a small amount of time each day, as the recipe (right) shows. Don't be tempted to hurry the process or the fruit will shrivel and become tough. To finish off the fruit, give it a sparkling crystallised finish or a smoother, shiny glacé coating.

Crystallised fruit

MAKES: 500 g (1 lb 2 oz)
PREPARATION TIME: 30 minutes initially, then 10 minutes a day for 7 - 8 days; plus 30 minutes finishing
COOKING TIME: 5 minutes a day for 7 - 8 days

500 g (1 lb 2 oz) canned fruit in syrup, such as apricots, peaches or pineapple
500 g (1 lb 2 oz) caster sugar or, for a clearer appearance to the fruit, use half caster sugar and half glucose syrup

1 Drain the fruit, reserving 300 ml (10 fl oz) of the syrup (top up with water if necessary). Remove any damaged fruit, then put the rest of the fruit into a heatproof bowl.
2 Put 250 g (9 oz) of the sugar in a pan with the fruit syrup. Stir the mixture well and heat it gently until the sugar has completely dissolved.

3 Bring the syrup to the boil and pour it over the fruit, which should now remain totally submerged in the syrup. Put a plate over the fruit, if necessary, to prevent it from floating up and being exposed to air. Leave the fruit to stand in a warm, but not hot, place for 24 hours.
4 Drain the syrup from the fruit into a saucepan and add 60 g (2 ¼ oz) of sugar. Bring it to the boil over a low heat, stirring until all the sugar has dissolved. Pour the hot syrup over the fruit again and leave to stand in a warm place for 24 hours. Repeat the next day and again the following day.
5 On the fifth day, strain the syrup into a saucepan and add 90 g (3 ¼ oz) of sugar. Heat gently, stirring, until the sugar has dissolved. Add the fruit to the pan and bring slowly to the boil, then simmer for 3 - 4 minutes. Gently pour the fruit and syrup into a bowl, cover and leave to stand at room temperature for 48 hours.

Ordinary canned fruit is transformed into an exquisite delicacy by a few days' total immersion in a sugar bath.

6 Repeat step 5 once. By the ninth day the cooled syrup should have the consistency of thick honey. (If it does not, boil the fruit and syrup together again until the syrup has thickened, then transfer them to a bowl, cover and leave to stand at room temperature for four days.)

7 Remove the pieces of fruit from the syrup and place them on a wire rack set over a tray to drain. (The leftover syrup can be used for fruit salads or cooking stewed fruit.)

8 The fruit now has to be dried. If the heat is continuous, such as in an airing cupboard or near a boiler, the fruit will dry out in a few hours. Drying can also be done in residual heat from the oven, but as the heat should be lower than 50°C (122°F), it is best to use it after you have finished cooking, when the oven is cooling down. (Remember to take the fruit out the next time you turn the oven on.) To help the drying process, turn the fruit over now and again. It is ready when it is dry and not sticky; it can then be eaten as it is or finished further.

9 For a crystallised finish, put a pan of water on to boil. First dip the fruit into the boiling water with a slotted spoon and drain well, then roll each piece in caster sugar and leave on a wire rack to dry for a few hours.

10 For a smooth and shiny glacé finish, put 500 g (1 lb 2 oz) of caster sugar and 150 ml (5 fl oz) of water into a saucepan over a gentle heat and stir until the sugar has dissolved. Bring the syrup to the boil and take it off the heat, then cover it to keep it hot and to stop evaporation. Bring a pan of water to the boil.

11 Pour a little of the syrup into a small bowl. With a skewer, spear one piece of dried crystallised fruit at a time. Dip it first into the boiling water, then drain and dip it into the syrup. Drain on a wire rack.

12 When the coating syrup in the bowl becomes cloudy, replace it with fresh warm syrup from the pan. When the process is completed, the fruit should be shiny but not sticky.

Layer the fruit in an airtight box, with nonstick paper between each layer. Eat within a month or two.

MULTIPLE CHOICE

Can all fruits be crystallised?

Strongly flavoured fruits such as apricots, cherries, peaches, pineapple, plums and slightly under-ripe pears are the best choice for crystallising. You can also treat orange, lemon and grapefruit peel, and angelica stems and chestnuts, in the same way. Soft fruits such as raspberries and strawberries are not suitable because they contain too much water and will break up and become mushy. Equally, the large amount of juice in whole oranges and lemons causes them to collapse easily, which makes them difficult to crystallise at home, but tiny clementines and kumquats can be preserved by this method.

You can use either canned or fresh fruit but canned fruit is easier to handle, with the exception of canned plums, which soften and disintegrate during the process.

Fresh fruit must be in perfect condition. The first step is to poach it lightly in sugar syrup until just tender. The second stage is to make a crystallising syrup from the cooking water and then the process is the same as for canned fruit (see recipe, left). It needs to be steeped for two to three days longer than canned fruit. Because fresh fruit can break up during the process, it is harder to see when enough sugar has been absorbed so the soaking may be stopped too soon, in which case the fruit could go mouldy.

TOUGH GINGER

Would you crystallise ginger in the same way as fruit?

Commercial preserved or stem ginger in syrup is made from the very youngest shoots of the ginger plant, and these contain very little fibre. The fresh root ginger we can buy is too fibrous to be used for home-made crystallised ginger. To give a subtle flavour of ginger to your own crystallised fruit, add a peeled piece of fresh ginger to the sugar syrup. Steep it with the fruit and discard it when done.

CUCUMBER

LESS WATER, MORE TASTE

Why do some recipes tell you to salt cucumbers before using?

Salt draws out the moisture which softens the crisp cucumber, resulting in a denser texture and a more concentrated flavour. This method is used for the tangy Greek salad or dip called tzaziki, in which the cucumber is coarsely grated and salted for 30 minutes; it is then rinsed, squeezed dry and mixed into yoghurt with plenty of garlic and a splash of olive oil.

QUICKLY COOKED

Can I cook cucumber and serve it as a vegetable with other dishes?

Hot cucumber makes a light, crisp vegetable dish to go with fish, but it shrinks during salting and cooking so you should allow a whole one to serve two people, or three at the most. You may have to use two pans if you are cooking for a larger number. Choose young cucumbers, which are smaller and have a thinner skin than older, outdoor-grown ones and are likely to have fewer seeds and softer, more edible flesh.

The recipe on the next page for Hot Buttered Cucumber, flavoured with dill, makes a good side dish for poached or grilled salmon.

Leftovers

Cooked or raw cucumber can easily be made into a quick cold and refreshing soup. Process or blend it with a clove of garlic, thick yoghurt, cream or crème fraîche, and mint or tarragon. Serve sprinkled with a tablespoon of the chopped herb and black pepper. A handful of tiny pink prawns adds colour and flavour.

Hot buttered cucumber with dill

SERVES: *2 - 3*
PREPARATION TIME: *5 minutes plus 30 minutes salting time*
COOKING TIME: *5 minutes*

1 large cucumber
2 teaspoons salt
50 g (1 ¾ oz) butter
A squeeze of lemon
Black pepper
2 tablespoons finely chopped dill

1 Peel the cucumber and cut it in half lengthways. Scoop out the seeds from the centre with a teaspoon and discard them. Cut the two halves in sections measuring 2 cm (¾ in) and toss them with the salt in a colander. Leave the pieces to drain in the sink for some 30 minutes, then rinse them under the cold tap and pat them dry.
2 Melt the butter in a wide pan or wok and stir-fry the cucumber until it is hot through. Season with lemon juice and black pepper and sprinkle on the dill; alternatively, try mint with mackerel, and chives, parsley or tarragon with fine white fish.

CURRY: see INDIAN COOKING and SOUTH-EAST ASIAN COOKING

Cucumber tossed in butter, accented with fresh dill and a sharpening dash of lemon, is a perfect partner for fish.

CUSTARD

GOOD AND EASY

I would like to move on from custard powder to the real thing. Is it difficult to make?

Custard is not really all that tricky but it does need to be cooked carefully. It is worthwhile mastering the technique because not only is the flavour of homemade custard much richer than that made with powder, but rich, smooth custard is the base on which many other desserts are built. For instance, it is essential for a superior trifle; when set with gelatine it turns into a bavarois; and frozen, it is the foundation of the very finest ice cream.

The most important thing when making custard is to cook it very gently and slowly. Trying to cook it in a rush is a mistake as it will almost invariably curdle. It must take its time and must never boil, so the choice of pan is important.

For best results, cook custard in a bain-marie, or water bath, which is a pan or tray of simmering water large enough to hold smaller pans or dishes. This makes it easier to control the temperature of delicate mixtures such as custard. A bain-marie is easy to improvise (see below, right). Alternatively, make the custard in the top of a double saucepan, or in a heavy-based pan on a very gentle heat. In addition, the custard must be stirred continuously while it is being cooked so that hot patches do not form against the side of the pan.

Custard is traditionally flavoured with vanilla. You can either infuse the milk with a split vanilla pod or add a few drops of vanilla essence. It does not have to be vanilla, however; try other flavourings, such as almond, nutmeg or mixed spice.

Once the custard has thickened, (it will never thicken as much as packet custard) take it off the heat and transfer it to a cold jug or bowl, so it does not continue cooking. Serve it immediately if you want it hot. To serve it cold, cover the custard closely to prevent a skin from forming on the top, leave it to cool completely, then refrigerate.

BAKED IN A MICROWAVE

Baked egg custard is the perfect dish to give to a convalescent, but it takes so long to make. Could I make it in the microwave?

Yes, it is very quick and easy to do, and because you cook the custard at a very low temperature, you do not need to use a bain-marie.

To make four individual custards, put 300 ml (10 fl oz) of milk in a microwave-safe jug and heat it on Medium for 1 ½ - 2 minutes. Whisk two medium eggs, 2 tablespoons of caster sugar and a few drops of vanilla essence together, then pour on the warm milk, whisking continuously. Strain into four ramekins and sprinkle with ground nutmeg. Microwave the ramekins on Low for 5 - 7 minutes, stirring occasionally until the custard is just set, then leave it to stand for a minute.

MAKING CUSTARD

To make perfect pouring custard, you need 600 ml (1 pint) of milk; 1 vanilla pod, cut into two lengthways; 2 eggs, size 3, plus 4 egg yolks; and 25 g (1 oz) of caster sugar.

1 Reserve 6 tablespoons of milk. Put the rest in a heavy pan or bain-marie and add the vanilla pod or a few drops of vanilla essence.

2 Heat the milk and vanilla until very hot but not boiling. Take it off the heat and set aside to infuse and cool for about 15 minutes. In a mixing bowl, lightly beat together the eggs, egg yolks and sugar.

3 Discard the vanilla pod and slowly pour the milk onto the egg mixture, whisking well. Then strain through a sieve into a clean heavy-based pan or double boiler.

4 Cook the mixture over a gentle heat, stirring continuously with a wooden spoon, until the custard thickens enough to thinly coat the back of the spoon. Do not allow the mixture to boil as this will make it curdle. Pour the custard into a cold jug and serve it hot or cold.

RESCUE OPERATION

Can I save a curdled custard?

There is no miracle remedy, but it will help to remove it from the heat immediately. You could try straining it into a cold dish sitting in a bowl of ice cubes and beating it vigorously, or you could try to rescue it by blending or processing it. This might restore some of the smoothness, and if it is not too overcooked it can be used, but the flavour will be affected. Another way of partially recovering curdled custard is to whiz it in the liquidiser with a small amount of cooled custard made quickly with about a tablespoon of custard powder.

EVEN COOKING

Why do my baked egg custards sometimes leak around the edges?

This is caused by too much heat and suggests the custard has been overcooked or cooked without the use of a bain-marie, or the oven temperature was too high. Any of these could result in pitting, so producing some moisture around the edges, and it cannot be rectified.

Check your oven temperature, and use a bain-marie. The simmering water beneath the dish lowers the temperature, ensuring a lower, even temperature during cooking.

A bain-marie is not necessary for the Plum Custard Tart, right, as the pastry protects the custard.

Improvising a bain-marie

A roasting tin can stand in for a bain-marie, either on the hob or in the oven. Always add the water to the bain-marie after you have put the dish in or it may overflow. When using the tin on the hob, put one end over the burner which is hot so the water bubbles; position the dish at the other end, away from the direct heat.

A double boiler can also be used on top of the stove to take the place of the bain-marie.

Plum custard tart

SERVES: 6
PREPARATION TIME: 40 minutes, plus 30 minutes resting for the pastry
COOKING TIME: 1¼ hours

---

75 g (2¾ oz) wholemeal plain flour
75 g (2¾ oz) plain flour
A pinch of salt
75 g (2¾ oz) salted butter or hard margarine, diced
500 g (1 lb 2 oz) plums, halved and stoned
300 ml (10 fl oz) milk (whole or semi-skimmed)
2 eggs, size 3, beaten
50 g (1¾ oz) caster sugar
A few drops of vanilla or almond essence

---

1 Put the flours and salt in a bowl. Rub the butter or margarine into the flour with your fingertips until the mixture resembles breadcrumbs.
2 Add 2 - 3 tablespoons of water and make a firm, smooth dough; you may need to add another tablespoon of water. Form the dough into a ball, wrap it in greaseproof paper or cling film and chill it for 30 minutes. In the meantime, preheat the oven to 190°C (375°F, gas mark 5) and lightly grease a 20 cm (8 in) flan dish.
3 Roll the chilled dough out on a lightly floured work surface and line the prepared flan dish with it. Bake the pastry blind for 15 minutes.
4 Remove the pastry from the oven and reduce the temperature to 160°C (325°F, gas mark 3). Put the plums, cut side down, in the pastry case.
5 In a saucepan, warm the milk gently until it is hot but not boiling. Quickly beat in the eggs, then beat in the sugar and vanilla or almond essence. Strain the mixture over the plums and bake the tart in the oven for about an hour until golden brown and just set. Serve warm or cold.
VARIATIONS
You can use other fruit, such as stoned apricots, cherries or sliced ripe pears, in place of the plums. For a spicy custard, add a teaspoon or two of ground mixed spice, some grated nutmeg or a pinch of ground coriander to the custard mixture.

DANISH PASTRIES

PATIENCE MAKES PERFECT

Are Danish pastries difficult to make at home?

Homemade Danish pastries require time and skill to make, but they are especially rich and luscious, as the recipe on the right shows. The yeast pastry is made in a similar way to puff pastry, by rolling butter in between layers of dough. Roll out the pastry so that butter does not break through the paste. If the butter escapes, the pastry will hold less fat and taste heavy.

Roll the pastry with short, light strokes, moving first forward and up (lifting the rolling pin slightly), and then backward and up. If your pastry seems too sticky, put it on a plate, dust it with flour then cover it with a polythene bag. Rest the pastry in the refrigerator until firm.

If you prefer, make the dough in advance, then place it in a plastic bag and leave it in the refrigerator for several hours or overnight.

TRICKY CROISSANTS

Why are there so few recipes for croissants?

It is hard to match the flavour and flakiness of a professional baker's croissants, even though homemade Danish pastries, which are similar, can be wonderful.

Croissants result from the special mix of the flour, butter and type of oven used. Any that are baked at home will probably disappoint. Be consoled that even the French rely on bakeries for croissants.

Danish pastries

MAKES: 8 windmills, or 16 small cartwheels, or 8 small crescents
PREPARATION TIME: 1 ½ hours plus about 2 hours resting, chilling and proving
COOKING TIME: 15 minutes

FOR THE PASTRY
175 g (6 oz) butter
15 g (½ oz) fresh yeast and 75 ml (2 ½ fl oz) warm milk, or 2 heaped teaspoons dried yeast and 1 teaspoon caster sugar plus 75 ml (2 ½ fl oz) warm milk, or 1 sachet easy-blend yeast
225 g (8 oz) plain flour
A pinch of salt
1 tablespoon caster sugar
1 egg, size 2, beaten

FOR THE ALMOND FILLING
25 g (1 oz) ground almonds
25 g (1 oz) caster sugar
1 drop almond essence
½ egg white, size 3
NOTE: for cartwheels, you should make double the quantity of almond filling and add 25 g (1 oz) currants for sprinkling
Icing sugar, sifted, for rolling out

FOR GLACE ICING AND DECORATION
125 g (4 ½ oz) icing sugar
1 tablespoon hot water
25 g (1 oz) almonds, hazelnuts or walnuts, chopped and blanched, optional
4 glacé cherries, quartered, optional

1 To make the pastry, put the butter between two sheets of greaseproof paper, then, using a rolling pin, roll it into a rectangle that measures about 25 × 7.5 cm (10 × 3 in). Chill the butter for 20 - 30 minutes.
2 If you are using fresh yeast, blend it with the milk. If you are using dried yeast, dissolve it with the sugar in the warm milk and leave the mixture until it is frothy, around 10 minutes. If you are using easy-blend yeast, add it directly to the flour.
3 Sift the flour and salt into a bowl then add the caster sugar. Make a well in the centre and add the yeasty liquid (if appropriate) and the egg. Using a knife, mix to a soft dough.

4 Add ½ - 1 tablespoon of water, if this helps the consistency, then knead the dough for 5 minutes until it is smooth and elastic. Place it in a polythene bag and let it rest in the refrigerator for about 10 minutes.
5 Lightly flour a work surface and roll the dough into a 25 cm (10 in) square. Place the chilled butter in the centre of the square.
6 Fold over the two sides of dough so that they overlap in the middle and press them together. Then roll the dough into a strip measuring approximately 46 × 15 cm (18 × 6 in).
7 Mark the dough into three equal portions. Bring the bottom third up over the middle and the top third down over the first to form a square. Seal the edges with a rolling pin, then place the dough in a polythene bag and chill for 10 minutes.
8 Put the dough on a board with the folded edge on the right. Roll it out into a strip and fold into three as before, then chill. Repeat a third time, again starting with the fold on the right, then chill for 30 minutes.
9 Meanwhile, make the filling: mix the ground almonds and caster sugar in a bowl, then stir in the almond essence and the egg white to make a stiff paste. If you are making pastry cartwheels, add the currants as well.
10 When you are ready to roll and shape the pastries, preheat the oven to 220°C (425°F, gas mark 7) and grease two baking sheets.
11 Shape and fill the pastries (see box, right). When they are ready, place them 6 cm (2 ½ in) apart on the baking sheets. Cover the pastries with a polythene bag and leave them to rise for 15 - 30 minutes at room temperature, until they are puffy.
12 Bake for 15 minutes until risen and golden. Cool on a wire tray.
13 To make the icing, sift the icing sugar into a bowl and add only just enough hot water to make a very smooth, glossy mixture.
14 Brush or spoon the icing over the pastries while they are still warm. Sprinkle with the chopped almonds or walnuts and top with the glacé cherries before the icing has fully set. Danish pastries are best if served while still very fresh.

SHAPING AND FILLING DANISH PASTRIES
MAKING WINDMILLS

Roll out the prepared pastry to a rectangle 40 × 20 cm (16 × 8 in) and then cut the dough into eight, neat 10 cm (4 in) squares. Then cut through the dough from each corner of the pastry to within 1 cm (½ in) of the centre.

1 Take a teaspoon of almond filling, roll it into a little ball and place in the centre of each pastry square.

2 Fold alternate corners of the pastry into the centre to form a windmill, firmly pressing down each corner.

MAKING CARTWHEELS

Start by cutting the prepared pastry in half. Set one portion aside and roll out the other to a rectangle that measures about 23 × 20 cm (9 × 8 in).

1 Spread the pastry with the almond filling and sprinkle it with currants. Roll the pastry up from the longest side, then cut the roll crossways into slices 2.5 cm (1 in) thick. Place the cartwheels on a greased baking tray.

2 Flatten the cartwheels lightly with your fingertips to make them about 5 cm (2 in) in diameter. Then roll out the other half of the pastry, and repeat the rolling up, slicing and flattening process to produce more cartwheels.

MAKING CRESCENTS

Cut the pastry in half and set one portion aside. On a work surface, roll the other portion into a rough circle only a little larger than a 20 cm (8 in) plate. Place the plate on top of the pastry and use it as a template to cut a neat pastry circle with a knife. Next, cut the circle into four triangles roughly equal in size.

1 Place a heaped teaspoon of the ground almond and sugar mixture on each of the four triangles, nearer to the curved edges than the centres.

2 Roll up each triangle from the long end, then bend it into a crescent. When all four have been filled, repeat with the other half of the pastry.

DATES

FRESH FROM FROZEN

In the supermarket I see packets labelled 'natural dates'. What does this mean and how should dates like these be used?

'Natural' or Hayani dates are not truly fresh in that they are frozen in a slightly underripe state, and then thawed and fully ripened while in transit to supermarkets. Because of their high natural sugar content, they thaw out perfectly well without any significant alteration to their original texture.

Natural dates are available all the year round, as are Medjool dates, which have crinkly skins and are partly dried in storage. Fresh dates are available only from mid August to the end of September, and then usually only in specialist shops.

When buying natural dates, you should ensure that they are deep brown, plump and moist. They will keep well in the refrigerator for up to a week. You can wash the fruit and eat them as they are, or cut the dates in half, remove the stones and chop them into salads.

Natural dates can be stuffed with soft cheese, almonds and various other fillings to serve as canapés. You can also offer them as sweetmeats with after-dinner coffee. Although the skin is edible, it can be removed, if you prefer, by squeezing the date at the stem end.

Healthy option

Natural dates are nutritious and well worth choosing. They contain only half as much sugar, and twice as much fibre (5.5 g per 100 g; ⅛ oz per 3½ oz) as the sun-dried boxed variety which appear in great profusion during the Christmas season.

DEEP-FRYING

CHOICE OF PANS

What kind of pan should I buy for deep-frying?

If you do a lot of deep-frying, an electric model has the advantage of thermostatic control as well as a charcoal-filter lid to prevent odours. Choose a pan with an automatic cut-off facility in case it is left on.

For occasional deep-frying, you can use a heavy-duty saucepan that is deep enough to hold a large amount of oil. You will also need a basket with mesh fine enough to keep the oil free of food particles. A close-fitting lid is essential for cutting off the air in emergencies (see SAFETY IN THE KITCHEN).

PROTECTIVE COATINGS

Why are some foods coated before they are deep-fried?

Foods are subjected to a very high temperature in the deep-fryer. A protective coating prevents a hard, unattractive skin forming on the food while allowing the inside to cook slowly and thoroughly.

If deep-frying is done properly, the coating also creates a seal that stops a food's flavour from tainting the oil, so it can be used again. Sealing has the added advantage of preventing any dangerous spluttering or bubbling of hot fat, which can happen if food juices leak out.

BATTER OR BREADCRUMBS

Recipes say to coat some foods in batter, others in breadcrumbs before they are deep-fried. Why?

Batter is best for wet foods, such as vegetable or fruit fritters, because it sticks to the surface of these foods once they have been floured. The batter will puff up and seal in the moisture without changing the lightness of the food inside.

Breadcrumbs, which are heavier, are best for foods such as fish and chicken which need to cook longer.

Shake these foods in flour first to dry the surface, then dip them in egg to give an initial seal. Finally, roll the food in breadcrumbs for an outer seal with a crunchy texture.

HEAT TEST

How do I know if the oil is at the right temperature?

The correct temperature for deep-frying is 190°C (375°F), which is moderately hot. If your fryer does not have a thermostat, you can test the oil by dropping in a cube of bread. It should take only about 40 seconds to brown.

If it browns in 10 seconds, the oil is dangerously hot and should be cooled. If it takes a minute, the oil is too cold and the batter will not crisp immediately. This causes the food inside to become soggy.

AVOIDING GREASE

How can I ensure that food inside the batter does not absorb grease?

Cook the food in small amounts. Adding too many pieces at one time to the pan lowers the temperature of the fat so that the coating does not form a crisp crust. The food then absorbs fat and loses its juices into the cooking oil.

WARMING THOUGHTS

How do I keep deep-fried food from cooling off quickly?

If the food must wait a short while before being served, spread it out in a single layer on a hot baking tray or dish. Keep the food warm and uncovered in the oven, with the door ajar to allow air to circulate freely. Do not cover or enclose the food, as this will only serve to make the crust soggy.

Keep it low

Fill a deep-fryer no more than one-third full of oil. The pan should be no more than half full after all the food has been added.

DINNER PARTIES

BALANCING TRICK

Can you give me guidelines on putting together a dinner menu?

Try to balance the menu. Include easy dishes as well as complicated ones and vary the ingredients.

Think of the textures, colours and tastes of the dishes you are planning and do not have the same dominant flavouring in more than one course. Also, avoid combining dishes that are similar in colour.

Aim for variety: follow food that is crunchy with something smooth, a mild dish with a sharp-flavoured one. If the main course is heavy, avoid a rich pudding and choose instead a light, simple recipe, such as one based on fruit.

Finally, keep the overall effect of the meal simple. Nothing can better the taste of fresh, well-prepared ingredients. (For detailed guidelines see also MENU PLANNING.)

RELAXED AND PREPARED

How can I give a great dinner party and still find time to enjoy the company of my guests?

Choose recipes that can be made largely in advance and need little last-minute attention. Avoid fiddly recipes that will keep you in the kitchen away from your visitors.

If you have the space, arrange the starter and dessert courses on plates ahead of time. Cover and put them in a cool place and set out cheeses to reach room temperature.

Lay out everything you will need in the way of cutlery and china for all of the courses, including coffee and after-dinner drinks. Make a simple timetable, wear a watch and work out a seating plan.

On the next pages are hot main course dishes that will delight your guests while still leaving you time to enjoy their company. Choose between the Fillet of Beef with Anchovy Butter (overleaf), and the vegetarian crêpe cake (opposite).

Triple-layered vegetable crêpe cake

SERVES: 6
PREPARATION TIME: 1 ½ hours
COOKING TIME: 1 ½ hours

FOR THE CREPES
150 g (5 ½ oz) plain flour
175 ml (6 fl oz) milk
175 ml (6 fl oz) water
A pinch of salt
3 eggs, size 3
3 tablespoons melted butter, plus
*   extra for greasing*

FOR THE VEGETABLE FILLINGS
500 g (1 lb 2 oz) courgettes, grated
500 g (1 lb 2 oz) carrots, cut into
*   matchsticks*
85 g (3 oz) butter
2 tablespoons chopped fresh
*   tarragon*
3 tablespoons olive oil
2 cloves garlic, finely chopped
4 shallots, finely chopped
500 g (1 lb 2 oz) mushrooms,
*   finely sliced*
Salt and black pepper

FOR THE CUSTARD
175 g (6 oz) ricotta cheese
4 eggs, size 3
75 g (2 ¾ oz) freshly grated
*   Parmesan cheese*
100 ml (3 ½ fl oz) milk
Salt and black pepper

FOR THE TOMATO SAUCE
1 shallot, chopped
2 tablespoons olive oil
500 g (1 lb 2 oz) tomatoes,
*   skinned, deseeded and chopped*
1 tablespoon chopped fresh basil
Salt and black pepper

1 Whisk all the crêpe ingredients together briefly then let the batter stand for about 10 minutes.
2 Heat a 20 cm (8 in) crêpe pan and grease it with butter. Pour a ladle of batter into the hot pan then swirl the pan to distribute it. Cook it until the underside is lightly browned.
3 Turn the crêpe over and cook the other side, then taste to check. Add a little more water to the batter if it seems too thick. Remove the cooked crêpe to a dish and repeat until you

have made at least ten more (any leftover crêpes can then be frozen).
4 To make the fillings, place the courgettes in a colander, sprinkle with salt and leave for 20 minutes.
5 Put the carrots in a heavy-based saucepan with two-thirds of the butter, 2 tablespoons of water and a pinch of salt. Cook, covered, over a very low heat until they are partially cooked. Add the tarragon to the carrots and set aside.
6 Heat the remaining butter along with 2 tablespoons of oil in a frying pan and add the garlic and two of the shallots. Stir for a minute before adding the mushrooms and cooking them until the juices are exuded. Turn up the heat and stir until the liquid has evaporated, then season. Put in a bowl and set aside.
7 Squeeze the courgettes to get rid of as much liquid as possible. Heat the rest of the oil in the frying pan, add the remaining shallots and the courgettes and cook, stirring, for a few minutes. Season and set aside.
8 Whisk the custard ingredients together and season. Preheat the oven to 180°C (350°F, gas mark 4).

9 Lightly grease a loose-bottomed cake tin 20 × 7.5 cm (8 × 3 in) and line the bottom with a crêpe. Space five more crêpes with their brown sides down around the sides of the cake tin. Arrange these so that they overlap and overhang the tin's edge.
10 Cover the bottom of the tin with the carrots, ladle about a third of the custard mixture over the carrots and top with another crêpe.
11 Next, add the mushrooms with another third of the custard and top with another crêpe. Finally add the courgettes. Pour over the remaining custard and fold the overhanging crêpes over the filling.
12 Top the cake with one or more crêpes, then cover loosely with foil. Stand the crêpe cake on a baking tray and bake for 1 ½ hours.
13 To make the tomato sauce, soften the shallot in the oil. Add the tomatoes, basil, salt and pepper then heat just enough to warm through.
14 Run a knife around the edge of the cake, turn it over and unmould onto an attractive serving plate.
15 Serve with the tomato sauce passed around the table separately.

Surprise your guests with a savoury layered cake. This vegetarian treat features colourful fillings of vegetables and cheese accompanied by tangy tomato sauce.

Fillet of beef with anchovy butter

SERVES: 6
PREPARATION TIME: 20 - 30 minutes
COOKING TIME: 25 minutes

1.3 kg (3 lb) piece of beef fillet,
  cut from the thick end, trimmed
  and tied
Black pepper
3 tablespoons sunflower oil

FOR THE ANCHOVY BUTTER
100 g (3 ½ oz) butter
6 anchovy fillets
1 teaspoon lemon juice
2 tablespoons finely chopped
  parsley
To garnish: fresh parsley, chopped

1 Preheat the oven to 230°C (450°F, gas mark 8). Sprinkle the meat with the pepper, heat the oil in a roasting tin and then brown the meat well on all sides. Place it in the oven and roast for just 10 minutes.
2 Remove from the oven and lay it on a rack to cool completely.
3 Purée the butter and anchovies in a blender, a processor or a pestle and mortar. Scrape the purée into a bowl and stir in the lemon juice, parsley and some pepper. Roll the mixture into a sausage shape, wrap it in cling film and refrigerate until it is firm.
4 When the meat is completely cold, place it on a piece of foil large enough to enclose it. Cut away the string and slice through the fillet of beef at 6 mm (¼ in) intervals, leaving just enough meat on the underside to hold all the slices together.
5 Cut the anchovy butter into slices and slip one in between every two slices of meat. Wrap the meat in the foil and refrigerate it until an hour before cooking, unless you intend to use it immediately.
6 Preheat the oven to 220°C (425°F, gas mark 7). Bring the meat to room temperature then roast it in the foil on a baking tray for 15 minutes.
7 Remove the meat from the foil, being careful not to lose the buttery juices. Sprinkle the fillet with some finely chopped parsley and arrange it on a warm serving platter. Serve with spinach and new potatoes.

DRIED BEANS

A SHORT SOAK

Do beans and pulses really need to be soaked before cooking?

Lentils, peas and many beans do not need soaking. For those beans that do, there are some basic rules to observe. First, rinse them in a sieve under the cold tap to wash off any loose, floury matter before cooking. This minimises the formation of scum during cooking.

Soak dried beans by pouring boiling water over them to quicken the process. In today's well-heated kitchens, a short soak is safer than leaving them to sit for a long time.

Although the beans absorb water, there is no evidence that they lose any nutrients. Nor do soaking and cooking methods affect flatulence: even ready-cooked canned beans can provoke wind.

BOILING FOR SAFETY

Why are we told to boil beans in one lot of water, then start again with fresh water?

Most dried beans need a preliminary period of fast-boiling because they contain toxins called protease inhibitors which interfere with the digestion of protein. While beans that have not had this preparation may taste palatable, the body will not benefit fully from their protein unless these toxins are neutralised.

Start by fast-boiling the beans, then discard the water and complete the cooking in a pan of fresh water (see chart, opposite).

This fast-boiling is particularly important for soya beans because they contain half as much protein again as most beans and many vegetarians rely on them as a source of protein. The toxins in soya beans will take an hour of fast-boiling to eliminate; they should then be simmered for another 80-90 minutes.

Raw kidney beans contain a substance that cannot be digested and which may cause serious food poisoning if the toxins are not extracted. It is absolutely essential that you fast-boil red kidney beans for 15 minutes before use, then change the water and simmer them for another 30 minutes until they are tender enough to eat.

TIMELY TIPS

Why do some beans and lentils cook in far less time than is recommended on the pack?

The recommended cooking times often reflect the fact that beans and lentils used to be stored for long periods before being cooked. This made them very dry and hard. Packets now feature 'best-before' dates, so the dried beans and lentils may become tender in a shorter cooking time, especially if you follow these guidelines.

To low-boil beans, cook them at a boil that is low but continuous, not at a simmer. The loss of water in the saucepan through evaporation can be minimised by partially covering the pan with a lid, but as water is being absorbed by the beans as well, you should be prepared to top up the level with boiling water when necessary.

The scum that rises to the surface during cooking is not dirt but a mixture of proteins and starches. It is best to skim it off, both for the sake of your pans and to prevent the liquid boiling over.

Do not salt dried beans during cooking, or cook them in a liquid containing salted meat for any longer than is necessary. This can toughen their skins and inhibit the swelling and softening of the beans you are aiming to achieve. Acidity also impedes their cooking, so do not add tomato sauces or any others

Record the date

When you store dried beans in a jar or tin, make a note of the 'best-before' date. Although older dried beans will still be quite edible, fresh ones need less cooking time.

that are acidic until the beans are already soft. Herbs and spices may be added early during cooking.

The acid to alkaline balance of local water can also affect cooking times. Use the chart (right) as a guide only. Keep testing the beans in the later stages of cooking.

CANS MAY SAVE TIME

Are canned beans as nutritious as dried ones, and which is more economical to use?

Canning does not reduce the nutritional value of beans but canned beans do cost considerably more than dried varieties. For example, 425 g (15 oz) of canned flageolet beans will give 225 g (8 oz) drained weight only while 100 g (3½ oz) of dried beans bulks up to the same weight after soaking and cooking.

Dried beans work out at less than a third of the price, but flageolet and some other beans require long cooking. The time and energy saved by using these beans canned may well justify the additional cost.

Whether you choose canned or dried, beans are a good source of protein, fibre and complex carbohydrates. They are low in fat and contain minerals as well as nearly all the vitamins we need.

PEAS AND LENTILS

Are the soaking and cooking instructions for dried peas and lentils the same as for beans?

No, on the whole the cooking process is simpler for peas and lentils. Only chickpeas (garbanzos) need soaking. Place them in cold water for 30 minutes, then change the water. Fast-boil for 15 minutes and low-boil for 80–90 minutes.

Neither soaking nor fast-boiling is required for cooking the peas and lentils listed below. They will require only low-boiling for the following times: marrowfat peas 90 minutes; split green or yellow peas 25–30 minutes; Egyptian or split red lentils 10–15 minutes; brown lentils 20–25 minutes; and Puy lentils 30–35 minutes.

SOAKING AND COOKING DRIED BEANS

Soaking needs plenty of water. Once the soaking and fast-boiling water is drained off and discarded, cooking should be continued in fresh, cold water. Use this chart as a guide for the timings needed for different kinds of beans:

BEANS	SOAKING	COOKING TIME
Aduki	No soaking needed	Fast-boil for 15 minutes Low-boil for 50–60 minutes
Black-eyed beans/ black-eyed peas/cowpeas	No soaking needed	Fast-boil for 15 minutes Low-boil for 30 minutes
Black kidney/black beans	No soaking needed	Fast-boil for 15 minutes Low-boil for 60–75 minutes
Butter beans	No soaking needed	Fast-boil for 15 minutes Low-boil for 40 minutes
Cannellini/ white kidney beans	Soak for 30 minutes	Fast-boil for 15 minutes Low-boil for 30–40 minutes
Flageolet/green haricot	Soak for 30 minutes	Fast-boil for 15 minutes Low-boil for 60–70 minutes
Ful medames	No soaking needed	Fast-boil for 15 minutes Low-boil for 90–100 minutes
Haricot/navy/Boston beans	Soak for 30 minutes	Fast-boil for 15 minutes Low-boil for 80–90 minutes
Mung beans	No soaking needed	Fast-boil for 15 minutes Low-boil for 25–30 minutes
Pinto beans	Soak for 30 minutes	Fast-boil for 15 minutes Low-boil for 45 minutes
Red kidney beans	No soaking needed	Fast-boil for 15 minutes Low-boil for 30 minutes
Soya beans	No soaking needed	Fast-boil for 60 minutes Low-boil for 80–90 minutes

GLORIOUS SALADS

How do I prepare beans for a mixed bean salad?

Beans make very good salads for parties, whether you use just one variety or decide to mix them. Combine dried beans with fresh or frozen peas or beans. Try to choose different sizes and colours for best effect, as in the recipe below.

Cook the beans according to the times in the chart on the previous page. Garlic, celery and spices – and woody herbs, such as bay and rosemary – can be added to the cooking water. Do not add salt but mix that into a dressing of olive oil and vinegar or lemon juice, with thin slices of red onion and garlic.

Gently toss the drained beans into the dressing while they are still hot, so they can absorb the flavour and wilt the onion slightly. Add the chopped fresh herbs, black pepper and other fresh ingredients when the beans are cold.

Butter, black-eyed and broad bean salad

SERVES: 10 – 12
PREPARATION TIME: 30 minutes
COOKING TIME: 50 minutes

---

200 g (7 oz) split butter beans
200 g (7 oz) black-eyed beans
1 stick celery, in 2 - 3 pieces
2 - 3 bay leaves
500 g (1 lb 2 oz) shelled broad
    beans (about 1.25 kg/2 lb 12 oz
    unshelled), or frozen broad
    beans, thawed
1 red onion
3 cloves garlic
100 ml (3 ½ fl oz) olive oil
Juice of 1 lemon
Salt and black pepper
1 teaspoon ground cumin
3 - 4 tablespoons chopped fresh
    herbs or herb sprigs (lemon
    balm, lovage, mint or parsley)

---

1 Fast-boil the butter beans and the black-eyed beans separately in two small pans of water for 15 minutes, then wash and drain separately.
2 Put the butter beans in a large pan of water, add the celery, bring to the

Combine butter beans, black-eyed beans and broad beans for a party salad. Onion, garlic, cumin and sprigs of herbs help to make plain beans special.

boil and cook for 40 minutes or until the beans are tender. Place the black-eyed beans in another pan of water, add the bay leaves, bring the beans to the boil and cook for 30 minutes.
3 Put the broad beans in a large pan of salted water, bring to the boil and simmer for 5 minutes. Drain and run under the cold tap. When they are cool, peel off the outer skins.
4 Slice the onion finely and chop or crush the garlic cloves. Mix with the olive oil, lemon juice, salt, pepper and ground cumin in a large bowl.
5 Drain the butter beans (removing the celery and bay leaves) and the black-eyed beans. Mix the two types of beans into the dressing and then add the broad bean kernels.
6 Sprinkle the salad with the herbs and serve at room temperature.

DRIED FRUIT

LOSING MOISTURE

Is all dried fruit produced in the same manner?

Most vine and tree fruits, including dried apples, apricots, figs, grapes, peaches and pears, are dehydrated in the sun. A few, such as prunes, are dried in ovens instead. All are dehydrated to about 20 per cent of their normal moisture content.

Using different kinds of grapes produces varied results. Currants are dried from a tiny, seedless black grape, sultanas are dried from a sweet, seedless green grape and raisins are dried from several types of grapes, muscat being the largest and sweetest. Store all of these dried fruits in airtight containers and they will keep for up to nine months in a cool, dry place.

Currants, dates, figs, raisins and sultanas are most commonly used in recipes in their dried form, while other dried fruits are rehydrated beforehand by soaking in cold water for at least 8 hours.

It is now increasingly common to find dried fruits that are labelled 'ready soaked', which means the same as 'ready-to-eat'. These are dried in their country of origin and then rehydrated in Britain to about a third of their moisture content. Once opened, the packets should be resealed, refrigerated and the fruit eaten within seven days.

Preservatives such as sorbic acid and potassium sorbate are sometimes added to fruits such as dates and figs to help prevent mould. Sulphur dioxide is usually added to dried fruits like apples, apricots, mangoes, papaya, peaches, pears and pineapple to retain colour.

CLEANING FRUIT

Do I need to wash dried fruit before using it?

It is advisable to wash any dried fruit that has been bought loose. Place it in a colander and rinse well under a cold, running tap before soaking in more cold water. Fruit that is bought in sealed vacuum packs does not need to be washed.

SHORT CUT

Can you suggest a speedy way to rehydrate dried fruit if you have forgotten to soak it for hours?

Rehydrating dried fruit in a bowl of cold water for at least 8 hours is easy and produces the best results. However, if you are rushed or have forgotten to soak the fruit, put it in a pan, cover it with boiling water and then soak it for 40 minutes before cooking normally. You can also cover dried fruit with water and heat it in the microwave on Medium for about 5 minutes.

WILD APRICOTS

I have eaten delicious dried wild apricots. Why are they so different from ordinary dried apricots and why are they so expensive?

Hunza apricots grow wild on trees in an area spanning Kashmir to Iran. They are left on the tree until completely dry and then harvested. As they are not treated with sulphur dioxide, they turn brown and have a deep, rich taste. Their relative scarcity makes them expensive.

An alternative is to buy cheaper unsulphured apricots, which have a similar rich flavour. Free from added preservatives, they turn a chestnut brown, differing from the usual orange fruit. Try any type of apricot you prefer in the tasty dried fruit compote recipe below.

Mixed dried fruit compote with star anise

SERVES: 8 – 10
PREPARATION TIME: 10 minutes plus overnight soaking
COOKING TIME: 30 minutes

---

115 g (4 oz) each dried apple rings, apricots, dates, figs, peaches, pears and prunes (not 'ready soaked')
150 g (5 ½ oz) dried mango slices
6 - 8 star anise
Thinly pared zest and strained juice of 1 large lemon
25 g (1 oz) caster sugar, optional

---

1 Put the dried apple, apricots, figs, peaches, pears and prunes into a large bowl, then pour over 1.4 litres (2 pints 10 fl oz) of cold water. Cover the bowl tightly and leave the fruit to soak overnight.
2 The following day, place the fruit and the water in a large saucepan. Add the dates, mango, star anise, lemon zest and juice and the caster sugar (if using). Stir them together gently and bring the pan to the boil.
3 Reduce the heat, cover the pan and simmer for 25 minutes. Remove the saucepan from the heat and pour the compote into a heatproof bowl.
4 Serve hot, or let cool, cover and refrigerate for up to seven days.

DUCK AND WILD DUCK

VARIATIONS OF DUCK

What is the difference between a duck and duckling, and what are the most common types?

A duckling has not yet reached its second-feather stage, which occurs around the age of two months. Nearly every oven-ready duck you buy in Britain is really a duckling, as it is the practice to slaughter commercial birds at about seven weeks old. The variations in oven-ready weight, 1.3–3.2 kg (3–7 lb), are related to differences in breeds rather than the level of maturity. Ducklings are available either fresh or frozen all the year round.

Nearly 90 per cent of ducklings that are now bought in Britain are a hybrid Lincolnshire duck, which is based on the white-feathered Pekin duck. The Lincolnshire duck has less fat than other Pekin-duck hybrids and skin that will crisp to a fine golden brown colour.

Substantial production of the British Aylesbury breed ended in the 1950s but hybrids descended from it are available. Other types of duck include the Gressingham, which is ideal for two as it weighs 700 g–1.3 kg (1 lb 9 oz–3 lb). It is lean and full of flavour. Nantais, which also has a strong flavour, is a popular French bird that weighs 1.8–2.25 kg (4–5 lb).

Barbary duck is also imported from France and these large birds are killed when the ducks have reached a weight of 1.3–3.2 kg (3–7 lb). The meat has a far more mature flavour and is less fatty than most other ducklings. Because of this, the Barbary duck must be regularly basted during cooking.

Few ducks of any kind are kept more than 12 months, except those that are used to produce foie gras de canard, a French delicacy made from duck liver. It is as good as the foie gras made from goose liver.

LOSING THE BONE

Can you bone a duck in the same way as chicken to make it easier to carve at the dinner table?

Yes. Boning a duck takes a bit of time and patience, but it can be done in advance and the stuffing gives you the chance to add texture and flavour, as in the recipe below. You can bone the duck in the same way as a chicken (see BONING), or ask the butcher to do it for you.

Boned stuffed duck

SERVES: 6 – 8
PREPARATION TIME: 20 minutes (not including boning), plus 4 hours soaking fruit
COOKING TIME: 2 1/2 hours

55 g (2 oz) dried apricots, chopped
55 g (2 oz) dried cherries
125 ml (4 fl oz) orange juice
75 g (2 3/4 oz) wild rice
2 tablespoons vegetable oil
2 shallots, chopped
2 cloves garlic, chopped
75 g (2 3/4 oz) dark flat mushrooms, roughly chopped
450 g (1 lb) pork or veal, finely minced
3 tablespoons chopped fresh thyme and parsley
A pinch of ground allspice
4 tablespoons brandy or Armagnac
Salt and black pepper
1 egg, beaten
1.6 kg (3 lb 8 oz) oven-ready duck, boned, and its liver, chopped

1 Soak the apricots and cherries in the orange juice for 4 hours. Cook the wild rice for 45 minutes or until tender. Drain, rinse and let cool.
2 Heat the oil in a small saucepan and cook the shallots and garlic gently for 3 - 4 minutes until soft but not coloured. Add the mushrooms and the duck liver, cooking for 2 - 3 minutes or until soft, then cool.
3 Preheat the oven to 180°C (350°F, gas mark 4). Combine the shallot mixture with the soaked dried fruit, juice, rice, minced meat, herbs, allspice and brandy or Armagnac.
4 Check the seasoning of the stuffing by frying a small patty of

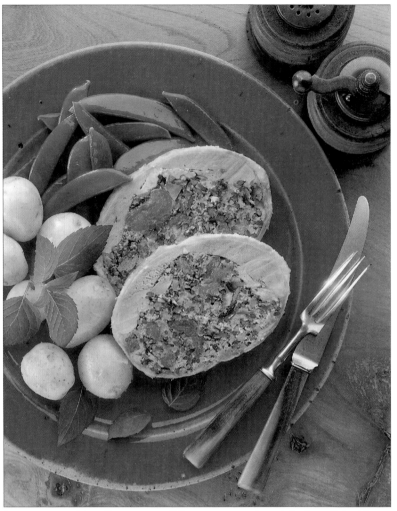

For an eye-catching dinner-party dish, serve a tasty boned duck stuffed with a delicious combination of dried apricots and cherries soaked in orange juice.

the mixture, then tasting it. Add salt and pepper to taste and just enough egg to bind the mixture.
5 Place the boned duck skin side down and lay the stuffing down the centre of the bird. Fold over the sides of the bird to form a neat roll and sew with a trussing needle and string, or a needle and strong thread.
6 Wrap the duck tightly in butter-soaked muslin or a clean J-cloth, tying both ends so that it looks like a Christmas cracker. Place the duck on a wire rack over a roasting tin and roast for 1 1/2 hours, basting often. After 1 1/4 hours, remove the cloth to help brown the skin.
7 Rest the duck for 15 minutes then serve hot, carved into thick slices, or allow to cool, chill and then slice.

A TASTE OF THE WILD

Does wild duck have a different taste from ordinary duck?

Wild ducks (such as the mallard, teal and wigeon) have a stronger, slightly oilier taste. They can range in size from less than 450 g (1 lb) to 4.5 kg (10 lb) but most are smaller than domesticated fowl.

The mallard is the largest and should be basted while cooking as they have a tendency to become dry. Wigeon are much sought after for their delicate flavour and each will serve one to two people. A teal is tiny and serves only one.

Ordinary duck recipes can be used for wild duck, but you will have to reduce the cooking times and temperatures as wild duck should be cooked rare. It is best roasted whole, at a high temperature of 220°C (425°F, gas mark 7). The bird should be roasted resting on each leg alternately, then on its back to ensure even cooking.

For a small duck such as teal, allow 12–20 minutes for the whole bird, depending on its size. For a larger mallard, allow 20–30 minutes for the whole bird. Do not prick a wild duck all over before roasting it, as they are leaner than domesticated ducks.

CRISP AND DRY

What is the best way to ensure duck skin becomes really crisp and the flesh is not too fatty?

Make sure the skin is thoroughly dry, as soggy duck skin will never become crisp. Leave the bird unwrapped in a cool place for a couple of hours before roasting to let the skin dry out, or blow air over it using a hair dryer on a hot setting until the moisture is gone. Prick the well-dried skin all over with a skewer or fork, being very careful not to pierce the flesh, then rub the bird with fine sea salt.

Weigh the duck and calculate the cooking time, allowing 40–50 minutes per kg (20–25 minutes per lb). Stand it on a rack in a roasting tin. Preheat the oven to 220°C (425°F, gas mark 7) and roast the bird for the first 30 minutes, then turn down the heat to 180°C (350°F, gas mark 4) and complete the cooking. Drain the fat at 20 minute intervals so that it does not burn.

BONY BIRD

How many will a duck feed?

It does not feed as many people as you might expect from the size (compared with chicken or turkey) because of the high proportion of bone to meat on a duck: a 1.8 kg (4 lb) duck will feed only two to three people, a 2.5 kg (5 lb 8 oz) bird will feed four. You will need a Barbary duck, or two smaller birds, to feed six to eight people.

FRENCH MAGRET

What exactly is a 'magret' and how should I cook it?

'Magret' is the French word for the breast meat from a duck that has been fattened to enlarge its liver to make foie gras. The bird grows much heavier than a normal duck, with breasts that are well flavoured and weigh about 350 g (12 oz) each.

To make sure the flesh is very tender before you grill it, rub the magret with salt and herbs and leave it refrigerated in this marinade for at least 12 hours. Wipe off the marinade, score the skin and fat diagonally and place the breast skin side down on a pan under a hot grill. Grill for 2 minutes, then turn and cook for a further 4–7 minutes, depending on how rare you like it. Duck is generally most appealing when served pink.

Alternatively, preheat the oven to 180°C (350°F, gas mark 4). Fry the magret skin side down in a little oil over high heat for 2–3 minutes to melt the fat and make the skin crisp. Then transfer the breast to the oven for 6–7 minutes. When cooked, take it out and allow it to rest for 5 minutes before carving it across the grain into thick slices.

See also: PEKING DUCK

DUMPLINGS

LIGHTER DUMPLINGS

What is the secret of making feather-light dumplings?

Unlike most pastries, which are made with plain flour, suet pastry for dumplings must be made with self-raising flour. The raising agent in the flour helps to produce light, fluffy dumplings which are then simmered on top of a casserole.

One way to help ensure lighter dumplings is to measure all the ingredients very carefully, being sure to add enough water to make the dough very soft. Once the water has been added, this type of pastry should be handled as little as possible. If the gluten in the flour develops, the dumplings will be tough when cooked. This is why suet pastry is best used immediately after it has been made.

Light, fluffy savoury dumplings, such as those in the following recipe, can help to make a main dish more substantial or stretch a casserole to serve more people.

Herb dumplings

MAKES: 8 dumplings
PREPARATION TIME: 5 minutes
COOKING TIME: 15 - 20 minutes

100 g (3 ½ oz) self-raising flour
A pinch of salt
50 g (1 ¾ oz) shredded suet
1 tablespoon chopped fresh chives
1 tablespoon chopped fresh parsley

1 Sift the flour and salt into a bowl, then add the suet and herbs and stir with a fork. Add 4 tablespoons of water and mix to make a soft, scone-like dough. Turn the dough out onto a lightly floured surface and divide it into eight equal portions.
2 Shape each portion of dough into a ball using lightly floured fingers. Roll each dumpling very lightly in flour, then shake off any excess.
3 Add the dumplings to your gently simmering stew or casserole, placing them lightly on top of the meat and ensuring that the dumplings are not submerged in the liquid.
4 Cover the pan or casserole with a lid and continue cooking for 15 - 20 minutes, or until the dumplings are cooked through. Serve immediately.
VARIATION
For dumplings to accompany a beef casserole, sift a teaspoon of English mustard powder and ½ teaspoon of dried mixed herbs with the flour and salt before adding the suet.

Use your loaf

To make really light dumplings, substitute white breadcrumbs for half of the flour. This will help to produce a firm but lighter result.

EGGS

FINE AND FRESH

What are the different grades of eggs and how are these decided?

Under European Community regulations, there are three grades of eggs. Grade A eggs (the top grade) are naturally clean and internally perfect, that is, they have no blood spots (which are harmless but spoil the appearance) and their shells are intact. The air sac inside the egg does not exceed 6 mm (just under ¼ in) in depth and the yolk does not move away from the centre of the egg when it is rotated.

Grade B eggs are less fresh and may have been refrigerated for several weeks – with the packaging indicating the length of time they have been stored. They are sometimes cleaned and contain an air sac that is a maximum of 9 mm (just under ½ in) deep. Grade C eggs are broken out of their shells and used by food and other manufacturers.

Hen's eggs are also graded from 1–7 according to size. Grade 1 is the heaviest egg and grade 7 is the lightest. Grade or size 3 eggs, which weigh around 60 g (2¼ oz), are the ones typically used in recipes.

An easy way to test for freshness is to put an egg in a bowl of water. If it sinks and lies on its side it is fresh. If it floats with its rounded end on the surface of the water it is stale. If an egg floats in the middle of the water with its rounded end up, it is not stale but it is probably two or three weeks old. Fresh eggs have thick whites that hold the yolks firmly in place.

SCRAMBLED NOT STUCK

How do you stop scrambled eggs from sticking to the pan?

For perfect unstuck eggs, first melt a small pat of butter in the pan and run it around to coat the base. Then pour in the eggs and cook them very gently and slowly, stirring all the time. Unlike omelettes (see page 265), where speed is of the essence, making scrambled eggs is a much more leisurely activity.

Add a knob of butter or a little cream or milk to the eggs at the end of cooking to reduce the temperature and keep the eggs moist. Take the eggs off the heat when they are still a little runny: they will finish cooking in their own heat while on the way to the table.

BEAT IN COPPER

What is the best way of whipping egg whites, and is a copper bowl better than anything else?

Egg whites can be whisked to as much as eight times their volume. It helps considerably if they are at room temperature and only a few days old: stale whites will never whip properly. Egg whites should always be whisked just before you want to use them otherwise they will begin to collapse and weep very quickly. Adding a pinch of salt or cream of tartar at the start of whisking will help to make the whisked whites stiff.

A balloon whisk and a copper bowl will produce the stiffest egg whites. The copper appears to have

To the rescue!

If you find you have whisked your egg whites too enthusiastically and they have collapsed, just add one extra white to every four whites already in the bowl. Then whisk them all together for 30 seconds until they are smooth.

an effect on the egg whites, making the beaten foam more stable. Why this is so is not completely understood but it does work.

Ensure that the copper bowl is very clean. If there are any spots, rub them with a mixture of salt and lemon juice to remove any traces of oxidised copper deposits, which may be toxic. The bowl should then be rinsed and dried.

If you do not have a copper bowl, use stainless steel, glass or china. Aluminium can cause the whisked egg whites to become grey, and plastic bowls are not recommended as it is quite difficult to remove every trace of oil or grease from the surface of the bowl. It is also important that whatever utensil you use to beat the eggs is free from grease and traces of egg yolk.

INVISIBLE BACTERIA

How can I tell if eggs contain salmonella bacteria?

It is not possible to judge if eggs contain the salmonella bacteria by looks alone. The best way to avoid the risk is to keep in mind a few sensible guidelines when buying and cooking them.

Hen's eggs and other types of eggs can be contaminated at any stage of production – through the bird's feed, in the laying process or even during handling of the eggs. These possibilities are reduced if high standards of cleanliness have been followed, so it is best to buy your eggs from a reputable source, with a rapid turnover. Salmonella bacteria may also penetrate the shell of a cracked egg, so don't buy any with broken or dirty shells.

Eggs should be cooked to a temperature of 71°C (160°F) whenever possible, as salmonella bacteria is destroyed at this temperature. Egg whites set at 60°C (140°F) and the yolks set at 71°C (160°F) so the risk of contracting salmonella bacteria is highest with soft-boiled, lightly cooked or raw eggs. These and dishes containing them should be avoided by the elderly, the infirm, pregnant women and children. If

KNOW YOUR EGGS

Some of the unusual eggs shown here are sold fresh at farm shops, specialist food halls, delicatessens and game dealers. | *Whites from hen's eggs are the best ones for whipping. They have a mild flavour and are the most economical.*

1 TURKEY Large and lightly speckled with a delicate flavour, available from some turkey farms. Use as hen's eggs.
2 HEN There is no difference in flavour or nutritional value between brown and white eggs. The colour of the shell depends entirely on the breed of hen.
3 GOOSE Available in spring and early summer, they are excellent for baking. They should be well cooked; hard boiled, they make fine devilled eggs.
4 DUCK Larger than hen's eggs, with a rich, assertive flavour, good for baking. They are best well cooked.

5 PHEASANT Not common but with a fine flavour, often served hard-boiled in salads. Their rich, distinct taste is also very good for baking.
6 BANTAM A breed of chicken, the eggs are similar to hen's, but about half the size, with an almost identical taste.
7 GUINEA FOWL These eggs with a slightly pitted shell are delicious and rich in flavour, available from farms.
8 QUAIL Tiny eggs, usually hard-boiled and served with celery salt, but they can be soft-boiled for 1 – 2 minutes, or fried to serve on small rounds of toast.

9 PARTRIDGE An uncommon delicacy with a good flavour. Like pheasant eggs, they are often hard-boiled and served in salads or used as a garnish.
• GULL (not shown) Collected from rocky cliffs and sometimes sold by traditional game dealers. Smaller than hen's eggs, they have a slightly fishy flavour and are always sold hard-boiled.
• OSTRICH (not shown) Farmed in South Africa, described as intensely rich and eggy, they take 45 minutes to soft-boil. One will make a dozen omelettes or scrambled egg for 12 people.

---

you are particularly anxious, eggs that have been pasteurised, a process which kills off any potentially harmful bacteria, are available dried or frozen, either as whole eggs or as separate whites or yolks. They are useful for many dishes but you cannot use them for mayonnaise, for example, or lemon curd, where the oily quality of fresh eggs is essential to the success of the dish.

SIMMER AND SUCCEED

How can I boil an egg without it cracking in the saucepan?

Do not boil the egg, simmer it. The egg should be at room temperature and the water should be gently simmering as you immerse it to avoid cracking the shell. Another precaution is to pierce the top of the rounded end with a sewing needle

before you put the egg in to simmer. It is the air inside the air sac expanding as it heats which causes it to crack. To save the egg, should it crack, quickly add 1 or 2 tablespoons of vinegar to the cooking water in the saucepan. This should help to seal the shell and stop the white leaking out of the cracks. The vinegar will not affect the taste of the cooked egg.

SEPARATING EGGS

The shell of the egg is a valuable and handy tool for separating eggs, as it cuts easily through the white.

1 Have two or three bowls ready. Tap the egg firmly on the side of one bowl. With your thumbs, break open the egg over the bowl, letting some of the white slip over the edge of the shell into the bowl.

2 Carefully tip the egg yolk back and forth from one half of the egg shell to the other, allowing as much white as possible to drop into the bowl underneath as you do so. Continue until all the egg white has been separated from the yolk.

Put the yolk in the second bowl. If you are separating more than one egg, use three bowls and break each white into the empty bowl before adding it to the others. Then if an egg is bad, you can discard it without ruining the others and if you break a yolk, only one white is spoiled.

3 If some of the yolk slips into the white, carefully remove it with the eggshell, a teaspoon or a piece of damp kitchen paper. The whites will not whip if any yolk is present.

EGG STORAGE

How should I store eggs and how long will they keep?

Eggs are best stored in the refrigerator as their freshness deteriorates at the warmer temperatures that are found in most modern kitchens. Store them pointed-end downward to help prevent breakage and minimise dehydration. Eggs are porous and will absorb strong flavours and odours, so store them well away from strong-smelling foods.

Eggs should be eaten within two weeks of purchase (many are now individually stamped with use-by dates) and should be removed from the refrigerator about 30 minutes before they are used. This helps to avoid curdling in cake mixtures and also helps to keep the eggs from cracking when they are put into simmering water.

Hard-boiled eggs can be stored in the refrigerator and used within two days. Egg yolks placed in a container and covered with water to prevent them from drying out will keep in the refrigerator for up to two days. Whites should be put in a covered container and will also keep well for up to two days when stored in the refrigerator.

Egg yolks can be frozen, but they must be creamed lightly with a little salt or sugar (½ – 1 teaspoon of salt or sugar per two yolks) before being frozen in a covered, rigid container: they will keep for up to three months. The addition of salt or sugar prevents the yolks from thickening and becoming hard.

To freeze egg whites, place them in a rigid container, cover them and they will keep for up to six months. Egg whites can also be frozen in ice cube trays covered with foil. When hard, remove the cubes from the tray and store in a freezer bag.

Once any frozen eggs have been thawed, use them on the same day and do not refreeze them. If you have frozen egg whites and cannot remember how many there were, you can weigh them. For use in recipes calculate that 25 g (1 oz) of egg white equals that of one egg.

POACHING IDEAS

I love poached eggs but find them rather stodgy served on toast. Can you suggest a more interesting way of using them?

Poached eggs make a rich foil for other savoury ingredients such as smoked fish. Serve this easy dish for brunch or a light supper.

Poached eggs with smoked salmon and mustard mayonnaise

SERVES: 4
PREPARATION TIME: 5 minutes
COOKING TIME: 4 minutes

150 ml (5 fl oz) mayonnaise
2 – 3 teaspoons whole-grain mustard
1 tablespoon chopped coriander
Salt and black pepper
75 g (2¾ oz) smoked salmon, cut into thin strips
8 eggs, size 3
To garnish: fresh coriander leaves or sprigs of watercress

1 Place the mayonnaise, whole-grain mustard, coriander and seasoning in a bowl and mix well. Stir in the smoked salmon, cover and set aside.
2 Poach the eggs in an egg poacher for about 3 minutes until they are just set. If you do not have an egg poacher, fill a large saucepan with water to a depth of 7.5 cm (3 in) and add 2 teaspoons of vinegar, which helps the eggs to keep their shape. Bring to a rolling boil. Break an egg into a cup, swirl a patch of water with a spoon and gently slip the egg into the whirlpool. Repeat with the remaining eggs. Reduce the heat to a simmer and cook for 4 minutes or until the eggs are lightly set.
3 Lift the eggs out with a slotted spoon and place one or two onto each serving plate. Spoon some of the flavoured mayonnaise over each egg and serve immediately, topped with fresh coriander or watercress.
VARIATIONS
For a lighter sauce, replace half the mayonnaise with soured cream or yoghurt. For a hotter flavour, stir in some Dijon mustard, cayenne pepper or another strong flavouring.

FAGGOTS

TRADITIONAL MEATBALLS

What sort of ingredients are used to make faggots? And how are they usually cooked?

Faggots are a traditional English and Welsh recipe for fried or baked balls of minced pork, pork fat and offal bound together with breadcrumbs and seasoned with onion, herbs and spices. (French crépinettes are similar.) The word faggot also refers to a bunch of flavouring herbs similar to a bouquet garni.

Faggots were originally wrapped in pig's caul, a white, lacy intestinal membrane, which held the meat together and also added flavour.

Today faggots are almost always bought already cooked and only need to be thoroughly reheated in the oven. The only advantage to making your own is that you know precisely what they contain. The usual accompaniment to faggots is pease pudding or mushy peas.

FATS

RICH TASTES

Which fat has the finest flavour?

Fats make many foods more palatable because they add flavour, texture, a smooth richness and variety. Goose and duck fat collected from a roasting bird will enrich any roast or fried dish, especially roast potatoes, and you can buy goose fat in tins. Beef dripping will add depth of flavour when roasting or frying other meats and vegetables, but lamb dripping has a very strong flavour and may leave a noticeable and undesirable aftertaste when it is used to fry other foods.

Lard is the rendered version of pork fat (see box, below), however, unrendered pork fat has a better flavour and is used in charcuterie, pâtés and for barding roast meat.

Different brands of butter, margarine and ghee have their own flavour: use the one you like best. Shortening is a hard fat most often made from vegetable oils but sometimes with animal fats added to it.

BUTTER IS BEST

Why do recipes tell you to use butter for greasing baking dishes? Is it better than oil?

Fats such as butter or lard are recommended because they do not break down at high temperatures, but will cling to the dish. Oils, and some margarines, become sticky when spread in a thin film so food might stick to them. Butter and lard will give a better result.

KEEPING DRIPPING

How long can meat dripping be kept in the fridge? Is it safe to use some of it and then top-up the dish with fat from the next roast?

Like many fats, dripping will turn rancid if it is kept for too long: fresh dripping may be kept in the refrigerator for up to two weeks and may be frozen for up to six months. If you collect the dripping fat from a roast, it should be poured into a suitable glass or china container: do not use plastic as elements from it could contaminate the hot fat. Allow it to cool, then cover and put it into a refrigerator.

Do not add the dripping taken from one roast to that from another. It will spoil the taste. Pour the second lot into a clean container, label it and store as before: this prevents any cross contamination and lets you keep track of how old the dripping is so there is less danger of keeping it too long.

CARDIAC ALERT

Are some cooking fats healthier to use than others?

Yes. The average British diet contains 40 per cent fat, of which 16 per cent is saturated fat, which has definitely been linked to heart disease. It is now recommended that not only should we reduce our overall intake of fat, but we should aim to replace saturated fats with healthier fats known as polyunsaturated and monounsaturated. One good way of doing this is by using a vegetable oil instead of butter or lard whenever you are frying or roasting.

Most vegetable oils are high in polyunsaturates, while olive and rapeseed oils are high in monounsaturates. Both these types of fats are considered to be healthier than saturated fats. Coconut and palm oils are high in saturated fats, so read the labels of blended oils and solid fats to see if any is included.

Today, margarine is usually made with pure vegetable oils, which makes it lower in saturated fat than butter. However, some margarines, particularly the harder varieties, have animal fats added to give them flavour, so if reducing your fat intake is a concern, read the labels carefully. (See also NUTRITION.)

HOW TO RENDER FAT

Rendering fat means melting it to separate it from the meat to which it is attached or from the impurities that are thrown off during cooking. Put the fat or meat trimmings in a baking tin and cook in the oven at 150°C (300°F, gas mark 2) until the fat turns to liquid. Carefully strain the melted fat through a fine metal sieve. Cover and cool the fat before storing it in the refrigerator.

FENNEL

VERSATILE BULB

How do I cook fennel? Does it go with anything other than fish?

Florence fennel, or fennel bulb, does not always have to be cooked; it may be thinly sliced and eaten raw, perhaps combined with some rémoulade sauce (see MAYONNAISE), or tossed with watercress. To prevent cut fennel from turning brown at the edges, put the slices in cold water acidulated with a little lemon juice until it is cooked.

Thin slices of fennel are delicious grilled and added to a warm mixed salad of Mediterranean vegetables, or battered and then fried as fritters. Fennel heads can be quartered and cooked in a sauce, or steamed, poached or braised. If there are any fresh leaves attached to the bulb, reserve them to use as a garnish or toss with salad leaves.

Fennel's mild aniseed flavour matches poultry as well as fish. The following recipe for coarsely chopped fennel cooked in a barley risotto could be served with either. Or it can be scattered with Parmesan cheese to make an original and attractive vegetarian dish that even meat eaters will appreciate.

Fennel with barley and leek

SERVES: 4
PREPARATION TIME: 20 minutes
COOKING TIME: 40 minutes

1 large head of fennel
Juice of 1 lemon
125 g (4½ oz) pearl barley
Salt and black pepper
3 tablespoons olive oil
2 slim leeks, sliced
2 cloves garlic, crushed or finely chopped
3 tomatoes, skinned and chopped
1 tablespoon chopped parsley

1 Roughly chop the head of fennel and put it into a bowl of cold water with half of the lemon juice.

A new twist on a risotto theme combines the faintly liquorice-like crunch of fennel with braised barley and, for extra colour, finely sliced leek and tomatoes.

2 Wash the barley in a sieve under a cold tap, put it into a saucepan and cover generously with cold water. Bring it to the boil, then drain the barley and discard the water.
3 Rinse the barley and return it to the pan with 1 litre (1 pint 15 fl oz) of cold water. Return to the boil, add salt and simmer for 30 - 35 minutes until the barley is tender. Drain, mix in the remaining lemon juice and keep warm in a serving bowl.
4 Drain the fennel and pat it dry. Heat the oil in a wok or large frying pan and stir-fry the fennel for a few minutes before adding the leeks and garlic. Continue stir-frying them for a further 2 minutes then add the tomatoes and cook for 3 - 4 minutes.
5 Mix the hot vegetable mixture into the barley, season to taste and scatter the chopped parsley all over.

FIGS

FIGGY COLOURS

Is there a difference between green and dark purple figs?

The figs seen most often have purplish-black skins, but they can also be brown, green, red or yellow, different colours inside and varying in flavour. Some figs are much sweeter and more aromatic than others. Ripe figs, with a powdery, white bloom on the surface, have plump, soft flesh and are eaten whole, skin and all. They are perishable and will only keep for a day or two. They are grown mainly in Greece and Turkey and are at their best from June until the end of September.

FILO PASTRY

LIGHT AND BRITTLE

If a recipe calls for filo pastry, can I use flaky pastry or puff pastry in the dish instead?

Not really. Even though filo pastry (also called phyllo or strudel pastry), flaky pastry and puff pastry are all made with the same basic ingredients of fat, flour and water, the proportion of fat to flour varies and this affects the amount of water used to form the dough and the type of pastry that results. If you use either flaky or puff pastry, both of which are sturdy, instead of the gossamer-thin sheets of filo for a recipe, the results, although they may be satisfactory, will be completely different in texture.

Filo pastry can be made at home but it is much easier to buy it ready-made, fresh or frozen, either from supermarkets or from delicatessens. It takes a great deal of time to beat, stretch, pull and roll the pastry into the characteristic sheets so thin you can read newsprint through them.

Ready-made filo pastry comes in very thin leaves of varying sizes. Thaw frozen filo pastry thoroughly according to the instructions on the packet and let it come to room temperature in its box before you try to use it. The sheets should then be brushed with butter or oil before they are baked to make the pastry layers light and crisp.

CRISPY WRAPPING

How do I make filo parcels?

Crisp, delicate filo pastry makes attractive casings for both sweet and savoury fillings. Cut the filo sheets as you need them and keep the pieces in a pile under a damp cloth so that the air does not get to them and dry them out.

Use filo in the following recipe for Prawn Triangles, filled with a spicy combination of prawns and coconut. They can be served either as a snack or as a first course.

Prawn triangles

MAKES: 10 starter-sized parcels
PREPARATION TIME: 35 minutes plus 15 minutes chilling time
COOKING TIME: 20 - 25 minutes

---

2 tablespoons sunflower oil, plus extra for greasing
1 clove garlic, crushed
4 spring onions, trimmed and chopped (use some of the green part as well as the white)
2.5 cm (1 in) piece ginger, peeled and grated
½ teaspoon chilli powder
A pinch each of ground cumin and turmeric
25 g (1 oz) creamed coconut, cut into chunks
125 g (4½ oz) peeled prawns, defrosted if frozen
5 sheets filo pastry
50 g (1¾ oz) butter, melted
1 teaspoon white or brown sesame seeds to sprinkle, optional

---

1 In a frying pan, heat the oil over a low heat and fry the garlic, spring onions and the ginger for 5 minutes, stirring occasionally. Add the spices and cook for 1 - 2 minutes more, stirring the mixture continuously.
2 Remove the frying pan from the heat and stir in the creamed coconut until it has melted. Allow to cool then stir in the peeled prawns.
3 Lightly oil a baking sheet. Take a sheet of filo then cut and fill the pastry triangles (see box, right). As each triangle is completed, brush the top with butter, and sprinkle it with a few sesame seeds, if you like. Repeat with the rest of the prawn filling and filo pastry to make ten triangles. Place them on a baking sheet and chill in the refrigerator for at least 15 minutes. Preheat the oven to 180°C (350°F, gas mark 4).
4 Bake the filo parcels in the oven for 20 - 25 minutes, or until they are crisp and golden brown, then remove them from the oven and drain the parcels on kitchen paper.
5 The cooked filo parcels should be served immediately, while they are still very crisp. Once cooked, the pastry quickly becomes soggy. Allow two parcels per person as a starter.

PREPARING FILO PASTRY PARCELS

This extremely brittle pastry dries out quickly, so work with one sheet at a time and keep it away from sunlight. As you work, keep the rest covered with a dampened tea towel. This will keep the waiting sheets of filo pastry moist and pliable until you are ready to use them.

1 Take a sheet of filo pastry and cut it lengthways into strips about 7.5 cm (3 in) wide. Brush one strip with melted butter, place the other on top and brush it with butter too.

2 Put a heaped teaspoon of filling on the end of the double-layered strip, about 2 cm (¾ in) from the end. Gently take hold of one corner of the pastry strip and fold it over the filling, making it into a neat and tidy triangular-shaped parcel.

3 Take hold of this portion and fold it over again. Keep folding the filled portion again and again until the whole strip of pastry is used up and folded over the filling.

FISH

CHOOSING FRESH FISH

I'm not sure I know what to look for when I am shopping for fish. What are the signs of freshness?

If the fish is whole, there are several things to look for: the eyes should be clear and bright, the scales should be shiny, the gills should be a healthy-looking pink or red and the flesh should feel firm and resilient to the touch. Fillets and steaks should also be firm and moist, and the flesh should have a fresh, translucent colour.

A fresh, clean smell is another good sign. Fresh fish should not in fact smell 'fishy', but saltwater fish should smell of the sea.

WHITE AND OILY FISH

What is the difference between white fish and oily fish?

White fish are saltwater fish with oil concentrated mainly in the liver. The two main groups are the cod family, which includes coley, haddock, hake, pollack and whiting as well as cod; and the flatfish family of brill, dab, halibut, plaice, sole and turbot. Other white fish are bass, grey mullet, gurnard, John Dory, monkfish, ray and skate (both of which are related to shark), sea bream and snapper.

The oil in oily fish is distributed throughout their flesh. This makes them more nutritious than white fish, but higher in calories. Saltwater oily fish include anchovies, herrings, mackerel, sardines, sprats and tuna while salmon and trout are oily freshwater fish.

KEEPING FISH

Must I cook fish the day I buy it?

All fish are highly perishable, especially once they have been cut. It is best to buy fish whole and have the fishmonger prepare it while you wait, or prepare it yourself just before cooking. Supermarkets often give long 'use by' dates, but fish is generally best eaten within 24 hours of purchase. Oily fish go off more quickly than white fish because their oils oxidise, causing the flesh to go rancid. Fish with their guts intact also deteriorate quickly, so gut fish before storing.

To store fish, remove it from its wrappings, rinse it under cold running water and pat it dry. Then rewrap the fish loosely in a polythene bag and store it in the coldest part of the refrigerator.

COOKED TO PERFECTION

How can I tell when a fish is ready to serve? I always seem to either undercook or overcook it.

One of the worst things you can do to fish is to overcook it, and as it cooks very quickly it needs to be carefully watched.

Properly cooked fish is moist, tender to the bite and full of flavour. Test the fish when it begins to look opaque. Gently prod it with the prongs of a fork: when the flesh will flake easily, the fish is done.

The moist, delicate flesh of fish becomes tough and loses flavour if overcooked. Keep testing the fish as it cooks for the moment when it will flake easily.

FISH FOR CHILDREN

The only fish my children will eat are fish fingers, because they are worried about bones. Can you recommend any non-bony fish?

Cod, haddock, salmon and whiting steaks have no small bones that would bother children, only large bones that can be easily seen and removed before cooking. Flatfish, such as fillets of plaice and sole, also have no small bones but have sweet flesh which appeals to children. Monkfish has one central bone which is easily removed.

Putting the fish into a pie or kedgeree is a good idea because you can check for bones when skinning and flaking it. Encasing boned fish in pastry is another option; try cutting the pastry into a fish shape and marking scales on it. Suitable fish are cod or haddock; salmon is particularly good as the rich colour contrasts well with the pastry.

STEAMING FISH

Which is the best fish to choose for steaming, and what's the best way to cook it in a steamer?

Any fish fillet, steak or small whole fish can be steamed – and this is the best way to retain all the natural goodness. Add richness of flavour by using a well-flavoured fish stock or court bouillon instead of plain water in the steamer, and rest the fish on a bed of herbs or seaweed.

Bring the liquid to the boil then turn the heat down to simmering point. Lay the fish in the top of the steamer, making sure they do not overlap or they will not cook evenly, place it over the liquid and cover. Steaming times vary with the size and quantity of fish: allow 5–8 minutes for fillets, 10–15 minutes for steaks and whole fish.

VERSATILE SALTED COD

We had baccalà on holiday in Spain. What is it?

Baccalà is dried salted cod, which is very popular in the Mediterranean and in the Caribbean. Because of its saltiness, it needs long soaking in water before cooking, and is usually served with pungent ingredients such as garlic.

You can buy baccalà in Britain from Spanish, Portuguese and Italian delicatessens, in Greek and Turkish stores and also in shops which sell ethnic foods from the West Indies. It is sold in grey fillets which are hard and dry, and have a light dusting of salt. You need to cut the fillets with a strong knife, then soak them in cold water for one to two days depending on the thickness of the fish, changing the water every 8 hours or so. After draining, baccalà can be cooked exactly like fresh fish, taking about 15–20 minutes to become tender.

In Portugal, baccalà is traditionally boiled, then skinned, flaked and served with boiled potatoes and garlic mayonnaise. It also has a good affinity with tomatoes, and in France it is boiled and puréed with milk, olive oil and garlic, when it is known as *brandade*. Baccalà is also delicious combined with fresh fish, so try adding a few pieces to your usual fish pies and stews.

SOLE DIFFERENCES

What is the difference between Dover sole and lemon sole?

Dover sole, *Solea solea*, is the only true sole. It is so named because it was once landed mainly around the town of Dover in Kent, but it is now caught widely in other European waters. Though expensive, Dover sole does have an exquisite flavour and delicate, firm flesh. It is delicious simply grilled, or fried in a little butter and lemon juice.

Lemon sole, *Microstomus kitt*, is not a true sole although it is similar in appearance. While lemon sole is considerably cheaper than Dover sole and not as fine either in texture or flavour, in recipes the two are interchangeable.

Dover sole is an exceptional fish in that it is best not eaten straight from the sea. It needs two or three days to 'relax' before cooking or the flesh can be tough and rubbery and the bones and skin will be difficult to remove.

PAN-DRESSING

My local supermarket has begun to stock 'pan-dressed' fish. Please explain what this means.

'Pan-dressed' simply means that the fish has been trimmed, scaled, gutted, boned or filleted and is ready for the pan. This type of

---

PREPARING FISH FOR COOKING

Most fish needs some preparation before cooking, even if it is going to be baked very plainly. Fish that is to be served whole is usually trimmed as retaining the fins makes handling and serving difficult. And if a scaly fish, such as grey or red mullet, is being served in its skin, it needs to have the scales removed.

All fish, except very tiny ones such as sprats and whitebait, must have their internal organs removed before cooking. Flatfish are usually gutted before being sold, but round fish are sometimes sold whole.

Whether or not you cut the head off the fish before cooking it is a matter of taste – and might depend on the size of your cooking vessels.

TRIMMING AND SCALING

1 Using kitchen scissors or a small sharp knife, cut off the fins from both sides of the belly (trout is shown here). Cut close to the skin.

2 Cut off the dorsal fins running along the back of the fish. Always discard the fins after trimming; they should not be used to make stock.

3 Put a large sheet of polythene (such as a cut-open bag) over the fish to catch the scales (grey mullet is shown here). Holding the tail of the fish in one hand and working from the tail towards the head, use a serrated knife to scrape the scales off. When finished, rinse the fish thoroughly under cold running water, then feel over the skin with your fingertips to ensure all the scales are removed.

GUTTING

1 Hold the fish on its side, then cut into the underside at the tail end and along the belly until you reach the head (mackerel is shown here).

2 Gently pull the opening apart to widen it, then scrape out the contents of the stomach with a knife or spoon. Discard the entrails.

3 Rinse the cavity thoroughly under cold running water while running the edge of a teaspoon along the backbone. Rinsing and scraping will remove any blood clots which would discolour the cooked fish if left in. Alternatively, rinse the inside of the fish then sprinkle salt in the cavity and, with your fingers, rub away any black skin within. Rinse the salt away under cold running water.

SKINNING A FLATFISH

If Dover sole is to be cooked whole, the dark skin is removed by ripping it off. Other fresh flatfish can be skinned this way or with a knife (see page 150).

1 Make a small cut in the dark skin at the tail end. With the point of the knife, ease the skin off the flesh until you can easily grasp it in your fingers.

2 Dip your fingers in salt to help you to grip, then grasp the skin in one hand and the tail in the other. Pull the skin away backwards, not upwards.

BONING A FLATFISH

A skinned fish can be cooked as it is, but it will be a more substantial dish if the bones are removed, leaving a pocket which makes an ideal container for stuffing. This technique is ideal for lemon sole. Narrower Dover sole, pictured here, can be boned provided it is meaty enough – choose one weighing at least 1 kg (2 lb 4 oz). Plaice is not suitable as the soft flesh tends to break when stuffed.

1 Cut along the backbone of the skinned side, then slide the flesh off the bones, leaving the edges attached.

2 Hold the fish firmly in both hands, then bend it in half lengthways and press tightly until the backbone snaps.

3 Slip the knife through the crack and slide it under the bones on one side, working towards the head.

4 With scissors, cut along the edge of the bones towards the head. Free the flesh and bones from the other side in the same way, then turn the fish around and repeat at the tail end.

5 Cut the backbone free at the head and tail ends and discard it. Check thoroughly for any small bones that may remain in the flesh and remove them, using tweezers if necessary.

preparation is common in supermarkets. Fishmongers will do all of these things as well, and should do them free of charge, but they may need notice at busy times. And you might need to explain your recipe because certain dishes, such as the Stuffed Lemon Sole below, require special boning (see box, left).

If you ask your fishmonger to bone a fish, remember to ask for the bones to use for stock, as these will not be included automatically.

Stuffed lemon sole

SERVES: 4
PREPARATION TIME: 1 hour
COOKING TIME: 20 minutes

2 lemon soles, each weighing at
    least 1 kg (2 lb 4 oz)
1 small bulb of fennel
1 leek
1 celery stalk
175 g (6 oz) cooked, peeled prawns
25 g (1 oz) butter
A good pinch of saffron threads
Salt and black pepper
250 ml (9 fl oz) dry white wine
125 ml (4 fl oz) fish stock
4 tablespoons mascarpone cheese,
    crème fraîche or double cream

1 Bone the soles (see left) and cut off the heads if you prefer. Preheat the oven to 190°C (375°F, gas mark 5).
2 Cut the fennel, leek and celery into julienne strips and chop the prawns if they are large.
3 Melt the butter in a frying pan, add the vegetables and saffron, and season to taste. Stir-fry them over a moderate to high heat for 5 minutes or until the vegetables just begin to soften. Remove the pan from the heat and stir in the prawns.
4 Put the boned soles into a lightly buttered baking dish and spoon the vegetable and prawn mixture into the cavities. Cover with a layer of buttered greaseproof paper or foil and bake for about 20 minutes, depending on the size of the fish.
5 When the fish are done, remove to a serving dish and keep warm.
6 Pour the cooking juices into the frying pan. Add the wine and stock and boil until the liquid is reduced

by about half. Add the cheese or cream and stir until thickened. Taste and season to taste.

7 To serve, bring the fish to the table whole and halve them there. Pass the sauce around separately.

PAPILLOTE AND PAUPIETTES

What is the difference between fish 'en papillote' and 'paupiettes'?

These French terms sound so similar many people confuse the two. Fish en papillote is baked in a parcel. It is traditionally wrapped in greaseproof paper, which puffs up full of steam in the oven, but nowadays foil is often used. Foil does the job just as well, but the finished dish looks less dramatic.

A paupiette is simply a rolled fillet of fish, usually sole, which is stuffed before being either baked, poached, or steamed. Paupiette is not a term confined to fish as fillets of beef, veal, chicken and turkey are also cooked in this way.

The following recipe for Sole Paupiettes can be prepared in advance up to the stage when the fish goes into the oven. The dish is quite rich and filling, and needs only a green vegetable or salad as an accompaniment.

Paupiettes of sole

SERVES: 4
PREPARATION TIME: 30 minutes
COOKING TIME: 10 - 12 minutes

---

1 shallot, finely chopped
1 clove garlic, crushed
125 g (4½ oz) wild mushrooms, such as chanterelles
50 g (1¾ oz) butter
50 g (1¾ oz) fresh white breadcrumbs
1 tablespoon chopped oregano
Salt and black pepper
8 sole fillets, skinned (see box, overleaf)
125 ml (4 fl oz) dry white wine
125 ml (4 fl oz) crème fraîche
To garnish: fresh oregano sprigs

---

1 Preheat the oven to 200°C (400°F, gas mark 6). Lightly grease a large, shallow ovenproof dish.

2 Finely chop half the mushrooms. Melt half the butter in a frying pan, add the shallot and garlic and soften. Add the chopped mushrooms and cook over a gentle heat, stirring all the time, until well softened.

3 Transfer the cooked mushroom mixture to a large bowl. Add the breadcrumbs and half the oregano, and season to taste. Mix well with your hands to make a stuffing.

4 Put the sole fillets skinned side up on a work surface, halve them lengthways and score them with a sharp knife. Put a heaped teaspoon of stuffing at the wide end of each piece, then roll up from that end.

5 Stand the rolls in the prepared dish, so that they are close together but not too squeezed. Dot each roll with a tablespoon of butter, sprinkle with the wine and pepper to taste. Bake for 10 - 12 minutes.

6 When the paupiettes are done, remove them from the dish and keep warm. Set aside the cooking liquid.

7 Melt the remaining butter gently in the frying pan, add the whole mushrooms and cook over a gentle heat for 1 - 2 minutes until slightly softened. Add the fish cooking liquid and the crème fraîche and stir over a high heat for 3 - 5 minutes until slightly reduced. Add the remaining oregano and adjust the seasoning to taste. Serve the fish with the sauce poured over and around it.

VARIATION

For an attractive swiss roll effect, spread the filling equally along the whole length of the fillet instead of heaping it at one end.

GRILLED FISH

I know that simple, grilled fish is healthy, but what is the best way to cook it so it stays moist?

Grilled fish is not only healthy, it is also very quick and easy to cook. Chopped fresh herbs, a couple of tablespoons of virgin olive oil and plenty of coarsely ground black pepper will greatly enhance the flavour – especially if you leave the fish to marinate in these ingredients for half an hour or so before cooking. Whole oily fish such as

---

MAKING PAUPIETTES

Paupiettes, sometimes described as turbans, transform simple fillets of fish into an impressive dish. The addition of a rich stuffing turns small pieces of fish into more substantial portions.

In France, the fish most typically cooked in this way is sole (pictured here), but any other white or oily fish fillet can be used in its place, provided it is thinly sliced.

1 Place skinned fillets on a board or work surface, skinned side up, and lightly score them with a sharp knife. Put a spoonful of stuffing at the widest end of the fillet and roll the fish up from that side.

2 Stand the filled rolls upright in a buttered dish, placing them close together so they do not unroll during cooking. Alternatively, the rolls can be secured after rolling with a thin strip of lightly oiled greaseproof paper, which is easily removed after cooking.

3 When making a large quantity of paupiettes, a quicker way of preparing them is to roll the fillets up without the stuffing, stand them in the dish and then pipe the stuffing in the centre. Paupiettes can also be made in long cylinder shapes, by rolling large escalopes of fish such as salmon spread with a stuffing. After cooking, the roll is sliced into attractive pinwheels.

BONING A WHOLE ROUND FISH

Fish can be cooked and served whole with the bones intact, but it makes for neater serving and eating if the bones are removed first. A filleting knife with a flexible blade makes *the task easier. The head can be removed if you prefer, but retaining it will help to keep the fish shape intact during cooking. In the pictures below, salmon is shown.*

1 Hold the fish with its open stomach cavity facing you. Taking care not to cut through to the skin, slide the tip of the knife between the rib cage and the flesh on both sides, so that all the ribs are freed down to the backbone.

2 With kitchen scissors, cut through each end of the backbone to release it from the fish. Then start to gently peel it away from the flesh, beginning at the head end. Keep the backbone: it may be used in fish stock.

3 Check that no small bones are still left in the flesh, especially around the edges. If necessary, pull the bones out with a pair of tweezers. The bigger the fish, the bigger the bones will be, so examine smaller fish very carefully.

FILLETING A WHOLE ROUND FISH

A round fish yields two meaty fillets, one on either side of the backbone. A flexible filleting knife is the best tool to use. *You will find it easier if you first remove the head and gills but leave the skin on. In these pictures, trout is shown.*

1 Lay the prepared fish on its side, with the tail facing you, and cut along the length of its back. Keep the knife parallel to the work surface and cut right through to the backbone, working from the head end to the tail.

2 Starting at the head end, cut the flesh free from the fine rib bones on one side of the fish, keeping the filleting knife close to the bones. Work down along the underside of the fish until the top fillet is detached.

3 Holding the exposed backbone, cut away the remaining lower fillet. Check for any small bones left in the flesh, especially around the edges, and pull these out with tweezers. The backbone may be used in fish stock.

SKINNING ROUND FISH FILLETS

Fish fillets are generally sold with their skins on, but any dark or tough skin is usually removed before cooking. You can ask the fishmonger to skin the fillets, but if you buy them in packets from a supermarket, or if you have filleted the fish yourself, you will have to tackle the skinning yourself at home.

Skinning is a job best done with a sharp, flexible filleting knife. In these pictures, haddock is shown.

1 Lay the fillet skin side down with the tail end towards you. Dip your fingers in salt and grip the tail end. Cut the flesh as close to the tail as possible.

2 Holding the knife flat on the board, work it between the skin and the flesh with a gentle sawing action. Fold the skinned flesh back as you go.

herring, mackerel, sardines and trout are easy to grill because their natural oils baste the fish and keep it moist, as the recipe below shows.

Thick, firm-textured fish fillets and steaks, from fish such as monkfish, salmon, swordfish and tuna, can also be grilled in the grill pan or in a ridged, cast-iron frying pan. Do not put them on the grill rack as they may break up.

Grilled fish

SERVES: 4
PREPARATION TIME: 5 minutes
COOKING TIME: 8 minutes

2 tablespoons virgin olive oil
2 tablespoons chopped fresh herbs
4 whole oily fish, each weighing
    375 - 500 g (13 oz - 1 lb 2 oz),
    trimmed, scaled and gutted
Salt and black pepper
To serve: lemon wedges

1 Preheat the grill for a minimum of 10 minutes. In a small bowl, turn the herbs in a tablespoon of oil until they are well soaked. With a sharp knife, make three deep slashes at regular intervals on both sides of each fish: this will help the heat to penetrate the flesh and facilitates even cooking. Brush the rack of the grill pan with vegetable oil.
2 Place the fish on the rack, brush with herb oil and season to taste. Put the fish under the very hot grill and cook one side for 4 - 5 minutes. Turn the fish over, brush that side with the remaining herb oil, season and cook for a further 4 - 5 minutes or until the flesh is opaque.
3 Serve with lemon wedges or a sauce such as the one to the right.

SAUCE FOR VARIETY

I have started grilling fish to be healthier but find it a bit dull. Can you suggest a tasty sauce?

The following recipe is based on the Mexican idea of serving hot grilled fish with a chilled fresh sauce (known as *salsa*). The sauce is very low in fat, and the contrast of colour and temperature rejuvenates tired tastebuds.

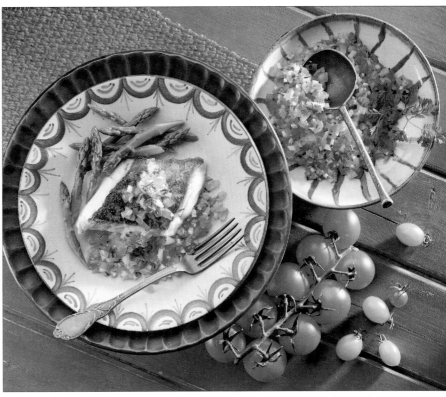

Fresh cherry tomato salsa, sweetened with a sprinkling of sugar to enhance the sun-ripened flavour, provides a pleasantly chilled contrast to grilled fish.

Sweet tomato salsa

SERVES: 4
PREPARATION TIME: 5 minutes, plus at least 30 minutes chilling time
COOKING TIME: none

250 g (9 oz) ripe cherry tomatoes
    (red and yellow if possible)
½ small onion
1 clove garlic
2 tablespoons virgin olive oil
1 tablespoon wine vinegar
1 teaspoon sugar
Salt and black pepper

1 Finely chop the tomatoes, onion, and garlic and put them in a bowl. Add the olive oil, vinegar and sugar, sprinkle on salt and pepper to taste and stir well to mix.
2 Chill for at least 30 minutes or until you are ready to serve it.
VARIATIONS
Add about six chopped and stoned black olives. Alternatively, flavour the salsa with 1 - 2 tablespoons of chopped fresh herbs, using whatever herbs were cooked with the fish.

MICROWAVING FISH

I've heard that fish is one of the easiest things to cook in the microwave. Which cuts of fish are the most suitable, and how do I go about cooking them?

Fish is excellent when cooked in the microwave, retaining all its delicate texture and shape as well as its natural juices. Because it is cooked with no or little added liquid, there is little loss of nutrients.

Fish steaks and fillets are most suitable to cook in the microwave, because they cook quickly and evenly, but whole fish such as whiting and trout weighing up to 500 g (1 lb 2 oz) are suitable, as are small whole fish such as sardines and herrings. Microwaved white fish can look bland, but can be made more appetising by basting it with soy or other flavoured sauces.

To microwave whole fish, slash the skin in two or three places on both sides so it does not burst during cooking. Then lay the fish in a microwave dish and shield the head and tail with small strips of foil. Steaks should be laid in a round dish with their thinner ends facing inwards. Fillets should be placed in a single layer, folding the thinner ends underneath so they do not overcook. Whole or cut, all fish should be covered with a microwave-safe top before cooking and turned over halfway through.

The following recipe for microwaving salmon steaks can be used for white fish as well and illustrates the simple technique of using soy sauce and similar flavours for a Japanese teriyaki-style marinade.

Fish steaks will cook more evenly in the microwave oven if you lay them in a circle, with the thicker end facing out.

Microwaved salmon

SERVES: 4
PREPARATION TIME: *10 minutes, plus 30 – 60 minutes marinating*
COOKING TIME: *5 minutes*

4 salmon steaks, each weighing about 175 g (6 oz)
2.5 cm (1 in) piece ginger, chopped
6 black peppercorns
1 clove garlic, chopped
2 tablespoons each vegetable oil, soy sauce and dry sherry

1 Lay the salmon steaks in a circle in a deep, round microwave-safe dish, with the thin ends pointing inwards.
2 Using a pestle and mortar, pound the ginger, peppercorns and garlic to a rough paste. Transfer the paste to a larger bowl, then mix in the oil, soy sauce and sherry.
3 Pour the sauce over the fish, cover with cling film and marinate for at least 30 minutes but no more than an hour, turning the fish over once.

4 Fold back an edge of the cling film so steam can escape then cook on High for 5 - 7 minutes, turning the steaks over once. Leave to stand for 2 minutes before serving.

CRISP AND LIGHT

Is there a lighter way of cooking crispy battered fish?

It is possible to make a light batter with egg whites rather than whole eggs or egg yolks, but the batter still needs to be deep-fried to be crisp. In the recipe below, breadcrumbs replace the batter and the fish steaks are baked, making them a healthy alternative to fried fish. The crust is crispier if the breaded fish is left to chill, uncovered, for up to 4 hours before cooking.

Oven-fried fish steaks

SERVES: 4
PREPARATION TIME: *15 - 20 minutes*
COOKING TIME: *10 minutes*

2 tablespoons plain flour
Pinch of cayenne pepper
Salt and pepper
150 ml (5 fl oz) fine breadcrumbs
2 tablespoons dried mixed herbs
1 egg white, size 1
4 thick white fish fillets or steaks, each weighing 175 - 250 g (6 - 9 oz), skinned
4 tablespoons groundnut oil
To serve: lemon wedges

1 Preheat the oven to 190°C (375°F, gas mark 5) and put a baking sheet in it to warm. Mix the flour with the cayenne and salt and pepper to taste. Stir the breadcrumbs into the herbs. Whisk the egg white lightly with a fork until just frothy.
2 Make sure the fish is dry. Coat it in the flour mixture first, then dip it into the egg whites and finally the herb-flavoured breadcrumbs.
3 Heat the oil in a large, nonstick frying pan until it is very hot but not smoking. Add the coated fish steaks and fry them over a moderate heat for about a minute each side.
4 Transfer the fish steaks to the hot baking sheet and bake for 8 minutes. Serve with lemon wedges.

MIXED FISH STEW

I often make the mixed fish stew called bouillabaisse, but the cod and haddock seem to disintegrate. Can you suggest other fish that might be more suitable?

The classic recipe for bouillabaisse from Marseilles in the south of France uses local fish, many of which cannot be found outside the Mediterranean. You can make a variation without them, as the recipe below shows. The secret is to prepare a rich broth first with trimmings from the fish you buy. Add the fish for the last 5–8 minutes only, to ensure that they will not overcook and disintegrate.

Firm-textured fish such as eel, gurnard, halibut, John Dory, mackerel, monkfish, mullet or weaver are best, but any similar white or oily fish that are in season will do. It is traditional to leave the fish on the bone as this helps to keep the flesh intact during cooking and also improves the flavour. For extra interest, you could also include squid, and shellfish such as mussels, prawns or scallops.

British bouillabaisse

SERVES: 4
PREPARATION TIME: *35 minutes*
COOKING TIME: *1 hour*

4 tablespoons virgin olive oil
1 small bulb of fennel, thinly sliced
1 onion, thinly sliced
4 cloves garlic, crushed
2 leeks, thinly sliced
4 tomatoes, skinned, seeded and chopped
1 tablespoon tomato purée
300 ml (10 fl oz) dry white wine
1 litre (1 pint 15 fl oz) fish stock
1 strip of orange rind
1 bouquet garni
A large pinch of saffron threads
Salt and black pepper
1.5 kg (3 lb 5 oz) mixed white and oily fish, cut into chunks
2 tablespoons Pernod

1 Heat the oil in a large, heavy-based saucepan and add the fennel, onion, garlic and leeks. Cook over a gentle heat, stirring frequently, for about 10 minutes until the vegetables are softened but not coloured.

2 Add the chopped tomatoes, purée and wine to the saucepan and stir well to mix with the vegetables. Add the stock and bring to the boil over a high heat, then lower the heat and add the strip of orange rind, bouquet garni and saffron. Sprinkle on some salt and pepper to taste.

3 Partially cover the pan and simmer gently for about 30 minutes, stirring from time to time, until the liquid has reduced slightly.

4 Remove the orange peel and the bouquet garni from the soup and discard. Add any firm-fleshed pieces of fish and simmer for 5 minutes, then add the more delicate fish and simmer for a further 2 - 3 minutes.

5 Pour in the Pernod and stir well. Check the seasoning and adjust if necessary before serving.

A dash of Pernod brings the flavour of the Mediterranean to chunky white and oily fish in a British Bouillabaisse.

SPICY ROUILLE

I was once served some fish stew which came with rouille. What is it, and can I make it myself?

Rouille is a rust-coloured sauce made with cayenne pepper, garlic and breadcrumbs blended with olive oil and fish stock. Spoon it into the soup to thicken it or spread it on toast and serve separately.

To make your own, sweat one or two crushed garlic cloves in a little olive oil, then add 15 g (1/2 oz) of crumbled white bread and 100 ml (3 1/2 fl oz) of the fish soup and reduce it all to a thick smooth pulp. Whisk in 100 ml (3 1/2 fl oz) of olive oil a little at a time, and season with salt, pepper and cayenne.

EXOTIC FISH

I sometimes see some unusual fish at my local fishmonger's. What could I do with them?

Exotic fish are generally very tasty, and are often best simply grilled or baked. However, they can be quite bony and this can put people off – as can their usually high price.

The recipe below can be used for any large whole fish such as grey mullet or sea bass, but many of the unusual fish shown overleaf could be cooked in this way. For smaller whole fish, such as red mullet, parrot fish and red tilapia, allow one fish per person and reduce the cooking time to 20 minutes.

Baked exotic fish

SERVES: 6
PREPARATION TIME: *20 minutes*
COOKING TIME: *60 - 70 minutes*

2 red onions, cut into wedges
2 fennel bulbs, cut into wedges
2 red peppers, deseeded and cut
    into wedges
4 large ripe tomatoes, quartered
2 cloves garlic, quartered
85 ml (3 fl oz) virgin olive oil
1 tablespoon lightly crushed
    fennel or coriander seeds
Salt and black pepper
2 kg (4 lb 8 oz) whole fish (see
    above), trimmed, scaled
    and cleaned
200 ml (7 fl oz) dry white wine
4 tablespoons Pernod, optional

1 Preheat the oven to 230°C (450°F, gas mark 8). Put all the vegetables in a large baking dish. Mix in the oil and crushed seeds and season to taste. Bake for 30 minutes, turning the vegetables over a few times.

2 Score the fish in two or three places on each side with a sharp knife, and sprinkle them inside and out with salt and pepper. Lay the fish on top of the vegetables, pour over the wine and Pernod, if using, and cover tightly with foil.

3 Reduce the oven temperature to 190°C (375°F, gas mark 5) and bake for 30 - 40 minutes until the flesh flakes easily when tested with a fork.

COOK'S GUIDE TO EXOTIC FISH

Brilliantly coloured fish from around the world and more unusual native fish are now becoming widely available. | *Cook them as you would more familiar fish or use the recipe for the richly flavoured baked fish on the previous page.*

1 SEA BREAM is inexpensive with firm, sweet flesh and comes from European and Atlantic waters. Gilt-head bream is called daurade in French. Whole fish can be baked and stuffed.

2 JOHN DORY, also known as St Peter's fish, has dark patterns said to be the apostle's fingermarks. Caught along the English south and south-west coasts, the Mediterranean and New Zealand, when filleted it resembles sole and turbot, and can be cooked in the same ways.

3 SNAPPER Many varieties and sizes of snapper come from the Far East and the Caribbean, and they are mostly red or orange in colour. The flesh is firm, white and tasty, and can be cooked most ways.

4 GREY MULLET, from British waters and the Mediterranean, has a good flavour and fairly firm texture. It is reasonably priced and versatile. It is good baked, steamed or braised, with or without stuffing; or grilled whole or cut into boneless pieces. It is also excellent cold.

5 EMPEROR is also called capitaine rouge, capitaine blanc or lascar. They are all tropical, and those from the Middle East and Australia are very colourful and have a strong taste. Baking is best for all varieties of emperor fish.

6 PARROT FISH These tropical fish have vivid, spectacular colours ranging from turquoise to violet, and can weigh up to 1 kg (2 lb 4 oz). They are best steamed, poached or baked whole; the colours fade on cooking and the bland flesh needs strong flavourings.

7 RED TILAPIA is also sometimes known as St Peter's fish. It is not the same as John Dory but is a Jamaican freshwater fish weighing up to 500 g (1 lb 2 oz). Its firm, white flesh is ideal for grilling, steaming, barbecuing or baking, either whole or cut into fillets.

8 GURNARD, from the Atlantic and the Mediterranean, has a large head and cone-shaped body and can be grey, yellow or red. The tasty, firm flesh (especially the red) is good in stews and soups. Although there is a lot of waste, it is inexpensive and the head can be used to make a very good stock.

9 SHARK are caught in the Atlantic and the Mediterranean. They have a strong flavour and meaty texture. Tails, middle cuts (pictured above), steaks and pieces are not bony and are relatively cheap. Shark holds its shape and is good for frying, barbecuing and using in chunky fish stews. Tope is a type of shark.

10 SWORDFISH is both temperate and tropical, and is abundant in the Mediterranean. It is dense and meaty, but swordfish steaks (pictured above) have a tendency to be dry, so need marinating and basting. Barbecuing and grilling are good cooking methods.

11 SEA BASS is a superior, expensive fish. It is caught in British waters and the Mediterranean, and the size varies from 1 - 9 kg (2 - 20 lb). The soft, delicate flesh is highly prized, especially for French and Oriental dishes. Whole fish are best steamed, poached or baked.

12 RED STRAWBERRY GROUPER belongs to the sea bass family and comes from the warm waters of the Caribbean and Mediterranean. It can be cooked as sole or turbot but its firm flesh needs strongly flavoured ingredients.

13 RED MULLET, from the Atlantic and Mediterranean, is superior in flavour to grey mullet (to which it is not related). It is traditionally cooked with fennel and tomatoes, and in bouillabaisse.

14 CARP is farmed in Eastern Europe, and has firm, sweet flesh and few bones. It is a favourite in China, and in Catholic countries is braised or baked and served on Christmas Eve.

FLAMBE

HOME FLAMES

My favourite restaurant serves a delicious dessert of fruit flambé. Can I make this at home?

Yes, flambéed food makes a spectacular show and is quite simple to prepare at home. The kirsch used to flambé the cherries in the recipe below intensifies the fruit flavour but if you prefer, use brandy, rum or whisky instead. Other fruits may be substituted for the cherries; for instance, try sliced apples, apricots, bananas, oranges or peaches.

To ensure ignition, heat the spirit before you light it, just long enough to warm it, but not so long that it allows the alcohol to evaporate. Keep your face and hair well away from the pan while you are setting fire to the alcohol and make sure that there is nothing else nearby or above that can catch fire. With practice, and a good spirit burner, you can even flambé the fruit while your guests are at the dinner table.

Cherries flambéed with kirsch

SERVES: 4
PREPARATION TIME: 25 minutes
COOKING TIME: 6 – 8 minutes

---

425 ml (15 fl oz) good-quality vanilla ice cream (either homemade or bought)
25 g (1 oz) unsalted butter
15 cm (6 in) strip lemon rind pared off with a vegetable peeler
3 tablespoons lemon juice
50 g (1¾ oz) caster sugar
500 g (1 lb 2 oz) ripe, plump and juicy cherries, washed and stoned
4 tablespoons kirsch, poured into a small bowl or teacup

---

1 Before cooking the cherries, divide the ice cream between four serving dishes and place these in the coldest part of your refrigerator. Take them out again just before flambéeing.
2 Put the butter, lemon rind, juice and sugar into a wide nonstick or enamel frying pan that is attractive enough to serve the fruit in. Put the pan over a moderate heat and stir until the butter melts and the sugar has dissolved completely. Increase the heat and let the syrup bubble gently until it has thickened slightly.
3 Add the cherries to the pan and cook them over a moderate to high heat for 2 - 3 minutes, stirring often, until they begin to soften.
4 If the cherries have produced a lot of juice, pour most of it off into a serving jug and set it aside to cool. Leave 2 - 3 tablespoons of juice in the pan, any more will dilute the spirit and prevent it from igniting.
5 Pour the kirsch into the pan, let it heat for a few seconds and then light it with a long match.
6 Shake the pan gently to and fro over the heat until the flames begin to die down. When all the flames have burnt out, spoon the cherries over the softened ice cream. Serve immediately. The reserved juice in the jug can be used as a sauce.

Dancing flames and lemon-scented cherries make an impressive finale for a dinner party. The dish is easy to set alight if the spirit is warmed first.

FLAN

SHORT FOR SAVOURY

What kind of pastry is best for making a savoury flan?

For a flan with a rich savoury filling like the Pissaladière overleaf, use a basic shortcrust pastry made with butter and plain flour. Pastry made with a mix of butter and lard is usually too short and crumbly for such a large flan. For pastry to use with sweet fillings, see TARTS.

To bake blind, line the uncooked pastry case with greaseproof paper and cover it with dried beans or rice. This weighs the pastry down and keeps it flat.

FLAN CASES IN ADVANCE

If I want to freeze flan cases to use later, should they be baked?

Bake them blind first, as shown above, then store them for up to three months in the freezer, packed in rigid containers, or keep them in an airtight tin in the refrigerator for a day or two. A prebaked pastry case will stay crisp during cooking, even with a moist filling.

WHICH DISH?

What material should a flan dish be made of for the best result?

A dish which heats up rapidly is best for making flans. Shortcrust pastry needs a quick burst of heat so the starch grains in the flour will swell and then burst and absorb the melting fat in the pastry mixture. Unless the fat is absorbed quickly the pastry will be limp and soggy. This is also true of pastry which is to be baked blind before being filled.

Metal is a better conductor of heat than ovenproof china or glass, and pastry will cook more quickly in a flan tin or in a metal ring placed on a baking sheet. A fluted flan tin with a loose base is easier to use than a fluted ring, which must be put on a baking sheet.

China flan dishes are attractive but are not as good for cooking. To make them more effective, put them on a baking sheet which has been preheated in a hot oven.

LINING A FLAN RING

If you and your family enjoy flans it is worth investing in a proper metal flan ring with a removable base. They are not very expensive and using one will make it much easier to remove the flan after it has been baked, when it is ready to be either filled or served.

1 Roll out the dough into a circle, using the flan tin as a guide for size. Allow for the depth of the side, plus an extra 1 cm (½ in).

2 Using a rolling pin, lift the rolled dough and drape it lightly over the base and side of the flan tin.

3 Gently ease the dough into the corners, being careful not to stretch it. Press it firmly against the side, then roll off the excess dough with the rolling pin to neaten the top edge. Alternatively, trim the edge with a small sharp knife so that it will look professional.

Pissaladière

SERVES: 4 - 6
PREPARATION TIME: 40 minutes, plus 40 minutes chilling time
COOKING TIME: 55 minutes

FOR THE PASTRY
175 g (6 oz) plain flour
A pinch of salt
90 g (3¼ oz) butter
1½ tablespoons water

FOR THE FILLING
3 tablespoons olive oil
1 large onion, finely chopped
2 cloves garlic, crushed
400 g (14 oz) canned chopped tomatoes in tomato juice
1 tablespoon tomato purée
2 tablespoons sun-dried tomatoes, marinated in oil, drained and thinly sliced
Salt and black pepper
8 fresh basil leaves
3 tablespoons freshly grated Parmesan cheese
50 g (1¾ oz) canned anchovy fillets, cut into thin strips
50 g (1¾ oz) black olives, pitted and cut in half

Sun-ripened tomatoes, anchovies, basil, olives and garlic bring the flavours of the Mediterranean to this simple flan.

1 Sift the flour and salt into a large mixing bowl and rub in the butter, adding enough water to make a firm dough. On a lightly floured surface, knead gently until smooth. Chill in a polythene bag for 20 minutes.
2 Preheat the oven to 200°C (400°F, gas mark 6).
3 Roll out the pastry and use it to line a 25 cm (10 in) flan case with a loose base. Put it on a baking sheet and prick the base in several places with a fork. Line the flan case with greaseproof paper and cover with dried beans. Bake for 10 minutes, then remove the paper and beans and bake for a further 10 minutes. Cool then chill for 15 - 20 minutes.
4 Heat 2 tablespoons of oil in a saucepan. Add the onion and garlic, cover and cook over a low heat until they are soft but not coloured. Stir in all the tomatoes with a little salt and pepper, bring to the boil, then simmer for about 20 minutes until the mixture is thick. Tear the basil into small pieces and stir it into the pan. Check the seasoning.
5 Spoon the vegetable mixture into the pastry case, sprinkle Parmesan cheese lightly over it and arrange anchovy strips and olives on top. Brush or drizzle carefully with the rest of the olive oil.

FLOUR

WHITE OR BROWN?

What is the difference between the various white and brown flours?

Flours are defined by the percentage of bran (the fibrous skin) and wheatgerm (the nutritious embryo of the wheat kernel) that remain after grains of wheat are milled. But most of what is left after grinding is the starchy endosperm, or inside of the wheat.

• WHOLEMEAL FLOUR is made from the whole grain, with nothing added to it or taken away.

• BROWN FLOUR generally has 85 per cent of the wheat grain intact.

• WHITE FLOUR has about 75 per cent of the wheat grain.

• WHEATGERM FLOUR is white or brown flour with at least 10 per cent added wheatgerm.

• MALTED FLOUR, which can be either brown or white, has been fortified with malted grains which have been sprouted.

BAKER'S CHOICE

Which type of flour should I choose for home baking?

Plain flour can be used for shortcrust pastry, sauces and gravies which do not need a raising agent. Self-raising flour, which includes added baking powder, is best for heavy mixes or cakes, scones, puddings and dumplings. It gives a better lift than plain flour with baking powder added at home, though that is suitable for lighter mixes or those with eggs or egg whites, which also encourage rising.

Gluten is a protein in flour that develops and becomes more elastic as the dough is kneaded. Strong flour has a large amount of protein, needed for pasta and bread making.

Use very finely milled flour, which has less gluten, for light cakes and pastries. Sponges, cakes and scones made with soft, fine flour have a more delicate texture and will rise higher.

LIGHTER BROWN

I'd like to use wholemeal flour, but find that my pastry turns out very dense when made with it. Is there anything I can do to make the texture lighter?

The fibre and bran in wholemeal flour, which add a nutty flavour to shortcrust pastry, also make it absorb more water, which produces a closer texture than pastry made with plain white flour.

By combining white flour with wholemeal, either half-and-half or up to a quarter white and three-quarters wholemeal, you retain the wholemeal flavour but the dough is more manageable and easier to roll out, as the following recipe shows.

Wholemeal pasties with vegetable filling

MAKES: *3 large pasties*
PREPARATION TIME: *40 minutes plus at least 30 minutes standing time*
COOKING TIME: *50 - 55 minutes*

FOR THE PASTRY
100 g (3 ½ oz) plain white flour
A pinch of salt
150 g (5 ½ oz) plain wholemeal flour
100 g (3 ½ oz) butter, diced
25 g (1 oz) white vegetable fat or lard, diced
Milk to glaze

FOR THE FILLING
2 tablespoons olive oil
1 large onion, finely chopped
1 clove garlic, crushed
1 medium potato, diced
1 medium carrot, diced
1 teaspoon ground coriander
½ teaspoon ground cumin
Salt and black pepper
3 tablespoons chopped parsley
1 tablespoon roughly chopped walnuts, optional
50 g (1 ¾ oz) mature or vegetarian Cheddar cheese, grated

1 Sift the plain flour and salt into a bowl and stir in the wholemeal flour. Add the fats and rub them in until the mixture resembles fine breadcrumbs. Sprinkle 3 tablespoons

of water over the mixture, then use a palette knife to draw it together and the fingertips of one hand to form a firm dough (you may need to add a little more water).

2 Turn the dough onto a lightly floured surface and knead it gently until smooth and free from cracks. Put it in a polythene bag and chill for at least 30 minutes.

3 To make the filling, heat the olive oil in a saucepan, add the onion and garlic, cover and cook for 5 minutes over a gentle heat. Add the potato and carrot, cover and cook for a further 6 - 8 minutes until they start to soften. Stir in the coriander and cumin and cook for another minute, then remove from the heat.

4 Turn the mixture into a bowl, season well, stir in the parsley and walnuts and leave to cool.

5 Preheat the oven to 200°C (400°F, gas mark 6) and grease a baking sheet. Divide the pastry into three equal portions. Using a plate as a guide, roll out a circle 18 cm (7 in) round, keeping the other portions covered to prevent them drying out. Repeat with the remaining pastry.

6 Divide the filling equally between the rounds, piling it in a strip along the centre of each. Sprinkle each strip with a teaspoon of cheese and reserve the remaining cheese.

7 Dampen the pastry edges with water, draw up both edges to meet at the top and press together. Flute the edges and place the pasties on the baking tray. Brush lightly with milk to glaze and sprinkle with the remaining cheese. Bake for about 30 minutes until the pastry is crisp.

To the rescue!

If you run out of self-raising flour you can make a substitute by sifting 2 ½ teaspoons of baking powder into 250 g (9 oz) of plain flour. But this will not give quite as high a lift to plain cakes, scones and puddings.

FOIL

FOIL SAFE

Is it safe to use foil for cooking and storing every kind of food?

In general yes, perfectly safe. But acid in food can eat into foil, so if you are wrapping, say, a cake laced with spirits, oiling the foil or wrapping the food in greaseproof paper first will prevent this. Food for freezing should be wrapped tightly in foil so it is completely airtight.

Foil should not be used in the microwave (see MICROWAVE OVENS), but is fine for using in conventional ovens, when you can put either side, matt or shiny, next to the food. Foil can be used to protect food from burning: for instance, place a piece over the head and tail of a fish, or the breast of a bird, while it is being roasted or baked. If you are wrapping food in foil for cooking, seal the parcel tightly but leave it loose to allow the air inside to circulate and cook the food evenly. And do not stretch foil tight across the top of a dish: put a pleat in the top to allow for expansion.

FOOD POISONING

HYGIENE RULES

How should I organise my kitchen to avoid food poisoning?

To avoid contamination of food, store it safely and take care that it is cooked thoroughly. There has been a five-fold rise in food poisoning cases in England and Wales from the mid 1980s to the mid 1990s. Possible causes range from the rise of giant food processing plants, in which a single infection can spread widely, through to declining cooking and hygiene skills in the home. To be safe, here are the golden rules to follow:

• Food should be stored in clean, dry, airtight containers, and raw and cooked foods kept separate.

• Food should be either cold or very hot, as bacteria multiply quickly at temperatures between 5°–65°C (40°–149°F).

• Discard any food that is past its 'use by' date, smells unpleasant or tastes as if it may be 'off'. If you have any doubts at all, get rid of it.

• Make sure meat and poultry are fully defrosted before cooking. When reheating food, make sure it is piping hot all the way through, and do not reheat it twice.

• Always wash your hands before handling food, and use separate bowls for washing up and for food preparation. Disinfect worktops, refrigerators and chopping boards often with an antibacterial cleaner.

CHICKEN AND EGG CARE

What are the common sources of salmonella poisoning, and how can I protect my family?

The foods which are most commonly infected with the salmonella group of bacteria are meat, poultry, eggs, milk and other dairy products. *Salmonella enteritidis PT4* is the most common food-poisoning bug. Symptoms usually appear in 12 to 48 hours and include tiredness, diarrhoea, high fever, severe abdominal pain and vomiting.

Cooking, providing the temperature at the centre of the food reaches 71°C (160°F), will destroy the salmonella bacteria. But as the bacteria reproduce, they produce toxins which will not be killed during cooking and which also cause food poisoning. This is why it is so important not to leave uncooked food lying around in the warm, moist conditions in which reproduction takes place. Store all food in cool, dry conditions, and take chilled and frozen food home quickly from the shop and put it in the refrigerator or freezer as soon as possible.

The Department of Health indicates that lightly cooked egg dishes are generally safe, but that foods which contain raw eggs should be avoided by the most vulnerable groups of people (see EGGS).

CLEAR, CLEAN WATER

Are water filters worth buying? Or should I use bottled water?

Mains tap water in Britain is safe to drink. If taste is a consideration, then both jug and on-line filters will reduce the taste and smell of chlorine, but it is very important to change the filters regularly.

Bottled water appears to be safe but it is not necessarily free of bacteria. There are standards for the maximum-permitted level of bacteria for the first 12 hours after bottling, but no clear rules for the period after that. The bottles may remain on supermarket shelves for up to 18 months in unrefrigerated conditions and tests have shown high levels of bacteria in many still waters. Sparkling waters generally contain fewer bacteria as the carbon dioxide in the bubbles inhibits the growth of these organisms.

Purchase only what you need at the time and finish it by the 'best before' date. Do not drink directly from the bottle as bacteria from your mouth could contaminate the rest of the water in the bottle.

All water given to babies should be boiled. Some bottled waters contain high levels of sodium which can cause damage to an infant's immature kidneys. Always check the label and choose one which lists a low level of sodium.

HIDDEN POISONS

Is it safe to cut mould off food and eat the unaffected part?

No. Throw away any mouldy food. Although not all moulds produce potentially harmful toxins, many do and it is best to be cautious as some moulds can be dangerous, even deadly. The only exception is mould added to foods deliberately, for example to the milk from which cheeses such as Brie are made.

By the time you see mould, what is obvious is the fruiting body of the organism. Spores that have not yet germinated are not visible, and if mould is visible elsewhere on the food, it may all be infected.

THE SAFE WAY TO STOCK YOUR FRIDGE

Below are basic guidelines regarding hygiene to keep in mind when stocking your refrigerator shelves. Remember that all food should be kept covered.

- The coldest parts of a refrigerator such as the one above are the lowest shelves. But if the fridge has a freezing compartment, the coldest shelves will be those immediately below it.
- Meat should be wrapped and put on the lowest shelf in the coldest area of the refrigerator. Never put raw meat on a shelf high in the refrigerator, in case it drips onto cooked food below. Cooked meat should be separated from raw meat. This is especially important if the cooked meat will not be heated again before it is served.
- Other foods which should be kept on the coldest, lower shelves are prepared salads, leftovers and desserts, in particular those made with cream.
- Foods which can be kept on the less cold shelves, or in the door, are dairy

products, including cheese, eggs, lard, opened jars, cartons and bottles, and salad dressings, both commercial and homemade.
- Salads and most vegetables should be kept in the salad drawer. Store them unwrapped so that air can circulate around them to keep them from spoiling too quickly. If salad greens are left in their plastic wrappings, the top should be opened enough to let air in.
- Fresh fruit will not ripen in the refrigerator, but fruit that is ripe can be stored in the salad drawer to inhibit further ripening and spoilage.
- Do not put hot food in the fridge as it will raise the temperature to an unsafe level. Cover the food to prevent contamination, cool quickly to room temperature and then refrigerate.

RARE BUG

What is listeriosis, and is it really such a serious risk?

Listeriosis is a food-borne disease caused by a listeria bacteria, but it is very rare. Foods most at risk include pâtés, soft mould-ripened cheeses such as Brie and Camembert and blue cheeses, ready-to-eat chickens and cook-chill foods.

As listeria can multiply at temperatures below that found in many domestic refrigerators, susceptible food should not be stored for more than four days. Listeria is also fairly heat-resistant, so cook-chill foods should be reheated to piping hot. Thorough cooking of susceptible foods is particularly important for pregnant women, who should also avoid unpasteurised (or raw) milk and any cheese made from it.

FOOD PROCESSORS

MIX AND CHOP

Which is the most useful machine for everyday domestic cooking, a food mixer or a food processor?

If a choice must be made, the food processor is the more useful. Processors are relatively lightweight and most of the functions are integral to, or built into, the machine. Food mixers tend to be more cumbersome and their attachments take up much more space.

Food processors make light work of laborious tasks such as chopping, grating and slicing, and some machines also have juice extractors. They make excellent pastry, provided the ingredients are not processed for too long. They do not whisk egg whites well because they do not incorporate enough air, but some machines have a separate whisking attachment. Care needs to be exercised with some models when mincing raw meat so that it is minced, not pulped to a mush.

Mixers are usually larger and are good for lengthy beating or kneading bread with the dough hook.

FREEZING

QUICK AND SLOW

Why are we told to freeze food quickly and thaw it slowly?

The quicker a food is frozen, the smaller the ice crystals that will form. Large ice crystals damage the cell walls of food so that when it is thawed, liquid is lost, including soluble nutrients. Meat especially loses so much moisture that it will be dry when cooked if frozen too slowly. This is why many freezers contain a fast-freeze compartment for the initial freezing process.

Thawing, however, should take place as slowly as possible since rapid thawing also leads to a loss of moisture and dry, tasteless food.

FULL SAVINGS

Is it more economical to keep the freezer full at all times?

Yes, a full freezer retains more cold when the door is opened. With a half-empty freezer, a lot of cold air will escape whenever the door is opened and more energy is then needed to bring the freezer back down to the right temperature.

Try to freeze small quantities of food at a time, separated out. Once frozen, pack them together closely. Remember to rotate food regularly and label it, or what you lose in wasted food will cancel out what you gain in energy savings.

FANTASTIC PLASTIC

What containers and wrappings are best for freezing food?

Heavyweight polythene bags are the cheapest and most effective wrappers because they take various shapes of food without creating too many air pockets.

The freezer atmosphere is very drying and direct contact with the icy air may cause 'freezer burn' (dry discoloured patches), so most foods need to be carefully wrapped before freezing. Whatever airtight container you use, it must be robust enough to withstand some rough handling in the freezer.

Pour liquids into polythene bags set in rectangular containers to freeze. Leave 2.5 cm (1 in) between the top of the liquid and the container to allow for expansion. Once solid, lift the polythene bags out of the containers (which allows the containers to be used elsewhere). The frozen bags of liquid can then be stacked neatly to save space.

Label frozen foods immediately with the contents and the date. Keep a record of what is in the freezer so that you remember what is there and can plan to use the food systematically in date order.

THE BIG THAW

What should I do if my freezer breaks down, or when there is an unexpected power cut?

Check first to see if the plug has been pulled out, a fuse has blown or the thermostat has been misset before calling for maintenance. And keep the freezer door closed while you check. If there has been a power cut, food remains solid and safe for 16–24 hours, providing the door has not been opened.

If you have advance warning of a cut in power, pack out any gaps in the freezer with crumpled newspaper and do not open the door during the cut, or for 2 hours afterwards. Food that is still solid with ice crystals is safe to eat. Foods that have defrosted may be cooked and eaten, but ice cream or foods that contain cream are best thrown away, as are ready-meals near their use-by date. If possible, insure your freezer contents.

If your freezer does break down and some of the contents deteriorate, leaving an unpleasant smell, you can remove it by wiping out the inside of the freezer with warm water to which you have added a little bicarbonate of soda or some vinegar. In addition, a small dish of bicarbonate of soda placed in the refrigerator will help to absorb the smell of strong foods.

THE FRUIT CROP

How should I freeze fruit?

Fruits for freezing must be just ripe, and of prime quality. Wash them only if necessary and dry well. Do not freeze fruit in contact with any metal, including foil.

Soft fruit such as blackberries, black and redcurrants, gooseberries and raspberries are best frozen separately on trays lined with baking paper as they will keep better and defrost easily. When solid, pack them into polythene bags or boxes.

Soft fruit can also be packed with sugar before freezing so that as it thaws, the fruit and sugar combine to become a syrup. Sprinkle 100 g (3 ½ oz) of sugar over each 450 g (1 lb) of soft fruit before freezing.

Fresh raspberries, frozen on lined baking trays then packed in polythene bags, extend the summer season.

Apples, apricots, peaches and pears tend to turn brown as they thaw, so freeze them in an acidulated syrup made from 450 g (1 lb) of sugar, 1 litre (1 pint 15 fl oz) of water and the juice of a lemon. Allow 300 ml (10 fl oz) of sugar syrup for each 450 g (1 lb) of fruit.

Bananas will turn brown in the freezer, however, you can mash them with lemon juice before freezing and defrost to use in cooking.

ONCE IS ENOUGH

Why should you not refreeze food once it has been defrosted?

Freezing will prevent bacteria from multiplying but it does not destroy them. Once frozen food has been thawed, the bacteria may multiply with renewed energy. If food is frozen and thawed repeatedly, bacteria could reach dangerous levels.

You can refreeze food safely if it has been cooked after thawing. However, freezing also results in some loss of moisture and if food is repeatedly frozen and thawed, it will become unpleasantly dry. Fibrous food like meat also loses its texture as it thaws, and will become flabby if it is refrozen and thawed again, say in a casserole.

BLANCH FIRST

Is it really necessary to blanch vegetables before freezing?

To preserve the colour, flavour, texture and nutritional content of vegetables, you must blanch them before freezing (see box, below).

Fresh vegetables contain natural enzymes which help them to grow and ripen. Blanching vegetables – plunging them briefly into boiling water then into cold – inhibits the action of these enzymes, which would otherwise cause deterioration during storage in the freezer.

BLANCHING FRESH VEGETABLES

Fresh vegetables should be trimmed and blanched before freezing. Use 3 litres (5 pints 5 fl oz) of boiling water and 2 teaspoons of salt per 500 g (1 lb 2 oz) of vegetables.

Place the trimmed vegetables in a wire basket and plunge it into the boiling, salted water. Quickly bring the water back to the boil and time the cooking according to the chart (right). Then plunge the basket into some water made very cold by the addition of ice cubes. Cool, drain and pack the vegetables for freezing.

BLANCHING FRESH VEGETABLES

VEGETABLE	VEGETABLE PREPARATION	BLANCHING TIME
Asparagus	Arrange stems of the same length and thickness in bundles.	Thin – 2 minutes Medium – 3 minutes Thick – 4 minutes
Beans	Wash and cut into 1 cm (½ in) slices. Leave french and string beans whole. Slice runner beans.	2 minutes
Broad beans	Use young beans only, and pod them.	2 minutes
Broccoli	Trim the heads into even-sized florets and cut away the tough stalks.	Thin – 3 minutes Thick – 4 minutes
Brussels sprouts	Wash, and trim away the outer leaves.	3 minutes
Carrots	Leave young carrots whole, but peel and slice larger ones.	Whole – 3 minutes Sliced – 2 minutes
Cauliflower	Wash and divide it into florets. Add a tablespoon of lemon juice to the boiling water.	3 minutes
Celeriac	Thickly peel off the skin and dice.	4 minutes
Corn-on-the-cob	Remove the husks and silk from the cobs and trim the ends.	Small – 4 minutes Large – 8 minutes
Courgettes	Cut into 1 cm (½ in) slices.	1 minute
Leeks	Remove the outer leaves. Wash the leeks well and slice if thick.	2 – 4 minutes, according to size
Parsnips	Choose young parsnips: scrape off the skin with a knife, wash and slice.	2 minutes
Peas	Use young peas only and shell.	1 minute
Spinach	Strip out the tough ribs and freeze only the tender leaves.	1 minute

ICED CREAM

Do cream and yoghurt freeze?

The higher the fat content of the cream, the better it will freeze. Jersey, clotted, double and whipping cream all freeze well and keep for three months. Half-whip the cream before freezing or it will separate on thawing. Adding a teaspoon of sugar to 150 ml (5 fl oz) of whipped cream before freezing will stabilise it. Single cream does not freeze but fruit flavoured yoghurts do. If they separate on thawing, simply whisk with a fork. Plain yoghurt mixed with honey also freezes well.

BARGAIN JOINT

My butcher is offering half a lamb at a bargain price - but will I be able to fit it into my freezer?

Meat sold at a good discount is worth having, and half a lamb will fit into a small freezer. Ask your butcher to cut the lamb into joints, trimming off the excess fat and removing bones where possible as these take up valuable space.

It is essential to wrap meat well to prevent the fat from turning rancid. Double-wrap the meat using some heavy-duty polythene bags and separate the chops and steaks with layers of freezer tissue.

FISHERMAN'S CATCH

I have been given a whole salmon. Should I gut and scale it before I put it in the freezer?

Yes, it is best to gut fresh fish before freezing. Wash and scale the fish, then gut it and wash the cavity thoroughly under running water. Pat the fish dry and wrap it in cling film or in a sealed polythene bag and freeze. Whole salmon, freshwater and oily fish can be stored for two months while white fish can be stored two to three months.

Whole fish are best when thawed slowly to retain their moisture and texture. Fish steaks and fillets are best thawed too, but they may be cooked from frozen if you increase the cooking time by a third.

LUNCH ON ICE

Is it safe to freeze a week's supply of sandwiches and take them to work frozen, letting them thaw out by lunchtime?

It is well worth making sandwiches for the freezer if you eat packed lunches regularly. Use firm, day-old slices of bread and spread them with softened butter right to the edges. Wrap filled sandwiches in freezer tissue to keep them separate, then pack in polythene bags.

Use cheese, meat, fish or pâté for the fillings and avoid hard-boiled eggs which can go rubbery, mayonnnaise which curdles and fresh salad which goes soggy.

Keep sandwiches in the freezer for no longer than two months. You can let them thaw in their wrappings for 3 hours or so during the morning. Transport them in a rigid, plastic box to avoid damage.

To the rescue!

Freezer burn is a greyish white patch that appears on frozen food when it is exposed to the air. Its development is due to inadequate packaging. While the burn causes dryness and some loss of colour and texture, the food is still perfectly safe to eat.

DON'T FREEZE THESE

Are there any foods that cannot be frozen satisfactorily?

Some foods do not freeze well because the texture is ruined. This is particularly true of fruit and vegetables with a high water content, such as bananas, cucumbers, lettuce and watercress, although some may be frozen in purée form.

Whole strawberries keep their colour and flavour well and are excellent for combining in mousses or fools, but the texture deteriorates and they become too soft to

be used whole when thawed. Full-fat milk separates after freezing, but skimmed and semi-skimmed milks that have been homogenised may be frozen for up to a month.

Eggs cannot be frozen in their shells; however, both whites and yolks will freeze well, either lightly beaten together or separated.

Emulsion sauces such as mayonnaise and hollandaise sauce do not tend to freeze well because they will separate when thawed.

Jellies, both savoury and sweet, lose their texture if frozen and would have to be reboiled and allowed to set again after thawing.

Curries freeze well, although after three to four months the spices will change flavour and may become peppery or fade. The flavour of garlic-laden foods, for example soups and casseroles, will intensify during freezing and can become unpleasantly strong.

FRUIT

ORGANIC IS FRESHER

Can I be sure that organic fruit is the same in every shop, and is it really a better purchase?

Fruit that is labelled organic has been grown without the use of artificial pesticides or fertilisers and will not have been irradiated. Regardless of where you shop, all the organic fruit sold in Britain, including any that is imported from abroad, is produced to the same European Community standards.

Growers of organic fruit claim their produce is safer, tastes better and is more nutritious. Other producers claim there is no difference.

For maximum nutritional benefit, fruit should be eaten soon after picking because its nutritional value declines over time. Organic fruit growers do not use fungicides to preserve their fruit, so it must reach customers quickly. Consequently, organic fruit is generally fresher and could therefore be described as more nutritious.

READY TO ENJOY

How can I tell when fruit is ripe?

A pleasing appearance is only one clue to the ripeness of fruit. Today, many fruits are artificially ripened without reaching their natural stage of maturity. Although these fruits may look attractive, they can nevertheless taste disappointing. It is important, therefore, to also use your senses of smell and touch when selecting the best fresh fruit.

Unwrinkled fruit that feels heavy for its size is likely to have a good juice content and a sweet flavour. Skins should be unblemished and free of bruises, splits and any signs of insect damage. Tough, dry and wrinkled skins on citrus fruits indicate that the rind has lost its essential oils and the zest will not be suitable for use in cooking.

The ripeness of many tree fruits, such as the juicier varieties of dessert pear, can be ascertained by a light squeeze with the thumb; if the fruit yields to this gentle pressure it should be pleasant to eat.

Soft fruit should be dry and undamaged. Check the packaging of berries for crushing, leakage or signs of mould or wetness.

Test melons and pineapples for ripeness by sniffing the base of the fruit. An attractive, sweet, fresh fragrance indicates the fruit is ripe.

Overripe fruit smells musty and often has soft, dark patches on the skin, indicating that the interior flesh also contains rotten patches.

DELIGHT IN STORE

Can you tell me the best way to store fresh fruit at home?

For the best flavour, you should buy or pick fruit that is ripe and ready to eat. But as fruit cannot always be bought daily, storing it under the right conditions will help to keep it fresh longer.

Apples, grapefruit, lemons, melons, oranges, pears and pineapple will keep well for several days in a fruit bowl at room temperature, especially if they are bought or picked slightly before they are ripe.

However, you must be sure to keep these fruits away from direct sunlight. Fresh bananas should also be stored at room temperature.

Slightly underripe apricots, nectarines and peaches can be stored at room temperature to help them ripen, but fruit that is already ripe should be refrigerated.

Loose lemons and limes can be kept for several weeks in the refrigerator. Place them unwrapped in the salad drawer ensuring that there is enough room so that air can circulate around the fruit.

All soft fruits are highly perishable and should be refrigerated as soon as you get them home. Put strawberries or currants in a colander standing on a plate and cover the top with another plate or foil. The holes in the colander will allow air to circulate around the fruit, keeping it dry. When berries become wet, their decomposition accelerates. Blackberries, loganberries and raspberries are best spread out in a single layer on a large plate. Cover them loosely with a lid, some kitchen foil or cling film.

Cherries will keep for up to ten days in the refrigerator. Keep them wrapped loosely in a perforated, polythene bag. Ripe, exotic tropical fruits and grapes are also best kept refrigerated. All refrigerated fruit should be brought back to room temperature before eating to bring out its full flavour.

Many supermarkets now sell fruit such as peaches and pears labelled 'ready to eat now'. However, if you do intend to serve the fruit that very day, it is still best to test it for ripeness before purchase.

SWEET ENOUGH

Is it really necessary for me to use a sugar syrup when making a fresh fruit salad?

No, although sugar syrup is useful when making a fruit salad that contains apples and pears. Adding them to a hot sugar syrup before adding the other fruits will help to soften their crisp texture and make them more pleasant to eat. Most

HOW TO STORE HOME-GROWN FRUIT

If you are lucky enough to have a glut of home-grown fruit, try storing some of it away carefully and enjoying it a few months later.

1 Late varieties of apples will keep for several months when placed individually in a plastic bag pierced with air holes (early varieties and windfalls do not store well). Place the wrapped apples, keeping them slightly apart, in single layers in wooden trays and store at an even temperature of about 4°C (40°F) in a cellar, garage, loft or garden shed.

2 Apples can otherwise be stored unwrapped, in the same storage conditions on slatted wooden trays or greengrocers' fibre trays. If you are using fibre trays, pierce them all over with air holes. Stacking the filled trays saves space and allows the fruit to be inspected easily.

3 Fresh pears, too, can be stored unwrapped and in a single layer on a tray or shelf, in a cool room or shed at 2°- 4°C (36°- 40°F). Ensure the pears do not touch each other.

fruits are naturally quite juicy and sweet, needing only a sprinkling of caster sugar to help draw out their juice. Or you can use a natural fruit juice such as apple, lemon, orange or passion fruit juice as an alternative to syrup. Fruit can also be macerated with red or white wine and spirits such as brandy or rum, or liqueurs such as Cointreau or kirsch. Whether you need to add sugar to the salad depends on the natural sweetness of the fruit.

There are no rigid rules for making a fruit salad, the combinations being limited only by the cook's imagination. Simplicity is the key to success, however, as the salads here show. Try to balance flavours, colours and textures. If you are using mainly soft fruit, add melon or pineapple for a contrasting texture. You could make a salad with a mixture of all citrus fruits, or try a selection of autumnal fruits such as apples, blackberries, pears and plums, or keep the range tropical. For details of how to select and prepare exotic fruits, see page 166.

Golden fruit salad

Serves: 6
Preparation time: 40 minutes
Cooking time: 10 minutes

For the caramel
225 g (8 oz) granulated sugar
4 tablespoons water

For the fruit salad
6 medium oranges
2 grapefruit
3 large, ripe peaches
3 large, ripe nectarines

1 To make the caramel, line a small baking tray with nonstick baking paper and set aside.
2 Make the sugar syrup by putting the sugar and water in a saucepan and heating gently until dissolved, without stirring. Brush down any sugar crystals on the sides of the pan with water. Bring it to the boil and cook until it turns a golden colour.
3 Immediately pour the caramel onto the lined baking tray and set it aside until cooled and set hard. As the caramel will have formed only a thin layer, it should set in 10 - 15 minutes in a cool place.
4 To make the fruit salad, peel the oranges and grapefruit (see box, page 106), cutting the oranges into thin slices and the grapefruit into segments. Halve, stone and skin the peaches and nectarines, if you wish (see box, opposite), then cut them into neat slices, cutting across the halves for a more attractive slice.
5 Lightly tap the set caramel all over with something heavy until it has broken into several small pieces. Put

Colour-coordinated fruit salads make a pretty dessert. The golden fruit salad is sprinkled with caramel, the green salad with sprigs of lemon balm.

a quarter of the caramel into an airtight container, seal well and set aside until it is needed.
6 Arrange a third of each prepared fruit in the bottom of the serving dish and sprinkle with a third of the remaining crushed caramel. Layer the dish twice more with the fruit and crushed caramel, ending with a layer of caramel pieces.
7 Pour over any remaining orange and grapefruit juice, then cover the dish with polythene food wrap. Set the fruit salad aside for 2 - 3 hours, or until the caramel has dissolved.
8 Just before serving, sprinkle the reserved caramel pieces over the top. Serve the fruit salad with whipped cream or Greek yoghurt.
Variations
Add a few tablespoons of fruit-based liqueur such as Cointreau, Grand Marnier or kirsch to the fruit salad.

Green fruit salad

SERVES: 6
PREPARATION TIME: 30 minutes
COOKING TIME: 5 minutes

---

70 g (2 ½ oz) granulated sugar
3 limes, well scrubbed under warm,
   running water
2 green dessert apples, washed
2 ripe, firm pears, washed
675 g (1 lb 8 oz) green-fleshed galia
   or honeydew melon
3 kiwi fruit
225 g (8 oz) seedless green grapes,
   washed (and halved, if large)
To decorate: sprigs of fresh lemon
   balm, optional

---

1 Pour 425 ml (15 fl oz) of cold water
into a small stainless-steel or enamel
saucepan and add the sugar. Pare the
rind from the limes using a zester or
peeler and add it to the pan.
2 Stir over a moderate heat until the
sugar has completely dissolved, then
bring the sugar syrup to the boil and
simmer it for 2 minutes. Remove the
saucepan from the heat.
3 Squeeze the juice from the pared
limes, stir it into the sugar syrup and
then pour the flavoured syrup into a
large serving bowl.
4 Working quickly, quarter and core
the apples and slice them directly
into the hot lime syrup. Then peel,
quarter and core the pears and slice
them into the syrup as well.
5 Cut the melon in half, remove the
seeds and then either scoop out the
flesh with a melon baller or cut it
into cubes. Add the melon and any
remaining juice to the bowl.
6 Peel and slice the kiwi fruit and
add them to the fruit salad with
the grapes. Stir the fruits together
gently, cover the bowl and leave to
stand for 2 - 3 hours before serving.
Serve the salad at room temperature
or slightly chilled, decorated with
lemon balm, if using.

VARIATIONS
As an alternative to lemon balm, stir
a handful of freshly chopped mint
leaves through the fruit salad just
before serving. For an alcoholic kick,
add a tablespoon of vodka, either
plain or lemon-flavoured, or sweet
white wine per person.

Tropical fruit salad

SERVES: 6
PREPARATION TIME: 30 minutes
COOKING TIME: none

---

60 g (2 ¼ oz) caster sugar
1 teaspoon ground cinnamon
½ teaspoon ground cardamom
2 passion fruit
1 large, ripe mango
1 large, ripe papaya
675 g (1 lb 8 oz) pineapple
225 g (8 oz) fresh dates
12 lychees
4 tablespoons rum
To garnish: a few physalis, optional

---

1 Put the sugar and spices into a
small bowl and mix together well.
2 Cut the passion fruit in half and
scoop the seeds out into a nylon
sieve placed over a bowl (see box,
overleaf). Work the seeds with the
back of a spoon to extract the juice.
Discard the seeds.
3 Peel and slice the mango and the
papaya. Skin, quarter and core the
pineapple then dice the flesh. Halve
and stone the dates, and peel and
stone the lychees (see box, overleaf).
4 Put all of the prepared fruits into
the bowl with the passion fruit juice,
sprinkle in the spicy sugar, pour in
the rum and gently mix together.
Cover and macerate for 2 - 3 hours.
5 Just before serving, transfer the
fruits and the flavoured juices to a
serving bowl and decorate with the
physalis, their leaves pulled back
(see box, overleaf). Serve at room
temperature or chilled.

WILD FRUITS

*Is it safe to use fruits which grow
wild in hedgerows? If so, should
you eat them raw or cooked?*

There are many edible fruits available for free in the hedgerows. You
can use them to make fruit pies and
flans, ice cream, jams and chutneys,
homemade wines, fruit syrups or
even infused spirits.

Depending on where you live,
you can find fruit such as wild bilberries (blueberries), blackberries,
cherries, cherry plums, crab apples,
elderberries, rosehips, sloes, wild

STONING FRUIT

*With some fruits, you must first
remove their stone before cutting
the flesh for use in a fruit salad.*

To remove the stone from tree fruits
such as apricots, nectarines, peaches
or plums, carefully cut around the
fruit following the natural groove.
Gently twist the halves in opposite
directions, separate and remove the
stone. This method can also be used
when stoning avocados.

strawberries and the berries (haws)
of the hawthorn bush. Cranberries
and bilberries are the hardest to
find. Bilberries, blackberries and
wild strawberries can be eaten raw
but the rest must be cooked.

Although these berries are all
safe to use, it is advisable to pick
them well away from the roadside
to ensure that they are not contaminated by exhaust fumes. Wild fruit
must also be washed before using,
especially those that were picked
from hedgerows surrounding land
that may have been sprayed with
fertilisers or pesticides.

Save it!

Overripe fruit need not
be thrown away. Simply purée it
with some caster sugar and a little
lemon juice to make a coulis.
You can then serve this as a
simple fruit sauce to accompany
desserts such as ice cream or fold
it into whipped cream, Greek
yoghurt or fromage frais to make
a delectable fruit fool.

EXOTIC FRUIT

The medical advice to eat fresh fruit every day has never been easier to follow as more and more mouth-watering tropical fruits arrive in the shops. Here we show some of the tastiest newcomers, and explain how to enjoy them.

Cinnamon, cardamom and rum add a Caribbean flavour to a salad made with sweet and fragrant tropical fruit (see page 165).

CHERIMOYA (CUSTARD APPLE)

A heart-shaped green or purple fruit with either smooth or scaly skin, cherimoya has sweet creamy flesh with large inedible seeds. It can be eaten spooned from the skin or used to make creamy desserts.

GUAVA

A good source of vitamin C, a guava can be round or pear-shaped. It is ready to eat when it is yellow and has a fragrant aroma. To eat the fruit, cut it in half lengthways and scoop out the flesh and edible seeds with a teaspoon. Eat it with cream, or poach it in sugar syrup, enhancing the flavour with a little lemon juice.

KIWANO (HORNED MELON)

Kiwano's subtle flavour resembles a blend of banana, lime and passion fruit. When ripe, the skin is golden orange.

To serve kiwanos, cut them into quarters lengthways and eat the flesh straight from the skin, as you would a slice of watermelon, or cut them in half and scoop the flesh out with a spoon. The seeds are edible. Kiwanos contain a lot of juice, which can be extracted in the same way as passion fruit juice (see opposite page), then sweetened to taste and drunk or used for desserts.

KIWANO

LYCHEE AND RAMBUTAN

The prickly shell of a ripe lychee can be reddish-brown, deep pink or white depending on the variety. The aromatic pearly white flesh tastes sweet yet slightly acidic. Rambutans, which have soft red or orange spines, are similar to lychees but have less flavour.

To eat lychees, peel away the rough prickly skin with your fingers and eat them like a cherry, discarding the stone. You can serve fresh lychees or rambutans with ice cream and sorbets to add an aromatic flavour, stone them and add them to exotic fruit salads, or liquidise the flesh to make a delicately perfumed drink.

MANGOSTEEN

One of the most delicious tropical fruits. The thick, dark-purple skin conceals segments of juicy, sweet white pulp.

Mangosteens are ripe to eat when their skin turns deep purple, almost black. Slice off the top of the mangosteen with a sharp knife, then cut down deeply through the skin on either side from stem to calyx. Pull the skin carefully away to expose the fruit inside and eat the segments like a small satsuma. Alternatively, the mangosteen may simply be cut in half and the flesh scooped out with a spoon.

PAPAYA (PAW PAW)

Papaya (sometimes known as paw paw) vary in size, colour and flavour depending on the variety. The dense, firm flesh is highly perfumed, juicy and sweet - something between a melon and a peach. The flesh may be orange, orange-yellow or red. The skin becomes yellow as the fruit ripens. Green fruit has a poor flavour.

To eat papaya, cut it in half lengthways and scoop out the black seeds, then eat the flesh straight from the skin with a spoon. For extra flavour, you can score the cut flesh with a knife and sprinkle lemon or lime juice over it before eating. Papaya can also be peeled and cut into slices or cubes to make a sweet addition to a fruit or vegetable salad.

The flesh can also be liquidised to make a rich, sweet drink. Papaya can also be used as a marinade to tenderise meat, as it contains an enzyme which breaks down tissue.

POMEGRANATE

PASSION FRUIT AND GRANADILLA

Passion fruit and granadilla come from the same botanical family. Purple passion fruit has a powerful flavour, yellow granadilla is more subtle and sweeter. Both are ripe when the skin begins to wrinkle.

To eat passion fruit or granadilla, slice off the top and spoon out the flesh with a teaspoon, or bite through the skin and suck out the flesh and edible seeds.

Passion fruit juice is very sweet (some would say cloying), and is often used to make drinks, ice creams, sorbets and other desserts. To extract the juice, scoop out the flesh into a stainless-steel or nylon sieve placed over a bowl, and push it through using the back of a wooden spoon, discarding the seeds. If you are putting the flesh into a liquidiser, you must pick out the seeds first, as they have a bitter, unpleasant taste when crushed.

PHYSALIS (CAPE GOOSEBERRY)

Pale and papery husks conceal shiny berries with a sweet-sharp flavour. When ripe, the berries are golden-orange.

To eat physalis, simply pull back the outer husks and bite off the whole fruit. But physalis are almost better used with their leaves curled back as a pretty garnish for cakes and desserts. They look prettier still, and taste even more delicious, if they are dipped first in a caramel, chocolate or fondant coating.

POMEGRANATE

The pomegranate has a tough, brightly coloured skin containing translucent, deep-pink kernels which have a specially refreshing sweet flavour.

To eat a pomegranate, slice off the top and bottom and score through the skin from top to bottom in four places with a sharp knife. Gently pull the pomegranate apart, still in its skin, to expose the kernels, and eat them with a spoon. Whether you swallow the seeds or spit them out is up to you, but the internal membrane separating the fruit into sections is not pleasant to eat. You can also use the brilliant ruby flesh as a garnish for sweet or savoury dishes.

To extract the juice, gently squeeze the whole pomegranate in your hand to crush and break down the kernels within. Then make a deep cut through the skin into the flesh and pour out the pomegranate juice into a bowl.

STAR FRUIT

Shiny and five-sided, the star fruit has a translucent pinkish-yellow colour and tart flesh.

To eat star fruit, wash and dry them and trim off the top edge of the ridges with a potato peeler. Then cut them cross-ways into thin, star-shaped slices. Star fruit is quite tart, so poach the slices gently for about 30 seconds in sugar syrup before adding to fruit salads or using as a garnish.

TAMARILLO

A shiny gold or red oval fruit, the tamarillo, or tree tomato, has yellow flesh like a plum and purple edible seeds. The sweet-sour flavour is rather an acquired taste, at its best when the fruit is ripe and soft to the touch. Cut it in half widthways and eat it with a spoon, but do not eat the outer skin.

GUAVA

MANGOSTEEN

LYCHEE

TAMARILLO

CHERIMOYA

RAMBUTAN

PAPAYA

FRUIT CAKES

SUNKEN FRUIT

Why does the fruit always sink to the bottom of my fruit cakes?

Dried fruits are heavy and will sink if a cake mixture is too soft and wet. If the fruit has been washed, spread it out to dry well on a cloth before adding it to the cake mixture. Glacé cherries are particularly heavy and covered in sticky syrup, so always wash, dry and quarter the cherries to make them lighter.

If you find the fruit still goes to the bottom of the tin, toss it first in a little flour or ground almonds, as in the following recipe. This technique should help to spread the fruit evenly throughout the cake.

Rich fruit cake

MAKES: 1 x 20 cm (8 in) round cake (suitable for a family Christmas or celebration cake)
PREPARATION TIME: about 1 hour, plus 6 weeks maturing time
COOKING TIME: 3 1/2 - 4 hours

---

100 g (3 1/2 oz) glacé cherries
100 g (3 1/2 oz) mixed peel, finely chopped
225 g (8 oz) currants
225 g (8 oz) large raisins
225 g (8 oz) sultanas
50 g (1 3/4 oz) ground almonds
50 g (1 3/4 oz) whole almonds
225 g (8 oz) plain flour
1/2 teaspoon salt
1 teaspoon mixed spice
225 g (8 oz) salted butter
225 g (8 oz) soft, dark muscovado sugar
4 eggs, size 3, lightly beaten
1 tablespoon black treacle
1/2 teaspoon vanilla essence
Finely grated zest of 1 orange or lemon
2 tablespoons milk
2 tablespoons brandy

---

1 Preheat the oven to 150°C (300°F, gas mark 2). Grease a 20 cm (8 in) round cake tin and line it with a double layer of greaseproof paper.

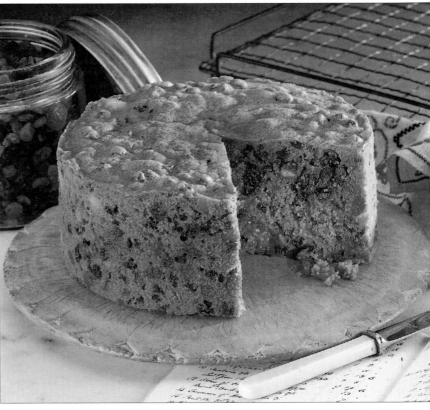

Dark from muscovado sugar and black treacle, this rich fruit cake is crammed with fruit, nuts and spices, then laced with brandy to keep it lusciously moist.

2 Wrap a layer of brown paper or newspaper around the outside of the tin and fix it tightly with string.
3 Wash the syrup from the cherries, then pat dry, quarter and place in a bowl. Add the mixed peel, dried fruits, ground and whole almonds.
4 Sift the flour, salt and mixed spice together then add 4 tablespoons to the fruit mixture and toss together.
5 Cream the butter and muscovado sugar together until very soft, light and fluffy. Then add the eggs to the creamed mixture a little at a time, adding a teaspoon of the flour with each addition to prevent curdling.
6 Fold in the remaining flour, then add the fruit mixture, treacle, vanilla, zest and milk. Mix well together then turn into the tin. Smooth the batter level and bake for 2 hours, then lower the temperature to 140°C (275°F, gas mark 1) for a further 1 1/2 - 2 hours, until a skewer or knife pushed into the centre comes out clean.
7 Leave the cake to cool in the tin for about an hour, then turn out onto a wire rack. When completely cooled, prick the surface with a fine skewer or fork, then brush or spoon the brandy evenly over the top.
8 Leave the cake for about an hour to allow the brandy to soak in.
9 Wrap the cake in a double layer of greaseproof paper, then foil, and seal the wrapping with tape to make it airtight. The paper protects the foil from the acid in the fruit, which can cause corrosion or mould. Store in a dark, dry place for at least six weeks, and leave for longer if possible.
10 Rich fruit cake is almost always covered with marzipan and then iced (see ICING). But if you prefer, you could simply brush a glaze of sieved apricot jam on the top and set whole almonds or glacé fruits into this. Clear honey is another possible base for decorative nuts.

VARIATION

For extra richness, soak the dried fruit in brandy for two to three days before baking, as well as brushing the cake with brandy afterwards.

ADDING SPIRIT

Does adding brandy to a fruit cake help it to keep longer?

Adding brandy or other spirits to a rich fruit cake does help it to keep, and gives it a moist texture and mellow flavour. When the cake is cool, skewer the top in several places and spoon or brush the spirit over. Wrap in greaseproof paper and foil, then store at a dry, even temperature. If you can, make the cake at least three months ahead, adding more spirit every month.

HOW MUCH CAKE?

How can I work out what size of wedding cake to make?

The table below shows how many small portions each size cake will usually yield. Use this to work out how many tiers you will need.

Portions	Square	Round
16	13 cm (5 in)	15 cm (6 in)
28	18 cm (7 in)	20 cm (8 in)
48	23 cm (9 in)	25 cm (10 in)
90	28 cm (11 in)	30 cm (12 in)
136	33 cm (13 in)	35 cm (14 in)

FRUIT DRINKS

KEEPING JUICE

If I squeeze oranges to make my own fresh juice, how long can I keep it in the refrigerator?

For maximum nutritional benefit, it is best to drink the juice as soon as possible. Orange juice can be kept for up to two days in an airtight container in the refrigerator, but the amount of vitamin C declines.

EXOTIC FRUIT DRINKS

I like unusual fruit juice drinks, but is it worth buying fresh fruit and juicing them at home?

Fruit juice drinks are not difficult to make with the help of an electric blender or a food processor. And they are superior to those you can buy, both in flavour and nutritionally, because you need not add any sugar and can avoid artificial preservatives, colours and flavours.

The flesh of mangoes, peaches, pineapples, raspberries and strawberries in different combinations make good drinks puréed in the blender, either alone or with added crushed ice. Dilute the juice to taste with mineral, soda or tonic water; use it for milkshakes; or add it to sparkling white wine or champagne. (See also JUICERS.)

CUTTING DOWN SUGAR

Can I make a fruit cordial that is not as sugary as the bottled ones?

Traditional fruit cordials and syrups are made with a high proportion of sugar which acts as a preservative and enables them to be kept for several months.

Homemade syrups and cordials using the traditional berry fruits can be made using less sugar than is usual. The Fruit Cordial recipe overleaf is a lower-sugar version which can be stored in the refrigerator for up to three months. It has a slightly sharp flavour but is still sweet enough for most tastes.

HOW TO ASSEMBLE A TIERED WEDDING CAKE

Wooden dowelling skewers are available from cake decorating shops, or you can cut your own. The skewers should go through the cake to the board, with enough above to reach the top of the decorative hollow pillars that cover them.

1 Cut a circle of greaseproof paper the size of the bottom tier, fold it into quarters and push a pin through about 8 cm (3¼ in) from the outer edge to make four evenly spaced pinpricks. Open out the circle on the cake and pierce through the pinholes to mark the position of the supporting pillars.

2 Push skewers into the cake at the marked positions and cover with the decorative pillars. Take another circle of paper the size of the second tier, and fold and mark it as before. It is important to locate the new pillars directly above the ones beneath, so that the cake has adequate support.

HOW TO CUT A CAKE

Use a serrated knife and cut half the cake at a time. Make the long cuts first, 8 cm (3¼ in) apart, then short cuts at right angles every 2 cm (¾ in). Have hot water on hand so you can rinse the knife, which will keep the slices neater.

Fruit cordial

MAKES: 725 ml (1 pint 5 fl oz)
PREPARATION TIME: 30 minutes
COOKING TIME: 20 - 30 minutes

675 g (1 lb 8 oz) prepared fruit,
* such as blackberries,*
* blackcurrants, cranberries,*
* loganberries, raspberries,*
* redcurrants or strawberries*
115 - 225 g (4 - 8 oz) caster sugar

1 Put all the prepared fruit into a
large heatproof bowl. If you are using
blackberries, loganberries, raspberries
or strawberries, add 90 ml (3¼ fl oz)
of cold water; if using redcurrants,
add 200 ml (7 fl oz) of water; and if
using blackcurrants or cranberries,
add 600 ml (1 pint) of water.
2 Place the bowl over a saucepan of
gently simmering water and heat for
some 20 - 30 minutes until the juice
flows freely. Occasionally crush the
fruit with a potato masher to help to
extract the juice. When the fruit is
very soft, take the bowl off the heat.
3 Scald a nylon or stainless-steel
sieve, a large bowl and a large square
of muslin with boiling water; drain
the bowl and sieve and wring out
the muslin. Place the sieve over the
bowl and line it with the muslin.
4 Pour the pulped fruit and syrup
into the sieve and leave it to drain
for about 20 minutes until almost all
of the juice has dripped through the
sieve into the bowl.
5 Take two opposite sides of the
muslin and fold them over the fruit
so that it forms a secure parcel. Twist
the ends of the muslin tightly in
opposite directions to squeeze out
all the remaining juice. Once the
juice has been extracted, discard the
pips and dry pulp remaining in the
muslin. This method produces a
clear, smooth syrup; for a grainier,
more textured juice, you can use a
nylon sieve without the muslin.
6 Pour the fruit juice into a clean,
stainless-steel or enamel saucepan.
Add the sugar gradually, a tablespoon
at a time, until sweetened to taste -
sweet fruits such as loganberries,
raspberries and strawberries will
need about 100 g (3½ oz) while the
other fruits will require more.

*Cordials need not be overly sweet. This pleasantly sharp thirst-quencher combines
blackberries, raspberries and redcurrants to make a sparkling summer drink.*

7 Place the saucepan over a low
heat and stir until the sugar has
completely dissolved, but do not
allow the syrup to become too hot.
8 Pour into clean and preferably
sterilised bottles (see CHUTNEY), seal
with a tight-fitting lid and store
refrigerated for up to three months.
9 To serve, pour the syrup onto ice
and dilute to taste, using about one
part syrup to two or three parts
mineral, soda, tap or tonic water.

Cordial and convenient

For long-term storage, pour the
syrup into ice-cube trays and freeze
it. Frozen cubes can be removed as
required, put into glasses or a jug,
allowed to melt and then diluted
to taste. Use three or four cubes
for each glass. The syrup will keep
in the freezer for up to six months.

Fresh lemonade

SERVES: 6
PREPARATION TIME: 20 minutes, plus
3 - 4 hours standing and chilling
COOKING TME: none

7 large lemons, well washed
1.2 litres (2 pints) boiling water
75 - 100 g (2 3/4 - 3 1/2 oz)
    caster sugar
To serve: ice cubes, optional
To decorate: sprigs of fresh lemon
    balm or mint, optional

1 Thinly pare the rind from six of
the lemons. Put the rind into a large
heatproof jug or bowl and pour in
the boiling water. Cover and leave to
infuse for an hour.
2 Squeeze and strain the juice from
the pared lemons and pour it into a
large serving jug. Strain the water
from the lemon rind into the jug,
add sugar to taste and stir until the
sugar has dissolved.
3 Thinly slice the remaining lemon,
and add the slices to the jug. Cover
the jug with cling film and chill in
the refrigerator for 2 - 3 hours.
4 Serve the lemonade as it is or add
some ice cubes and decorate with a
few leaves of lemon balm or mint.

FRYING

SMALL LEAPS

What is the difference between frying and sautéing?

They are similar ways of frying
food in a little oil over a high heat.
In frying, the food is turned with
a spatula; in sautéing the pan is
shaken so the food 'jumps' (the
French verb *sauter* means to leap).
Both are quick cooking methods
suitable for small, tender pieces of
meat and other foods.

The fat you use for frying or
sautéing food is important, as its
flavour, or lack of it, will affect the
taste. Olive oil, butter, lard and
beef or bacon dripping all add their
particular flavour to fried foods;
corn, peanut, safflower and most
other vegetable oils have relatively
little flavour. When choosing a fat,
remember that some fats can be
heated to much higher temperatures than others before they start
to break down and burn. For example, bacon or beef dripping, lard,
and solid cooking fat can withstand
more heat than butter, margarine or
vegetable oil, while clarified butter
(see BUTTER) can be heated higher
than untreated butter. All fats tend
to break down if they are heated
too long, causing them to smoke
and give an unpleasant flavour to
any food that is fried in them.

STAY CRISP

What can I do to prevent fried food from becoming soggy?

Use a wide, uncovered pan because
a lid traps the steam so that the
food stews or steams instead of frying crisply. Preheat the fat so that
the food forms a crisp coat straightaway and does not absorb the fat
and become greasy.

Fry only a little food at a time,
and cook meat quickly so that the
outside browns all over. Then
lower the heat to moderate and
cook until the inside is cooked
through. To keep fried food crisp,
always serve it as soon as you possibly can after it has been cooked.
(See also DEEP-FRYING.)

SEASONING SURFACES

What is the best way to season a new frying pan?

Seasoning, or proving, a pan gives
a relatively nonstick surface to pans
that do not have a nonstick coating.
The easiest method is to wash and
dry the pan thoroughly and then
put it on a high heat with a tablespoon of salt and one of oil. Heat
it until the oil is smoking, then
wipe the pan clean with a large
piece of crumpled kitchen paper,
using any remaining salt as an
abrasive. When the pan is clean, it
is seasoned. A new pan may need
several attempts to create a perfect
surface. A wok improves greatly by
this treatment and may need to be
seasoned again if food begins to
stick. If possible, use an omelette
pan only for omelettes, or season
the pan every time you make one.
After use, wash a seasoned pan in
soapy water, avoiding anything that
would scratch the surface.

DEGLAZING THE PAN

When a recipe mentions the term deglazing, what does it mean?

Deglazing is a term for loosening
the browned juices stuck on the
bottom of a pan after frying meat.
Tip off the fat, add a few tablespoons of liquid such as cream,
stock, water or wine and bring to
the boil, stirring and scraping to
dissolve the sediment. The juice
will be full of flavour and can be
poured over meat, added to a sauce
or stirred into a casserole.

SHAKING NEWS

What exactly is dry-frying? Surely food will stick if there is no fat in the pan to keep it loose?

In these health-conscious times,
dry-frying has become a popular
way of cooking fish and meat. First
heat a frying pan with a heavy
bottom on a high flame until it is
hot. Meanwhile, prepare the meat
or fish. If it has little fat of its own,
drizzle a small amount of oil over
the surface and rub it in. However,
if the meat has natural fat or the
fish is oily, simply season with
freshly ground black pepper.

When the pan is hot, add the
meat or fish and leave it. Do not be
tempted to move it around in the
pan until a crust has formed. You
will then be able to slide a spatula
or palette knife underneath and
turn it to cook on the other side.

Dry-frying is commonly used to
extract and bring out the flavour of
whole spices, seeds or nuts before
they are used in recipes. Fry them
without fat in a heavy-bottomed
frying pan over a high heat, shaking
the pan from time to time. Continue cooking until they give off a
distinct aroma, and then tip them
onto a cold plate. Watch them carefully, as they can all easily burn.

GAME

SPORTING FARE

What does the term 'game' mean?

The word game refers to any wild animal, bird or fish hunted for sport or for food, and their flesh. Laws restrict the hunting seasons, to allow the animals time to breed.

Feathered game is at its best during the winter, although the shooting season begins on August 12 for grouse and snipe; partridge and wild duck on September 1; pheasant and woodcock in October. The grouse season ends in mid December, most others finish at the end of January, pheasant and partridge on February 1.

The season for the different varieties of venison overlaps across most of the year. Hare may not be sold between March and August. Pigeon and rabbit, both considered pests, are always available, and almost all quail are farmed.

HANGING MATTER

Does all game need to be hung and, if so, for how long?

All game birds are hung before being plucked, which helps to tenderise the meat and develop the flavour. They are suspended by the neck in a cool airy place, not touching, until the tail feathers can be pulled out. Game sold by butchers is already hung.

The hanging time depends on the weather, type of bird and personal taste. If it is warm and humid, two days is usually enough. In cool weather, allow two to four days for grouse; three to five days for a young partridge and up to ten days for older birds. Three days hanging

---

KNOW YOUR GAME BIRDS

Feathered game is a great delicacy and very nutritious since it is low in fat and high in flavour. Though most game birds are quite small, their meat is dense and filling so that a little goes a long way, further if you add a tasty stuffing.

1 HEN (left) and COCK PHEASANT: a brace (two birds) serves three to four. Flavour resembles gamy chicken or guinea fowl.
2 MALLARD: serves two. Very lean and a little oily. Teal and wigeon (not shown) have a more delicate duck flavour.
3 GROUSE: serves one to two. The flesh is dark with a strong, gamy flavour.
4 PARTRIDGE: serves one. Pale flesh with a very delicate gamy flavour.
5 SNIPE: serves one. Very strong, slightly fishy flavour as it is cooked ungutted.
6 QUAIL: serves one as a starter. It has a very delicate flavour without hanging.
7 SQUAB (left) and WOOD PIGEON: both serve one. Squab, a young pigeon, is pale and tender; wood pigeon has dark flesh and an almost liverish flavour.

is enough for a young pheasant but allow up to ten days for an older bird. Wild duck needs only one or two days or it can turn rancid, but wild geese can be hung for one to three weeks, depending on taste. Woodcock and snipe are hung for only two to three days. Pigeon need only for the crop to be emptied as soon as this is possible.

Venison less than three years, whether farmed or wild, does not need long hanging to tenderise it, but ten days hanging develops the flavour. Older venison, when hung long enough to tenderise it, has a strong gamy taste. Supermarket venison, which is briefly hung, can be marinated to give it more character.

TELLTALE SIGN

Is there any way you can tell the age of a game bird?

It is difficult, but all young game birds have more pliable beaks, skin and feet than older birds. Should the head and feet be missing, an alternative is to measure the blind-ended passage, called the bursa, above the vent under the tail. If you can insert a matchstick into the bursa to a depth up to 2.5 cm (1 in) this indicates the bird is young. A completely closed bursa means the bird is much older.

An alternative method (except with pheasant) is to inspect the two outer primaries or flight feathers on the wings: on a young bird they look pointed, not blunt. Young cock pheasants can be identified early in the season by blunt, short spurs on their legs.

If you are in any doubt about how old a bird is, it is best to braise or casserole it as only a young bird is tender enough for roasting.

BETTER SOURCE

Is game bought ready-prepared from a supermarket as good as game bought from a butcher?

Ready-prepared game birds can be bought in season in many supermarkets but will usually taste quite mild. If you prefer a more gamy taste, buy your game from a reputable butcher or poulterer who will probably have hung it for longer. A game dealer will hang game to your specifications, will pluck game birds and will also be able to tell you the approximate age of the bird when it was shot.

GAME PIG

Can you buy joints of wild boar and, if so, what does it taste like?

Boar is bred in this country from stock that came originally from Poland, and you can buy it through a 'Q Guild' butcher or other reputable source, but it is not widely sold. The meat is more dense and a little darker than pork and tastes similar but gamier. Almost any pork recipe can be used for boar, but it will stand up to more robust treatment, and marries well with other strong flavours such as wild mushrooms, garlic and hefty red wines.

GAMMON: see BACON

GARLIC

KNIFE OR CRUSHER?

Why do some cookery experts prefer not to use a garlic crusher?

Many experienced cooks prefer to use a knife to crush garlic because garlic crushers can be hard to clean and may harbour stale remnants that can taint the next dish. Crushing garlic also releases acrid-tasting chemicals. This is not a problem if the garlic is to be heated, as it is mellowed by cooking, but garlic to be eaten raw has a more refined flavour if it is carefully minced by hand (see box, right).

EAT MORE, SMELL LESS

Is it true that removing the green shoot from an old clove of garlic prevents 'garlic breath'?

Not necessarily, but the green tip is strong and bitter and should be removed anyway. Some people who

---

CHOPPING AND CRUSHING GARLIC

For many dishes garlic does not need to be finely chopped. Whole cloves, skinned, can be added and will disintegrate during cooking.

1 To pop the clove out of its papery skin, simply put it on a chopping board and press down firmly with the flat of a large heavy knife.

2 To mince or finely chop a clove of garlic, cut it lengthways into thin strips, then cut widthways.

3 To crush a garlic clove to a pulp, sprinkle it with coarse salt and alternately chop with the blade then mash it with the flat of the knife.

---

eat a lot of garlic claim their digestive system adapts and the smell of garlic no longer lingers, but this is not proven. The theory that only raw garlic smells, not cooked garlic, is also folklore. Scientists do agree, however, that garlic, a traditional folk remedy to 'cleanse the blood', does have anti-clogging properties. They recommend eating it often for a healthy heart.

SEASONAL SENSATION

Are there different types of garlic, as some bulbs seem to be much more pungent than others?

There are several types of garlic: most is pearly white, but other varieties are streaked with pink and mauve. However, the colour does not noticeably affect the flavour.

The more important distinction is seasonal. The most familiar garlic is sold from late summer, sometimes plaited into skeins to hang in a cool place for winter. It has been dried in the sun, which has firmed up the heads and transformed the skin into a tissue-like wrapping, and the garlic is good if it is firm. It will get stronger in taste as green shoots begin to germinate and sprout in the individual cloves.

Towards the end of April, the first of the new season's young and juicy garlic begins to arrive from Cyprus and Italy. The cloves are unseparated within a moist, fresh skin and the stem is thick and fleshy. This new-season garlic is sweet and mild enough to be treated as a vegetable, and is very good roasted whole with fresh herbs, such as thyme (below).

Serve the roasted heads as a starter, with bread and mild goat's cheese, or as an accompaniment to chicken or lamb. Diners squeeze the cloves out with their fingers.

Roast garlic with thyme

SERVES: 4 - 6
PREPARATION TIME: 20 minutes (for oven to preheat)
COOKING TIME: 45 minutes - 1 hour

6 large heads of young garlic
100 ml (3 ½ fl oz) olive oil
Flaky sea salt
6 sprigs fresh thyme

1 Preheat the oven to 200°C (400°F, gas mark 6).
2 Cut the top third from each head of garlic to expose the flesh, then trim off the roots. Pack the whole heads, cut side up, in an ovenproof dish that will hold them quite tightly in a single layer. Trickle the olive oil all over, sprinkle with salt and tuck sprigs of thyme among the heads.
3 Roast, uncovered, for 45 minutes to an hour, basting once or twice with the pan juices. The garlic is done if it feels soft when pressed.

Whole heads of sweet young garlic roasted with aromatic thyme are a feast for garlic lovers, especially seductive in the spring when the new crop appears.

GELATINE

LEAF OR POWDER?

Which is easier to use, leaf or powdered gelatine?

This is a matter of personal preference. Leaf gelatine is sold in sheets which need to be softened in water before being dissolved in a hot liquid. Put the required number of leaves into a bowl of cold water and leave for 5 minutes to soften. Take them from the water, squeeze out excess water and put the sheets in a small pan. Place the pan in a bain-marie, a larger pan half-full of simmering water, and heat until the gelatine has completely dissolved.

Powdered gelatine needs to be reconstituted before use. Measure the liquid into a small bowl and sprinkle the gelatine over the surface. Leave it to soak for 5 minutes, during which time the gelatine will absorb the liquid and the mixture will become spongy. Place the bowl in a bain-marie and heat until the gelatine is runny and clear.

Whichever you use, make sure it does not get too hot. Overheating makes gelatine stringy and can cause it to lose its setting power.

HOW MUCH IS ENOUGH?

If a recipe calls for powdered gelatine and I find that I only have leaves, how do I make up the same quantity of gelatine?

Powdered gelatine is usually sold in boxes of individual envelopes, each holding just over 11 g (about ⅓ oz), which sets 600 ml (1 pint) of liquid. Leaf gelatine varies in weight. You need about 7 g (less than ¼ oz) to set 600 ml (1 pint);

check the instructions on the pack. If the liquid to be set will contain solid pieces of food, or if the jelly is to stay in a warm room for any length of time, you will need more gelatine. Conversely, if the mixture is going to be served well chilled, or is already fairly stiff, less gelatine is needed. Note that kiwi, papaya and pineapple contain an enzyme which prevents setting.

SWIRLED NOT STIRRED

Should you stir gelatine if it does not dissolve immediately?

Never stir gelatine as the quantities used are so tiny you will lose half on the spoon. If one or two patches do not absorb the liquid at once, swirl the bowl gently, taking care not to lose gelatine up the sides.

A VEGETARIAN SET

I am a vegetarian. I have always wanted to make savoury set terrines, but cannot use gelatine because it is an animal product. Is there anything else I can use?

Gelatine is derived from the bones of beef. Agar-agar, which is based on seaweed and is used a great deal in commercial food processing for thickening and as a stabiliser, is a common alternative. It is sold in many of the large supermarkets.

Two teaspoons of agar-agar sets 600 ml (1 pint) of liquid, but you will never achieve a firm set if your mixture is acidic, for example a mousse with citrus; or if a mixture contains some chocolate or spinach. Always dissolve the agar-agar first, then boil it rapidly to activate the setting process. It sets at a higher temperature than gelatine, but the end result does not melt so well in the mouth and feels quite different.

Another vegetarian product that can be used as a substitute for gelatine is Gelozone, which is made from locust bean, guar gum and carrageen, or Irish moss. Follow the instructions on the packet which will tell you how much to use and always heat it gently before adding it to the mixture.

GINGER

VENERABLE ORIENTAL

Where does ginger come from, and how is it used?

Ginger comes from Asia where it has been cultivated since ancient times for its warm flavour and is valued as an aid to digestion. The edible part is the rhizome, or root, and it may be used either fresh, dried, pickled or preserved.

The British have used dried ginger for hundreds of years to flavour sweet dishes such as gingerbread, biscuits and puddings. In China, India, Japan and South-east Asia, fresh ginger is more common and used for a wide variety of savoury dishes such as soups, curries, marinades, pickles and relishes.

Fresh ginger is now becoming increasingly available in Britain. To use it, first peel the root, then chop it very finely or grate it on a fine grater. If you only want the juice and not the ginger itself for flavouring, crush it in a garlic press.

Fresh ginger is used mostly in conjunction with other flavourings such as garlic, spring onions and chilli peppers, for example in stir-fried dishes. It also goes well with broccoli, chicken, noodles, rice and shellfish. The following recipe for Ginger Butter uses fresh ginger juice to make a spicy accompaniment to vegetables, pasta or grills.

Ginger butter

SERVES: 8
PREPARATION TIME: 10 minutes, plus 30 minutes chilling
COOKING TIME: none

250 g (9 oz) unsalted butter, softened to room temperature
50 g (1 3/4 oz) fresh ginger, peeled
2 large cloves garlic, crushed
2 tablespoons lemon juice
Sea salt and black pepper

1 Put the butter in a food processor. Crush the fresh ginger in a garlic press held over the butter to release its juice, then discard the ginger. Add the garlic and lemon juice and season to taste, then process till smooth. Transfer the butter to a small bowl and chill for 30 minutes.
2 Form the butter into a sausage shape, wrap it in foil and return it to the refrigerator to harden. (The butter can also be stored in the freezer for up to two months; to defrost, transfer it to the refrigerator overnight.) To serve, remove the foil and cut into thick slices.

ONE OR THE OTHER

Can dried ginger be used in a recipe that calls for fresh ginger?

No, they are not interchangeable. Their flavour is completely different, and one cannot be used as a substitute for the other.

GOAT

TASTY AND TENDER

I have seen goat in Indian recipes and kid on the menu in France. What are they like to eat?

Goat can have a strong taste, but the flavour is mellowed by being cooked slowly with spices, as it is in Indian and Caribbean recipes. This slow cooking also helps to make the meat more tender.

In Britain you are more likely to find lean young goat, called kid. It is very tasty and has the fat on the outside rather than being marbled throughout the flesh. Kid can be ordered from high street butchers and may also be available from Indian and Middle Eastern suppliers. (In the Middle East roasted kid is served with rice and hard-boiled eggs.) If the meat is labelled 'halal', the animal has been slaughtered in accordance with Muslim law, just as 'kosher' meat is killed according to orthodox Jewish religious law.

Cook young goat in the same way you would cook young lamb. Kid is a favourite for spring festivals in France, roasted with herbs over an open fire or cooked in a stew.

GOOSE

PERFECT PARTNERS

How should you cook a goose, and what are some other dishes that are good to serve with it?

The recipe for roast goose (below) includes the traditional sage and onion stuffing. Stuff the neck end only, as any stuffing placed in the cavity will absorb too much fat. Gooseberry sauce, roasted apples, braised red cabbage, mashed or roast potatoes and gravy are also usually served with goose.

Roast goose with roasted apples

SERVES: 6 - 8
PREPARATION TIME: 1 1/4 hours
COOKING TIME: 2 1/4 - 2 3/4 hours

Fresh or frozen goose, thawed,
  3.5 - 4.5 kg (8 - 10 lb) to feed 6 or
  4.5 - 5.5 kg (10 - 12 lb) to feed 8
Sea salt and black pepper
1 red eating apple per person
2 - 4 tablespoons melted butter
2 tablespoons plain flour
600 ml (1 pint) good poultry stock

FOR THE STUFFING
50 g (1 3/4 oz) butter
4 onions, finely chopped
2 tablespoons chopped fresh sage
125 g (4 1/2 oz) white breadcrumbs
1 egg yolk

1 Pull out the bag of giblets from the cavity of the goose. Dice the liver and set it aside, reserving the rest of the giblets. Remove any large lumps of fat from inside the goose and set them aside, and make sure the cavity is thoroughly dry.
2 With a hair dryer, blow-dry the skin slightly for 15 minutes. Or leave the bird, uncovered, in a very cool place for a couple of hours. When it has dried, prick the skin all over so that the fat, which is mainly just beneath the skin, can run off during cooking (do not pierce through to the flesh or you will loose the juices). Rub the skin with fine sea salt.

This beautifully roasted goose has a depth of flavour no other bird can match and is splendidly garnished with baked red apples and sage and onion stuffing.

3 Preheat the oven to 220°C (425°F, gas mark 7). To make the stuffing, melt the butter in a frying pan, add the onions and cook for 5 minutes until soft. Remove from the heat, stir in the diced liver and the rest of the stuffing ingredients and season well. Allow the mixture to cool then use it to stuff the neck of the bird. Put any remaining stuffing in a separate ovenproof dish and cook it beneath the bird for 25 minutes.
4 Lay the bird on a wire rack in a roasting tin. Cover the breast with the reserved goose fat. Add the remaining giblets and a little water to the roasting tin. Roast the goose for 45 minutes, then reduce the heat to 180°C (350°F, gas mark 4); if a bird is to serve six people, cook for a further 1 1/2 - 1 3/4 hours; cook a larger bird for 1 3/4 - 2 hours. Baste and drain off the fat regularly. If you find that the goose is browning too quickly, cover it loosely with a layer of foil.
5 Half an hour before the meat is ready, make a slit around each apple, brush with melted butter and place

on a baking tray. Roast them on the top shelf for 25 - 30 minutes until they are soft but not collapsed.
6 Put goose and apples on a warm serving dish. Keep them warm while you make the gravy.
7 Leave the sediment, 2 tablespoons of fat and the giblets in the tin, add the flour and cook on the hob until brown, scraping up all the sediment. Whisk in the stock, bring to the boil and simmer for about 5 minutes. Check the seasoning then strain the finished sauce into a gravy boat.

MICHAELMAS TREAT

What is the best time of year to buy a goose, and how can I work out how many people it will feed?

The best time to buy a goose is from late September, when it is six months old, through to December. At six months it weighs 4.5–6 kg (10–14 lb), rising to some 8.5 kg (about 18 lb). There is a high proportion of bone to flesh so allow 750 g (1 lb 10 oz) per person.

GOOSEBERRIES

SHARP SAUCE

How is gooseberry sauce served?

Gooseberry Sauce (right) is a traditional and particularly English accompaniment to fatty, savoury foods such as pork, mackerel and goose, which may be how the fruit got its name. It is still fashionable, and is often seen on smart restaurant menus accompanying fried mackerel or fried Camembert. The sharpness of the tart gooseberries should counteract the oiliness of the food. To keep the sauce tart, use either green gooseberries with only a tiny pinch of sugar added, or the larger, sweeter dessert varieties before they are completely ripe and cook them without any sugar.

A refreshing, pale green sauce of ripe gooseberries makes a pleasantly sharp contrast to creamy deep-fried cheese.

Gooseberry sauce

SERVES: 4
PREPARATION TIME: 10 minutes
COOKING TIME: 15 minutes

250 g (9 oz) green gooseberries,
 topped and tailed
15 g (½ oz) butter
15 g (½ oz) sugar
1 tablespoon chopped fennel leaves,
 optional

1 Place the prepared gooseberries in a saucepan with a tablespoon of water, and add the butter, sugar and fennel. Cover and cook them gently, stirring occasionally with a wooden spoon, for about 15 minutes until the gooseberries are soft. (Add another tablespoon of water if it seems dry.)
2 Beat well with a wooden spoon to a pulpy consistency and add a little more sugar, if wanted. Serve warm.
VARIATIONS
Retaining the skin and pulpy pieces of fruit adds texture and colour, but if you prefer a smooth sauce, it can be pressed through a sieve after cooking. And if you use defrosted frozen gooseberries, you should not need to add any additional water. They will cook in about 10 minutes; do not overcook them.

COLOUR FAST

How can I keep the green colour when making gooseberry jam?

How green the jam will be depends on the variety and maturity of the gooseberries you use and on the length of boiling time needed to reach the setting point. The longer the jam is boiled, the redder it will become, ending up deep pink.

If you are lucky enough to have an old-fashioned brass preserving pan, use it for making gooseberry jam. The acid in the fruit reacts with the brass and keeps them green. Using modern preserving sugar with added pectin will also help to retain the colour of the gooseberries because jam made with this sugar needs only a short boiling time to reach a set.

GREEN FOR FOOLS

What type of gooseberries are best for making gooseberry fool?

The sharper green gooseberries are the best complement to the rich custard and cream in a fool (see recipe, below). The larger yellow and red gooseberries are sweetest and best kept for eating raw. If you think your ripe green gooseberries are too bland, taste them after cooking and add the custard and cream in stages until they taste right. Adding lemon juice may help as well. To serve, stand each glass on a small plate and arrange one or two shortbread biscuits on the side.

Gooseberry fool

SERVES: 4
PREPARATION TIME: 30 minutes plus about 4 hours chilling time
COOKING TIME: 20 - 25 minutes

550 g (1 lb 4 oz) gooseberries, topped, tailed and rinsed
115 g (4 oz) sugar
150 ml (5 fl oz) double cream, thoroughly chilled

FOR THE CUSTARD
2 eggs, size 2
1 tablespoon caster sugar
200 ml (7 fl oz) full-cream milk
1 teaspoon vanilla extract or essence
To garnish: shortbread biscuits

1 Put the gooseberries and sugar into a stainless-steel or enamel pan, add 2 tablespoons of water, then cover and cook over a moderate heat for 20 - 25 minutes until the fruit are soft and their skins break.
2 Pour the fruit into a nylon sieve over a bowl and drain it just long enough to remove the excess juice, but do not drain dry. Transfer the gooseberries to a bowl and leave to cool, then chill in the refrigerator.
3 To make the custard, break the eggs into a bowl, add the caster sugar and whisk together lightly.
4 Put the milk into a small pan and heat it almost to boiling point. Whisk it into the eggs, then pour the whole mixture back into the pan. Stir the custard over a low heat (or over a pan of boiling water) until thick enough to coat the back of the spoon.
5 As soon as the custard thickens, pour it through a nylon sieve into a small bowl and stir in the vanilla. Cover the surface of the custard closely with cling film to prevent a skin forming, then allow it to cool and chill it until set.
6 Mash the chilled gooseberries with a fork and fold in the chilled custard. For a smoother texture, sieve the fruit pulp, or purée it in a blender or food processor, before adding it to the chilled custard.
7 Whisk the double cream until it forms soft peaks and fold it into the gooseberry mixture.
8 Spoon the fool into four stemmed glasses holding about 225 ml (8 fl oz) each, then cover and chill for at least 2 hours before serving. It needs to be very cold to bring out the flavour.

GRAPEFRUIT: see CITRUS FRUIT

GRAPES

WAIT TO WASH

Does washing grapes make them rot more quickly?

Grapes should be washed, but only just before they are served or eaten. The pressure grapes put on each other when in bunches can cause bruising which creates moisture, encouraging the fruit to spoil. If they are washed before storing, water is likely to remain between the grapes and can accelerate rotting which will create soft spots.

It is best to buy grapes in small quantities, checking carefully to make sure they are not bruised. Store them, unwashed, in a colander in the refrigerator, which allows the air to circulate and keeps them dry. Use them within two to three days. If you want to serve perfect grapes for a party and you do not have much room in the refrigerator, the best way of making sure they are in perfect condition is to find the time to buy them on the day.

EASY DESEEDING

I find removing the pips from grapes tedious. Should I just use the seedless varieties?

Seedless grapes are wonderful for eating but are not always what you need for cooking. Some recipes, such as the Sole Véronique below, require a sharper tasting grape to counterbalance a rich sauce. You can remove the seeds by inserting a cocktail stick into the top of the grape and fishing them out.

When making a dessert jelly with grapes, it is better to use fruit that has been peeled. Seedless grapes can have quite tough skin and if you used them unpeeled, their texture would spoil a smooth jelly. To remove grape skins, simply prick each end, cover with boiling water and leave to stand for 45 seconds. Then plunge the grapes into cold water to cool, peel and cut in half.

Sole Véronique

SERVES: 8 as a first course or 4 as a main course
PREPARATION TIME: 30 minutes if the fish is filleted and skinned by the fishmonger, 1 hour if preparing the soles yourself
COOKING TIME: 30 - 35 minutes

175 g (6 oz) large green grapes
4 large Dover soles, each weighing at least 450 g (1 lb), skinned and filleted
200 ml (7 fl oz) dry white wine
Salt and black pepper
2 sprigs fresh parsley
1 small onion, finely sliced
6 allspice berries
6 black peppercorns
600 ml (1 pint) fish stock
35 g (1 1/4 oz) butter
35 g (1 1/4 oz) plain flour
150 ml (5 fl oz) double cream

1 Skin the grapes and remove any seeds. Cut them in half if they seem very large, then set aside. Check the fillets carefully for any small bones and remove them. Preheat the oven to 220°C (425°F, gas mark 7).
2 Starting at the head end, and with the skinned side uppermost, roll up

each sole fillet towards the tail to form a neat roll or paupiette. Stand the rolls upright in an ovenproof dish and pour the wine over them. Season with salt and black pepper then add the parsley, onion, allspice berries and peppercorns.

3 Cover the dish well with a tight-fitting lid or thick foil and cook the rolls for 15 - 20 minutes, until they are almost but not quite cooked. The cooking time will vary according to the thickness of the dish you use.

4 While the fish is cooking, pour the fish stock into a saucepan and bring to the boil, then reduce the heat and boil gently for 20 minutes or until the stock is reduced by about half. Remove the pan from the heat and set aside to cool.

5 Remove the fish from the oven, leaving the oven on, and pour the cooking juices into a small pan.

6 Leave the fish in the dish, covered, and set it aside in a warm place. The rolls will complete their cooking in the heat remaining in the dish. Do not put them back into the oven or there is a risk they will overcook.

7 Put the grapes on a large serving dish and put it in the oven to warm. Preheat the grill to a medium heat.

8 Boil the cooking juices rapidly until they are reduced to 150 ml (5 fl oz), then strain them into the reduced fish stock.

9 Melt the butter in a saucepan and stir in the flour. Cook this roux over a moderate heat for a minute, then stir in the blended fish stock a little

In elegant Sole Véronique, juicy grapes are lavishly coated in a creamy fish stock sauce with a hint of allspice.

at a time. Bring the sauce to the boil, stirring continuously until it thickens, then stir in the cream. Reduce the heat, season to taste and simmer for a further 5 minutes.

10 Transfer the paupiettes to the warm serving dish. Strain any juices left behind in the cooking dish into the sauce and stir well. Coat the paupiettes with the sauce, put them under the grill for a minute or two to glaze, then serve immediately.

As a first course, serve with warm Melba toast. For a main course, serve with new potatoes, sprinkled with chopped mint, and a green salad.

GRAVY

TRADITIONAL WAY

What is the best way to make really delicious gravy?

Well-flavoured gravy incorporates both the juices and sediment of roasted meat and should be made in the roasting pan after the meat has been removed and left to rest on a serving dish.

Once you have moved the joint, pour off most of the fat, except for 1–2 tablespoons which you should leave in the tin with the dark sediment from the roast.

Stir in 1–2 tablespoons of flour, stirring and browning it slowly to the colour you prefer. Then gradually pour in meat stock or vegetable water and stir until the gravy is thick and smooth. Any lumps can be sieved out afterwards.

If any fat remains on top of the finished gravy you can remove it by laying sheets of absorbent paper on the surface of the gravy.

A thinner gravy can be made by reducing the flour to a teaspoon. If it is then too thin, the gravy can be reduced by rapid boiling for a few minutes. Season to taste, transfer to a gravy boat and serve hot.

If you prefer meat gravy to have a slightly lighter texture, you can thicken it with cornflour or arrowroot instead of ordinary flour.

DASH OF FLAVOUR

What can I add to gravy to make its flavour more interesting?

The best guarantee of a good gravy is well-flavoured stock. If this is lacking, there are several additions you can make to give the gravy colour as well as flavour.

For children, try a little Marmite or Bovril. Adults may prefer some red or white wine, sherry, Martini, or a dash of liqueur or port.

Adding acidic or sweet flavours in small quantities to gravy will also enhance its flavour. You could try a squeeze of orange or lemon juice, vinegar (in particular a few drops of rich balsamic or sherry vinegar) or even jellies made from herbs, redcurrants, cranberries or gooseberries. If you are serving gravy with game or goose, meats which benefit from a little sweetness, add a teaspoon or so of plum, redcurrant, rowan, sloe or similarly sharp-flavoured jam to the reduced gravy. The jam melts very quickly when stirred into the hot gravy and gives it an impressive smoothness.

Fresh or dried herbs and spices such as allspice, cayenne, horseradish, mustard, nutmeg and thyme can add a distinctive taste to gravy.

When you are adding alcohol, reduce it first by rapid boiling to eliminate any harsh flavour, then use this to replace some of the water or stock in the recipe.

An excellent way of improving gravy is to pour a glass or two of red wine over the joint halfway through the roasting period. The alcohol will evaporate during the rest of the cooking, the flavour of the meat will improve and the wine will amalgamate with the juices and sediment in the pan.

STOCK QUESTION

What type of stock will make the most successful gravy?

A good homemade stock will taste best. It should ideally match the meat you are roasting, but chicken stock can be used for most gravies.

Giblet stock can be made quickly by simmering the poultry giblets (neck, heart, gizzard, liver) in water for 30 minutes. For a richer gravy, do not add the liver to the stock but instead fry it, finely chopped, in the roasting tin before adding the flour.

Supermarkets now sell readymade chilled stock, which is a good alternative to homemade, and a can of consommé is a good standby. Commercial stock cubes or granules are usually heavily seasoned and should be used only as a last resort. If you have to use a stock cube, use only half a cube to the amount of water suggested on the pack to reduce the saltiness.

FASTER GRAVY

What can I use to make gravy when I am in a hurry?

The quickest homemade gravy is a *jus* (see box, below) made from stock and the roasted meat's natural juices. Unlike gravy, it is not thickened with flour. Remove the joint from the roasting tin and pour off the fat into a separating jug. Then pour the stock into the tin and bring to the boil, scraping in all the sediment from around the tin. Add the meat juices that have separated from the fat in the jug and simmer for several minutes. Strain the jus into a gravy boat, season and serve.

DEGLAZING FOR JUS

Jus is an unthickened meat juice gravy made by deglazing the pan in which meat has been roasted. If the juices are not dark enough at the end of the cooking time, reduce them until they are caramelised.

1 Pour the fat from the joint into a jug. A separating jug is ideal for this as it allows you to pour out the meat juices from beneath the fat.

2 With a wooden spoon, scrape all the crusty bits of sediment from the sides and base of the tin. Pour in some stock, vegetable water or wine and continue stirring over a moderate heat. Add any meat juice that has separated from the fat and simmer until rich brown in colour.

GRIDDLE

ANCIENT PAN

What is a griddle?

It is a heavy, flat, cast-iron pan with a small rim and a handle that can be laid flat. It can be used for frying meat and vegetables or cooking pancakes, drop scones, griddle cakes and unleavened bread.

The griddle is an ancient piece of cooking equipment and was originally a large, flat stone heated from below by a fire with the surface used for baking called a griddle, girdle or bakestone.

BEST WITHOUT SIDES

Do I have to buy a griddle pan to make drop scones, or can I use a normal frying pan?

Bannocks, drop scones, oatcakes, tattie scones and Welsh cakes are all best made on a griddle, although it is possible to improvise. You can use a large heavy-duty or nonstick frying pan, but if the sides are too deep, you may have a little difficulty in turning the food.

CHARRED LINES

How can I create at home those wonderful brown charred lines that I see on restaurant food?

The brown charred lines on restaurant food are created either by cooking the food on a chargrill or by placing very hot skewers on the cooked food in a trellis pattern.

Charcoal-fuelled chargrills, similar to indoor barbecues, are offered for home use by some manufacturers of high quality ovens. These slot into the kitchen bench alongside the stove top. Portable electric 'chargrills' are also now available from department stores.

A similar effect can be created by using a ridged griddle or frying pan (see box, above right). Chicken, fish, steaks and vegetables such as aubergines, courgettes and peppers are delicious cooked in this way.

USING A GRIDDLE

The griddle, a heavy, metal plate or pan, stands over a hot ring for frying. The traditional griddle is flat and is used for drop scones, but some griddles now have ridges, which give an attractive stripe to meat and vegetables as they cook.

Heat the griddle slowly until very hot, then place lightly oiled food onto the surface. Move it after a few seconds, so it does not stick, then leave to brown. Turn and repeat.

GRILLING

NECESSARY HEAT

I want to do more grilling as I believe it is healthier than frying. What do I need to know?

Intense heat is the secret of successful grilling. Although this method of cooking requires close attention, the advantages are that the food cooks quickly and the charred surface gives an excellent flavour.

To produce succulent meat that is crisply brown outside and juicy pink inside, it is essential to preheat the grill to its highest setting. This may take 10 or even 20 minutes on a domestic cooker.

Under a cooler grill, the meat's surface will not brown quickly and juices will leak out, leaving the meat dry, tasteless and unattractive by the time it is cooked through. If the grill cannot be adequately preheated to ensure that the meat and fish are quickly sealed, it would be better to fry the food instead.

Unlike slow methods of cooking such as braising, grilling will not tenderise meat, so use only tender,

choice cuts. For best results, these should not be much more than 5 cm (2 in) or so thick, otherwise the outside of the meat will be burnt before the inside is cooked.

Ensure the meat is at room temperature before you start grilling otherwise a chilled steak will still be cold inside when the outside is brown and sizzling. This is particularly important if the steak is to be served very rare.

Once the meat has been sealed, you can reduce the fierceness of the grilling process. It is best to do this, if possible, by lowering the grill pan a little to increase the distance of the food from the heat rather than by reducing the temperature of the grill itself.

Grilling is considered healthier than frying as the excess fat can drip away during cooking so it is good for bacon, chicken fillets, chops, kebabs, sausages and steak.

A GOOD TURN

How should you turn food while it is being grilled?

Turn the grilling food with tongs or spoons, not a sharp instrument, which would pierce the meat and allow the juices to escape.

DELAY THE SALT

Why do my cookery books say not to salt meat before grilling?

Salt draws moisture from the meat's cells, so salting in advance may make it dry and tough. Instead, salt meat during or after grilling.

To the rescue!

Brush food for grilling with butter, oil or a mixture of the two to keep it moist and to speed the browning process. This oiling is essential with delicate foods such as fish to prevent them from sticking to the grill pan.

GROUSE

GOOD TIMING

When is the best time of year to enjoy fresh grouse?

The season for shooting grouse is from August 12 until December 10, but those bred in that year and shot before mid October are the most succulent. Young grouse can be shot and eaten on the same day or hung for two to four days, depending on the weather and how you like the taste. As with all game, it is best eaten in season to appreciate fully its individual flavour.

BEWARE OF PELLETS

Sometimes the wrapping on a game bird warns you to beware of the lead shot. Is this poisonous?

The warning is to prevent you from breaking your teeth on the tiny dark-grey pellets. You will usually be able to spot the shot holes if you examine the bird carefully.

Take out any noticeable shots with your fingers. Marinating the bird may help to ease them out. If any are missed, you are unlikely to consume enough lead to poison yourself from one bird. The pellets are easy to detect in the mouth so simply remove any shot you find and put it on the side of your plate.

SIGNS OF YOUTH

How do you tell if a grouse is young? Should you cook young and old birds differently?

Young birds are best roasted, while those over six months old are better casseroled, made into soups or potted. Young grouse have downy breast feathers and pointed flight feathers on their wing tips, while the feathers on the wing tips of older birds are rounded. Tender plump breasts and soft, rounded spurs on the back of the legs are other signs of young grouse. The recipe (right) is for a young bird; an older bird would be too tough.

Young grouse roasted to perfection is a delicacy. Enjoy it with seasonal fruit tucked inside, plus traditional game chips, rowan jelly and bread sauce.

Roast young grouse

SERVES: 2
PREPARATION TIME: 10 minutes
COOKING TIME: 40 minutes

A brace of grouse (a male and a female), plucked and drawn
75 g (2¾ oz) softened butter
Salt and black pepper
A few raspberries or blueberries
4 slices green rindless streaky bacon

1 Preheat the oven to 190°C (375°F, gas mark 5). Place a small knob of butter in the cavity of each bird. Season with salt and pepper and place the raspberries or blueberries in the cavity as well.
2 Liberally rub the birds all over with the remaining butter, set them in a roasting pan and cover their breasts with bacon. Roast for 35 - 40 minutes, depending on the size.
3 Ten minutes before the birds are ready, remove the bacon to allow the breasts to brown and discard it, then baste and return to the oven to finish. Grouse is traditionally served on a croûte of bread fried in butter and spread with the lightly fried liver of the bird. Use the pan juices as a gravy for the birds.

GUINEA FOWL

SPOTTED BIRD

What is a guinea fowl? Is it the same as the 'pintade' bird I have seen on menus in France?

The guinea fowl, which is a similar bird to pheasant, originated in West Africa and was known as a 'turkey' during the Middle Ages. The female bird is known as a guinea hen. *Pintade* is the French name. The species, which is characterised by a blackish plumage marked with small white spots, is now battery farmed but free range birds retain a gamy flavour and darker flesh.

You can use any chicken recipe for guinea fowl and it is especially good roasted. The lean, golden-fleshed birds weigh about 1 - 1.8 kg (2 - 4 lb) and will feed four. Bard first with a layer of fat or bacon to keep the breast moist and allow 30 minutes per kg (13 minutes per lb) at 200°C (400°F, gas mark 6) plus an extra 15 minutes. Roast for the last 15 minutes without the fat or bacon and dust with a little flour to make the skin brown and crisp.

HAGGIS

SCOTTISH DELICACY

What exactly is haggis, and how should it be cooked?

Haggis, a popular Scottish speciality, is a large, spicy sausage encased by a sheep's stomach. It is made from the animal's liver, lungs and heart, minced and mixed with oatmeal, onion, suet and seasonings.

By tradition, haggis is served accompanied by mashed potatoes and bashed neeps (swedes) on festive occasions such as Burns Night. The taste is rich and meaty.

Haggis bought in a supermarket or at a butcher's is already cooked but needs reheating by boiling for around 40 minutes. To serve the haggis, cut a hole in the skin and scoop out the contents.

NO-MEAT TREAT

Is it true that you can buy haggis that is suitable for vegetarians?

Yes. Macsween, the Edinburgh haggis makers, have been selling a vegetarian version since the early 1980s which is available in health food shops and some butchers.

It contains an aromatic mixture of kidney beans, lentils, nuts, oatmeal, onion, vegetables and spices designed to approximate both the texture and flavour of a traditionally prepared meat haggis.

The vegetarian version of the sausage has a plastic casing which must be discarded after reheating and before the haggis is eaten. Macsween's haggis is approved by the Vegetarian Society.

HAM

PRESERVATION TECHNIQUE

What is the difference between ham and gammon?

Ham is a pig's hind leg, first cut off the carcass and then smoked, salted or dried (or a combination of these) for preservation.

Gammon also comes from the hind leg but it is cured as part of a side of bacon and cut off afterwards. (Bacon itself comes from the central body meat of the pig.)

Gammon may be smoked separately or left unsmoked but it is not matured long enough to have a strong ham flavour and does not keep for as long as ham, which is generally cured more slowly. While some hams are meant for further cooking, some such as Parma and Bayonne hams are simply eaten in the 'raw' cured state, having been salted and then dried over several months to preserve the flesh.

Hams may also be smoked over a slow fire, and the different types of wood used, such as beech, juniper or oak, will each produce a distinctive flavour. Unsmoked hams are also known as green hams and have a milder flavour.

You can buy an uncooked whole ham to bake as a special dish, but in Britain most ham is sold cooked and sliced, and can be grilled, or included in recipes where it just needs to be heated through. Gammon is sold in joints, rashers or steaks for cooking at home.

HOW TO CARVE A HAM

Because a ham is so large, you need a special long, slim ham knife with a rounded tip to carve it properly. Make sure that it is razor sharp.

1 With the ham lying flat, fat side up, on a board and the knuckle bone pointing towards you, cut even slices along the side of the ham, parallel to the main bone of the leg, using a ham carving knife and fork.

2 After cutting a few slices, you will meet resistance from a small bone located near the knuckle end. Remove this bone with a small pointed knife, then continue cutting slices until you almost reach the main bone.

3 With the ham still lying flat on the surface, cut slices from the large end of the ham - the end opposite the knuckle bone. Continue cutting slices in this direction until the leg's ball and cartilage are fully exposed.

4 Stand the ham on its cut side and slice vertically towards the bone, then horizontally along the bone to release the slices. Grasp the knuckle and trim off the remaining meat by cutting parallel to the main bone.

HOW TO MAKE A PAPER FRILL FOR BAKED HAM

A crisp white frill adds the final touch to a party ham. Use an A4 sheet of paper. The same technique can be used to make smaller frills for lamb cutlets and crown roasts.

1 Lightly fold the paper into halves lengthways. Make 5 mm (¼ in) parallel cuts along the folded edge, cutting two-thirds of the way down.

2 Unfold the cut paper, then fold it back on itself the other way to make the loops open out.

3 Wind the base of the frill round your fingers. Slip off and push up from inside to stagger the loops.

4 Secure the join in the base with a pin or non-toxic glue. Slip the frill over the end of the ham bone.

BOIL OR BAKE

What is the best way to cook a whole ham at home?

If you want to cook a ham yourself, you will have to order a whole or half joint from a specialist supplier. If the ham is dry-cured and salty it may need soaking overnight in cold water before you cook it, so consult your supplier when you take delivery of the ham. Most hams you can buy will come with appropriate cooking instructions from the company that cured it.

Hams can be boiled or baked. To boil, put the ham in a large pan of fresh clean water, bring it to the boil and then simmer it gently for 40 minutes per kg (17 minutes per lb) plus 20 minutes extra.

If serving hot, rest the joint for 30 minutes before carving (see box, previous page). To serve cold, cool in the water, drain and then remove the skin and press brown breadcrumbs into the fat.

To bake a ham, wrap the joint loosely in foil and place in a roasting tin. Cook in a 160°C (325°F, gas mark 3) oven for 40 minutes per kg (17 minutes per lb). Thirty minutes before the end of the time, take out the tin and raise the oven temperature to 220°C (425°F, gas mark 7). Drain off the juices, cut off the skin and score the fat in a diamond pattern. Stud with cloves, spread with English mustard and then press demerara sugar all over. Return to the oven to finish cooking and then rest for 30 minutes before carving or cool overnight. Add a paper frill (see box, left) and serve with Cumberland sauce.

MAKING THE MOST OF IT

Can you suggest some interesting ways for me to make use of any leftover baked ham?

The full-flavoured salt savour of baked ham is delicious when simply layered with slices of Cheddar or Cheshire cheese into a raised hot water pie crust (see MEAT PIE) and served hot or cold with salad. Parsley is another good match for baked ham. Try flavouring aspic or a light jellied stock with parsley and white wine, then pour into a terrine which you have filled with rugged pieces of baked ham. Leave to set in the refrigerator for a few hours, turn out, then slice and serve cold with a green herb sauce.

You could also stir some pieces of leftover ham into a German-style stew of sausage, beans, cabbage and onion for a hearty family supper.

COSTLY PROCESS

Why are some hams so much more expensive than others?

It is the way ham is produced and cured that most affects the cost. Dry-cured hams are generally more expensive than hams cured in brine as dry-curing takes longer. After salting, the ham may be smoked over fragrant wood and left to age for three months to two years. Traditionally produced Continental dry-cured hams such as Parma and Bayonne are particularly costly as they take great skill to produce and need more than a year to mature.

The pigs' feed is another factor affecting the cost and flavour of the finished ham. For example, peaches are used for feed in Georgia and peanuts in Virginia, making these hams more expensive.

These hams are some of the most famous and readily available varieties from around the world:
• BAYONNE: French dry-cured ham similar to Parma, eaten raw.

Save it!

To prevent cooked ham from discolouring or drying out, wrap it closely in cling film. Joints will keep for up to ten days in the refrigerator, but slices should be eaten within a few days. Alternatively, use the ham to fill sandwiches generously, wrap in polythene and freeze to use later for packed lunches.

- BRADENHAM: dark red English ham pickled in molasses, juniper berries and spices until the skin turns a distinctive black; strong, sweet flavour; sold cooked.
- JAMBON D'ARDENNES: Belgian ham best sliced thinly; eaten raw.
- KENTUCKY: American ham that is smoked over apple, sassafras or hickory wood; eaten raw.
- PICNIC HAM: not a true ham as it is cut from the shoulder of the pig, but cured in the same way; less expensive; sold cooked.
- PRAGUE: ham from the Czech Republic; smoked over beech; good in hot dishes; sold cooked.
- PRESUNTO: lightly cured smoked ham from Portugal; eaten raw.
- PROSCIUTTO DI PARMA: Italian ham from pigs fattened on the whey left over after Parmesan cheese is made; eaten raw.
- SAN DANIELE: Italian ham made on a small scale with a flat shape and sweet flavour; eaten raw.

- SERRANO: Spanish ham matured for about ten months, stronger in flavour than Parma; eaten raw.
- SMITHFIELD: originally from pigs fed on peanuts then cured and processed in Smithfield, Virginia, USA; hickory-smoked and covered with pepper; sold cooked.
- SPECK: smoked ham from Italy; similar to Westphalian; eaten raw.
- SUFFOLK: sweet-cured English ham similar to Bradenham; blue-black skin and rich red-brown meat; sold cooked.
- SUGAR-GLAZED: boneless ham that has been coated with sugar, honey or treacle; sold cooked.
- WESTPHALIAN: German raw ham with a dark coloured rind created by long smoking over beech and juniper twigs; eaten raw.
- WILTSHIRE: really gammon rather than ham; English; sold cooked.
- YORK: the best-known English ham; mild and usually coated in breadcrumbs; sold cooked.

JUST FOR STARTERS

What can I do with Parma ham besides serve it with melon?

Parma ham, and the other air-dried hams such as Bayonne, can also be served with figs, or as part of a mixed hors d'oeuvre. Try wrapping the paper-thin slices around bread sticks to serve with drinks.

A very simple Italian-style starter involves laying the ham slices flat on each plate, sprinkling them with flakes of Parmesan and dressing with a vinaigrette made of olive oil, lemon juice and seasonings.

Parma ham is generally wasted in cooked dishes except where it adds a hint of flavour. Try it puréed with ricotta as a filling for home-made ravioli or tortellini.

Thin slices of sweet, salty Parma ham paired with fruit, asparagus, olives, Parmesan cheese or bread sticks, makes sophisticated canapés or starters.

HAMBURGERS

HOMEMADE VERSION

My children will insist on eating hamburgers. Could you give me a recipe for a healthy version?

The best way to guarantee healthy hamburgers is to make them yourself from whole meat. Homemade mince has a better flavour and texture than bought mince and you can cut off the fat first. The result will be fresher so you need not add anything to enhance the taste.

Making your own mince for hamburgers gives you the opportunity to choose the type of meat you want to include. Lean beef steak is

---

CHOPPING UP MEAT FOR A HAMBURGER

Producing top quality hamburger mince in your own kitchen is easy using the two-knife technique.

1 On a chopping board, chop the lean meat finely using two large cook's knives (they do not have to be identical), holding them loosely and parallel to each other. Lift each knife up and down in turn, using a smooth, rhythmic movement.

2 Occasionally lift and turn the meat with the flat of the knives. Continue chopping until the meat resembles a fine mince.

---

preferable to tougher, cheaper cuts as the burgers will be cooked quickly and so need to be tender. Alternatively, try high quality cuts of lamb, or venison, which has a lower fat content than other red meats. Buying your own meat to make into hamburgers also means you can enjoy organic or free-range burgers if that is what you prefer.

Use the coarse blade of a mincer, or chop the meat using two knives (see box, left). This produces a better texture and more of the tasty meat juices will be retained than if you use a food processor. The recipe below does not include cereal, so there is no need to use an egg to bind the mixture.

Hamburgers

SERVES: 4
PREPARATION TIME: 15 minutes
COOKING TIME: about 10 minutes

---

675 g (1 lb 8 oz) lean chuck steak, trimmed of fat
Salt and black pepper
1 small onion, optional
2 tablespoons chopped parsley or a large pinch of mixed herbs, optional
1 tablespoon Worcestershire sauce

---

1 Preheat the grill and brush the grill rack with oil. Chop the meat using the coarse blade of a mincer, or pile it onto a chopping board and chop it finely using two knives.
2 Put the minced meat into a bowl and add salt and pepper.
3 Grate the onion and allow it to sweat lightly in a little oil or butter before adding it to the meat.
4 Add your chosen herbs then the Worcestershire sauce and mix well.
5 With wet hands, form the mixture into even-sized patties 2.5 cm (1 in) thick, without pressing them firmly together. The mixture will make four to eight hamburgers, depending on the size of the patties.
6 Grill for 4-6 minutes on each side, depending on the thickness of the burgers and how well you like them cooked. Serve with salad and toasted white or wholemeal rolls, baps or hamburger buns.

HARE

ALL YEAR ROUND

Is hare always in season?

Hare is available year-round and is a darker, more gamy tasting meat than rabbit. Young hares (up to a year old) can simply be roasted, however, older hares require long, slow, moist cooking.

BLOOD THICKENING

Is it true that hare's blood can be used to thicken a sauce?

Yes. When hanging a freshly killed hare, suspend it upside-down and place a bowl under the head to catch any blood lost during the hanging period. The bowl should contain a teaspoon of wine vinegar to prevent the blood from coagulating. Then, when skinning and paunching the hare, add the blood found behind the membrane in the chest cavity to the blood in the bowl. Store the blood in the fridge or freezer for later use.

For best results when adding blood to thicken a sauce, stir it in for only about the last 5 minutes and do not allow the sauce to boil.

HARE VARIATIONS

What exactly is jugged hare, and are there any other good ways of cooking hare?

Jugged or casseroled hare is an old English dish using the hind legs of the hare, which are first marinated in vinegar and wine with bay leaf, onion and peppercorns. The joints are then dried and well browned then placed in a deep earthenware pot or jug with some browned, diced carrot, celery and onion, plus allspice and lemon rind. The marinade and some stock is poured over to cover and the jug is sealed with a lid of flour and water paste.

The meat is cooked slowly for about 3 hours until it is really tender. When cooking is complete, the liquid is strained off, reduced with a little redcurrant jelly, thickened with hare blood and poured back over the hare. The dish can be made easily in a heavy casserole and the sauce thickened with a beurre manié instead of blood.

Other ways of cooking this strong-flavoured meat include hare soup with celeriac and dumplings. In many European countries, the saddle of hare is served roasted very rare and sliced thinly into long strips. The legs, which are rather tough, are generally made into pies or used in stocks and sauces.

In Germany, hare is cooked as a spicy stew called *Hasenpfeffer*, while in Belgium it is cooked with beer or prunes. The Spanish casserole hare with a little chocolate. In Tuscany, chopped hare is the basis of a wonderfully rich sauce for a dish of pasta known as *Pappardelle alla lepre* (see recipe, right).

The richness of hare cooked with red wine, garlic, herbs and pasta makes this an inexpensive gourmet meal.

Hare sauce for noodles (Pappardelle alla lepre)

SERVES: 8
PREPARATION TIME: 30 minutes
COOKING TIME: 2½ hours

1 hare, skinned and jointed
1 tablespoon olive oil
40 g (1½ oz) butter
1 medium onion, finely diced
1 medium carrot, finely diced
1 stick of celery, finely diced
2 cloves garlic, chopped
75 g (2¾ oz) green bacon, diced
Salt and black pepper
2 tablespoons plain flour
300 ml (10 fl oz) dry red wine
2 bay leaves
1 teaspoon chopped fresh rosemary
1 tablespoon chopped fresh sage
600 ml (1 pint) game or chicken stock
450 g (1 lb) dry pappardelle or flat noodles

1 Cut all the meat from the hare joints with a sharp knife, then cut again into small dice.

2 Heat the oil and butter in a sauté pan and add the diced onion, carrot, celery and garlic. Stir well and cook the vegetables gently for 10 minutes until they have softened and are beginning to turn brown.

3 Add the bacon and hare, stir well and cook for a couple of minutes until the meat is browned. Season the sauce generously.

4 Stir in the flour, then the wine and half of the stock. Mix well, scraping off any sediment that has lodged on the base of the pan and stirring it into the sauce.

5 Add the herbs, bring to the boil then turn down the heat and half cover the pan with a lid. Simmer the sauce gently for 2 hours, topping up with more stock if necessary, and cook until the meat is very tender and the sauce is thick and reduced.

6 Taste the hare sauce and adjust the seasoning as necessary. Remove the bay leaves and serve the sauce tossed with buttered pappardelle pasta.

HAZELNUTS: see NUTS

HERBS

◆

Nothing improves food so simply and dramatically as a leaf or two of fresh herbs. They offer every sort of flavour from grassy to peppery, aromatic to pungent. They will boost a casserole, add summer to a salad and enhance a sauce. Study this guide to the best culinary herbs for great ideas and partnerships.

GREEN BASIL

PURPLE BASIL

BAY

CHERVIL

CHIVES

CORIANDER

DILL

A yoghurt sauce crammed with aromatic dill and spiced with mustard balances the richness of smoked salmon (see page 192).

ANGELICA

Angelica is rarely used fresh these days, as it cannot be bought raw. The young stems and leaf stalks are picked in the second year to be crystallised and used to decorate cakes and trifles, and this is now done commercially.

You could grow your own, but it is such a large plant, 1.8 - 3 m (6 - 10 ft), it can easily take over a small garden.

BASIL

The three main varieties of basil are the sweet green basil most familiar in Britain, Greek basil which has tiny green leaves, and purple basil. These share a rich, peppery flavour and a powerful aroma.

You can also purchase basils scented with lemon, anise and cinnamon. Basil is particularly good with tomatoes and is frequently used in Italian dishes and in other Mediterranean-style recipes, especially those made with vegetables.

BAY

Unlike most herbs, aromatic bay leaves are equally good fresh and dried. Bay forms part of the classic bouquet garni, which is added to fish or meat stocks, soups and casseroles.

BORAGE

The most common use for borage is as a garnish for Pimms. Its vivid blue flowers contribute visual appeal as well as the faint flavour of cucumber to this summer drink.

CHERVIL

This delicate summer herb goes well with eggs, fish, chicken and boiled potatoes. It is a traditional part of the fines herbes mixture.

CHIVES

These bright-green stems have a fresh, oniony flavour and are delicious sprinkled on potato salad, baked potatoes and on vichyssoise soup. They provide a slightly hot contrast for bland creamy dishes.

CORIANDER

A powerfully flavoured herb that looks like flat-leaf parsley, coriander has a special affinity with chilli peppers, garlic, ginger and spring onions, and often adds its heat to exotic dishes such as guacamole, stir-fries and salsas.

DILL

The delicate flavour of dill means it goes splendidly with fish, shellfish, boiled potatoes and cream cheese. It is also good in sauces and dips made with mustard or soured cream, and it is traditionally used when curing salmon, as in the Scandinavian dish, gravad lax.

FENNEL
Fennel is very similar to dill but with a coarser, stronger flavour. It is most often paired with fish and is often burnt under red mullet when it is being barbecued to add an unusual smoky flavour.

LEMON BALM
Lemon balm may be used as a substitute for lemongrass or for making tisanes. Its strongly perfumed flavour can be an acquired taste.

LOVAGE
Lovage is a robust plant with an assertive flavour, a little like celery. It is best used sparingly in hearty dishes such as tomato soup or a pasta sauce.

MARJORAM/OREGANO
These two herbs are actually different varieties of the same plant. Sweet or knotted marjoram is the variety usually grown in Britain, while wild marjoram (oregano) is used in the Mediterranean for such dishes as pizzas and tomato sauces served with pasta. The British variety of marjoram has a milder flavour.

MINT
Mint is frequently used in the Middle East in yoghurt sauces and salads such as tabbouleh. Tea flavoured with mint is a popular drink throughout North Africa and the Middle East. The use of mint in Britain is limited by comparison as it is used mostly for sauces or jellies to serve with roast lamb, new potatoes and green peas.

PARSLEY
There are two types of parsley, curly and flat. Choose curly parsley for traditional British dishes such as salmon fishcakes and parsley sauce, and for deep-frying to serve as a garnish with goujons of sole. Use the flat variety in Middle Eastern dishes, soups, salads and as a garnish.

ROSEMARY
This has a very pronounced flavour and should be used sparingly. It is best kept for roast or baked lamb, chicken and potato dishes.

SAGE
The dominant flavour of sage goes well with pork, liver, onions and pasta, and the herb is a prime ingredient of the Italian dish of fried calf's liver and onions called *fegato alla Veneziana*. Whole fresh leaves may be fried in butter and scattered over dishes of grilled or baked vegetables.

SALAD BURNET
Less well known than other herbs, salad burnet makes a wonderful flavouring for wine vinegar. It is also good used in salads made with tomato, cucumber and lettuce.

SAVORY
Savory is much used in France, especially with broad beans. It also acts as a flavour enhancer for other vegetables. Unlike most herbs, its robust flavour develops with long cooking and it is one of the handful of herbs that dries well.

SWEET CICELY
Used mainly in cooking sweet dishes, sweet cicely reduces the acidity of food such as rhubarb and cooking apples without the use of sugar.

TARRAGON
Fresh tarragon has a sweet and spicy flavour well suited to eggs, white fish, chicken, potatoes and cream sauces. The French variety is the one to use; Russian tarragon has little value as a flavouring and tarragon preserved in vinegar makes a better substitute.

THYME
Thyme is easy to grow and can be dried or frozen without any loss of flavour. It is best in Provençal-type dishes, meat or poultry casseroles and with tomatoes, cheese and mustard.

SPECIAL COLLECTIONS
- Bouquet garni consists of three sprigs of parsley, two of thyme and a bay leaf, often tied up in a celery stick or a section of leek, and added to casseroles and stocks.
- Fines herbes is a mixture of four fresh herbs: chervil, chives, parsley and tarragon, and is best used for quickly cooked foods such as eggs.
- Herbes de provence is a mixture of five or six dried herbs. Rosemary and thyme are always present, plus some marjoram, savory, tarragon and/or basil. It is used in slow-cooked stews.

TARRAGON

THYME

SAGE

LEMON BALM

ROSEMARY

MARJORAM

MINT

BOUQUET GARNI

HERBS

STORING FRESH HERBS

Freshly cut herbs seem to wilt fast. What's the best way to store them?

Wrap herbs loosely in paper or in a plastic bag left open, and put them in the refrigerator salad drawer. They will keep for five to six days.

SOFT-FROZEN

Can herbs be frozen?

All the tender herbs, such as basil, chervil and tarragon, freeze well, with the exception of parsley which turns to slush when defrosted. The tougher woody herbs, such as bay, rosemary, sage and thyme tend to splinter, so it is better to dry these.

To freeze herbs, wrap them in foil or small plastic bags and seal well. It is useful to label the parcels if you cannot see inside them.

PRESERVING IN OIL

Can some herbs be preserved in olive oil instead of being dried?

This used to be done with basil before people owned freezers, but freezing is much more effective.

HOME DRYING

Can I dry my own fresh herbs, and should all herbs be dried in the same way?

Most fresh herbs are easily dried, and the same method applies to all of them, but bay, marjoram, mint, rosemary, sage, savory and thyme dry particularly well.

They should be freshly picked, then quickly rinsed and patted dry before being spread on racks and covered lightly with muslin. Then put them in a warm, dry place out of direct sunlight. They will take about a week to dry.

Most herbs are best stripped off their stems before being stored in sealed jars, but some herbs, such as thyme, may be left on the branch and stored upright in the jar.

TIME TO HARVEST

Can herbs be picked at any time for use in the kitchen?

No, they can be picked only up to the point of flowering. Once herbs have developed buds and flowered, all their energy goes into producing seeds and woody stems, and consequently their flavour is dissipated. For freezing or drying, herbs are best picked immediately before they flower, when their flavour is at its most potent.

Small pots of fresh-growing herbs are frequently available in supermarkets throughout the year.

DRIED INSTEAD OF FRESH

Can I substitute dried herbs for fresh ones, and if so, should I use them in the same amounts?

It is hard to give an exact formula for using dried herbs instead of fresh, as the flavour of both is such a variable factor. With fresh herbs, the flavour depends on how fresh they are and how they have been grown: the soil, climate and time of picking. With dried herbs, it depends on how long and in what conditions they have been kept. Assuming both supplies are fresh and in good condition, allow one-third of a tablespoon of dried herbs for each tablespoon of fresh.

In some cases, it is possible to replace one fresh herb with a different, dried one. Dried mint can often be used to replace fresh coriander, for instance, as both herbs marry well with cool, sharp, juicy flavours such as cucumber, garlic, tomatoes and yoghurt.

Freshness test

Dried herbs lose their aroma and their flavour quickly. If you think yours may be too old to use in cooking, test with a sniff. Musty herbs do not need to be thrown out, however: you can sprinkle them over the soil of house plants to give a fertilising boost.

HERBS IN SALAD

Can you give me a good recipe for a fresh herb salad?

Scatter a mixture of four or five tender herbs – chives, chervil, salad burnet, flat parsley or tarragon, for instance – over the small, crisp leaves of Little Gem lettuce. Edible flowers such as borage or nasturtium add a dash of colour (see also CRYSTALLISED FLOWERS). Complement the fresh flavours with a light dressing of olive oil and lemon juice.

CORIANDER: TWO IN ONE

Do the seeds of coriander give the same flavour as the fresh leaf?

Absolutely not. Their flavours are totally different, and they cannot be used as substitutes for each other. Coriander seeds have a gentle, citrus-like aroma, while the leaves are somewhat bitter. The seeds survive long heating well, but the fresh leaves should be added near the end of cooking or sprinkled over the finished dish.

To enjoy the full spicy flavour of the fresh herb, try the following salsa. Its clear, sharp flavour goes well with grilled mixed vegetables, chicken, fish or shellfish.

Coriander salsa

SERVES: 4
PREPARATION TIME: **15 minutes**
COOKING TIME: *none*

---

4 - 5 tomatoes, unskinned, cut
  into quarters
1 bunch spring onions, thinly sliced
1 - 2 red chillies, deseeded and
  finely chopped
2 tablespoons lemon juice
2 tablespoons chopped fresh
  coriander
Sea salt and black pepper

---

1 Put the quartered tomatoes in a food processor and process until they are reduced to a lumpy hash.
2 Turn the purée out into a bowl and stir in all the other ingredients. Taste the salsa; if it seems too spicy, add another chopped tomato. Serve cool but not chilled.

FRAGILE BASIL

Why do some people say that it is not advisable to cook basil?

Basil is a fragile herb which suffers some loss of flavour when subjected to heat or drying. In most recipes, you can minimise the loss of flavour by adding basil near the end of the cooking time. However, it is most flavourful when used fresh, as in the Italian sauce pesto, or as a garnish added after cooking, as in this recipe for Grilled Vegetable Salad. The salad is served at room temperature, and is delicious as a starter with some crusty bread to mop up the dressing.

Grilled vegetable salad with basil

SERVES: 4 as a starter
PREPARATION TIME: 45 minutes
COOKING TIME: 50 minutes

1 red pepper
1 yellow pepper
1 aubergine
1 head fennel
2 red onions
4 tablespoons olive oil
1 clove garlic, finely chopped
Sea salt and black pepper

FOR THE DRESSING
3 tablespoons virgin olive oil
½ tablespoon white wine vinegar
To garnish: 6 - 8 leaves basil

1 Preheat the grill for 10 minutes. Quarter the peppers and scrape out the seeds. Put the wedges under the grill, skin side up, until the skins have blackened and blistered evenly all over. Let them cool slightly, peel off the skin then set aside.
2 Cut the aubergine lengthways in 1 cm (½ in) slices, leaving the skin on, and brush with olive oil. Grill until golden brown, turning once. Drain on kitchen paper.
3 Cut the fennel lengthways in 1 cm (½ in) slices. Brush one side with oil and grill until coloured, then oil the other side and grill that.
4 Peel the onions, cut each one into four wedges and brush with oil. Grill until soft and well browned.

The warm flavours of a salad of grilled vegetables are brought to life with a scattering of purple basil leaves and a side dish of spicy coriander salsa.

5 Arrange all the vegetables on a flat dish and scatter the chopped garlic over them, then season with salt and plenty of pepper. Mix the oil and vinegar together and spoon over. If the basil leaves are small, tuck them among the vegetables. If large, tear them in pieces and scatter on top.

SEEDS FOR LONG COOKING

Which are best for using in dishes that require lengthy cooking, fresh herbs or seeds?

Seeds are often better in dishes such as casseroles as most fresh herbs lose their taste when subjected to heat. However, the taste of seeds will be somewhat different. Instead, try finishing the dish with fresh herbs just before serving.

VEGETABLE PARTNERS

How do I choose which herbs to put with vegetables?

All herbs go well with vegetables. It is the nature of the dish, rather than the ingredients, that determines which herb to use. For example, a robust herb such as thyme is a good choice in oily Provençal-type stews or casseroles of mixed vegetables. Dill will add freshness to boiled or steamed carrots, lovage is excellent in hearty vegetable soups, while rosemary goes well with roast potatoes. Basil is the obvious choice for tomatoes and oregano is traditional with mixed Greek salads.

FISHY HERBS

Which herbs go best with fish?

Fennel is often served with fish in France, while, for the British, curly parsley is the most popular choice.

The Scandinavians usually pair fish with dill, for instance in simple butter sauces or a mustard sauce such as the one below. This usually accompanies cured salmon (*gravad lax*), but is also delicious with any cured or cooked fish, with chicken, and even cold boiled beef.

Dill and mustard sauce

SERVES: *4*
PREPARATION TIME: *12 minutes*
COOKING TIME: *none*

1 tablespoon Dijon mustard
1 tablespoon olive oil
125 ml (4 fl oz) yoghurt
Juice of 1 lemon
4 tablespoons chopped dill

1 Put the mustard in a bowl and whisk in the olive oil drop by drop, as if making mayonnaise.
2 When all the oil is amalgamated, gradually stir in the yoghurt. Add lemon juice to taste, sprinkle on the chopped dill and mix well.

VERSATILE PARSLEY

Can curly and flat-leaf parsley be substituted for each other?

Both are used as a garnish, but curly parsley is easier to chop. Flat-leaf parsley, sometimes called French parsley, has a slightly mellower, fuller flavour than curly, and is best used in Middle Eastern dishes and in soups and salads. Choose curly parsley for parsley sauce to accompany fishcakes, or deep-fry it, as in the recipe below, and use as a garnish for fish dishes.

Fried parsley

SERVES: *4*
PREPARATION TIME: *5 minutes*
COOKING TIME: *1 minute*

10 - 12 large sprigs very fine
   curly parsley
Frying oil

1 Fill a deep pan or wok half full with clean oil. Heat the oil to 180°C (350°F). Drop in half the parsley and fry for 20 - 30 seconds until it turns a bright emerald green; it should turn crisp and brittle almost immediately.
2 Lift the parsley out with a slotted spoon and drain it well on several layers of kitchen paper.
3 Keep the first batch of parsley warm while you fry the second batch. Drain this on kitchen paper, mix with the first batch and serve warm.

HERBS FOR CHICKEN

Which herbs go well with chicken?

Rosemary is as good with roast chicken as it is with lamb. Simply tuck a few branches between the wings and the body of the bird, and baste well with oil while roasting. Cook in a fairly hot oven so that the chicken browns well. Serve with roast potatoes and a crisp green salad, sprinkling on a few more rosemary leaves.

Other herbs that go well with chicken are lemon balm, sage, tarragon and thyme. They can either be cooked with the meat or added to a sauce served with it.

HERBAL TEAS

Which are the best herbs to use when making herbal teas?

The most popular herbs to infuse are camomile, hibiscus and peppermint. A mixture of mint and lime flower is very common in France, as is lemon verbena.

An unusual tea can be made with fresh sage. Simply put a handful of freshly gathered sage leaves in a small teapot and pour over about 500 ml (18 fl oz) of nearly boiling water. Then let it stand, covered, for 4–5 minutes, before pouring into cups. Sage tea is reputed to act as a digestive aid, an antiseptic and a slight stimulant. See also TISANES.

FINELY CHOPPING FRESH HERBS

Herbs can be chopped with a kitchen knife, a two-handled mincing knife, or in a food processor. If using a blade, *ensure it is sharp or you will crush and bruise the herbs. If using a machine, take care not to overchop into a purée.*

1 Wash and dry the herbs (parsley is shown here) and compress them into a ball in the palms of your hands.

2 Chop the leaves coarsely, keeping your fingertips tucked well under, then scrape into a pile with the blade.

3 Hold the knife down at its tip and lever the handle up and down. Keep piling and slicing until finely chopped.

HOLLANDAISE SAUCE

CURDLE-FREE SAUCE

How do I stop hollandaise sauce from curdling during cooking?

This butter sauce will curdle if it overheats, so it must be cooked over a very gentle heat, if possible in a bain-marie (see panel, right).

If the hollandaise becomes granular during cooking, immediately remove the basin from the heat, place it in a bowl of cold water and stir the sauce to cool it quickly. Or, remove it from the heat at once and stir in a tablespoon of warm water.

To save a curdled sauce, break a fresh egg yolk into a basin. Stir in a teaspoon of water, add a knob of butter and place the basin over a pan of hot water. Stir the mixture gently until the butter has melted and the egg thickens slightly, then gradually add the curdled sauce, beating until smooth.

QUICKER METHODS

Is there a quick and easy way to make hollandaise sauce?

You can make hollandaise in a food processor or liquidiser: lightly blend the egg yolks and vinegar reduction in the bowl then pour in the warm melted butter in a thin stream while the motor is running and process until thick and smooth.

Hollandaise can also be made in the microwave. Heat the butter, egg yolks and vinegar reduction together on High for 10 seconds. Remove from the oven and whisk. Repeat the 10 second cooking followed by whisking until the sauce is thickened and smooth.

SAUCY DIFFERENCE

What is the difference between hollandaise and béarnaise sauce?

Both butter sauces are based on egg yolks but hollandaise is lightly flavoured with wine vinegar, while béarnaise has shallot and tarragon added for a stronger flavour. The béarnaise sauce below is delicious with steak or other grilled food.

Béarnaise sauce

SERVES: 2 - 4
PREPARATION TIME: 10 minutes
COOKING TIME: 15 minutes

---

4 tablespoons tarragon or white wine vinegar (or half dry white wine and half vinegar)
1 shallot, chopped
6 peppercorns, crushed
1 bay leaf
1 sprig tarragon
2 egg yolks, size 2
100 g (3 ½ oz) butter, diced
1 teaspoon chopped tarragon leaves

---

1 Put the vinegar in a small pan and add the shallot, peppercorns, bay leaf and sprig of tarragon. Boil until reduced to a tablespoon.
2 Put the egg yolks in a small bowl, strain in the flavoured vinegar and whisk to a light foam. Place the bowl over a small pan of hot (but not boiling) water off the heat, making sure the bowl does not touch the water. Beat the mixture with a hand whisk until slightly thickened.
3 Put the pan and the bowl over a gentle heat. Gradually add the cubes of butter to the mixture, stirring continuously until all the fat has been incorporated and the sauce is thick and glossy. Stir in the chopped tarragon and serve the sauce warm, or at room temperature.

WAITING TIME

How long ahead can hollandaise or béarnaise be made?

Either sauce can be kept warm for up to an hour. Cover the bowl with cling film or foil and stand it over a pan of hot but not boiling water, removed from the heat. Before serving, beat the sauce well as it will have thickened as it cools. If the sauce has cooled too much, reheat the water in the saucepan, then replace the basin of sauce and whisk it continuously until it is the required temperature.

MAKING
HOLLANDAISE SAUCE

Rich and smooth hollandaise sauce is traditionally served warm with delicately flavoured fish, shellfish, asparagus and artichoke.

To make enough sauce for two people, you need a tablespoon each of wine vinegar and water, 1 bay leaf, 6 peppercorns, 100 g (3 ½ oz) of butter and 2 egg yolks, size 3.

1 Boil the vinegar, water, bay leaf and peppercorns together until the liquid is reduced by half. Strain into a bowl or the top of a double saucepan. Gently melt the butter.

2 Put the bowl with the vinegar reduction over a pan of very hot (but not boiling) water, and, using a wooden spoon, mix in the yolks.

3 Remove the pan from the heat and gradually stir in the melted butter to give a creamy texture.

4 Return the pan to the heat and continue stirring over a very gentle heat for 8 - 10 minutes until the sauce becomes light, airy and glossy, and is just thick enough to drip off the spoon. Season to taste.

HONEY

HONEY AND SUGAR

Is it true that honey is a healthier sweetener than sugar?

Honey contains a small amount of B-group vitamins and some minerals (calcium, chlorine, potassium and sodium), making it marginally healthier than white sugar, which contains some calcium and potassium but no vitamins at all. Golden demerara sugar contains slightly more minerals than honey does, but fewer vitamins.

Regarding calorie content, 100 g (3½ oz) of honey has 280–290 Calories, while the same amount of sugar has about 395 Calories. And as honey tastes sweeter than sugar, it is usually used in smaller quantities, reducing the calories further.

HONEY FOR COOKING

Can honey be used as a substitute for sugar in recipes?

Honey is good to use in cooking, especially baking, because it absorbs moisture better than sugar. This means that honey will keep breads and cakes moist for longer.

To substitute honey for sugar, use a spoonful of honey to every one-and-a-quarter spoons of sugar stated in the recipe. Note that as honey contains some water, the amount of liquid used in the recipe needs to be reduced slightly.

ORGANIC PRODUCTION

What is organic honey?

Organic honey is produced in areas remote from chemical and artificial sprays, the most notable places being in New Zealand and some forests in Africa, and the hives are not treated with chemicals.

In Britain, hives may be set in relatively pure land, but there can be no guarantees as to its 'organic' quality as bees fly great distances – up to a 8 km (5 mile) radius – in their search for nectar.

SWEET VARIATIONS

Can I use a thick, set honey where a recipe says to use clear honey, and are some honeys better to cook with than others?

You can use any honey in cooking, but cloudy or set honey should be warmed first to liquefy it so it can be mixed in evenly.

It is generally best to use a light-coloured honey for cooking, as the flavour of darker honeys is too strong. Both the colour and flavour of different honeys are determined by the nectar the bees collect. Acacia honey, for instance, is thin, runny and pale, honey made from heather is thicker and sometimes cloudy, while clover honey is thick and pale amber. Mexican alcahual is almost pure white. Sage honey is very dark and strongly flavoured, as is lavender honey, which is amber with a green caste. Greek Hymettus has aromatic flavours of marjoram, savory and thyme.

A clear, light honey is the best choice for the following ice cream, where it adds richness and depth to a caramelised sugar syrup.

Burnt honey ice cream

SERVES: 4
PREPARATION TIME: 50 minutes, plus cooling and freezing time
COOKING TIME: 15 - 20 minutes

4 egg yolks, size 3
125 g (4½ oz) caster sugar
300 ml (10 fl oz) milk
300 ml (10 fl oz) double cream, lightly whipped
125 g (4½ oz) granulated sugar
4 tablespoons water
4 tablespoons clear honey

1 Beat the egg yolks and the caster sugar together briskly. Heat the milk until it just comes to boiling point and immediately pour it onto the egg and sugar mixture, whisking well.
2 Return the custard to the pan and heat it gently, stirring continuously until it thickens and just coats the back of the spoon. Strain the custard through a sieve and leave to cool completely, then stir in the cream.

3 Put the granulated sugar into a small saucepan, add 2 tablespoons of water and heat gently until the sugar has dissolved. Then bring the syrup to the boil and boil rapidly until it becomes a dark golden brown.
4 Remove the pan from the heat, cover your hands well with cloths to protect them and carefully add the remaining 2 tablespoons of water. The mixture will hiss and spit rather fiercely for a few seconds. Stir well, return the pan to the heat and cook for a further 1 - 2 minutes.

The syrup is ready when a small drop put onto a plate forms a soft ball when rolled between your fingers (dip your finger and thumb into iced water immediately before and after testing). You can also test it with a sugar thermometer, heating until the syrup reaches 115°C (240°F).
5 Remove the pan from the heat and allow the mixture to cool slightly, then stir in the honey.
6 When the honeyed syrup has cooled but is still liquid, stir it into the custard. Pour the mixture into a metal or plastic container, cover it, then freeze it for 1 - 2 hours until it begins to harden to a depth of about 2.5 cm (1 in) around the edges. Whisk the mixture well, then return it to the freezer. Repeat the freezing and whisking process twice more.

CRYSTAL CLEAR

Is crystallised honey usable?

Yes. Crystallisation does not affect either the taste or the nutritional value of honey. If there is only a little crystallisation, a good stir may solve the problem. If most of, or all the honey has become unpleasantly gritty, put the jar in a pan of very hot water and leave it for an hour. For quicker results, gently heat the pan of water containing the jar of honey on the hob. Use the honey while still warm, as it will recrystallise on cooling.

The following recipe for Baklava, the eastern Mediterranean sweetmeat, is a good way to use up gritty honey. The honey is added to a hot syrup which is then poured onto the pastry to seep through.

Baklava

MAKES: *16 pieces*
PREPARATION TIME: *45 minutes*
COOKING TIME: *1 hour*

FOR THE SYRUP
450 g (1 lb) caster sugar
300 ml (10 fl oz) water
1 tablespoon rosewater
1 tablespoon orange flower water
2 tablespoons lemon juice
*4 tablespoons clear, strongly
  flavoured honey such as the
  Greek Hymettus*

FOR THE FILLING
*400 g (14 oz) shelled walnuts,
  finely chopped*
25 g (1 oz) sugar
1 tablespoon ground cinnamon

FOR THE PASTRY
400 g (14 oz) prepared filo pastry
225 g (8 oz) unsalted butter, melted

1 To make the syrup, put the sugar and water into a pan and heat gently until the sugar has dissolved. Bring the mixture to a gentle boil and simmer for about 5 minutes until the syrup is still clear but has thickened enough to coat the back of a spoon.
2 Remove the saucepan from the heat and stir in the rosewater, orange flower water, lemon juice and honey. Leave the syrup to cool thoroughly then chill in the refrigerator.
3 To make the baklava filling, mix together the chopped walnuts, sugar and cinnamon in a small bowl to make a rough paste.
4 Lightly brush a shallow baking tin measuring 33 × 23 cm (13 × 9 in) with melted butter. Take out the filo pastry but keep the sheets covered with a damp cloth or upturned bowl until you are ready for them as they dry out very quickly. Preheat the oven to 150°C (300°F, gas mark 2).
5 Place a sheet of filo in the bottom of the tin and brush it well with melted butter, then repeat until there are five or six stacked sheets. Spoon on about a quarter of the filling, cover with another five or six layers of buttered pastry sheets and then add more filling. Continue layering and filling in this way until you end with a layer of filo.
6 With a sharp knife, cut the top layer of pastry into strips about 4 cm (1 ½ in) wide. Cut the strips with diagonal parallel lines 4 cm (1 ½ in) apart to form diamond shapes.
7 Bake for 45 minutes, then turn the temperature up to 200°C (400°F, gas mark 6). Cook the baklava for a further 5 - 10 minutes or until the pastry is golden brown and puffed.
8 Remove from the oven and pour the cold syrup all over the baklava. Leave in the tin for at least 24 hours for the syrup to be absorbed. When ready to serve, cut into pieces along the original lines. Baklava will keep for up to a week in the refrigerator.

A fragrant honey syrup makes a rich treat of Baklava, a Greek speciality in which a sweet, nutty filling is layered between crisp sheets of paper-thin filo pastry.

HORSERADISH

FRESH OR PROCESSED

Can you buy fresh horseradish?

The edible part of the horseradish plant, the small buff-coloured root, is usually found fresh only in good greengrocers, specialist food shops and large supermarkets, throughout autumn and winter. It is more commonly available already processed, finely grated and mixed with citric acid. Horseradish, which is rich in vitamin C, is almost always used in cold sauces like the recipe below, served with hot or cold roast or braised beef or smoked fish such as eel, mackerel and trout.

Horseradish sauce

SERVES: *4*
PREPARATION TIME: *10 minutes*
COOKING TIME: *none*

*2 tablespoons fresh horseradish,
  peeled and grated*
*150 ml (5 fl oz) lightly whipped
  double cream*
1 - 2 teaspoons lemon juice
Salt and white pepper

Stir the horseradish into the cream, add the lemon juice and season to taste. Eat within three days.

ICE CREAM AND SORBETS

HAND-BEATEN

Is an ice cream machine essential for a really good result?

The short answer is no, although machines do make the job considerably easier, as it is essential to beat air into the mixture while it is freezing to break up the ice crystals and create a rich, smooth texture.

To make ice cream by hand, pour the mixture into a metal or plastic container and put it into the freezer for about 1½ hours. When it has started to freeze around the edges, you can either whizz it in a food processor for 20 seconds, or tip it into a bowl and beat vigorously by hand or with an electric whisk.

Return the slushy ice cream to the container and pop it back into the freezer, and repeat the process another two or three times until you achieve the right consistency.

MECHANICAL HELP

There are so many different types of ice cream machine. Can you advise on which one to choose?

The simplest type of machine consists of a container set inside a bucket, which you pack with ice and salt. The ice cream is then churned either by hand or electrically. These machines make very successful ice cream, but they can be messy to clean up.

Sorbetières, used for both sorbets and ice cream, have electric motors; they are designed for use in the

---

MAKING VANILLA CUSTARD ICE CREAM

Ice cream is easy to make without an electric ice cream machine. The following vanilla ice cream, made with a thick custard base, will serve up to six people. You will need 4 egg yolks, 125 g (4½ oz) of caster sugar, 300 ml (10 fl oz) of milk, 300 ml (10 fl oz) of thick or lightly whipped double cream and 1½ teaspoons of vanilla extract.

1 Beat the egg yolks with the caster sugar. Heat the milk to just under boiling point then whisk it into the egg mixture. Heat the custard gently, without boiling, in a heavy-based pan.

2 Stir the custard continuously with a wooden spoon until the mixture thickens and lightly coats the back of the spoon. Strain it through a sieve into a bowl and leave until cold.

3 With a metal spoon, stir the cream and vanilla extract into the cold custard. Pour the mixture into a metal or plastic container and freeze for an hour or two until the edges are frozen but give when pressed with a finger.

4 Tip the mixture into a bowl and whisk well, or put into a food processor and beat. Pour the ice cream back into the container and return it to the freezer. Repeat the freezing and whisking process twice more.

---

freezer, and have a thin power supply cord to enable you to shut the freezer door. Another version has a removable coolant-filled canister which you freeze overnight before churning. These machines are usually quite small.

For people who make ice cream regularly and in large quantities, a large machine with integral refrigeration is worth considering – they are excellent but expensive and take up a lot of space in the kitchen.

SMOOTHER RESULTS

What is the best way to make fresh fruit ice cream?

Ice cream can be made with cream, custard, or a mixture of the two, and recipes with a large amount of butterfat produce the best results when made by hand. Most fruit ice creams are made with a cream rather than a custard base as cream

allows more of the fruit flavour to come through. However, a custard base produces smaller ice crystals and will result in a smoother ice cream. If using strawberries, their flavour may be diminished slightly, but can be intensified by adding half a jar of strawberry jam.

You can use any soft fruits in the following recipe for cream-based Summer Fruit Ice Cream, but raspberries on their own are watery; it is best to add some other fruit, such as strawberries or blackberries.

Soft fruits such as these need no cooking before being incorporated into ice cream, but you could also use fruit that needs cooking first, such as apples, greengages, pears, plums or rhubarb. Simmer them in a little water, with sugar to taste, until they are just tender, or longer for a purée (depending on how smooth you want your ice cream to be), then continue with the recipe.

A glorious fruit ice cream, made with a mixture of summer berries, is a feast for both the eyes and the palate.

Summer fruit ice cream

SERVES: 8
PREPARATION TIME: 20 minutes plus at least 6 hours freezing
COOKING TIME: none

1 kg (2 lb 4 oz) prepared fresh fruit such as blackberries, raspberries or strawberries
2 tablespoons lemon juice
350 g (12 oz) icing sugar
600 ml (1 pint) double cream

1 Put the fruit, lemon juice and icing sugar into a food processor and blend until smooth. With a wooden spoon, press the mixture through a nylon sieve into a large bowl, then discard the seeds. Alternatively, if you have no food processor, start by pushing the fruit through a nylon sieve set over a large bowl. Then mix the fruit purée with the lemon juice and icing sugar, stirring well.

2 Whip the cream until it forms very soft peaks, then fold it gently into the fruit mixture.

3 To freeze the mixture without an ice cream machine, pour it into a metal or plastic container, cover and freeze for about 1½ hours until the edges of the ice cream are frozen and the centre is soft. Remove from the freezer and beat until the whole mixture is slushy then return to the freezer. Repeat this process at least twice more. For maximum flavour, eat within two weeks.

VARIATION

For a smoother custard base, mix a few drops of vanilla essence into 500 ml (18 fl oz) of milk and heat gently. Whisk 5 egg yolks with 60 g (2¼ oz) of sugar and stir this into the hot milk. Heat gently until it thickens then leave it to cool. Fold the custard instead of the cream into the fruit purée then freeze.

SMART TURNOUT

What is the best way of turning out a finished ice cream smoothly from a metal mould?

Simply dip a tea towel in hot water, wring it out and wrap it around the mould for a few seconds. Then invert the mould over a plate, give it a good shake and the ice cream should be released. Metal is the best material for ice cream moulds as it conducts cold and heat well.

LUSCIOUS SAUCE

How can I make a fruit sauce to pour over ice cream?

Soft fruits such as blueberries and raspberries are especially good to make into a sauce. Stew the fruit gently in a tablespoon or two of water, with added sugar and a liqueur if you like, until the juices

MAKING A LEMON AND LIME SORBET

Sorbets are made with fruit and a sugar syrup; egg whites can be added to help prevent crystals from forming. For six people, you need 200g (7oz) of caster sugar, the rind and juice of 2 lemons and 4 limes, and 2 egg whites.

1 Put the sugar into a pan with 125 ml (4 fl oz) of water and heat gently, stirring continuously, until the sugar dissolves. Then bring the liquid to the boil and immediately remove the pan from the heat.

2 Add the lemon and lime rind to the hot sugar syrup, then cool the syrup to room temperature.

3 Strain the cooled syrup into a bowl, stir in the fruit juice then pour the mixture into a container and freeze until it resembles slush.

4 Whisk the egg whites to soft peak stage, then add the slushy sorbet in large spoonfuls and gently whisk. Return the mixture to the freezer until it is icy and half-frozen. Remove and stir gently with a fork, then return to the freezer until solid.

run. Then purée the fruit, by hand or in a food processor, and push through a sieve to remove the pips. Serve warm or cold.

WATER ICES

What is the difference between a granita and a sorbet?

Both are based on a sugar syrup but a granita is much coarser, with a consistency somewhat like fluffy snow, whereas a sorbet is smooth-textured. A granita contains much less sugar than a sorbet and should be eaten on the day it is made as the texture deteriorates.

ADDING EGGS TO SORBETS

Is it common for sorbet recipes to include a meringue mixture?

A sorbet does not usually contain any milk or egg. However, some recipes add lightly whipped egg whites (see box, left) to smooth the texture and lighten the mixture. This also helps to prevent the formation of crystals and adds an opaque look to the finished ice.

Generally, sorbets are made from a mix of fruit juice or purée and a sugar syrup. The denser the sugar syrup, the smoother and sweeter the sorbet will be.

ADDING YOGHURT

Can you add yoghurt to sorbet?

You can make delicious low-fat ice creams by making a fruit sorbet and adding low-fat yoghurt to the mixture before freezing. Greek yoghurt is particularly good for this but has a slightly higher fat content.

SORBETS AS STARTERS

Can you make savoury sorbets?

Savoury sorbets are easy to make from such ingredients as avocados, cucumbers, red peppers and tomatoes. Use virtually any ingredient that will blend well with a sugar syrup, as in the Tomato and Red Pepper Sorbet, right. These savoury sorbets are delicious as starters or as refreshers between courses.

Tomato and red pepper sorbet

SERVES: 8
PREPARATION TIME: 40 minutes plus at least 5 hours freezing
COOKING TIME: 10 minutes

---

2 large red peppers
2 tablespoons sunflower oil
100g (3 ½ oz) caster sugar
300 ml (10 fl oz) water
500g (1 lb 2 oz) tomato passata
½ teaspoon salt
Juice of ½ large lemon
1 teaspoon Worcestershire sauce
1 teaspoon soy sauce
A few drops Tabasco
White pepper

---

1 Preheat the grill to medium hot. Cut the peppers into quarters and remove the seeds and membranes. Brush them with a tablespoon of oil, place skin side up on a grill rack, then grill until the skin is blistered and blackened and the flesh is soft. Allow to cool. Peel off and discard the skin and set the peppers aside.
2 To make the syrup, put the sugar and water into a pan and heat gently, stirring from time to time, until the sugar has dissolved. Bring to the boil and simmer for 4 - 5 minutes until a thick syrup forms that reaches 115°C (240°F) on a sugar thermometer. (If you do not have a thermometer, drop a little ball of syrup into a small bowl of very cold water. When gathered together with your fingertips, it should form a soft ball.) Then leave the syrup to cool completely.
3 Put the cold syrup, along with the peppers, remaining oil and all the remaining ingredients into a food processor and blend until smooth.
4 Pour the mixture into a shallow freezer container, cover and freeze for about 1½ hours or until mushy.
5 Remove the soft sorbet from the freezer and beat well, then return to the freezer. Repeat the freezing and beating process twice more.
6 About 30 minutes before serving, move the sorbet into the refrigerator to allow it to soften a little. Serve small scoops in hollowed-out tomato halves or avocado halves, or with a salad garnish and thin crisp toast.

ICE CREAM BISCUITS

How do I make biscuit 'baskets' to use as a container for ice cream?

The easiest way to do this is to make thin, lacy biscuits and press them over oranges while they are still warm and pliable. In the recipe below, chopped almonds add a crunchy texture which is a pleasant contrast to the softness of the ice cream. Note that small shells are most successful as the weight of a larger biscuit can break the shape.

Ice cream shells

MAKES: 16 – 18 shells
PREPARATION TIME: 25 minutes
COOKING TIME: 8 minutes per batch

75 g (2 3/4 oz) caster sugar
75 g (2 3/4 oz) softened butter
40 g (1 1/2 oz) plain flour
60 g (2 1/4 oz) chopped almonds
3 - 4 small oranges for shaping

1 Preheat the oven to 200°C (400°F, gas mark 6) and line two baking sheets with baking paper.
2 Put the sugar, butter and flour in a bowl, beat for 2 - 3 minutes until well mixed, then stir in the almonds.
3 Put a few rounded teaspoons of the mixture onto the baking sheets, leaving a large gap between each one, and flatten with the back of a wet fork. Bake for 7 - 8 minutes until golden but still slightly pale in the centre, then leave on the sheets for no more than a minute to set a little.
4 While the biscuits are still warm, carefully remove them with a palette knife and drape each one gently over a lightly oiled orange, then mould the biscuits around the oranges. (If a shell is now too firm, return it to the oven for a few seconds to soften.)
5 Leave the shells draped over the oranges for a few minutes to let them harden, then lift them off gently and transfer to a wire tray.
6 Repeat the process with the rest of the mixture, then store the shells in an airtight container until ready to use. They will keep for up to ten days. Just before serving, carefully fill each biscuit with a small scoop of ice cream or sorbet and soft fruit.

ICING

CHOOSING WISELY

What is the difference between royal, glacé, sugarpaste and fondant icing?

Royal icing is a thick paste made from egg whites and sifted icing sugar. It is spread over marzipan-covered fruit cakes, or piped into decorations, and left to dry out. It is mainly used on rich, highly decorated celebration cakes.

Glacé icing is a smooth paste of icing sugar dissolved in a little water, which is spread straight onto the cake and left to dry out. It is ideal for covering cup cakes, tea breads and simple sponges.

Sugarpaste and fondant icing are the same thing: icing sugar, egg whites and liquid glucose are mixed and kneaded to a soft dough which is rolled out before being smoothed over a cake. Use it on simple cakes, novelty or celebration cakes.

There are many other types of icing, including the rich and creamy frosting in the recipe for Frosted Walnut Cake in CAKES.

KEEPING ICING SOFT

How do I stop royal icing from going rock-hard after a few days?

Royal icing becomes hard if it has not been beaten for long enough: it needs at least 15 minutes of beating with an electric mixer (or 20 minutes with a wooden spoon). The mixture should form soft peaks, and a palette knife run through it should leave a clean mark.

Then leave the icing to stand, covered with a damp cloth or in a sealed plastic container, for about 24 hours. This alters the structure of the sugar and makes it easier to spread and pipe. The icing can then be kept in a covered plastic container in the refrigerator for up to a fortnight, but may need further beating to restore to the right consistency. Another way of ensuring that royal icing is soft and spreads

COVERING A CAKE WITH ROYAL ICING

To achieve a good finish, give the cake two or three thin coats of icing as described below, and leave the icing to dry thoroughly each time.

1 For the first coat, put three large spoonfuls of icing on the top of the cake. Spread the icing roughly with a palette knife, ensuring there are no trapped air bubbles.

2 Hold an icing ruler or other firm, flat ruler at an angle of 45° over the cake. Smooth the icing by sweeping the ruler back and forth across the cake until the top is perfectly flat. With a palette knife, trim off excess icing around the edge and leave to dry for 24 hours.

3 Place the cake on a turntable, or on a plate placed on a bowl, and spread a layer of icing evenly around the side with a palette knife.

4 Gently but firmly hold a cake scraper at the side of the cake, then pull the turntable around in an even sweep. Leave the icing to dry overnight. When dry, trim off the ridge of icing from the rim with a small, sharp knife. Smooth out any bumps with fine sandpaper.

5 Apply a second, thinner coat of icing over the top and sides and leave it to dry for 48 hours. Trim and gently sand the icing then apply a third thin coat and leave to dry for 24 hours before decorating.

easily is to add a teaspoon of glycerine to each 500 g (1 lb 2 oz) of icing sugar, as in the recipe below.

Royal icing

MAKES: *enough to cover a 20 cm (8 in) cake*
PREPARATION TIME: *35 minutes*
COOKING TIME: *none*

2 egg whites, size 3
500 g (1 lb 2 oz) icing sugar, sifted
1 teaspoon glycerine

1 Put the egg whites in a bowl and whisk with a fork until just frothy. Gradually beat in the sugar until the mixture becomes white and smooth.
2 Whisk for 15 minutes at a slow speed with an electric mixer, or beat for 20 minutes with a wooden spoon. Add the glycerine, then cover with a damp cloth and leave to stand in a cool place for 24 hours before using.

To the rescue!

If your royal icing dries in the bowl and goes hard, leave it covered with two damp cloths for a few hours or overnight. Pass the dampened icing through a sieve to remove any lumps, then beat briefly to restore the consistency.

DIRECT ACTION

Marzipan is not popular in our family. Could I put royal icing directly onto fruit cake?

Not really. Marzipan, or almond paste (see following recipe), provides a smooth surface for the icing and stops moisture from the fruit coming through to stain the icing. However, you can spread glacé icing (see recipe, right) or sugarpaste straight onto a cake that is to be eaten soon after being made.

Marzipan is rolled out, cut to fit the top and sides of the cake and pressed onto the surface. Because it is so smooth, marzipan will not stick unless the cake is covered with a glaze first, traditionally of apricot jam or marmalade. Once pressed onto the cake, marzipan should be left to dry out for at least 24 hours, and preferably a week, before being covered in icing.

Almond paste (Marzipan)

MAKES: *enough to cover a 20 cm (8 in) cake*
PREPARATION TIME: *20 minutes*
COOKING TIME: *none*

100 g (3 ½ oz) icing sugar
100 g (3 ½ oz) caster sugar
225 g (8 oz) ground almonds
1 teaspoon lemon juice
A few drops of almond essence
1 egg, size 3, beaten

1 Sift the sugars and almonds into a bowl and make a well in the centre. Add all the remaining ingredients and mix to a soft dough.
2 Turn onto a surface that has been lightly dusted with icing or caster sugar and knead briefly until smooth. Wrap tightly in cling film and store in a cool place until needed.

Glacé icing

MAKES: *enough to cover a 20 cm (8 in) cake*
PREPARATION TIME: *5 minutes*
COOKING TIME: *none*

100 g (3 ½ oz) icing sugar
1 tablespoon warm water

Sift the icing sugar into a bowl and gradually mix in the water, or any variations, until the icing is smooth.
VARIATIONS
● CHOCOLATE ICING: mix 2 teaspoons of cocoa powder in a tablespoon of boiling water, cool slightly and mix a little at a time into the icing sugar.
● CITRUS ICING: replace the water with a tablespoon of strained lemon or orange juice, and add a few drops of yellow food colouring.
● COFFEE ICING: dissolve a teaspoon of instant coffee in a tablespoon of boiling water, cool slightly and mix a little at a time into the icing sugar.
● ROSE ICING: replace the water with a tablespoon of rosewater.

SIMPLE SUGARPASTE

What is the easiest, quickest and neatest way to ice a cake?

Using glacé icing is very simple, as it is quick and easy to make and is spread over cakes with a palette knife. However, if you prefer a smooth, neat finish, use bought, ready-to-roll fondant or sugarpaste icing. It is rolled out like pastry and can be smoothed over a cake in just a few minutes, either straight onto the cake itself or over a layer of marzipan. It can also be used for modelling decorations or can be cut into letters or numbers for special occasion cakes.

To cover a cake with sugarpaste, knead the icing until soft and roll it out onto a surface that has been lightly covered with sieved icing sugar, moving the icing continually to prevent it from sticking. Measure across the top and sides of the cake with string and roll the icing out to a circle 2.5 cm (1 in) larger.

If you have covered the cake with marzipan first, brush it lightly with boiled water or alcoholic spirit such as brandy so the icing sticks. If you are putting the icing straight onto the cake, brush it with a jam glaze first to enable it to stick.

Holding the rolled icing with both hands, lift it carefully onto the cake and into position. Flute the bottom edges out like fabric but do not pleat or this will leave a line. Smooth the icing over the cake with your palms to remove any air bubbles, then trim the edges with a knife. The scraps can be rolled into a ball and used for decorations.

COLOUR TO PLEASE

What is the best way to add colour to sugarpaste icing?

Sugarpaste icing is sold in a range of colours and also in plain white, which can be coloured or painted with edible paste food colouring. Liquid food colouring would make the icing dull and limp because you would need so much colouring to achieve the right depth of colour. Thicker paste food colouring is available at bakers' supply shops and some larger supermarkets and major department stores.

To colour the icing, knead in the colouring until it is mixed through. Blend it in a little at a time until you achieve the right shade: it is very concentrated. To paint colouring onto icing, put a drop of the colouring onto a saucer, then mix in a teaspoon of water.

SHAPING DECORATIONS

I have tried to make fondant cake decorations but the paste turned brittle. Can this be avoided?

Sugarpaste icing is rolled out to a smooth dough-like paste which can be spread over cakes or moulded into shapes such as flowers (see box, right), but, like Plasticine, it will dry if left exposed to air.

When covering and decorating cakes, keep the scraps fresh until you are ready to make the trimmings. Roll the scraps into a ball and keep this airtight in a freezer bag or strong plastic bag. When you are ready to make some decorations, break off some icing and return the rest to the airtight bag.

UNBROKEN LINES

When I try to pipe icing, the lines always break and look ragged. What am I doing wrong?

Piping is usually done with royal icing, and the problem most people have is making it to the right consistency. Stiff icing will be difficult to press out for piping, the strands will break and you will have an aching arm. For best results, use less sugar than you would for a covering icing: beat in only three-quarters of the sugar, until the mixture is like thick cream, and add the rest a little at a time, stopping when the icing is thick but not too stiff.

The easiest way to pipe icing is to place small amounts in a small piping bag (see box, right) or in a cone made from a rolled-up sheet of greaseproof paper. Piping in small amounts requires less pressure so you have more control.

MOULDING AND PIPING DECORATIVE ICING

Pretty decorations can be made very easily with sugarpaste icing, using flower cutters. These can be bought at specialist cake decorating shops or through mail order; look for the addresses in specialist cake magazines or books. To make the flowers pictured here, you will also need royal icing for piping.

Piping decorative shapes onto a cake can take a bit of practice. Success comes from getting the pressure right when pressing out the icing and experimenting with the best angle for holding the bag. Use a small icing bag, as that is easier to handle; if you only have a large bag, fill it halfway.

MAKING FLOWERS

1 Colour some bought, ready-to-roll sugarpaste icing with edible paste food colouring and roll it out thinly. Stamp out with flower cutters. To make it easier to bend and shape the flowers, make cuts starting from the side of each rounded 'petal' to within 5 mm (¼ in) of the centre.

2 Holding a flower gently in one hand, mould the petals with the fingertips of the other hand. Place some crumpled foil in the cavities of an egg carton and place the flower in one of the cavities. Shape the petals of another flower and press its centre gently inside the first one to make a double-layered flower head. Shape and assemble the rest of the flowers.

3 Put some royal icing into a piping bag and press out dots of icing into the centre of each flower. Leave the flowers to dry for several hours, preferably overnight. When dry, gently lift each flower out of the egg carton with a palette knife. Arrange them on the cake immediately, or store in an airtight box for up to two months.

PIPING STARS

Put a little royal icing into a small piping bag fitted with a star nozzle, hold the bag vertically and gently pipe out a small amount of icing. Stop pressing and lift the piping bag away.

PIPING SHELLS

Put some icing into a small piping bag fitted with a star nozzle. Hold the bag at a 45° angle, press out a rounded shape, release pressure and pull the bag away sideways. Pipe the next shell about 5 mm (¼ in) away from the first one. As you press out the icing, the shells will touch.

PIPING STRAIGHT LINES

Using a small piping bag fitted with a plain nozzle, press out some icing and gently push it down to secure it to the cake. Then pipe a line, allowing the icing to fall into position.

INDIAN COOKING

POWDER AND PASTE

What is the difference between curry powder and curry paste?

Both are blends of many spices, but they are used differently. Dry curry powder cannot be fried in hot oil because it burns and turns acrid, so it must be added to foods that are already simmering in liquid.

For fried dishes it is best to use a curry paste. If you don't have curry paste on hand, you can make your own by adding a few teaspoons of water to curry powder and stirring vigorously until it has absorbed the water and the mixture is moist.

SPICY DECISION

What is curry powder, and could I make it myself rather than buy it ready-made?

There is no single recipe for curry powder. It was invented by the British in India as a quick substitute for the thousands of different spice blends that Indian cooks make for themselves. A basic curry powder includes black pepper, chilli, coriander, cumin, ginger and turmeric in varying proportions; it often has fenugreek and oily spices such as cardamom, cinnamon, cloves and mace, and can include asafoetida, cassia leaves, curry leaves, mustard and poppy seeds too. To make your own, experiment until you find a mixture you like.

Some whole spices such as coriander, cumin seed, dried chillies, fenugreek seed and peppercorns, need to be roasted before being ground and mixed (oily spices do not need roasting). Use a dry pan in the oven, or dry-fry them in a frying pan. Use a small coffee grinder or pestle and mortar to grind the spices individually, then mix them together. Store in an airtight bottle.

South-east Asian curries, which derive mainly from southern India, will often have fresh ingredients such as lemongrass, sweet basil and galangal (an aromatic root of the ginger family) added to the ground spices. For example, red and green curry pastes, using fresh chillies with other ingredients, are a central feature of many Thai dishes (see SOUTH-EAST ASIAN COOKING).

HEALTHIER POPPADOMS

Is there a low-fat way of cooking poppadoms so that they are crisp?

The microwave is a blessing for the greaseless cooking of cracker-like poppadoms. Place them one at a time on the turntable of the microwave and cook for 40–60 seconds on High until puffed and crisp. They will not be as fluffy as those that are traditionally fried in oil, but they are considerably healthier.

MYSTERIOUS LASSI

What is in the yoghurt drink that Indian restaurants serve?

Lassi, a traditional Indian drink, used to be made from buttermilk poured into earthenware crocks, with salt added to combat dehydration in the hot climate. It is now made from thin yoghurt, with salt or sugar. To make your own, dilute plain yoghurt with water or milk, add salt or sugar to taste, then blend vigorously with crushed ice.

BALANCED INDIAN MEAL

Are there any rules about what Indian dishes are served together?

Most Indian meals are not formally structured and there are usually a number of dishes for balance. There may be a meat dish, a seafood dish, at least one vegetable dish and perhaps a lentil dish as well. All would be served with fluffy rice and probably a bread such as chapati.

A typical meal you can cook at home includes Chicken Vindaloo and Prawn Korma served with Ghee Rice (see recipes, right). Serve them with mango chutney and cucumber raita, made from sliced cucumbers in yoghurt with lemon, cumin and fresh mint. A vindaloo is traditionally rather sharp and fiery. The amount of chilli used in the recipe below makes a medium-hot curry. You can add more or less according to your own personal taste, but keep in mind that a chilli powder made in India is often hotter than a European brand.

Chicken vindaloo

SERVES: 4
PREPARATION TIME: 30 minutes, plus 2 hours to marinate
COOKING TIME: 30 minutes

---

1 kg (2 lb 4 oz) chicken breasts, skinned
300 ml (10 fl oz) plain yoghurt
1 large onion, sliced
1 tablespoon honey
1 teaspoon salt

FOR THE SPICE BLEND
1 tablespoon ghee or vegetable oil
3 tablespoons chopped onions
1 tablespoon finely chopped garlic
1 tablespoon grated ginger
1 tablespoon hot chilli powder or 3 – 4 dried red chillies
1 tablespoon ground coriander
1 teaspoon ground cumin
4 cardamom pods, crushed
4 cm (1 ½ in) cinnamon stick
2 tablespoons tomato purée
1 tablespoon malt vinegar

---

1 Cut the chicken into large chunks. Mix the yoghurt, sliced onion, honey and salt in a large bowl to make a marinade and soak the chicken in it for 2 hours, turning occasionally.
2 To make the spice blend, heat the ghee or oil in a saucepan and fry the chopped onions, garlic and ginger for 5 minutes. Add the chilli powder or grind in the dried chillies, then add all the other spices to the pan. Stir-fry for a minute or two.
3 Add 300 ml (10 fl oz) of water, plus the tomato purée, vinegar, the chicken and its marinade and mix them together well.
4 Cover and simmer for 30 minutes until the sauce has thickened.
VARIATION
For a more substantial dish, you can add a large potato, peeled and diced, to the vindaloo during the last 15 minutes of cooking.

Prawn korma

SERVES: 4
*PREPARATION TIME: 5 minutes, plus
30 minutes for prawns to marinate*
COOKING TIME: 20 minutes

12 large raw tiger prawns, peeled
1 teaspoon ground turmeric
2 tablespoons vegetable oil
2 tablespoons chopped onion
1 teaspoon grated ginger
1 tablespoon raisins
1 tablespoon ground almonds
2 teaspoons sugar
300 ml (10 fl oz) plain yoghurt
1 teaspoon salt

FOR THE SPICE BLEND
1 teaspoon ground cumin
2 teaspoons ground chilli
1 tablespoon ground coriander
3 cardamom pods, crushed

1 Devein the prawns, rub them with turmeric and leave for 30 minutes.

2 Meanwhile, make up the spice blend with a teaspoon or so of cold water and stir to a soft paste.
3 Heat the oil and fry the onion and ginger for a minute until they have just softened. Add the spice blend and fry for a further 2 minutes.
4 Add the remaining ingredients except the prawns and simmer for about 10 minutes until the sauce thickens. Add the prawns and cook for 5 minutes until they turn pink.

Ghee rice

SERVES: 4
PREPARATION TIME: 5 minutes
COOKING TIME: 20 minutes

250 g (9 oz) long-grain rice
2 tablespoons vegetable ghee
1 - 2 teaspoons salt

1 Wash the rice in several changes of water until the water runs clear, then put it in a saucepan. Add 500 ml (18 fl oz) of water, bring to the boil then simmer for 10 minutes.
2 Add the ghee and salt and rake the rice with a fork. Cover, cook for a further 5 minutes until dry, then rake again to loosen the grains.
VARIATION
To cook in a microwave, prepare as above but add the ghee and the salt at the beginning. Then cook the rice, uncovered, for 12 minutes on High or until the water has been absorbed.

STYLISH VARIATIONS

What is the difference between balti, karahi and tandoori?

Balti and karahi are the same style of cooking, originating in Kashmir, where the curries are made in a cast-iron pan with a rounded bottom and two handles, rather like a Chinese wok. You can use a wok to cook Balti-style dishes at home.

Typical spices used in balti curries are aniseed, cardamom, cassia bark, cloves, coriander, cumin, fennel, ginger and the spice blend called garam masala (see SPICES). Balti curries are often eaten without rice or cutlery, using large, flat breads such as naan instead.

Tandoori cooking, from the Punjab, is named after the tandoor, a clay oven used for roasting or baking. It is shaped like a large jug, and is traditionally sunk into the ground up to its neck. The ovens used today have a plaster layer on the outer walls for added insulation. Burning charcoal is placed in the bottom of the oven and the food to be cooked is hung inside on long spits over the coals.

Before cooking, tandoori meats and seafood are usually marinated in a mixture of chilli, garlic, ghee, ginger, onions, paprika, peppers, salt, spices, and yoghurt. The characteristic red stain of tandoori meats once came from cochineal, but now a vegetable colouring is used.

Cooling drinks of lassi are the perfect accompaniment for a fiery Chicken Vindaloo (top), made with spices fried in ghee (right), or a Prawn Korma sweetened with almonds and raisins.

JAM

RIPENESS OF FRUIT

When is fresh fruit at its best for making jam?

Use the fruit when it is just ripe or slightly underripe. The pectose in underripe fruit changes to pectin as it becomes ripe. Pectin is a gummy substance produced by the flesh, skins and pips of fruit and it must be present if jam is to set properly. The amount varies from fruit to fruit, and there is little pectin in any that are overripe.

STONY PROBLEM

Do I need to stone fruit before preparing jam?

No, simply pick over the fruit and wash it carefully. Simmer gently with water in a preserving pan, and stir and crush it occasionally until it is tender. The stones will float to the surface and can be lifted out.

STRAWBERRY SOLUTION

How can I prevent strawberries from disintegrating when cooked?

To preserve soft-skinned fruit, such as raspberries and strawberries, whole, they should first be covered in sugar. This draws out their juices, leaving them firm enough not to disintegrate during fast boiling.

Hull the strawberries and wipe each one with kitchen paper. Do not wash them as extra moisture dilutes pectin, making the setting more difficult. Layer the fruit in the preserving pan, sprinkle with an equal weight of sugar and leave

them overnight. Next day, cook the fruit over a low heat until the sugar has dissolved completely. Then bring the mixture to the boil and cook it rapidly until it sets.

FROZEN SOFT FRUITS

Can I use frozen raspberries and strawberries to make jam?

Yes, but the pectin level falls after a few months, so use 10 per cent more frozen fruit than specified in your jam recipe to compensate for this loss. Take the fruit straight from the freezer, heating it gently in a pan to defrost (see also FREEZING).

VARYING TEXTURES

What are the differences between jams, jellies and conserves?

Jam is basically a cooked mixture of fruit and sugar, made from whole berries or larger fruit that has been chopped. It is usually set, but not hard, and has a very spreadable consistency. Jellies are made from strained fruit juice and should be firm, but still quivering gently, when spooned from the jar.

Conserves are generally richer, sweeter and much more syrupy than jams. Strawberries, raspberries and loganberries are good fruits to use. The fruit is layered with an equal quantity of sugar and left overnight to extract the juices before boiling for a short time. They are superb with cream, thick yoghurt or fromage frais.

RISING PEEL

What can I do to stop the fruit or peel from rising to the top of the jar when I make jam?

Chunky marmalade and whole fruit jams are particularly susceptible to this problem. After removing the pan containing the mixture from the heat, you should leave it to stand for about 15 minutes.

When it has begun to set, give the blend a stir to distribute the fruit or peel. This precaution will help to ensure that the fruit or peel stays suspended throughout the jar.

TIGHT COVER

What is the best method to use for sealing jam jars?

The best way to seal a jar for long storage is to fill it with hot jam and cover it immediately, using a screw-top or spring-clamp lid.

If the jam is being stored in a cool, dry, well-ventilated place, you can use sealing lids instead. Put a waxed paper disc, waxed side down, on the surface of the jam and smooth it over with your finger to remove any air pockets. Then cover the jar with a cellophane circle made moist by wiping with a damp cloth. Place the cellophane round damp side up over the jar lid and secure it with a rubber band.

Don't wait until the jam is luke-warm before you seal the jar, or moisture will collect inside the lid and the jam may become mouldy. Jams will generally keep for about a year in a dry, cool, dark place.

SUGAR THAT BINDS

What is the difference between preserving sugar and 'jam sugar'?

Preserving sugar has large white crystals which dissolve more easily than ordinary sugar, is less likely to burn and needs less stirring. It also makes the finished preserve appear clearer and brighter.

Sugar with pectin, also known as jam sugar, is ordinary sugar that has had natural apple pectin and citric acid added to it, to ensure a good set to the jam.

TESTING TIME

How should I test for a set?

Once the sugar has dissolved and the jam is boiling rapidly, it will start to look like jam in about 10 minutes. Test it as soon as you think it is ready as you must not overboil the jam, which could make it dark. If you think it is ready, take the pan off the heat and test with a jam thermometer or in a saucer (see box, right). Clear jam or jelly will fall from a spoon in a wavy curtain, not a stream, when it is ready.

PREDICTING A SET

How can I tell if my fruit will set?

If you are not sure of the setting qualities of the fruit you are using, take a teaspoon of juice from the pan of soft, cooked fruit (before the sugar is added) and put it in a small glass. Add a tablespoon of methylated spirit to the cooled juice, shake gently and leave for a minute. If a jelly-like clot develops, the fruit has plenty of pectin. If it does not form a clot, the pectin content is low and extra pectin is needed.

ADDING PECTIN

Which fruits need to have pectin added when making jam?

Fruits that are low in pectin and in natural fruit acid, which helps the pectin to gel, include cherries, elderberries, peaches, pineapples, rhubarb and strawberries. Adding lemon juice and pectin, either in liquid form or as sugar with pectin, helps the jam to set.

You can buy bottled pectin, or make your own pectin extract from sour cooking apples or crab apples, gooseberries or redcurrants. Wash the fruit, then chop apples roughly but leave berries whole. Cover with cold water, simmer for 45 minutes and then strain through a scalded jelly bag. Add 125 ml (4 fl oz) of this pectin extract to every 1.5 kg (3 lb 5 oz) of fresh fruit.

The recipe for Soft-fruit Freezer Jam (below) uses liquid pectin, but it is meant to be rather sloppy, and is lovely on crumpets, sinking lusciously into the holes. The Rhubarb and Orange Jam (below, right) is made using sugar with pectin.

Soft-fruit freezer jam

MAKES: about 3.25 kg (7 lb)
PREPARATION TIME: 1 1/4 – 2 1/4 hours, plus overnight standing
COOKING TIME: none

1.5 kg (3 lb 5 oz) raspberries or small strawberries, hulled, or raspberries and redcurrants
1.75 kg (3 lb 13 oz) caster sugar
4 tablespoons lemon juice
250 ml (9 fl oz) bottled liquid pectin

---

1 Layer the fruit and sugar in a large bowl, crushing the fruit lightly with a potato masher. Pour on the lemon juice, cover and leave the mixture at room temperature for 1 - 2 hours, stirring frequently, until the sugar has completely dissolved.
2 Add the liquid pectin and stir it into the crushed blend of fruit and sugar and stir it for 2 - 3 minutes.
3 Pour the fruit mixture into small, clean, freezerproof containers; leave enough space to allow for the jam to expand as it freezes. Leave them in a cool place for 24 hours for the jam to thicken, then label and freeze. The jam can be stored in the freezer for as long as six months.
4 When ready to use, remove one of the containers from the freezer and allow the jam to defrost in the fridge before serving. Once thawed, the jam must be stored in the fridge, where it will keep for up to a week. It is delicious stirred into thick Greek yoghurt or served on ice cream with shavings of bitter chocolate.

Rhubarb and orange jam

MAKES: about 1.3 kg (3 lb)
PREPARATION TIME: 15 minutes, plus overnight standing
COOKING TIME: 30 - 35 minutes

---

1 kg (2 lb 4 oz) rhubarb, weighed after being washed, trimmed and cut into 2.5 cm (1 in) pieces
Grated rind and juice of 2 large oranges, washed gently
1 kg (2 lb 4 oz) sugar with pectin

---

1 Put the prepared rhubarb in a large bowl and mix in the orange rind, orange juice and sugar. Cover and leave to macerate overnight.
2 Next day, tip the mixture into a preserving pan and cook it very gently for 15 - 20 minutes until the rhubarb has softened and the sugar has dissolved completely. Then increase the heat and bring the jam to a rolling boil for 4 minutes or until the setting point is reached (see the box on the left for ways to test if the jam is ready).
3 Remove the pan from the heat and skim off any surface scum with a slotted spoon. Let the mixture stand for 15 minutes. Stir to distribute the fruit and put into clean jars.
4 Seal, label and store the jam in a cool, dry place for up to a year.

TESTING THE SETTING POINT FOR JAM

The acid, pectin and sugar must all be in the right proportions for jam to become firm. Use one of these two methods to see if yours is ready to set.

TEMPERATURE TEST

1 The most accurate method for testing a set is to stir the jam and then insert a sugar thermometer. Do not let the thermometer touch the bottom or sides of the pan.

2 Keep testing while the jam boils. A proper set should be obtained when the temperature of the jam reaches 105°C (221°F).

COLD-SAUCER TEST

1 Remove the pan from the heat to prevent the contents overcooking. Put a small quantity of jam onto a pre-chilled plate and place it in the refrigerator to rest for a few minutes.

2 As soon as the jam is cold enough, push a finger gently through it. If the surface of the jam shows wrinkles, the setting point has been reached.

FIRM AND FRUITY

What is the difference between fruit butters, cheeses and curds?

Fruit butters and cheeses are made by cooking fruit to a purée and then adding sugar. They are thicker than jam and often spiced.

Fruit butters, like the Plum Butter (right), are very tasty spread over toast. Keep unopened jars in a cool place for up to two months. Once open, refrigerate them and eat within two weeks.

Fruit cheeses have a firmer texture than butters, but should be kept in the same way. Blackberry and Apple Cheese (far right), can be potted in small jars and served as a relish with meat, game and cheese.

Curds cannot be called true preserves because they have added eggs and butter, and for this reason they do not keep as well as jam. The Honeyed Lemon Curd, below, should be made in small quantities, kept in the refrigerator and used within two or three weeks.

Honeyed lemon curd

MAKES: about 675 g (1 lb 8 oz)
PREPARATION TIME: 20 minutes
COOKING TIME: 25 minutes

Finely grated rind and juice of
4 large juicy lemons, preferably
unwaxed, gently washed
4 eggs, size 1, lightly beaten
100 g (3 1/2 oz) unsalted butter,
diced
225 g (8 oz) caster sugar
2 tablespoons thick honey

1 Put all the ingredients into a double or heavy-bottomed saucepan. Stir continuously with a wooden spoon over a medium heat until the sugar has dissolved, then continue cooking for a further 25 minutes, stirring all the while, until the curd will coat the back of the spoon (see picture, above right). Be careful not to let the mixture come to a boil.
2 When the mixture has thickened, remove the pan immediately from the heat to prevent it overcooking.
3 Pour into clean, warm jars, cover with waxed discs and seal.

Curd is ready when it is thick enough to coat the back of a wooden spoon.

Plum butter

MAKES: about 1.3 - 1.6 kg
(3 - 3 lb 8 oz)
PREPARATION TIME: 30 minutes
COOKING TIME: 50 - 60 minutes

1.25 kg (2 lb 12 oz) ripe plums
Finely grated rind and juice of
1 lemon, preferably unwaxed,
gently washed
1 kg (2 lb 4 oz) granulated sugar

1 Put the plums, lemon rind, lemon juice and 450 ml (16 fl oz) of water into a preserving pan and simmer gently for 15 - 20 minutes or until the fruit is very soft and pulpy.
2 Working in batches, spoon the cooked fruit and juice into a nylon sieve set over a bowl. With the back of a spoon, rub the fruit through the sieve. Discard the skins and stones.
3 Measure the purée and for each 600 ml (1 pint) add 350 g (12 oz) of sugar, then return both to the pan.
4 Stir over a low heat until the sugar has dissolved, then bring the mixture to the boil and simmer for about 25 - 30 minutes, stirring it frequently until it reaches setting point (see picture, below). Spoon into clean, warm jars, cover with waxed discs and seal.

Fruit butter is set when a spoonful on a saucer does not exude any liquid.

Blackberry and apple cheese

MAKES: about 900 g (2 lb)
PREPARATION TIME: 20 - 30 minutes
COOKING TIME: 1 1/2 hours

1 kg (2 lb 4 oz) blackberries
450 g (1 lb) cooking apples, peeled,
cored and finely chopped
1.3 kg (3 lb) granulated sugar
(approximately)

1 Put the fruit into a preserving pan with 600 ml (1 pint) of water and cook gently for about 30 minutes until it is very soft.
2 Press the pulp through a nylon sieve set over a bowl. Measure the resulting purée and return it to the pan, adding 500 g (1 lb 2 oz) of sugar for each 500 ml (18 fl oz) of purée.
3 Stir over a low heat until the sugar has dissolved, then bring the mixture to the boil and simmer, stirring often, for 40 - 60 minutes. Check that the cheese is ready (see picture, below).

Fruit cheese is ready when a wooden spoon drawn across the bottom of the preserving pan leaves a clean line.

4 As soon as it is done, spoon the cheese into warmed, clean, small jars, cover with waxed discs and seal. Alternatively, the fruit cheese can be poured into ramekins, left to set and then unmoulded for serving.

PREPARING JARS

Is it true you should warm jars in the oven before pouring in jam?

Yes. Warm the jars to ensure that the glass does not crack when you pour in the hot jam. Oven warming also helps to ensure that freshly washed jars are absolutely dry.

Once the jars have been washed, arrange them without their lids in

Fruity preserves (clockwise from top centre): Soft-fruit Freezer Jam, Blackberry and Apple Cheese, Honeyed Lemon Curd, Blackcurrant Jelly and Plum Butter.

an oven preheated to 140°C (275°F, gas mark 1). Leave them to warm for about 5 minutes before you take them out and ladle in the hot jam.

Jam jars should be clean, but are usually not sterilised since the strong concentration of sugar has a dehydrating effect which will inhibit the development of potentially dangerous micro-organisms. However, if you want greater protection against bacteria, you can sterilise all the jars you want to use for preserves. Follow the instructions which are given in CHUTNEY.

SET JELLIES

Why will my bramble jelly not set?

Jellies will set only if there are sufficient quantities of pectin, acid and sugar present. Some fruit, such as the blackberries in bramble jelly, or apricots and raspberries, contain only a moderate level of pectin so must be combined with other fruit higher in pectin, or the jelly must be made using sugar with pectin.

Fruits such as cooking apples, blackcurrants, citrus fruits, gooseberries, quinces and redcurrants are naturally high in both pectin and acid and, with the addition of sugar, they can be relied on to produce firm jellies.

The Blackcurrant Jelly recipe below needs no additional help to become a firm favourite and the added lemon sharpens the flavour.

Blackcurrant jelly

*MAKES: about 1.3 - 1.6 kg
(3 - 3 lb 8 oz)
PREPARATION TIME: 10 minutes, plus
12 hours straining juice
COOKING TIME: 50 - 60 minutes*

---

*1.5 kg (3 lb 5 oz) blackcurrants
Pared rind of 1 lemon and
  2 tablespoons of lemon juice
900 g (2 lb) granulated sugar*

---

1 Rinse the fruit and put it into a preserving pan, then add the lemon rind and juice and 850 ml (1½ pints) of water. Bring to the boil and simmer for about 30 minutes, stirring and mashing with a wooden spoon until the fruit is very soft.

2 Prepare the jelly bag by pouring boiling water through it. Squeeze it dry then attach it to its stand or to the legs of an upturned stool with a bowl below. Ladle in the pulp and leave for at least 12 hours or until it has finished dripping. Do not squeeze the bag or the jelly will be cloudy.

3 Discard the pulp, then measure the strained juice back into the preserving pan. Add 450 g (1 lb) of sugar for each 600 ml (1 pint) of juice. Heat gently, stirring until the sugar has dissolved, then boil rapidly for 5 - 10 minutes or until the setting point is reached.

4 Remove any surface scum with a slotted spoon, then pot up and seal.

A jelly bag allows the clear juice to drain away from the mashed fruit.

JAPANESE COOKING

SUSHI FOR BEGINNERS

Japanese food looks exquisite but appears to be difficult to prepare. Is there anything quick and easy that I could make at home?

Yes, there is. Sushi is made from rice flavoured with *mirin*, or sweetened rice wine, and formed into finger-sized mounds topped with raw seafood or pickled vegetables. It is an art form in Japan, but the basic technique is simple. Sushi rice can also be rolled around a filling and wrapped in sheets of seaweed called *nori*, then cut into bite-sized pieces – but the moulded sushi (right) are easier to make. The seafood toppings are raw and must be absolutely fresh. For the most authentic taste and texture, use Japanese sticky rice.

Sushi rice

MAKES: *about 24 individual pieces*
PREPARATION TIME: *30 minutes, plus 30 minutes soaking rice*
COOKING TIME: *12 – 15 minutes*

---

400 g (14 oz) Japanese glutinous rice, or pudding or risotto rice
2 tablespoons rice vinegar or white wine vinegar
2 tablespoons sugar
1 teaspoon salt
2 tablespoons mirin (sweet sake) or dry sherry
To serve: 1 – 2 tablespoons wasabi (Japanese horseradish), powdered and blended, or ready-prepared; plus soy sauce, pickled ginger and grated mooli (white radish)

FOR THE TOPPINGS
4 medium prawns, uncooked
100 g (3 ½ oz) raw tuna, sliced
100 g (3 ½ oz) raw squid, sliced
100 g (3 ½ oz) raw or smoked salmon, sliced
100 g (3 ½ oz) red caviar or salmon roe

---

1 Put the rice in a saucepan and cover it with cold water up to 4 cm (1 ½ in) above the level of the grains. Soak for 30 minutes.
2 Combine the vinegar, sugar, salt and mirin in a small saucepan and bring to the boil. Remove and cool.
3 Make a slit along the back of the prawns from head to tail, then put them in boiling water and simmer for 2 – 3 minutes until they turn pink and open out in a butterfly shape. Drain and set aside to cool.
4 When the rice has soaked, bring it to the boil without changing the water and simmer for 10 minutes until the water is absorbed. Transfer to a bowl and add the cooled vinegar dressing. Stir for about 10 minutes to release the starch and allow to cool.
5 Take handfuls of rice and mould it by patting it firmly into bite-sized oblongs about 4 cm (1 ½ in) long, 2 cm (¾ in) wide and 3 cm (1 ¼ in) high. Dab wasabi paste on top.
6 Trim the toppings to fit and press them gently down on each piece of moulded rice, using the wasabi to hold them in place.
7 Serve with individual side dishes of soy sauce and wasabi, which each diner mixes according to personal preference as a spicy dip, and dishes of pickled ginger and grated mooli.

TEXTURE AND HARMONY

What is distinctive about the style of Japanese food?

Japanese food covers a much wider spectrum than most people realise. The raw fish, called *sashimi*, do not dominate the menu. Japanese cuisine is characterised more by methods of cooking than by particular flavours. There are soups, steamed dishes, raw salads, dishes cooked at the table, deep-fried and quick-fried foods as well as boiled

From top to bottom, sushi on the large dish are topped with raw squid, salmon, butterfly prawns and salmon roe. Serve with spicy green wasabi and soy sauce for dipping, bright-pink pickled ginger shoots and raw, grated mooli.

and pickled dishes. There are some complicated recipes and also artful blends of seasonings, but the Japanese generally prefer a stylised minimalist presentation.

The Japanese respect and value freshness above all, so the integrity of each ingredient is enhanced by few strong condiments or spices, only a little soy sauce, perhaps some grated mooli (white radish) and subtle seasonings such as bonito flakes and some delicate herbs. The strongest condiment is wasabi.

In the 16th century the Portuguese brought beef-eating to Japan and this became *sukiyaki*: finely sliced grilled or barbecued beef served with piquant dips. Japanese foods fried in batter are called *tempura* and are also of Portuguese origin. Noodles are one of the many dishes of Chinese origin, adopted by the Japanese in the 7th century.

JELLY

HEALTHIER JELLY

Packet jelly always seems to taste artificial. Is there any easy way I could use fresh fruit to make a healthier, more natural jelly?

Yes, fresh oranges, lemons, and all soft fruit can be easily converted into jelly and the result has a flavour much nicer than any from a packet. Children who may resist eating fresh fruit often love to eat jelly and making your own helps to ensure that some vitamins are retained. Fresh fruit jellies should be eaten on the day they are made.

Jellies made with loganberry, raspberry, strawberry or tayberry will still contain a few seeds even after the purée has been sieved. If this coarser texture is not to your liking, you can remove all the seeds by straining the purée through a muslin cloth (see the technique in the recipe for Blackcurrant Jelly on page 207). Try making fruit jellies with as little sugar as you can so they are really healthy, and the taste of the fruit comes through.

Fresh berry jelly

SERVES: 4 – 6
PREPARATION TIME: 30 minutes, plus an hour standing time
SETTING TIME: about 3 hours for moulded jelly; 1 – 2 hours if set in individual dishes

---

500 g (1 lb 2 oz) loganberries, raspberries, strawberries or tayberries, hulled and sliced
Strained juice of 1 lemon
100 – 140 g (3 1/2 – 5 oz) caster sugar
2 sachets powdered gelatine

---

1 Put your chosen fruit into a bowl and add the lemon juice and sugar. Stir well, cover and leave it all to macerate for about an hour.
2 Pour the fruit and lemon juice into a food processor or blender and add 300 ml (10 fl oz) of water. (If the goblet isn't large enough, the water can be added later.)
3 Process or blend the fruit into a smooth purée then pass this through a fine nylon or stainless-steel sieve to remove the seeds. If you have not already added it, stir the water into the berry purée now.
4 Measure the sieved fruit mixture. The fruit should have produced

This cool strawberry jelly requires no cooking, which means it retains all the flavour and goodness of the fresh fruit.

about 850 ml (1 1/2 pints) of purée, but if the fruit is very juicy you may have up to 1.2 litres (2 pints). Taste for sweetness and add a little more sugar if necessary.
5 Dissolve the gelatine in 100 ml (3 1/2 fl oz) of water, using one whole sachet plus 1 1/2 level teaspoons of the other for 850 ml (1 1/2 pints) of fruit mixture; if you have a larger quantity of purée, use two sachets of gelatine. Leave it to stand for 3 – 4 minutes, until it has absorbed all the water and looks opaque.
6 Whisk the dissolved gelatine into the fruit mixture and pour the jelly into a 1.2 litre (2 pint) dampened mould, small ramekins or stemmed glasses. Chill for 3 hours or until set.
7 To turn the chilled jelly out, dip the mould up to the rim in hot water for 5 seconds only. Put a plate on top of the mould then invert the two together and give the mould a quick, sharp shake. If the jelly does not come out the first time, repeat the process as many times as necessary. Serve with cream and thin biscuits.

JERUSALEM ARTICHOKE

NO RELATION

Are Jerusalem artichokes related to globe artichokes?

No, they are not. Jerusalem artichokes, also called root artichokes or sunchokes, are actually members of the sunflower family. The name Jerusalem is a mispronunciation of the Spanish *girasol*, meaning 'turn to the sun'. Globe artichokes are members of the thistle family. The sharing of the name 'artichoke' refers to some similarity of flavour, but they have little in common beyond being pleasantly sweet.

VARIOUS USES

What can I do with Jerusalem artichokes besides make soup?

Jerusalem artichokes are popular for soup as they have a tendency to collapse when cooked. Their sweet chestnutty flavour also makes them good partners for salty foods such as ham or smoked fish, as in the following recipe. You could also lightly poach some slices of Jerusalem artichoke and use them in salads, or try mashing them with potato to serve as an accompanying vegetable or as a topping for shepherd's and fish pies.

Jerusalem artichoke and smoked haddock chowder

SERVES: 6 as a starter
PREPARATION TIME: 30 minutes
COOKING TIME: 30 minutes

3 medium-sized floury potatoes
450 g (1 lb) smoked haddock
1 onion, roughly chopped
500 g (1 lb 2 oz) Jerusalem artichokes
Juice of ½ lemon
2 sticks celery, destrung and diced
50 g (1 ¾ oz) butter
600 ml (1 pint) milk
Black pepper
To garnish: spring onions, snipped

1 Peel the potatoes, boil until soft, then drain, mash and set them aside.
2 Put the haddock into a pan with the onion and enough cold water to cover. Bring to the boil and skim. Simmer the fish for 5 - 7 minutes or until it is just beginning to flake.
3 Drain the fish through a sieve, keeping the liquor and making it up to 500 ml (18 fl oz) with some fresh cold water. Discard the onion.
4 When the fish is cool, skin, bone and roughly flake it. Stir half of the cooking liquor into the potatoes.
5 Peel the artichokes and slice them thinly into a small bowl of cold water acidulated with the lemon juice.
6 Fry the celery for 2 - 3 minutes in butter, then add the milk, drained artichokes and the rest of the fish stock. Bring to simmering point, then partially cover and cook for 10 - 15 minutes until the artichokes are soft.
7 Mix the mashed potato and flaked fish into the vegetable mixture and grind in some black pepper.
8 Heat the soup again, garnish with the spring onions and serve with hot wholemeal toast and butter.

JUICERS

ENDLESS VARIETY

I would like to use my juicer for more than fresh orange juice. Can you suggest some ideas?

Juicers capable of pulping hard vegetables such as carrots and celery will produce highly nutritious, easily digested fruit and vegetable juices very economically and the variety of combinations is endless, depending on your imagination.

Some carrot, celery and tomato seasoned with Worcestershire and Tabasco sauces makes a particularly good version of tomato juice, perfect for Bloody Marys. Cucumber and melon juiced together with a little fresh mint is a refreshing summer drink served with ice.

Juicers also make good bases for milkshakes: try mango and banana, strawberry and peach or papaya and kiwi fruit, mixed with equal quantities of vanilla ice cream.

Use the pulp left over from juicing fresh carrots as the basis of a delicious carrot cake. You can also use vegetable juices to add flavour to casseroles, risottos and soups instead of adding stock or water.

A chunky chowder of sweet Jerusalem artichokes makes a filling meal. Here the creaminess of milk and mashed potatoes is offset by the smoky flavour of the fish.

KIDNEYS

FROM GRILL TO PIE

Are all types of kidney equally suitable for grilling and frying, or for using in steak and kidney pie?

Lamb's and pig's kidneys are both tender and after preparation (see box, right) can be grilled, fried, casseroled or used in pies. Lamb's kidney has the more subtle flavour; pig's kidney is somewhat stronger.

Large, multilobed veal kidneys are lightly coloured and delicately flavoured but expensive. They are best quickly grilled or fried in order to optimise their tenderness.

Ox kidneys from mature animals are strongly flavoured and best cooked slowly with other ingredients in casseroles and pies.

The flavour of kidneys combines well with herbs, mushrooms, mustard, olives, peppers, tomatoes and strongly flavoured wines.

SOAK NO MORE

Is it necessary to soak kidneys before cooking them?

In the past, kidneys were often stronger in flavour and soaked to soften their taste. Modern breeding and husbandry methods mean that it is unnecessary to soak calf's or lamb's kidneys. Whether or not you soak the stronger-tasting pig's kidneys is a matter of personal choice. Many people prefer to soak ox kidneys in milk, generally for at least an hour, especially if they are a prominent ingredient in a recipe.

KIPPER: see SMOKED FISH

PREPARING LAMB'S KIDNEYS

Lamb's kidneys, with their lighter flavour, are the most versatile and easily available kidneys. The larger ox and pig's kidneys are sliced into chunks before cooking.

1 Cut the lamb's kidneys in half lengthways through the core.

2 Snip out the white core of the kidney with scissors.

3 Using your fingers, peel off the kidney's fine covering skin.

4 To fry a kidney, cut it right through into two. To grill, cut the kidney only three-quarters of the way through so that it can be opened out like a book. Then push a skewer through both halves of the kidney to hold it flat while cooking.

KIWI FRUIT

VITAMIN RICH

Is it true that kiwi fruit have more vitamin C than oranges?

Yes, kiwi fruit contain 59 mg of vitamin C per 100 g (3½ oz) compared with 54 mg for oranges. So, eating a single kiwi fruit or just one medium orange will supply you with more than the recommended daily intake of 40 mg of vitamin C. Raw blackcurrants are even better, averaging 200 mg of vitamin C per 100 g (3½ oz).

Sometimes known as Chinese gooseberry, kiwi fruit is an acidic fruit with dark-green flesh and edible black seeds. It has a distinctive flavour and makes a conventional fruit mixture more exciting.

Kiwi fruit are ready to eat if they yield slightly when lightly pressed. Cut the kiwi fruit in half, scoop the flesh out with a teaspoon and eat it straight from the skin. Kiwi fruit can also be peeled with a small sharp knife and cut into slices to add to fruit salads or use as a decoration for cakes and desserts.

KNIVES

ESSENTIAL UTENSILS

I want to buy some new kitchen knives. What should I look for?

Always buy the best quality knives that you can afford. A good set of knives will not only last a lifetime, but will pay for themselves many times over in saved labour. Choose knives that feel comfortable in the hand, are heavy and well balanced. Carefully place the junction of the blade and handle on the side of your open hand. The handle should fall back gently into your palm.

Knives that have a tang (the part of the blade that extends into the handle of the knife) running along the whole length of the handle give the best overall balance and the

HOLDING A KNIFE CORRECTLY

Sharpness is crucial in knives and it is important to choose the correct type of knife for each job. Learning to hold knives correctly will not only improve cutting efficiency but will promote safety in the kitchen as well.

CHOPPING AND SLICING

Hold the knife with your thumb and forefinger either side of the blade just below the handle to prevent it rolling in your hand. Bend the fingertips of the other hand out of harm's way and cut smoothly through the vegetable.

HEAVY-PRESSURE CUTTING

For heavy-pressure cutting of tough vegetables such as cabbage, hold the knife with your hand close to the blade and use the other hand to keep the vegetable steady. Cut through the vegetable firmly, without sawing.

CRUSHING

To use the knife as a mallet to crush foods like lemongrass or garlic, use the flat of the blade and press it down firmly with your fingers.

PRECISION CUTTING

For cutting requiring careful control, or when scraping vegetables, use a small knife and keep your hand low down on the handle.

blunt readily. Carbon-steel knives are easier to sharpen and will stay sharp for a long time. However, they rust easily so they must be wiped clean and dried immediately after use. They also discolour, particularly by contact with onions and highly acidic foods, which can then become tainted.

Knives made from high-carbon stainless-steel have the advantages of both carbon-steel and stainless-steel knives and yet none of the disadvantages, but they cost more.

CLEAN AND DRY

Should I treat my knives with any special care?

All knives must be looked after carefully. Always wipe them clean and dry immediately after use. When carbon-steel knives get very stained, clean them with half a lemon sprinkled with salt. If that does not work, use a scouring pad, but only occasionally. To remove rust from a carbon-steel knife, rub the blade with a burnt cork.

Sharpen your knives regularly and do not store them in a drawer, where their blades will get damaged and you may inadvertently cut your hands when reaching for them. Use a wooden knife block or knife magnet to store them instead.

longest life – blades that are not riveted in place this way invariably come loose. The heads of the rivets should be flush with the surface of the handle for easy cleaning.

The best handles tend to be those that are made of wood impregnated with plastic to seal it. Plain wooden handles are nonslip, tough and attractive; the less expensive plastic handles are easier to keep clean but do not provide the same grip.

You can never have too many knives in the kitchen, and there is one for every job you undertake. Build up your selection gradually and, when you can afford it, add specialist knives such as boning and fish filleting knives to your collection. The following are essential knives that should be bought first:

- A large cook's knife with a blade at least 20 cm (8 in) long.
- A fruit knife with a serrated edge and stainless-steel blade.
- A paring knife with a 8–10 cm (3¼–4 in) stainless-steel blade.
- A bread knife with a rigid 20–25 cm (8–10 in) serrated blade.
- A carving knife with a rigid blade at least 20 cm (8 in) long.
- A palette knife with a flat, round-ended blade.

STEELY LIFESPAN

Are stainless-steel kitchen knives better than carbon-steel ones?

Stainless-steel knives are strong, do not rust and can be used on onions and acidic foods. Unfortunately, they are difficult to sharpen and

STAY SHARP

What is the best way to use a steel to sharpen my knives?

There are two methods for using a steel. Try both of them to see which is most successful for you.

The first method is arguably the easiest as you have more control of the steel and the angle of the knife. Hold the steel vertically with the tip on a nonslip surface. Put the knife edge where it joins the handle at the top of the steel, with the blade pointing downwards, at an angle of 45 degrees. Bring the knife down the steel, keeping the angle constant and drawing the blade across the steel so that when you reach the bottom of the steel you are sharpening the tip of the blade.

Move the knife smoothly along the length of the steel, parting your hands so that the entire blade is sharpened.

Repeat the procedure, dragging the other side of the blade down the steel, always keeping the angle at 45 degrees. Repeat both sequences until the blade is sharp.

Alternatively, hold the steel in one hand, the knife in the other and place the handle ends of each together at an angle of 45 degrees. Keeping your elbows against your sides, raise the steel and the knife, parting your hands so that the blade travels up the steel. Finish with the knife tip near the tip of the steel. Repeat, holding the other side of the knife blade against the other side of the steel. Continue this sequence until the knife is sharp.

KOHL RABI

SPICY CABBAGE

What exactly is kohl rabi and how can I best use it?

Kohl rabi is a swollen, round stem that looks like a turnip. The leaves, which can be cooked in the same way as spinach, are often trimmed off before the vegetable is sold.

Look for small kohl rabi that are not much bigger than a tennis ball and steam to serve as a hot vegetable accompaniment. If you find leaves attached, trim and shred them, then steam briefly to serve as a garnish over the halved or quartered globes of the cooked stem.

As it is a member of the cabbage family, the spicy warmth of kohl rabi is best brought out by blanching. The recipe for Kohl Rabi and Cress Salad (right) would go well with pork chops or sausages.

Kohl rabi and cress salad

SERVES: 4
PREPARATION TIME: 15 minutes
COOKING TIME: 1 minute

---

450 g (1 lb) kohl rabi
Juice of ½ lemon
1 red-skinned apple
4 slim spring onions
Black pepper
1 carton mustard and cress

FOR THE DRESSING
1 tablespoon grainy mustard
2 teaspoons cider vinegar
Salt
4 tablespoons olive oil
4 tablespoons yoghurt

---

1 Peel the kohl rabi, then grate it coarsely into a saucepan. Pour on boiling water and cook it just until it returns to the boil. Drain and refresh immediately under a cold tap.

2 Squeeze the lemon juice into a small bowl and half fill it with cold water. Quarter and core the apple then coarsely grate it into the bowl.
3 Drain the apple, mix it with the kohl rabi and dry thoroughly, either in a salad spinner or with a tea towel before transferring it to a salad bowl.
4 Finely slice the spring onions and add to the bowl with some coarsely ground black pepper.
5 Mix the mustard, vinegar and salt in a small screw-top jar and shake until combined. Add the olive oil and yoghurt, shake vigorously again and toss into the salad with another good grinding of black pepper.
6 Cut the mustard and cress and spread over the salad, tossing again immediately before serving.

A dressing of yoghurt and mustard lends piquancy, while the apple adds sweetness to this simple kohl rabi salad.

LAMB

RAISING STANDARDS

Is all lamb free-range?

Yes, all lamb is reared naturally outdoors although the sheep are brought inside for lambing. Lamb that has been organically reared or is labelled Conservation Grade will have had especially humane treatment, in slaughtering methods for instance. Several schemes apply special standards to meat produced in Britain, such as Freedom Food, which is backed by the RSPCA.

GOOD SIGNS

How do I recognise good lamb?

New season lamb should be pale pink in colour while older lamb should be brownish-pink, although the colour can vary according to the breed. The colour should never be greyish and the fat should be white, silky and resilient, so avoid buying cuts where the fat is brittle, crumbly or discoloured. The flesh should be fine-grained and lean.

Most lamb is reared on grass, but if you like lamb that has a slightly more gamy flavour look for hill lamb. Lamb that has roamed on salt marshes, such as Romney Marsh or French pré-salé lamb, and Shetland lamb, which is fed predominantly on heather, also have unusual and slightly more pronounced flavours.

YOUTH AND AGE

Is young lamb better than larger, older lamb or mutton?

It depends on the dish. Young lamb (under 3–4 months) has a more delicate flavour and is leaner than older lamb (4 months – 1 year). It is excellent for roasts or cooked quickly as grilled and fried chops, cutlets and noisettes. The stronger flavoured older lamb is more suitable for rich dishes where the mild taste of young lamb would be lost.

When a lamb reaches one year of age, its meat is sold as mutton. This is less popular and so less widely available than young lamb, however, you should be able to obtain it easily from a good independent or specialist halal butcher.

DIFFERENT PARTS

What's the difference between a chop, a cutlet and a noisette?

Chops, cutlets and noisettes are all suitable for grilling and frying but are different cuts of meat.

There are two types of chops: chump chops (taken from just above the hind leg), which have a round central bone, and the smaller loin chops (from the middle carcass) with a good eye of meat plus a tail of meat and fat curling round it. Double loin chops, or butterfly chops, are thick chops cut across both loins, split lengthways and opened out to form one large chop.

Cutlets come from the best end of neck joint. They have an eye of meat with a short bone on one side and a long one on the other. They are smaller than chops, so you usually need two per portion.

Noisettes are cut from the eye of the loin (see box, below) and are usually about 2–2.5 cm (¾–1 in) thick. The tender meat of noisettes is best eaten when still slightly pink. Grill or fry the noisettes until browned on the outside but still pink in the centre. The following recipe partners noisettes with a rich sauce of mushrooms, tarragon and crème fraîche that would be equally delicious served with other cuts of lamb, or with chicken.

PREPARING AND ROLLING LAMB NOISETTES

Noisettes are the eye of the loin, boned, rolled and sliced. They may seem quite expensive, but they generate no waste because they are boneless. Ask the butcher for a chined, skinned loin, which will supply four to six noisettes.

1 Cut through the meat on either side of each bone then cut beneath the bone to release and remove it. Cut off the flap at the thin end of the joint.

2 Trim away any excess fat that is on the outer side of the loin, then grip the fleshy end of the joint and roll up the meat tightly towards the thin end.

3 Tie the roll in shape with string at 2.5 cm (1 in) intervals, knotting each loop separately. Slice it midway between each tie to make the noisettes.

Noisettes of lamb with mushrooms

SERVES: 4
PREPARATION TIME: 5 minutes
COOKING TIME: 15 minutes

---

225 g (8 oz) mixed shiitake, oyster
    and cultivated mushrooms, cut
    or broken into large pieces
40 g (1 ½ oz) butter
1 tablespoon olive oil
8 noisettes of lamb, each about
    2.5 cm (1 in) thick
2 - 3 teaspoons chopped fresh
    tarragon
1 - 2 tablespoons wine, red or white
90 ml (3 ¼ fl oz) crème fraîche or
    double cream
Salt and black pepper
1 tablespoon lemon juice, optional

---

1 Fry the mixed mushrooms in the
butter for about **5** minutes, stirring
occasionally. Using a slotted spoon,
transfer the mushrooms to a plate
and keep them warm.
2 Add the oil to the frying pan and
heat to a moderate temperature. Add
the noisettes and fry for 3 minutes
on each side until they are browned
on the outside but still pink in the
centre. Using a fish slice, transfer to
a warm plate, season and keep warm.
3 Add 2 teaspoons of tarragon and
a little wine to the pan and stir to
dislodge the sediment, then add the
crème fraîche or double cream and
bring to the boil. Season.
4 Add the mushrooms and any
excess meat juices on the plate and
stir over a moderate heat until it is
heated through. Add more tarragon,
if preferred, and some lemon juice if
necessary to lift the flavour. Serve
with the cooked noisettes.

STUFFINGS FOR LAMB

*Most stuffings seem to be geared
toward poultry. Can you suggest
one that would go with lamb?*

Lamb is a very popular dish in the
Middle East where it is often served
with apricots and spices. This is the
basis for the stuffing used with a
boned leg (right). Bone the leg of
lamb yourself (see BONING) or have
the butcher do it for you.

*Quickly fried lamb noisettes are served accompanied by a rich, chunky sauce of
mushrooms and crème fraîche, spiked with the aniseed bite of tarragon.*

Stuffed leg of lamb

SERVES: 6
PREPARATION TIME: 1 hour if boning
leg otherwise 15 - 20 minutes, plus
overnight soaking of apricots
COOKING TIME: 2 hours

---

75 g (2 ¾ oz) dried apricots,
    chopped and soaked overnight
1 tablespoon olive oil
1 onion, finely chopped
1 clove garlic, chopped or crushed
Finely grated zest of 2 oranges, plus
    the juice of 1 orange
Juice of ½ lemon
75 g (2 ¾ oz) chopped hazelnuts,
    toasted
1 tablespoon ground allspice
50 g (1 ¾ oz) fresh breadcrumbs
50 g (1 ¾ oz) bulgur wheat
Salt and black pepper
1 boned leg of lamb weighing
    about 2 kg (4 lb 8 oz)

FOR THE GRAVY
175 ml (6 fl oz) dry white wine
300 ml (10 fl oz) chicken stock

---

1 To make the stuffing, drain the
apricots, reserving 100 ml (3 ½ fl oz)
of juice and add it to the stock. Heat
the oil in a pan and fry the onion
and garlic until softened. Remove
from the heat and add the remaining
ingredients, bar the lamb.
2 Preheat the oven to 180°C (350°F,
gas mark 4). Pack the majority of the
stuffing lengthways down the leg,
then roll the meat up and tie it with
string at intervals of 2.5 cm (1 in).
Put the remaining stuffing into a
heatproof dish, add a tablespoon of
hot water, stir and set aside.
3 Weigh the joint and calculate the
cooking time, allowing 55 minutes
per kg (25 minutes per lb), plus an
extra 20 - 30 minutes for well-done
lamb. Place on a rack in a roasting
tin, sprinkle with pepper and roast.
4 About 30 minutes before the end
of cooking, put the dish of stuffing
in the oven. When the lamb is done,
transfer it to a carving dish, cover
and keep warm in the oven, with
the heat turned off, for 20 minutes.
5 To make the sauce, pour off the
fat from the roasting tin. Place the
tin over a moderate heat and stir in
the wine to dislodge the sediment.
Bring to the boil, add the stock, and
boil briskly until slightly thickened.
Season and serve with the lamb.

ON YOUR HONOUR

I have always admired guard of honour. How do I prepare it?

Guard of honour is one of the most impressive ways to cook new season's tender lamb and it allows you to cut any excess fat off the joint before roasting (see box, below). Do not overcook the lamb, as it should be served slightly pink. Garnish with a selection of vegetables roasted with the lamb for extra flavour, as in the recipe (right).

PREPARING A GUARD OF HONOUR

The upper rib section (containing seven to nine ribs on each side) is called the best end of neck, or rack of lamb. A single line of ribs may be shaped into a circular crown roast, or two racks of lamb may be interlinked to form a guard of honour.

1 Cut the fat and meat in a straight line across the first rack down to the rib bones, about 2.5 cm (1 in) from the ends, then remove the fat.

2 Cut the meat from the ends and scrape the bones clean with a knife. Repeat with the second rack.

3 Interlock the two racks of meat with the fat on the outside, and weave string tightly between each set of bones to secure the racks together firmly. Cover the ends of the bones with foil during roasting.

Guard of honour with roast vegetables

SERVES: 6
PREPARATION TIME: 20 minutes
COOKING TIME: 50 - 70 minutes

---

2 racks of lamb weighing 700 - 900 g (1 lb 9 oz - 2lb) each
115 g (4 oz) fresh breadcrumbs
1 egg, size 3, beaten
Finely grated rind of 1 lemon
4 tablespoons chopped fresh mixed herbs such as basil, parsley, rosemary and thyme
1 tablespoon finely chopped black olives
4 tablespoons olive oil
Salt and black pepper
6 cloves garlic
2 red peppers, deseeded and cut into thick slices
2 aubergines weighing about 225 - 300 g (8 - 10 oz) each, cut into chunks
1 small butternut squash, peeled, deseeded and cut into chunks, or 2 courgettes, cut into chunks
6 plum tomatoes, halved and deseeded
3 sprigs of thyme
3 - 4 tablespoons olive oil, or oil from a jar of sun-dried tomatoes, or a mixture of both
3 tablespoons chopped fresh basil or oregano

---

1 Preheat the oven to 180°C (350°F, gas mark 4). Weigh the lamb and calculate the cooking time: allow 35 minutes per kg (15 minutes per lb) plus 15 minutes for pink lamb, or 55 minutes per kg (25 minutes per lb) plus 25 minutes for well done.
2 Prepare the racks of lamb and tie them together (see box, left).
3 Mix together the breadcrumbs, egg, lemon rind, mixed herbs, olives, a tablespoon of the oil, and some salt and pepper. Carefully press the mixture in an even layer on the fatty side of the lamb then set aside.
4 Put all the vegetables and thyme into a roasting tin, season and pour over the olive or sun-dried tomato oil. Stir to coat all the vegetables.
5 If you prefer your meat well done, place the interlinked racks of lamb upright on top of the vegetables and

trickle 2 tablespoons of oil evenly over the coating, then roast for around 45 - 50 minutes. If you prefer pink lamb, put the vegetables in the oven for 10 - 15 minutes, then add the meat and oil and cook for 35 - 40 minutes. Baste two or three times while cooking and cover with foil if the coating becomes too brown.
6 To test, pierce the eye of the meat with a metal skewer. If the juices are red, the meat is rare and if they are clear, the meat is well done.
7 When cooked, sprinkle the basil or oregano over the vegetables, then cover the lamb and vegetables and leave them to stand in the oven, with the heat turned off and the door propped open, for 15 minutes.
8 To carve the guard of honour, remove the string, then separate the racks and cut down between the lamb bones, cutting portions of two or three cutlets per person. Serve with the herb-flavoured vegetables.

LANGOUSTINE

TWIST IN THE TAIL

Are langoustines the same as langoustes?

No, langoustines are not related to langoustes (see CRAWFISH). Sometimes known as Dublin Bay prawns or Norway lobsters, langoustines are found in the Mediterranean and in the Atlantic waters from Iceland to Morocco. It was as scampi that they became familiar in Britain.

Although they typically weigh about 50 g (1¾ oz), langoustines are not as meaty as their size might indicate. They are actually tiny lobsters, but their claws contain no meat and often only the fleshy tails are found on sale. Whole langoustines, however, are a favourite garnish of restaurants for seafood platters and other fish dishes.

The flesh is sweet when freshly cooked, but langoustines are usually sold frozen and ready-breaded for the deep-fryer, in which case they will need much help from a tasty tartare or similar sauce.

LASAGNE

LESS SAUCE

My lasagne always seems too sloppy. Should I use less sauce?

Yes. Many people enjoy a lasagne that has plenty of sauce but it is not really necessary and can dilute the flavours of the other ingredients.

It is important to use a filling that has a strong taste of its own, such as the ham and mushrooms in the *Lasagne con Prosciutto e Fungi* (below). Add plenty of seasoning because the pasta can also neutralise the flavour of the filling.

Lasagne with ham and mushrooms (Lasagne con prosciutto e fungi)

SERVES: 6
PREPARATION TIME: 1 hour
COOKING TIME: 50 minutes

FOR THE BÉCHAMEL SAUCE
85 g (3 oz) butter, plus extra for
*   greasing*
70 g (2 ½ oz) flour
1.2 litres (2 pints) milk
1 bay leaf
A few gratings of nutmeg
Salt and black pepper

FOR THE FILLING
40 g (1 ½ oz) dried porcini
*   mushrooms*
70 g (2 ½ oz) butter
2 tablespoons olive oil
2 shallots, finely chopped
675 g (1 lb 8 oz) fresh mixed
*   mushrooms, thinly sliced*
Juice of ½ lemon
500 g (1 lb 2 oz) lasagne sheets
225 g (8 oz) cooked ham, cut into
*   thin matchsticks*
100 g (3 ½ oz) Parmesan cheese,
*   freshly grated*

1 To make the béchamel sauce, melt the butter in a saucepan, then stir in the flour and cook for a few minutes without allowing the roux to colour.
2 Pour in the milk and whisk until the sauce is thick and smooth. Add the bay leaf, simmer for 15 minutes then season with nutmeg, salt and pepper. Remove the bay leaf and dot the surface of the sauce with butter to prevent a skin forming. Set the sauce aside until needed. Preheat the oven to 190°C (375°F, gas mark 5).
3 To make the mushroom filling, cover the dried mushrooms with boiling water. Leave for 30 minutes, then rinse if they are gritty and chop finely. Strain the mushroom water through a clean cloth and reserve.
4 Heat 40 g (1 ½ oz) of the butter with the oil in a large frying pan, sauté the shallots for a few minutes, then add both the sliced and dried mushrooms and lemon juice. Cook, uncovered, until they start to exude juices. Raise the heat to evaporate most of the liquid, add the strained water from the mushrooms, boil for a few minutes, season and set aside.
5 Cook the lasagne sheets, a few at a time, in boiling salted water then remove with a slotted spoon and place in a bowl of cold water. Drain on clean, dry cloths and continue until all the pasta sheets are cooked.
6 Mix the cooked mushrooms with the béchamel sauce. Lightly grease a shallow, rectangular ovenproof dish about 33 × 25 cm (13 × 10 in) with some of the butter then add a thin layer of mushroom sauce. This makes it easier to get a spatula under the lasagne when you serve it.
7 Arrange a layer of lasagne sheets over the top of the sauce, sprinkle some ham and grated cheese over this layer, then top with some more lasagne and cover it with the sauce (see box, right). Repeat, finishing with a layer of mushroom sauce, then cover with the remaining cheese and dot with the rest of the butter.
8 Bake for 45 - 50 minutes, or until well browned and bubbling. Allow to rest for 5 minutes before serving.

SOFT TOUCH

I have tried using those 'no cook' lasagne sheets but they stayed stiff after baking. Why?

'No cook' lasagne sheets will stay stiff unless you layer them with a great deal of fairly thin sauce, and even though they absorb it, they can still taste heavy and pasty. In a traditional lasagne, the sauce would be béchamel, but a tomato sauce would also work. Although the lasagne sheets that need precooking are more trouble, the results are superior and demand less sauce. Fresh sheets are now available that need only a little precooking and these are excellent.

LAYERING LASAGNE

Building up layers of pasta sheets, meat sauce, ham and cheese adds to the varied texture and delicious flavour of this old Italian favourite.

1 Butter a shallow ovenproof dish and cover the base with a layer of mushroom sauce. Arrange a layer of cooked lasagne sheets over the top, without overlapping.

2 Sprinkle a thin layer of ham and cheese over the pasta sheets and cover with another layer of lasagne.

3 Continue to build up the dish, repeating the layers as above and finishing with a layer of the sauce. Cover with grated Parmesan cheese and dot the top with butter.

The simplest dish to make for guests who arrive without warning, or for friends who linger on until they need to be offered a meal, is individual omelettes. They take only a minute or two to make and there is plenty of scope for fillings from things you probably have to hand, such as fresh herbs, grated cheese, chopped tomatoes or crispy bacon.

Another speedy option is pasta, which everyone seems to like, and it is wise to keep a selection of dried pasta in your cupboard. If you also keep cans of chopped tomatoes or passata on hand, you have the foundation of an impromptu pasta sauce. Just add a can of drained clams, a few olives, anchovies or capers, or small jars of artichoke hearts, wild mushrooms in oil, sun-dried tomatoes, or tapenade.

The contents of these cans and jars can also be turned quickly into spreads for toast to serve with drinks, or as a starter, while you make the next course. For instance, try a can of salmon whizzed up in the food processor with a little mayonnaise and sharpened with a few gherkins.

Here are some other recipes for fine-tasting meals you can improvise in a hurry.

*L*AST-MINUTE GUESTS

◆

Friends who turn up unexpectedly are one of life's pleasures – but a challenge to the cook who wants to offer them a welcoming meal. All these simple dishes, however, can be made up in minutes from a well-stocked store cupboard.

Grated potato becomes a star in this gratin mixed with cheese, eggs and herbs, and sandwiched between onions and crispy bacon.

Tuna and bean salad

Tuna and Bean Salad is an Italian classic that fills the bill when you want a nourishing dish that needs no cooking. Keep a variety of ready-to-bake loaves in your freezer and serve it with warm ciabatta.

If you don't have cannellini beans to hand, you can use other beans such as flageolet or red kidney beans, or leave them out altogether and add some hard-boiled eggs instead. Or turn the dish into a salade Niçoise: toss the tuna with green beans, tomatoes, canned new potatoes and black olives in a salad dressing.

SERVES: 4
PREPARATION TIME:
10 minutes
COOKING TIME: none

400 g (14 oz) canned tuna
550 g (1 lb 4 oz) canned
  cannellini beans
½ mild red onion or
  several spring onions,
  finely chopped
Juice of 1 lemon
4 tablespoons olive oil
Finely chopped fresh parsley
  or other herb, if available
Salt and black pepper

1 Drain the tuna and tip it out into a wide serving bowl, then break the chunks into small pieces with a fork.
2 Drain and rinse the beans and mix them in with the tuna. Add the onion, lemon juice, olive oil and herb. Stir well to mix then season to taste with salt and pepper.

TUNA AND BEAN SALAD

BUTTERBEAN AND SPINACH SOUP

Butterbean and spinach soup

Nourishing Butterbean and Spinach Soup uses frozen leaf spinach, which is handy to keep as it makes a great addition to a variety of soups, used in the way shown here. Good homemade stock is another invaluable freezer item as it upgrades any soup or sauce.

Follow the soup with some cheese and biscuits, and fresh fruit. Or, if you can find a late-night delicatessen open, buy an array of various cold meats and serve them with bread, pickles and salad to make a more substantial meal.

SERVES: 4
PREPARATION TIME: 5 minutes
COOKING TIME: 15 minutes

2 tablespoons olive oil
1 large onion, chopped
425 g (15 oz) canned butter
    beans
600 ml (1 pint) chicken
    stock
300 g (10½ oz) frozen
    leaf spinach
A squeeze of lemon juice
A pinch of grated nutmeg
Salt and black pepper
To serve: grated mature
    Cheddar or Parmesan

1 Heat the oil in a saucepan and gently cook the onion until soft. Rinse the butter beans and add them to the onion along with the stock and frozen spinach. Cover the pan and leave to simmer for about 12 minutes until the spinach is thawed.
2 Season to taste with lemon juice, nutmeg, salt and pepper then mash or blend, leaving some texture to the soup. (A hand-held blender that does its work in the saucepan is useful for this.)
3 Serve the soup sprinkled with a generous handful of grated cheese.

Cheese and bacon potato gratin

This recipe uses the ingredients almost everyone has to hand in the kitchen: bacon, eggs, an onion, potatoes. Even if you don't have cream, you may have a cream stick in the freezer, or you can use milk. If you've run out of bacon, you could dice some ham or other cold meat and add that to the grated potato mixture instead.

The gratin does not take long to prepare; then, while it is baking, you can go back to your guests and offer them a drink and a simple starter.

SERVES: 4 – 6
PREPARATION TIME:
15 minutes
COOKING TIME: 40 minutes

3 eggs
150 ml (5 fl oz) cream or
    milk
125 g (4½ oz) grated sharp
    Cheddar or Parmesan
750 g (1 lb 10 oz) potatoes
½ teaspoon dried thyme
½ teaspoon dried chives
Salt and black pepper
1 onion, thinly sliced
250 g (9 oz) bacon

1 Preheat the oven to 200°C (400°F, gas mark 6). Butter the bottom and sides of a large gratin dish.
2 Beat together the eggs, the cream or milk, and the cheese in a large mixing bowl with a balloon whisk.
3 Peel the potatoes and grate them in a food processor using the coarsest grating disc. Add them immediately to the egg mixture. Add the herbs and season with lots of salt and pepper. Turn the mixture over a few times to mix everything thoroughly.
4 Scatter the onion slices over the bottom of the dish and spoon the egg and potato mixture over them, spreading it into an even layer with a knife or spatula. Put it on the top shelf of the oven and bake for 35 - 40 minutes.
5 Check the gratin is nicely browned, then grill or fry the bacon until crisp (microwave it if you like) and sprinkle it over the top to serve.

Couscous with prawns and peas

Couscous is a versatile grain that is sold already processed and needs only to be moistened and warmed through, rather than cooked. If you have a microwave, the frozen peas and prawns can be defrosted quickly; otherwise, allow an extra 30 minutes.

SERVES: 4
PREPARATION TIME:
10 minutes
COOKING TIME: 10 minutes

350 ml (12 fl oz) stock
250 g (9 oz) couscous
3 tablespoons olive oil
1 shallot, finely chopped
1 dried chilli, crumbled
200 g (7 oz) frozen peas or
    broad beans, defrosted
300 g (10½ oz) frozen
    prawns, defrosted
A squeeze of lemon juice
2 tablespoons fresh mint
Salt and black pepper

1 Bring the stock to the boil, pour in the couscous and give it a quick stir with a fork before covering it and setting it to one side, off the heat.
2 Heat the olive oil in a frying pan, add the shallot and the chilli and stir them together for a few minutes. Add the peas or beans and the prawns and stir until they are heated through.
3 Run a fork through the couscous several times to separate the grains then turn it out into a large bowl. Add the contents of the frying pan along with the mint, then mix well together. Add a generous sprinkling of salt and pepper and serve warm.
VARIATIONS
Couscous can be an almost instant base for a variety of ingredients. For instance, try leftover meat instead of the prawns, and use canned sweetcorn or mushrooms in place of peas or beans.

COUSCOUS WITH
PRAWNS AND PEAS

LEEKS

AUTUMNAL TREAT

What can I do with the slimline leeks that are sold in the shops in autumn and early winter?

They are young and tender and can be quickly steamed or boiled for a salad dressed with a vinaigrette, as in the recipe, right. This is a good starter salad served at room temperature with warm French bread, or an interesting side salad served lukewarm with poached white fish.

You can also cut young leeks into short lengths and add them to mixed vegetable soups, vegetarian casseroles or Oriental stir-fries.

Young leeks braised in a peppery dressing, sprinkled with capers and currants, make a tempting side dish.

Braised leeks with capers and currants

SERVES: 4
PREPARATION TIME: 10 minutes
COOKING TIME: 25 minutes

---

75 ml (2 1/2 fl oz) olive oil
4 tablespoons white wine
1 tablespoon white wine vinegar
Salt and black pepper
8 slim leeks
1 tablespoon capers, rinsed
25 g (1 oz) currants
A pinch of cayenne pepper

---

1 Mix the oil, wine, vinegar, salt and pepper in a pan wide enough to hold the leeks in one layer. Add the leeks, scattering the capers and currants in among them.
2 Bring to the boil, cover and then simmer for 15 minutes, basting once or twice with cooking liquor. The leeks are done when their centres can be pierced easily with a knife.

3 Uncover the pan, raise the heat and boil for 5 minutes to reduce the liquor, basting the leeks regularly. Transfer the leeks and the dressing to a serving dish and sprinkle with a light dusting of cayenne to serve.

GOODBYE GRIT

I wash leeks under the tap but there always seems to be some grit remaining. How should I wash them to get rid of it all?

Supermarket leeks usually come washed and trimmed but home-grown ones can be difficult to clean properly. Remove most of the green tops and make slits in the outer layers to enable you to flush out any grit under the cold tap. If more cleaning seems necessary after you have sliced the leeks, rinse them thoroughly under a running tap or stand them in a bowl of cold water for 15–20 minutes.

VEGETABLE RIBBONS

What is a chiffonade of leeks?

Chiffonade is an old French word for ribbons and refers to finely shredded vegetables used as a bed for fish, lamb or poultry, or as a garnish. Leaves such as endive, lettuce or sorrel are rolled up and cut across to make a chiffonade. Leeks can be cut lengthways (see box, below) and cooked in a cheese or tomato sauce to serve with pasta.

SLICING LEEKS FOR A CHIFFONADE

This method of cutting leeks results in a coarse shred which makes a useful garnish. The technique can also be applied to rolled up leaves such as lettuce, sorrel or spinach.

1 Cut the washed and trimmed leeks in half lengthways, then cut into 7.5 cm (3 in) lengths.

2 With the cut side down, slice into strips 6 mm (¼ in) wide.

3 Blanch the leek strips in boiling, salted water for a few seconds and drain to create the chiffonade.

LEFTOVERS

COLD MEATS

Is it safe to freeze leftover meat and poultry and, if so, what is the best way to do this?

Leftover meat can be frozen but do not keep it at room temperature for any longer than necessary. If the meat is still warm, put the plate on a bed of ice cubes to cool it quickly and then freeze it immediately so the bacteria that might cause food poisoning have no time to grow.

To freeze a leftover joint, carve the meat and pack the portions separately in foil or airtight polythene bags, or cover the slices in gravy and store in freezer boxes.

Freeze casseroles or curries in plastic boxes or bags. They will keep for up to two months. It is not advisable to refreeze meat that was frozen before being cooked as the texture suffers considerably.

SUPERFLUOUS SAUCE

If I have leftover sauces or gravy is it all right to freeze them?

Yes, most sauces freeze very well and frozen blocks of sauce or gravy can be reheated in a saucepan straight from the freezer. Egg-based emulsions, however, such as béarnaise, hollandaise and mayonnaise, will separate if they are frozen. Flour-based sauces, gravy and meat sauces such as Bolognese will keep for three months, while vegetable sauces, such as tomato, keep for three to four months. Frozen sauces are good timesavers so it is worth making twice as much as the recipe calls for and freezing half.

NO TO FREEZING

If I don't use all of a can of tuna fish can I freeze the rest?

It is not advisable to freeze canned fish or any other canned foods as these products have already undergone heat processing and their structure is affected by cooling treatments. Canned fish that has been frozen breaks down and becomes flabby and limp when thawed. But canned fish that has been mashed with other ingredients, in a pâté for example, can be frozen successfully as the flesh has already been broken down.

RECYCLING TIPS

Can you suggest some good ways of using leftover vegetables?

Leftover vegetables can be stored, covered, in the fridge for a couple of days and reheated, for instance in a tomato or curry sauce, or sautéed in herb butter or olive oil. For a supper dish, mix them with cooked pasta and cheese sauce in an ovenproof dish, top with breadcrumbs and some grated cheese and bake. Make vegetables such as green beans, peas or potatoes into a salad by tossing them in a mayonnaise dressing with fresh herbs.

The remains of a Sunday lunch can be turned into bubble and squeak. To make eight triangles, mash 500 g (1 lb 2 oz) of cooked potatoes with 100 g (3½ oz) of cabbage, carrots or peas, 225 g (8 oz) of minced cooked meat, a grated raw onion and 25 g (1 oz) of butter. Add 2 tablespoons of mustard and salt and pepper to taste. Shape the mixture into pieces, coat with flour and fry for 2 minutes each side.

SECOND APPEARANCE

It seems such a shame to throw away party cakes. How can I use them in interesting ways?

Start by removing any icing and almond paste. Rich fruit cake can be fried in butter and brown sugar and served hot with ice cream. Slices of panettone, or yeasted cakes which are only slightly stale, make an excellent base for a very special bread and butter pudding. And stale sponge cake can be used to make a good base for trifles. Put slices in a dish and spread with jam, sprinkle over sherry or fruit juice to moisten, and top with canned fruit, fresh custard and whipped cream.

USING UP EGGS

What can I do with leftover egg yolks and whites, and how long is it safe to keep them?

Separated egg yolks and whites are always worth keeping. Spare yolks can be used to enrich such dishes as omelettes, scrambled eggs or stir-fried rice, as well as to thicken soups or sauces. Leftover whites can be used for a variety of recipes such as meringues and soufflés.

Store egg yolks in a small dish, covered with cold water to stop them drying out, and whites in a lidded plastic box; both can be refrigerated this way for up to two days. You can also freeze whites and yolks and they will keep for three to six months (see EGGS).

LEMON: see CITRUS FRUIT
LENTILS: see DRIED BEANS
LETTUCE: see SALAD LEAVES
LIME: see CITRUS FRUIT

LIVER

OPTIONAL SOAKING

Why do some recipes tell you to soak liver in milk before cooking?

In the past, liver often had a stronger taste than it does now and it was soaked to soften the flavour. Modern breeding produces liver that has a milder flavour, and lamb's or calf's liver does not need soaking. Whether to soak stronger-tasting pig's and ox liver is a matter of personal taste.

FLASH IN THE PAN

In Italian restaurants the liver is always tender but mine is always tough. What am I doing wrong?

For a start, they always use calf's liver, which is the most tender liver. But it also needs to be cooked correctly, and quickly toughens if it is overcooked. For best results, slice the liver thinly (see box, right) and cook briefly over quite a high heat. When the blood bubbles through

on one side, turn it over and cook until it bubbles through on the other side, then serve it straightaway. Try the recipe below for a truly tender dish.

Italian liver and onions

SERVES: 4
PREPARATION TIME: 15 minutes
COOKING TIME: 45 minutes

---

4 tablespoons olive oil
675 g (1 lb 8 oz) large onions, thinly sliced
Salt and black pepper
500 g (1 lb 2 oz) calf's liver, prepared and very thinly sliced

---

1 Heat 3 tablespoons of the olive oil in a large frying pan. Add the onions and a little salt and black pepper. Cover the pan with a lid or a sheet of foil and cook gently, stirring from time to time, for 25 - 30 minutes until the onions are very soft.
2 Put a bowl and a plate to warm. When the onions are soft, remove the cover from the pan, increase the heat to moderate and cook, stirring, until the onions are golden brown and caramelised, but be careful not to let them stick to the bottom of the pan. Transfer the onions to the warmed bowl, using a slotted spoon, and leave the excess oil in the pan.
3 Add the remaining oil to the pan and heat over a high heat. Add half the liver in a single layer and cook for 45 seconds - 1 minute until it is just browned. Turn the slices over using a fish slice and brown the other side for 45 seconds - 1 minute; the liver should still be pink in the centre. Using the fish slice, transfer the slices to the warmed plate.
4 Fry the remaining liver in the same way. Return the onions and the first batch of liver to the pan alongside it and stir both over a high heat for 30 - 45 seconds to warm through.

TENDER FOR TOTS

Is there any way to cook liver so that my children will eat it?

Most children dislike the strong flavour of liver, and will find it even less appetising if it is tough

PREPARING LIVER

Very strongly flavoured liver, such as ox liver, can be soaked overnight in milk to make the flavour more mellow before it is to be cooked.

1 Carefully snip and peel away the fine membrane covering the liver (calf's liver is shown here).

2 With a sharp knife, cut the liver diagonally into even, thin slices.

3 Snip out any tough internal tubes with some sharp scissors.

and overcooked. To lessen both these problems, it is best to braise it very slowly in a casserole with vegetables and flavourings so it is very tender and the flavour is mellowed. Or disguise it by combining the liver with other meats and flavourings. Liver can be buried in meat loaves, patties, burgers, shepherd's pie or with pasta in a tomato sauce.

In any case, children should not eat liver too often; it is such a rich source of vitamin A that just 100 g (3½ oz) supplies more than ten times the daily adult requirement, which is too much for children.

OUT OF STOCK

Why should you not include the liver of a bird in giblet stock? What can you do with it?

Poultry livers make stocks cloudy, though this is not a problem if you are using the stock for gravy, and the liver can be mashed up after cooking in the stock to add richness. There are many other ways to use poultry livers; they can be added to stuffing, used to make pâtés, or quickly fried with mushrooms and onions for serving on toast. They can also be used to make an unusual warm salad, as in the recipe below.

Chicken or duck liver and grape salad

SERVES: 4 as a starter
PREPARATION TIME: 5 minutes
COOKING TIME: 5 minutes

4 large handfuls of mixed salad leaves such as curly endive, rocket, ruby chard and spinach
500 g (1 lb 2 oz) chicken or duck livers
4 tablespoons olive oil
A sprig of thyme
1 tablespoon red wine vinegar
2 teaspoons balsamic vinegar
2 tablespoons walnut oil
115 g (4 oz) seedless grapes, halved
Salt and black pepper
To garnish: fresh herbs or flowers

1 Divide the salad leaves between four individual salad bowls or plates.
2 Remove any membranes from the chicken livers and slice them into pieces of roughly equal size.
3 Heat 2 tablespoons of the olive oil in a frying pan, add the livers and thyme and cook briskly, shaking the pan occasionally, for about 2 minutes on each side so the livers are slightly caramelised on the outside but still pink inside. Using a slotted spoon, transfer the livers to the salads.
4 Stir the vinegars and oils into the pan, dislodging the sediment. Add the grapes and gently heat the sauce through. Then pour a little warm dressing over each of the salads and garnish with fresh herbs or flowers.

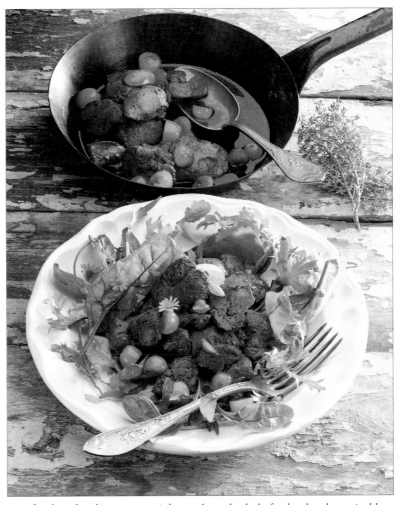

Pan-fried poultry livers on a rainbow-coloured salad of ruby chard, marigolds and basil are served with a warm walnut oil and balsamic vinegar dressing.

ENLARGED LIVER

What is foie gras and do you have any suggestions on how to use it?

Foie gras is the enlarged liver of a force-fed goose or duck. Some connoisseurs think goose foie gras has a smoother, more subtle flavour than that of duck, others prefer the more complex flavour of duck, which also has slightly less fat.

Fresh raw foie gras is available vacuum-packed. It should be firm and evenly coloured, the colour ranging from pink to ochre. Fresh foie gras needs to be prepared before cooking: cut out all traces of the green gall bladder, then separate the two lobes with your hands. Slit each lobe lengthways, cut out the tubes, slice it thickly and sauté quickly at a high temperature until brown on the outside but still pink inside. Gentle baking in a terrine is also a good way of cooking it.

Cooked foie gras is widely available. When labelled *mi cuit* (half-cooked), the liver has been cooked but not sterilised, has a limited shelf life and must be kept refrigerated. It will taste almost as good as the freshly home-cooked liver.

Foie gras in cans with no such labelling has been sterilised at a high temperature so will not have such a good flavour or texture; *entier* on the label indicates that the liver is whole; pieces of liver are just labelled foie gras.

Truffe on the label means that it contains black truffle, and *pâté de foie gras* contains minced pork.

LOBSTER

KINDLY KILLING

Is there a relatively kind way to kill and cook a lobster?

The traditional way to kill and cook a lobster is to drop it into a large pot with 100 g (3½ oz) of salt per litre (1 pint 15 fl oz) of boiling water. Crustaceans die within a few seconds of being immersed.

The RSPCA suggests that a more humane method is to place the live lobster in a plastic bag and freeze it for at least 2 hours before cooking. This will stun the cold-blooded creature so that it is unconscious when it goes into the boiling water.

HEAT AGAIN

Lobster meat is cold by the time you have got it out of its shell, so how do I serve a hot lobster dish?

A lobster can be killed by splitting it open, then grilling or roasting it in olive oil and herbs, and this method of cooking means the meat is brought to the table hot. But most home cooks would flinch from chopping up a live lobster. Many of the rich classical treatments, however, such as the recipe for Lobster Thermidor on the right, use lobster meat that is cut up when cold and then reheated. A sauce is built around the lobster flesh, which is then returned to its shell for a final blaze under a very hot grill to brown the top.

Lobster thermidor

SERVES: 2 as a starter
PREPARATION TIME: 40 minutes
COOKING TIME: 10 - 12 minutes

1 × 750 g (1 lb 10 oz) cooked
   lobster
50 g (1 ¾ oz) butter
2 shallots, finely chopped
1 tablespoon white wine
1 tablespoon dry sherry
100 ml (3 ½ fl oz) fish stock
4 tablespoons double cream
4 tablespoons finely grated
   Parmesan cheese
1 tablespoon chopped parsley
Salt and black pepper
1 teaspoon dry English mustard

1 Twist the head off the lobster, then pull away the claws and crack them open. With a heavy knife, cut the tail in two lengthways. Remove all the flesh from both claws and tail, scraping out the tomalley and any coral you find in the shell. Cut the meat into slices about 2 cm (¾ in) thick. Scrub the halved shell clean and leave it upside-down to drain. Preheat the grill to red hot.
2 Melt the butter in a saucepan and fry the shallots gently for 3 minutes until softened but not browned. Add the lobster meat and tomalley and crumble in any coral. Take the pan off the heat and gradually stir in the wine, sherry and fish stock. Return the pan to the heat and simmer the sauce for 3 - 4 minutes, stirring often, until it is smooth and thick.
3 Pour in the cream and half the Parmesan. Heat gently, stirring often, until the lobster is heated through and the cheese has melted smoothly into the sauce. Add the parsley and season to taste, then sprinkle on the mustard powder and stir well.
4 Spoon the mixture into the halved shells, sprinkle over the remaining Parmesan and grill until the surface is bubbling and has turned golden brown. Serve immediately.
VARIATION
For Lobster Newburg, the sauce is made with cream thickened with egg yolk and flavoured with Madeira or sherry. It is sometimes sharpened with a pinch of cayenne powder.

COOKING AND DRESSING A LOBSTER

Cook lobsters for 12 minutes for the first 500 g (1 lb 2 oz) of weight, 10 minutes for the next 500 g and 5 minutes for each additional 500 g. Remove and hold under the cold tap. Place the cooled lobster on its back and pull away the claws and legs. Break the legs at the central joint and pick out the meat.

1 Crack the claws with either a small hammer or heavy weight and then remove the meat. Twist off the head and set aside to use as a garnish.

2 With a heavy knife, cut along either side of the underside of the tail, pulling away the covering shell and prising out the column of flesh.

3 Remove the transparent stomach sac and gills from below the head and pick out the thin line of intestine running the length of the tail meat. Discard the feathery gills, but keep the grey-green tomalley (liver) from inside the head, and any pink coral (roe).

4 Slice the tail meat into medallions. Crack open the claws and remove the meat in one piece if possible. The cold lobster meat can then be arranged decoratively on an attractive bed of mixed salad leaves and accompanied by fresh homemade mayonnaise.

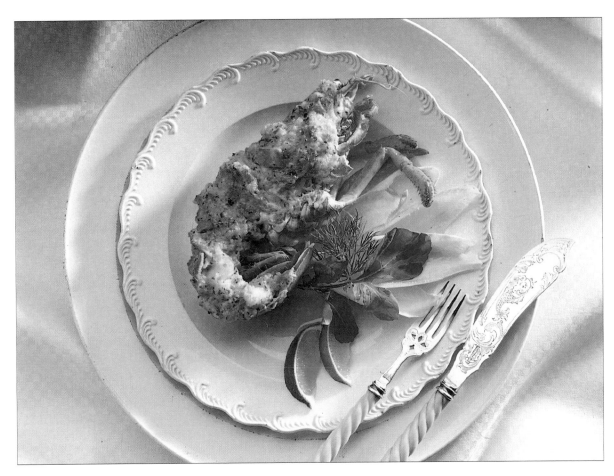

Lobster, sherry, Parmesan cheese, cream and a whiff of fiery mustard make Lobster Thermidor irresistible.

BEST BUY

How do I choose the best lobster?

If the lobster is cooked, look for a firm, springy tail and reject any with tails that are limp. Imported North American lobsters are usually cheaper than native lobsters.

Obtaining live lobsters is not easy unless you live near the sea or a good fishmonger, but they can usually be ordered in advance. Look for one that is moving and feels heavy for its size. Lobsters cast their shells to grow larger ones and you don't want to buy a small lobster in a large new shell. A worn shell, and white tracery on the top, are signs of an old shell, which the lobster is likely to have filled out.

LOGANBERRY: see SOFT FRUIT

LOW-FAT CHEESES

SOFT AND LOW

Which cheeses have the lowest natural fat content?

In general, softer cheeses have a lower fat content than hard cheeses because they have a higher percentage of water. Cream cheeses and cheeses labelled triple-crème are the exceptions as they are particularly high in fat, containing about 47 per cent fat. Hard cheeses made from goat's and ewe's milk are likely to be higher in fat than similar cheeses made from cow's milk, as both goat's and ewe's milk have a naturally higher fat content.

If you are aiming to cut down on your fat intake, it is best to stay with cottage cheese or soft, fresh cheeses such as Brie, Camembert, ricotta and feta. Of the harder cheeses, Edam is a better low-fat choice than Cheddar. Blue Vinney (Dorset Blue), made of skimmed cow's milk, is the lowest in fat of the blue cheeses but is now rare and difficult to find.

An increasing number of shops stock a selection of lower-fat alternatives to full-fat cheese in which the saturated butter fat has been removed and replaced with polyunsaturated vegetable oils. These are particularly useful for those people who want to reduce their saturated fat intake.

The nutritional information supplied by manufacturers can be misleading. The fat content is often expressed as 'fat in dry matter', which means the fat content of the cheese solids after the water has been removed. An ordinary Brie which is labelled a '60 per cent' Brie is not as rich as it sounds because it actually contains half the fat of a regular cream cheese.

CHEESES BY FAT CONTENT

CHEESE	% OF FAT PER 100g (3½ OZ)
Quark	trace
Cottage cheese (plain)	3.9
Fromage frais (plain)	7.1
Ricotta	11.0
Reduced-fat Cheddar	15.0
Goat's milk, soft	15.8
Feta	20.2
Mozzarella	21.0
Port Salut	23.0
Saint Paulin	23.0
Camembert	23.7
Edam	25.4
Brie	26.9
Processed cheese	27.0
Bel Paese	29.0
Danish Blue	29.6
Emmental	29.7
Full-fat soft cheese	31.0
Gouda	31.0
Lancashire	31.0
Caerphilly	31.3
Cheshire	31.4
Wensleydale	31.5
Parmesan	32.7
Roquefort	32.9
Gruyère	33.3
Leicester	33.7
Red Windsor	33.7
Derby	33.9
Double Gloucester	34.0
Cheddar	34.4
Stilton	35.5
Cheddar (vegetarian)	35.7
Gorgonzola	47.0
Cream cheese	47.4
Dolcelatte	48.0

LEANER CUISINE

Can I use a reduced-fat Cheddar cheese in my usual recipes, or will it behave and taste differently when I try to cook with it?

Modern manufacturing techniques for reduced-fat cheeses are increasingly sophisticated, nevertheless in some situations the performance of these cheeses in cooking is not the same as their full-fat equivalents. A reduced-fat, Cheddar-style hard cheese will melt under the grill, but it will not brown properly. If you want a crusty topping for a baked dish, add breadcrumbs to these reduced-fat hard cheeses.

But in most dishes in which reduced-fat hard cheese is used (such as quiche or pastry), you can expect it to perform in much the same way as its full-fat equivalent.

When making cheese sauces with reduced-fat cheese, make sure you remove the pan from the heat first, and stir the cheese through at the last minute so it doesn't overheat. And when using a reduced-fat cheese for sauces, you may also find it necessary to add a little mustard or some herbs to boost the flavour, as it is usually less rich.

LOW-FAT DESSERTS

Can I use reduced-fat soft cheeses for making desserts?

You can, but be wary as they will work only in some dishes. While hard cheeses made with vegetable oil can be used in cooking like their fattier equivalents, reduced-fat soft cheeses tend to perform poorly in cooking. In particular, they should not be used for icings or dips as the process of stirring will break down the texture of the cheese and the finished product will be disappointingly runny.

Reduced-fat soft cheeses can, however, be used in recipes such as cheesecakes and mousses which contain several other ingredients, but remember to check the flavour level carefully as these cheeses have a less assertive flavour than their full-fat equivalents.

LOW-FAT SPREADS

WHEN THEY WORK

Can all low-fat spreads be used successfully in cooking, or do some of them not work?

All low-fat, reduced-fat or half-fat spreads contain half the fat of butter or margarine and a great deal more water. This means that while they can be used like butter or margarine as a spread on bread, they are not always suitable for cooking.

They can be used successfully for all-in-one sauces and cakes, for choux pastry and, if mixed with full-fat butter or margarine, can sometimes be used for other sorts of pastry. To make a cheesecake base, normally done by mixing butter with biscuit crumbs, melt the low-fat spread carefully over a low heat and then add the crumbs.

Low-fat spreads are generally not suitable for shallow or deep-fat frying because they contain too much water. However, they can be used in a nonstick saucepan to fry foods such as onions or mushrooms, as long as it is gently done over a low heat. They are also unsuitable for some biscuits and cakes, and preserves such as lemon curd, because they do not set firm.

Very low-fat spreads, which have an even higher proportion of water and contain less than 25 per cent fat, are quite unsuitable for frying or sautéing because they will spit and are liable to burn very easily.

Healthy option

You can use a low-fat spread instead of butter or margarine to make crisp and light choux pastry. Melt the spread with the water over a low heat then add it to the other ingredients and continue with the recipe (see page 103).

LOW-FAT POURING SAUCE

Preparing and cooking this all-in-one sauce will only take about 10 minutes: 5 minutes for preparation and 5 minutes for cooking. It can be flavoured with ingredients such as grated reduced-fat cheese, finely chopped fresh parsley or chopped capers. Stir the chosen flavouring into the sauce after it is cooked.

1 Place 15 g (½ oz) of low or half-fat spread and 15 g (½ oz) of plain flour in a pan with 250 ml (9 fl oz) of milk. Heat the mixture, stirring often, until the sauce comes to the boil.

2 Simmer gently for 2 - 3 minutes, whisking all the time until the sauce has become thick, smooth and glossy. Season, add any flavouring and pour into a jug, or over a cooked dish.

FRUITY FAT SUBSTITUTE

Is there any way to lower the fat content of dishes usually made with full-fat ingredients?

Reduced-fat products such as low-fat cheeses and creams may be used to replace full-fat varieties in some recipes. Even more surprisingly, you can reduce the fat, calorie and cholesterol contents of some cakes and biscuits by replacing part or all of the butter or margarine with a purée of dried fruit, such as apricot or prune. This will add flavour and texture, as well as reducing the fat.

To make 275 g (9½ oz) of purée, place 225 g (8 oz) of ready-to-eat dried apricots or prunes in a food processor or blender with 90 ml (3 fl oz) of water. Blend until the mixture is smooth, then use it in place of the butter or margarine.

With many recipes you can replace all the fat with purée, using the same number of grams or ounces of purée. But with other recipes you may find it works better to have half fat and half purée. And note that the purée is not suitable for replacing fat in pastry. The recipe for Apricot and Cinnamon Fruit Bars (right) uses prune purée instead of butter or margarine to make a healthier sweet snack.

Apricot and cinnamon fruit bars

MAKES: 16 bars
PREPARATION TIME: 35 minutes
COOKING TIME: 35 - 40 minutes

175 g (6 oz) rolled oats
175 g (6 oz) plain flour
175 g (6 oz) soft brown sugar
2 teaspoons ground cinnamon
1 egg, size 3, lightly beaten
275 g (9½ oz) prune purée
125 g (4½ oz) ready-to-eat dried apricots
125 g (4½ oz) sultanas or raisins
225 ml (8 fl oz) orange juice

1 Preheat the oven to 180°C (350°F, gas mark 4). Grease a shallow cake tin measuring 28 × 18 cm (11 × 7 in).
2 Put the oats in a bowl and add the flour, sugar, cinnamon, the egg and three-quarters of the prune purée. Rub the mixture with your fingertips until all is well combined. Spoon half the mixture into the prepared cake tin and spread it evenly.
3 Chop the apricots and put them in a saucepan then add the sultanas or raisins, the orange juice and the rest of the prune purée. Cook over a medium heat for about 5 minutes until the fruit has softened. Take the pan off the heat and allow to cool.
4 Mix the cooled fruit into the remaining oat mixture and spoon it

over what is already in the tin. Bake for about 35 - 40 minutes or until the mixture is crisp on top.
5 Leave to cool completely in the tin before cutting it into bars.
VARIATIONS
Use muesli instead of rolled oats (or a mixture of half and half), and make the purée from dried apricots.

LOW-FAT SANDWICHES

Can you give me some ideas for tasty, low-fat sandwich fillings?

You can cut calories and reduce the fat content of sandwiches by using a low-fat spread and, if you include powerfully flavoured ingredients, still make a filling that is satisfying and appealing. You may also find that wholewheat bread sandwiches not only have more flavour but more staying power.

For example, you can use a low-fat spread on brown bread, top it with soft cheese, scatter chopped sliced canned pineapple over the cheese and then sprinkle it with chopped chives or spring onions. Add a final generous seasoning of sea salt and black pepper.

Another successful combination is flaked cooked or canned salmon and chopped watercress, bound with 2 tablespoons of reduced calorie mayonnaise, garnished with a sliced tomato and sprinkled with lemon juice to finish. You can also use canned tuna or crabmeat with a handful of freshly chopped herbs and use finely shredded lettuce instead of watercress. Chopped red pepper or canned sweetcorn adds a crunchy texture.

Instead of sliced bread use baps, lightly toasted ciabatta, a walnut or tomato bread or halved French sticks. To give reduced-fat mayonnaise more zest, stir in a teaspoon or two of good strong mustard. And the addition of fresh herbs, such as basil, coriander or flat-leafed parsley, will help to make sandwiches much more attractive and tempting. Pungently flavoured foods in unusual combinations can be so interesting and delicious that no one will ever miss the fat.

MACAROONS

FRESHLY GROUND

Should I grind my own almonds for macaroons or marzipan?

Yes, because fresh whole almonds usually have more flavour than ground or blanched almonds. To grind your own, first blanch the unskinned almonds in a pan of boiling water, plunge them in cold water, slip off the skins and then grind them in a blender, food processor or coffee mill. You can also pulverise them in a pestle and mortar, but this will take much longer and they will not be as fine.

TINY MACAROONS

What is the difference between macaroons and ratafias?

The only difference is their size. A ratafia is a tiny almond-flavoured macaroon, but in the 18th century, almond-flavoured biscuits, cakes and some homemade liqueurs were also known as ratafias.

A handful of ratafias are a good addition to the base of a traditional English trifle or lemon syllabub. For emergency puddings, sprinkle ratafias with kirsch or brandy, then serve them topped with soft red fruits and cream. They also go well with ice cream and rich chocolate sauce. Finely crushed ratafias can be pressed onto the sides of cold soufflés, or used whole to decorate the tops of creamy mousses.

The recipe for Almond Macaroons on the right can be made into ratafias, but use almond essence, not vanilla, to flavour them.

Almond macaroons

MAKES: about 15 macaroons
PREPARATION TIME: 30 minutes
COOKING TIME: 20 minutes

2 - 3 sheets edible rice paper
90 g (3 ¼ oz) ground almonds
90 g (3 ¼ oz) caster sugar
1 egg white, size 2
2 drops almond or vanilla essence
To decorate: flaked almonds

1 Preheat the oven to 180°C (350°F, gas mark 4) and line a large baking sheet with rice paper.
2 Mix the ground almonds with the caster sugar in a bowl.
3 Whisk the egg white to soft peaks. Using a large metal spoon, carefully fold the ground almonds and sugar mixture plus the almond or vanilla essence into the egg white, stirring until the mixture is smooth.
4 Place a large piping bag fitted with a 2 cm (¾ in) plain nozzle over a jug and turn down the cuff. Spoon in the almond mixture and pipe as many rounds, 4 cm (1 ½ in) across, as will fit on the lined baking sheet. Press a flaked almond on top of each round. Cook the macaroons in the oven for around 20 minutes or until they are very lightly browned then cool them on the baking sheet.
5 When the macaroons are cold, lift them and tear away the spare rice paper so that just the base is covered. You can store the cold macaroons in an airtight tin for up to ten days.
VARIATIONS
Instead of a plain nozzle, you can use a straight star nozzle for a fluted appearance. For tiny ratafias, about 1 - 2 cm (¾ in), use the recipe above but cook for only 10 - 12 minutes.

Crunchy macaroons piped into neat rounds only need a simple flaked almond on top for crisp decoration.

MANGOES

TOUCH TESTING

How can you tell when a mango is ripe and ready to eat?

The colour of a mango is no guide to ripeness as the skins vary from one variety to another. A green mango can be as ripe as one that is bright red. You test for ripeness by touch: they should yield when gently pressed. Mangoes that are to be shipped are picked unripe and these can be encouraged to ripen by leaving them out in a warm room or by putting them in a bowl with other fruit: fully ripe bananas are especially effective.

Mangoes can vary considerably in flavour, sweetness, aroma and texture. There are hundreds of varieties, and they are not always labelled, but if they are, one of the most popular Indian mangoes is the small fragrant, exceptionally sweet Alfonso. Others to look for are Kent, Palmer and Van Dyke, all of which are rich and melting. The Haden and Tommy Atkins varieties, which are tougher and more fibrous, are best used for chutney.

MULTIPLE USES

I have often used mangoes in desserts, but is there anything else I can do with them?

Mangoes are more versatile than some other exotic fruits and can be used in many dishes, both sweet and savoury. Diced mangoes can be added to a salad made with rice or vegetables. They also make fine raw and cooked chutneys. Ripe mangoes, sliced or cut into chunks, dressed with a squeeze of lime, or fried until slightly caramelised, go well with smoked meats, chicken and turkey. They can be blended with yoghurt, honey and a squeeze of lemon or lime for a revitalising drink. The luxurious salad opposite is another original way of serving a luscious ripe mango. Serve it as a special dinner party starter.

Mango and wild strawberry salad

SERVES: 4
*PREPARATION TIME: 15 minutes plus
30 minutes chilling time*
COOKING TIME: none

---

1 large ripe mango
*A few mixed salad leaves, such as
    oak leaf and lamb's lettuce*
115 g (4 oz) wild strawberries

FOR THE DRESSING
1 teaspoon Dijon mustard
Salt and black pepper
2 tablespoons red wine vinegar
1 tablespoon hazelnut oil
5 tablespoons virgin olive oil
2 spring onions, very thinly sliced
*25 g (1 oz) hazelnuts, skinned,
    lightly toasted and chopped*
*2 tablespoons very finely chopped
    fresh chives or parsley*

*Rich mango, wild strawberries and
decorative salad leaves start a summer
meal with vivid colour and flavour.*

1 To make the salad dressing, put
the mustard, a little salt and pepper,
plus the vinegar, hazelnut and olive
oil into a small bowl and whisk them
together. Stir in the spring onions,
hazelnuts and the chives or parsley.
2 Peel and slice the mango (see box,
right). Arrange the salad leaves on
four plates, place the mango on top
and sprinkle with wild strawberries.
3 Spoon the hazelnut dressing over
the fruit, then chill the salads for 30
minutes before serving.
VARIATION
Use quartered large strawberries
instead of tiny wild ones and add a
sprinkling of finely chopped mint.

MARGARINE: see FATS

HOW TO CUT UP A MANGO

*Fresh mangoes can be as small as
a peach or as large as a melon.
Inside the tough, leathery skin is
sweetly scented, juicy flesh that can
be sliced or diced for using fresh or
in cooked dishes, sweet or savoury.*

1 With a small sharp knife, score
through the skin lengthways,
dividing the mango into four equal
sections without slicing deeply
enough to cut into the flesh.

2 To make the mango easier to
handle and to prevent the ripe
flesh from bruising, insert a fork
into the stalk end. Lift the end of
each section of skin with the tip of
a knife, grip it with your thumb and
peel off the skin in large strips.

3 With the mango still held on the
fork, slice off the flesh from one
side of the stone. Turn it over and
cut off the other side, discarding
the stone. The flesh may now be cut
up into slices, either lengthways or
widthways, or cut into cubes. Any
flesh that remains attached to the
skin can be sucked off as a cook's
perk, very messy but delicious.

MARINADE

SOAKED IN FLAVOUR

What is a marinade?

A marinade is a mixture of ingredients in which food is soaked before cooking. It can include fruit juice, herbs, oil, spices, vinegar, wine, yoghurt and other seasonings. Marinades for meat should not contain salt as this draws out too much of the natural juice and colour.

Originally used as a way of preserving meat for a few days, before domestic fridges were common, marinades are now used only to heighten the flavour of food, help to prevent it from drying out and also to have a tenderising effect. The choice of ingredients depends on the food and the type of dish, and how it will be cooked. When grilling, for instance, the marinade is either basted on the food during cooking or reduced and thickened separately to make a sauce.

RAW, COOKED AND DRY

What types of marinade can I use?

There are three main types: raw, cooked and dry. Raw marinades of oils and vinegar, or yoghurt, are used for relatively tender foods such as chicken or fish that only require a short marination time.

An uncooked marinade composed of wine, brandy, vegetables and/or herbs can be used for large joints, game and poultry. Cooked marinades, such as those using red or white wine, are used to give food a fairly strong flavour. They should be properly cooled before being poured over the meat, which is then covered and refrigerated until you are ready to cook it.

The term dry marinades is a slight misnomer, as a little oil and vinegar (or lemon juice or wine) is included. But the spices and other flavourings mixed with the liquid are rubbed into the dry meat and not used as a bath in which the meat is immersed. Dry marinades are more economical, as very little oil or vinegar is used, and the marinade, plus any juices that run from the meat, is frequently used in the final dish. The function of the dry marinade is simply to flavour the meat, through prolonged contact.

Whatever method you choose, turn the food frequently while it is marinating for even absorption.

THE RIGHT DISH

What kind of containers should be used for marinades?

Marinades usually contain an acid, such as vinegar or wine, to break down tough food fibres and this affects metals other than stainless steel, including copper and aluminium. Glass or ceramic dishes or bowls or plastic boxes are suitable containers for marinades. Use cling film or a plate to cover them.

OILS FOR MARINADES

Which oil is best for a marinade?

Any oil with a pleasant but not too strong flavour, such as a mild olive oil, sunflower or rapeseed oil, is fine for a marinade. Oils with a very positive flavour, such as sesame, could drown the flavour of the meat. If the food to be marinated is particularly bland and needs help, try one of the herb or spice-flavoured oils, such as garlic or chilli, for extra flavour.

BENEFITS OF YOGHURT

When yoghurt is included in a marinade, does it tenderise the meat or simply add flavour?

Both. The yoghurt adds flavour but it also contains active enzymes that act as a tenderiser. Using yoghurt as a marinade is very popular in Indian cookery. The recipe (right) for Chicken Tikka is a typically Indian way of preparing pieces of chicken so that they are tender and aromatic after cooking. In an Indian restaurant this dish would most often be cooked in a tandoor, an extremely hot traditional clay oven, and served with naan bread.

Chicken tikka

SERVES: 4
PREPARATION TIME: 25 minutes, plus overnight marination
COOKING TIME: 15 - 20 minutes

150 ml (5 fl oz) plain yoghurt
1 teaspoon cornflour
1 small onion, chopped
1 clove garlic, crushed
1 tablespoon finely chopped fresh root ginger
1 fresh chilli, finely chopped
Juice of 1 lemon
2 tablespoons olive oil
2 teaspoons paprika
1 teaspoon garam masala
1 teaspoon ground cumin
2 tablespoons chopped fresh coriander
Salt and black pepper
500 g (1 lb 2 oz) boned, skinned chicken breasts, cubed

1 Put all the ingredients, except the chicken, into a food processor or a blender and process until smooth.
2 Put the chicken pieces into a nonmetallic dish, pour the blended flavourings over them and mix well, ensuring that all the chicken pieces are coated thoroughly. Cover the mixture and leave it to marinate in the refrigerator overnight.
3 Heat the grill to medium. Thread the chicken onto skewers and cook it for 15 - 20 minutes, turning the skewers occasionally and brushing the chicken from time to time with the remaining marinade until the meat is cooked and tender.
4 Serve the chicken tikka hot or cold with warm naan or pitta bread and a cucumber and yoghurt raita.

VARIATION
The chicken pieces and marinade can be cooked in a roasting tin in a preheated oven at 200°C (400°F, gas mark 6) for 30 minutes, turned every 10 minutes or so while they cook. If there is any marinade left over when the chicken is done, it can be reduced to a thick sauce by cooking it in the roasting tin over a high heat while you scrape up all of the sediment and pan juices. Stir the sauce until it has thickened then pour it over the chicken just before serving.

Tuna steaks taste fresh and tender if they are marinated in olive oil, lime and basil before being quickly grilled.

TENDERISING TACTICS

If I marinate a tough steak for a few hours, will it become tender? Is this a clever way of turning cheap steak into tender food?

While the acid content of the marinade will penetrate the meat fibres and make a tough steak softer, it would have to marinate for days to become as tender as fillet steak and this would have a detrimental affect on the flavour of the meat.

FOODS TO MARINATE

Are there any foods other than meat that can be marinated?

Fish and shellfish, game, offal, poultry and vegetables can all be marinated. Thin slices of fish, such as monkfish, salmon, trout and turbot are often marinated on a plate for 15 minutes and served without

cooking. The tuna recipe below shows how a simple marinade can add a subtle flavour to grilled fish.

Marinated fresh tuna steaks with basil

SERVES: 4
PREPARATION TIME: 15 minutes, plus 2 hours marination
COOKING TIME: 10 - 14 minutes

3 tablespoons olive oil
Finely grated zest and juice of 1 lime
3 tablespoons chopped fresh basil
Salt and black pepper
4 × 175 g (6 oz) tuna steaks

1 Put the oil, lime zest and juice, basil and seasoning in a bowl and whisk together until well blended.
2 Put the tuna steaks in a shallow, nonmetallic dish and then pour the marinade over them. Turn the tuna

steaks over in the marinade so they are evenly coated. Cover and leave to marinate for at least 2 hours in the refrigerator, turning occasionally.
3 Heat the grill to a medium heat. Remove the tuna from the marinade and cook for 5 - 7 minutes on each side until the fish is lightly cooked and tender. Serve with a spicy salsa or uncooked chutney, and some boiled new potatoes or fresh bread.
VARIATIONS
You can also chargrill the tuna over a barbecue or in a ridged iron grill pan over a very high heat.

To bake the fish, loosely wrap the marinated steaks individually in foil, then seal them (with or without a little of the marinade) and cook in a preheated oven at 180°C (350°F, gas mark 4) for 20 - 30 minutes, until the steaks are just cooked and tender. Allow the tuna steaks to stand in the foil for 10 minutes before serving.

MARMALADE

PEEL AND PARE

How should you prepare fruit for making marmalade?

Choose ripe fruit with smooth skin, preferably unwaxed, then scrub and dry them. For fine-shred marmalade, pare off the zest and slice it into very thin strips. For thin-cut and coarse-cut marmalade, cut off and discard the ends, stand the fruit upright and cut away the peel, avoiding the inner pith. Cut each strip of peel into thin strips for thin marmalade or short 3 mm (⅛ in) thick strips for coarse-cut.

Cut up the flesh roughly, reserving the juice, pith and pips. You can speed up the job by chopping unpeeled oranges straight into a food processor but the processed peel will be chunky and uneven.

The Pink Grapefruit Marmalade recipe on the right uses thin-cut peel and is surprisingly sweet.

Cooking the pips and pith in a muslin bag with the fruit releases their pectin and helps the marmalade to set.

Pink grapefruit marmalade

MAKES: *about 1.8 kg (4 lb)*
PREPARATION TIME: *30 minutes*
COOKING TIME: *2½ hours*

2 large pink grapefruit
4 lemons
1.3 kg (3 lb) granulated sugar

1 Scrub the grapefruit and pat them dry. Pare the rind from the fruit and slice it into thin, even strips.
2 Remove the pith and roughly cut up the flesh, reserving the pips and any juice. Put the pips and pith on a square of muslin and tie it up into a bag with a long piece of string.
3 Put the grapefruit flesh, the juice, rind and 1.7 litres (3 pints) of water in a preserving pan. Add the muslin bag and tie the string to the handle. Bring the mixture to the boil, then simmer gently for 1 - 2 hours or until the pared rind is very tender and the pan's contents has reduced by half.
4 Warm the sugar by spreading it on a baking tray and placing it in a very low oven for about 10 minutes.
5 Lift out the muslin bag, squeeze it well to allow the juices to run back into the pan, then discard it. Add the warmed sugar to the pan and stir it over a low heat until it has dissolved.
6 Bring the marmalade to the boil and continue to boil rapidly for 15 minutes or until the setting point is reached. It is ready when your finger leaves a furrow in a spoonful placed on a chilled saucer.
7 Skim the marmalade then leave it to stand for 15 minutes. Stir it well and then pour it into clean, warm jars. Cover immediately with waxed discs, waxed side down, and seal.

Pink grapefruit flesh and thin-cut peel make a delectable marmalade to brighten up even a mid-winter morning.

MAYONNAISE

SAFETY RULES

Is it safe to eat mayonnaise after all the scares about raw eggs?

It is quite safe as long as strict rules of hygiene and safety are observed. Always use fresh, undamaged eggs from a reputable source, store them in the refrigerator and use them well before their 'use by' date (so the finished mayonnaise can then be stored for up to three days). Bring them up to room temperature by taking them out of the refrigerator about 30 minutes before using.

While eating mayonnaise is safe for most people, raw egg products are not recommended for vulnerable people such as babies, the elderly, pregnant women or anyone who is unwell.

KEEPING MAYONNAISE

For how long is it safe to keep homemade mayonnaise?

Homemade mayonnaise will keep for up to three days in the refrigerator. The freshly made mayonnaise should be covered immediately to prevent a skin forming, or transferred to a covered container or screw-top jar. Be sure to label it with the date before storing. The flavour will not be satisfactory if it is not warmed to room temperature by removing it from the refrigerator 30 minutes before serving. Mayonnaise does not freeze well as it almost always curdles.

SEPARATE SOLUTION

What can I do if mayonnaise begins to separate?

Rescue it by quickly whisking in a tablespoon of warm water. If this fails, the mixture can still be salvaged by starting again. Put a fresh egg yolk, a teaspoon of cold water or a teaspoon of mustard into a clean bowl then very slowly start whisking in the curdled mixture and carry on until it is smooth.

CHOOSING THE OIL

Is one oil any better than the others for making mayonnaise?

Virtually any edible oil, apart from pumpkin seed oil and sesame oil, can be used as long as the flavour and price are acceptable. Olive oil, as used in the recipe below, is the traditional choice, but some people find the flavour too strong. Instead you can use a mix of olive oil and a milder vegetable oil, or try a light olive oil with a little extra virgin for flavour. Alternatively, mix half nut oil and half mild vegetable oil.

Mayonnaise

MAKES: 300 ml (10 fl oz)
PREPARATION TIME: 10 minutes
COOKING TIME: none

2 egg yolks, size 2
½ teaspoon Dijon mustard
* or a pinch of dried mustard*
Salt
300 ml (10 fl oz) olive oil (or olive
* and vegetable oil mixed)*
2 tablespoons white wine vinegar
* or 1 - 2 tablespoons lemon juice*

1 Put the egg yolks in a medium-sized mixing bowl, add the mustard and a pinch of salt and beat it well with a wooden spoon or wire whisk, standing the bowl on a damp cloth to prevent it from slipping.
2 Add the oil, drop by drop, beating continuously until the mixture has begun to thicken. Continue to add the oil half a teaspoon at a time, still beating well. When half of the oil has been added, beat in the vinegar or lemon juice and keep on adding the remaining oil in a thin stream, whisking the mixture all the time.
VARIATIONS
Add what is listed to the 300 ml (10 fl oz) of mayonnaise (above):
• CHANTILLY MAYONNAISE: add 75 ml (2½ fl oz) whipped double cream.
• GREEN MAYONNAISE: add 75 ml (2½ fl oz) chopped fresh herbs such as basil, dill, marjoram, parsley, watercress or blanched and finely chopped fresh raw spinach.
• PRAWN COCKTAIL SAUCE: add 2 - 4 tablespoons of tomato ketchup,

---

MAKING MAYONNAISE IN A BLENDER

This is a quick and easy method for making mayonnaise when it is not so important for the mixture to be really thick and stiff.

Put the two egg yolks (or one whole egg) in the blender, then add the mustard, vinegar or lemon juice and blend for a few seconds. With the motor running, start pouring in the oil through the hole in the lid, drop-by-drop at first, and then in a thin stream until the mixture appears to be thick. This method will produce a slightly thinner and lighter result than hand-mixed mayonnaise.

---

2 tablespoons of cream, yoghurt or fromage frais, and a dash each of brandy and Worcestershire sauce.
• TARTARE SAUCE: add 2 tablespoons each of chopped capers, gherkins and finely chopped chives, parsley, shallots or spring onions to taste.

SAUCE REMOULADE

Is it possible to make mayonnaise without using raw eggs?

Yes. Sauce rémoulade is made with hard-boiled egg yolk, which makes it particularly suitable for anyone hesitant about eating raw eggs.

Mash a sieved size 2 yolk thoroughly, add a tablespoon of boiling water and stir it to a smooth paste. Gradually add 225 ml (8 fl oz) of olive oil, beating the mixture continuously. When the mayonnaise has thickened, add 2 tablespoons each of finely chopped gherkins and parsley, a tablespoon of drained capers and a dash of anchovy essence. This sauce is often combined with celeriac, as in the recipe for Celeriac Rémoulade, overleaf.

Celeriac rémoulade

SERVES: 4 - 6
PREPARATION TIME: 35 minutes
COOKING TIME: 30 seconds

525 g (1 lb 3 oz) celeriac
250 ml (9 fl oz) rémoulade sauce
   (see previous page)
1 teaspoon lemon juice or
   wine vinegar
2 tablespoons single cream
Salt and black pepper
1 tablespoon chopped parsley

1 Peel the celeriac and cut into thin, julienne sticks, dropping them into water with some added lemon juice as you go, to prevent browning.
2 Blanch the julienne of celeriac in boiling salted water for 30 seconds, then drain and leave the sticks to cool in the sieve or colander.

3 Stir the lemon juice or vinegar and cream into the rémoulade sauce.
4 Place the celeriac in a bowl and toss in the mayonnaise until it is well coated. Season to taste and serve it sprinkled with the chopped parsley.
VARIATIONS
Rémoulade sauce goes well with fish and shellfish or cold meats. It can also be added to mixed salads of other grated or sliced vegetables.

GARLIC MAYONNAISE

What is aïoli and how is it made?

Aïoli is a garlic-flavoured mayonnaise that is traditionally served with Mediterranean fish soups. But it also goes very well with other foods such as eggs, fish, salads and vegetables. Follow the recipe on the right to make this superb sauce.

Aïoli

MAKES: 300 ml (10 fl oz)
PREPARATION TIME: 15 minutes
COOKING TIME: none

2 egg yolks, size 2
2 - 4 large cloves garlic, to taste
A pinch of salt
300 ml (10 fl oz) olive oil, or olive
   and vegetable oil, mixed
1 teaspoon lemon juice

1 Put the egg yolks in a bowl. Crush the garlic with the pinch of salt, add it to the eggs and beat or whisk well.
2 Start adding the oil, beating all the time. When half of the oil has been incorporated, add the lemon juice, then the remaining oil, whisking all the time until the aïoli is thick and smooth. Aïoli should be stored in the same way as a mayonnaise.

Variations on a mayonnaise theme. Clockwise from left: tangy tartare sauce, green herb mayonnaise and a garlicky aïoli.

MEAT

KNOWING YOUR MEAT

What should I look for when choosing a good joint of meat?

It should look and smell fresh, the flesh should be silky, not wet, and the fat should be creamy white. Bright red flesh is not necessarily a sign of freshness or of quality, although many people think it is, and some supermarkets even put extra lights over the meat cabinet to make the flesh look a brighter red. Well-hung meat will be darker, and properly aged beef has a purple tinge. Meat with a greyish tinge should always be avoided.

When choosing boned, rolled and tied joints, you need to look for a neat appearance. They should also be of a uniform thickness so that they will cook evenly. If the meat is still on the bones they should have been cleanly sawn through and not jaggedly chopped.

All meat, but especially chops and steaks, should be neat and well trimmed of surplus fat. Any tough sinew should be removed, either by the butcher or at home.

CUTTING TECHNIQUE

Why should you cut across the grain of the meat rather than in the same direction?

Because the meat fibres will be shorter and a piece of meat cut across will be easier to chew, and so seem to be more tender.

LEAN IS BEST

Are more expensive cuts of meat more nutritious or lower in fat?

The nutritional value of all lean meat is absolutely the same no matter what it costs, but weight for weight the cheaper cuts of meat are not quite as good because they contain a smaller amount of nourishing lean meat and more gristle and fat. However, you can buy more of the cheaper cuts for the same money, to allow for wastage, and although they are tough, careful cooking will tenderise them.

GOOD VALUE CUTS

Which cuts of meat offer the best value for a family meal?

Those that come from the parts of the animal which have done a certain amount of work, such as the legs, are the best value for money. They have developed flavour but not too much waste in the form of fat, gristle or bone; for example, beef chuck and blade steaks, and top rump or thick flank; lamb shoulder and best end of neck chops; pork hand and spring (from the front leg), spare ribs and cuts of shoulder or blade.

However, because these parts of the animal contain the main muscles, they can be tough. To increase their tenderness, beat them or soak for a few hours in a marinade containing an acid, such as lemon juice, vinegar, wine, plain yoghurt or pulped tomatoes. Cook them slowly without too much moisture.

JOINTS TO ROAST

Which joints of meat are best for roasting and which for braising or pot roasting? Is size a factor?

The best cuts for roasting are those that come from the parts of the animal that have done the least work, mainly the body, which produces beef fillet, rib, sirloin and top rump; lamb best end of neck and loin; and pork chump end, fillet and loin. But legs of lamb and pork, although they contain muscle, are also roasted, since they come from young animals. Large joints roast more successfully than small ones.

Small joints, and joints from the parts of the animal that have been more active, are less expensive and are better suited to more gentle pot roasting, which makes the meat more tender. Suitable joints are beef brisket, silverside, topside and top rump; lamb shoulder, shanks and shank end of leg; and pork shoulder, hand and spring.

NATURAL REARING

What does it mean when meat is labelled conservation grade?

This means that the meat has been reared using traditional husbandry techniques, which reflect proper care and concern for animal welfare. This means no restriction on their movement, development at a natural pace, and medication only when absolutely necessary. These animals are slaughtered humanely. Organic meat is reared and slaughtered in the same way but is also fed organically grown food.

QUALITY BUTCHERS

My friend buys from the Q Guild of butchers. Who are they?

A group of independent butchers established the Q Guild in 1986. The group has members in Britain and Eire. Some of the Q Guild's members rear and sell their own animals, others are butchers and buy their meat from farmers or wholesalers whose good methods of breeding, rearing and slaughtering meet the Guild's standards. The Guild's logo is a guarantee of high-quality meat with superior flavour.

FRENCH CUTTING

Is French trimming the same as Continental butchery?

Do not confuse the two. French trimming (which almost always applies to lamb) exposes the bone of either a leg, to make carving easier, or a cutlet, to make it easier and cleaner to pick up and chew. For cutlets, the chine bone is removed and the long ends of the cutlet bones are scraped of all fat and meat about 2.5 cm (1 in) from the tip of the bone.

Continental butchery, which is also known as seam butchery, produces pieces of meat which are sometimes described as 'French cuts'. It is different from the English method in that French butchers separate the tissues along each muscle whereas we cut across the meat and through the joints in order to make smaller and more manageable pieces. The exception in Britain is fillet steaks, which are always seam cut, beef rump and sometimes pork leg steaks.

The terms high lean and extra trim, usually found on pork leg steaks or beef rump steaks, almost always mean they were seam cut.

RARE BUT SAFE

With all the worries about food poisoning, is it safe to eat meat which has been cooked rare?

The toxins produced by bacteria prior to cooking are the cause of food poisoning, so storing meat at the correct temperature is the vital factor in food safety. If the meat has been properly stored, it is safe to leave it rare in the centre. However, if the meat has been pierced or cut in any way, and particularly if it has been boned and rolled, bacteria will have been able to enter the meat, so it should be well cooked right through.

TAKING THE TEMPERATURE

How can I tell when meat is cooked through?

The only way to be absolutely sure that meat has been cooked to your liking is to use a meat thermometer. It should be inserted into the thickest part of the joint, without touching any bones, just before the end of the cooking time. When cooking beef and lamb, the meat will be rare when the temperature reaches 60°C (140°F), medium rare when it is 71°C (160°F) and well done when the temperature reads 80°C (180°F). Pork and veal should only be served well done, which means that the temperature should reach 75°C (170°F) for pork, and 71°C (160°F) for veal.

If you do not have a meat thermometer, you can insert a metal skewer into the thickest part of the cooked joint and wait for 30 seconds. If the skewer feels cold to the touch when it is withdrawn, the meat is not done; if it feels warm the meat is rare, and if it is hot the meat is well done.

It is wise to take the resting time into consideration when you are testing for doneness because the meat will continue to cook while it is sitting. This is more important for a piece of meat that you wish to serve rare or medium and less crucial if the meat is going to be eaten when it is well done.

COOKING FROM FROZEN

Is it safe to cook meat while it is still frozen?

No, meat should always be completely thawed before it is cooked, as otherwise the centre may not be cooked by the time the outside of the meat looks done, which could be dangerous. This is especially true of large joints of meat, but even small pieces could be hazardous.

Whenever possible it is better for meat to thaw slowly in the refrigerator, allowing 6-8 hours per kg (3-4 hours per lb) for large joints of meat and 5-6 hours overall for steaks and chops. If you have a microwave oven, follow the manufacturer's instructions.

Another consideration is that the taste and texture of meat, even quite small pieces, cooked from frozen is not very palatable. It is a waste of an expensive item of food to try to cook it without thawing.

DELICATE MINCE

I find mince often goes grey and rubbery when I cook it - what is it that I am doing wrong?

The most probable explanation for pallid rubbery mince is that you are cooking the meat for too long at a temperature that is too high. For better results, the mince should be started over a moderate heat in a large frying pan. If you use a pan that is too small the mince will steam in the moisture it exudes as it cooks and the texture will not be as firm as it should be. Stir it to break up any lumps and cook it just until it is no longer raw but has not taken on any colour. Then reduce the heat and add the liquid, if you are using any, and continue to cook the meat, keeping it just below the simmering point.

The colour of mince is also determined by the amount of fat it contains. If it is pale it has more fat; lean mince is darker in colour.

For perfectly cooked mince, use the recipe on the right for Mexican Beef with Cornmeal Topping. It is a good dish for a family supper.

A crunchy cornmeal topping and spicy Latin American seasoning make minced chuck steak into a warming supper.

Mexican beef with cornmeal topping

SERVES: 4
PREPARATION TIME: 15 minutes
COOKING TIME: 1 hour 10 minutes

FOR THE SAUCE
1 - 2 tablespoons olive or
*   sunflower oil*
2 sticks celery, chopped
3 cloves garlic, finely chopped
1 onion, finely chopped
1 red pepper, diced
2 teaspoons cumin seeds
675 g (1 lb 8 oz) chuck steak, fat
*   removed and minced*
150 ml (5 fl oz) beef or vegetable
*   stock or water*
A few drops Tabasco sauce
425 g (15 oz) canned
*   chopped tomatoes*
2 - 3 tablespoons tomato purée
1 tablespoon chopped fresh
*   oregano or marjoram*
A pinch each of salt, cayenne
*   pepper and chilli powder*

FOR THE TOPPING
150 g (5 ½ oz) cornmeal
40 g (1 ½ oz) self-raising flour
2 teaspoons baking powder
Salt and black pepper
1 egg, size 3, beaten
50 g (1 ¾ oz) butter, melted
175 ml (6 fl oz) milk

1 To make the sauce, heat the oil in a flameproof casserole over a moderate heat. Add the celery, garlic, onion and red pepper and cook until soft and lightly coloured.
2 Stir in the cumin seeds and heat until fragrant, about 30 - 60 seconds. Stir in the beef and cook it, stirring, over a medium heat until it is no longer pink, but do not let it brown.
3 Stir the stock or water, Tabasco sauce, tomatoes, tomato purée and oregano or marjoram into the meat and heat until bubbles just begin to appear. Cover the casserole tightly and cook the beef at a very gentle simmer for 30 - 40 minutes, stirring it every so often. Preheat the oven to 220°C (425°F, gas mark 7).
4 To make the topping, mix the cornmeal, flour, baking powder and seasoning together in a bowl. Stir in the egg, melted butter and milk and stir until it is smooth.
5 When the meat sauce is cooked, season it to taste with salt, cayenne pepper and chilli powder. Spoon on the cornmeal topping. Smooth the top with a spatula and bake the dish for about 15 - 20 minutes, or until the cornmeal has set. This dish can be made ahead of time and reheated.

Spicy fried patties

Leftover Mexican Beef can be rejuvenated by mixing the meat and topping together in a bowl with a chopped raw onion and a beaten egg. Form the mixture into patties and fry them gently.

MEAT FROM THE DELICATESSEN

Cold meats are a blessing for the busy cook, served thinly sliced in a plate of cold cuts or cut into strips or chunks to boost salads and hot dishes. Here is our guide to the most popular smoked or dried meats and sausages.

Continental meats from the delicatessen counter offer a marvellous range of flavours from mild liver sausage or mortadella to fiery chorizo, spicy pastrami or sweet roast ham, and are ready to use in seconds. Some are made with raw meats, some are cooked, but even those made from raw ingredients have usually been cured, dried or smoked so they need no further cooking.

Heavily smoked or air-dried meats like salami keep almost indefinitely when whole, but dry out once sliced. Lightly smoked meats like bierwurst and mortadella keep less well. Unless you buy a whole pepperoni, salami or teewurst, it is best to eat cold cuts within a day or two of purchase. Keep them in the refrigerator, well wrapped in cling film.

BIERSCHINKEN (Germany)
Made from pork and chunks of ham, bierschinken is studded with peppercorns and pistachio nuts.

BIERWURST (Germany)
Coarse-textured pork, or pork and beef, goes into a bierwurst, which is then highly seasoned with juniper berries and cardamom and sometimes with garlic too.

BILTONG (South Africa)
Biltong or jerky was originally strips of game dried in the sun to provide long-lasting rations for travellers. Now you can buy beef and venison varieties

Make perfect antipasto from a selection of cold meats sharpened with olives, gherkins, radishes, celery and a shaving of Parmesan.

as well. To eat, simply cut off thin slices and chew hard.

BOLOGNA (Multinational)
Based on mortadella (from Bologna), this smoked pork sausage is known as polony in Britain and boloney in the United States.

BRESAOLA (Italy)
A speciality of Lombardy in Italy, bresaola, and the Swiss bundnerfleisch, are both air-dried cuts of tender lean beef, very thinly sliced. They are served raw with a vinaigrette dressing or with a squeeze of lemon, some olive oil and freshly ground black pepper.

CHORIZO (Spain)
A pork sausage, chorizo's hot taste and deep red colour come from a seasoning of paprika. There are different types and it is often added to dishes of beans. Hungary and France also make chorizo.

COPPA (France)
This large sausage is made from smoked pig's shoulder marbled with extra fat.

GARLIC SAUSAGE (Multinational)
This widely made, inexpensive mixture of pork and beef is strongly flavoured with garlic.

GYULAI (Hungary)
Pork is mixed with sweet red peppers to make gyulai.

HAM (Multinational)
Ham, simply the cured hind leg of the pig, often air-dried; many countries have their particular versions (see HAM).

JAGDWURST, SCHINKENJAGDWURST (Germany)
Minced pork with chunks of ham, produces a sausage similar to bierschinken.

KABANOS (Poland)
Smoked and spicy, kabanos is very long and thin, and traditionally cooked with lentils.

KATENRAUCHWURST (Germany)
A large, coarsely cut smoked pork sausage that is similar to salami, but with a black skin.

CHORIZO

GARLIC SAUSAGE

GYULAI

KABANOS

MORTADELLA

LIVER SAUSAGE

KIELBASA (Poland)
A highly seasoned mixture of pork and beef, kielbasa can be smoked or fresh, cooked or uncooked. It is used in *bigos*, a Polish hunters' stew.

LANDJAGER (Germany)
Air-dried or smoked, this sausage is made of beef with a little pork, and flavoured with caraway seeds and garlic.

LIVER SAUSAGE (Multinational)
German leberwurst is the best known, but many other countries have their own. It is a smooth spreadable mixture of well-seasoned pork and pig's liver, steamed inside a thick casing. Finer but more expensive liver sausages are made with calf's or goose liver.

LOUKANIKA (Greece)
Small and knobbly loukanika is made from minced pork seasoned with coriander and marinated in red wine. It is a popular ingredient of Greek hors d'oeuvre.

METTWURST (Germany)
A lightly smoked mixture of pork and beef, mettwurst can be either a smooth uniform pink or coarsely minced to resemble salami.

MORTADELLA (Italy)
Much bigger than other sausages, mortadella is made from pork and contains large chunks of fat, whole black peppercorns and sometimes green pistachio nuts.

PASTRAMI (Italy)
Pastrami is brisket of beef cured in a dry mixture of sugar, spices and garlic, then smoked – which gives it a dark exterior. Like salt beef, it is excellent in sandwiches made with rye bread.

PEPPERONI (Italy)
Coarsely chopped pork and beef flavoured with red pepper and fennel, pepperoni is often served on pizza.

PLOCKWURST (Germany)
Also known as schinkenplockwurst, this is a large, coarsely chopped smoked ham. It is also sold in another version known as pfefferplockwurst, which is square and coated with crushed peppercorns.

SALAMI (Italy/EC)
There are countless different salami, all made from coarsely minced pork and pork fat, with beef and veal sometimes included. Flavourings include coriander, fennel, garlic, paprika, peppercorns and wine.

They are slowly air-dried or smoked to produce a long, mottled sausage. The casing may be smoke-blackened, covered in white mould or coated with herbs or crushed peppercorns. Italian salami are often considered the finest. Danish salami is cheaper but is fatty, salty, and an artificial red colour.

SALCHICHON (Spain)
These salami lookalikes are made from minced smoked pork and spices. Mildly flavoured Salchichon de Vich is highly esteemed.

SALT BEEF (UK)
Salt beef is brisket of beef; the joint is first wet-cured in a spiced brine and then cooked.

SAUCISSON FUME, SEC (France)
The French equivalent of salami is made with smoked or dried pork, pork fat and garlic. The best-known are saucisson Jésus and Rosette de Lyon.

SMOKED CHICKEN (Multinational)
Smoked chicken is ready-to-eat and has a mild, bacony flavour. It is good dressed in mayonnaise in sandwiches or salads. Smoked duck or turkey, also available, can be used in the same way.

TEEWURST (Germany)
This highly spiced sausage combines pork and beef finely ground together to make a pink spreadable paste. It looks small and stubby and comes in a smooth, shiny casing.

WIEJSKA (Poland)
A pure pork sausage with a hint of garlic, tied into a horseshoe. Typically sold cut into chunks, wiejska is eaten cold, or boiled, grilled or stewed.

ZUNGENWURST (Germany)
A large reddish blood sausage, zungenwurst contains substantial chunks of fat and slices of tongue (zunge).

ZWYIEKA (Poland)
Pork and beef slicing sausages formed into long thin links.

SMOKED CHICKEN

MILANO SALAMI

SAUCISSON

PARMA HAM

PASTRAMI

HONEY ROAST HAM

MEAT PIE

STRONGER PASTRY

What is a hot-water crust?

It is a particular type of pastry that is used exclusively for cold meat and game pies. The dough is made by adding boiling water to lard and this mixture is then poured into the flour. As the gluten in the flour starts to develop, it makes the dough more elastic and easier to mould into a tall pie.

The high proportion of water used also helps to bind the pastry so that it is strong and will hold a substantial filling. After kneading, the dough should be kept warm for 15 minutes or so to allow the gluten to develop completely.

LUSCIOUS JELLY

Why are the meat pies that are made with hot-water crust pastry filled with jelly after cooking?

Jellied stock keeps the pie moist and adds flavour to the filling. It takes practice to judge when the stock is ready. If it is too thin, it may soak through the pastry and leak. If it is too thick, it will not trickle down and fill the gaps between the pastry and filling. The stock should be added when cool and just on the point of setting.

Gradually add as much stock as the pie will hold: the exact amount will vary. Do not rush this stage or you may flood the hole. Once it is added, the stock will take 3 hours or longer to set into a jelly.

SIMPLE EQUIPMENT

Do you need to use a special tin for making a raised meat pie?

No. Traditional raised pies were shaped by hand over a wooden mould, a large jar or a straight-sided container, and the pastry was left to set firm before the container was removed. In the recipe for Pork Pie (right) the dough is moulded inside a loose-based, deep, round tin. But if you make a lot of pies, it will be worth buying a pretty and practical fluted, hinged pie frame.

Pork pie

SERVES: 8 – 10
PREPARATION TIME: 1 hour plus several hours resting, standing, cooling and setting
COOKING TIME: 2 ½ hours

FOR THE FILLING
900 g (2 lb) lean boneless pork, such as fillet or shoulder
225 g (8 oz) sausage meat
1 small onion, chopped
1 tablespoon finely chopped fresh sage
Salt and black pepper

FOR THE PASTRY
450 g (1 lb) plain flour
¾ teaspoon salt
150 g (5 ½ oz) lard, diced
2 eggs, size 4, beaten
A pinch of salt, extra

FOR THE JELLY
150 ml (5 fl oz) well-flavoured chicken stock
1 teaspoon gelatine

1 To make the filling, trim the pork and cut it neatly into 1 cm (½ in) cubes. Place the pork, sausage meat, onion, sage, salt and pepper in a bowl and mix well, then set aside.
2 To make the pastry, sift the flour and salt into a warm bowl, making a well in the centre.
3 Put 200 ml (7 fl oz) of water and the lard into a saucepan. Heat them over a moderate heat until the lard has melted, then quickly bring the mixture to the boil and immediately pour it into the well you have made in the middle of the flour mixture.
4 Stir quickly with a wooden spoon until the mixture clings together in a ball, leaving the sides of the basin clean. It will come together quickly.
5 Turn the dough onto a floured surface and knead it until smooth. Place the dough under an upturned basin and leave it for 15 minutes.
6 To make the pie, lightly grease a deep, round cake tin with a loose base 18 cm (7 in) in diameter and a depth of 7.5 cm (3 in). Preheat the oven to 200°C (400°F, gas mark 6). When the dough is ready to shape, cut off two-thirds and return the smaller piece to the bowl.
7 Working quickly with the larger piece of dough, mould it evenly over the base and sides of the tin, bringing the pastry right up to the top edge. Carefully smooth out any air pockets or creases with your fingers. Make sure there is not a thick layer of dough between the base and sides of the tin, and that the pastry is not too thin.
8 Spoon the pork mixture into the pastry-lined tin. Reserve a quarter of the remaining dough and roll out the rest into a circle 18 cm (7 in) in diameter to make the pie lid. Brush lightly around the top edge of the dough with a little water.

Using a pastry brush to dampen the edge of the pie with water will help to secure the pastry lid firmly to the sides.

9 Cover the pie with the dough circle, pressing the outside down on the dampened edge to seal. Flute the edges to form a decorative border (see box on page 279). Cut a small cross in the centre of the lid, then moisten around it with a little of the beaten egg and fold back each point, pressing it against the top. This hole allows steam to escape and will be used later for pouring in the stock.
10 Roll out half of the remaining dough and make four or six pastry leaves. Brush around the hole in the lid with some beaten egg and arrange the leaves around the hole.
11 With the remaining dough, make a tassel by rolling out the dough to a strip 13 × 2.5 cm (5 × 1 in) and making a series of cuts widthways to within 5 mm (¼ in) of one edge. Dampen a short end and roll it up to

form a hollow tassel to be placed over the centre hole.

12 To make a shiny glaze, whisk a pinch of salt into the remaining egg and brush some of it over the pastry.

13 Bake the pie for 45 minutes, then reduce the oven temperature to 180°C (350°F, gas mark 4). Cover the pie lightly with foil to prevent overbrowning and then cook for a further hour. Remove it from the oven, turning the heat down to low to keep the oven warm, and leave the pie to stand for 30 minutes.

14 Turn the oven temperature back up to 180°C (350°F, gas mark 4). Lift the pie carefully in its tin and put it on top of a large flat-topped can.

15 Carefully ease down the sides of the baking tin, leaving the pie on its base on top of the can. Brush the sides with the rest of the beaten egg, then cover the top with foil to prevent overbrowning. Put the pie, on its base, onto a baking sheet, and cook it for 35 - 45 minutes, or until the sides are golden. Remove the pie from the oven and leave it to cool.

16 Meanwhile, make the jellied stock: place the stock in a heatproof jug, sprinkle over the gelatine and leave to soften for 5 minutes. Stand the jug in a pan of simmering water and stir until the gelatine dissolves.

17 Remove the jug and set it aside for about 30 minutes, until the stock begins to thicken but not set.

18 When the jelly is ready, remove the tassel from the top of the pie, insert a funnel into the hole and pour in the jelly, stopping when the cavity is full. Replace the tassel and refrigerate the pie for several hours.

19 Serve cold, with salad. The pie can be kept refrigerated for two

A small plastic funnel is useful to help you pour the jellied stock through the hole made in the top of the pie.

days, but is not suitable for freezing as the jelly would crystallise and the pastry would lose its crispness.

VARIATIONS

For a spicier filling, add ½ teaspoon each of ground allspice and freshly grated nutmeg to the finely chopped fresh sage. You could also use fresh thyme, lemon thyme or some winter savory instead of the sage.

MELONS

TEST FOR RIPENESS

When buying melons, how can I tell if they are ripe and sweet?

A ripe melon should give slightly when pressed gently at one end. For charentais, galia and ogen melons, press at the stalk end. For honeydew and piel de sapo, press at the end opposite the stalk. You should also sniff the melon: a ripe one has a strong scent and there will be little or no scent if it is unripe. Another test is to weigh several melons of the same size in your hand and choose the heaviest.

Watermelon is not so easy to test for ripeness, but it should sound hollow when tapped. If you are buying watermelon by the slice, choose those that are bright red with shiny black seeds. Although quite bland, watermelon is refreshing when eaten chilled on a hot day. It can add a cool taste to salads or a contrast to hot, spicy foods.

COLOUR GUIDE

If I want a green-fleshed melon for a green fruit salad, which melon should I choose?

Many supermarkets specify on the label the interior colour of the melon. If there is no guide, look for galia, ogen or piel de sapo (a type of honeydew), all of which have green flesh. Other honeydews can be pale or golden. Cantaloupes will have pale green or orange flesh. Charentais (a type of cantaloupe) have a deep orange flesh. Watermelon flesh is red or deep pink.

INTENSIFYING FLAVOUR

When I make melon sorbet, the delicate taste almost disappears after it has been frozen. Is there a way to maintain the flavour?

Freezing can dull the flavour of any melon so it is best to begin with a strongly flavoured variety such as cantaloupe or ogen. Charentais has a rough, pale green skin and when ripe a delightfully fragrant peachy orange flesh which is highly successful used in sorbets. Honeydew melons and watermelons are not particularly good for making into sorbets because their flavours are much more delicate.

Whatever melon you decide to use, adding a little lemon juice to the mixture will help to enhance and sustain the melon flavour, as shown in the recipe on the next page for a superb melon granita.

MAKING MELON BALLS

Shaping melon flesh into balls is an attractive way to present the fruit.

1 Cut the melon in half and scoop out the seeds with a spoon. To catch any juice retained among the seeds, put them into a stainless-steel or nylon sieve placed over a bowl to drain. The recovered juice can then be added to a fruit salad.

2 Press a melon baller, open side down, into the flesh and twist it to remove a neat, round sphere of melon. Tap the melon ball out into the bowl. Repeat this process until all the flesh of the melon has been removed. Each time you insert the baller, place it as close as you can to the previous cavity.

Scrape out the ragged pieces of melon with a spoon and liquidise them to make a refreshing drink.

Melon granita with raspberries soaked in kirsch

SERVES: 4
PREPARATION TIME: 30 minutes plus 4 - 5 hours freezing plus 20 minutes to assemble
COOKING TIME: 5 minutes

FOR THE GRANITA
60 g (2¼ oz) granulated sugar
1 cantaloupe or charentais melon, weighing about 550 g (1 lb 4 oz)
2 tablespoons lemon juice
90 ml (3¼ fl oz) medium-sweet white wine

TO SERVE
1 medium galia melon
175 g (6 oz) fresh raspberries
1 tablespoon caster sugar
1 - 2 tablespoons kirsch
Fresh mint leaves
1 teaspoon icing sugar, for sifting

1 To make the melon granita, put the sugar into a saucepan with 90 ml (3¼ fl oz) of water, and stir over a moderate heat until the sugar has dissolved. Bring it to the boil and continue boiling for a minute, then remove it from the heat and allow the mixture to cool.

2 Cut the canteloupe or charentais melon in half and discard the seeds. Scoop out all the flesh, put it into a food processor and blend it to a purée. Add the cooled sugar syrup, lemon juice and wine. Blend the mixture together for a few seconds, pour it into a plastic or metal bowl then put it into the freezer to harden.

3 After an hour, stir the granita with a balloon whisk to break up the stiff, crunchy crystals that have appeared around the edge. Freeze it for another hour and whisk it again, then cover the granita and return it to the freezer until it is completely frozen. (Although granita is frozen, it is best served as soon as it is ready so that the texture is light.)

4 Twenty minutes before serving, remove the granita from the freezer and leave it at room temperature to soften and reach a more acceptable temperature for eating.

A scintillating granita made with lush, ripe melon and white wine is layered with kirsch-soaked raspberries, scoops of perfumed galia and cool mint.

5 Cut the galia melon in half and dice the flesh or shape it into melon balls. Chill four large serving glasses in the freezer for a few minutes.

6 Put the raspberries into a small bowl, sprinkle with the caster sugar, add the kirsch and mix them gently. Cover and set aside.

7 Just before serving, break up the granita with a fork and spoon it into the chilled glasses, alternating the granita with the pieces or balls of melon and the macerated raspberries.

8 Decorate each glass with a few sprigs of mint, sift icing sugar over the leaves and serve immediately.

MENU PLANNING

KEEP IT SIMPLE

Although there are many dishes I can cook, I find it difficult to put together a successful menu. Can you suggest some tips?

However large or small the occasion, try to keep the menu simple. Do not attempt to cook so much that you risk doing it badly, and aim to have at least two-thirds of the cooking and preparation done in advance. The meal should also be feasible. It is no use planning two courses which will require oven space at different temperatures if there is only one oven, or trying to stir-fry all the vegetables while at the same time assembling a complicated main course.

Match the food to the guests and try to stay with one style. For example, serving an Italian starter, followed by a main course from southern France, and ending with a Spanish dessert is fine as these are all Mediterranean. It would be considerably less appealing to serve French moules marinière, followed by Thai green curry, and ending with an American pecan pie for dessert. These flavours create an unhappy, unharmonious mix.

Balance is also crucial because you do not want your guests to feel bloated after the meal. If the first and second courses contain little fat, then an indulgent coffee cream pudding or a meringue that tastes wickedly rich will be greeted with sighs of pleasure instead of half-hearted enthusiasm.

Avoid repetition. For example, do not have a melon starter and then fruit salad as the dessert. No two courses should contain similar meat or fish, and try to vary the colours, textures and cooking processes as well. If a first course is vichyssoise or pâté, do not then serve mashed potato or puréed parsnips with the main course, or stewed apple for the pudding as all of them have a similar smooth texture and rather bland colour.

Aim to keep your menus as seasonal as possible. The flavour of vegetables and fruit is always best when they are meant to be harvested. On the whole, sauces tend to be very popular, so be generous in the amounts being offered, and if they are served separately the guests can help themselves.

Check that the wines, if served, are in the right order, so that more dominant flavours follow delicate ones and match the food. In general: red wines should follow white wines, older wines should follow younger ones and strong wines should follow light ones. Usually, white wines are a good match to fish, white meats and poultry, while reds go with cheese, game, red meats and robust poultry dishes.

COLOUR AND TEXTURE

Should you always offer two or three vegetables with the main course, or is one enough?

Offering a varied selection of vegetables adds colour and texture to meals, but is not always necessary. Try to achieve a balance by offering one starchy dish, such as pasta, polenta, potatoes or rice, and one crisp, fresh vegetable.

Alternatively, serve a mixture of vegetables cooked in advance, such as roasted root vegetables, or braised fennel and celery, plus a quickly cooked green vegetable or a green salad. If your main course consists mainly of vegetables (a vegetarian stew, for example) you may decide potatoes or rice, plus a salad, is more than enough.

MULTIPLYING A RECIPE

If I am using a recipe meant for four people to feed 20, do I simply multiply the quantities by five?

Common sense is needed. If, for example, your recipe is for grilled chicken breasts with Mediterranean vegetables, you need one chicken breast per person whatever the number being served. However, you may reduce the quantity of vegetables to what is sufficient for 16-18 people and still provide a generous and appetising meal.

PLANNING QUANTITIES

How can I work out how much food people will probably eat?

Professional caterers work on the basis that the more people there are being served, the less food per person is needed. With a larger group, everyone has more people to talk to and there is less time to eat; people also tend to eat less when they are standing up. Here are some guidelines on how much raw food to allow per person for a gathering of four to six people:

- CHICKEN AND TURKEY: 450 g (1 lb) if it is on the bone.
- CUTS OF MEAT: **Lamb cutlets:** three or four. **Loin chops:** two. **Pork chops:** one. **Fillets:** two for three or four people.
- ROAST MEAT: **Beef, on the bone:** 350 g (12 oz). **Beef, boned and rolled:** 175-225 g (6-8 oz). **Beef, fillet:** a 2 kg (4 lb 8 oz) piece will feed ten people. **Leg of lamb:** 1.5 kg (3 lb 5 oz) for three or four people, 2 kg (4 lb 8 oz) serves four or five people, 3 kg (6 lb 8 oz) for seven or eight people. **Crown roast:** 3 cutlets. **Leg of pork:** 200 g (7 oz) loin, off the bone.
- STEWED MEAT: **Beef and lamb:** 225 g (8 oz) boneless and trimmed. **Venison:** 175 g (6 oz) lean meat.
- FISH: **Whole large:** uncleaned, with head, 350-450 g (12 oz-1 lb). **Whole small,** with head, 225-350 g (8-12 oz). **Cutlets and steaks:** 175 g (6 oz). **Prawns:** 50-85 g (1¾-3 oz).
- VEGETABLES: assuming that two vegetables, as well as potatoes, are being served with a main course: 125 g (4½ oz) of each vegetable, except french beans and peas: 85 g (3 oz); spinach: 350 g (12 oz).
- SOUP: 250 ml (9 fl oz).
- CHEESE: 50-55 g (1¾-2 oz).
- SANDWICHES: **Bread:** assume an average 20 slices of bread in a medium sliced loaf. **Butter:** 25 g (1 oz) butter will cover eight large slices of bread. **Cucumber:** one makes 15 rounds. **Egg:** one hard-boiled egg per round. **Tomatoes:** 450 g (1 lb) for nine rounds. **Smoked salmon:** 20 g (¾ oz) per round. **Canned tuna:** 200 g (7 oz) plus 4 tablespoons mayonnaise for five sandwich rounds.

Buffet parties

As a general principle, aim to offer two or three main-course dishes, including one that is vegetarian, plus three or four salads, and a selection of two or three desserts.

MERINGUES

PERFECT RESULTS

How can I make wonderful, foolproof meringues?

Begin with a bowl that is clean and completely free of grease. It should be either copper, stainless steel, glass or china, not aluminium or plastic. Using either an electric or a balloon whisk, beat the egg whites until they are very stiff. Gradually blend in half the sugar, whisking well after each addition and then, using a metal spoon, lightly fold in the rest of the sugar.

Use the frothy meringue mixture immediately, piping or spooning it onto baking paper placed on baking sheets. Bake in a low oven, 110°C (225°F, gas mark ¼) for 2½–3 hours. The meringues will be firm and crisp but still white. They will actually be drying out in the oven rather than cooking. Leave the meringues to cool on a wire rack, then carefully remove the baking paper. Once cooled, the meringues should keep fresh and moist for up to three weeks if stored in an airtight container.

WEEP NO MORE

I use the same recipe every time, but sometimes my meringues weep terribly. Why is this?

Meringues tend to weep if the uncooked meringue mixture is left standing too long before baking. The meringue then begins to liquefy or separate and this may result in the meringues exuding droplets which stick to the upper surface and edges and look unsightly. Once you have made the meringue mixture, especially a simple one of egg whites and caster sugar, you should bake it immediately.

Meringues that are baked at too high a temperature may also weep. Always ensure that they are baked at a very low heat for the correct amount of time, which will be indicated in your particular recipe.

SOFTENING THE MIXTURE

Why is vinegar added to some meringue recipes?

In meringue recipes such as the Late Summer Pavlova (below), a small amount of vinegar and cornflour is added so that the baked meringue has a crisp outside and a soft, sticky centre, which makes a soft bed for the mixed fruit.

Late summer pavlova

SERVES: 6-8
PREPARATION TIME: 30 minutes
COOKING TIME: 1 hour

3 egg whites, size 3
175 g (6 oz) caster sugar
A few drops of vanilla essence
½ teaspoon white wine vinegar
1 teaspoon cornflour
300 ml (10 fl oz) double cream
350 g (12 oz) fresh, mixed soft
    fruits such as blackberries,
    blackcurrants, raspberries
    and strawberries

1 Preheat the oven to 150°C (300°F, gas mark 2). Draw an 18 cm (7 in) circle on a piece of baking paper and place this on a baking sheet with the marked side of the paper down.
2 In a large bowl, whisk the egg whites until stiff. Gradually add half the sugar, whisking well. Fold in the remaining sugar with the vanilla, vinegar and cornflour.
3 Spread or pipe the meringue over the circle on the paper, piling it up at the edges to form a rim. Bake for about an hour until the meringue is crisp and dry. Transfer to a wire rack to cool, then remove the paper and place the pavlova on a serving plate.
4 Whip the cream until it is stiff, then pile or pipe it on top of the pavlova. Arrange the fruit over the top and serve immediately.

VARIATIONS
Use other fruits such as apricots, nectarines, peaches or plums in place of the mixed berries.

Muscovado sugar may be used to make the meringue instead of caster sugar and will turn it brown. You can also add a teaspoon or two of ground mixed spice to the mixture.

Benefits of maturity

Egg whites that are a few days old whisk better than egg whites that are very fresh, as some of the water in the white will have evaporated. The drying makes the albumen stronger. Egg whites that have been frozen also whisk well.

VARIATIONS ON A THEME

What is the difference between Swiss meringue, Italian meringue and meringue cuite?

- SWISS MERINGUE: also known as plain or simple meringue, is made by whisking and folding caster sugar into stiffly whisked egg whites at a ratio of 50 g (1¾ oz) per egg. This mixture has to be used immediately. The resulting meringues are light and fragile but have a delicious, sticky texture.
- ITALIAN MERINGUE: is made by beating hot sugar syrup, boiled to the hard ball stage, into whisked egg whites. The hot syrup partially cooks the whites, enabling them to hold their shape for much longer. Italian meringue is impossible to overwhisk and, when uncooked, is more stable than a Swiss meringue, holding its shape well for as long as two days. Italian meringue also cooks faster than Swiss meringue, making brilliant white meringue which forms a powder when the meringue is crushed. Because it holds its shape in the oven, Italian meringue is suitable for shaping as baskets and vacherins (shells).
- MERINGUE CUITE: also known as cooked meringue, is the most robust. It is made by beating egg whites and sugar together over a pan of steaming water to form a smooth, fluffy paste. This process, used mainly by professional chefs, takes time and is hard work when performed by hand. It is used for intricate work and as an uncooked frosting for various pies and cakes.

The Hazelnut Meringues recipe that follows shows how easy Swiss meringues can be to make.

Hazelnut meringues

MAKES: either 20 single meringues or 10 pairs
PREPARATION TIME: 30 minutes
COOKING TIME: 2 ½ - 3 hours

50 g (1 ¾ oz) hazelnuts, toasted
3 egg whites, size 3
150 g (5 ½ oz) caster sugar
150 ml (5 fl oz) double or
  whipping cream

1 Chop the toasted nuts by hand as using a food processor would make them very oily which will affect the meringue. Preheat the oven to 110°C (225°F, gas mark ¼).
2 In a large bowl, whisk the egg whites until they are stiff. Gradually blend in half of the sugar, whisking well after each addition. Lightly fold in the remaining sugar and the chopped nuts, using a metal spoon.
3 Pipe 20 small mounds of the meringue onto baking sheets lined with baking paper and cook them for 2 ½ - 3 hours until crisp.
4 Transfer them to a wire rack to cool, then whip the cream until it is quite thick. Sandwich the meringues together in pairs with the cream and then serve immediately.

VARIATIONS
You can use other varieties of nut, such as chopped or ground almonds, in place of the toasted hazelnuts.

Light soft brown sugar may be substituted for the caster sugar.

If you prefer, the meringues may be sandwiched together with plain fromage frais or thick Greek yoghurt in place of the cream.

Chopped hazelnuts add a light crunch to these delectable meringues.

MICROWAVE OVENS

VIBRATING MOLECULES

How do microwave ovens differ from conventional cookers?

A microwave oven uses an electronic device, the magnetron, to convert electrical energy into high-speed waves. These are deflected off the oven's metal walls directly into food to a depth of about 4 cm (1 ½ in). These microwaves are then absorbed by molecules of moisture in the food, causing them to vibrate rapidly, which creates intense cooking heat. With larger pieces of food, the centre is cooked by conduction, in the same way as in an ordinary oven.

Microwaves pass through china, glass, paper, pottery and some plastics, but metal deflects the microwaves so metal containers are not suitable for cooking.

PROS AND CONS

What are the good and bad features of a microwave oven?

Apart from reheating cooked food, thawing frozen food and cooking raw foods like fish and vegetables, the microwave is an invaluable cook's mate. Use it to soften butter, heat sauces and melt chocolate. Microwaving is very fuel-efficient and fast, taking a quarter to a third of the time needed in conventional cooking. Both oven cleaning and washing up are usually reduced.

As microwaves stop when the oven door is open, and the oven itself is not hot, there is less risk of anyone being burnt. This is especially helpful with children, the elderly and the disabled. The chances of food boiling over or burning are reduced as the oven is set to switch off. Microwaving is also healthier in that less fat, oil and liquid is needed and more nutrients are kept in the food.

Microwave ovens are very useful but have disadvantages with some types of recipes. Anything which needs hot air to rise, such as puff pastry, will fail as the air inside a microwave does not get hot. Roasting is also less successful, but you can brown meat by frying or grilling it briefly before or after microwaving. A combination oven can work as a microwave and convection oven simultaneously, and speeds up cooking while also giving food a brown, crisp finish.

LEARN THE RULES

How can I be sure to use my microwave oven safely?

Do not use metal containers, china with a metallic trim or wire twists as metal may cause damage to the component parts. However, very small pieces of foil can be used, as on a chicken where the wings are cooking too quickly. Secure the foil with cocktail sticks as it must not touch the walls.

Use only microwave-safe plastic containers, as some other plastics would buckle. You can use cooking bags designed to withstand boiling or freezing, but make a slit in the bag to allow steam to escape. To cover food, use a perforated plastic lid or microwave-safe cling film folded back at one corner.

Cooking eggs in their shells causes a build-up of pressure and they may explode unless cooked in a special microwave egg-boiler. Foods such as potatoes or apples should be pricked all over for cooking in their skins. Membranes like egg yolks need pricking too.

BASIC TECHNIQUES

What is the best way to arrange food in a microwave oven?

Microwaves are generally focused around the oven edges with less energy present in the centre. Arrange individual items around the outside of the turntable in a circular fashion, with thinner parts placed towards the centre.

Any food containing liquid needs to be stirred occasionally to redistribute the heat. Bulky foods, such as roasts and whole chickens, must be turned over during cooking so that the top and bottom cook evenly. Raise food on a plastic trivet so that the microwaves can be absorbed underneath. The standing time is crucial, for meat especially, as cooking continues after the oven is turned off. Leaving food to stand allows heat to travel to the centre without overcooking the outside.

When reheating, spread the food in shallow containers so that the microwaves will penetrate easily. Covering the containers helps to keep food moist and also speeds up the process. Ensure that any food being reheated in a microwave becomes piping hot throughout.

SHARING SPACE

When microwaving two packet dinners at once, how do you work out the cooking time?

Microwave them for one-and-a-half times the recommended time for one. As with all microwaving, the more food you cook at a time, the longer it takes. When doubling any recipe, allow a third to a half extra time. Use a plastic stacking ring to separate the dinners or place them side-by-side, if they will fit.

REHEATING DRINKS

Can you reheat cups of cold tea or coffee in a microwave oven?

You can reheat coffee and tea by microwaving for a minute or two (check the booklet with your machine). For best results, use a safe cup with a sloping side and stir it midway. Do not boil or the drink will become bitter.

ADAPTING RECIPES

I have just bought a microwave. How can I adapt my favourite recipes to cook in it?

There are no simple conversion charts to follow and some dishes, such as soufflés, simply do not microwave well. Be guided by the instruction manual for your oven and consult microwave cookbooks for examples of similar recipes.

MILK

PROCESSING TECHNIQUES

In what way do pasteurised and homogenised milk differ?

They are two different processes. Many countries have laws that require milk to be pasteurised so that any harmful bacteria are destroyed. The milk is heated to almost boiling, held at this temperature for several seconds then cooled.

After being pasteurised, some milk is homogenised, which disperses the fat evenly throughout the milk. If it is not homogenised, the cream will float to the top.

GREEN-CAPPED MILK

Is unpasteurised milk available for sale in Britain?

Yes, you can buy unpasteurised, or raw, milk in England, Northern Ireland and Wales – but it is banned in Scotland. The milk can be sold only by a farmer who holds a valid licence issued by the Ministry of Agriculture, Fisheries and Food. It must be labelled clearly and you will find unpasteurised milk in bottles with a green foil cap.

The milk comes from cows that have been certified brucellosis-free and it is filtered before bottling. Nevertheless, pregnant women, the ill, babies and the elderly should be using the widely available pasteurised variety for greater safety.

Healthy option

Fortified milk, which can be used just like ordinary milk, has been boosted by the addition of vitamins A and D and/or calcium. Fortified skimmed milk is made by adding extra vitamins and calcium to the milk after the fat has been skimmed off.

LONGER LIFE

What is UHT milk and can I use it in my cooking?

UHT, ultra heat treated or long-life, milk has been ultra-pasteurised by being heated in a sealed container to 138°C (280°F) for a few seconds. It is packaged in sealed cartons and can be stored without any refrigeration for up to three months.

The ultra-pasteurisation affects the taste, making it less appealing to drink. It is probably best used for cooking, where it will behave just like ordinary milk. Once it is open, UHT milk must be kept in the refrigerator like fresh milk.

CONDENSED VERSION

What is the difference between evaporated and condensed milk and does it affect how I use them?

In Britain, evaporated milk (available either whole or skimmed) has had its water content reduced so that it is almost twice as concentrated as ordinary milk. Condensed milk is simply evaporated milk with added sugar, which makes it thicker. Both evaporated and condensed milks may be used in cooking, but some recipes are clearly better made with one or the other.

On the Continent, there is no milk called evaporated but rather a type described as condensed (which is the same as evaporated milk in Britain). There is also a variety with added sugar which is called sweetened condensed milk.

The high heat of the canning process gives evaporated milk its very distinctive cooked flavour. Evaporated milk may be whipped like double cream for use in desserts, poured over fruit and other desserts as a topping, or made into a tasty fudge.

Condensed milk is rich, thick and syrupy and is especially suited to making toffee and other kinds of confectionery, including the sticky coconut sweetmeats made in India.

The toffee and banana pie which follows makes delicious use of the special taste of condensed milk.

Banoffee pie

SERVES: 6 - 8
PREPARATION TIME: 20 minutes, plus 45 minutes cooling and chilling
COOKING TIME: 10 minutes

150 g (5 ½ oz) butter
175 g (6 oz) digestive biscuits, crushed
1 teaspoon ground mixed spice
50 g (1 ¾ oz) soft light brown sugar
2 tablespoons milk
225 g (8 oz) condensed milk
5 small bananas
Juice of ½ lemon
150 ml (5 fl oz) double or whipping cream
To decorate: grated chocolate

1 Carefully melt half the butter, remove it from the heat and stir in the crushed biscuits and mixed spice. Press evenly into the base of a 20 cm (8 in) flan dish and then refrigerate for at least 30 minutes.
2 Put the other half of the butter and the sugar in a small, heavy-based pan and heat it gently until the butter melts and the sugar dissolves. Bring the mixture to the boil and allow it to simmer for a minute.

3 Take the pan off the heat and stir in the milk and the condensed milk. Bring back to the boil and bubble for 2 minutes or until the mixture turns to a very thick golden sauce, stirring continuously so that it does not burn. Remove it from the heat.
4 Peel and slice four of the bananas and then brush them lightly with some of the lemon juice.
5 Arrange the banana slices over the prepared biscuit base, then spread the warm toffee over the banana slices and leave it to cool.
6 Whip the cream until it is stiff and spread or pipe it over the filling.
7 Peel and slice the last banana, brush the slices with lemon juice and arrange them decoratively over the cream. Sprinkle the chocolate over the top and serve.

VARIATIONS
Use crushed chocolate digestive biscuits or gingernuts in place of the digestive biscuits. You can also leave out the mixed spice if you prefer a pie shell with a milder flavour.

Sliced bananas and grated chocolate crown this regal Banoffee Pie in style. Condensed milk is the key ingredient.

BUTTERMILK OPTIONS

What is buttermilk and is there a substitute I could use in cooking?

Traditional buttermilk is the liquid whey left behind when milk has been churned and all the fat is extracted as butter. Commercial buttermilk is produced by adding a special bacterial culture to either low-fat or skimmed milk.

Buttermilk contains an acid that reacts with bicarbonate of soda and releases gas to raise the dough in soda bread, scones, biscuits and some pancakes. If no buttermilk is available, use half soured cream or yoghurt with half ordinary milk. Alternatively, you can mix a teaspoon of lemon juice with ordinary milk and the dry ingredients.

REDUCING THE FAT

If I use skimmed milk or semi-skimmed milk in place of whole milk in recipes, will the reduced-fat content affect the result?

Skimmed milk has a much thinner consistency than whole milk and both semi-skimmed and skimmed milk have a flavour that is less full and rich than whole milk. All three varieties perform acceptably in cooking but the dish will have a thinner flavour if either skimmed or semi-skimmed milk are used.

If you would like to give your family a milkshake with less fat but without losing its popular appeal, boost the flavour with fresh fruit. Try this simple but luscious recipe for Strawberry Milkshake.

Strawberry milkshake

SERVES: 1
PREPARATION TIME: 5 minutes

300 ml (10 fl oz) semi-skimmed milk
75 g (2 3/4 oz) strawberries, hulled
2 tablespoons vanilla ice cream (low-fat, if preferred)

Place all the ingredients in a blender or food processor and blend until smooth. Pour the milkshake into a large glass and serve it immediately.

AVOIDING BURNING

How do I stop my milk-based recipes from burning?

Milk scorches easily because of the sugars and proteins which fall to the bottom of the pan when it is heated. To avoid scorching, place the milk in either a heavy-based saucepan or a double-boiler and cook over a low or moderate heat. You can also try rinsing the pan in cold water before adding the milk.

FREEZING MILK

Is it all right to freeze milk?

Milk can be frozen in either waxed cartons or plastic containers (not bottles) that allow enough space for expansion. Skimmed and semi-skimmed milk freeze better than whole fat milk, which tends to separate on thawing. They can all be frozen for up to a month and then thawed slowly in the refrigerator. If the milk is going to be heated, the thawing process may be speeded up by heating it slowly from frozen.

MILLET

TASTY TREAT

I thought millet was simply birdseed. Is it also for cooking?

Yes, it can be used to thicken soups, cooked in milk to make a breakfast cereal or added to breads and tea breads to boost their texture and flavour. While it is not a gourmet ingredient, millet can be tasty and is a good source of proteins as well as carbohydrates.

Since Roman times at least, millet has been widely grown in North Africa, Asia and the Mediterranean countries. It is an important food for many of the world's poor, and is often fermented to make beers.

The dried grains are tiny, about the size of a pinhead, and coloured pale yellow with a darker brown spot on one side. They swell considerably during cooking so it is important not to add too much to

dishes such as soups. Millet flakes cook faster than the whole grains and are also used to thicken soups.

Unless whole millet grains are cooked in plenty of liquid, they should be presoaked as shown in the following recipe for griddle cakes. The millet adds a fine texture to these delicious drop scones from the United States, and the smoky flavour is enhanced by toasting the moistened grains until they become aromatic. Serve the griddle cakes warm with lusciously melting strawberry butter as a sweet surprise for high tea.

Griddle cakes with strawberry butter

MAKES: 6 cakes
PREPARATION TIME: 10 minutes
COOKING TIME: 45 minutes

GRIDDLE CAKES
15 g (1/2 oz) millet grains
225 g (8 oz) plain white flour
1/2 teaspoon cream of tartar
1/2 teaspoon bicarbonate of soda
25 g (1 oz) caster sugar
1 egg, size 2
350 ml (12 fl oz) milk
Vegetable oil, for frying
To serve: fresh strawberries and crème fraîche

STRAWBERRY BUTTER
115 g (4 oz) unsalted butter, softened
1 tablespoon good quality strawberry preserve

1 Wash the millet, place it in a small pan and cover well with cold water. Bring to the boil and simmer for about 25 - 30 minutes until the grains are swollen and tender. Drain the millet well and set aside.
2 Meanwhile, make the strawberry butter by beating together the butter and the strawberry preserve until they are thoroughly combined. (It is worth using a good quality preserve to add maximum flavour.) Chill this mixture well until it is required.
3 Sift the flour, cream of tartar and bicarbonate of soda together into a bowl. Stir in the sugar and gradually beat in the egg and milk to form a

Fresh strawberries and crème fraîche brighten these griddle cakes made with millet. Spread them with strawberry butter for an unusual sweet treat.

smooth batter. Stir in the cooked millet and mix thoroughly.

4 Lightly brush a griddle with the oil and bring it to a medium heat. Using a ladle, pour on a spoonful of batter. Cook for about a minute until very small bubbles begin to appear on the surface. Gently flip the cake and cook it on the other side for a further minute, or until the pancake is puffed and looks golden.

5 After cooking, keep each griddle cake warm in a low oven and repeat the frying process with the rest of the batter until you have made a total of six pancakes.

6 Serve the griddle cakes at once, each of them spread with some of the strawberry butter and decorated with a few fresh strawberries. Add some generous spoonfuls of crème fraîche to the warm griddle cakes for a delicious creamy topping.

MINCEMEAT

SAFE KEEPING

How long can I store mincemeat that I have made at home?

Mincemeat stored in sterilised, air-tight jars will keep for a year in a cool, dark, dry place. It should be made at least a month before it is needed so that the flavour has time to mature. If it becomes dry, add a dash of sherry or brandy.

VEGETARIAN OPTION

I am a vegetarian. Could I make mincemeat without suet?

Shredded vegetarian suet, which is widely available, can be used to replace beef suet in any mincemeat

recipe – the quantities needed and cooking method are exactly the same. The Vegetarian Mincemeat recipe (below) should be bottled and stored in the same way as mincemeat made with beef suet.

There are also vegetarian mincemeat recipes that contain no suet or sugar and simply combine dried fruits, nuts, fresh fruit or vegetables. This sugar-less mincemeat will not keep well unless it has a little spirit added. It should then be stored in the refrigerator and used up within a week. It makes a good topping for ice cream or yoghurt.

Vegetarian mincemeat

MAKES: about 2.25 kg (5 lb)
PREPARATION TIME: 30 minutes, plus maturing time of at least 4 weeks
COOKING: none

---

350 g (12 oz) seedless raisins
350 g (12 oz) sultanas
225 g (8 oz) currants
175 g (6 oz) chopped mixed peel
450 g (1 lb) cooking apples (peeled, cored and coarsely grated)
225 g (8 oz) vegetarian suet
350 g (12 oz) soft brown sugar
50 g (1 ¾ oz) blanched almonds, chopped, optional
Finely grated rind and juice of 1 lemon and 1 orange
15 g (½ oz) ground mixed spice
1 teaspoon ground nutmeg
150 ml (5 fl oz) brandy

---

1 Place all the ingredients in a large bowl and mix together thoroughly. Cover and leave in a cool place for two days, stirring occasionally and replacing the cover each time.

2 Pot the mixture in clean, sterilised jars then cover, seal tightly and store in a cool, dark, dry place.

3 Allow the mincemeat to stand for at least four weeks before it is used; this gives it time to mature.

VARIATION

For alcohol-free mincemeat, replace the brandy with unsweetened apple juice. This will taste fine, but it will not have the preservative power of the brandy, making it necessary to keep the mincemeat refrigerated. It should be eaten within a few days.

MOUSSE

SEPARATE PROBLEM

My mousses always separate while chilling. What am I doing wrong?

If you are using gelatine to set the mousse, do not fold the gelatine mixture into the cream until it is cool, as this may cause the mousse to separate. The thickened mixture should be of a similar consistency to the cream before the two are stirred together. Stir the mousse gently but continuously as the gelatine sets so it does not sink to the bottom, giving a layered effect.

If the mousse is being made with whisked egg white instead of, or as well as, gelatine, fold it in gently so as not to lose the air bubbles which hold up the mousse.

If a mousse does separate, there is no remedy. However, it should be perfectly edible, even if it is less attractive than intended.

FISHY CHOICE

What is the best fish for mousses?

Fresh salmon is a popular choice because it has a good flavour and an attractive colour. It is particularly nice combined with shellfish for a luxurious dinner party starter.

Smoked fish such as mackerel, salmon, trout and even kippers work well because they, too, are strongly flavoured. They can be combined with some cream, cream cheese or mayonnaise and lemon to make a rich, tasty mousse.

Be careful when preparing fish to remove all the bones before working the flesh in a food processor. The resulting purée should also be checked for small bones before being combined with other ingredients. Fish bones in mousse are unpleasant and can be dangerous.

Try this quick recipe for Smoked Salmon and Taramasalata Mousse (right) which has no fish bones at all. Buy a good quality, mild and creamy taramasalata, or make your own (see recipe on page 345).

Smoked salmon and taramasalata mousse

SERVES: 4
PREPARATION TIME: 20 minutes, plus 4 hours chilling
COOKING TIME: none

1 teaspoon powdered gelatine
250 g (9 oz) taramasalata
Black pepper
350 g (12 oz) thinly sliced smoked salmon
To garnish: black olives, lemon wedges and coriander sprigs
To serve: hot pitta bread

1 Sprinkle the powdered gelatine over 2 tablespoons of water in a heatproof bowl and let it soak for about 5 minutes until spongy.

2 Stand the bowl in a small pan of gently simmering water and heat until the gelatine dissolves. Leave it to cool slightly, then slowly stir the gelatine into the taramasalata in a thin stream. Add pepper to taste and stir again until evenly mixed.

3 Line four small ramekins or timbale moulds with the smoked salmon slices, allowing them to hang over the edges a little. Spoon in the taramasalata, dividing it equally between the ramekins, and fold the salmon slices neatly over the top.

4 Leave to chill in the refrigerator for at least 4 hours, then turn the mousses out onto plates and serve with hot pitta bread. Garnish, if you like, with some black olives, lemon wedges and sprigs of coriander.

This stunning parcel of taramasalata with smoked salmon wrapping will impress dinner guests. It looks complicated to make but in reality is quick and simple.

MOUSSES AND FOOLS

What is the difference between a mousse and a fool?

A mousse is a light, foamy mixture which usually contains a cold set mixture made with egg yolks, cream, whisked egg white or gelatine, and flavouring. A fool is a cold dessert of sweet fruit purée mixed with whipped cream. It does not contain eggs and is not set.

In the following recipe for a Minted Blackcurrant Mousse, the mixture is lightened with whipped cream and set with gelatine.

Minted blackcurrant mousse

SERVES: 6
PREPARATION TIME: 45 minutes, plus 3 - 4 hours chilling time
COOKING TIME: none

---

*450 g (1 lb) fresh blackcurrants,
 poached lightly and cooled, or
 frozen blackcurrants, defrosted*
A large bunch of fresh mint sprigs
1 tablespoon powdered gelatine
3 eggs, size 3
100 g (3 ½ oz) caster sugar
300 ml (10 fl oz) double cream
To decorate: mint sprigs

---

1 Put the blackcurrants in a blender or food processor. Strip the leaves off the mint sprigs, add them to the blender and process until smooth. Press the fruit mixture through a fine nylon sieve, then discard the seeds and any skins.
2 Sprinkle the powdered gelatine over 3 tablespoons of cold water in a small bowl and leave it to soak for about 5 minutes. Place the bowl over a pan of simmering water until the gelatine has dissolved, then set aside until it has cooled.
3 In a large bowl, whisk the eggs and sugar until they are thick, pale and creamy. Gradually whisk the blackcurrant purée into the egg mixture, then stir in the gelatine.
4 Whip the cream until softly stiff and fold with a metal spoon into the egg and fruit mixture carefully but thoroughly. Pour the mousse into one large serving dish, or into six

individual dishes and chill for 3 - 4 hours or until it has set. Decorate the blackcurrant mousse with the fresh mint sprigs before serving.
VARIATION
For an alcoholic kick, try folding 2 or 3 tablespoons of a blackcurrant liqueur into the egg mixture just before adding the cream.

Healthy option

When making a mousse you can replace the double cream with plain fromage frais (with 8 per cent fat), a mixture of fromage frais and Greek yoghurt, or whipped reduced-fat double cream to create a healthier version.

MUFFINS

CAKE CONFUSION

What is the difference between an American muffin, an English muffin and a fairy cake?

Fairy cakes are small, light sponge cakes topped with coloured icing, and best eaten within a few days of baking. American muffins are a cross between a scone and a fairy cake, but bigger. They are made with a thick batter rather than a dough and are raised with baking powder. American muffins are not as sweet or as rich as fairy cakes.

Americans use the term 'English muffins' to describe what the English call crumpets; however, the authentic traditional English muffin is different and uses dough made from strong white flour and yeast cooked on a griddle or hot plate. The muffin is torn apart when cooked and eaten immediately with sweet or savoury toppings.

American Muffins are both quick and easy to make, as the following recipe shows. They are best eaten the day they are baked.

American muffins

MAKES: 10 - 12 muffins
PREPARATION TIME: 10 minutes
COOKING TIME: 20 minutes

---

225 g (8 oz) plain flour
1 tablespoon baking powder
½ teaspoon bicarbonate of soda
*75 g (2 ¾ oz) soft light brown
 sugar*
1 egg, size 3
250 ml (9 fl oz) milk
A pinch of salt
*50 g (1 ¾ oz) butter, melted and
 cooled*

---

1 Preheat the oven to 200°C (400°F, gas mark 6). Place 10 - 12 large, deep, paper cases in muffin tins.
2 Sift the dry ingredients into a bowl and make a well in the centre.
3 Beat together the egg, milk and salt and add to the dry ingredients with the melted butter. Lightly stir the mixture together with a fork.
4 Fill the paper cases three-quarters full, then bake for 20 minutes until the muffins are well risen, golden brown and cooked through. Leave them in their tins for a few minutes then transfer to a wire rack to cool.
VARIATIONS
For blackberry, blueberry, cranberry or raspberry muffins, add 75 g (2 ¾ oz) of fresh or partly thawed frozen berries and a few drops of vanilla essence to the mixture after adding the melted butter.

For double chocolate chip muffins, add 4 tablespoons of cocoa powder and 100 g (3 ½ oz) chopped dark, milk or white chocolate.

For banana, bran and cinnamon muffins, add two mashed bananas, 50 g (1 ¾ oz) of natural bran and ½ teaspoon of ground cinnamon.

BERRY CHOICE

My favourite muffins contain blueberries, which are expensive. Can I use blackberries instead?

You can include any other berry fruit such as raspberries or blackberries in muffins, but use them half-thawed if they have been frozen. This will keep them firm when baked and give better results.

MUSHROOMS

CAREFUL STORAGE

What's the best way to store and prepare mushrooms?

Fresh mushrooms have a sponge-like density that either absorbs moisture or sweats it out to become slimy in storage, so it is important to keep them dry. Wrap mushrooms in kitchen paper and store in a greaseproof paper bag, brown paper bag or sealed plastic container in the salad drawer.

Washing mushrooms impairs their texture and peeling diminishes their flavour: there is no need to do either. Brush off any surface grit or growing medium with some kitchen paper if necessary.

WILD AND CULTIVATED

Can wild mushrooms be used in place of cultivated ones in recipes, and when is it best to use field mushrooms rather than the smaller button variety?

Wild mushrooms are a rare treat. Although they can always be substituted for other mushrooms in recipes, they are best when simply fried in bacon fat with shallots, or in olive oil with garlic.

Button mushrooms make dainty garnishes and have a firm texture that is good thinly sliced and served raw or marinated in salads, however, they can also look attractive when cooked whole in stews.

Large field mushrooms have a much fuller flavour that makes them the best choice for a breakfast fry-up, or to use in meaty stews or creamy sauces as in the paprika-spiced Hungarian recipe (above right). This can be served on toast as a snack for four, or with rice as a vegetarian supper dish for two, or as a vegetable accompaniment to some plainly grilled meat or fish.

Chunky paprika-spiced mushrooms gently pan-fried make a deliciously creamy topping for hot toast.

Mushroom paprika

SERVES: 4
PREPARATION TIME: 10 minutes
COOKING TIME: 20 minutes

1 large, sweet onion, finely chopped
A good pinch of dried thyme,
    optional
3 tablespoons olive oil
2 teaspoons paprika
250 g (9 oz) field or large
    cultivated mushrooms, sliced
Salt
300 ml (10 fl oz) soured cream or
    Greek yoghurt

1 Fry the onion, with the dried thyme if using, gently in the oil over a very low heat for at least 10 minutes or until the onion is soft and golden, stirring occasionally. Stir in the paprika, sliced mushrooms and salt. Add 200 ml (7 fl oz) of water.
2 Raise the heat a little and bring the sauce to the boil. Cover and cook for 2 - 3 minutes until the mushrooms collapse, releasing their liquor.

3 Remove the lid, raise the heat higher still and cook the mushrooms for around 5 - 6 minutes, shaking the pan regularly (stirring would break up the mushrooms), until the sauce is thick and sticky.
4 Carefully stir in the soured cream or yoghurt. Taste, season, then spoon the mushrooms over hot toast.

HOME DRYING

Can I dry wild mushrooms myself, and how should they be stored?

Yes, you can dry mushrooms and they are a useful addition to the store cupboard. To dry your own, place the mushrooms on racks in a very low oven for several hours or overnight. Very large, fleshy mushrooms can be sliced before drying.

The dried mushrooms are ready for storage when they are dry but still just pliable rather than crisp. If stored in airtight containers, the dried mushrooms can be kept and used until the next picking season.

COOKING FROM DRIED

How do I cook dried mushrooms?

Dried mushrooms should be reconstituted before use: soak them in warm water, perhaps with a splash of sherry or wine in it, for up to 20 minutes depending on their size, then use in stews, risottos or pasta sauces. The liquid in which they were reconstituted can be incorporated into sauces and stock.

MUSSELS

STAYING SAFE

How can I tell when is it safe to eat fresh mussels, and how do you prepare and cook them?

Traditionally mussels were eaten during months with the letter 'R' in their name because they were at their cheapest and best in the cool months from late September to early April. However, mussel farming and air transportation have made them available, at a price, virtually throughout the year, and refrigeration keeps them safe.

Mussels are sold while still alive, and although they are now sold much cleaner than they used to be, it is important to follow careful preparation procedures (see box, right), and particularly to ensure you discard uncooked mussels that gape open or have chipped shells.

REQUIRED CLEANSING

What are the 'purified' mussels I have seen sold in packets?

Most shop-bought mussels are now purified by being kept for days in cleansing tanks to allow them to purge themselves of anything nasty inside. If you gather your own mussels, you must make sure they come from safe sites, facing out to sea and away from sewage outfalls or other possible sources of pollution. It is best to take local advice if you do not know the area, and safest of all to buy mussels in the market or from fishmongers.

CLEANING AND COOKING MUSSELS

Before mussels can be opened, they must be properly cleaned. Once the shell has been opened, the mollusc must be cooked or eaten immediately.

1 Scrub the mussels in a sinkful of cold water, scraping off barnacles with the back of a small knife. Pull away the beards. Discard any mussels with broken shells or open mussels that don't close when tapped sharply.

2 Cover the bottom of a large pan with white wine then add parsley stems and garlic if you like. Bring the wine to the boil, throw in the cleaned mussels, then cover and cook them for 2 – 3 minutes over a high heat.

3 Transfer the opened mussels with a slotted spoon to a sieve placed over a bowl. Cook any that have not yet opened for another minute, then discard if they are still closed. Dish up the mussels, straining the liquid from both the pan and the bowl over them.

4 Eat the mussels with your fingers, using an empty mussel shell to scoop out the meat. Accompany the mussels with French bread and place a large bowl on the table for discarded shells. When you have finished eating the mussels, drink the broth.

VARIETY OF RECIPES

I see moules marinière on many menus, but what are some other ways of cooking mussels?

Mussels are found in many of the world's waters so there are plenty of different treatments for them. Mussels spill delicious juices as they open and most of the popular cooking methods incorporate this liquor in the sauce.

When mussels are to be served in their shells to eat with the fingers, it is best not to include sticky or fatty ingredients, but mussels can be shelled and their juices then enriched with cream.

For an excellent starter, large mussels can be opened over heat (see box, above), shelled and then returned to their half shells, topped with some garlic butter and breadcrumbs, then grilled and served hot. Eat the mussels with a fork.

Alternatively, try using the technique from the basic recipe for moules marinière (overleaf) but adapt the ingredients to create several simple, well-flavoured mussel dishes. Add some chopped fennel and shallots, for instance, or for a Provençal flavour, add tomatoes, garlic and thyme with white wine and a dash of an anise-flavoured liqueur such as pastis. You could also thicken the juices slightly with beurre manié or a little cream.

Mussels with similar cream, wine or tomato-based sauces are highly delicious when served with freshly cooked pasta such as spaghetti.

Moules marinière

SERVES: 4
PREPARATION TIME: 30 minutes
COOKING TIME: 6 - 8 minutes

2 kg (4 lb 8 oz) live mussels
2 onions, chopped
2 cloves garlic, chopped
4 large sprigs parsley
200 ml (7 fl oz) dry white wine
Salt and black pepper

1 Clean the mussels (see details in box on previous page).
2 Put the onions and garlic into a large pan with the parsley stalks (not the leaves) and the wine. Bring to the boil and simmer for 5 minutes.
3 Raise the heat and add half of the mussels. Cover the pan with a lid and cook the mussels for 3 minutes.
4 Use a slotted spoon to transfer the opened mussels to a sieve placed over a bowl. Cook any unopened mussels for a minute more, but if any remain shut they must be discarded. Warm a serving bowl while cooking the next batch of mussels.
5 Chop the parsley leaves. Transfer the mussels to the serving bowl. When you have transferred them all, season the cooking liquor to taste.
6 Allow the liquid to stand for 1–2 minutes so that any grit settles on the bottom of the pan, then strain it over the mussels. Scatter with the chopped parsley and serve.

Fresh mussels from the market are a gourmet treat best cooked simply, as in this recipe for Moules Marinière.

MUSTARD

SPICY PLANT

What is mustard made of?

Mustard is made from the crushed seeds of a family of plants. Some mustard plants are grown for their leaves, which are widely eaten as a vegetable in the East; others for their seedlings, often eaten with cress as a salad or sandwich garnish.

Three sorts of seed – black, brown and white – were once used in the manufacture of mustard powder but black seeds are no longer grown commercially. Mustard powder has been used in Britain for centuries, however, French-style whole-grain mustard has become popular in recent years and is now made by manufacturers in Britain as well as France.

FEEL THE HEAT

Why is English mustard so much hotter than other mustards?

Largely because this is what the English desire of it. English mustard is made with equal quantities of white and brown mustard seeds; while the white give heat on the tongue, the brown give a volatile heat in the back of the throat. It is usually sold dry and then simply mixed with cold water, which adds to its strength of flavour.

French Dijon mustard is made from brown mustard seeds only, diluted with white wine and spices to make it less hot than English mustard. The sweeter, smoother German and American mustards are made with white mustard seeds, their flavour softened by additions such as sugar or herbs.

FLAVOUR IMPROVER

Is it true that a pinch of dry mustard added to cheese recipes makes the cheese easier to digest?

True or not, it certainly improves the flavour. Mustard has been credited with digestive powers, and it has always been eaten with rich, fatty foods, such as pork, sausages or cooked cheese. The simple Mustard Sauce below adds spice to grilled pork or veal chops, chicken, rabbit or hard-boiled eggs.

Mustard sauce

SERVES: 4
PREPARATION TIME: 5 minutes
COOKING TIME: 30 minutes

40 g (1 ½ oz) butter
2 tablespoons plain flour
300 ml (10 fl oz) chicken stock, hot
1 - 2 tablespoons smooth Dijon
    mustard, to taste
150 ml (5 fl oz) soured cream
Salt and black pepper
2 tablespoons freshly chopped
    chives

1 In a saucepan, melt the butter, add the flour and cook for a minute, stirring continuously.
2 Add the stock and bring to the boil, stirring until blended. Simmer gently for 20 minutes, then whisk in the mustard and soured cream.
3 Season to taste then cook gently for 1 - 2 minutes without boiling. Remove from the heat and add the chopped chives before serving.

NOODLES

IN THE SOUP

What sort of noodles should I use in chicken noodle soup?

The traditional noodle for chicken noodle soup is a narrow, square tube rather than a rounded noodle, but any small, narrow egg pasta would be an acceptable substitute.

The word 'noodle' is confusing because although it was used in the past to describe hollow, macaroni-type pasta, today it is used when referring to long, flat Italian pasta such as fettuccine, pappardelle, tagliarini, tagliatelle or tagliolini.

To complicate matters further, Chinese noodles are generally thin and round, like spaghetti.

WORLDWIDE STAPLE

What are Chinese noodles?

There are two basic types of Chinese noodles, wheat flour noodles which are yellow, and rice flour noodles which are white. Many shapes are available and their texture varies, with the addition of egg for instance. The translucent vermicelli or cellophane noodles are made from mung bean flour.

Throughout the Oriental world, noodle dishes take on myriad guises. There are curried noodles (such as Singapore's *laksa*), plus Indonesian spicy fried noodles (*bahmi goreng*), Vietnamese beef noodles (*pho*), complex recipes cooked with choice ingredients, and humble vegetarian dishes. There are also dozens of varieties of instant noodles available.

SIMPLE COOKING

What is the best way to cook Chinese noodles?

This depends very much on the type of noodle you are using. Generally, all dry noodles, whether made from wheat, rice or mung bean flour, should be softened by blanching or boiling before cooking them with other ingredients. Fresh noodles, such as rice sticks and yellow wheat noodles, can be cooked without any preparation.

Throughout Asia, noodles are eaten as much for symbolic reasons as for taste, texture and their versatility – which explains why they are always disconcertingly long. It will not do to cut them as the action shortens your life span!

Perhaps the best-known dish in the West is chow mein (literally, 'fried noodles'). Leftover cooked beef, chicken and pork are excellent ingredients to use with fresh vegetables in the following recipe, which could be served as a meal in itself or as part of a Chinese menu.

Leftovers are never more enticing than when fried with Chinese noodles to produce the popular chow mein.

Quick chow mein

SERVES: 4
PREPARATION TIME: 10 minutes
COOKING TIME: 10 minutes

500 g (1 lb 2 oz) wheat or rice noodles
2 tablespoons vegetable oil
1 large onion, sliced
125 g (4½ oz) bean sprouts
125 g (4½ oz) fresh vegetables, such as baby corn, peppers (sliced or chopped) and sugar snap peas
250 g (9 oz) roast chicken, beef or pork, shredded
2 tablespoons light soy sauce
2 tablespoons oyster sauce
300 ml (10 fl oz) stock
To garnish: 2 tablespoons chopped fresh coriander or spring onions

1 Cook the noodles according to the packet instructions and drain.
2 Heat the oil in a wok and stir-fry the onions for 5 minutes until soft.
3 Add the vegetables and stir-fry for around 2 – 3 minutes. Add the meat, noodles and remaining ingredients and stir-fry for 5 minutes until well blended and the stock is nearly all absorbed. When cooked, the noodles should be moist. Serve garnished with coriander or spring onions.

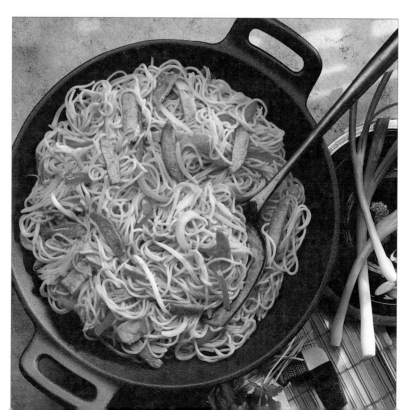

NUTRITION

VARIETY IS THE KEY

I feel battered by the conflicting advice on healthy eating. Are there some simple rules to follow?

Yes. Eat a variety of different types of food and try to regulate your intake to keep your weight within the healthy range for your height.

Study the chart opposite, which is based on the National Food Guide prepared by the Health Education Authority, the Department of Health and the Ministry of Agriculture, Fisheries and Food. Most important is to eat plenty of fruit and vegetables, and plenty of starchy foods such as whole-grain bread, cereals, pasta, potatoes and rice, plus beans, lentils and peas.

Make the most of poultry and fish, choose lean cuts of red meat and limit fried foods, snacks, pastries and biscuits. Take advantage of lower-fat alternatives, use salt sparingly and if you drink alcohol, enjoy it in moderation.

A GOOD DIET IS BEST

Do my children really need to take multivitamin pills?

Although children do not generally need larger amounts of vitamins in absolute terms, they have high requirements in relation to their energy needs and body weight. Vitamin supplements may be a convenient 'insurance policy' but are not really a substitute for a good diet, in children or adults.

PRESERVING VITAMINS

What is the best way to cook fresh fruit and vegetables with the least possible loss of vitamins?

The cooking of fruit and vegetables always results in some loss of vitamins: water-soluble vitamins may be leached into the cooking water and some vitamins are destroyed when exposed to air. The loss of water-soluble vitamins can be very large if the vegetables are completely covered in water while being cooked – they may lose up to 80 per cent of their vitamin C.

Steaming reduces this loss, but the destruction of vitamin C due to the action of oxygen may be increased. Microwaving and pressure cooking both help to reduce the loss of essential vitamins, as less water is used in these methods and the cooking time is shorter.

FAT IN PERSPECTIVE

Would it be harmful to cut fat from my family's diet completely?

Although we need to avoid eating too much fat, cutting all the fat from your diet is not wise. We need fat because it gives us energy, provides the essential fatty acids which enable the body to absorb the fat-soluble vitamins, A, D, E and K, and makes foods more palatable.

Fats are particularly important for children under the age of five, who need to have sufficient energy and nutrients for rapid growth. If very young children are given the bulky, low-fat diets recommended for adults, their small stomachs are quickly filled without providing them with the amounts of energy and nutrients they need.

BUTTER OR MARGARINE?

What are the pros and cons of butter and margarine?

Butter and margarine contain the same number of calories and by law the vitamins A and D, which occur naturally in butter, must be added to margarine. But they differ in other ways. Butter contains more saturated fat (54 per cent) and less polyunsaturated fat (2.6 per cent) than soft margarine (which contains 16.2 per cent saturates and 41.1 per cent polyunsaturates).

As most people need to limit their consumption of saturated fats while increasing their intake of polyunsaturates, margarine is the healthier choice. However, cheap, hard margarines can contain up to 35 per cent saturated fat and only a small amount of polyunsaturates, making them less healthy than the more expensive soft margarines.

The differing cholesterol contents of butter and margarine may also be important to people concerned about heart disease. Soft margarines made from vegetable oils are almost cholesterol-free.

TRANS FATTY ACIDS

Some margarines list the amount of 'trans fatty acids' they contain. What are they and should I be concerned about them?

Trans fatty acids have been linked to heart disease because they appear to raise blood cholesterol levels. They are created when polyunsaturated and monounsaturated oils are heated, as they are during the manufacture of margarines. Trans fatty acids are also found, in smaller amounts, in natural animal products such as meat and butter.

If you are concerned about heart disease and your blood cholesterol level, choose food products that are low in trans fatty acids.

OILY FISH

What are omega-3 and omega-6 fatty acids?

Omega-3 and omega-6 are generally known as essential fatty acids and are found in some foods such as oily fish, seeds and seed oils.

Believed to be essential for brain and eye development, omega-3 is also useful to the body for reducing inflammation and lowering the tendency for blood to clot.

Omega-6 appears to help regulate blood pressure and the body's water balance. It also improves our nerve and immune functions.

There is some evidence to suggest that people who eat oily fish, such as herring, mackerel and sardines, twice a week may have lower rates of heart disease. Certainly, it is an easy and inexpensive way of increasing your intake of omega-3 fatty acids. The seeds of pumpkin, sesame and sunflower are good, tasty sources of omega-6.

JUICE IS BETTER

Is it true that drinking tea with food, or shortly before eating, inhibits our absorption of iron?

Yes. Only a small amount of the iron in the foods we eat is absorbed and it varies according to the type of food, and whether other factors help or hinder its absorption. For example, about 20–40 per cent of the iron in red meat is absorbed, compared with only 5 per cent from some vegetable sources.

Vitamin C improves the body's absorption of iron while the tannins in tea and, to a lesser extent, coffee interfere with this process. So to boost iron absorption, a glass of orange juice is a better accompaniment to a meal than tea or coffee.

IRRADIATION WORRIES

Is irradiated food harmful? And is there any danger of my buying it without knowing?

Irradiation involves exposing food to a source of radioactivity which inhibits the continued growth or ripening of the food. This makes it an effective preservation process, but it does cause chemical changes in the food, and some destruction of vitamins may occur.

The irradiation process can form new compounds called 'radiolytic products' in the food. Even though these may be present in very small amounts (one or two parts per million), questions have been raised about the possible harmful effects.

The flavour and texture of foods can also be adversely affected by irradiation; for instance, vegetables may become soft and spongy, and irradiated meats have often been described as having an unpleasant 'goaty' or 'wet dog' flavour.

The Advisory Committee on Irradiated and Novel Foods, appointed by the Department of Health and the Ministry of Agriculture, Fisheries and Food, concluded in 1986 that there are no health hazards associated with eating food that has been irradiated to a specified level. In Britain, food may only be

THE BALANCE OF GOOD HEALTH

This chart is based on one compiled by British government bodies to show the foods we should eat in the recommended daily proportions to maintain health.

- Eat plenty of fruit and vegetables every day, choosing a wide variety, including fresh, frozen and canned.
- Emphasise bread, other cereal foods and potatoes. Eat all types and choose high fibre varieties whenever you can.
- Enjoy meat, poultry, fish and other protein sources in moderation, opting for low-fat varieties wherever possible.
- Milk and all other dairy products should be consumed in moderation. Choose low-fat varieties when you can.
- Limit your intake of fatty and sugary foods such as biscuits and desserts.

irradiated under licence, and the types of food and permitted dosage of radiation are specified in Government regulations. By law, any irradiated food on sale in shops must be labelled, but irradiated restaurant food need not be.

SALT AND BLOOD PRESSURE

Why is the consumption of salt said to be bad for you?

There is some concern about the amount of salt used in Western diets because of the links between sodium and high blood pressure (hypertension), a condition which increases the risk of heart attack, stroke and kidney failure.

We need sodium (salt is sodium chloride) for proper cell, nerve and muscle function, but the danger of consuming too much comes partly from the hidden salt in processed foods and the habit of oversalting

food. Britons consume around 9 g of salt a day when the World Health Organisation recommends just 6 g.

There are two ways of reducing your salt intake. Limit your intake of high-salt foods, such as smoked and cured meats or fish, cheese, salty snacks, packet soups and stock cubes. Secondly, reduce the amount of salt you add to your food during cooking and at the table.

POTASSIUM CONCERN

Is reduced-sodium salt better for you than ordinary salt?

While using reduced-sodium salt can help you eat less sodium, the amount of potassium in these products makes them unsuitable for diabetics, and sufferers of kidney disease. Moreover, the level of salt we use is largely a matter of habit and using substitutes does not help to re-educate our taste buds.

NUTS

STORING NUTS

What is the best way to keep nuts really fresh and full of flavour?

Because of their high fat content, nuts turn rancid quite quickly in warm or damp conditions and they are best bought only when you intend to use them, and in small quantities. They can be stored in the refrigerator or freezer, providing they are kept very dry, or in airtight plastic containers.

Nuts sold in vacuum-sealed packs showing a 'use-by' date are the best to buy, as they will keep in a cool, dry cupboard until you are ready to use them. Once the packet has been opened, however, the nuts should be kept in an airtight container and eaten quite quickly.

RICH IN PROTEIN AND FAT

Some people say nuts are very healthy, while others say they are high in fat: who is right?

Both statements are correct. All nuts, but particularly peanuts and almonds, are a good source of protein, and play an important part in a vegetarian diet. They are also a good source of B-group vitamins.

However, all nuts except chestnuts are high in fat and therefore high in calories, so anyone on a low-calorie diet should avoid them. Macadamia, pine nuts and walnuts have the highest overall fat content; pine nuts and hazelnuts contain less saturated fat than other nuts.

NUTS OR SEEDS?

Are pine nuts really nuts?

No. Although pine nuts resemble nuts and are used like nuts, they are in fact the seeds, or kernels, of the stone pine, a tree native to Mediterranean countries and especially common in Italy. In that country, pine nuts are an essential ingredient for the basil, garlic and Parmesan sauce, pesto (see OILS).

SHELLING AND SKINNING NUTS

Nuts that are to be used in cooking should have their thin inner skin removed first. Prepared nuts in packets are available, but nuts are best when used fresh.

BLANCHING AND SKINNING ALMONDS

1 Crack open the shells and remove the kernels. Put the almonds into a saucepan and cover with cold water. Bring to the boil and immediately pour the almonds into a sieve to drain.

2 As soon as the blanched almonds have drained and while they are still warm, pop the nuts out of their thin papery skins by squeezing them between your thumb and forefinger.

ROASTING AND SKINNING HAZELNUTS

1 Crack open the shells, remove the kernels and put the hazelnuts on a baking tray. Roast them in a moderate oven for 5 - 10 minutes or until their skins begin to split open and the nuts turn golden brown. Remove from the oven and tip onto a clean tea towel.

2 Rub the roasted hazelnuts together firmly in the tea towel to remove their thin papery skins, then pick the skinless nuts out of the tea towel. If necessary, put any nuts still covered in their skin back into a moderate oven for a few more minutes.

MELLOWING WALNUTS

I find the flavour of some walnuts rather bitter. Is there anything I can do to counteract this?

The flavour of walnuts can vary depending on their freshness and country of origin. If you have bought some which you find bitter, their flavour can be mellowed by blanching them. Crack open the nuts and put the kernels in a small saucepan of boiling water. Boil gently for a minute, then drain and dry before using.

For the best flavour, make sure that walnuts are absolutely fresh. To test the freshness of shell-on nuts, weigh them in your hand individually – each one should feel heavy and not rattle when shaken. If the nut rattles, the kernel inside will have dried and shrivelled.

If, after blanching, you still find the flavour too bitter, you could use mellower pecan nuts instead, which are from the same family.

NUT-FREE STUFFING

I have an allergy to all types of nuts; can you suggest an easy alternative to add to a stuffing?

Bulgur wheat makes a great alternative to nuts as it has a similar taste and texture. First soak the uncooked grains in cold water for 30 minutes to swell and soften them, then add them to the stuffing and cook as stated in the recipe.

OATS

FABULOUS FIBRE

I have heard that oats are good for the heart. Is this true?

Generally speaking, oat grains are a highly nutritious food: they contain carbohydrates, protein and fat as well as iron, potassium and most B-group vitamins. Oats also contain soluble fibres that turn into a jelly-like consistency when cooked; these have been connected in various studies to cholesterol-lowering activity in the body. Though there is not enough firm evidence to confirm this, oats are regarded as very beneficial in the diet.

GROUND OR ROLLED

What is the difference between oatmeal and oatflakes?

Both are processed from the oat cereal, but oatmeal is ground from the whole kernel while oatflakes are made from steamed and rolled oats. Oatmeal is graded according to how finely it is ground; the largest is pinhead oatmeal, followed by coarse, medium and fine.

Both oatmeal and oatflakes can be used in sweet or savoury dishes. Because oatflakes (also known as jumbo oats or porridge oats) have been lightly steamed, they cook faster than oatmeal. Oatmeal is used in biscuits, stuffings and coatings instead of breadcrumbs; it is also added to breads, although it cannot be used on its own for this purpose as the gluten content of oats is too low. Traditionally, oatflakes are used in flapjacks (right).

Rich and crumbly oatflake flapjacks are some of the easiest biscuits to make. They are always a favourite with children and anyone with a sweet tooth.

Flapjacks

MAKES: 8 - 12 fingers
PREPARATION TIME: 5 minutes
COOKING TIME: 15 - 20 minutes

100 g (3 ½ oz) butter
3 tablespoons golden syrup
40 g (1 ½ oz) caster sugar
175 g (6 oz) oatflakes

1 Preheat the oven to 190°C (375°F, gas mark 5). Grease a shallow 18 cm (7 in) square baking tin.
2 Put the butter, golden syrup and sugar in a small pan and heat gently until the butter is melted. Stir in the oatflakes until evenly combined.
3 Spoon the warm mixture into the prepared tin and smooth the surface level. Bake for 15 - 20 minutes until bubbling and golden.
4 Remove from the oven and leave to cool for a few minutes, then mark the top into fingers. Leave to cool in the tin before turning out.
5 When thoroughly cool and crisp, cut out the individual portions and serve. Flapjacks will keep in an airtight tin for three to four days.

SUPERIOR PORRIDGE

I have always made porridge with oatflakes, but on a recent trip to Scotland I had delicious porridge made with oatmeal instead. Which is best?

The easiest and quickest way to make porridge is to use oatflakes, as they cook in only 3–4 minutes against 20 minutes or more for oatmeal. To make two generous portions, put 125 g (4 ½ oz) of oatflakes into a pan. Pour in 600 ml (1 pint) of cold water, or, for a richer consistency, half water and half milk. Bring to the boil and continue simmering, stirring continuously, for 3–4 minutes. When the porridge is as thick as you like it, season with a little salt. Serve with milk, butter or cream and brown sugar or honey.

In Scotland, where it originates, porridge is traditionally made with oatmeal. Although it takes longer to cook, the flavour and texture of oatmeal are far superior so it is worth trying the Oatmeal Porridge recipe below. To avoid small lumps forming, stir the porridge from time to time as it simmers.

Oatmeal porridge with fresh apricot compote

SERVES: 2 – 4
PREPARATION TIME: 10 minutes
COOKING TIME: 20 – 25 minutes

FOR THE PORRIDGE
50 g (1 ¾ oz) medium oatmeal
300 ml (10 fl oz) milk
A pinch of salt

FOR THE COMPOTE
225 g (8 oz) fresh apricots, halved and stoned
25 g (1 oz) caster sugar
2 tablespoons water
1 teaspoon lemon juice
A pinch of ground cinnamon
To serve: 50 g (1 ¾ oz) caster sugar, 25 g (1 oz) unsalted butter and extra milk

1 Put the oatmeal in a heavy-based pan, pour on the milk, add 300 ml (10 fl oz) of water and sprinkle on some salt. Bring the mixture slowly to the boil, stirring continuously. Partially cover with a lid and simmer very gently for 20 minutes, stirring from time to time, until the oatmeal is softened and the mixture thick.
2 While the oatmeal is cooking, make the compote. Roughly chop the prepared apricots, put them into a small pan and add the remaining ingredients. Bring gently to the boil, cover and simmer for 5 minutes.
3 Remove the lid from the apricots and cook for a further 3 - 4 minutes until they are soft and the liquid syrupy. Pour into a serving bowl and set aside to cool slightly.
4 Before serving the porridge, stir in the sugar and the butter. Serve with a dessertspoon of the apricot compote and a little extra milk.
VARIATION
Dried apricots can be used for the compote instead of fresh. Soak 225 g (8 oz) of dried ready-to-eat apricots overnight in 300 ml (10 fl oz) of cold water. Cook them in this water, with the lemon juice and cinnamon, for 20 minutes, then roughly purée.

OFFAL

INTERNAL PARTS

What does the term 'offal' include?

It covers all edible, internal parts of animals, such as the kidneys and liver, as well as brains, cheeks, ears, stomachs, sweetbreads, tripe and tongue. (You can no longer buy bovine brains in Britain because of the outbreak of bovine spongiform encephalopathy; see BEEF.)

FRESHNESS TEST

How do I know if offal is fresh?

Look for moist, shiny offal, and avoid buying any that has a greenish colour, slimy surface or an unpleasantly strong smell. Freshness is crucial with offal, as it spoils quickly and should be eaten within two or three days of slaughter.

BLANCHING NEEDS

Which kinds of offal should be blanched before cooking and why?

Brains, sweetbreads and tripe have to be immersed in boiling water before cooking to remove all traces of blood and to give them a better texture. First soak the offal in cold water for 1 – 2 hours. Then put it in a pan of fresh cold water and bring to a gentle boil, skimming off any froth. Simmer for a few minutes, drain and rinse well.

COOKING CHOICE

What is the best way to cook each type of offal?

Brains and parts of the stomach are poached in a well-flavoured court bouillon (water, sometimes with added white wine, and herbs), with vinegar or lemon juice to tenderise the meat. The poaching liquid can be strained and reduced to make a

---

PREPARING SWEETBREADS

Sweetbreads are usually fried quickly and served with a sauce. They should be soaked and briefly poached first, and their membranes should be removed.

1 Soak the sweetbreads in cold water for 2 - 4 hours until white (lamb's sweetbreads are shown here). Drain and cut away any discoloured parts.

2 Add them to a pan of cold, salted water and heat to simmering point. Poach for 5 minutes (3 minutes for calves' sweetbreads). Drain and refresh.

3 Pull away the sweetbreads' tubes, covering membrane and skin. They then fall into pieces for cooking.

4 Or put the pieces between two plates, weighted down. Chill for 2 hours until firm. Then slice and cook.

sauce. Braising in the oven, using a low, even temperature, is better for tougher, heartier types of offal, such as heart and tongue.

More tender offal such as sweetbreads, kidneys and liver can be sliced and sautéed in butter (see also KIDNEYS and LIVER). Grilling can be used for kidneys but tends to dry out other types of offal.

HARMFUL RESIDUES

I have heard that residues of illegal growth-promoting drugs are higher in offal than in muscle meat. Should I be concerned?

A 1994 survey conducted by the Belgian consumer group VU and funded by the European Commission, suggests we are much more likely to eat residues of illegal growth-promoting drugs in offal than in muscle meat such as steak. The synthetic hormones and similar drugs were still being used in a number of European countries, despite being banned in 1988 by the European Community as a potential risk to human health.

The risk appears to be very small for animals produced in Britain, but greater in some other European countries. Spain and Belgium seem to have quite high levels of illegal drug residues in their beef and the specific advice from VU is to avoid eating Spanish calf's or ox liver.

TENDER SWEETBREADS

What are sweetbreads, and how are they prepared and cooked?

Sweetbreads, which are low in calories but high in cholesterol, are the thymus (neck) glands or pancreatic (stomach) glands of young animals. Those from calves are best, and may need to be ordered from your butcher. Thymus-gland sweetbreads come in a pair and have a more pronounced flavour, while pancreatic sweetbreads are more tender and luscious. After preparation (see box, left) they can be braised, poached or fried, as in the following recipe. Serve them as a starter, with crusty bread.

For a filling yet delicate dish, pressed sweetbreads are sliced, dusted with flour and briefly fried, then served with a sharp caper and lemon butter sauce.

Sweetbreads with capers and lemon butter sauce

SERVES: 4
PREPARATION TIME: 5 minutes, not including preparing sweetbreads
COOKING TIME: 10 minutes

---

500 g (1 lb 2 oz) calf's or lamb's sweetbreads, blanched, prepared and thinly sliced
1 tablespoon plain flour, seasoned with salt and black pepper
1 tablespoon mild olive oil
40 g (1 1/2 oz) unsalted butter
25 g (1 oz) capers, rinsed if salt-packed, drained if in vinegar
Juice of 1 lemon
To serve: 1 tablespoon chopped parsley

---

1 Dust the sliced sweetbreads with the seasoned flour, gently shaking off any excess covering.
2 Heat the oil and half the butter together in a large frying pan until the mixture begins to sizzle then add the sweetbreads and fry over a moderate heat for 2 - 3 minutes each side until golden. Remove the slices from the pan and keep warm.
3 Gently heat the remaining butter in the frying pan until it becomes golden brown but not burnt. Add the capers, stir in the lemon juice and heat briefly. Put the sweetbreads onto warmed plates, pour over the butter sauce and sprinkle with parsley.

FREEZING OFFAL

Can you freeze fresh offal?

Yes, but it must be absolutely fresh. Liver can be frozen either in large pieces or sliced. Calf's kidneys should be chopped up, but lamb's kidneys can be frozen either whole or halved. Sweetbreads are best frozen whole, after blanching.

Pack the offal in usable weights, interleaving the pieces with cling film, and freeze for up to three months. Thaw on a rack in a shallow dish in the refrigerator, then rinse and pat dry before cooking.

OILS

BEST FOR COOKING

Can I use any variety of oil in cooking, or are some unsuitable?

There are more than 20 different culinary oils available, including avocado and pumpkin seed oils; in addition, there are many varieties of olive and flavoured oils. Some oils are best used for cooking and others for flavouring.

Oils which are fairly neutral in flavour and can withstand high temperatures, such as those made from corn, grapeseed, groundnut or peanut, rapeseed and sunflower, are best for cooking. Others, such as almond, hazelnut, sesame and walnut oils, are more suitable for flavouring foods. Some oils, such as olive, may be used for both.

STORING OILS

What is the best way to store oils?

They should be stored, well sealed, in a cool, dark, dry place to prevent the oil from oxidising and developing a rancid taste. Exposure to air, light and constant warmth will encourage oxidation. Some oils are now sold in dark glass jars which help to prevent oxidation. Some deterioration is inevitable over a period of time, so buy oil in small amounts and replace it frequently.

Refrigeration may cause oils to congeal and go cloudy. Some oils, such as olive and walnut, may even solidify if refrigerated and must be brought back to room temperature before using. They will clear again as they become warm. In warm climates, it is often necessary to refrigerate delicately flavoured oils.

REHEATING OIL

How long can I keep reheating frying oil before it goes off or becomes dangerous?

Oil that is frequently reheated in a deep-fryer is likely to become rancid in time. Its vitamin content also reduces, the flavour may become unpleasant, and it is possible for harmful substances to be produced if the oil is overheated. Discard any frying oil that smells unpleasant, produces too much foam when heated, creates smoke easily and has become dark in colour.

In general, you should reheat oil two or three times only before discarding it. Each time it is used, the oil should be allowed to cool completely, then filtered through a fine sieve, preferably lined with a piece of muslin, to get rid of any sediment. Once you have cooked a specific type of food in a batch of oil, re-use the oil for that food only, to avoid tainting flavours. Store it, covered, in a cool, dark place.

DELICATE GRAPESEED

What, if any, are the advantages of grapeseed oil over other oils?

Grapeseed oil is a pale, delicate oil, extracted from grape pips. It is able to withstand a wide range of temperatures and has a high smoking point, which makes it ideal for frying. In addition, it does not turn cloudy when refrigerated.

Excellent in most salad dressings, grapeseed oil is also suitable for making mayonnaise, and can be used for diluting strong-flavoured oils such as hazelnut or walnut.

QUALITY OLIVE OILS

There are many types of olive oil. Which countries make the best?

Most olive oil is produced around the Mediterranean. Spain is the world's largest producer of olive oil, and Spanish oils are usually of a high quality. Italy is the second largest producer, and some Italian oils are generally regarded as the finest, particularly those produced in Tuscany and Umbria.

Greece is another major producer of olive oils, but the quality tends to vary as the controls are less strict than in other countries. In the south of France, the amount of olive oil produced is relatively small but the quality is high.

EXTRA PURE

What is the difference between ordinary and virgin olive oil?

Olive oils are classified according to their level of acidity. The first cold pressing of a high grade of olives produces the finest olive oil, with a maximum acidity level of only 1 per cent and this is called

---

MAKING PESTO

Pesto sauce, usually served with pasta, blends the aromatic flavours of basil, garlic, pine nuts, Parmesan cheese and virgin olive oil.

1 In a mortar, put 50 g (1 ¾ oz) of torn fresh basil leaves, 3 chopped garlic cloves, 2 tablespoons of pine nuts and some salt and pepper.

2 Grind the mixture with a pestle until it forms a rough paste. Add 50 g (1 ¾ oz) of finely grated fresh Parmesan cheese and mix well.

3 Gradually trickle over and beat in 100 ml (3 ½ fl oz) of virgin olive oil, using the pestle or a wooden spoon. Pesto can be kept for up to a week; store it in a sealed jar in the refrigerator. It also freezes well.

VARIATION: pesto may be made using a blender or food processor instead. Put all the ingredients except the Parmesan cheese in a blender or processor and blend at high speed until creamy. Transfer to a bowl, fold in the Parmesan and mix well.

extra-virgin olive oil. Further processing by heat produces more oil, which decreases in quality and flavour. Fine virgin olive oil contains a maximum acidity level of 1.5 per cent; ordinary virgin olive oil of 3 per cent. Plain olive oil, sometimes called pure olive oil, is made from a blend of refined oil and one of the grades of virgin oil.

Olive oil is healthy and versatile, and it is worth buying the best quality that you can afford. It is important to use virgin olive oil in sauces such as pesto (see panel, left). The following recipe for Bruschetta, a simple crispy snack or starter, calls for the best extra-virgin olive oil, but this may be too strong for some other recipes.

Bruschetta

SERVES: 4 as a starter
PREPARATION TIME: 10 minutes
COOKING TIME: 10 minutes

4 thick slices of Italian or French
  country bread
2 large cloves garlic
Extra-virgin olive oil
Sea salt
To serve: slices of Parma ham or
  grilled tomato slices, optional

1 Preheat the grill and toast the bread on both sides.
2 While the bread is hot, rub cut garlic over both sides of each slice. Drizzle some oil over each slice and sprinkle with sea salt. If you like, top with Parma ham or slices of grilled tomatoes. Serve immediately.

ADDING FLAVOUR

Flavoured oils are lovely but quite expensive. Could I make my own?

Oils can easily be infused with a variety of herbs or spices to add extra taste and colour, as the following recipes show.

Chilli Oil is strongly flavoured, good for stir-fries, marinades, and for drizzling over noodles. The Herb and Saffron Oil makes a light and subtle salad dressing, or it can be brushed onto fish or chicken before grilling or barbecuing.

Chilli oil

MAKES: about 225 ml (8 fl oz)
PREPARATION TIME: 5 minutes, plus
12 hours infusing
COOKING TIME: 11 – 12 minutes

2 teaspoons Sichuan or whole
  mixed peppercorns
8 – 10 dried red chillies
225 ml (8 fl oz) groundnut oil
1 tablespoon sesame oil

1 Heat a heavy-based pan, then add the peppercorns and eight of the chillies. Dry-fry them over a medium heat for a minute or two, stirring all the while so they do not catch and burn. Reduce the heat to very low, pour in the groundnut oil and cook for 10 minutes more. Leave to cool.
2 When cold, stir in the sesame oil. Cover the pan and set aside to infuse for about 12 hours or overnight.
3 Strain the flavoured oil through a muslin-lined sieve into a sterilised jar or bottle. Add the two remaining chillies if you like, for decoration. Seal well then store in a cool, dark place for up to three months.

Herb and saffron oil

MAKES: about 750 ml (1 pint 7 fl oz)
PREPARATION TIME: 10 minutes
COOKING TIME: none

2 sprigs fresh rosemary
2 – 4 sprigs fresh thyme
1 teaspoon dried oregano
2 cloves garlic
1 teaspoon fennel seeds, crushed
A generous pinch of saffron strands
750 ml (1 pint 7 fl oz) extra-virgin
  olive oil

1 Wash the fresh herbs, pat them dry thoroughly with kitchen paper, then lightly bruise them with the flat side of a knife to release their aroma.
2 Place all the dry ingredients in a sterilised jar or bottle and cover them completely with oil. Seal well, then shake to mix. Store in the refrigerator for at least a week and use within two weeks. You might prefer to strain the oil before using.

Oils flavoured with herbs and spices such as chilli, garlic and rosemary add a touch of drama to simple dishes.

OKRA

JUICY FINGERS

Is okra the same as the 'ladies' fingers' I have eaten in Indian restaurants? If so, are there any other ways of cooking it?

'Ladies' fingers' does refer to the tapering shape of okra's seed pods. Inside the pods, the seeds are set in sticky juices and this is what thickens the soups and stews that are part of southern American cuisine. In the Cajun dishes of Louisiana okra is usually sliced up so the sticky juices are released, and it is often smothered in a peppery tomato sauce like the one on the right. Lard would probably be used instead of olive oil. However, in this recipe the pods are left uncut.

Choose okra that is bright green and velvety, with no brown tinge along the outside ridges. Serve this dish as a hot accompaniment to grilled meat or oily fish. Or, for a vegetarian meal, offer it with bean dishes and corn bread or corn muffins made with green chillies.

Cajun smothered okra

SERVES: 6
PREPARATION TIME: 10 minutes
COOKING TIME: 35 - 40 minutes

500 g (1 lb 2 oz) okra
3 tablespoons olive oil
1 red onion, thinly sliced
1 - 2 cloves garlic, crushed
1 teaspoon dried oregano
400 g (14 oz) canned chopped tomatoes in juice
3 tablespoons red wine
Salt, black pepper and cayenne pepper or Tabasco sauce

1 Trim off the stem ends of the okra. Avoid cutting into the seed pod, as this would make the dish very sticky.
2 Heat the oil in a frying pan then fry the onion, garlic and oregano for 2 - 3 minutes. Add the tomatoes with all their juices, and the wine. Gently stir the mixture and cook at a low boil for about 10 minutes until it becomes a thick sauce.
3 Season the tomato sauce with salt, then stir in the okra. Put a lid on the pan and continue cooking over a low heat for about 25 minutes. Check halfway through the cooking and add a little hot water if the sauce seems to be drying out.
4 When the okra are soft, season with black pepper and sprinkle on cayenne pepper or Tabasco sauce.

A colourful dish of spicy okra from the southern United States is smothered in a garlic, tomato and red wine sauce.

OLIVES

COLOUR DIFFERENTIAL

What is the difference between black and green olives?

They are essentially the same fruit, picked at different stages of ripeness: unripe olives are green, black are fully ripe, and those with a violet tinge are picked sometime in-between. Black olives have a fruitier taste than the green and are more often used in cooking.

Olives are one of the oldest processed foods known to man, and there are many regional varieties and preferences. In Spain, there are smooth, green table varieties, from large queen olives to the refined manzanilla often sold stoned and stuffed with red pepper, anchovy, orange rind or almonds. Purple-black Kalamata olives from Greece have an intense flavour, especially those allowed to ripen on the tree. The shiny Niçoise olives from Provence are small, black and wrinkled with an almost creamy taste and are often sold in jars. Kalamata and Niçoise olives are the ones most often used in cooking.

HOW TO STORE

How long do olives keep, and how should they be stored?

Fresh olives are very bitter and must be 'cured' or pickled in brine to render them edible, so they are naturally long-keeping. However, when removed from their brine they will begin to go soft and deteriorate in flavour.

Once the jar or can has been opened, or if bought loose in their brine, olives should be stored in the refrigerator and eaten within a few days. Those stored in olive or some other cooking oil will keep for about two weeks in the refrigerator, as long as they are completely submerged in the oil. The oil will take on some flavour from the olives and this delicately flavoured oil is very pleasant for cooking.

OMELETTE

SECRET INGREDIENTS

Is the secret of a good omelette in the cooking or in the pan?

Both. Omelettes, to be soft and runny in the centre while smooth on the surface, should be cooked very quickly over a heat that is brisk but not too fierce. If cooked slowly, they become flat and tough and similar to scrambled eggs.

To ensure even cooking, use a small, heavy-based nonstick frying pan. Better still, invest in an omelette pan, in which the base meets the side in a gentle curve to make it easier to fold the omelette and slide it out. After use, do not wash an omelette pan but simply wipe it clean with kitchen paper.

LIGHTEN UP

How do I make an omelette that is really light and fluffy?

Traditional omelettes are not fluffy, but a fluffy soufflé omelette can be made by folding whisked egg whites into beaten egg yolks. These soufflé omelettes may be savoury, like the bacon, cheese and tomato recipe overleaf, or sweetened by whisking sugar into the egg whites before they are added to the yolks.

MAKING AN OMELETTE

Heat and speed are essential to make perfect, soft omelettes. To serve several people, make individual omelettes like the one below rather than one large one.

1 Break two eggs into a bowl, add salt and black pepper to taste and beat lightly with a fork until the egg just passes through the prongs.

2 Place the pan over a brisk heat and add a little oil or some clarified butter. When the oil or butter is very hot, quickly pour in the beaten eggs.

3 Shake the pan to and fro and stir the eggs with the back of the fork until they start to thicken. Then tilt the pan, lifting the cooked egg at the side and allowing the uncooked egg to flow underneath. When the eggs have cooked enough so that only the centre is still just moist (about 1 - 2 minutes), draw the pan off the heat.

4 To transfer the omelette to the plate, fold a third of the egg from the side to the centre, sliding the omelette towards the edge of the pan. Fold the open third back towards the centre, forming a cigar shape. Press the ends together so that all the juice remains in the omelette and does not leak when it is turned onto the plate.

Smoked bacon, cheese and tomato soufflé omelette

SERVES: 1
PREPARATION TIME: 20 minutes
COOKING TIME: 15 minutes

---

50 g (1 3/4 oz) smoked bacon, diced
1 tomato, peeled, deseeded and
    roughly chopped
2 teaspoons chopped fresh mixed
    herbs or spring onions
2 eggs, size 3, separated
Salt and black pepper
15 g (1/2 oz) salted butter
50 g (1 3/4 oz) Cheddar cheese,
    grated or finely chopped

---

1 Cook the bacon in a saucepan or small frying pan for about 5 minutes until crisp, then add the tomato and cook for a further minute to soften. Stir in the herbs or spring onions, then keep the mixture warm while you make the omelette.

2 Put 2 tablespoons of water with the egg yolks, whisk well and season. Whisk the egg whites until stiff.

3 Preheat the grill. Melt the butter in an omelette pan over a gentle heat. Meanwhile, fold the egg whites into the yolks, using a metal spoon.

4 Pour the mixture into the pan and cook over a moderate heat until the underside is golden brown. Then put the pan under the heated grill and cook until the omelette is puffed up, set and pale gold on top.

5 Loosen the omelette around the edges and make an indented line across the middle to help you fold it. Spoon the bacon mixture over the omelette, sprinkle the cheese on top, then fold the omelette in half and slide it onto a warmed plate.

FRITTATAS AND TORTILLAS

What is the difference between a frittata and a tortilla?

They are very similar: both are flat, round, firm omelettes in which the eggs are cooked without stirring over a low heat and served hot or cold. Tortillas are from Spain and Mexico, while frittatas come from Italy, but both make excellent fare for picnics or packed lunches as they are chunky, sturdy and very easily transported. They also make good family suppers and are usually cut into wedges for serving. Choose a lively red or white wine from the Mediterranean, their home ground, to drink with them.

Tuna and courgette tortilla

SERVES: 4
PREPARATION TIME: 20 minutes
COOKING TIME: 20 minutes

---

1 tablespoon olive oil
1 onion, sliced
1 clove garlic, crushed
275 g (9 1/2 oz) courgettes, thinly
    sliced
350 g (12 oz) boiled potatoes, diced
4 eggs, size 3
3 tablespoons milk
2 teaspoons chopped tarragon
Salt and black pepper
215 g (7 1/2 oz) canned tuna in oil,
    drained and flaked
75 g (2 3/4 oz) Red Leicester or
    Cheddar cheese, grated

---

1 Preheat the grill. Heat the oil in a large nonstick frying pan, then add the onion, garlic and courgettes and cook for 5 minutes, stirring once in a while. Add the potatoes and cook for 3 minutes, still stirring.

2 Meanwhile, beat the eggs, milk, tarragon and seasoning together, add the tuna and mix well. Add the egg mixture to the frying pan and cook over a medium heat, without stirring, until the eggs begin to set and the tortilla is golden brown underneath.

3 Sprinkle the cheese over the top and place the tortilla under a very hot grill until the cheese has melted and the top is golden brown.

4 Cut the tortilla into wedges and serve it with crusty bread. A good accompaniment would be a salad of mixed leaves topped with a garlic dressing and croutons, and perhaps some capers, olives or anchovies.

A substantial tortilla with eggs, tuna, courgette, potato and tarragon is given a golden glaze of grilled cheese.

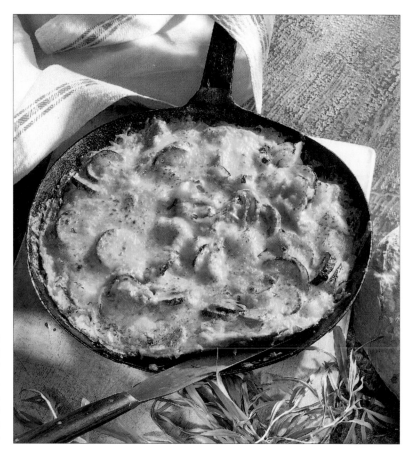

The other tortilla

In Latin America, tortillas are also a popular form of flatbread. These thin pancakes are made from corn or maize flour and are dry-fried on a griddle. Fresh, they are served sprinkled with salt or folded, fried and filled. Small stale pieces are deep-fried to make tortilla chips.

SERIAL COOKING

Could I make omelettes for a supper party one at a time and let them sit while I make more?

No. If omelettes are left to stand, or kept warm for even a short period of time, they will dry out and be tough and leathery. Have everything prepared, and warm a plate ready to serve the omelette as soon as it has been cooked. Make them in swift succession for your guests and insist that they start eating the omelettes as soon as they are done.

ONIONS

VARIOUS TYPES

Are some kinds of onion better suited to certain methods of cooking than others?

Yes. Red onions and big, sweet golden Spanish onions have the mildest taste and can be sliced raw into salads or gently fried. Spring or salad onions are also excellent raw, or cooked very quickly in stir-fries so that they do not collapse.

Medium-sized onions, which have a stronger flavour, are delicious roasted whole in their skins, basted with fat and stock or water as they cook. This will transform their flavour into a mellow sweetness. Shallots are usually fried briefly and then finished in wine or stock.

For braising, choose pickling or small, evenly sized onions no larger than a golf ball, so that they all cook at the same rate, as they do in the recipe on the right.

Succulent braised onions, cooked with raisins, fresh rosemary and bay leaves, have a hint of sweet and sour flavour that goes well with roast meat or poultry.

Onions braised with raisins and rosemary

SERVES: 4 - 6 as an accompaniment
PREPARATION TIME: 10 minutes
COOKING TIME: 40 - 45 minutes

12 - 18 small onions, peeled
3 tablespoons olive oil
3 tablespoons red wine vinegar
Salt and black pepper
1 teaspoon sugar
2 bay leaves
6 - 8 short sprigs rosemary
2 tablespoons raisins
1 teaspoon balsamic vinegar

1 Put the onions in a pan in a single layer. Add the oil and fry gently for about 5 - 8 minutes, shaking them regularly, until patched with brown.
2 Pour in cold water almost to cover the onions and add the vinegar, some salt, the sugar, bay leaves, four sprigs of rosemary and the raisins. Partially cover and simmer for 10 minutes. Then remove the lid, increase the heat and cook just below the boil for 25 - 35 minutes, shaking the pan regularly to turn the onions. They are done when they look translucent and feel soft when pierced with a knife. The braising liquid will have reduced to a sticky brown sauce.
3 Sprinkle on the balsamic vinegar and pepper to taste. Serve garnished with the remaining rosemary sprigs.

NO TEARS

What is the best way to chop an onion without crying?

The trick is not to stand over the onion, where the rising fumes can enter your nose and tear ducts. Sitting down to slice or chop your onion is the simple answer.

TAKE YOUR TIME

Why do fried onions sometimes taste terribly bitter?

They taste bitter if they are not fully cooked. Many cooks do not realise that it takes a good 10 minutes of slow frying and stirring to caramelise and soften one medium onion; allow 20–30 minutes for two or three onions. And frying onions for only 5 minutes before adding any liquid will result in slimy pieces of half-cooked onion lurking in the finished dish.

Skinning small onions easily

Small onions can be fiddly to peel. Pouring boiling water over them in a heatproof container and draining them after a minute or two will make the skins slip off more easily.

ORANGE: see CITRUS FRUIT

OVENS AND HOBS

FUEL FOR THOUGHT

I am trying to decide whether to cook by gas, electricity or solid fuel. What factors should I take into account when I choose?

• GAS produces heat quickest and is easiest to control: when you turn down the flame on the gas hob there is an instant reduction in temperature. Gas ovens are hotter at the top than the bottom, which is preferable when it is convenient to bake several dishes in the oven at the same time but at slightly different temperatures.

The central shelf is usually closest to the temperature the oven is set at, while the top shelf is about one gas mark hotter and the bottom shelf one gas mark cooler.

• ELECTRIC COOKERS AND HOBS create no fumes, and ceramic halogen hobs are almost as quick to heat and easy to control as gas hobs are. Some electric hobs can be set at a hand-hot temperature for long periods of time, without the fear, which you have with a gas hob, of the flame going out. Like gas ovens, conventional electric ovens do not provide an even heat, but the difference is less acute than with gas. Some electric ovens also offer the option of an automatic timer, which can be set to turn the oven on and off when you are away from the kitchen.

• FAN OVENS give perfectly even heat throughout an electric oven by means of a fan mounted on the back wall of the oven (which is not practical with gas). This makes the transfer of heat to the food more efficient, so it is in fact cooking at a higher temperature than in a conventional oven. Take this into account when setting the oven temperature.

• CAST-IRON COOKERS such as Agas and Rayburns use solid fuel, gas or electricity. They are usually left on all day, ready for use.

WIDE RANGE

What sorts of features should I be looking for in a new oven?

After deciding on the fuel to use, the choice is between a traditional, free-standing cooker or a separate hob and oven. An all-in-one cooker is often cheapest. The advantage of separate units is that you can install them in different parts of the kitchen; the oven can be positioned higher than it is in a free-standing cooker to eliminate stooping; and you also have the option of using different fuels, possibly gas for the hob and electricity for the oven.

With a separate oven, the grill may be placed either above the cooker hob at eye-level, below it or

inside the oven itself. Decide how much grilling you do and how inconvenient it would be if the grill were inside the oven. If you have only one oven, it cannot be used for any other cooking, such as baking, while you are using the grill.

There are useful extras which are worth having. You might want a self-cleaning or stay-clean oven, a motorised rotisserie or an integral charcoal-style grill. There are also built-in deep-fryers connected to extraction units which eliminate smells. Some cookers have optional bread or pizza stones which fit exactly into the oven, heat up with it and provide an ideal surface for baking rustic breads and pizza.

DOUBLE THE CHOICE

Is it worth having a double oven?

If you do a lot of cooking, a double oven is more useful than a single one because you can bake and roast at different temperatures at the same time. Fitted oven units with a lower main oven and smaller top oven housing the grill allow the grill and oven to be used at the same time. But you may have to reconsider cooking the Christmas turkey, as double ovens are often smaller than single ones.

TEMPERATURE CHECK

I have an old cooker, and lately a lot of my dishes have come out of the oven not properly cooked. Could it be the oven's fault?

In an old cooker, the temperature control may well have become less accurate over the years. If you have doubts, use an oven thermometer to check the heat being produced at a specific setting on your oven so you can then adjust the cooking times in recipes accordingly.

You need a thermometer able to withstand temperatures as high as 260°C (500°F). While thermometers with dials are tougher, they have fewer markings and give less precise readings than those of spirit thermometers. To test an oven, put the thermometer on a middle shelf while preheating it and take the reading when the oven is up to temperature. Check with the manufacturer if you have any queries.

HOBS CHOICE

What are the different types of hobs to choose from, and what are their various advantages?

Electric hobs that have sealed hotplates with the electric element embedded in them are easier to clean than radiant rings, but you may not be able to tell at a glance when the plate is hot. Ceramic hobs, which hold the radiant elements under glass, often have 'hob hot' signals which stay on until it is safe to touch the rings.

Some hobs have halogen areas which heat up and cool rapidly, but they must be used with saucepans that have dull, flat bases because shiny bases reflect the light back into the hob. Another type, the induction hob, can heat the contents of a steel or iron pan while the hob itself stays cool to the touch.

Most gas hobs still have the traditional burners, but with different sizes and innovations such as a revolving oval burner that produces a gentle, simmering heat. And several manufacturers offer a special wok ring which produces the very high heat needed to stir-fry. Some gas hobs also have a long central plate, which is used mainly for cooking in a fish kettle.

SAFETY FIRST

I worry about grilling in my oven with the children playing in the kitchen. Is there any oven that is considerably safer to use?

Some fan ovens have a system that lets you keep the door closed while grilling, which is useful for homes with young children. There are also ovens with doors that stay cool while the oven is hot inside, which is another useful safety feature. These options often do not add anything to the cost of the cooker.

See also: MICROWAVE OVENS

OYSTERS

WHEN TO EAT OYSTERS

What is the difference between native and Pacific oysters? Is it still true that you should only eat native oysters when there is a letter 'R' in the month?

The native oyster (*Ostrea edulis*), also known as the flat or European oyster, has a smoother, flatter, rounder shell than the Pacific or Japanese oyster (*Crassostrea gigas*). Native oysters, unlike the Pacific variety, are not good to eat in the summer months while they are spawning, during which time they taste unpleasant. This is why they have the best flavour in the cooler months with the letter 'R' in them, and they are not available in the shops in the summer. Pacific oysters breed differently, so they taste agreeable all year round.

CLEAN LIVING

Is eating oysters ever risky?

There is very little chance of eating a contaminated oyster as long as you choose ones with their shells tightly shut. Oysters sold commercially are safe to eat fresh and raw as they undergo a cleansing period in purified water for 42 hours. This eliminates any bacteria that the oyster may have imbibed. (The public cannot buy oysters that have not been treated this way.)

Fresh oysters that are tightly shut can be kept in the refrigerator for up to a few days. Wash off any mud before storing them, but do not soak them. Oysters that have been opened are best eaten straightaway but can be stored in the refrigerator for up to 2 to 3 hours.

Oysters are a very concentrated form of protein and some people find them difficult to digest for this reason. As oysters are often eaten on festive occasions, they may be consumed with more alcohol than usual, which can also contribute to adverse side effects. Oysters do seem to cause particularly severe problems if mixed with spirits, so it is better to drink chilled white wine or champagne, or even cool dark stout, with them. These are better suited to their taste anyway.

Oysters are most often served raw, topped with cayenne pepper and a squeeze of lemon juice. They may also be grilled lightly in the half-shell so that they just curl, or topped with breadcrumbs or garlic butter. They can also be gently cooked in soups and chowders.

THE SAFE AND EASY WAY TO OPEN AN OYSTER

When opening or 'shucking' oysters, use a knife with a finger guard and take care to hold it and the shell securely. This job needs concentration, not speed.

1 To open native oysters, hold the oyster firmly on a board, rounded shell down, with a tea towel wrapped around your hand in case the knife slips. Using an oyster knife, work the point into the hinged end, then twist the knife and break the shell open.

2 Cut through the muscle holding the shell closed and the muscle fixing the meat to the shell. Serve in the deep shell, with its liquor. Pacific oysters are harder to open because of the crumbly 'apron frill' around the shell but the same rules apply.

PACKED LUNCHES

Just a few simple touches in preparation and presentation can make all the difference to a successful carry-out lunch. For instance, make or buy whole small pies or quiches: they are more robust than a slice from a larger one. To accompany a flask of soup or a carefully packed salad, rolls travel better than slices of bread. And sandwiches will stay fresh for longer if they are lined with lettuce and parcelled in cling film.

Always add some refreshing extras to the meal, such as a clutch of cherry tomatoes or a stick of celery, and a whole fresh fruit. And if you know the lunch will be eaten alone, include a cheering sweet treat, even if it is only a chocolate bar or some biscuits.

Wide-mouthed flasks are best for hot stews, but bear in mind that the food will go on cooking. This suits some soups and curries, but is not kind to fresh herbs, fish, pasta or rice, and has a specially bad effect on anything creamy. Soups thickened with pulses or a vegetable purée are best.

Wrap cutlery in a paper napkin so it doesn't stray into the depths of the box, and pack twists of salt and pepper so you can season to taste.

Whether you are filling a child's lunch box, snatching a bite at your desk, or setting off into the outdoors, a well-planned packed lunch can become a personal treat. Here are great ideas for recipes that are portable and memorable.

Hot peanut soup from a flask, a granary roll with cress and crunchy crudité to dip, make a filling lunch for a hungry child.

A CHILD'S LUNCH BOX
Nourishing vegetable soup can be thickened with peanut butter, preferably crunchy for added interest. Make enough soup for two servings and freeze half for another day.

Pack a small, buttered granary roll with some peppery cress as a contrast to eat with it. Cut some crisp raw vegetables into little sticks and, for a dip, add a small plastic tub of mayonnaise, coloured a rich pink with tomato ketchup to make it more tempting. Finish off the meal with a few chocolate digestive biscuits.

(This menu is suitable for vegetarian children.)

Peanut flask soup

SERVES: 2
PREPARATION TIME:
10 minutes
COOKING TIME:
30 - 40 minutes

1 tablespoon vegetable oil
1 medium onion, chopped
1 medium carrot, diced
1 large potato, diced
2 sticks celery, destrung and diced
500 ml (18 fl oz) vegetable stock
2 tablespoons crunchy peanut butter
Salt and black pepper
2 tablespoons salted peanuts (not dry-roasted), crushed

1 Heat the oil in a saucepan and cook all the prepared vegetables over a low heat for about 7 - 8 minutes, shaking the pan occasionally.
2 Add the stock to the pan and bring it to the boil, then partially cover the pan and simmer for 15 - 20 minutes until the vegetables have become very soft.
3 Leave the vegetables in the cooking stock and mash them thoroughly with a potato masher, or purée them in a food processor. Gently stir in the peanut butter until it is fully incorporated, then season to taste.
4 Stir in the crushed peanuts and reheat the soup just to boiling point. Pour half into a flask and freeze the rest.

MANGETOUT AND BACON
SALAD WITH HAZELNUTS

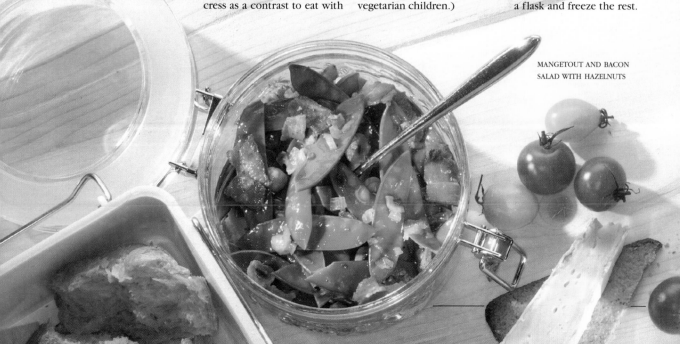

THE OFFICE LUNCH PACK

Salads are often favoured by office workers who don't want to gain more calories than they can work off in the course of a day at the desk.

Green salads wilt if dressed too long in advance, but some salads actually improve in their dressing. Try grated carrot and sultanas, dressed in olive oil and orange juice and scattered with sesame seeds; potato salad with chopped onion and a little mayonnaise, eaten with some separately wrapped slices of salami or smoked fish; or a well-herbed pea salad, like the one below.

Pack cherry tomatoes and a ciabatta roll to eat with the salad. Add some Brie, sandwiched between crackers, and finish with a fruit yoghurt.

Mangetout and bacon salad with hazelnuts

SERVES: 1
PREPARATION TIME:
10 minutes
COOKING TIME: 10 minutes

1 tablespoon olive oil
2 rashers streaky bacon, cut
  into small strips
1 shallot, chopped
125 g (4 ½ oz) mangetout,
  topped and tailed
1 teaspoon hazelnut oil
1 teaspoon red wine vinegar
Salt and black pepper
1 tablespoon roughly
  chopped hazelnuts

1 Heat the oil in a frying pan and fry the bacon strips until the fat runs off and the bacon becomes crispy. Before the bacon is fully cooked, add the shallot and fry for 2 minutes.
2 Meanwhile, bring a small pan of salted water to the boil and cook the mangetout for about 3 minutes. Drain well and tip them into a bowl.
3 When the bacon is cooked, remove the frying pan from the heat. Add the hazelnut oil and vinegar, stir to scrape off any sediment then pour the mixture over the mangetout.
4 Season to taste, toss in the chopped hazelnuts and leave the salad to cool.
5 When cold, transfer to a covered container.

BACKPACKER'S PICNIC

Spending a day in the fresh air is a hungry business and, more than any other packed lunch, backpackers' food should be satisfying, tasty and easy to eat in the hand.

For a hearty treat, cook and cool a couple of fat sausages, split them open and smear with mustard or chutney. Then cut the thick ends from four sticks of celery and sandwich each sausage between a pair for transit. Add a few spring onions, a beef tomato and a hard-boiled egg.

To follow, pack a big square of fortifying sticky Ginger Cake (see right) wrapped in kitchen paper. Add a small jar of moist and refreshing home-made apple sauce, to spread over it before eating.

Remember to include some trail munchies that will fit in the pocket for an accessible nibble: make up small packets of nuts, dried fruit or a couple of sturdy biscuits. And don't forget to pack plenty of liquid, as exercise is thirsty work.

Ginger cake

SERVES: 4 - 6
PREPARATION TIME:
20 minutes
COOKING TIME: 45 minutes

175 g (6 oz) plain flour
2 teaspoons ground ginger
2 teaspoons baking powder
200 ml (7 fl oz) milk
1 teaspoon bicarbonate of
  soda
50 g (1 ¾ oz) soft brown
  sugar
50 g (1 ¾ oz) soft margarine
1 tablespoon black treacle
1 tablespoon golden syrup
2 eggs, size 2 or 3

1 Preheat the oven to 160°C (325°F, gas mark 3). Line an 18 - 20 cm (7 - 8 in) square cake tin with baking paper, letting it stand 2.5 cm (1 in) above the rim of the tin.
2 Sift the flour, ginger and baking powder together.
3 Put the milk into a pan, sprinkle the bicarbonate of soda over it and swirl over a low heat until it dissolves and the milk is warm.

4 In a bowl, beat together the sugar, margarine, treacle and syrup and keep beating until the mixture is much paler. Beat in the eggs one at a time, adding a tablespoon of the spiced flour mixture after each egg.
5 Add the remaining flour mixture and the milk, and beat briefly until smooth. Pour into the prepared tin and bake in the centre of the oven for 45 minutes or until springy in the middle.
6 Gently turn the cake out onto a rack and leave it to cool in its wrapping.
7 When the cake has cooled completely, peel off the paper wrapping. Cut into slices and wrap them individually.

GINGER CAKE
AND APPLE SAUCE

PANCAKES

THIN AND LIGHT

My pancakes always seem to turn out stodgy. How can I make a really light batter?

Pancake batter can be used as soon as it is made, but it is best to allow it to stand in a cool place for 15–30 minutes before being used. This makes the starch grains in the flour soften and expand in the liquid, which results in lighter pancakes. The following recipe is for some delicious stuffed pancakes, which are sprinkled with cheese and then baked for an ideal supper dish.

Chicken, mushroom and broccoli pancakes

SERVES: *4 (2 pancakes per person)*
PREPARATION TIME: *20 minutes, plus 15 - 30 minutes standing time*
COOKING TIME: *45 minutes*

8 pancakes
100 g (3 ½ oz) broccoli florets
50 g (1 ¾ oz) salted butter
100 g (3 ½ oz) mushrooms, sliced
25 g (1 oz) plain flour
300 ml (10 fl oz) whole milk
175 g (6 oz) boneless chicken breast, cooked and diced
2 teaspoons fresh or dried tarragon
Salt and black pepper
75 g (2 ¾ oz) Cheddar or Gruyère cheese, grated

1 Prepare the batter and cook the pancakes (see box, right). Preheat the oven to 180°C (350°F, gas mark 4).
2 Cook the broccoli in a saucepan of boiling water for 5 minutes, then drain the florets and set aside.

3 Melt one-third of the butter in a pan and cook the sliced mushrooms for 3 minutes, stirring occasionally. Remove from the heat and set aside.
4 Melt the remaining butter in a saucepan, stir in the flour and cook for a minute, stirring continuously. Remove the pan from the heat and gradually add the milk, stirring until the mixture is smooth. Return to the heat and bring slowly to the boil. Stir until the sauce thickens, then simmer gently, stirring occasionally, for a further 20 minutes.
5 Stir in the broccoli, mushrooms, chicken, tarragon and seasoning.
6 Fill the cooked pancakes one by one with the mixture and fold or roll them up. Place in an ovenproof dish. Sprinkle with grated cheese and bake for 20 minutes, or until the cheese is melted and bubbling.

CROSS-CHANNEL NAMES

Is 'crêpe' just a fancy French word for ordinary pancakes?

Crêpes is the French term for delicate pancakes, which are thinner than ordinary pancakes. They may be served on their own or rolled or folded with a sweet or savoury filling. A little sugar is often added to the batter for sweet crêpes.

Crêpes are best cooked quickly in a crêpe pan for about a minute on each side. If cooked slowly, they will become tough and leathery.

Unfilled crêpes can be layered in between sheets of greaseproof paper, then covered and stored in the refrigerator for up to three days or in the freezer for two months. Filled crêpes can be kept covered in the refrigerator for two days and frozen for up to two months.

FRENCH LESSON

What is the difference between a crêpe and a galette?

A crêpe is the French term for a thin pancake while a galette is a sturdier pancake made from buckwheat or brown flour. Thin, round biscuits or cakes, large and small, sweet and savoury, are also sometimes called galettes.

MAKING PANCAKES

To make enough batter for eight pancakes you need 115 g (4 oz) of plain flour, a pinch of salt, a size 3 egg and 300 ml (10 fl oz) of milk.

1 Mix the flour and salt in a bowl and make a well in the centre. Add the egg and beat it well with a whisk. Gradually beat in the milk, incorporating all the flour to make a smooth batter. Cover and chill the mixture for 15 - 30 minutes.

2 Pour a little oil into an 18 cm (7 in) heavy-based frying pan, running it round the base and sides. When it is hot, pour off any surplus.

3 Ladle in just enough of the batter to coat the base of the pan. Cook it for 1 - 2 minutes, until it is golden brown underneath and set on top.

4 Turn the pancake with a palette knife, or toss it, and then cook the second side until it is golden.

5 Transfer the cooked pancake to a plate and keep it warm. Make more pancakes with the remaining batter, layering them when cooked with greaseproof or nonstick paper.

PARSNIP

HARD CENTRE

Do I need to remove the core of a parsnip before cooking it?

Parsnips, especially when they are large, can be woody in the middle towards the end of their season in March or April. Then it is wise to cut them into chunks and remove the woody centres. During the rest of the year, when they are smaller, removing the core is not necessary.

NEW IDEAS

Are there better ways of cooking a parsnip than to purée it?

Being sweet, parsnips are excellent roasted, a process that caramelises their sugars. They also make good alternative chips, or can be layered with other root vegetables to form a stylish wheel-shaped centrepiece dish such as the one below.

Mashed parsnips are useful but do need rich additions to improve both the texture and flavour. Dry the pieces carefully before mashing, then add plenty of butter or cream, black pepper and sweet spices such as nutmeg. Some dry mashed potato can also be mixed into mashed parsnip to lighten it and this makes a good topping for shepherd's or cottage pie.

Parsnip and carrot wheel

SERVES: 6 - 8
PREPARATION TIME: 20 minutes
COOKING TIME: 1 1/4 hours

125 g (4 1/2 oz) butter, melted
1.5 kg (3 lb 5 oz) parsnips
500 g (1 lb 2 oz) carrots
A pinch of ground allspice
Salt and black pepper
To garnish: sprigs of fresh parsley and sage

1 Preheat the oven to 190°C (375°F, gas mark 5). Line a 25 cm (10 in) diameter fixed-bottom cake tin, at least 5 cm (2 in) deep, with foil and paint it lavishly with melted butter.

2 Try to choose parsnips and carrots of a similar medium size. Peel the parsnips and slice them thickly lengthways, then drop them into a large pan of salted, boiling water and after the water returns to the boil, cook them for 3 minutes. Drain the parsnips thoroughly. Peel the carrots and halve them lengthways.

3 Line the tin with parsnips, tips inwards, sprinkle them with melted butter and season with the allspice, salt and pepper. Put a layer of carrots of the same thickness on top of the parsnips, then butter and season. Continue layering the vegetables, making the top layer parsnips.

4 Cover the wheel with foil and bake for about 1 - 1 1/4 hours, or until the vegetables feel soft when pierced with the point of a knife. Remove the wheel from the oven and allow it to stand for 5 - 10 minutes.

5 Remove the foil cover, place a plate larger than the tin on the top, grip both firmly and invert. Slide the tin off and peel away the lining foil. Decorate the wheel with fresh sprigs of parsley and sage.

A pretty presentation of root vegetables, Parsnip and Carrot Wheel is garnished with parsley and sage and tastes sweetly of caramelised butter and spices.

PARTRIDGE

FINE GAME BIRD

Is there a difference between English and French partridges, and how are they best cooked?

Partridge has a very subtle flavour, and many people consider it to be the king of game birds. The common English or grey partridge has a more delicate flavour than the larger French red-legged partridge, but in both the meat is pale.

One bird usually feeds one or two people, and the birds are hung for three to five days only, so as not to make the meat too gamy.

Young birds are in season in October and November, and they are best plainly roasted to highlight their delicate flavour. Older birds have to be casseroled or braised to tenderise them. Ask your butcher to advise you, or check the recommended cooking method on the label. In the following recipe for older birds, they are wrapped in vine leaves to impart flavour and to keep the flesh moist. This dish goes very well with braised red cabbage mixed with cooked chestnuts, and steamed Brussels sprouts puréed with a little cream and nutmeg.

Partridge braised in vine leaves

SERVES: 2
PREPARATION TIME: 20 minutes
COOKING TIME: 1 1/4 hours

2 older partridges
Salt and black pepper
4 slices lemon
50 g (1 3/4 oz) butter, softened
4 rashers unsmoked streaky bacon
4 fresh or preserved vine leaves, rinsed and patted dry
2 tablespoons vegetable oil
4 shallots, finely chopped
1 carrot, finely chopped
1 stick celery, finely diced
150 ml (5 fl oz) medium-dry white wine
90 ml (3 1/4 fl oz) sweet white wine
2 tablespoons brandy
150 ml (5 fl oz) chicken consommé or chicken stock
2 sprigs thyme
1 bay leaf
350 g (12 oz) seedless grapes, halved if large
4 tablespoons crème fraîche
To garnish: extra grapes

1 Season the insides of the partridges with salt and pepper and tuck in the lemon slices. Spread the butter all over the breasts of the birds.
2 Stretch the bacon with the back of a knife and wrap two rashers around each partridge. Then wrap each bird in two vine leaves and tie with fine string. Preheat the oven to 190°C (375°F, gas mark 5).
3 Heat the oil in a small casserole. Add the birds, brown them well all over and transfer to a plate.
4 Put the chopped vegetables in the casserole and cook for 5 - 10 minutes until golden. Pour in the wine and brandy and boil for 10 minutes, or until reduced by half.
5 Add the consommé or stock, the thyme and bay leaf and set the birds

Sometimes called the king of game birds, partridge looks spectacular when prepared along this vineyard theme using grapes, wine and vine leaves.

on top. Cover tightly and braise for around 45 - 60 minutes, or until the juices run clear when the birds are pricked through the thigh. Remove the birds and keep them warm.
6 Strain the casserole contents, reserving the stock. Skim off any fat, then return the stock to the pan and boil until reduced by half.
7 Add the grapes and crème fraîche and boil for 2 minutes until slightly thickened. Season to taste. Spoon the sauce onto warmed plates and sit a partridge on top of each. Surround the birds with extra grapes.

MOPPING UP THE JUICES

How do I make the delicious croutons I have been served with roast partridge? Do I just cook a piece of bread under the bird?

These croutons are more correctly termed 'croûtes' as they are bigger than the crispy cubes served in salads and soups. A classic accompaniment to roast game birds, they are not cooked with the birds but fried separately and served to catch any juices from the bird after it is roasted. Croûtes are most delicious when fried in butter, but olive oil or vegetable oil could be used. They can also be toasted, but then will not be so crisp or so tasty.

To make croûtes, take medium slices from a day-old white loaf and cut each into an oval to fit the base of the bird. Fry the bread in a generous amount of foaming butter or oil over a high heat until it is crisp and golden on both sides. Drain on kitchen paper (or not, if you prefer) and then place a roasted bird on top of each slice before serving.

If you are given a fresh partridge, make sure you reserve the liver. It is considered a treat cooked and mashed then spread on the croûte before the bird is placed on top.

PASTA

WELL WORTH IT

Is it worth making fresh pasta when it is widely available from shops? And is it difficult to make?

Using commercial fresh pasta is fine when you need tagliatelle or other noodles. But homemade pasta is worth the effort when preparing a stuffed or baked dish such as ravioli or lasagne, because you can achieve a lightness and texture no commercial product can match. It is not difficult to make fresh pasta at home if you have a hand-cranking machine (see box, below).

WHAT TYPE OF FLOUR?

Do I have to use a special flour to make pasta?

You can make pasta with a variety of flours including plain white flour or strong white flour. In Italy they would use flour made from durum (or hard) wheat and you can find this in Italian delicatessens and some supermarkets.

You may also find '00' (double zero) flour, otherwise known as farina 00. This is a specially refined durum wheat flour and is used for the most delicate, handmade egg pasta. You can use ordinary plain flour if you cannot find it, but plain flour makes a fluffier pasta. The recipe below lets you choose.

DRYING OUT

Should I let homemade pasta rest for a while before cooking?

Just-made pasta can be sticky and should be left to dry out slightly before being cut and cooked.

Once cut, fresh pasta can be cooked immediately but you can also make pasta in advance and lay the cut strips on a baking tray in between some sheets of grease-proof paper. Alternatively, sprinkle the fresh pasta with a few table-spoons of semolina and refrigerate for 24 hours or so. You can also freeze strips of cut pasta, first loose on trays, then packed together.

Homemade egg pasta

MAKES: 350 g (12 oz)
PREPARATION TIME: 20 minutes
COOKING TIME: 5 minutes

---

3 eggs, size 2
300 g (10½ oz) plain, strong or
*   farina 00 flour*
A pinch of salt

---

1 Mix the eggs, flour and salt in a bowl, using a fork, and then working with your hands until it just forms a mass. The dough should not be too moist – if it is, add a little more flour.

2 Take a lump of dough the size of a lemon and feed it through the rollers, which should be set at the widest opening (see steps, below). Crank the piece through. Fold it in half, end to end, and feed it through again six or seven times until it is smooth and quite rectangular. If the dough sticks to the machine, brush it with flour.
3 Lay the pasta sheet on a clean cloth or lightly floured surface and repeat with the remaining dough.
4 Reset the rollers to the next setting (narrower) and starting with the first strip, crank it through the rollers once. Do the same with the other pasta strips, keeping them in the same order to allow them to dry.
5 When you have fed all the dough through, reset the machine to the next setting and repeat. Do this twice more, resetting the machine on each occasion. The strips of pasta will become longer and will need to be cut in half to facilitate handling.
6 When the strips have reached the desired thinness, they are ready to be cut into the required shape, or to be fed through the cutters and made into noodle shapes such as spaghetti or tagliatelle. Be sure the strips have dried enough (without becoming brittle) to prevent them sticking once they have been cut. If you are using sheets of pasta for lasagne or stuffed pasta, proceed without drying.
7 Cook the pasta for 2 - 3 minutes or until it is al dente (cooked but firm).

ROLLING FRESH PASTA BY MACHINE

As a general rule, use 100 g (3½ oz) of flour per egg to make pasta. You will need 300 g (10½ oz) of flour and 3 eggs to make enough pasta for four people. To prevent the dough sticking to the machine, dust the rollers with flour before use.

1 Set the rollers of the machine fully open and crank the dough through six or seven times until it is smooth.

2 Reset the machine to the narrower setting and crank again. Repeat three times, lowering the setting each time.

3 To make the pasta strips (tagliatelle is shown here), feed the dough through the appropriate cutters.

HEALTHY PASTA

Is pasta fattening?

Not necessarily: 25 g (1 oz) of dried pasta contains about 28 Calories. A generous 75 g (2¾ oz) helping of cooked pasta with a tomato and cheese sauce makes a satisfying dish of about 250 Calories. Served with a salad and fruit for dessert, it makes a well-balanced meal. And pasta's low fat content means it is useful for people on diets. Remember, however, the richer the sauce, the more fattening the dish will be.

SHAPES AND SAUCES

How do I know what shaped pasta to add to what sauce?

Thick pasta shapes are best with heavy sauces which contain meat or cheese. Long thin pasta, such as spaghetti, goes well with olive-oil based sauces that allow the strands to remain separate. If you are layering a dish with a sauce, large flat sheets of lasagne are the obvious choice. There are, however, no strict rules, and you can use whichever pasta is your favourite to go with the quick sauces below made from handy store cupboard items.

Pasta with sardines

SERVES: 4
PREPARATION TIME: 5 minutes
COOKING TIME: 20 minutes

---

4 tablespoons olive oil
½ small onion, finely chopped
50 g (1¾ oz) anchovy fillets, drained
400 g (14 oz) fresh or canned chopped tomatoes
25 g (1 oz) raisins
250 g (9 oz) sardines in oil, drained
350 g (12 oz) dried pasta
2 tablespoons finely chopped parsley, optional
50 g (1¾ oz) dried breadcrumbs

---

1 Heat the oil in a large frying pan and sauté the onion and anchovies until softened but not browned.

2 Add the tomatoes and raisins and cook for 10 minutes. Then add the sardines, simmer the sauce gently for 5 minutes and season to taste.
3 Cook and drain the pasta, add to the sauce and toss together. Stir in the parsley, breadcrumbs and serve.

Pasta with sun-dried tomato sauce

SERVES: 2
PREPARATION TIME: 15 minutes
COOKING TIME: 15 minutes

---

2 tablespoons olive oil
5 ripe tomatoes, chopped
12 sun-dried tomatoes in olive oil
A handful of stoned olives, sliced
1 fresh green chilli, deseeded and chopped
175 g (6 oz) dried pasta

---

1 Simmer the olive oil, fresh and sun-dried tomatoes, olives and chilli for 10 minutes in a small saucepan.
2 Bring a large pan of salted water to the boil. Cook the pasta, drain and serve it with the sauce.

The robustly flavoured sardine pasta sauce (left) and sun-dried tomato sauce (right) are quick and easy to make.

PLENTY OF WATER

How much water do I need for cooking pasta, and is it the same for dried and fresh pasta?

Allow 1.5 litres (2¾ pints) of water and a tablespoon of salt for each 100 g (3½ oz) of dried pasta, and remember that you will need a large saucepan, even if you are cooking a small amount of pasta. Once the water has come to the boil, add the salt and then the dried pasta.

This large amount of water will prevent the pasta sticking together and enable it to return to the boil more quickly once the pasta has been added – this is important to achieve a firm yet cooked result.

If you leave the lid off while the pasta boils it will be easier to prevent the water boiling over. Use the timing instructions on the package as a guide but test the pasta a few minutes before the given time. Remove a piece of pasta and bite into it. It should be tender yet still have a slight resistance.

The rules for cooking fresh pasta are the same except that it will cook in just a few minutes and requires about 25 per cent less water because fresh pasta does not expand to the same degree.

If you are cooking pasta for a salad, do not let it drain too thoroughly, and immediately toss it with a few tablespoons of olive oil. For hot pasta dishes, add the sauce just before serving so the pasta does not sit in it and become soft.

PASTA WILL WAIT

What is the best way of keeping pasta warm if I have to wait for my guests? I usually keep it warm over a very gentle heat, but it sometimes sticks together.

Pasta can be kept warm, covered, in a low oven. It can be reheated in a microwave or conventional oven, also covered, or over a low flame with a little added water to prevent it from sticking together. If you have to keep it for some time, leave a little of the cooking water with it, as you do with pasta for salad.

QUICK AND CONVENIENT

Is fresh pasta always better than dried? What is the difference between fresh and dry pasta?

Each kind has its virtues. Fresh pasta has more flavour because it always contains eggs, but dried pasta, which except for noodles is made without eggs so is more neutrally flavoured, is preferable for some dishes. Fresh pasta is quicker to cook but dried pasta is more versatile as it comes in many different shapes. Dried pasta can be stored indefinitely and is therefore a very convenient store cupboard item.

WHEN AND HOW?

If I am adding pasta shapes to soup, what sort of soup should I add them to, when do I add them and in what quantity?

Thick vegetable-based soups such as minestrones are enhanced by shapes such as shells, bows or macaroni. They should be added to the simmering soup, allowing enough time for them to cook as if in water. Pastina is the general term for a group of tiny pasta varieties normally used in clear broths.

Pasta expands with cooking so you need only very small amounts: a tablespoon or two is enough for a soup that feeds four or six people.

HOLD THE CHEESE

Should I always sprinkle pasta with grated cheese? A waiter once told me that you don't put it on fish sauces like vongole.

There are many pasta sauces that are served on their own without the addition of grated cheese. Seafood sauces are traditionally served plain, as are many of the sauces based on olive oil, such as *olio, aglio e peperoncino* (oil, garlic and chilli). Pesto sauce, which contains Parmesan, does not require additional cheese, although you can always add more if you enjoy the flavour.

See also: CANNELLONI, LASAGNE, RAVIOLI, SPAGHETTI, TAGLIATELLE

PASTRY

CHILL OUT

I don't have the cool hands needed for shortcrust pastry nor a mixer. What can I do?

You do need to keep everything cool when you are rubbing fat into flour for shortcrust pastry, but even if your hands are not naturally cool (and few people's are) you can keep everything else cool. Chill the mixing bowl for about 30 minutes beforehand and use iced water to make the dough. A marble slab is excellent for rolling out pastry as the surface remains cold.

You could also buy an inexpensive gadget called a pastry blender that rubs in the fat for you. Hold the handle and draw the rack of rounded metal blades across the flour and fat: the blades will cut and blend the fat into the flour to make it resemble breadcrumbs. The water can then be added and mixed in with a knife or fork. Grating the chilled butter directly into the flour also reduces the rubbing time and hence the heat generated.

Or try a quick-mix pastry where you do not have to use your fingers. Sift 225 g (8 oz) of plain flour into a bowl with a pinch of salt. Using a fork, cream 140 g (5 oz) of block margarine at room temperature with 2 tablespoons of water and half the flour until well mixed. It takes about 30 seconds. Stir in the remaining flour to form a firm dough, then knead it on a lightly floured work surface until smooth.

Fast shortcrust

To make shortcrust pastry in a food processor or mixer, sift the flour into the bowl. Add the salt, sugar and diced butter. Process until mixed, then add the water and process until the mixture just binds together to form a firm dough. Chill for 20 minutes.

SHORT WORK

Which makes the better pastry: butter, margarine or lard?

Butter gives pastry a fine flavour and a crisp texture. For rich pastries, such as puff or pâte sucrée, where flavour is important, it is always best to use butter.

Firm margarine can be used to make plain types of pastries such as shortcrust pastry. Some soft polyunsaturated margarines can also be used for pastry: check the label and follow the manufacturer's instructions. Use them straight from the fridge for easy handling.

Lard or vegetable fat gives shortness to pastry but not much flavour so a mixture of equal quantities of butter and lard is often preferred.

DELAYED REACTION

Why should pastry be rested?

Gluten, the protein present in flour, begins to react when it comes into contact with water during mixing, and during resting it becomes firm and elastic. This makes the dough much easier to roll out.

Resting pastry in the refrigerator is particularly important during the folding and rolling process of rich layered pastries such as puff and flaky, because it firms up the fat in the pastry, making it easier to roll, and protects the layers so they will rise evenly during cooking.

LIQUIDATE THE LIQUID

How do I stop pies going soggy?

There are several possible causes of soggy pastry. One is that oven temperatures vary and the only way to be sure your oven is the correct temperature is to use an oven thermometer. A pie that is soggy inside may not have been cooked for long enough; or a precooked filling may not have cooled sufficiently before being covered with pastry.

Too much liquid in the filling can wet the pastry lid. Fruits combined with sugar require only a little water as they will exude juice during cooking. If you are layering

Save it!

You can save time by making your pastry in advance, or making double quantities and freezing half. Wrap and freeze it in convenient 225 g (8 oz) quantities. Allow to thaw for 1 - 2 hours at room temperature or overnight in the refrigerator.

fruit with sugar, make sure the last layer is fruit before the pastry lid is added: if the sugar comes directly into contact with the pastry, it will make it soggy. A hole or cross cut in the top of the pie allows steam to escape from a covered pie and keeps the pastry crisp.

QUANTITY MATTERS

If a recipe states that I should use 225 g (8 oz) of pastry, is this the amount of flour I should use, or the quantity of finished pastry?

Pastry quantities given in recipes indicate the amount of flour used to make the pastry. Care should be taken when using bought puff pastry in a recipe. It is sold by weight, so a 450 g (1 lb) pack of puff pastry will be equivalent to 225 g (8 oz) of homemade pastry made with equal quantities of flour and butter.

HEALTHY CRUST

Is it possible to make a healthy pastry, one low in saturated fat?

Yes, you can make a flan case using light, mild olive oil. This pastry is not as short as traditional shortcrust and will have a firm texture that needs careful handling.

Sift 225 g (8 oz) of plain flour into a bowl with a pinch of salt and make a well in the centre. Whisk 5 tablespoons of light, mild olive oil and 4½ tablespoons of water in another bowl until blended.

Gradually add the oil to the flour, mixing until it forms a firm dough. Knead quickly until smooth and

use to line a 23 cm (9 in) flan tin and bake it blind. Should a slight crack appear during baking, brush it over with a little lightly beaten egg white and return to a hot oven for 1 - 2 minutes to dry out. This helps to seal the crack and prevent the filling seeping out.

STAY PUT

What makes the tops of single-crust pies come away from the side and slip into the filling?

It happens because the lids have shrunk during cooking. Pastry that has been chilled for 20 - 30 minutes before rolling will relax and shrink less. Short, light strokes are also important when rolling out pastry as pushing the rolling pin heavily will stretch the pastry and it will shrink during baking.

Pies made in deep oval dishes are always made with a single crust as the shape makes it difficult to line the dish properly. But there must be sufficient filling to mound above the rim of the dish and support the pastry lid. The fruit pie below is baked in just such a deep dish with just a single crust, so there is more of the luscious fruit filling than pastry.

Nectarine and redcurrant single-crust pie

SERVES: 5 - 6
PREPARATION TIME: 40 - 45 minutes, plus 30 minutes resting
COOKING TIME: 45 - 50 minutes

FOR THE PASTRY
175 g (6 oz) plain flour
A pinch of salt
40 g (1½ oz) butter or margarine, diced
40 g (1½ oz) lard, diced
To glaze: 1 egg white, beaten, and caster sugar

FOR THE FILLING
7 ripe nectarines, peeled, stoned and cut into thick wedges
125 g (4½ oz) redcurrants, rinsed and stripped off their stalks
60 g (2¼ oz) caster sugar
1 tablespoon lemon juice

Deep dish fruit pies with a buttery pastry crust are a traditional favourite. Add a twist with unusual fruit combinations, such as nectarines and redcurrants.

1 Preheat the oven to 200°C (400°F, gas mark 6). Sift the flour into a bowl, add the salt and fats and rub them into the flour until the mixture looks like breadcrumbs. Add 1½ tablespoons of cold water and using a knife, mix to form a dough.

2 Using your fingertips, knead the dough gently on a lightly floured board until smooth. Then place it in a polythene bag and leave it to rest in the refrigerator for 30 minutes.

3 Have ready a 1 litre (1¾ pint) oval pie dish. On a floured surface, roll the pastry to a shape 4 cm (1½ in) larger all around than the top of the dish. Then cut out the centre of the pastry about 2.5 cm (1 in) in from the edge. Reserve the outer strip to line the rim of the dish.

4 Spread layers of nectarines and redcurrants into the dish, sprinkling each with a little caster sugar and finishing with a layer of fruit. Add the lemon juice. The fruit should be piled well above the top of the dish to hold up the pastry lid.

5 Lightly brush the rim of the dish with beaten egg and lay the pastry strip on it neatly with no overlap. Dampen the edging strip with water or beaten egg then lift up the pastry lid on a rolling pin and cover the pie, pressing gently to seal.

6 Trim then knock up the pastry edge by making horizontal dents on the outside edge with the back of a knife, and decorate by pinching (see box, right). Make a small hole in the centre to let the steam escape.

7 Roll out the pastry trimmings, cut three or four leaves, draw on veins with a knife and arrange on the pie.

8 Brush the pie with egg white and sprinkle with caster sugar. Put the pie dish on a baking sheet and cook the pie for 20 minutes. Then reduce the heat to 180°C (350°F, gas mark 4) and continue baking for a further 25 - 30 minutes until golden brown.

DECORATING A PIE

After sealing, the edges of pies can be decorated using a fork, pastry pincer, knife or even your fingers. Deep fluting is the most appropriate technique to use for fruit-filled pies, which might leak juice.

1 Cut off the pastry edge level with the edge of the dish, using a sharp knife. Hold the knife at an angle, with the handle pointing towards the edge of the dish.

2 Gently mark the pastry edges with the back of a knife to neaten them and give an attractive flaky finish to pies and tarts.

3 To decorate, pinch around the outer edge of the pastry lid with your fingers to shape the dough.

4 Or press your thumb on the top outer edge, then draw the edge towards the centre using the back of a knife. Repeat around the edge.

ROLLING AND FOLDING PUFF PASTRY

The rolling and folding process is a simple one and creates the light layers characteristic of puff pastry.

1 Roll out the dough into a strip 38 × 13 cm (15 × 5 in), then form the butter into a rectangle around 13 × 10 cm (5 × 4 in) and place it in the middle. Fold the bottom third of dough up and the top third down to enclose the butter. Press the edges firmly with the rolling pin to seal.

2 Give the dough a half turn clockwise so that the folded edge of the dough is on your right. Roll into a strip three times as long as it is wide. Mark the strip into three. Fold the bottom third of the dough up and the top third down.

3 Seal the edges again with the rolling pin and give the dough a half turn clockwise. Roll the pastry into a strip then fold and seal again.

4 Press the top of the dough with your fingertips to remind you of how many rolls and folds the pastry has had. It is easy to forget! Then chill the pastry and repeat twice.

LAYERED FOR LIGHTNESS

What is the difference between puff and rough puff pastry?

The aim with both pastries is to form thin layers of fat between very thin layers of dough to produce a pastry which rises well.

Puff pastry is the richest and lightest of the two, and usually uses equal quantities of fat to flour. Some of the fat is rubbed into the flour, as in shortcrust pastry, but then the rest is added in a single piece and distributed through the dough by a lengthy process of rolling and folding, which builds up the number of layers and the subsequent lightness of the pastry.

If the butter is cut into pieces instead of formed into a compact slab, and if the folding process is shortened, the result is flaky pastry, which does not rise quite as effectively as puff pastry.

Rough puff pastry uses less fat than puff pastry and is easier to make. The fat is cut into small pieces and added all at once to the flour. Rough puff pastry also needs less rolling and folding.

COOK'S CHOICE

Is it really worth the effort of making homemade puff pastry when you can buy it prepared?

Making puff pastry takes time and practice, but once you have the skill, making puff pastry may be fitted in with other cooking and will seem less of a chore.

Is it worth the effort? That is for you to decide. Homemade puff pastry will taste rich, light and buttery because it is usually made with equal quantities of butter and flour. Chilled or frozen puff pastry tastes less rich but is convenient to store, easy to use and gives good results.

STEAM HEAT

Is there any way to make sure puff pastry will rise evenly?

A steamy atmosphere inside the oven will help the layers of puff pastry to rise evenly. Half fill a roasting tin with hot water and place on the bottom of the oven during cooking. This and a wetted baking sheet will create the steam to help the pastry rise evenly. Try this method with the following recipes for homemade puff pastry made into a giant vol-au-vent case filled with mixed mushrooms.

Puff pastry

SERVES: 4 - 6

PREPARATION TIME: 1 hour plus 1 ½ hours chilling time, plus overnight chilling; then from 30 - 60 minutes resting time

COOKING TIME: 65 minutes

225 g (8 oz) strong plain flour
A pinch of salt
225 g (8 oz) butter, at room temperature
About 8 - 10 tablespoons iced water
2 teaspoons lemon juice

1 Sift the flour and salt into a large mixing bowl. Work the butter on a plate with a palette knife until it is softened. Cut off about 15 g (½ oz) of butter and rub it into the flour until it resembles breadcrumbs.
2 Sprinkle the surface of the dough with 8 tablespoons of the iced water and the lemon juice. Mix to a soft but not sticky dough – add the extra water if the mixture is dry.
3 Transfer the dough to a lightly floured surface and knead for it for about 5 minutes or until smooth and elastic. Sprinkle it with flour, place it inside a large polythene bag and leave to rest in the refrigerator until cool and firm, about 20 minutes.
4 Lightly flour a work surface. Shape the dough into a small rectangle and then roll and fold it as described in steps 1 - 4 in the box on the left. For best results, always roll the dough away from you using short, sharp strokes of the rolling pin.
5 Roll and fold the pastry four more times, putting the pastry to chill for around 20 - 30 minutes after each two rollings and foldings, or after each if the pastry becomes sticky.
6 Wrap and chill the finished pastry for at least 20 minutes before using, or refrigerate overnight.

A selection of earthy mushrooms glistening with Madeira sauce makes a superb chunky filling for a mammoth vol-au-vent case made with buttery puff pastry.

Giant mixed mushroom vol-au-vent

SERVES: 4 – 6
PREPARATION TIME: 30 minutes, plus 2¹/₂ hours resting time
COOKING TIME: 40 minutes

FOR THE VOL-AU-VENT
225 g (8 oz) homemade puff pastry, (see left), or 450 g (1 lb) frozen puff pastry, defrosted
1 egg, size 3, beaten with a pinch of salt for brushing

FOR THE MUSHROOM FILLING
15 g (¹/₂ oz) dried wild mushrooms
150 ml (5 fl oz) Madeira
50 g (1 ³/₄ oz) unsalted butter
3 shallots, finely chopped
450 g (1 lb) mixed fresh mushrooms cleaned, quartered or sliced
Juice of ¹/₂ lemon
1 tablespoon arrowroot
100 g (3 ¹/₂ oz) crème fraîche
Salt and black pepper

1 Remove the puff pastry from the refrigerator and leave it to rest for an hour before rolling out.
2 Roll the pastry out to about 1 cm (¹/₂ in) thick. Using a sharp knife, cut two circles from the pastry using an 18 cm (7 in) plate as a guide.
3 Cut a 10 cm (4 in) circle from the centre of one of the circles: this will be the lid. Leave the uncut circle, the circle with the hole and the lid, covered with some polythene, in the fridge to rest for 30 minutes.
4 Put the uncut pastry circle on a wetted baking sheet. Brush the edge with beaten egg and carefully place the cut ring of pastry on top.
5 Knock up the sides of the pastry. Brush the top of the ring with the beaten egg, avoiding the knocked up edges or they will stick together and prevent the pastry rising properly.
6 With the back of a knife, mark lines to form a star pattern around the border of the pastry ring.

7 Place the lid on another wetted baking sheet and knock up or flake the edges. Brush with beaten egg and mark a trellis pattern on the top of the pastry with the back of a knife. Cover each piece of cut pastry with a polythene bag and leave them in the refrigerator to rest for an hour.
8 Preheat the oven to 220°C (425°F, gas mark 7). Half fill a roasting tin with hot water and place it in the bottom of the oven.
9 Put the pastry case near the middle of the oven and the lid on the shelf below, allowing room for it to rise, and bake for 30 - 35 minutes or until the case and lid are well risen, cooked and golden brown.
10 Meanwhile, start to make the filling. Rinse the dried mushrooms to remove any grit then soak them in warm water for 20 minutes, or until they are plump and soft. Drain the mushrooms and reserve the liquid.
11 Pour the Madeira into a small saucepan and boil for 5 minutes or until reduced by half.
12 Melt the butter in a frying pan, add the shallots and fry gently for around 2 - 3 minutes until softened but not browned. Add the dried and fresh mushrooms, sprinkle with the lemon juice, then cover and cook for about 5 minutes until softened.
13 Measure out 150 ml (5 fl oz) of the reserved mushroom water, blend with the arrowroot and add to the mushroom mixture. Cook gently, stirring, for 3 minutes or until the sauce has thickened.
14 Remove the vol-au-vent from the oven and cool slightly. Remove any soggy pastry from the centre of the case and return the vol-au-vent to the oven for 5 minutes to dry off.
15 Add the reduced Madeira and crème fraîche to the mushrooms and cook the mixture over a low heat for about 2 - 3 minutes. Season to taste.
16 To serve, pour the mushrooms into the hot pastry case and put the lid on top at an angle. Use a large knife to cut the vol-au-vent into four wedges at the table and place on serving plates, ensuring each person has a generous portion of pastry and mushroom filling. Accompany the vol-au-vent with a spinach salad.

LEAVE IT OUT

Should the fat be used straight from the fridge when making flaky or puff pastry?

No. To make flaky or puff pastry easy to roll, the fat should be the same temperature and consistency as the dough, at normal room temperature. (Do not attempt this type of pastry in hot weather as it can become sticky.) If the fat is hard it can break through the dough, and if it is too soft it will not keep the pastry layers apart, making the rolling sticky and hard to manage. If the dough becomes sticky, put it in a polythene bag in the refrigerator until firm enough to continue.

Save it!

Rolled trimmings of puff or flaky pastry can be rerolled two or three times but you must not roll them into a ball as this will destroy the light layers of the pastry. Instead, stack the trimmings on top of each other as neatly as possible and then roll.

BETTER BOUGHT PASTRY

How can I get the best out of bought puff pastry?

There are times when you want to serve a puff pastry dish but have neither the time nor the inclination to make pastry from scratch. Be prepared and keep some frozen puff pastry in the freezer.

Some frozen packs of pastry contain 250–280 g (9–10 oz) portions, which are convenient to use. If you need a larger quantity, buy 450 g (1 lb) blocks. If you cannot find the larger size and have to combine two smaller packs, be sure to lay one on top of the other and roll them out flat to preserve the layers.

You can make bought pastry richer by adding extra butter. Roll out a 250 g (9 oz) portion of pastry

to make a rectangle three times as long as it is wide. Mark it into three equal parts. Cover the top two-thirds with 25 g (1 oz) of butter cut into flakes. Bring the bottom third of pastry up over the middle section and the top third down to form a square. Seal the edges with a rolling pin and give the pastry a half turn clockwise so that the folded edge is on your right. Roll out the pastry to the same size as before, fold it into three, seal the edges and place the dough in a polythene bag. Chill for 30 minutes until firm, then use as required.

RAISE THE HEAT

How can I prevent fat seeping out of my puff pastry during cooking?

You need to use a hot or very hot oven, usually 220°C (425°F, gas mark 7). If the oven is not hot enough, the fat will run out of the pastry layers before it is absorbed by the starch. If the fat runs at this oven setting, check the temperature of your oven or use a higher setting. If you are using bought pastry, check the instructions for oven temperature on the pack and be sure you preheat the oven for long enough: at least 20 minutes.

Some recipes advise reducing the oven temperature after the initial cooking. This allows time for the filling of the dish to cook sufficiently while preventing the pastry from cooking too quickly.

SWEETER PASTRY

The pastry used in French tarts seems to taste richer than my normal shortcrust. What is it?

For fine pâtisserie the French often use pâte sablée, which is enriched with egg and sugar, instead of shortcrust. It is traditionally made on a flat surface and mixed by hand. To make pâte sablée, add an egg, 125 g (4½ oz) of caster sugar and a few drops of vanilla essence to 250 g (9 oz) of sifted plain flour and 125 g (4½ oz) of softened butter. Draw into a ball with your hands and chill for an hour before rolling.

WEIGH THE FLOUR

How much pastry do I need to make if I want to line a 25 cm (10 in) tart tin?

For a 25 cm (10 in) tart tin you will need 225 g (8 oz) of shortcrust pastry – that is, pastry made with 225 g (8 oz) of plain flour. This will also do for a 28 cm (11 in) tart tin. For a 23 cm (9 in) tin you will require a 175 g (6 oz) quantity of pastry.

SEASONAL ZEST

I would like to jazz up my mince pies this year. What kind of pastry would complement the flavour of the mincemeat?

Oranges are frequently associated with Christmas time. Try this recipe which uses orange juice instead of water to make the basic shortcrust pastry, traditional for mince pies. The grated zest of the orange is then added to the mincemeat. For an extra kick, you could add a few tablespoons of an orange liqueur.

Orange mince pies

MAKES: *about 18 pies*
PREPARATION TIME: *30 – 35 minutes plus 20 – 25 minutes resting time for the pastry*
COOKING TIME: *25 minutes*

---

350 g (12 oz) plain flour
A pinch of salt
75 g (2¾ oz) butter or margarine, diced
75 g (2¾ oz) lard or vegetable fat, diced
3 tablespoons orange juice
Grated rind of 1 small orange
450 g (1 lb) mincemeat
Milk for brushing pastry
To decorate: icing or caster sugar

---

1 Sift the flour and salt into a bowl. Add both the fats and rub them into the flour until the mixture resembles fine breadcrumbs.
2 Add the orange juice and, using a knife, mix to a firm dough.
3 Using your fingertips, knead the dough gently on a lightly floured board until smooth, then put it in a polythene bag and leave it to rest in

Save it!

To freeze mince pies, layer cold, cooked pies in rigid containers between sheets of nonstick baking paper. To serve warm: preheat the oven to 180°C (350°F, gas mark 4), place the frozen pies on a baking tray, cover with foil and bake for 20 minutes.

the refrigerator for at least 20 - 25 minutes before using.

4 Preheat the oven to 200°C (400°F, gas mark 6). Lightly grease two tartlet tins, enough for about 18 pies.

5 On a lightly floured surface, roll out two-thirds of the dough thinly. Using a 7.5 cm (3 in) round fluted cutter, stamp out as many rounds as you can. Reroll the pastry trimmings and cut out more rounds.

6 Carefully line the tartlet tins with the cut rounds of pastry.

7 Roll out the remaining portion of pastry and cut out 6 cm (2½ in) rounds to make lids. Using a small star-shaped cutter, 3 cm (1¼ in) in diameter, cut out shapes from each pastry lid. Or, if you prefer plain lids, cut two slits in the top of each lid with a sharp knife or scissors.

8 Stir the grated orange rind into the prepared mincemeat and put a teaspoon of the mixture in the centre of each lined tartlet case.

9 Dab some water onto the pastry edges. Place the lids over the filled tartlets and press the edges together to seal. Glaze the lids with milk.

10 Bake the pies for 25 minutes or until the pastry is golden.

11 Sprinkle the cooked pies lightly with sifted icing or caster sugar and serve warm with some brandy butter or cream. Alternatively, cool the pies on a wire tray and when cold, store in an airtight tin. They will keep for up to ten days in a cool place.

To reheat mince pies, preheat the oven to 180°C (350°F, gas mark 4). Put the mince pies on a baking sheet and heat for 8 - 10 minutes or until they are warmed through.

PATES AND TERRINES

ROUGH OR SMOOTH?

What is the difference between a pâté and a terrine?

The line dividing pâtés and terrines is a very thin one. They are both most commonly made with minced or pounded meat, poultry or vegetables, highly seasoned and then cooked in a very slow oven. Pâtés tend to have a smoother texture and, apart from fish and vegetable pâtés, are predominantly made of liver, served from the container in which they are cooked, and eaten spread on bread or toast.

Terrines often, but not always, have a coarser texture than pâtés, with definite pieces. They are usually pressed after cooking and then served sliced as a first course. Terrines do not have to be made from meat. Layered terrines of seafood or vegetables set with aspic are very attractive. The word terrine is also used to describe some very smooth fish, seafood or vegetable mixtures that are set in a terrine tin, turned out and served sliced.

SEALED WITH BUTTER

What does it mean when a food is described as 'potted'?

Cooks have been potting meat and fish since the 16th century as a way of preserving it. Potted meat or fish is seasoned and cooked until tender, then either pounded to a paste, pressed into a pot and covered with melted butter, or left whole in its cooking pot and covered with melted butter. The butter sets into an airtight seal so that the contents can be stored in a cool larder or refrigerator for up to two months.

Once the seal is broken, potted food should be eaten within two days. This method of preserving food is largely a thing of the past, but potted shrimps are still popular. (See recipe in PRESERVING.)

PEACHES AND NECTARINES

SUMMER SEASON

At what time of year are peaches and nectarines at their best?

The best time to buy peaches and nectarines is during the summer months, from late June through to the end of August, when those from France, Italy and Spain are available. Peaches that appear in the shops around Christmas time can have a woolly texture and little flavour. Look out for white-fleshed peaches in the stores as these are considered to have a better flavour than the yellow-fleshed varieties.

Peaches and nectarines are close relations: the nectarine is not, as is widely believed, a cross between a plum and a peach. The only difference between them is that peaches have a fuzzy skin while nectarines are smooth. Before they are eaten, peaches and nectarines should be rinsed under a cold running tap to rid them of any fungicides.

SWEET RELATIONS

Can peaches and nectarines be used interchangeably in recipes?

Yes. Peaches and nectarines are completely interchangeable in recipes, although nectarines can be a little sweeter so may require less additional sugar than peaches.

Raw and ripe, both peaches and nectarines are perfect for making fruit salads – combined with just one other fruit such as fresh raspberries (with which peaches and nectarines have a natural affinity) or with a mixture of other fruits.

Poached in a light sugar syrup, they can be served hot with cream or ice cream, or chilled and used in ice cream sundaes, or to top a flan or gâteau. They can also be spiced, baked, or grilled, cooked with pan-fried steaks and gammon, or added to casseroles, curries and stews. (See also recipe in PASTRY.)

PEARS

COOKING AND EATING

Which varieties of pears are best for cooked recipes?

Virtually any variety of pear can be used for cooking, provided the pears are firm and not too ripe. For eating, it is best to buy pears that are not quite ripe unless you want to eat them immediately as they deteriorate quickly after reaching their peak. Keep them in a warm place to ripen and they should be ready to eat in two to three days. For the Boozy Pears recipe below, choose a large, firm variety of pear.

Boozy pears

SERVES: 8
PREPARATION TIME: 30 minutes
COOKING TIME: 30 - 40 minutes, plus overnight standing; next day: 15 minutes plus 2 - 3 hours chilling

---

1 large orange and 1 large lemon
175 g (6 oz) granulated sugar
750 ml (1 pint 7 fl oz) sweet white
    wine
8 large, ripe Comice, Conference
    or Williams pears
2 - 3 tablespoons Grand Marnier
1 tablespoon chopped pistachio nuts
To serve: whipped cream, optional

---

1 Wash the orange and lemon and pare off the rinds in thin strips. Put these into a large stainless-steel or enamel saucepan that will hold all the pears comfortably.
2 Add the granulated sugar and the wine, then stir over a moderate heat until the sugar dissolves.
3 Bring to the boil and remove from the heat. Squeeze the orange and lemon, adding the juice to the pan.
4 Cut off the dried flower bud from the bottom of each pear and peel them, leaving the stalks. Place the pears in the wine syrup and return the saucepan to the heat.
5 Bring to the boil, then reduce the heat. Cover the pan and gently cook the pears for 30 - 40 minutes until only a slight resistance is felt when

Thin strips of orange and lemon rind make a colourful garnish for this pear bathed in white wine and Grand Marnier. Pistachio nuts provide some crunch.

they are pierced with a knife. Turn the pears frequently to ensure they are well coated with wine syrup.
6 When the pears are cooked and translucent, take the pan off the heat and let the pears stand in the syrup overnight at room temperature.
7 Next day, remove the pears from the wine syrup with a slotted spoon and arrange them upright on a serving dish. Cover and set aside.
8 Bring the wine syrup to the boil and simmer it for 15 - 20 minutes or

until it has reduced by about half and become rich and heavy. Remove the saucepan from the heat and allow the wine syrup to cool.
9 Stir the Grand Marnier into the cooled syrup, then pour it over the pears. Cover the dish with cling film and chill for 2 - 3 hours.
10 Just before serving, spoon the syrup from the bottom of the dish over the pears and sprinkle with the chopped nuts and strips of rind. Serve with whipped cream, if liked.

KEEPING GOOD COLOUR

How do I stop pears from turning brown during preparation?

Use a stainless-steel potato peeler and put the peeled pears into a bowl of cold water. Add the juice of a large lemon or 2–3 tablespoons of bottled lemon juice.

Alternatively, depending on the recipe you have chosen, the pears can be put directly into a wine or sugar syrup to keep them from discolouring. For the most appealing presentation, try to choose either Comice, Conference or Williams varieties that are a standard size and have a true pear shape.

Peeled pears may be poached, stewed, baked or even pickled in a wide variety of recipes. They are delicious with fish and poultry.

PEAS

CLOSE RELATIVES

Are mangetout and sugarsnap peas similar to garden peas?

They are all the same family of pea, but they are sold at different stages of maturity. Mangetout are flat with barely formed peas inside. Sugarsnaps contain more developed, plump peas, but are not as mature as garden peas. Both mangetout and sugarsnap are grown for their crisp, sweet edible pods.

For peas eaten whole, a good helping is about 100 g (3½ oz) for each person. Garden peas should yield just under half their unshelled weight. For two, allow about 500 g (1 lb 2 oz) of unshelled peas, unless you are serving them with other vegetables or using them in a salad, such as the one on the right.

This is a good salad for a summer buffet table or barbecue because the peas and lentils stay firm in the dressing. Soft fruits are in season at the same time as peas, so you can sprinkle over some redcurrants as a colourful decoration. A splash of raspberry vinegar will lend another subtle summer aroma to this salad.

Pea and Puy lentil salad in mint dressing

SERVES: 6 - 8
PREPARATION TIME: 15 minutes
COOKING TIME: 30 - 35 minutes

---

350 g (12 oz) Puy lentils
2 bay leaves
700 g (1 lb 9 oz) unshelled peas
1 teaspoon sugar
Salt and black pepper
1 teaspoon ground cumin
4 - 6 spring onions
3 - 4 sprigs mint
2 - 3 sprays redcurrants, optional

FOR THE DRESSING
90 ml (3¼ fl oz) olive oil
1 tablespoon sherry vinegar
1 teaspoon raspberry vinegar

---

1 Put the lentils into a pan with the bay leaves and cover them well with cold water. Bring to the boil, skim, then turn down the heat and simmer for about 30 - 35 minutes or until tender. Drain, rinse and leave them to drain further in a colander.

2 Meanwhile, shell the peas and put them in a small pan. Add the sugar and enough water to cover. Simmer the peas for 7 - 10 minutes, or until they are soft and sweet.

3 While the peas are cooking, put the ingredients for the dressing into a small screw-top jar and shake well.

4 When the peas and lentils are done, mix them together in a bowl. Season with the salt, black pepper and ground cumin and toss in the salad dressing. This can be done a few hours in advance if you like.

5 Shortly before serving, wash, trim and shred the spring onions, then shred the mint and toss them both into the pea and lentil salad. Garnish with redcurrants if you like, or add an extra sprig of mint to decorate.

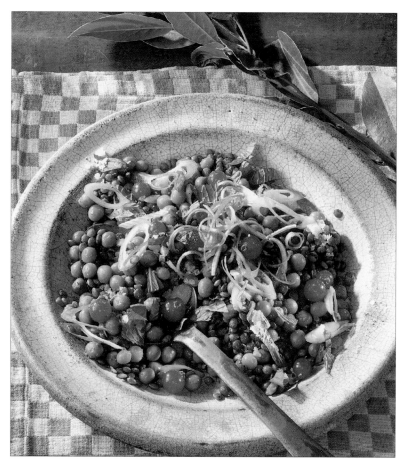

Bright redcurrants enliven the green peas, spring onions and Puy lentils in this distinctive salad. Fresh mint and ground cumin add an exotic flavour.

PEKING DUCK

AUTHENTICALLY CRISP

Is it possible to cook Peking Duck at home or is it too complicated?

True Peking duck uses a special species of bird bred in north China which is roasted and traditionally eaten in three courses. The crispy skin is served first with pancakes, then the meat is stir-fried as a main course and the bones are served next, in a soup. Such a meal is not easy to produce at home. However, even in China, the meat is now usually served with the pancakes, making life easier for the cook.

It is most important that the skin is thoroughly dried before roasting to achieve perfect crispness, which is fundamental to this dish.

The traditional way to dry the duck is to hang it outdoors in the sun for up to 12 hours, but this is not always practical in the British climate. You can also suspend the duck in a warm place, such as an airing cupboard, for 6–8 hours, with a dish beneath it to catch any drips. A surer solution is to use a hair dryer (see box, right).

When making Peking Duck (see recipe right), choose an oven-ready Lincolnshire farmhouse duckling, which is the most similar breed to that used in China. The thin, pale Mandarin pancakes are an essential accompaniment to Peking Duck. These may be bought from Oriental stores and some supermarkets.

See also: DUCK

Microwave pancakes

To save steaming the pancakes, you can spread four at a time on a large plate and microwave them on High for a minute. They must be served quickly as they become brittle and dry after 10 minutes. It helps to keep them well covered with a warm, damp cloth.

Peking duck

SERVES: 4 - 6
PREPARATION TIME: 1 hour, including 45 minutes drying time
COOKING TIME: 1 3/4 hours

2 spring onions
1/2 cucumber
1 oven-ready duck, 2 - 2.5 kg (4 lb 8 oz - 5 lb 8 oz), dried (see box, right)
1 tablespoon honey diluted with 75 ml (2 1/2 fl oz) water
20 - 30 Mandarin pancakes
Hoisin sauce

1 Slice the spring onions very finely on the diagonal. Peel and core the cucumber, chop it into chunks and then into very fine strips. Soak both in cold water until required.

2 Preheat the oven to 230°C (450°F, gas mark 8). Rub the prepared duck with the diluted honey and leave it to dry for about 15 minutes.

3 Place the duck on a trivet in a roasting tin in the centre of the oven. Cook for 30 - 45 minutes, depending on whether you prefer your duck slightly pink or well done. Reduce the temperature to 150°C (300°F, gas mark 2) and cook the duck for a further 30 - 45 minutes. When it is done, the skin should be reddish-brown and extremely crisp.

4 Leave the duck to rest while you heat the pancakes. Steam four to six at a time for 5 minutes in a steamer basket set over a wok or a large pan of boiling water. Transfer them to a plate and cover with a cloth. They will keep warm for 15 minutes.

5 Drain the spring onions and the cucumber then pat them dry.

6 To serve the Peking Duck, carve pieces of skin with a thin layer of meat about 2.5 cm (1 in) square, then cut the rest of the duck meat into manageable pieces. Arrange it on a platter with the spring onions and the cucumber and place a couple of dishes of hoisin sauce on the table.

7 Before eating, place a teaspoon of hoisin sauce in the centre of a pancake then top with a few strips of onion and cucumber and a piece of duck. The pancake is then rolled up and eaten with the fingers.

DRYING THE DUCK

The duck used in Peking Duck has to be dried thoroughly so the skin becomes crisp when it is cooked. The best way is to use a hair dryer.

1 Remove the giblets from the cavity of the duck and discard, or store them for use another day. Loop a length of strong string under the wing joints of the duck then wrap it once around the upper body. Be sure to knot the ends of the string.

2 Holding the duck by the ends of the string, plunge it into a large pot of rapidly boiling water for a few minutes. This will shrink the skin and slightly reduce the fat content of the duck before the drying begins. Remove the blanched duck from the pot and place it on a plate or trivet deep enough to catch the drips of fat and moisture during drying.

3 Turn your hair dryer to High and blast the duck all over, from a distance of about 15 cm (6 in) to prevent any scorching. Dry the inside of the duck cavity as well.

A 2.25 kg (5 lb) duck will take at least 30 minutes to dry, so place the duck on a table. You can then sit down and perform this process with the minimum of arm fatigue. When the skin begins to look reasonably parched, the duck is ready to roast. Remove the string before cooking.

PEPPERCORNS

COLOUR VARIATIONS

What is the difference between black, white, green and pink peppercorns?

Black, white and green peppercorns all come from the fruit of the same Asian tropical vine. However, they are picked at different stages and processed differently, which affects their flavour. Black peppercorns are the most pungent variety, followed by white, then green.

The vine bears green berries, which may be canned in their unripe state. These green peppercorns give a pepper flavour but without much heat. They can be used in subtle ways, such as scattered over strawberries, and will not overpower poultry or fish.

If these green berries are dried rather than canned, they darken to form the familiar black peppercorns. If, instead, they are left for longer on the vine to ripen, they turn bright red. White peppercorns are made by taking the ripe, red berries and removing the skin and pulp. The inner white seeds are then dried in the sun. White pepper is more expensive and less aromatic than black, but it is preferred for use in some sauces where black pepper would look unattractive.

Pink peppercorns are the berries of a different tropical bush. They are picked ripe and then dried. Pink peppercorns have a fruity heat and spicy flavour that is reminiscent of both cinnamon and allspice, but must be used sparingly as they are toxic when eaten in large quantities. Try a smattering of pink peppercorns in a recipe such as pickled peaches (see PICKLING), to add colour to the presentation.

All dried peppercorns should be freshly ground in a mill to maintain their flavour, which is quickly lost after processing. An opened can of green peppercorns can be transferred to an airtight jar and stored for six weeks in the refrigerator.

DAMPEN THE FIRE

What can I do if I have added too much pepper to a dish?

There is not much to be done, beyond trying to lessen the impact of the pepper by increasing the other ingredients. In some cases, you may be able to add a bland ingredient to the dish such as mashed potato, rice or cream. There are some recipes, however, where pepper is the primary flavouring ingredient, such as in the classic French dish Steak au Poivre.

Steak au poivre

SERVES: 2
PREPARATION TIME: 3 minutes
COOKING TIME: 6 minutes

2 teaspoons black peppercorns
2 sirloin steaks, cut 1.5 cm
   (around ½ in) thick
1½ teaspoons olive oil
Sea salt

1 Crush the peppercorns briefly with a pestle and mortar until they are broken but still quite large.
2 Rub the steaks lightly with the oil then press the crushed peppercorns firmly into the meat.
3 Heat the grill, or grill pan, until very hot. Cook the steaks quickly for about 2 minutes on each side.
4 Sprinkle the steaks with coarse sea salt and serve immediately with Coriander Salsa (see page 190).

PEPPERS

SWEETER WHEN SKINNED

Do all peppers taste the same regardless of their colour?

No, they do not. They are all members of the same capsicum family, however, red peppers are distinctly sweeter than green, which are simply unripened red peppers. Yellow peppers are the mildest of all.

The flavour of all peppers will be even smoother and sweeter if they are grilled or roasted (see box, right). As the skin blisters, it can be

GRILLING AND ROASTING PEPPERS

Grilling or roasting peppers makes them sweeter, more succulent and considerably easier to digest.

1 Put the peppers under a hot grill, until they are well blistered and browned. Or, put them in the oven at 200° C (400°F, gas mark 6) for about an hour, turning once. When cooked, put them in a covered dish.

2 When they are cool, pull away the skin with your fingers.

3 Halve the peppers on a plate to catch as much juice as possible. Remove the core, seeds and pith then slice the peppers as required. It is worth saving the juices to add to the salad dressing. Or, put the roasted peppers into containers, cover with their juices and freeze.

flaked off. If you want to peel the peppers but do not want to cook them, a very sharp potato peeler will take off almost all of their slightly bitter skin. The following salad recipe shows how delicious sweet roasted peppers can be.

Salad of roasted peppers and shallots

SERVES: 6
PREPARATION TIME: 20 minutes
COOKING TIME: 1 hour

6 peppers of assorted colours
12 shallots
8 large cloves garlic, unpeeled
3 bay leaves
2 - 3 tablespoons olive oil
2 canned anchovy fillets
2 tablespoons walnut oil
1 tablespoon red wine vinegar
Salt and black pepper
2 tablespoons coarsely chopped
   walnut kernels
To garnish: fresh bay leaves,
   optional

1 Preheat the oven to 200°C (400°F, gas mark 6). Halve the peppers and place them, cut side down, on a baking sheet in the top of the oven.
2 Peel the shallots, letting them fall into their natural segments. Place in an ovenproof dish with the garlic.
3 Halve the bay leaves lengthways and scatter them over the shallots, then sprinkle with a tablespoon of olive oil. Place the shallots on the shelf beneath the peppers and roast both for about 30 minutes until the peppers are blistered and brown.
4 Remove the skin, seeds and pith from the peppers, saving as much juice as possible. Slice the peppers into long strips, on a plate to collect their juices, then transfer the strips and juices to a shallow serving dish. Add the roasted shallots, discarding the cooked strips of bay leaves.
5 Squeeze the garlic pulp out of the skins, mash it into the anchovies and beat in the remaining oils and vinegar, adding more vinegar if there is a lot of sweet pepper juice. Pour the dressing over the salad, scatter with walnuts and toss gently. Season and garnish with bay leaves, if using.

PICKING PEPPERS

Peppers are available all year but are they better in some months?

As peppers respond well to indoor cultivation, they are grown all year round. However, their natural season is late summer, when they are at their tastiest and cheapest. Look for bright, shiny peppers and avoid any peppers that are wrinkled, limp or brown around the stem.

PESTLE AND MORTAR

STILL GOOD

Is a pestle and mortar still useful as kitchen equipment?

A pestle and mortar is invaluable for jobs like crushing and grinding small amounts of spice. You are able to control the grinding very accurately and the weight of the pestle helps with the process. This fine grinding is used in Indian and Far Eastern cookery where freshly ground spices are preferred.

A pestle and mortar is excellent for lightly crushing soft herb leaves such as mint and basil to release their fragrance for use in dressings and pestos (see OILS).

Making garlic mayonnaise is also easier with a pestle and mortar. Soak a slice of white bread in water, squeeze and then crush it in the mortar. Add two cloves of garlic, a pinch of coarse rock salt and pound into a smooth paste. Gradually add a lightly flavoured olive oil in drops, mixing vigorously with the pestle. When the mayonnaise has become sufficiently thick, season it with a little lemon juice.

The better bowls

Marble, glass and porcelain are good materials for mortars as they do not absorb flavours. All will work best when less than half full.

HOW TO USE A PESTLE AND MORTAR

The ancient pestle and mortar is one of the best tools for pounding spices to release their aroma.

Hold the pestle upright and push down firmly, moving it in a circular motion around the mortar bowl.

PHEASANT

PLUCKY BIRD

A friend who lives in the country is bringing me some pheasants. What should I do with them?

Check with your friend if the birds have been hung and are ready to eat. If not, you will have to hang them yourself (see GAME).

For pheasants that are still 'in the feather', the simplest solution is for you to take them to a game dealer or butcher and pay them to prepare the birds. If you do not know a suitable butcher, you will have to prepare them yourself.

First, pluck the feathers (see box, opposite) and cut off the head. Make a slit in the neck lengthways, take hold of the neck bone and twist it, then cut off the neck very close to the body of the bird.

Turn the pheasant around and make a slit at the rear vent. Push your fingers inside the cut and work around the cavity loosening the innards, which you should draw out in one motion. Take care not to break the gall bladder, which is the green sac attached to the liver, as its bitter juice would taint the meat. Do not rinse the cavity as you would lose much flavour. Simply wipe the inside with damp kitchen paper. Discard the lungs, intestines and cut the gall bladder away from the liver. Keep the neck, gizzard, heart and liver to make giblet stock.

Finally, cut through the feet and pull them off, twisting to pull out the sinews from the legs. The bird can be frozen at this stage.

SEX DISCRIMINATION

Why do recipes often specify a hen pheasant rather than a cock?

The hen pheasant is smaller than the male but has a plumper breast and finer flavour. If you buy a brace of pheasant, you usually get a cock and a hen. One pheasant will serve two people.

Pheasant can be used in robust recipes for chicken and guinea fowl and using a chicken brick gives good results. Cook the pheasant for 1½ hours, putting the brick into the cold oven and then setting the temperature to 230°C (450°F, gas mark 8). Young, tender birds are best plainly roasted, while older birds are best made into pâté or casseroled, as in this recipe.

Pheasant casserole with apple and walnuts

SERVES: 4
PREPARATION TIME: 25 minutes
COOKING TIME: 1 hour 35 minutes

6 dessert apples
225 g (8 oz) seedless red grapes
300 ml (10 fl oz) red grape juice
1 tablespoon green tea leaves
300 ml (10 fl oz) boiling water
2 tablespoons olive oil or butter
2 older pheasants
1 tablespoon dark soy sauce
200 ml (7 fl oz) red wine
2 teaspoons balsamic or sherry
    vinegar
Salt and black pepper
175 g (6 oz) walnut halves
To garnish: sautéed apple slices and
    extra grapes

1 Peel, core and roughly chop the apples into a bowl. Whizz the grapes roughly in a food processor with the grape juice and mix with the apples.

2 Put the green tea leaves in a bowl, pour over the boiling water and leave it to steep for about 5 minutes. Strain the tea, reserving the liquid.
3 Preheat the oven to 180°C (350°F, gas mark 4). Heat the oil or butter in a casserole and fry the birds until browned. Pour on the fruit mixture, soy sauce, tea, wine and vinegar. Season and bring to the boil.
4 Cover tightly and transfer to the oven for 1¼ hours or until one of the birds' legs will wobble when pushed. Alternatively, test them by pushing a skewer into the meatiest part of a thigh. If the pheasants are cooked, the juices should flow clear.
5 Transfer the birds to a warmed serving platter and keep warm in the oven while you finish the sauce.
6 Bring the juices in the casserole to the boil and then fast-boil them for about 10 minutes. Strain the liquid into a saucepan, pressing the juice through with a wooden spoon.
7 Stir the walnuts into the sauce, then bring it to the boil and simmer for 10 minutes or until it has reduced to about 450 ml (16 fl oz). The sauce should be slightly syrupy. If it is not, reduce further then season to taste.
8 Joint the pheasants into four and arrange on a dish. Spoon the walnuts around the birds and garnish with sautéed apple slices and grapes. Pour the sauce into a warmed sauceboat.

FATTY PROTECTION

How do you keep the tender breast meat from drying out when you are roasting a pheasant?

As the flesh of game birds is very lean, the breast must be protected. Cover it with a layer of pork fat or streaky bacon to prevent it drying out in the oven. The birds should also be basted from time to time during roasting with the cooking juices and melted fat. Remove the pork fat or bacon 10 minutes before the end of cooking to let the breast brown. If the skin is not brown and crisp enough at the end of cooking, put the bird under a hot grill for a minute or two before serving. Using roasting bags also helps to retain the moisture in a bird.

PLUCKING A PHEASANT

To stop soft breast feathers flying about, use wet hands and start plucking the pheasant inside a large plastic bag. If the bird is hard to pluck, plunge it into boiling water for 30 seconds, then into cold.

1 Start at the neck end of the bird's breast. Press the skin taut at the base of the quills and pull out the feathers in the direction in which they grow. Work from the neck end, moving along towards the tail, then pluck the sides, back and legs.

2 Stretch out a wing to spread the feathers, and pluck the inside of the wing to its tip joint. Turn the bird over and pluck the back of the wing. Repeat with the pheasant's other wing and cut off the tips.

3 Pluck the neck, then pull out the tail feathers. Once plucked, the bird should be singed to remove any stray fluffy feathers. Do this by turning the bird over a gas flame for a few seconds until the little feathers have become frizzled.

PICKLING

WELL PRESERVED

Does it really matter what type of vinegar I use to make pickles?

You should use only high quality vinegar with an acetic acid content of at least 5 per cent, which includes all wine vinegars and most others. Malt vinegar, which was once the staple of the traditional English pickle, is the most economical but it has a distinctive taste. Brown malt vinegar has the best flavour.

White distilled malt vinegar, with its concentrated acidity, is useful for pickling watery vegetables such as cucumber, but there are more subtle, less harsh alternatives you can use as well, such as cider vinegar and red or white wine vinegar. Sherry vinegar and balsamic vinegar can be used half and half with wine or cider vinegar in order to impart their special flavours.

When choosing a vinegar, try to complement the vegetable or fruit that is being preserved. Think about the colour and flavour you wish to create. For example, white vinegar gives a better appearance to light coloured pickles, such as those made from gherkins, cauliflower or cucumber, whereas dark red wine vinegar is best for pickled beetroot or red cabbage. Cider vinegar, with its apple base, is particularly good for sweet pickles. Sherry vinegar, which is a deep caramel colour, has a very mellow flavour. It is perfect for giving a boost to pickled shallots.

ADDING SPICE

What else besides vinegar can I use to give pickles more flavour?

Sugar, herbs, and hot and sweet spices can be added to pickling vinegar to give extra flavour. Sweet pickles are produced by adding a spiced sugar and vinegar syrup to the ingredients. The vinegar must rise above the pickling ingredients by 1–2.5 cm (½–1 in) to allow for evaporation. When crisp vegetables such as onions are pickled, cold vinegar is used. For softer pickles, such as peaches or walnuts, the vinegar should be heated.

CAREFULLY SEALED

What is the best way to seal jars used for pickles?

Lids with plastic-coated linings or specialised preserving jars with glass tops and rubber sealing rings are essential. Never use paper or cellophane covers for pickles (or chutneys) as the jars need to be completely airtight. If the jars are not adequately covered, the vinegar will evaporate and expose the ingredients to the air and harmful bacteria. The preserve will shrink and the top will dry out.

Avoid using metal tops for jars as the vinegar in pickles will corrode them, leading to possible rust and contamination. If the vinegar does evaporate during storage, top it up with more as the ingredients in the container should stay covered.

GIFT WRAPPING

Can you give me some ideas for pretty or unusual pickles I could make as Christmas presents?

Homemade preserves, like Pickled Quail's Eggs, Pickled Shallots and Sweet Pickled Peaches (see recipes, following) make good Christmas presents. They taste superb with ham and cold meats, cheese, pork pies or freshly baked sausages. The best time to make them is when you can obtain a large quantity of ingredients at bargain prices, which is usually late in the summer.

Put the pickles into attractive jars and decorate with labels that state the contents, when the pickles were made, how they should be stored, the date by which they should be eaten and some serving suggestions. Make little hats or collars for the jars and tie the tops with pretty coloured ribbon. The following recipe for Pickled Quail's Eggs would make an especially dainty and sophisticated present.

Pickled quail's eggs

Fills: 500 ml (18 fl oz) jar
Preparation: 20 minutes, plus 2 hours infusing
Cooking time: 10 minutes

1 teaspoon whole mixed peppercorns
2 dried red chillies
Small piece fresh ginger, peeled and finely chopped
1 blade mace
A pared strip of orange zest
1 teaspoon yellow mustard seeds
1 teaspoon sea salt
600 ml (1 pint) white wine vinegar
24 fresh quail's eggs

1 Put all the ingredients except the eggs into a pan. Bring them to the boil, then remove from the heat and leave for about 2 hours or until cold.
2 Hard-boil the eggs for 3 minutes, plunge them into cold water, and peel them when cool. Pack the eggs into a sterilised jar (see CHUTNEY).
3 Strain the spiced vinegar through muslin, then pour it over the eggs so that it covers them completely.
4 Seal with nonmetallic vinegar-proof lids and store in a cool, dark place for a week before using. It is best to use them within a month but they will keep for a year or more.

Pickled shallots

Fills: 2 × 1 litre (1 pint 15 fl oz) jars
Preparation time: 30 – 40 minutes, plus 2 days wet brining and 2 hours infusing
Cooking time: 10 minutes

115 g (4 oz) sea salt
900 g (2 lb) shallots
600 ml (1 pint) white wine vinegar
300 ml (10 fl oz) sherry vinegar
2 blades mace
2 dried red chillies
4 allspice berries, lightly crushed
1 cinnamon stick
1 bay leaf
6 black peppercorns

1 Using a large, nonmetallic bowl, dissolve the salt in 1.2 litres (2 pints) of water, then add the trimmed and peeled shallots with the root end intact. Rest a weighted plate on top

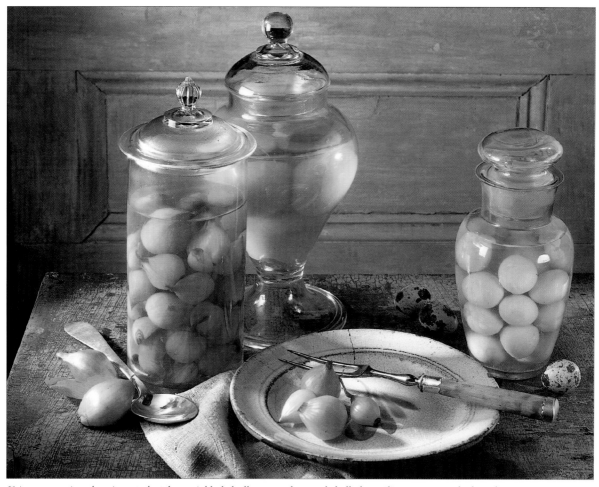

Using attractive glass jars makes these pickled shallots, peaches and shelled quail's eggs particularly welcome presents.

of the bowl to keep the shallots submerged. Leave them for two days, stirring the shallots occasionally.

2 About 2 hours before you are ready to start pickling, bring the vinegars, spices and bay leaf slowly to the boil in a large pan. Remove from the heat and leave the mixture to stand for 2 hours or until cold.

3 Rinse the shallots under cold running water, drain well and pat them dry with kitchen paper. Pack the shallots into sterilised jars.

4 Strain the spiced vinegar through muslin, then pour over the shallots so that it covers them completely.

5 Seal the jars with nonmetallic vinegarproof lids then leave them in a cool, dark place for at least a month before using. This resting period will allow the flavours to develop. The shallots will be at their best when eaten within a year.

Sweet pickled peaches

FILLS: 1 litre (1 pint 15 oz) jar
PREPARATION TIME: 30 minutes
COOKING TIME: 25 minutes

---

350 g (12 oz) granulated sugar
2 teapoons coriander seeds
1 teaspoon whole mixed
  peppercorns
5 cm (2 in) piece cinnamon stick
8 cloves
4 green cardamom pods, lightly
  crushed
2 tablespoons lime juice
600 ml (1 pint) white wine vinegar
10 ripe but firm peaches

---

1 Put all of the ingredients, except the peaches, into a large saucepan or preserving pan. Heat gently, stirring, until the sugar has dissolved.

2 Meanwhile, bring a saucepan of water to the boil. Halve the peaches,

remove the stones, then drop them into the boiling water a few at a time for 30 - 40 seconds, depending on their ripeness. Remove them with a slotted spoon and slip off the skins, using a potato peeler if necessary.

3 Add the peeled peach halves to the vinegar and sugar mixture, bring them to a simmer then poach for about 5 - 10 minutes, or until tender when pierced. Transfer the peaches to a warmed, sterilised jar.

4 Boil the syrup rapidly over a high heat to reduce it by half. Strain the syrup and pour it over the peaches, making sure the fruit is completely covered and there are no air pockets. If necessary, weigh the peaches down with crumpled greaseproof paper, removing it after a week.

5 Seal with a nonmetallic vinegar-proof lid and store in a cool, dark place for six weeks before using.

PIGEON

PIGEON VARIETIES

What is the difference between pigeon, wood pigeon and squab?

Wood pigeon is one of several breeds of pigeon and is the one most commonly available for eating. It is meatier than other pigeons, each bird weighing about 450 g (1 lb), and inexpensive as wood pigeon is in plentiful supply and is available throughout the year.

A squab is a young pigeon which has not yet been fed on whole grain or learned to fly. Squabs are bred for the table in small numbers

Succulent pieces of tender grilled pigeon are accompanied by a herby tomato sauce and polenta slices.

and hence are quite expensive. Each squab weighs approximately 375 g (13 oz) and will serve only one person. The flesh is pale red, tender and flavoursome. It is not as strong-tasting as pigeon, and has a good plump shape.

Most of the meat on a pigeon is on the breast and it is easier to remove it before cooking rather than after. It is also easier to eat as a separate piece rather than attacking a small bird on the plate! The remaining legs and carcass of a raw bird from which the breast has been removed can be used for making game stock, as can the bones from a whole roasted bird.

Pigeon can become tough when overcooked, and for this reason the breast is often cut into smaller pieces and cooked quickly, as in the following recipe, in which the meat is presented on skewers.

Grilled wood pigeon on polenta

SERVES: 4
PREPARATION TIME: *50 minutes plus 1 hour setting time for the polenta*
COOKING TIME: *55 minutes if using coarse polenta or 15 minutes if using instant polenta*

---

175 g (6 oz) coarse polenta or instant polenta
2 tablespoons chopped fresh sage
1 tablespoon chopped fresh rosemary
1 teaspoon chilli flakes
Salt and black pepper
4 large ripe tomatoes
2 cloves garlic, finely chopped
4 tablespoons chopped fresh herbs such as basil, oregano or parsley
150 ml (5 fl oz) olive oil, plus extra for basting
4 wood pigeons
50 g (1 ¾ oz) butter
To garnish: sprigs of rosemary and sage

---

1 To make the polenta, bring 850 ml (1 pint 10 fl oz) of water to the boil and add a good pinch of salt. Sprinkle in the coarse polenta, whisking all the time to prevent lumps forming. Turn down the heat and simmer the mixture for 40 – 45 minutes, stirring continuously, or until the polenta leaves the side of the saucepan when it is stirred (it should be very thick). Alternatively, use instant polenta and simmer for about 5 minutes.
2 Stir in the sage, rosemary, chilli and plenty of salt and pepper.
3 Turn out onto a wooden board and shape into a rough loaf with a spatula. Leave for an hour to set, then cut into four triangular slices. Cover the polenta slices with cling film and set aside until needed.
4 To make the sauce, skin and deseed the tomatoes, then chop them into 5 mm (¼ in) cubes. In a nonmetallic bowl, mix the tomatoes with the garlic, herbs, oil and some salt and pepper. Cover and allow to macerate for 30 minutes.
5 To cook the pigeons, cut down along the breast bone on each side of the birds with a sharp knife and gently ease the breasts off. Cut each

breast in half crossways and season with salt and pepper. Cover and set aside. (Freeze the carcasses to use in stock later.)

6 Preheat the grill to very hot. Melt the butter in a frying pan and, when foaming, add the polenta slices and fry for 2 – 3 minutes each side or until golden. Keep them warm in a low oven with the door ajar so they retain their crispness, and put four plates in to warm.

7 Brush the pieces of pigeon breast with oil and thread four pieces onto each of four metal skewers. Place the skewers on a foil-lined grill pan and grill for 2 – 3 minutes on each side.

8 Place the slices of polenta onto the four heated plates, top each slice with a skewer of pigeon and serve, garnished with the fresh herbs and accompanied by the tomato sauce.

PINEAPPLES

SWEET SMELL OF RIPENESS

How can I tell if a pineapple is ripe before I buy it?

The easiest way is to smell it – a ripe pineapple will have a sweet yet distinctive smell. Another test is to pull one of the inner leaves of the spiky plume; if it comes away easily, the pineapple is ready to eat. Avoid pineapples that are beginning to turn brown on the outside, or any that feel soft.

SIMPLE PREPARATION

How do you prepare a fresh pineapple?

First cut off the top with its spiky green plume and then take a thin slice from the base of the pineapple and stand it upright.

With a large knife, cut the skin downwards, away from the pineapple flesh, in wide strips. Then, with the tip of a knife, remove the hard brown eyes from the surface of the pineapple flesh.

If you want to serve the pineapple in rings, cut it into slices of the required thickness, then remove the hard, woody centre core from each slice with a small knife or biscuit cutter. For wedges or cubes, cut the fruit lengthways into quarters, slice off the core from each piece, then cut up the flesh.

Pineapples can also be hollowed out to act as a container for sorbet, ice cream or fruit salad. First, slice off the top of the pineapple leaving a good wedge of skin attached to the green plume, then cut a sliver from the base and stand it upright. With a pointed stainless-steel knife, carefully cut down into the pineapple just inside the skin and as far as you can go, without puncturing the skin. Work the knife right round the pineapple, then cut around the central core. Make several cuts across the flesh and remove as much of it as you can. Continue cutting until all the flesh has been removed and only the centre core remains, then cut away and discard the core. The pineapple case and its lid can now be put into a polythene bag and frozen until needed.

> ### A note of caution
>
> If you are adding fresh pineapple to dessert mixtures that contain gelatine, such as cheesecake, jelly or mousses, poach the fruit gently in a little sugar syrup beforehand. Otherwise the pineapple's enzymes will break down the gelatine and prevent the mixture from setting.

PINE NUTS, PISTACHIO: see NUTS

PIZZA

MORE HEAT

Why does my homemade pizza base come out soft and not crisp?

The most likely reason is that the baking surface in the preheated oven was not hot enough when you slid the uncooked pizza onto it. The oven and the cooking surface must be preheated to the highest possible temperature. Experienced pizza makers put the dough with its topping straight onto a preheated pizza stone or tile (many kitchen shops sell them) or a large, preheated, unglazed tile. This is the closest home cooks can get to a traditional wood-fired pizza oven, which is extremely hot.

A wooden pizza paddle with a long handle can make manoeuvring the pizza onto the hot surface easier. If you do not have a pizza paddle, put a baking sheet (or tile) on the top rack of the oven and preheat it. Then put the dough on a round, thin pizza tin, lightly oiled and floured, and put it on the preheated surface to bake.

You can also buy a special non-stick two-piece pizza pan which has a perforated disc on which the pizza cooks, so that air circulates underneath ensuring a crisp crust.

QUICK AND WHOLESOME

Can you give me some easy ideas for healthy pizza toppings?

Well-flavoured sliced tomatoes seasoned with fresh basil, salt and a sprinkling of olive oil make a good, simple, low-fat pizza. A mixture of grilled vegetables such as aubergines, courgettes and peppers, arranged decoratively with a drizzle of olive oil, a sprinkling of fresh chopped herbs (such as basil, mint, oregano, or rosemary) and sea salt is another easy option. This pizza could also include some sliced fresh tomatoes. Or simply place thin stalks of fresh asparagus on top of a tomato-based pizza sauce.

CHEESE CHOICE

Are there any cheeses I can use on pizza that will melt well but make a change from mozzarella?

Yes, there are several. Cheddar, Fontina, goat's cheese, Gorgonzola and Gruyère all melt well and are very suitable for pizzas. Smoked Scamorza, another good choice, is similar in texture to mozzarella but slightly firmer and well flavoured. Or try placing spoons of ricotta on top of a pizza and sprinkle them with a little Parmesan. The recipe below uses a stylish combination of tangy goat's cheese and walnuts.

Basic pizza dough

MAKES: 2 x 30 cm (12 in) pizzas
PREPARATION TIME: 20 minutes
COOKING TIME: 15 minutes

10 g (¼ oz) fresh yeast or
  5 g (⅛ oz) dried yeast or
  1 sachet easy-blend yeast
125 ml (4 fl oz) lukewarm water
225 g (8 oz) plain flour
½ teaspoon salt
1 tablespoon olive oil

1 Preheat the oven to 240°C (475°F, gas mark 9). Put a pizza tile, a layer of unglazed ceramic tiles or a flat baking sheet on the oven's top rack.
2 Dissolve the fresh or dried yeast in the lukewarm water. Put the flour into a large bowl with the salt and the easy-blend yeast, if using. Make a well in the centre, then add the oil and the yeast mixture or water. Stir the mixture first with a fork, then by hand, until a dough is formed.
3 Knead on a floured surface for around 5 minutes or until soft and smooth. Divide into two balls, put them on a floured board, cover with a clean cloth and leave to rise for 15 minutes or until doubled in volume.
4 Roll out one ball of dough on a floured surface, rolling it from the centre until you have a circle about 30 cm (12 in) in diameter. Flour a pizza paddle and put the pizza round on top. Or shape the pizza with your hands on a round, lightly oiled and floured tin, or press gently into a nonstick pizza pan.
5 Quickly add the topping (see right) and if you are using a pan, put it immediately into the hot oven. If you are using a pizza paddle give it a few shakes, back and forth, to be sure the dough is not sticking and then slide the pizza from the paddle onto the hot tiles or baking sheet with a sharp jerk. Bake the pizza for about 15 minutes.

If you want to make more than one pizza at a time, you can partially bake each one separately first for about 7 minutes with a thin layer of thick tomato sauce, if using, and set them aside. Then, when you need the pizzas, add the various toppings, and finish off the baking, together if you have room, or one at a time.

Pizza with onions, goat's cheese and rosemary

MAKES: 2 x 30 cm (12 in) pizzas
PREPARATION TIME: 40 minutes,
including making pizza dough
COOKING TIME: 45 minutes

Basic Pizza Dough (see recipe,
  above left)
25 g (1 oz) butter
2 tablespoons olive oil
4 large mild Spanish onions, thinly
  sliced
A pinch of sugar
Salt and black pepper
175 g (6 oz) firm goat's cheese,
  chopped
85 g (3 oz) walnuts, chopped
1 teaspoon very finely chopped
  rosemary

1 Heat the butter and oil in a large frying pan. Add the onions and sugar, season with salt and pepper and stir for several minutes.
2 Cover and cook over a gentle heat for about 30 minutes. Uncover and continue to cook until the onions start to take on a little colour. Taste and adjust the seasoning.
3 Preheat the oven to 240°C (475°F, gas mark 9). Make the pizza dough and leave it to rise for 15 minutes.
4 Roll out one ball of dough into a circle about 30 cm (12 in) in diameter. Spread half the onions over the pizza base and sprinkle with half of the cheese, walnuts and rosemary. Bake as for the Basic Pizza Dough recipe, about 15 minutes. Repeat with the remaining dough for a second pizza.

Mild Spanish onions add an attractive colour and delicious sweetness to this pizza baked with goat's cheese, walnuts and rosemary.

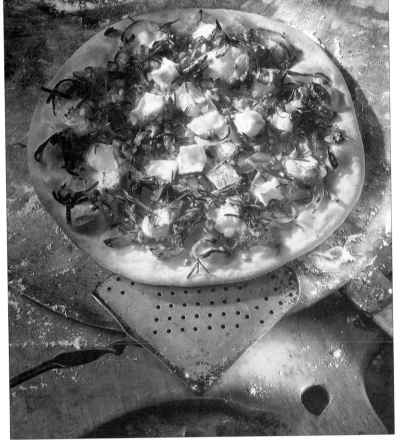

PLANTAIN

GOOD FOR COOKING

Is a plantain the same as a banana, and can I substitute bananas in savoury recipes?

Plantain, often known as green banana, is certainly a member of the banana family, but is bigger and coarser than the familiar dessert varieties. Ordinary sweet bananas are too soft to stand up to much cooking, and their sweetness can be quite cloying in savoury recipes, whereas the plantain is higher in starch, with less natural sugar.

In Britain, the plantain has long been available in the markets of cities with African, Caribbean and Indian communities, and it is now increasingly found on sale in super-markets. Plantains are quite simple to prepare: peel, slice then cook in salted water for 15–45 minutes, depending on ripeness. Then mash and serve with African, Caribbean, Indian or South American dishes.

A QUESTION OF RIPENESS

Does it matter whether the plantains I use in cooking are green or yellow-skinned?

Yes. Green plantains are consider-ably firmer. In addition, they often need to be peeled with a knife, take longer to cook and are less sweet and more vegetable-like than the riper yellow plantains. Never-theless, the sweetness of yellow plantain can be used to good effect in a lemony sweet-and-sour curry like the one featured on the right.

Spicy crisps

Green plantains make delicious spicy 'crisps' to serve with drinks. Peel them with a knife, cut into coin-thick slices and shallow-fry in hot oil. Drain on kitchen paper and sprinkle with salt and black or cayenne pepper. Serve hot.

Tropical spices such as cumin, turmeric and coriander lend savoury interest to the riper yellow variety of plantain in this highly flavoured curry.

Plantain curry

SERVES: 4
PREPARATION TIME: 10 minutes
COOKING TIME: 12 - 15 minutes

500 g (1 lb 2 oz) yellow plantain
1 ½ teaspoons coriander seeds
5 cloves garlic
1 teaspoon salt
1 small dried red chilli
2 teaspoons ground cumin
½ teaspoon ground turmeric
1 teaspoon mustard seeds
4 tablespoons vegetable oil
1 teaspoon sugar
Juice of ½ a large lemon
1 tablespoon shredded coriander leaves

1 Peel and cut the yellow plantain into 1 cm (½ in) slices.
2 Grind the coriander seeds roughly in a pestle and mortar, then add the garlic and salt, break in the chilli and grind. Mix in the cumin and turmeric and add 1 or 2 tablespoons of the water to make it into a paste.
3 Heat the mustard seeds in a wok or frying pan over a moderate heat, shaking and covering the pan when the seeds begin to pop. When the popping slows down, add the oil and the spice paste to the pan, and heat until the mixture begins to darken and release its fragrance.
4 Add the sugar, lemon juice, sliced plantain and 75 - 85 ml (2½ - 3 fl oz) of water, turning to coat the plantain with the spices. When the mixture starts to bubble, lower the heat, cover the pan and cook for 7 - 8 minutes, stirring gently occasionally to turn the plantain slices over.
5 When the plantain is quite tender, uncover the pan, raise the heat and cook the curry for 2 - 3 minutes, shaking the pan occasionally. When the sauce has reduced, serve the plantain curry sprinkled with some shredded coriander leaves.

PLUMS, DAMSONS, GAGES AND SLOES

PLUM JOBS

Which are the best plums to eat fresh and which need cooking?

Most plums can be eaten fresh; only a few are too tart to be eaten raw and are best used for cooking.

Dessert plums are at their best when they have a bloom on their skin and are plump and firm to the touch. Disregard any that are damaged, shrivelled or poor in colour.

Varieties to look out for include the British-grown Victoria plums (imported Victoria plums do not have as good a flavour), Coe's Golden Drop, Kirke's Blue and the Santa Rosa. Dessert varieties of plum, such as the greengage, can also be used for cooking if they are bought slightly underripe.

Of the cooking plums, damsons are the best known, especially for making jam with a deep, tangy flavour. Purple Pershore is another cooking variety, not usually found in supermarkets – look out for these in farm shops, or where you can pick your own fruit. The Mirabelle, a yellow variety of cooking plum, is a little smaller than a greengage and also very fragrant.

SKIM THE STONES

Is it necessary for me to remove the stones of the fruit when making plum or damson jam?

No. After the sugar has been added and the jam is brought to a full boil, the stones will rise to the surface and can be skimmed off easily with a slotted spoon. Remove the stones before potting the jam. This method applies to any stone fruit.

LUCKY FIND

What is the difference between plums and greengages?

The greengage is one of several varieties of plum. It is said to have been named after the Gage family of Hengrave Hall in Suffolk by their gardener, when an unlabelled tree from a collection imported from the Chartreuse monastery in Paris in the middle of the 18th century produced particularly fine fruit.

In France the greengage is called Reine Claude (it was named after the queen of Francis I). It is an old variety of plum, more tender and lavishly scented than others. Gages can be either this original green-skinned variety with green flesh, or the newer yellow-skinned gage with yellow flesh.

Gages are a dessert plum but also used for cooking. They are particularly good in French-style tarts, fruit pies and compotes but also make excellent preserves – try them in bottling and jam making.

WILD PLUMS

Are sloes and bullace both related to plums?

Yes, in that they are both native to Britain and members of the *Prunus* family. Bullaces are either purple or golden green, smaller than damsons and with softer skin. Although just sweet enough to be eaten raw, they are mainly used for cooking and jam making. They grow in hedgerows, as do dark purple sloes, the fruit of the blackthorn bush. Sloes are smaller than bullaces and have a flavour that is quite tart, but they are a good flavouring for gin (see SPIRITS). They can also be used for making chutney and jam.

POACHING

GENTLE COOKING

What is the difference between poaching and boiling?

Poached chicken or fish has a juicy tenderness not found in boiled food. For food to be poached it must be submerged, or partly submerged, in a flavoured liquid (such as syrup or stock), and cooked so that the liquid barely moves. It is an excellent method of cooking delicate foods such as fish or soft fruit.

Foods can be cooled in their poaching liquid, which stops them drying out, but the poaching pan should be stood in cold water so that the contents cool quickly. This is to prevent the food going bad, as it might if kept too long in a warm, steamy atmosphere.

Plum harvest (clockwise from top left): red Victoria plums, traditional green and newer golden gages, purple and gold bullaces, damsons and purple sloes.

PORK

SAFE STORAGE

Does pork go off quicker than other types of meat? If so, how should I store a Sunday joint of pork before cooking?

The only pork which might go off slightly quicker than other types of meat is very fatty pork, but most modern pork is so lean that there is no risk of the fat becoming rancid. In the past pork was particularly susceptible to being contaminated by trichinella cysts, rather than the usual food poisoning bacteria. But today modern husbandry and stringent inspection ensure that British pork is unlikely to be infected.

As with all meat, pork should be stored loosely wrapped in the coldest part of the refrigerator, where the temperature should be 0–5°C (32–41°F). If it is wrapped in a rigid plastic container with a sealed top, this should not be opened until required. Otherwise, discard the original wrapping from the meat, rewrap it loosely in greaseproof paper or foil, and put it on a plate to catch any blood that comes out of the meat. You can then keep the joint for two or three days. Always store raw meat well away from cooked foods in the refrigerator.

LESS FAT

When I tried grilling lean pork leg steak, it turned out tough. What's the best way to cook it?

Lean cuts, such as pork steaks, which do not have much natural fat, need some lubrication if they are not to be dry, tasteless and tough. This is best done by marinating them in oil and vinegar so that you replace some of the missing pork fat with a healthier fat. Add other ingredients to give extra flavour, such as fruit juice, wine or yoghurt, plus herbs or spices.

Pork leg steaks, or escalopes cut from a lean leg, can be first beaten and then quickly flash-fried.

WELL COOKED

How long should you fry or grill a pork chop to make sure it is cooked through?

It depends on the chop's thickness, shape and size, the temperature of the grill, and the temperature of the chop. For best results, meat should always be cooked from room temperature rather than straight from the refrigerator, so take it out of the fridge 5–10 minutes beforehand.

Allow 4–5 minutes a side for a chop that is 2.5 cm (1 in) thick and at room temperature before cooking. To test whether the pork is cooked, pierce the thickest part with the point of a thin knife or a fine skewer – when the juices run clear the meat is done.

Another way of cooking pork chops that takes longer, but is a reliable way of making sure they are well cooked, is to bake them, as in the recipe below. It also provides an opportunity to give the chops a strongly flavoured spinach and mushroom filling.

Pork chops stuffed with spinach and mushrooms

SERVES: 4
PREPARATION TIME: 25 minutes
COOKING TIME: 20 – 25 minutes

4 pork chops 4 – 4.5 cm (1 ½ – 1 ¾ in) thick, each weighing about 225 g (8 oz)
1 tablespoon oil
1 small onion, finely chopped
1 clove garlic, crushed
100 g (3 ½ oz) large flat mushrooms, finely chopped
350 g (12 oz) frozen leaf spinach, thawed
50 g (1 ¾ oz) full-fat soft cheese with garlic and herbs
1 teaspoon whole-grain mustard
1 tablespoon fresh breadcrumbs
Salt and black pepper

1 Preheat the oven to 180°C (350°F, gas mark 4). Cut a deep large pocket in each chop (see box, above).
2 Heat the oil in a frying pan, add the onion and garlic and fry until softened. Add the mushrooms and

STUFFING PORK CHOPS

As pork is becoming leaner all the time, a stuffing is useful to help keep the meat moist and tender while it is baking in the oven.

1 Trim off any excess fat from the chops, then cut horizontally into the fat side to make a pocket.

2 Pack the stuffing into the pocket you have made, then tie some string around the chop to hold in the filling during cooking.

continue to cook the mixture until the mushrooms are tender.
3 Drain the spinach and squeeze out as much water as possible. Stir into the frying pan and continue cooking for about 2 minutes.
4 Remove the pan from the heat and stir in the cheese, mustard, breadcrumbs and seasoning.
5 Divide the mixture between the pockets in the chops. Season the outside of the meat, then place the chops in a shallow baking dish and bake for 20 – 25 minutes.

VARIATIONS
Make an apricot-flavoured stuffing with a small onion, six reconstituted dried apricots, 2 tablespoons of pine nuts, 4 tablespoons of fresh white breadcrumbs, a clove of garlic and some fresh sage, chopped and mixed together. Or try prunes and walnuts instead of apricots and pine nuts.

DRY AND CRISP

How do you get perfect crackling?

Make sure the skin is completely dry and if necessary, remove any remaining hairs by singeing the rind with a flame or shaving it with a disposable razor. Just before roasting the joint, score the rind.

Carefully scoring the skin and fat of the pork joint at regular intervals before roasting it will help to give delicious, crispy pieces of golden crackling.

Rub the rind generously with salt. Cook the meat on a rack in a shallow roasting tin and refrain from basting it during cooking.

For crackling that is particularly crisp, remove the whole rind about 30–45 minutes before the end of cooking and continue cooking it beside the joint, as in the recipe below, which includes an unusual accompaniment of baked apples.

Roast leg of pork

SERVES: 6
PREPARATION TIME: 20 minutes
COOKING TIME: about 2 hours

*Fillet end of pork leg weighing
    about 2 kg (4 lb 8 oz)*
Salt
3 crisp dessert apples, washed
2 tablespoons lemon juice
2 tablespoons clear honey
6 small sprigs of fresh sage

1 Preheat the oven to 200°C (400°F, gas mark 6). Score the rind of the pork and rub it generously with salt.
2 Put the pork leg onto a rack in a shallow roasting tin and then roast it, without basting, for 55 minutes per kg (25 minutes per lb).
3 About 30–45 minutes before the end of the cooking, take the pork

Liven up a simple roast leg of pork with accompaniments such as apples baked with honey and sage, sugar snap peas and a parsnip and carrot purée.

out of the oven. Using a sharp knife, slice off the rind. Put the rind next to the pork on the rack and return them to the oven to finish cooking.
4 Halve and core the apples. Place the halves cut side down on the work surface and slice them thinly without cutting completely through.
5 Place each half on a square of foil and spoon over the lemon and honey. Add a sage sprig then bring up the edges of the foil and twist the edges together to seal. Place the parcels

on a baking tray and cook for 5–10 minutes, until the apples are tender. Test by opening one of the parcels and piercing the apple with a knife.
6 Transfer the pork joint to a warm carving plate and leave it to rest in the oven with the heat turned off and the door propped open, for about 10 minutes. Carve the pork, cut the crackling into pieces, and serve it with the baked apples, sugar snap peas, parsnip and carrot purée and gravy, if you care to make it.

POT-ROASTING

BAKED IN A POT

What is the difference between pot-roasting and roasting?

Pot-roasting is not really roasting at all, but an old, economical way of baking food in a pot, either over a low heat or in the oven. Roasting proper is a faster, dry method, used for cooking choice, tender cuts of meat, poultry and sometimes fish.

Pot-roasting is used for cheaper cuts that are cooked in their own juices and it could be considered a simpler version of braising. The meat is first browned in oil or butter to give a 'roasted' appearance and then cooked with little or no extra liquid in a casserole with a tight-fitting lid. Moisture from the meat provides the liquid during cooking, though with poultry, a few spoons of liquid are usually added after browning.

A traditional technique in pot-roasting is to cook the browned meat on a piece of pork rind. This adds flavour and richness, and prevents the meat scorching on the bottom of the pot. Coarsely cut root vegetables are sometimes put under the meat for the same purpose. They can be raw, or browned in the same fat as the meat, though the meat should be removed while you are browning the vegetables. When cooked, the vegetables are served alongside the meat.

For more tender and subtly flavoured meats, try this variation on pot-roasting that could be called 'gentle roasting'. Small cuts, such as best ends of lamb or even whole small birds, are seasoned, rubbed with butter and set on a bed of root vegetables in a deep pot with a lid. The lid is removed in the latter stages of cooking to brown the meat lightly, and a sauce is made by pouring off the fat and adding a good stock and some wine or spirit to the meat juices. The sauce is then simmered and thickened with arrowroot if necessary.

POTATOES

WHAT YOU SEE

Is there any way to tell simply by looking at a potato whether it will be waxy or floury?

Alas no, but retailers are increasingly offering advice as to the suitability of potatoes for various cooking methods. The new or first early varieties available in spring and summer are waxy and good for boiling to eat hot or in salads. Winter maincrop potatoes tend to be floury and good for mashing, but the red-skinned Desirée and Romano varieties and Santé, with its pale yellow skin and flesh, are firmer and better for boiling.

Good waxy potatoes to look for in winter are our home-grown Pink Fir Apple potatoes and Ratte, both of which have a fine flavour, and Charlotte or Belle de Fontenay, which are imported from France.

In early spring, before the welcome arrival of the first Jersey potatoes and later our own new potatoes, the Mediterranean varieties from Cyprus, Majorca and Egypt, are reliably waxy and good for salads such as the one below.

New potatoes in watercress and walnut vinaigrette

SERVES: 4
PREPARATION TIME: 10 minutes
COOKING TIME: 20 - 30 minutes

50 g (1 3/4 oz) walnut kernels
1 bunch watercress
4 spring onions
400 g (14 oz) small, waxy potatoes
3 tablespoons olive oil
2 tablespoons walnut oil
1 tablespoon red wine vinegar
Salt and black pepper

1 Crush half the walnut kernels in a mortar or food processor. Trim and chop the watercress and then finely shred the spring onions.
2 Wash the potatoes but do not scrape them. Leave the tiniest ones

whole but cut larger ones to the same size as the smaller ones. Cook in salted water until tender.
3 Put the crushed walnuts into a jar with the oils, vinegar, salt and pepper and shake it well to combine.
4 Drain the cooked potatoes. Shake the dressing again and toss it gently through the potatoes. Leave to cool.
5 Scatter the watercress and spring onions over the salad, toss again and then serve the salad scattered with the uncrushed walnut kernels.

SUPERB ROAST SPUDS

What is the secret of perfect roast potatoes, brown and crunchy outside and meltingly soft inside?

There are three golden rules to perfect, crunchy roast potatoes. First, choose a floury, maincrop variety such as King Edward, Maris Piper or, when you can get them, Golden Wonder or Kerr's Pink. Then parboil the potatoes for 5–7 minutes before roasting, shaking them gently in the pan after draining so that the outside surface becomes soft and flaky. This will allow them to absorb the fat better, essential for a good crust. Alternatively, you can rough up the surface of parboiled potatoes with the tines of a fork.

Roast the potatoes in meat fat rather than oil and start them in a little lard or dripping, adding fat from the joint as it collects in the roasting tin. Regular turning of the potatoes in the fat is important for a good crust – do this every 20 minutes, when you baste the meat.

It is a sad fact that there is no vegetarian alternative to perfect roast potatoes; oil tends to toughen the skins more than animal fats.

Temperature and timing are not crucial – both can be adapted to suit what is required for the meat the potatoes will accompany. If they are to go with small joints it may be advisable to start roasting the potatoes before the meat and allow at least an hour in all.

The most luxurious potatoes of all are those roasted in goose fat. Keep the fat from the tin in which you have roasted a goose or if you remove any solid fat from the bird before roasting, melt it slowly and then store it in a covered container in the refrigerator. Goose fat is also sold in cans, and you can save the surplus fat from a can or jar of Confit d'Oie (goose preserved in its own fat). Duck and pork fat are almost as good as goose fat. The recipe here for roasted potatoes is excellent with roast chicken.

Roast potatoes with a sesame seed crust

SERVES: 6
PREPARATION TIME: 20 minutes (while oven preheats)
COOKING TIME: about 1 1/2 hours

1 kg (2 lb 4 oz) floury maincrop
    potatoes, peeled
Salt
3 tablespoons sesame seeds
100 g (3 1/2 oz) lard, dripping, meat
    fat or vegetable fat

1 Preheat the oven to 200°C (400°F, gas mark 6). Cut the potatoes into evenly sized pieces then bring them to the boil in a large pan of salted water and keep at a low, rolling boil for 5 minutes. Drain and leave until cool enough to handle.
2 Pull the tines of a fork over the surface of each potato to score it. Roll each potato in sesame seeds.
3 Melt the fat in a large roasting tin in the hot oven. Turn the potatoes in the fat a few times then roast them for about 1 1/2 hours, turning the potatoes again every 20 minutes or so until they are brown and crispy.

FEWER CALORIES

Are there any low-fat fillings for baked potatoes that sink into the flesh instead of just sitting on top?

Sadly, no. It is fat that sinks into the flesh, softening it and giving flavour. Low-fat yoghurts or cottage cheese are just not as effective or as delicious as butter. However, there are some good fillings that turn a baked potato into a meal.
• A poached or a soft-boiled egg slipped inside a split baked potato makes a satisfying supper, as the

yolk spills nicely into the flesh. For a more elaborate treatment, spoon out the cooked potato flesh, then season and mash it. Separate a raw egg, beat the yolk into the mashed potato (with some cheese, too, if you like), then whisk the egg white firmly and fold in. Spoon back into the potato shells and return to a hot oven to rise soufflé-style.
• For vegetarians, baked potatoes can be topped with cucumber and celery in soured cream or yoghurt and sprinkled with chopped nuts.
• Smoked haddock in white sauce is good in baked potatoes, so is taramasalata with diced cucumber.
• Scoop out the flesh from split baked potatoes, then mash corned beef into it plus some chopped red onion. Spoon back into the shells, top with grated cheese and return to the oven to heat through and melt the cheese. Serve with hot beetroot or green vegetables.
• Baked potatoes to accompany a stew can be split and served with a spoonful of the meat juices or gravy to moisten and flavour them.
• Olive oil and mashed anchovy makes a pungent filling, or try soured cream with some chopped onion in it and a topping of caviar.

QUICK OR CRISP?

Why are potatoes baked in the microwave so disappointing?

It is not possible to truly bake a potato in a microwave oven. When a potato is properly baked, the heat of the oven reaches the skin first, drying it and sealing in the potato's natural moisture so that the flesh steams as the skin crisps. This delicious contrast of textures cannot be achieved in a microwave oven, which merely cooks the potato.
    You can bake small-sized baking potatoes relatively quickly, in about 30 minutes, in a hot oven; they will cook even quicker if you push a metal skewer through them. Alternatively, if you own a convection microwave, compromise and use the combination facility. For best results and to achieve a delicious contrast between crisp skin and

soft interior, rub the potato skins with sea salt while they are still damp from washing. Baked potatoes are done when you can press them and feel that the flesh inside is soft and yielding.

TWICE-COOKED POTATOES

What are the potato skins I see on restaurant menus, and can I make them at home?

Dishes based on potato skins are a good way for restaurants to make use of the skins left over from making mashed potatoes. It is time-consuming to make potato skins at home, but they are delicious.
    A good method is to bake potatoes in the oven until soft, let them cool, then cut them in half and scoop out most of the flesh. The skins can then be cut into pieces and shallow fried until crisp, or oven-roasted in a little oil until well browned. Serve with salsa, cheese or soured cream and chives.

SKINS ON

What is the best way to boil potatoes?

It is always best to boil potatoes in their skins, even if they are to be mashed. Not only does this help to prevent the flesh from absorbing too much cooking water, it also conserves vitamins which are concentrated in or just below the skin. Serve the potatoes whole in their skins or, for mashing, peel them as soon as the cooked potatoes are cool enough to handle.
    An alternative, particularly at the end of the season when they tend to absorb more moisture, is to oven-bake the potatoes in their skins and then mash them. This is a common practice commercially.
    It is always worth making extra mashed potatoes as the leftovers are very good for thickening soups, making potato scones, fishcakes, bubble and squeak or hashes, or for topping shepherd's and fish pies. Alternatively, blend leftover mashed potato into the following small, hot, savoury cheese puffs.

Whisked egg whites lighten this savoury mixture of cheese, potatoes and spring onions, which is cooked in bun tins.

Cheese potato puffs

SERVES: 4 - 6 as a snack, with salad garnish as a first course, or with fried sausages for supper
PREPARATION TIME: 20 minutes
COOKING TIME: 15 minutes

---

450 g (1 lb) mashed potatoes
4 spring onions, finely shredded
50 g (1 ¾ oz) mature Cheddar
   cheese, finely grated
3 tablespoons milk
25 g (1 oz) butter
Salt and black pepper
Grated nutmeg, to taste
2 eggs, size 1 - 2, separated

---

1 Preheat the oven to 220°C (425°F, gas mark 7) and generously butter a nonstick bun tin, also greasing the sections between the holes.
2 Mix the mashed potatoes, spring onions and cheese in a bowl.
3 Warm the milk and butter with salt, pepper and nutmeg, swirling the saucepan to help melt the butter. Heat to just below boiling point, then beat the milk into the potato mixture and beat in the egg yolks.
4 Whisk the egg whites to form soft peaks, mix a spoonful or two into the potato mixture to loosen it, then fold in the rest as lightly as possible.
5 Spoon the mixture into the bun tins and bake for about 15 minutes until golden brown and well risen.

HAND BEATEN

What is the secret of perfect mash with no lumpy bits? Can I use a blender or processor to keep my arms from aching?

No, unfortunately all electric tools seem to produce mashed potatoes with the gluey texture of wallpaper paste. The easiest way to a lump-free mash is some hard work with a potato masher, or to put the potatoes through a food mill. Additions such as olive oil, cream, butter and milk should be added while the potatoes are warm, along with seasonings of salt (try celery salt for a change), pepper and nutmeg. Vigorous beating is what lightens the mash and at the final stage you could possibly use an electric beater set on a slow speed.

As an alternative to mashing, try riced potatoes, positively lump-free. A potato ricer, available from catering shops and good kitchenware departments, looks rather like a giant garlic press and crushes whole, cooked potatoes, extruding them in a light snow.

Rice the potatoes directly into the serving bowl, adding butter and seasonings to the layers as you go. Riced potatoes can be reheated in their bowl, but stirring will sacrifice their lightness. You can mash or rice the potatoes for the light-as-a-feather gnocchi recipe overleaf.

Potato gnocchi in Gorgonzola sauce

SERVES: 4
PREPARATION TIME: 15 minutes
COOKING TIME: 30 - 40 minutes

500 g (1 lb 2 oz) King Edward or other floury maincrop potatoes
Salt
1 egg, size 2 - 3, lightly beaten
140 g (5 oz) plain flour
3 tablespoons milk
25 g (1 oz) butter
140 g (5 oz) Gorgonzola cheese, cubed
125 ml (4 fl oz) double cream
4 tablespoons finely grated Parmesan cheese
Black pepper and grated nutmeg
To garnish: basil leaves

1 Boil the potatoes in their skins in salted water, or bake in the oven until tender. Drain and skin as soon as they are cool enough to handle.
2 Mash or rice the potatoes and beat in the egg and most of the flour.
3 Spread the remaining flour thickly on a work surface and gently knead the potato dough on it, gradually incorporating all of the flour.
4 Divide the kneaded dough into two and lightly roll each section into a cylinder about 36 cm (14 in) long.
5 Cut each cylinder of dough into pieces 1.5 cm (generous ½ in) long. Flatten each one slightly with the tines of a fork to create some ridges.
6 In a small saucepan warm the milk, butter and Gorgonzola, stirring steadily, swirling the pan to melt the cubed cheese. Add the cream and half the Parmesan. Bring to the boil, season with pepper and nutmeg, reduce the heat and keep warm.
7 Heat a serving dish in the oven. Bring a large pan of water just to simmering point (do not let it boil). Cook the gnocchi in two or three batches, lifting them out using a slotted spoon 15 - 20 seconds after they float to the surface.
8 Transfer to the warmed serving dish and trickle some sauce over each batch, stacking them on the dish as they are cooked. Scatter over the remaining Parmesan and garnish the dish with basil before serving.

TROPICAL TUBERS

Is there a difference between a sweet potato and a yam?

Yes. Sweet potatoes and yams are members of two different botanical families. Sweet potatoes (*Ipomoea batatus*) come from the tropical areas of the Americas and have a distinctive sweetness, particularly the pink-skinned, orange-fleshed variety. There are also some sweeter white or yellow-fleshed varieties grown in the tropics.

Though sweet potatoes are native to tropical America, they also found their way to the Far East, and hot baked sweet potatoes are sold in winter on the streets of many Chinese and Japanese cities.

The yam (*Dioscorea*), is a large, brown-skinned starchy root that can weigh over 5 kg (about 12 lb). Its bland yellow or white flesh is a perfect partner for spicy stews in the parts of Africa, Asia and the Caribbean, where yams are a staple ingredient in cooking.

NICE AND SWEET

When I boil sweet potatoes, why do they sometimes go mushy and taste disappointing?

Sweet potatoes are less firm than ordinary white potatoes and lose much of their flavour into the cooking water when boiled. They also have a tendency to absorb a lot of water when cooked this way, making them heavy and soggy.

They are much better when they are baked like ordinary baked potatoes, although sweet potatoes will cook more quickly. Split them and serve oozing with butter, salt and plenty of black pepper or paprika. Baked sweet potatoes also tend to benefit from the addition of a little cinnamon and brown sugar. Try baking then mashing them to make a topping for shepherd's pie.

Sweet potatoes make very good chips, either deep-fried or oven-baked, and can be sliced thickly, brushed with butter and grilled, a treatment which is very good with venison steaks or duck breasts.

PRAWNS

RAW PRAWNS

I thought all prawns were sold already cooked; is this true?

Not always. Cold-water prawns are always cooked and you can buy them either still in their shells or peeled. Warm-water prawns are sold uncooked, either whole or as tails (without their heads). They are also sold cooked and shelled.

All the prawns we buy have been frozen, unless they are purchased straight from a fishing boat. They are often sold thawed and kept on ice to prevent them dehydrating.

Prawns which have already been cooked only need heating through when they are added to a dish.

WHOLE DELICACY

Peeling shrimps seems very fiddly. Is it always necessary?

Not always. One of the nicest ways to eat small brown or pink shrimps is as the French do: whole with French bread and unsalted butter. You bite off the whole body and eat it shell and all, discarding only the head. Shrimps must be peeled for potted shrimps, which are sealed under a thick layer of clarified butter (see recipe in PRESERVING).

NICE LOOKS, FINE TASTE

Is it better to buy large imported prawns for Oriental recipes?

It depends on the recipe you have chosen. If visual impact is important, the large sea-water prawns of South-east Asia, usually called giant or tiger prawns, and large Mediterranean prawns, look spectacular and are impressive grilled.

However, Britain's smaller cold-water prawns have a finer flavour. Use them in fish stews and curries where size is less of an issue, such as in the following recipe for Thai Prawn Curry. Here the prawn shells are also used to contribute to the flavour of the stock.

Thai prawn curry

SERVES: 4
PREPARATION TIME: 25 minutes
COOKING TIME: 30 minutes

700 g (1 lb 9 oz) cooked prawns
  in their shells
7.5 cm (3 in) root ginger
2 stems lemongrass, bruised and
  chopped
Salt
100 g (3 ½ oz) creamed coconut
  block, grated or chopped
1 onion, chopped
3 cloves garlic
1 teaspoon ground coriander
1 teaspoon ground cumin
1 teaspoon ground turmeric
3 tablespoons cooking oil
3 large green chillies, deseeded
  and shredded into long, thin
  strips
Juice of 1 lime
2 tablespoons chopped coriander
  leaves
To serve: boiled rice, prawn crackers

1 Shell the prawns and put the shells into a small saucepan. Peel the ginger and add the peel to the prawns. Set the remaining ginger aside.

2 Add the lemongrass and a little salt to the prawn shells with cold water just to cover. Bring to the boil and simmer the shells, uncovered, for 15 minutes. Strain the stock through a sieve, mashing the solids with a spoon to extract the flavour before you discard them.

3 Put the creamed coconut into a measuring jug and stir in enough hot stock to make 500 ml (18 fl oz). Stir the mixture to make a milk.

4 Put the onion, peeled ginger, garlic, coriander, cumin, turmeric and half the oil, plus 3 tablespoons of cold water, into a food processor and blend to a paste.

5 Put the remaining oil into a large pan. Add the chillies and spice paste, and stir-fry gently for 2 - 3 minutes until it becomes more aromatic.

6 Stir in the coconut milk and lime juice and cook the sauce at a low boil, stirring it regularly, for 10 - 15 minutes until the sauce has reduced and thickened. Add the prawns and cook just until they are hot through.

Choose full-flavoured cold-water prawns for this spicy blend of green chillies, coriander and coconut. Accompany the curry with rice and prawn crackers.

7 Adjust the seasoning and serve the prawn curry scattered with some chopped coriander and accompanied by rice and prawn crackers.

NEW IDEAS

I enjoy prawns in starters but would like a change from prawn cocktail. Have you got any ideas?

Prawns work very well with Oriental ingredients and can be quickly stir-fried or grilled on skewers with flavourings such as chilli, garlic, honey and soy sauce. A seafood kebab, perhaps with added bacon, is another way the flavour and colour of prawns can be highlighted.

Stirred with a few tablespoons of tomato-flavoured mayonnaise, prawns make a good filling for avocados or omelettes. Alternatively, scatter them over a fanned avocado half and serve with a vinaigrette dressing, or use in a salad with eggs, lettuce and tomato.

PRESENTATION

Simply presented food that looks fresh and uncluttered is what pleases the eye best. And since we look before we taste, we are predisposed to like a dish when it is presented attractively. Follow the simple guidelines given here: they will help you to make every meal a feast for the eye as well as for the tastebuds.

The first rule of presentation is: keep it simple. Even grand buffet pieces like whole salmons are more effective if the design is restrained and the fish is not buried under a garish jumble of cucumber curls and tomato water lilies.

Secondly, bear in mind that nothing looks sadder than tired food. Salads wilt when dressed in advance, sautéed potatoes become dull and dry when kept warm for hours, and whipped cream goes buttery in a warm room. The minor inconvenience of last-minute salad-tossing or dishing up is a price worth paying.

Thirdly, choose accompaniments and garnishes that are appropriate to the main dish. A sprig of watercress complements lamb cutlets because the texture, taste and colour all do something for the lamb. Sprigs of parsley, though the right colour, are scratchy and unpleasant to eat. Here are a few ideas to help you to present your food in the best possible light.

STARTERS

Small items of food such as canapés, sandwiches or sushi rolls look neat and professional if they are arranged in rows rather than dotted about the serving dish at random. Make each row of one variety, contrasting the colours.

Pâtés and terrines can look flat and colourless. If you want to serve individual portions, instead of one thick slice, cut three thin ones and lay them overlapping, to one side of the plate. Add a few dressed green leaves and the plate becomes colourful and attractive.

If you are serving a starter in a ramekin or cocotte dish, put a colourful plate underneath it so it does not look small and insignificant.

If you are serving smoked salmon or gravad lax, lay it on the plate slightly rumpled to give it a little height. Do not sprinkle it with lemon juice in advance as this discolours the fish and makes it spotty.

A bowl of soup can be garnished with a swirl of double cream or crème fraîche just

Small items such as canapés look most professional set out in neat lines, each of a different kind. Try tomatoes stuffed with pesto and ricotta; Parma ham and soft cheese pinwheels; prawn croustades; smoked halibut and salmon triangles; and filo pastry purses.

before serving: pour a small amount into the centre of the soup bowl and then gently stir it in with a teaspoon. Single cream is too thin and will bleed into the soup. Croutons, crumbled crispy bacon, finely chopped herbs and grated cheese are other suitable garnishes for soup. Remember not to overfill the soup bowl to avoid unattractive slops on the way to the table.

MAIN COURSES

There is a fashion, spurred on by the example set by chefs, for serving main courses on the plate. Remember that the chefs have the time, the space and the experience to get it right, and don't attempt too much if you are a novice.

Do not try to serve dishes on the plate for more than six people or the food is likely to get cold. Sketch out a rough design with the various elements at 12 o'clock, 3 o'clock and so on around the plate so you know exactly where to put what. Make sure your plates are hot and

A starter of feta cheese, watercress and watermelon will look more imposing if the small plate sits on a larger one.

smear-free before you begin. If you are serving roast meat, do not cut the slices too thin. Odd numbers of slices look better than even, and should be overlapped to add height. Carefully pour the sauce over the meat using a small ladle, pouring away from you and ending in a puddle of sauce at the top of the plate. Have ready some dampened kitchen paper to wipe away spills. Add the vegetables and any garnish and carry the plates to the table, setting each plate down in the same relative position for each diner.

If you prefer to use serving dishes, consider the needs of individual foods. Sliced meats, chops and steaks look best overlapping evenly, and more will fit comfortably on the serving dish than if placed side by side. Round slices of meat, or chicken breasts, look particularly good laid in concentric circles. With steaks or cutlets of fish or meat, the side that was grilled or fried first usually looks best and should be laid uppermost.

Think about serving all the food on a single large platter rather than on two or three smaller ones. If you are serving grilled chicken joints with roast vegetables, for example, they will look more dramatic if you pile the vegetables into a large colourful dish and put the chicken on top, with no unsightly bones sticking out and served on its best side.

Pasta needs only simple presentation, but should not look as if you have simply shoved it onto the dish. Get ready by warming your serving dish in advance and mixing the pasta and sauce in the saucepan. Then pile it into the warm serving dish, or onto individual plates, creating height in the centre, and arrange one or two of the sauce ingredients on the top so everyone knows what they are about to eat. Shavings of Parmesan cheese made with a vegetable peeler look better than grated cheese.

Oven-to-table dishes are a blessing to the home cook, but even the most delicious casserole looks off-putting if it is served in a dish with burnt-on spills. Keep a hot cloth to hand to wipe off any dribbles and perhaps sprinkle freshly chopped herbs over the dish before you carry it in.

A dish of vegetables looks at its best if the food is higher in the middle with the sides sloping down. Coat carefully with the sauce if there is one. But do not overload the plate,

Lamb chops look best sitting on the sauce, not under it. Two vegetables, of different colours, are sufficient.

because this makes dishing up the vegetables difficult and, once breached, an over-large pile of food looks unattractive.

DESSERTS

Desserts lend themselves to attractive decoration, but you must be careful not to make them look fussy. Plated cold desserts are useful if you have room in your refrigerator as they can be done in advance, leaving only the final garnish to add before serving.

If your dessert has a sauce and you want to flood the plate with it, put a ladleful in the centre of the plate and swirl the sauce towards the edge in an even circle. It is then ready for you to place the dessert on top, remembering that once done it will be difficult to move it, so think where you want to put it first. Very often it will look better, and be easier to position, if you place it off-centre, with a decoration to the side.

Fruit tarts and tartlets look more inviting if they are first glazed with warmed apricot or redcurrant jam. Alternatively, for a quicker but effective finish that covers a

multitude of sins, dust the tart on the serving plate using icing sugar and a fine sieve.

Finally, when setting out a number of items, such as lamb cutlets on a plate or rosettes of cream on a cake, odd numbers look better than even. This is especially true of small numbers: three and five almost always look better than four.

A dessert such as this plum custard tart looks prettiest placed slightly off centre, with a small garnish of the fresh fruit on one side.

PRESERVING

PRESERVING IN OIL

I love red peppers preserved in oil; is it safe to preserve my own?

Vegetables preserved in the Mediterranean fashion, using olive oil, are safe provided you take strict precautions as there is a slight risk of botulism with food preserved in oil. Botulism is caused by a bacteria that lives in the soil; it does not penetrate the vegetable, but could be present in any soil particle clinging to it and thrives in the absence of air. So foods to be preserved in oil must first be washed carefully. Any that grow underground, such as garlic, are most at risk of being contaminated.

After washing, the foods must be processed in some way to remove their excess water, otherwise they will deteriorate. Baby artichokes are cooked in a vinegar solution; aubergines are salted then cooked in a vinegar solution; mushrooms can be dried or cooked; olives are salted; peppers are roasted; and tomatoes are dried.

Even after the foods have been processed, it is important to bring all the ingredients to boiling point. A squeeze of lemon juice or splash of vinegar, which are acidic, also lowers the risk of contamination. Commercial preparations, such as sun-dried tomatoes in oil, are all ultra heat treated (UHT).

Always use sterilised jars (see CHUTNEY) and seal them tightly, and store the preserves in the refrigerator, for no more than two months. Refrigeration may cause the oil to solidify, but it will clear again when left at room temperature. Once the preserve has been eaten, the flavoured oil can be used for drizzling over bread or salads, or for basting grilled meats and fish.

Unlike vegetables, cheese does not need cooking before being preserved; feta and goat's cheeses are favourites for preserving in this way, as the following recipe shows.

Goat's cheese with herbs

MAKES: 2 × 750 ml (1 pint 7 fl oz) preserving jars
PREPARATION TIME: 10 - 15 minutes
COOKING TIME: none

---

750 g (1 lb 10 oz) fresh, firm
   goat's cheese
½ teaspoon finely crushed
   black peppercorns
4 teaspoons herbes de Provence
Whole peppercorns, sprigs of herbs
   and 1 - 2 bay leaves, optional
750 ml (1 pint 7 fl oz) olive oil
150 ml (5 fl oz) walnut oil

---

1 Cut the cheese into 2.5 cm (1 in) chunks. Sprinkle over the crushed peppercorns and herbs and pat them lightly onto the cheese. Transfer the cheese into sterilised jars, adding more peppercorns, mixed herbs and a bay leaf or two if you like.

2 Mix the olive and walnut oils well, then pour over the cheese, making sure it is completely covered.

3 Seal the jars tightly and store them in the refrigerator. Eat the cheese within a month. Take the jars out of the refrigerator about an hour before you are ready to serve the cheese to bring it to room temperature.

POTTED FOR STORAGE

What exactly are potted meats?

Potting is a technique in which cooked meat, fish and shellfish are preserved in fat in small earthenware pots or glass jars. The meat or fish is usually spiced and then puréed or finely chopped before potting. It is then encased in clarified butter or fat to exclude air and moisture, which would encourage the growth of bacteria. Unopened

Herb-dusted goat's cheese preserved in olive oil brings a touch of sunshine to the table. Mixed peppercorns, sprigs of herbs and bay leaves add extra piquancy.

jars can be stored in the refrigerator for up to a fortnight depending on the meat or fish used. Once the fatty seal has been broken, eat within one or two days.

Although most potted meat or fish is puréed, brown shrimps are often left whole, as in the recipe below. If you cannot get brown shrimps, use the larger pink ones and chop them roughly.

Potted shrimps

SERVES: 4
PREPARATION TIME: 5 minutes, plus 1 - 2 hours cooling and chilling
COOKING TIME: 15 minutes

300 g (10 ½ oz) unsalted butter
350 g (12 oz) small brown shrimps, or prawns, cooked and peeled
½ teaspoon ground mace
A generous pinch each of cayenne pepper and freshly grated nutmeg
A pinch of salt

1 Melt 175 g (6 oz) of the butter in a saucepan. Remove from the heat and leave to stand for a few minutes to allow the sediment to settle. Pour off the clear liquid into a clean pan, leaving as much of the sediment as possible in the first pan.
2 Stir the shrimps or prawns and the spices into the clarified butter, cover and heat gently for 10 minutes to allow them to soak up some of the spiced butter. Check the seasoning and sprinkle on some salt to taste.
3 Put an equal amount of shrimps and clarified butter into four sterilised ramekins and set them aside to cool thoroughly. When completely cold, chill until the butter is firm.
4 Melt the remaining butter, let it stand for a few minutes to allow the sediment to settle and pour the clear liquid over the shrimps to seal. Leave to cool, then chill once more until the butter is completely set. Cover with foil or cling film, then store in the refrigerator for up to two weeks.
5 Before serving, leave the mixture to soften at room temperature for about 30 minutes. Serve the potted shrimps with thinly sliced buttered brown bread, Melba toast or warm soda bread, and lemon wedges.

FRENCH PRESERVES
What are rillettes?

Rillettes are a type of preserved meat. The meat is gently cooked in fat, strained, shredded into a coarse pâté, packed into jars and covered with a fresh layer of fat. Originally from south-western France, rillettes may be made from pork, goose, rabbit, or even hare, though pork is the most common. Rillettes will keep for a month unopened in the refrigerator, and improve in flavour during that time. Eat with French bread and small pickled gherkins.

PUMPKINS AND SQUASHES

SEASONAL VARIATIONS
How do you cook squashes?

This large family of vegetables has both summer and winter varieties. Summer squashes such as courgettes, marrows and the small patty pan squashes generally have thin, green or yellow skins and moist, subtly flavoured white flesh. They need only light steaming, grilling or shallow-frying and a sprinkling of salt, pepper and fresh herbs.

Winter varieties, which range in size from small acorn squashes to enormous pumpkins, have dense yellow or orange flesh within their hard skins. They respond well to vigorous flavours. Add chunks to a meat or vegetable casserole, or use in well-spiced, thick winter soups, such as the one that follows.

Scoop out the seeds and fibre of small winter squashes, then cut up and peel the flesh for adding to soups and stews.

Spiced butternut and millet soup

SERVES: 6
PREPARATION TIME: 20 - 25 minutes
COOKING TIME: 35 minutes

1 kg (2 lb 4 oz) butternut squash or other winter squash or pumpkin
3 tablespoons cooking oil
1 large onion, finely chopped
2 - 3 cloves garlic, finely chopped
5 cm (2 in) piece of ginger, grated
2 dried red chillies, crumbled
2 bay leaves
1 teaspoon mustard seeds
1 teaspoon cumin seeds
50 g (1 ¾ oz) millet
Salt and black pepper
3 tablespoons tomato ketchup
Juice of ½ lemon
2 teaspoons garam masala
To garnish: 1 bunch watercress, chopped

1 Cut the squash in half, remove and discard the seeds and fibre, chop the flesh into chunks and peel them.
2 Heat the cooking oil in a deep pan and fry the onion, garlic, ginger and chillies over a low heat for 5 minutes.
3 Add 1.7 litres (3 pints) of water to the pan. Grate in the squash and add the bay leaves. Bring to the boil and simmer for about 10 minutes until the squash is soft, then mash it well.
4 Dry-fry the mustard, cumin and millet over a moderate heat until the millet looks mildly toasted and the mustard seeds have mostly popped.
5 Tip the spiced millet into the soup, sprinkle on some salt and simmer for about 15 minutes until the millet is soft. Remove from the heat and leave to stand for at least 10 minutes.
6 When you are ready to serve the soup, remove the bay leaves and stir in the ketchup, lemon juice, garam masala and a generous sprinkling of pepper. Reheat, stir in the watercress and serve with hot bread.

VEGETABLE PASTA
What is spaghetti squash?

Spaghetti squash, sometimes also called vegetable spaghetti, looks like a yellow-skinned marrow with a harder rind. When it is cooked and split open the flesh falls into a mass of tangled strands. To cook it, break off the stem and pierce that end deeply to stop the squash bursting during cooking, then boil or bake for about 40 minutes until the flesh feels tender when pierced with a skewer. Split the squash lengthways and fork out the flesh. Dress with a meat or tomato-based sauce as you would pasta.

YOUNG, TENDER MARROW

A neighbour occasionally gives me one of his home-grown marrows, but I can't find any interesting recipes for them. Can you advise?

Marrows are often allowed to grow too large, and end up watery and bland. Smaller marrows, measuring less than 30 cm (12 in), have much more flavour. They can be stuffed with rice or minced meat and baked in a moderate oven for 30–45 minutes, or cut into small pieces, gently fried in olive oil with some garlic and sprinkled with parsley. Large marrows can be made into well-spiced and fruited chutneys or combined with ginger to make a surprisingly good jam.

SWEET AND FILLING

What vegetables go best with squash and pumpkin?

A green vegetable, such as spinach or leek, would balance the sweet flavour of squash and pumpkin. In the Americas squash is often combined with other vegetables for a thick, filling stew, and the following recipe uses three ingredients to come from the New World: squash, sweetcorn and tomatoes. Serve it with bread or as an accompaniment to grills or roast meat.

Native American trinity

SERVES: 6
PREPARATION TIME: 25 – 30 minutes, plus 30 minutes soaking for beans
COOKING TIME: about 2 hours

200 g (7 oz) dried haricot beans, soaked in boiling water for 30 minutes
3 tablespoons olive oil
2 onions, finely chopped
1 teaspoon dried oregano
1 large butternut squash, weighing about 800 g (1 lb 12 oz)
2 green chillies, deseeded and finely chopped
500 g (1 lb 2 oz) tomatoes, peeled and chopped
2 cobs of corn
Salt and black pepper
3 tablespoons chopped parsley

1 Drain the soaked beans, put them into a pan of fresh water, bring to the boil and cook fast for 10 minutes. Drain and put the beans into fresh water, bring to the boil then simmer for a further 1 hour 20 minutes or until tender. Drain and set aside.
2 Heat the oil in a large saucepan, add the onions and oregano and cook over a low heat for about 10 minutes, stirring them regularly.
3 Cut the squash into quarters and cut away and discard the central seeds and fibre. Peel the flesh and cut it into 2.5 cm (1 in) cubes.
4 Add the cut-up squash, chillies and 125 ml (4 fl oz) of water to the onions in the pan. Cover and leave to simmer for 10 minutes.
5 Add the tomatoes and simmer, covered, for a further 20 - 25 minutes, until the squash is very soft and the tomatoes have reduced to a sauce.
6 Pull away the husks and silk from the corn cobs. Strip off the kernels with a strong, sharp knife, holding the cobs upright on a board and cutting downwards.
7 Add the corn and drained beans to the stew and simmer gently for a further 5 minutes. Season, sprinkle with chopped parsley and serve.

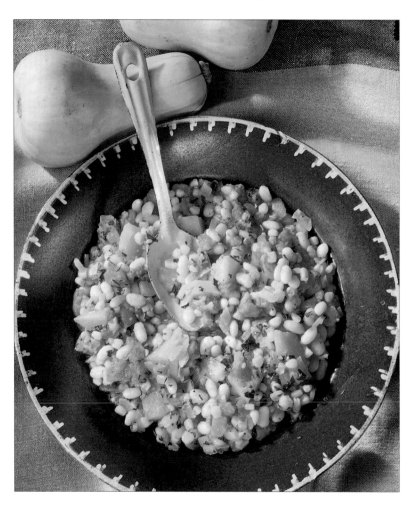

Tuck into a filling vegetarian stew of squash, tomatoes, corn and beans, spiced up with green chillies and herbs.

PUNCH

WELL-MIXED DRINK

How much punch should I allow per person, and what will the alcohol content of each glass be?

When punch is served as a welcoming drink to arriving guests, one or two 225 ml (8 fl oz) glasses will be sufficient. If punch is to be the only alcoholic drink served, guests will probably drink three to four glasses each. But because most punches are sweetened, people tend not to go on drinking them all night, usually preferring to switch to wine, beer or spirits, given the chance.

The alcohol content will depend on whether the punch is made with wine alone or has added spirits, and on how much – or how little – the alcohol has been diluted. Note that a cold punch, such as the one below, will be more intoxicating than a hot one made with the same amount of alcohol, as some of the alcohol will have cooked off the hot one during the heating.

Chilled, as above, or mulled, this fruity and powerful punch is welcome at any time of the year. Cinnamon and cloves spice the blend of brandy, rum and wine.

Chilled wine punch

SERVES: 8 glasses
PREPARATION TIME: 30 minutes, plus 3 hours chilling time
COOKING TIME: 5 minutes

1 large orange
2 large lemons
600 ml (1 pint) water
140 g (5 oz) granulated sugar
7.5 cm (3 in) stick cinnamon
4 cloves
175 g (6 oz) fresh pineapple, cubed or cut into wedges
150 ml (5 fl oz) brandy
150 ml (5 fl oz) rum
1 lime, thinly sliced
750 ml (1 pint 7 fl oz) full-bodied red wine, such as a Fitou, chilled
12 ice cubes

1 Wash the orange and lemons under warm running water. Pare the rind of the orange and one of the lemons finely, then squeeze and strain their juice. Thinly slice the other lemon.

2 Pour the water into a stainless-steel or enamel pan. Add the orange and lemon rind, sugar, cinnamon and cloves and stir over a moderate heat until the sugar has dissolved, then bring to the boil and boil for 2 minutes. Take the saucepan off the heat, cover and allow to cool. When cold, chill for 3 hours.

3 Put the pineapple into a jug. Add the orange and lemon juice, brandy, rum and the lemon and lime slices, and stir well. Cover the jug with cling film and chill.

4 One hour before serving, strain the spiced sugar syrup through a nylon sieve into the jug. Pour in the wine, stir and chill. Just before you serve the punch, add the ice cubes.

VARIATIONS

For an alcohol-free version, use the juice of two lemons instead of one, and 1 litre (1 pint 15 fl oz) of grape juice instead of wine and spirits.

For a hot punch, allow the sugar syrup to infuse at room temperature for an hour then strain it into a large saucepan. Add all the remaining ingredients, stir well and heat until the punch becomes very hot, but do not allow it to boil. Serve in punch cups or heatproof glasses.

If you do not have any heatproof glasses, put a metal teaspoon into ordinary glasses before pouring the hot punch: the metal will absorb the heat and prevent the glass cracking.

COCKTAIL EGGS

What is the difference between eggnog and egg flip?

Eggnog is a very rich, chilled punch made with egg, sugar, whisky (or rum and whisky), milk and cream (or all cream), with the egg whites whisked separately and folded in. In the United States, it is traditionally served at Thanksgiving and Christmas, topped with grated nutmeg. Egg flip is a much simpler drink: a whole egg is mixed with sugar and some wine or spirit, and is then strained into a glass and topped with grated nutmeg. It can be made with brandy, gin, Madeira, port, rum, vodka or whisky.

WINTER WARMER

What is a hot toddy?

It is a hot drink made from whisky, brandy or rum and boiling water, with or without added spice, sugar, lemon or orange rind and juice.

Hot toddies are normally thought of as a remedy for colds and flu, but they make a wonderful warming drink to have on any chilly evening. You certainly should not wait until you get a cold to make the following toddy.

A twist of lemon and a cinnamon stick add a sharp bite to sweet hot toddy, the ultimate alcoholic winter warmer.

Hot toddy

SERVES: 2
PREPARATION TIME: 5 minutes
COOKING TIME: none

---

90 ml (3 ¼ fl oz) brandy, whisky or rum
2 teaspoons soft dark brown sugar
2 teaspoons runny honey
2 cinnamon sticks, each measuring about 7.5 cm (3 in)
A strip of thinly pared rind and strained juice of 1 lemon or orange
600 ml (1 pint) boiling water

Pour the spirit into two heatproof glasses. Add a teaspoon of sugar, a teaspoon of honey and a cinnamon stick to each glass. Cut the rind in half and add a piece to each glass. Divide the juice between the glasses and top up with boiling water. Stir and serve immediately.

PUREES

VEGETABLE VARIATIONS

I love parsnip purée. Can you give me some ideas for other interesting vegetable purées?

Almost any cooked vegetable may be puréed, and the resulting dishes are often lighter, and more attractive and sophisticated than the whole ingredients. First cook the vegetables, either by boiling, steaming, roasting, frying or sweating, then purée them in a food processor or blender, or work them through a sieve. Season well and beat in some butter, cream, white sauce or another vegetable purée.

You can create some interesting combinations, but cook the vegetables separately to retain their full flavour, then purée each individually before mixing together. Some purées, for example carrot, celeriac or spinach, can be rather wet; drive off the excess moisture by cooking them gently while stirring, or add a little mashed potato to stiffen. Purées reheat very well and can be made in advance. Try some of the following combinations:
- BROAD BEAN with butter and chopped fresh summer savory.
- CARROT with pepper, sugar and a touch of grated ginger.
- CAULIFLOWER AND POTATO with a light sprinkling of curry powder, or with cream and nutmeg, baked in a dish with a cheese topping.
- CELERIAC AND POTATO with an added trickle of rich truffle oil.
- MUSHROOM AND ONION mixed with breadcrumbs and baked in scooped-out tomatoes.
- PEAS with sweated onion, garlic, mint and sugar.
- PUMPKIN or squash with garlic, pepper and soured cream.
- SPINACH with nutmeg and double cream, heated to reduce it a little.
- SWEETCORN AND POTATO, mixed with egg and grated cheese and fried as pancakes.
- TURNIP, CARROT AND POTATO with butter and garlic.

QUAIL

TINY TREAT

Quail are so tiny, are they really worth preparing and eating?

The flesh of quail is pale and delicate, and is certainly worth trying. The birds, which are tender and juicy, weigh 115–150 g (4–5½ oz) each. They look small but, like pigeon, have a lot of meat on the breast. Some people find eating whole quail very fiddly, and some butchers and supermarkets are selling part-boned quail, ready for stuffing or already stuffed, which makes them a bigger mouthful. These part-boned quails have the breast bone and rib cage removed but have the legs intact so that when stuffed they will retain the original shape of the bird.

WORKING OUT PORTIONS

How many quails should I allow per person as a main course - or are they simply unsuitable for a main course?

A boned stuffed quail would serve one person, as there really is quite a lot of meat on the breast. However, if not stuffed, allow two per person as a main course. It is worth being generous as quail is equally delicious served cold as a leftover.

Quails are suitable for roasting, casseroling, grilling and barbecuing (most chicken recipes will suit them), and will cook in 25 minutes. Serve them with a rich, wild mushroom sauce and a purée of potato mixed with mashed parsnip or carrot, or golden potato croquettes.

QUENELLES

SOFT AND TENDER

What are quenelles?

Traditionally, quenelles were small portions of savoury fish mousse, poached in stock or plain water and served as a starter or light meal. The term is now occasionally used for sweet confections, but is usually reserved for savoury mixtures of fish, poultry or vegetables. In the recipe below, delicate spinach and cheese quenelles are served on a robust tomato sauce.

When cooking quenelles, it is important to poach them gently so that they will not break up. They are traditionally shaped like an elongated rugby ball with a flat bottom, but they can also be made in a simpler egg or sausage shape.

Spinach and ricotta quenelles

SERVES: 6 as a starter
PREPARATION TIME: 20 minutes, plus infusing time
COOKING TIME: 10 minutes

FOR THE QUENELLES
175 g (6 oz) spinach
225 g (8 oz) ricotta cheese
50 g (1 ¾ oz) Parmesan cheese, finely grated
1 egg, size 3
Salt and black pepper
A pinch of freshly ground nutmeg

FOR THE SAUCE
150 ml (5 fl oz) virgin olive oil
2 cloves garlic, flattened but not crushed
8 plum tomatoes, peeled, deseeded and finely chopped
1 bunch basil, finely chopped, reserving a few leaves for garnish
Salt and black pepper

1 To make the sauce, gently heat the oil and garlic together in a pan. Before the oil gets very hot, remove it from the heat and leave to infuse for 10 minutes - 1 hour, depending on how strong you want the flavour.

2 To make the quenelles, rinse the spinach, put it into a pan with no added water and cook for 3 minutes. Drain well, pressing out as much liquid as possible, and chop finely.
3 Put a large pan of salted water to heat and bring up to simmering point. Mix the spinach, cheeses and egg together in a bowl and add salt, pepper and nutmeg to taste.
4 Using two dessertspoons, form the mixture into 12 ovals resembling small Cornish pasties. Lower them gently into the barely simmering water until the pan is comfortably full (poach two batches if you need to). Poach them very gently until they float back up to the surface, in about 3 - 4 minutes. Remove from the pan with a slotted spoon, drain off any excess liquid, and keep warm.
5 To complete the sauce, remove the garlic from the oil. Stir in the tomato and basil and season to taste.
6 Pour the sauce onto six plates and lay the quenelles on top. Garnish with the reserved basil and serve.

QUINCES

MYSTERIOUS FRUIT

What are quinces, and what can you do with them? Can you buy them in the shops, or do you have to grow them yourself?

The large, golden-yellow, apple or pear-shaped quince is thought to have originated in western Asia, although it is now also grown in Europe. It has yellow flesh that is slightly tart and turns pink when cooked. Because the flesh is too hard to eat raw, quinces must be cooked for about 45 minutes in a sugar syrup. They can be eaten as plain poached fruit or used as a pie filling. Quinces are very high in pectin, so are ideal for jam and jelly making. Quince jelly is an excellent accompaniment to pork, poultry and game, or cold meats.

When they are in season, in late September and October, quinces can be bought from good greengrocers and large supermarkets.

QUINOA

HIGH-PROTEIN SUPERGRAIN

I have recently seen a food I did not know called quinoa. What is it, and how is it cooked?

Quinoa is a small grain indigenous to South America. It has a very high protein content, which has led to it being described as a 'supergrain', but you might find its flavour slightly bitter. When cooked, the grains swell to double their size.

Quinoa makes a good substitute for rice, can be added to stuffings, served in a salad (as in the recipe, right) or sweetened with sugar as a breakfast cereal. It tends to become soggy when cooked immersed in boiling water. It is best to soak the grains for a few hours, preferably overnight, and then steam them for 8–12 minutes depending on how long they have been soaked.

Spiced quinoa salad with grilled peppers

SERVES: 4
PREPARATION TIME: 20 minutes, plus overnight soaking
COOKING TIME: 25 minutes

225 g (8 oz) quinoa
2 large red or yellow peppers
90 ml (3 1/4 fl oz) olive oil
1 onion, chopped
1 clove garlic, crushed
1 small red chilli, deseeded and chopped
1 teaspoon ground coriander
1 teaspoon ground cumin
1/2 teaspoon ground cinnamon
2 tomatoes, peeled, deseeded and chopped
2 tablespoons red wine vinegar
2 tablespoons chopped fresh coriander
Salt and black pepper

1 Wash the quinoa, then transfer it to a bowl, cover it well with cold water and leave to soak overnight.

2 The next day, grill the peppers for about 15 - 20 minutes, turning them often until charred all over. Transfer them to a dish, cover and set aside until cool enough to handle.

3 While the peppers are under the grill, drain the quinoa and transfer it to a muslin-lined steamer. Cook it, covered, over simmering water for about 10 minutes until the grains are puffed up and tender, then set aside.

4 Heat 2 tablespoons of the oil in a frying pan and fry the onion, garlic, chilli and spices for 5 minutes until tender. Transfer to a bowl and stir in the tomatoes and quinoa.

5 Peel and deseed the peppers over a bowl to catch the juices. Chop the flesh and stir it into the quinoa, then add the pepper juices, the rest of the olive oil, the vinegar and chopped coriander, and season to taste. Serve warm or allow to cool.

Protein-rich quinoa is the basis for an aromatic salad, where the grain's slight bitterness is balanced by sweet peppers.

QUORN

MEAT SUBSTITUTES

Is Quorn the same as TVP, and if not, what is the difference?

No, they are not the same. TVP, or textured vegetable protein, is derived from soya flour and resembles tofu, which is soya bean curd. (See also TOFU and TVP.)

Quorn is a newer foodstuff called a mycoprotein, made from a commercially grown fungus. Oxygen, nitrogen, glucose, minerals and vitamins are added and the resulting fungal mycelium is mixed with egg white to bind it. Colouring and flavouring may be added and the mycoprotein can be textured like meat before it is diced or shredded.

Quorn is low in fat, low in calories and cholesterol-free. It is used in manufactured ready-meals and is on sale from supermarket chill counters. While it does not need to be cooked, it is best used as a meat substitute in mixtures such as the one below, where it takes on flavours from the other ingredients.

East meets West in a Quorn stir-fry: soft cubes of this meat substitute contrast with crunchy vegetables and cashew nuts in a soy and sherry sauce.

Stir-fried Quorn

SERVES: 4
PREPARATION TIME: 20 minutes
COOKING TIME: 8 minutes

4 tablespoons cooking oil
2 sticks celery, sliced
2 cloves garlic, crushed
5 cm (2 in) piece of ginger, grated
350 g (12 oz) Quorn pieces
100 g (3 ½ oz) unsalted cashew nuts
1 small red pepper, deseeded and thinly sliced
200 g (7 oz) bean sprouts
125 g (4 ½ oz) Chinese leaves, finely shredded
6 spring onions, sliced diagonally
3 - 4 tablespoons soy sauce
4 tablespoons dry sherry
Black and cayenne peppers

1 Heat the oil in a wok or wide pan and stir-fry the celery, garlic, ginger, Quorn and cashews until the Quorn and nuts are patched with brown.

2 Add the red pepper, bean sprouts, Chinese leaves and spring onions to the Quorn mixture in the wok and toss them about. Mix the soy sauce and sherry together and pour over the vegetables, stirring.

3 Cover the wok and cook over a brisk heat for 3 - 4 minutes until the Chinese leaves are just beginning to wilt, then season with black and cayenne peppers. Serve with steamed rice or other grain.

VARIATION
If you have a bit of time to spare, marinate the Quorn before stir-frying it with the vegetables. Mix the soy sauce and sherry together and add a dash of lemon or lime juice if you like. Toss the Quorn in this sauce and leave it to marinate for about an hour. When you are ready to cook it, drain the Quorn over a small bowl and reserve the marinating liquid, then use this for the stir-fry sauce as above.

QUORN VERSUS TOFU

Is Quorn better or more suitable for cooking than tofu?

Not really. Although the texture of Quorn may be preferable in some dishes, tofu (soya bean curd) is more versatile: the creamy version, silken tofu, can be used in sauces, dips and desserts; a block of firm tofu can be cut into chunks or slices to be deep-fried, sautéed or added to salads and casseroles.

NOT QUITE VEGETARIAN

Is Quorn an acceptable foodstuff for all vegetarians?

To enable Quorn to hold its shape, the vegetable protein is bound with whites of battery eggs, which is not acceptable to all vegetarians, and the Vegetarian Society has withheld approval for this reason. The product does not fit into a vegan diet.

RABBIT

PORTION SIZE

How much meat is there on a rabbit? How much do I need to buy to feed four people?

A medium-sized farmed rabbit will weigh around 1.25 kg (2 lb 12 oz) and will serve up to three people. If you want to serve four generously, allow 350 g (12 oz) of meat on the bone for each person. If you cannot find a large enough rabbit, cook two small ones, or buy extra joints. Wild rabbits are usually slightly smaller than farmed ones.

STRENGTH OF FLAVOUR

How can I make the most of the strong flavour of rabbit?

Farmed rabbit does not have a strong taste at all but tastes rather like chicken and can be cooked using most chicken recipes. Rabbit also cooks very well in a chicken brick where it will benefit tremendously by being cooked with strong flavourings such as garlic, herbs, onions, red wine and tomatoes. Mustard is another good partner, as the recipe on the right shows.

Wild rabbit, however, has a more gamy flavour and is better suited to long, slow, gentle cooking with strongly flavoured sauces. As wild rabbit tends to be dry, it is wise to marinate it in ingredients such as olive oil, red wine and herbs for at least 4 hours before cooking.

Tender fresh rabbit makes a warming casserole with shallots, fresh thyme and a creamy French mustard sauce.

Mustard rabbit

SERVES: 4
PREPARATION TIME: 10 minutes, plus 1 hour marinating
COOKING TIME: 1 ½ hours

1.25 - 1.5 kg (2 lb 12 oz - 3 lb 5 oz) rabbit joints, skinned
4 tablespoons Dijon mustard
600 ml (1 pint) dry white wine
1 bay leaf
2 teaspoons chopped fresh thyme
60 g (2 ¼ oz) butter
12 shallots, skinned and quartered
300 ml (10 fl oz) double cream or crème fraîche
Salt and black pepper
2 tablespoons chopped fresh parsley

---

1 Spread the rabbit joints with half the mustard, then cover and leave them to marinate for at least an hour.
2 Preheat the oven to 220°C (425°F, gas mark 7). Place the rabbit pieces in a shallow flameproof casserole (it is not necessary to add any oil) and roast, uncovered, for 30 minutes.

3 Remove from the oven and turn it down to 180°C (350°F, gas mark 4). Pour the wine over the rabbit and stir well to loosen any sediment. Add the bay leaf and thyme, bring to the boil, cover and return the casserole to the oven for 30 - 40 minutes, or until the meat is very tender.
4 Meanwhile, in a separate pan, melt the butter and fry the shallots until golden. Set aside.
5 With a slotted spoon, remove the rabbit from the casserole, put it on a warm serving dish, cover and keep warm while you make the sauce.
6 Bring the casserole juices to a boil and cook for 10 minutes or until reduced by half. Lower the heat and stir in the shallots, the remaining mustard and the cream. Simmer the sauce for 10 minutes, or until it has thickened, then remove the bay leaf. Season, stir in half the parsley and pour over the rabbit.
7 Sprinkle the dish with the rest of the parsley then serve with buttered noodles and steamed broccoli.

RADISHES

LOOK AT THE LEAVES

Which are the best radishes?

Radishes are at their best during their natural season, summer. They can be red and round, or elongated and white-tipped. The latter are widely preferred for their peppery crunchiness. Solid red radishes can be good if they are not too bloated.

Choose bunched radishes with their leaves attached, as the leaves are a good indicator of freshness. Radishes can be sliced thinly over a green salad, but are perhaps best served in the French manner, as a first course with French bread, unsalted butter and flaky sea salt. They also go well with charcuterie.

VERSATILE DAIKON

What is daikon? How is it used?

Daikon is a variety of radish and tastes similar to the red varieties. Also called mooli, white or winter radish, in size and appearance it is more like a slim parsnip.

Peel and grate or shave it into very thin slices to eat raw in salads. Serve daikon as a hot vegetable by cutting it into slices or chunks, sprinkling it with salt and draining it for 30 minutes to remove some of the harshness. Then steam or simmer it until tender and, while still warm, toss it with butter or olive oil.

RASPBERRY: see SOFT FRUIT

Save it!

Radishes that are just beginning to become soft can be firmed up by a short soak in a bowl of iced water. But if the radishes are very limp, starting to wrinkle and losing their lustre, they are beyond redemption.

RAVIOLI

SIMPLE BUT NECESSARY

Do ravioli need a sauce?

Ravioli, even with a fairly robust stuffing, do benefit from being served with a sauce, as otherwise they can be rather dry. The sauce need only be as simple as melted butter to which you have added a few chopped fresh sage leaves, or it can be a combination of cream and butter melted together. This can be made richer with a little cheese, such as Gorgonzola, which has a very pungent flavour and creamy texture. A light tomato sauce is also good and goes with most stuffings. The hearty ravioli in the recipe below, however, stuffed with butternut squash, have enough flavour in themselves to need only a simple sauce of melted butter and some freshly grated Parmesan cheese.

Ravioli stuffed with butternut squash

SERVES: 4 – 6
PREPARATION TIME: 1 hour
COOKING TIME: 10 minutes

FOR THE FILLING
450 g (1 lb) butternut or acorn
   squash, peeled, deseeded and diced
50 g (1 ³/4 oz) Parmesan cheese,
   freshly grated
1 egg yolk, size 3
¹/2 teaspoon freshly grated nutmeg
1 tablespoon fresh white
   breadcrumbs
¹/2 teaspoon salt
Black pepper

FOR THE PASTA
350 g (12 oz) homemade pasta
   thinly rolled into sheets (see PASTA)
To serve: melted butter and freshly
   grated Parmesan cheese

1 Steam the squash for 5 minutes or microwave it until tender. Drain and press out as much liquid as possible.
2 Put the squash in a bowl and mix it with the cheese, egg yolk, nutmeg, breadcrumbs, salt and pepper.

FILLING RAVIOLI

Making your own fresh ravioli with homemade pasta is easy once you have mastered the technique.

1 Lay a sheet of pasta on the work surface and place half-teaspoons of filling at 5 cm (2 in) intervals.

2 Brush around the filling with water before laying a second sheet of pasta over the top.

3 Press down between the mounds of filling with the side of your hand and cut the sheets into squares using a special fluted pastry cutter.

3 Depending on the size of your pasta sheets, you can either make two rows of small ravioli or one row of bigger ravioli. Fill the ravioli as shown in the box above.
4 Cook the ravioli uncovered in a large saucepan of boiling salted water for about 5 minutes or until tender. Remove with a slotted spoon and serve with melted butter and grated Parmesan cheese.

VARIATION
Make pumpkin ravioli by replacing the squash with pumpkin which you have steamed, microwaved, or baked, skin side up, at 190°C (375°F, gas mark 5) for about 20 minutes, or until the skin is soft. Scoop the flesh away from the skin with a spoon. If the pumpkin is too soft, add a tablespoon of dried breadcrumbs to the filling mixture to make it firmer.

LEAKPROOF RAVIOLI

If I increase the size of my ravioli, are they more likely to fall apart while they are cooking?

If you seal the edges of your ravioli well, by using water and pressing the edges together firmly, it will help to keep them intact and the size should not make any difference. It is also helpful to roll the pasta as thin as you can and use a fairly thick stuffing. You can always add a few dried breadcrumbs, if necessary, to firm up the filling.

The most usual size for ravioli, and the most practical, is 4–5 cm (1½–2 in) square. If possible, have the salted water gently boiling in a wide shallow pan and cook the ravioli uncovered. When they are ready, carefully remove them with a slotted spoon rather than roughly turning them out into a colander.

INSIDE INFORMATION

Could you suggest some simple fillings I could make for ravioli?

A popular Italian combination that will fill 350 g (12 oz) of pasta is made with 300 g (10½ oz) of fresh spinach and 150 g (5½ oz) of ricotta cheese, 2 tablespoons of grated Parmesan cheese and ½ teaspoon of salt. Wash the spinach and cook it covered, with only the water that is still clinging to the leaves, for 5 minutes. When cool, squeeze out as much liquid as you can and chop finely. Mix with the other ingredients and then use. Any leftovers can be used to stuff large, ripe tomatoes or flat field mushrooms and then baked in the oven.

Another simple filling is made with 150 g (5½ oz) of ricotta, 40 g (1½ oz) grated Parmesan cheese, an egg yolk and 2 tablespoons of finely chopped parsley, all mixed together. If you have any left over once the ravioli have been filled, the mixture can be made into patties or small sausage shapes and gently fried in a little olive oil that has been heated with a garlic clove.

REDCURRANT: see SOFT FRUIT

REFRIGERATORS

NEVER ENOUGH

What is the best way to choose and use a new refrigerator?

Buy the largest model that you can afford and that will fit into your kitchen; you can never have enough refrigerator space. Models that defrost automatically are a tremendous bonus, as are frost-free ones where cold air is constantly circulated so frost is never deposited.

• The ideal internal temperature of a refrigerator is 4°C (40°F). Some models have different temperature zones to store different foods. For example, the fruit and vegetable section has a higher temperature than the area for meat.

• Most kitchens have only one refrigerator, so it is important that you observe some basic rules of elementary hygiene.

• Always store raw meat and fish on the bottom shelf so that if there are any drips or leaks they will not contaminate food stored below it.

• Cover all food, to avoid cross-contamination. This will also stop strong-smelling food from tainting any other foods stored nearby.

• Do not put hot food into the fridge, it warms up the interior and encourages any bacteria to breed. (See also FOOD POISONING.)

HOW TO CHILL

If a recipe says to chill something after cooking, how can I do this as safely as possible?

Food cools more quickly when fresh air can circulate around it, so do not leave it to cool in its hot cooking vessel covered with a tightly fitting lid. Transfer the food to a cold dish and cover it loosely with a kitchen cloth until cold, or put a large upturned bowl over it. If you want to stop it drying out or prevent a skin from forming, put wet greaseproof paper, which is thin enough not to hinder cooling, flat on the surface of the food. Do not wrap hot food in cling film, as this can leave spaces between the food and the film which create pockets of hot air where the climate is ideal for bacteria to breed.

Cool casseroles and large pans of food fast by standing the container in a bowl of ice or cold water or stand the bowl in the sink with the cold tap running to keep it cool.

RHUBARB

LIGHT AND DARK

What is the difference between the pink rhubarb we buy early in the year and darker rhubarb?

Bright pink, early forced rhubarb is tender and considered to be superior in quality and flavour to later maincrop rhubarb, which is grown outdoors, is far tougher and has a stronger flavour. Maincrop rhubarb often has a stringy covering that is best peeled and discarded.

Forced rhubarb is available from the end of December until the end of March and is produced using horticultural techniques that have hardly changed since the Victorian times. The plants are grown outside for two to three years and are then replanted in huge sheds and grown in the dark, because with too much light, the stems would not be so pale and fragile. As the stems are so tender, early rhubarb does not require stringing: simply cut off the leaves and the root end of each stalk, then wash them and cut into pieces ready for cooking.

When buying rhubarb at any time look for firm, bright stems and avoid those that are clearly limp, bruised or split. The part of the plant that we eat is the leaf stem (rhubarb is actually a vegetable and not a fruit) and when it is limp, can be refreshed by standing the stems, root end down, in cold water.

It is imperative that you always remove and discard the leaves from rhubarb. They must not be eaten as they contain oxalic acid and are extremely poisonous.

PINK AND SWEET

I know rhubarb is usually made into a tart, but is there any other way of making it into a pudding?

The following stately pudding is a brilliant combination of rhubarb and cooking apples. During late summer, when the first British cooking apples are available, you will still be able to find some slender stalks of pink rhubarb. In the early spring you can make the charlotte with forced rhubarb and imported or stored apples.

Rhubarb charlotte

SERVES: 8
PREPARATION TIME: 1 ½ hours
COOKING TIME: 1 - 1 ¼ hours

1 kg (2 lb 4 oz) trimmed rhubarb,
   cut into 2.5 cm (1 in) pieces
300 g (10 ½ oz) demerara sugar
1 kg (2 lb 4 oz) cooking apples,
   peeled, cored and sliced
175 g (6 oz) granulated sugar
225 g (8 oz) white breadcrumbs
125 g (4 ½ oz) unsalted butter
1 level teaspoon ground cinnamon
1 level tablespoon icing sugar
To serve: whipped cream

1 Preheat the oven to 180°C (350°F, gas mark 4).
2 Put the rhubarb and 225 g (8 oz) of the demerara sugar into a heavy-based, stainless-steel or nonstick saucepan and cover with a tightly fitting lid. Put the sliced apples with the granulated sugar into a similar, separate saucepan. Cook them both over moderate heat for about 25 - 30 minutes until both fruits have been cooked enough to soften, but have not completely broken up. Stir them occasionally to prevent sticking. (The apples will not exude much juice as they cook but the rhubarb will.)
3 Meanwhile, put the breadcrumbs on a baking tray and dry them in the oven, without browning, for 10 - 15 minutes. Stir them gently with a fork occasionally. Remove the crumbs from the oven and set aside to cool.
4 Put two large nylon sieves over two large bowls. Pour the cooked rhubarb into one of the sieves and

the apples into the other then leave the fruit to drain for 20 minutes so that the juice drains off, but the fruit does not become too dry.
5 Mix the drained rhubarb and the apples together gently and set aside. Pour the rhubarb juice into a jug and reserve to serve as a sauce.
6 Melt the butter in a large frying pan, add the dried breadcrumbs and cook them over a gentle heat, stirring constantly, until they turn a golden brown colour. Take the breadcrumb mixture from the heat and stir in the cinnamon and the remaining sugar.
7 Butter a 20 cm (8 in) round, spring-clip cake tin and line the base with a circle of baking paper. Spread a third of the buttered crumbs in the bottom of the tin and spoon on half of the fruit mixture. Add another third of the crumbs and then the remaining fruit. Cover the charlotte with the rest of the crumbs.
8 Place the cake tin on a baking tray and cook in the centre of the oven for 50 minutes - if the crumbs start to overbrown, cover the cake

tin loosely with foil. Remove the charlotte from the oven and allow it to cool for about an hour to room temperature before serving it or, alternatively, allow it to cool then cover and chill it overnight.
9 Run a palette knife around the charlotte to loosen it from the tin, then open out and remove the side of the cake tin. Put the charlotte on a flat serving plate and sift the icing sugar evenly over the top. Cut the charlotte into wedges and serve it on individual plates.
10 Thicken the rhubarb juice with a tablespoon of arrowroot blended with 2 tablespoons of cold water. Put the sauce into a jug to serve with the charlotte. Pass around a bowl of whipped cream to accompany.

LESSEN LEAKS

Why does my rhubarb pie always leak all over the oven?

Rhubarb has a high water content and exudes considerable juice as it cooks. To help prevent the juice

Buttery toasted breadcrumbs with dark brown sugar and cinnamon form crunchy layers for a charlotte of pink rhubarb and tangy cooking apples.

overflowing, toss the cut rhubarb in a little flour before putting it into the pie dish: the flour will thicken the juice as the pie cooks and help to keep it contained. Use a level tablespoon of plain flour to each 500 g (1 lb 2 oz) of prepared fruit, and mix it with the sugar before tossing with the rhubarb.

Also, when making the pie, ensure that the pastry edges are well sealed. Make a small hole in the top of the pie to let the steam escape – this will prevent the steam forcing the sealed edges apart and will allow some of the juice to evaporate. Always stand the pie dish on a baking tray to catch any juice that could overflow and burn on the bottom of the oven.

RICE

UNSTICKING THE GRAINS

What do I do if I lift the lid and find my rice has stuck together?

Transfer the rice to a large sieve and rinse it thoroughly with boiling water over the sink. Shake off the excess liquid, return the rice to the saucepan, cover and leave undisturbed for 5 minutes. Remove the lid, fork through the rice and serve. If you like, the rice can be enriched with a few tablespoons of butter. Stir it in gently so that the rice does not turn sticky. As the butter melts, it will colour and coat the rice.

EASY PERFECTION

Is there a fail-safe method for cooking light, fluffy rice?

There are many different types of rice grown all over the world and each of them requires a slightly different method of cooking. If you use more than one type of rice in the kitchen, you may have to experiment to find the exact proportion of rice, water and cooking time that works for each variety as they all have different absorption qualities. The following recipes for cooking white and brown rice are

very reliable. The most widely available variety of rice is American long grain. White rice has been polished to remove the outer husk. Brown rice is considerably more nutritious as the outer layer of bran is left on the grain, adding valuable fibre and more vitamins and protein to the diet than white rice.

Perfect white rice

SERVES: 4
PREPARATION TIME: 2 minutes
COOKING TIME: 15 minutes, plus
10 minutes standing time

250 g (9 oz) white long-grain rice
A pinch of salt

1 Put the rice into a heavy-based saucepan (you will need one with a tight-fitting lid), add 500 ml (18 fl oz) of cold water plus the salt and bring the pan to the boil. Stir the rice once, return it to a gentle simmer, then cover and simmer it over a very low heat for 10 minutes.
2 Remove the pan from the heat but do not remove the lid. Leave the pan undisturbed for 10 minutes, then remove the lid, fork through the rice and serve it immediately.

VARIATIONS
If you are using white basmati rice, put the rice in a deep bowl and add plenty of cold water. Drain off the water and repeat this process four or five times until the water in the bowl is clear, then drain off all the water. When you are cooking white basmati rice, boil it for only 8 minutes before letting it sit for another 10 minutes.

Perfect brown rice

SERVES: 4
PREPARATION TIME: 2 minutes
COOKING TIME: 35 – 40 minutes

250 g (9 oz) brown rice
Boiling water, for topping up the
 saucepan as necessary
A pinch of salt

1 Place the rice in a large saucepan, cover with 500 ml (18 fl oz) of cold water and add the salt. Stir the rice once to prevent it from sticking to the bottom of the pan.

2 Bring the rice to the boil and then simmer it, uncovered, for 30 - 35 minutes, or until the rice is cooked through, adding more boiling water if the pan becomes too dry. When the rice is cooked, drain and serve.

PRESTEAMED RICE

Is easy-cook rice really easy?

Easy-cook rice, which is sometimes called parboiled or prefluffed rice, is steamed before it is milled. The whole grain is steamed under pressure, which hardens it so that it will not break down during cooking.

Easy-cook rice cannot be overcooked and the grains will always remain separate. But in general, this rice is considered inferior in taste to ordinary long-grain rice varieties because some people find the texture unpleasantly chewy.

There are, however, some nutritional benefits to this process: all the mineral and vitamin content of the outer layers of the grain that are normally removed in the milling process are pushed into the centre of the grains. This applies to both brown and white easy-cook rice.

INDIAN SPECIALITIES

Which is the best rice to serve with an Indian curry?

In India two main types of rice are used to accompany curries. The rice chosen will depend on the region, the dish and the occasion.

Basmati rice, the most superior, grows in the foothills of the Himalayan mountains in both India and Pakistan. It is often served on special occasions because of its lovely aromatic flavour. Basmati is usually aged for a year in order to develop its special fragrance before sale. It is therefore relatively expensive.

All-purpose long-grain rice, usually the patna variety, is used in many Indian dishes where herbs, spices and other flavourings may be added to the rice for extra flavour. Whenever possible, spend a little more and use basmati rice, which is widely available in both brown and white varieties.

WHEN TO RINSE

Some books say you should wash all rice, some say never wash it. Which of these is correct?

The reason for washing rice is to remove any excess starch from the grains; it is the starch in the grain that gives the rice a sticky quality, so whether or not you need to wash it will depend on the type of rice you use and the recipe.

Basmati rice needs to be washed before cooking in plenty of water. Stir the rice well then drain off the cloudy water. Repeat until the water that runs off the rice is clear.

Risotto, on the other hand, needs starch to give a creamy texture to the finished dish so risotto rice should never be washed.

All-purpose long-grain rice is processed and does not generally need washing, though it may need to be soaked if the cooking method in the recipe requires it.

STIRRING STORY

Why are you warned not to stir rice while it is cooking?

Stirring rice while it is cooking makes it more sticky as the action releases the starch in the grain. You should only stir rice once, at the beginning of cooking, to prevent it from sticking to the bottom of the pan. However, when you cook a risotto, which needs to be sticky, it is important to stir the grains continually, which releases the starch as the rice cooks and absorbs the liquid in which it is cooking.

NOT THE SAME

Are risotto and pilau the same dish with different names?

No, there is very little similarity between risotto and pilau dishes, although both are savoury and often combined with a mixture of meat or fish, spices and vegetables.

The Italian risotto is authentically made with a long, large-grained Italian rice called superfino, a variety that includes the arborio and canaroli rices, though a fino rice called vialone, a long and tapering grain, is also used. These can be found in well-stocked delicatessens and some supermarkets.

Risottos, such as the one on the right, are cooked in a heavy-based pan to which simmering stock is added a little at a time. The rice is stirred continually as it cooks so that it absorbs the liquid, becoming creamier and stickier as the starch in the grain is released. The risotto is cooked when the rice grains have swollen to about three times their original size and are still slightly crunchy in the centre.

Pilau is Indian in origin although many Middle Eastern and North African countries cook pilaf, which is similar. The rice (usually basmati) for a pilau or pilaf should be washed and then left to soak in plenty of cold water for an hour or so before cooking to remove the excess starch and soften the grains, so that they do not stick together. The rice is first fried in butter or oil, then as soon as the liquid is added the rice is left undisturbed until the grains are cooked through.

Pilaf can be cooked either in a pan on top of the stove, as in the recipe overleaf, or in a casserole dish in the oven, with the ingredients arranged in layers so that they cook evenly. In either case, use a pan with a tight-fitting lid.

Simple basil risotto

SERVES: 4
PREPARATION TIME: 5 minutes
COOKING TIME: 35 - 40 minutes

---

4 tablespoons olive oil
1 onion, chopped
2 cloves garlic, crushed
350 g (12 oz) Italian risotto rice
1.2 litres (2 pints) chicken or
* vegetable stock*
150 ml (5 fl oz) white wine
50 g (1 ¾ oz) Parmesan cheese,
* freshly grated*
2 tablespoons double cream
4 tablespoons chopped fresh basil
Black pepper

---

1 Heat the oil in a deep frying pan or large saucepan, fry the onion and garlic until soft but not coloured, then add the rice. Continue frying for a minute, stirring all the time, until the rice is translucent and each grain is well coated in oil.
2 Bring the stock up to a steady simmer. Add the white wine to the rice and boil until reduced. Add a ladleful of the simmering stock to the rice, stirring constantly over a low heat until the liquid is absorbed.
3 Continue adding the stock to the rice, one ladleful at a time, and stir constantly for about 25 minutes until the rice is al dente. Just before serving, stir in the Parmesan cheese, double cream, basil and pepper.

MAKING AN ITALIAN RISOTTO

Start the risotto by gently frying first the flavouring ingredients and then the rice. Stir the rice until it is transparent and then begin to add the stock, which should be just simmering and close by the pan so that it can be added easily.

1 Add the simmering stock a ladleful at a time, stirring constantly until most of the liquid has been absorbed. Then repeat with the remaining stock.

2 After about 25 minutes, when the risotto has thickened and the rice is cooked but al dente, quickly stir in the Parmesan cheese and basil.

Layered pilaf

SERVES: 4
PREPARATION TIME: 20 minutes,
plus 30 minutes soaking and
15 minutes standing time
COOKING TIME: 55 minutes

250 g (9 oz) long-grain rice
50 g (1 ¾ oz) raisins
2 tablespoons olive oil
500 g (1 lb 2 oz) lamb, diced
1 onion, chopped
2 cloves garlic, crushed
2 carrots, diced
2 sticks celery, sliced
2 teaspoons ground mixed spice
25 g (1 oz) almonds, blanched
    and lightly toasted
850 ml (1 pint 10 fl oz) lamb or
    chicken stock
To garnish: toasted pine nuts or
    flaked almonds, and chopped
    coriander, mint or parsley

1 Soak the rice and the raisins,
separately, in water for 30 minutes.
Drain the rice and rinse it under
running water until the water runs
clear. Drain the raisins and set aside.
2 Heat the oil in a frying pan and
fry the lamb over a high heat for a
few minutes until browned. Remove
from the pan to a plate.
3 Fry the onion, garlic, carrots,
celery and mixed spice in the pan
for 5 minutes. Add the raisins and
almonds to the pan and stir well.
4 In a straight-sided, heavy-based
saucepan, stir a quarter of the rice
into the meat. Add a layer of one-third
of the vegetables, then one-third of
the remaining rice, and repeat the
layers ending with a layer of rice.
5 Bring the stock to the boil. Pour it
slowly down the side of the pan.

*When making pilaf, pour the stock
down the side of the pan carefully to
avoid disturbing the layers.*

6 Cover the pan and cook, without
stirring, over a low heat for 35 - 40
minutes until the liquid is absorbed.
7 Remove the lid and cover the pan
with a layer of foil. Replace the lid
and allow the pilaf to sit undisturbed
for another 15 minutes. Invert onto a
serving dish. Sprinkle pine nuts or
flaked almonds over the top of the
pilaf and finish with a scattering of
chopped parsley, mint or coriander.

WARM UP

*How can I keep rice fluffy if it has
to be kept warm for some time?
And can I heat up leftover rice?*

One of the best methods of keeping cooked rice warm is to put it in
a large heatproof dish or platter,
fork it through well, cover it with a
tent of foil and keep it warm in a
preheated oven at 140°C (275°F, gas
mark 1) until ready to serve.

Leftover rice can be steamed in a
muslin-lined steamer for 5 minutes
or so, stirring regularly until it is
hot through, or put into a large pan
of boiling water, brought back to
the boil and drained immediately.
Alternatively, stir-fry the rice for a
few minutes or heat it in a microwave just before serving.

CALCULATING QUANTITIES

*Should I allow the same amount
of rice per person for different
dishes, or does it vary?*

As an accompaniment to a curry or
a stew, 60–85 g (2¼ – 3 oz) of rice
per person is the accepted norm.
A rice salad for two people will
require a greater quantity of rice, as
much as 115 g (4 oz) per person.

For a risotto or a paella, such as
the one on the right, where the rice
makes up the greatest part of the
dish with extra meat, fish and vegetables added, the quantity of rice
required could also be as much as
115 g (4 oz) per person. In Spain the
rice traditionally used for paella is a
creamy variety from Valencia. It is
not easy to find outside the region,
although some supermarkets and
specialist food stores stock it. You
can use arborio rice instead.

Seafood paella

SERVES: 4 - 6
PREPARATION TIME: 40 minutes
COOKING TIME: 1 ½ hours

225 g (8 oz) large raw
    Mediterranean prawns
850 ml (1 ½ pints) fish stock
A pinch of saffron strands
4 tablespoons olive oil
1 large onion, chopped
1 large red pepper, deseeded and
    chopped
2 cloves garlic, crushed
1 small red chilli, deseeded and
    chopped
2 teaspoons paprika
350 g (12 oz) Valencia or arborio
    rice
150 ml (5 fl oz) dry white wine
225 g (8 oz) skinless cod fillet,
    cubed
12 fresh mussels, scrubbed
225 g (8 oz) squid, cleaned and
    sliced into rings
115 g (4 oz) frozen peas
2 tablespoons chopped fresh parsley
Salt and black pepper
To garnish: lemon wedges

1 Shell and clean the prawns, then
put the prawn heads and shells into
a saucepan with the stock. Bring to
the boil, cover and simmer for 30
minutes. Strain the stock, add the
saffron strands and set aside.
2 Heat the oil in a large wide frying
pan and fry the onion, pepper, garlic
and chilli for about 5 minutes. Add
the paprika and rice and stir-fry for 2
minutes. Pour in the wine and boil
rapidly until evaporated.
3 Reheat the stock until simmering,
then add 150 ml (5 fl oz) to the rice
and simmer gently, uncovered, for 10
minutes or until absorbed. Add the
remaining stock to the pan and leave
to simmer for 20 minutes, stirring
occasionally. Add extra stock or hot
water if the pan becomes too dry.
4 Add the prawns, cod, mussels,
squid and peas to the pan. Cover the
pan loosely with foil and cook for a
further 10 - 12 minutes or until the
rice is tender, the liquid is absorbed
and the seafood is cooked through.
Sprinkle the top with parsley, season
and garnish with lemon wedges.

NO ORDINARY RICE

What makes wild rice different from ordinary rice?

Wild rice is actually not a rice at all. It is an aquatic grass with thin black grains that is indigenous to Canada and the northern United States.

Wild rice absorbs four times its volume of liquid during cooking and takes longer to cook than ordinary rice; anything from 35–60 minutes. It has an intriguing nutty flavour and is extremely nutritious as it contains all nine of the essential amino acids. Wild rice is also a good source of fibre, is gluten free and low in calories and cholesterol.

In the following recipe for an exotic salad inspired by the exciting flavours of Californian cooking, wild and white rice are combined with fresh crab meat and diced papaya. If you use a freshly cooked crab then you will need one weighing about 1.3 kg (3 lb). Reserve the brown meat to use in another dish. Some fishmongers will sell vacuum packed fresh crab meat or frozen crab meat. You could also use well-drained canned white crab meat.

Another unusual, colourful rice is the red rice from the Camargue region of France, which is stocked by health food stores and specialist food shops. Cooked in the same way as brown rice, it has a distinctive flavour that makes it a good alternative to wild rice in recipes.

Wild rice salad with crab and papaya

SERVES: 6
PREPARATION TIME: 15 minutes
COOKING TIME: 40 minutes

---

85 g (3 oz) wild rice
115 g (4 oz) white long-grain rice
100 ml (3 ½ fl oz) extra virgin
   olive oil
1 clove garlic, crushed
2 tablespoons lime juice
½ teaspoon clear honey
Salt and black pepper
450 g (1 lb) white crab meat
1 ripe papaya, deseeded and diced
1 small red onion, thinly sliced
50 g (1 ¾ oz) flaked almonds, very
   lightly toasted
2 tablespoons finely chopped
   fresh coriander

---

1 Cook the wild rice for 35 – 40 minutes in plenty of boiling water until just tender. Meanwhile, cook the long-grain rice separately in salted water for 12 – 15 minutes.
2 In a small bowl, combine the oil, garlic, lime juice, honey, salt and pepper to make the dressing.
3 Drain the cooked rices and mix together in a bowl, then add the crab meat. Stir in the dressing and leave the mixture to cool.
4 Add the papaya to the rice and crab mixture along with the onion, almonds and coriander. Stir until well combined and serve at once.

VARIATIONS

Use Camargue red rice, boiled for 35 – 40 minutes, instead of wild rice. Or replace the fresh coriander with mint, chervil, wild garlic leaves or the green tops of spring onions.

Wild rice, white crab meat, sharp red onion and vivid papaya are tossed in a colourful salad with a zesty lime and honey dressing.

RICE PUDDING

SOFTLY SOFTLY

Is there a quick way of cooking a smooth rice pudding?

Rice pudding is best cooked slowly, so the rice will absorb all the milk and soften, and is normally baked at a low temperature for a couple of hours. It may also be simmered on the hob in a covered pan, as long as the heat is kept very low and the mixture is stirred frequently.

The only way to speed up the process is to use a microwave oven but it will still take about an hour, and care must be taken as milky puddings have a tendency to boil over in the microwave.

The following recipe is a lovely example of a creamy rice pudding baked in the oven, and may be eaten hot or cold.

Fresh lemon rice pudding

SERVES: 4
PREPARATION TIME: 15 minutes, plus 30 minutes standing time
COOKING TIME: 2 - 2½ hours

50 g (1¾ oz) pudding rice
600 ml (1 pint) whole milk
Finely grated rind of 1 lemon
25 g (1 oz) caster sugar
15 g (½ oz) butter

1 Grease an 850 ml (1 pint 10 fl oz) ovenproof dish. Wash and drain the rice, then put it in the prepared dish. Pour on the milk and gently mix in the lemon rind, and allow the mixture to stand for 30 minutes. While the rice softens, preheat the oven to 150°C (300°F, gas mark 2).
2 Stir the sugar into the milky rice and dot the surface of the pudding with shavings of butter.
3 Bake for 2 - 2½ hours, stirring after 30 minutes, until the pudding is thick, creamy and golden brown on top. For a creamier pudding without a skin, fold the skin in after about 1½ hours cooking. Serve hot or cold with fresh or canned fruit such as peach slices or raspberries.

Spoon through the crisp, golden skin to reach a soft and creamy sweet rice pudding. A hint of lemon brightens up this traditional dessert and teatime treat.

CREAMY SUCCESS

My rice puddings tend to be a bit thin. How can I rectify this?

Too much milk can make the pudding thin and runny. You may also be using the wrong rice. Pudding rice, also known as pearl, round or short-grain rice, contains more starch than long or medium-grain rice so that it absorbs a large quantity of liquid and becomes quite sticky and very soft.

To enrich the mixture, replace some of the milk with the same quantity of double cream, and dot half a tablespoon of butter over the top before baking. You will also achieve a creamier result if you stir in the skin 30 minutes into the cooking time, and again about two-thirds of the way through.

RISSOLES

CRISPY COATING

What is the difference between a rissole and a croquette?

They are very similar: both are made with chopped or minced ingredients bound together, often with a well-seasoned white sauce (in the case of croquettes) or a thick brown sauce (rissoles) but sometimes with mashed potato. The mixture is then coated with egg and breadcrumbs and fried.

The terms are sometimes used interchangeably, but rissoles are generally thought to have meat or poultry as their main ingredient, while croquettes are more often made with vegetables. Mixtures containing fish as a main ingredient are mostly called fishcakes.

Whatever they are called, when cooked they should be crisp and golden on the outside yet remain moist and creamy inside. The mixture should be thick enough to hold together during cooking, but not so thick that the finished result is dry, so it is advisable to chill rissoles and croquettes thoroughly before cooking to firm the mixture up.

VERSATILE DISH

What sort of ingredients could I use to make rissoles?

Rissoles are a good way of using up leftover meat or vegetables, but they are also worth making from scratch. Served on a bed of salad, or with a spicy sauce, they make a good starter or light supper dish.

A few simple ideas might include a mixture of chopped ham, grated cheese and finely chopped sage; a selection of cooked, diced root vegetables sprinkled with crumbled goat's cheese and finely chopped celery; or pieces of crispy bacon with Stilton cheese.

Season the mixture to taste, mix with a white sauce and shape into patties (see box, above right). Alternatively, shape teaspoons of the mixture into flat rounds and cover them with stiff mashed potato. In either case, dust them with flour, dip them in egg and coat in breadcrumbs, and fry gently to ensure that the inside gets heated through.

LUSCIOUS FISHCAKES

What kind of fish should I use for making fishcakes?

Any firm white fish is suitable, and you can use either raw or cooked fish, though raw will take a little longer to cook. First flake the fish and mix it with mashed potato, or with a strongly flavoured cheese sauce and plenty of chopped parsley. Then shape, coat and cook.

For a more unusual flavour, add some chopped garlic, grated ginger, lemongrass and spring onion.

SHAPING RISSOLES

Creamy rissoles or croquettes are shaped by hand, dusted with flour, dipped into egg and breadcrumbs then fried for a crisp exterior.

1 For every 500 g (1 lb 2 oz) of minced dry ingredients (minced poultry is shown here), mix in some 200 ml (7 fl oz) of thick white sauce.

2 Shape the mixture, using wet hands, into flattened balls. Dust with flour, coat in beaten egg and breadcrumbs, chill thoroughly till firm, then fry gently until golden.

ROASTING

TURNING POINT

What is the difference between roasting and spit-roasting?

Roasting is a method of cooking food, usually meat, in the oven with no liquid other than fat. The food is regularly basted to prevent the upper part of the meat drying out, and to enhance the flavour.

In spit-roasting, meat is skewered onto a rod and cooked in front of or above an open fire, being turned regularly to ensure cooking throughout and to run the fat and meat juices over the surface. Nowadays some ovens or grills have electrically operated spits, known as rotisseries, built into them.

RELAXING MEAT

Why should meat and poultry be rested after cooking, and how long should they be rested for?

Resting meat after cooking allows the fibres of the meat to relax. The juices, which expand during roasting, shrink as the meat cools so the joint deflates and the fibres consolidate. The meat is then firmer and easier to carve. If you try to carve it straight from the oven, the slices will be ragged and steam from the hot juices can cause scalding.

Large joints weighing more than 2 kg (4 lb 8 oz) should be covered in foil and rested for 20–30 minutes. Small roasts need 10–15 minutes and can be rested uncovered.

SMALL IS BEAUTIFUL

I enjoy a roast, but there are only two of us in our household. Are small joints worth cooking?

Joints of meat and poultry weighing under 1.5 kg (3 lb 5 oz) are now commonly available, reflecting the growing number of small households. These joints need extra care to be successfully roasted. Although small, they still need time to cook through, and as there is not enough fat and juices to keep the meat moist, they could become dry and tough. The answer is to bard them (see overleaf), and baste often.

Making gravy from small joints is another problem, because they will not provide enough of the vital sticky juices. But you can create the basis of a good gravy by roasting the meat on a bed of sliced onion and carrot and pouring 150 ml (5 fl oz) of stock, wine or water into the roasting tin at the start.

TROUBLE-FREE ROASTING

How do I ensure my roasts are always successful?

Roasting should be trouble-free, but here are some general rules:
• Weigh the meat to calculate the cooking time (see chart, overleaf), but remember that cooking times are meant only as a general guide,

and a long, thin piece of meat will take less time to cook than a thick, round one of the same weight.

• Before putting the meat to cook, allow time to preheat the oven to the required temperature: this may take 15 minutes or more.

• Put the meat on a roasting rack or trivet in a roasting pan. This keeps the meat off the bottom of the pan where the melting fat accumulates, and allows the heat to penetrate the meat more evenly as it circulates around it.

• Beef and lamb should be cooked at 230°C (450°F, gas mark 8) for 20 minutes first, to brown them. The temperature is then reduced and roasting completed according to the chart below. Roast pork does not need this initial browning as it is cooked at a higher temperature to ensure crisp crackling.

• Halfway through the cooking time, check the meat. If it is well browned on top, turn it over and baste it with the melted fat and juices in the bottom of the pan.

• The meat must reach an internal temperature of 60°C (140°F) to be rare, 71°C (160°F) to be medium pink and 80°C (176°F) to be well done. A meat thermometer inserted directly into the centre of the meat eliminates guesswork. It should be positioned when the roasting is almost complete, and should not touch any bones or the roasting tin as both of these conduct heat and give a false reading.

• When the cooking time is up, stand the roast on a warm serving platter in a warm place to relax and firm up, or leave it to rest in the turned-off oven with the door ajar while you make the gravy.

ADDING FAT AND FLAVOUR

What is the advantage of barding and larding over basting?

Very lean meats, such as veal and game birds, and very small joints of any meat, need extra fat when they are roasted or they become dry and tough. Continual basting is time consuming, and opening the oven door lowers the temperature. The answer is to make a roast 'self-basting', by barding or larding it.

Barding involves covering the joint with a layer of fat, which melts over the meat as it cooks. Pork back fat is the most suitable as it does not have a strong flavour, but some game birds are barded with streaky bacon, tied into place.

Larding involves threading strips of pork back fat through the meat with a larding needle. It is particularly suitable for large joints which need a long cooking time as the fat slowly dissolves, basting the meat internally and adding extra richness to the meat juices.

Barding dry meat, such as quail, with bacon keeps the flesh moist, enriches the flavour and produces rich juices.

ROASTING CHART

Bear in mind that long, narrow joints need less roasting time weight for weight than large round ones, and joints on the bone cook faster than boned joints.

MEAT	OVEN TEMPERATURE / COOKING TIME	INTERNAL TEMPERATURE
Beef (Sirloin, Rib or Topside)	180°C (350°F, gas mark 4)	
Rare	35 min per kg (15 min per lb) + 15 min	60°C (140°F)
Medium	45 min per kg (20 min per lb) + 20 min	71°C (160°F)
Well done	55 min per kg (25 min per lb) + 25 min	80°C (176°F)
Lamb (Leg, Loin or Shoulder)	180°C (350°F, gas mark 4)	
Rare	35 min per kg (15 min per lb) + 15 min	60°C (140°F)
Medium	45 min per kg (20 min per lb) + 20 min	71°C (160°F)
Well done	55 min per kg (25 min per lb) + 25 min	80°C (176°F)
Pork (Leg or Loin)	200°C (400°F, gas mark 6) 55 min per kg (25 min per lb)	75°C (167°F)
Chicken	200°C (400°F, gas mark 6) 35–45 min per kg (15–20 min per lb) + 15–20 min	71°C (160°F)
Turkey	180°C (350°F, gas mark 4) 45 min per kg (20 min per lb) + 20 min	71°C (160°F)

ROLLS

HOMEMADE READY-BAKE

I find the 'ready-bake' rolls I buy from the supermarket invaluable. Could I make my own?

Ready-bake rolls, or prepared but undercooked rolls that need only brief reheating or baking, are easy to make: simply bake any roll recipe in the usual way but remove them from the oven about 15 minutes before the total baking time. They can be made in the morning and finished off that evening, or frozen and kept for a later date, then cooked straight out of the freezer as required.

The following unusual savoury rolls have the advantage of being different from most 'ready-bake' rolls you can buy.

Sun-dried tomatoes and chopped black olives give a Mediterranean flavour to a cluster of rolls, the perfect foundation for a filling snack or cheese course.

Sun-dried tomato and olive rolls

MAKES: 8 rolls
PREPARATION TIME: 20 minutes
RISING AND COOKING TIME: 3 hours

400 g (14 oz) strong, unbleached white flour, plus extra for kneading
1 sachet easy-blend yeast
2 teaspoons salt
225 ml (8 fl oz) lukewarm water
6 sun-dried tomatoes packed in olive oil, finely chopped
12 black olives, stoned and finely chopped
40 g (1 ½ oz) butter, melted

1 Mix together the flour, yeast and salt in a bowl. Make a well in the centre and stir in the water, first with a spoon and then with your hand until a soft dough is formed. Do not knead the dough at this stage; just cover with a cloth or cling film and set in a warm place for 1 - 2 hours, until doubled in volume.
2 When the dough has risen, knock it down and knead until it is smooth. Knead in the tomatoes and olives,

sprinkling on more flour if the dough becomes sticky.
3 Form the dough into a long tube and cut it into eight equal pieces. To shape the rolls, cup the palm of your hand over each piece of dough and rotate your hand continuously until it gathers up into a small ball. Repeat with the other portions.
4 Grease a 23 cm (9 in) shallow cake tin and dust it with flour. Set the balls in the tin, cover and leave to rise for 30 - 40 minutes until doubled in volume. Meanwhile, preheat the oven to 230°C (450°F, gas mark 8).
5 When the rolls have risen, brush them with melted butter and bake for about 15 minutes or until lightly browned. Remove the tin from the oven and leave the rolls in the tin to cool. Cover with a cloth if the baking is to be completed later that day. To freeze, seal the rolls in a plastic bag. They can be cooked from frozen.
6 When ready to serve, preheat the oven to 230°C (450°F, gas mark 8) and cook for 10 - 15 minutes until crisp and browned. Cool on a rack before serving. To serve, pull off individual rolls by hand as needed.

ROSEWATER

DELIGHTFULLY DELICATE

What is rosewater, and what dishes would I use it in?

Rosewater is a clear liquid with a delicate flavouring derived from scented rose petals. When made for its scent, to freshen pillows and sheets for instance, it is made from plain water, but for cooking purposes it is made from the distilled essence of rose petals.

Rosewater is used a great deal in Middle Eastern dishes and Balkan confectionery, and in some Indian cooking. It can be added to sweet syrups for poaching fruit, serving with fritters or pouring over sponge cakes to moisten them, or mixed into icings, milk puddings, cream, ice creams and cold soufflés. Some savoury rice dishes, such as pilau, also contain rosewater.

The other commercially available flower water is orange flower water, which is made from the flowers of the bitter Seville orange. It is used in the same way as rosewater. Commercial rosewater and orange flower water are both distilled, so it is not possible to make your own at home.

ROULADE: see SWISS ROLL

RYE

FOREIGN FLOUR

I like the sharp taste of rye bread. Could I make my own?

The rye grain is ground to produce a dark greyish flour, used in various sour-tasting Eastern European breads. You can make a successful light rye bread by using a mixture of half rye flour and half plain flour, adding some caraway seeds for extra flavour and consistency. You can also use rye flour to make pancakes similar in appearance and taste to buckwheat pancakes.

SAFETY IN THE KITCHEN

BURN TREATMENT

What is the best thing to do if I burn myself in the kitchen?

Never apply butter, lotions or ointment to a burn, as these trap the heat and intensify the problem. Instead, run cold water over the affected area for at least 10 minutes. Remove any rings, watches or tight clothing before any swelling starts, then cover the burn with a sterile dressing or any other clean, non-fluffy covering.

If the burn is large, or the skin looks charred and grey, or there is clothing stuck to the burnt area, the injury may be serious. Cover it with cling film or a clean plastic bag to prevent infection and reduce dehydration of the area, and cool the burn by running cold water over the film or bag. Do not touch the affected area, burst any blisters or remove anything sticking to the burn. Seek medical help for any burn larger than a 10p coin.

MOUTH BURNS

I am terrified that my young child will get hold of something very hot and put it in his mouth. What should I do if this happens?

This type of accident can result in rapid swelling of the throat and inflammation of the air passages, leading to a serious risk of suffocation. Loosen clothing around the neck, give the child cold water to sip and call for an ambulance.

CHEMICAL DANGERS

I am aware that some common household cleaning agents contain potentially dangerous chemicals. What should I do if one of these comes into contact with the skin, or if my child swallows some?

Chemical burns are different from other burns: the onset is slower and there is a fierce stinging pain. Look for redness or staining of the skin, and blistering followed by peeling. Wash the affected area under cold running water to remove traces of the chemical and reduce the heat, then the person should be taken to hospital immediately.

Dangerous chemicals should be kept out of the reach of children. However, even seemingly innocuous substances, such as liquid soap, can be dangerous if swallowed. If the child swallows a household substance, such as bleach or cleaning fluid, and is conscious, give milk or water to sip. An unconscious victim should be laid on their front, face sideways and chin tilted up to keep the airway open. In either case, call an ambulance and, if possible, take a sample of the chemical with you to the hospital.

CUTS IN THE KITCHEN

What should I do if I cut myself while preparing food?

If possible, your hands should be clean before dealing with a wound. Rinse the cut under cold water then gently dry it with a clean or sterile swab and apply a plaster. A kitchen cut is most likely to affect a finger or hand, which you should then keep covered to prevent infection getting in. Your hands are likely to become wet and dirty as you cook, so change the dressing regularly and use water-resistant plasters.

COPING WITH GAS LEAKS

What should I do if I walk into my kitchen and smell gas?

If you smell gas, extinguish any naked flames immediately, but do not turn any electrical switches on

To the rescue!

Make your kitchen safe by keeping this equipment to hand:
- First-aid kit containing plasters, sterile dressings and bandages, safety pins, scissors and tweezers.
- Cling film or large plastic bags in case of large burns.
- Fire blanket to smother flames.
- Dry-powder fire extinguisher labelled 'for kitchen use'.

or off. Open the door and windows to let the gas disperse. Turn off the gas supply to the cooker and any other gas appliances such as a gas fire, either at the tap that supplies it, or if it does not have one, at the main tap next to the meter. When the lever is parallel with the pipe the gas is on, when it is at right angles to the pipe the gas is off.

If you cannot turn off the supply, or the smell continues after the gas has been turned off, ring British Gas immediately. Their 24-hour emergency service number is listed in the phone book under Gas.

OIL FIRE

What should I do if oil catches fire in a deep-fryer or saucepan?

Never throw water on an oil fire as it will cause an explosion of hot fat. Turn off the heat but do not move the pan as the flames could blow towards you. To deprive the flames of oxygen, cover the pan with a fire blanket, or use a damp towel or a metal lid or tray. When approaching the burning pan, keep the cloth or lid between you and the flames.

Leave the pan covered for at least 30 minutes; do not uncover it sooner as it could reignite. To minimise the risk of an oil fire, never fill a pan more than half full of oil.

If you feel unable to cope with fire, shut the doors and windows to contain the flames, leave the room and call the fire brigade. Do not go back into the room.

ELECTRICAL FIRE

What should I do if there is an electrical fire in the kitchen?

Turn off the power and pull out the plug, if possible. A small fire will probably go out once the power is cut. If it persists, it is best to use a dry-powder fire extinguisher on a small electrical fire: conveniently sized extinguishers of dry chemical powder marked 'for kitchen use' are sold by ironmongers. Never use water on an electrical fire.

If the source of a fire is in the socket rather than the appliance, it may indicate a fault in the wiring. In the event of a socket fire, do not attempt to fight it yourself. Close the doors and windows, leave the room and call the fire brigade.

SAFFRON

FLOWER POWER

Is saffron added directly to dishes, or do you have to prepare it first?

Saffron, which comes from a flower of the crocus family, is sold either as whole strands or in powdered form. Strands should be toasted briefly, just for a few seconds, in a dry frying pan over a gentle heat, then pounded in a mortar and steeped in a little hot liquid, stock, milk or water, in order to disseminate their flavour and colour more freely. Powdered saffron can be added directly to dishes.

LIMITED ALTERNATIVES

Saffron is very expensive. Is there any other way to give dishes that wonderful, warm colour?

Nothing can duplicate the orange hue of saffron, or its subtle and aromatic flavour. Turmeric produces a vivid yellow colour, has an agreeable flavour and is cheaper and easier to find, but it cannot be fairly compared with saffron.

Saffron is essential for this cool, golden, spicy sauce, which makes any fish dish very special.

A light and fragrant mayonnaise, made with added yoghurt and flavoured with saffron and other spices, is perfect with egg dishes, fish and vegetables.

Cold saffron sauce

SERVES: 4
PREPARATION TIME: 10 minutes
COOKING TIME: none

1 egg yolk, size 3
A pinch of sea salt
⅛ teaspoon powdered saffron
¼ teaspoon ground cumin
¼ teaspoon ground coriander
150 ml (5 fl oz) sunflower oil
1½ teaspoons white wine vinegar
1½ teaspoons lemon juice
150 ml (5 fl oz) yoghurt

1 Beat the egg yolk in a bowl, then mix in the salt and spices.

2 Pour in the oil drop by drop as if making mayonnaise, beating with a wooden spoon until each addition had been amalgamated. After half the oil has been beaten in, the rest can be added a little more quickly.
3 When all the oil is amalgamated, stir in the vinegar and lemon juice, then fold in the yoghurt. Serve with grilled salmon steaks, Dover sole, or poached white fish.

VARIATION

For a more robust flavour, replace the ground cumin and coriander with ½ teaspoon of mild curry powder. Toast it briefly in a metal spoon over a flame before adding it to the egg.

$\mathscr{S}$ALAD LEAVES

Healthy food has never been as quick to prepare or as pretty to look at as it is now with all these gorgeous salad leaves. Balance colours and flavours and add a simple garnish, and your own salad dressing for a feast of fresh goodness.

COS/ROMAINE

RED AND YELLOW CHICORY

CRISP LETTUCE

Leaves of different colours and flavours, dressed with nut oil and fruity raspberry vinegar, draw the eye and tempt the palate.

You only need one salad leaf to make a plain green side salad: cos, for example, with a few shavings of Parmesan cheese. For a more elaborate salad bowl, three different leaves are usually enough: try to balance taste and shapes, mixing a crunchy leaf like iceberg with sharp rocket, chicory or watercress and a pretty leaf like lollo biondo.

Keep a selection of toppings in the refrigerator to add a sharp taste or crunchy texture to salads: fresh herbs, olives, slivers of roasted pepper, lardons, croutons, toasted pine nuts or sesame seeds.

The best way to keep salad leaves fresh is to leave them unwashed and still attached to their stem, in a plastic box or polythene bag in the salad drawer of the fridge. Use a sharp knife to cut the leaves as it minimises damage to the cell structure and the consequent loss of vitamins.

There is a great deal of name-switching in salad stuffs, with American terms usurping the names of traditional British varieties, and supermarkets giving their own 'brand names' to identical lettuces. Here are the leaves you are most likely to find.

BATAVIA
Sometimes known as escarole, this began life as a coarse-leaved winter salad, but what the supermarkets call batavia today is a tender, loose-leaved lettuce with well-flavoured, crimp-edged leaves.

CHICORY
In Britain, chicory means the tight, pointed heads that the French call endive. They are sold blanched and pale, or occasionally red. The mildly bitter leaves cook well and are especially good with citrus.

CHINESE LEAVES
A refined member of the cabbage family, the tender, juicy leaves can be used all year round - it is much the best cabbage to use for coleslaw. Heads are large, but they keep well and leftovers can be used up in a stir-fry.

COS
Also known as romaine, cos is a classic long-leaved lettuce, whose head plumps out considerably in summer though it does not have much heart. The leaves are packed with assertive flavour, and it is essential for Caesar salad.

CRISP LETTUCE
This has leaves that bend over backwards to show off its big heart. It is a junior member of the iceberg clan, weighing in at about 200 g (7 oz).

DANDELION
Dandelion leaves are a feature of salads in many parts of Europe in spring, when youth softens their bitterness. But gather them from your own garden, where you can be sure they are not polluted.

CHINESE LEAF

FRISEE

ICEBERG

FRISEE

A raggedy-leaved salad, frisée is the bistro favourite topped with bacon bits and croutons. Called chicorée in France and chicory in the United States, frisée has a pleasing bitterness and a texture sturdy enough to stand up to hot dressings.

ICEBERG

This is subsuming older names such as Webb's Wonderful as the generic term for all crisp, tightly packed, pale green lettuces. Its juicy leaves keep better than most. Iceberg makes a big bowlful of salad for a buffet, but needs other elements added to compensate for its unassertive flavour.

LAMB'S LETTUCE

Also known as mâche and corn salad, lamb's lettuce is related neither to lettuce nor corn. It is expensive, but a few sweet, little leaves will go a long way as a garnish for first courses or incorporated into a mixed salad. It is best bought with its root attached because it revives well in iced water.

LINCOLN

First developed in the United States and now also grown in Britain, this is like a slim cos, with the crisp invulnerability of iceberg and 7 per cent more sugar. Also sold as baby cos or sweet romaine, it is a family sized, all-purpose lettuce.

LITTLE GEM

A miniature cos, this little lettuce is usually sold prepacked in pairs or threes. Its leaves are so densely packed you can slice straight across the head for salads, while the single leaves are just the right size to fit into a sandwich.

LOLLO BIONDO AND LOLLO ROSSO

Both have wonderfully pretty frilled leaves; the biondo (Italian for blonde) is a dainty pale green, while the leaves of the red-headed rosso are flushed with bronze at the edges. Glamorous but delicate, these leaves are best included for their looks alongside others with more texture and flavour.

OAK LEAF LETTUCE OR FEUILLE DE CHENE

This is tender, mild flavoured and handsome, with serrated and variegated leaves coloured from brownish green through to deepest bronze. It makes a highly pleasing salad mixed with peppery greenery such as rocket or watercress.

RADICCHIO

A ruby-leaved Italian chicory that is now grown in Britain as well as imported, radicchio is firm, bitter and beautiful, and mixes particularly well with pale green contrasting additions such as sliced avocado. It is sometimes cooked, but this darkens its leaves to brown.

ROCKET

Halfway between a herb and a salad leaf, rocket has a strong, peppery flavour that goes a long way. Mix a few leaves into green salads to add piquancy, or use as a garnish.

ROUND OR BUTTERHEAD

Once the lettuce of our summer salad patch but now available all year, it has soft, green leaves and is an ideal garnish for lining a dish of sandwiches or cold meats. It is also good inside sandwiches, keeping them moist without drawing attention to itself.

SALAD DRESSING (VINAIGRETTE)

• PROPORTIONS: traditionally, a salad dressing comprises four parts of oil to one part of vinegar (or other acid element such as lemon juice), but you can use up to six parts oil. Measure the ingredients into a screw-top jar, or pour them through a funnel into a bottle and shake hard to emulsify.

Green salads will wilt if they are left sitting in a salad dressing too long. Either offer the dressing at the table, or toss it in at the last minute.

• OILS: use your best oils, such as extra virgin olive oil for simple vinaigrettes; but if you find this too heavy, mix it with a lighter oil such as grapeseed. For a nut-flavoured dressing, one part of hazelnut or walnut oil can be mixed to two or three parts of olive oil. For an Oriental dressing, use one part of sesame oil to four parts of bland oil, and season with soy sauce instead of salt.

• VINEGAR: the classic acid element of salad dressing is red or white wine vinegar. Balsamic vinegar has a strong, sweet flavour and, like sherry vinegar, is rich and powerful; use both in small quantities. Cider vinegar is assertive and good for winter salads. Fruit and herb-flavoured vinegars can be added by the teaspoon for an elusive background flavour, while for an Oriental dressing try using rice wine vinegar. Or don't use vinegar at all - lemon juice makes a refreshing change.

• FLAVOURINGS: add sea salt, pepper, crushed garlic, some finely chopped shallot or a pinch of sugar to taste, and a teaspoon of French mustard to thicken the dressing.

ROUND LETTUCE

RADICCHIO

ROCKET

OAK LEAF LETTUCE

OLIVE OIL

BALSAMIC VINEGAR

LOLLO BIONDO

LAMB'S LETTUCE

LITTLE GEM

HAZELNUT OIL AND RASPBERRY VINEGAR DRESSING WITH MUSTARD

LOLLO ROSSO

SALMON

HOT AND COLD

When poaching whole salmon, how do I calculate the cooking time? Some books say 2 minutes, some say 20. Which is right?

A whole poached salmon can be served either hot or cold, and the cooking method varies accordingly. This accounts for the wide variation in cooking times given for whole salmon in recipe books.

For a salmon that is to be served cold, as in the recipe on the right, put the fish into cold water or court bouillon, cover and then bring it to the boil, skimming off any scum that forms. Turn off the heat as soon as it reaches the boil and leave the salmon in the liquid to cool completely before dressing it with your chosen garnishes. It is not necessary to set the trimmings in an aspic glaze. If preferred, fresh herbs can simply be laid on top.

For a salmon that is to be served hot, pour enough court bouillon or water to cover the fish into a fish kettle, but do not add the salmon. Bring the liquid to the boil, and then add the fish. Return it to simmering point and poach the salmon gently, allowing 11 minutes per kg (5 minutes per lb). Remove the fish from the liquid, then cover and leave it to rest for 5 minutes.

To accompany the salmon, serve tiny new potatoes, freshly made mayonnaise, and a cucumber salad made with fresh dill or mint, thick plain yoghurt and black pepper.

Whole dressed salmon

SERVES: 8 as a main course
PREPARATION TIME: 20 minutes, plus cooling time for court bouillon
COOKING TIME: 40 - 45 minutes, plus several hours or overnight cooling

Whole salmon, about 2.5 kg (5 lb 8 oz), gutted and cleaned

COURT BOUILLON
6 litres (10 pints 10 fl oz) cold water
150 ml (5 fl oz) white wine vinegar
1 onion, sliced
1 carrot, sliced
1 stick celery, sliced
2 strips lemon zest
3 bay leaves
A small bunch each of thyme sprigs and parsley stalks
A pinch of peppercorns
To garnish: sprigs of fresh tarragon, thinly sliced radishes, aspic jelly (optional), plus radish roses, pansies and sprigs of fresh dill to decorate the serving platter

1 To make the court bouillon, put all the ingredients in a fish kettle and bring them to the boil. Cover and simmer gently for 15 minutes.
2 Leave the court bouillon to cool and then strain off the flavourings, reserving the liquid.
3 To cook the salmon, lower the fish into the cold court bouillon (cut the head off to fit, if necessary, but add it to the pan for flavour). Bring to the boil over a medium heat, skim off any scum, then turn off the heat, cover the pan and leave to cool for a few hours or overnight.

TO DRESS THE SALMON
1 Remove the fish from the liquid then trim off the skin, fins and grey flesh, and the head if you wish.
2 Transfer the salmon to a serving dish or board. Decorate the top of the fish with sprigs of tarragon and radish slices. The fish may then be coated in a layer of aspic jelly made with the court bouillon, to keep it moist and to set the decoration.
3 Cover and leave the fish in a cold place until required. It is better not to chill it if possible, however, if the fish has to be prepared more than several hours in advance, or if it is being served on a hot day, keep it refrigerated until about 30 minutes before serving. Do not add the fresh garnishes until just before you are ready to serve the salmon.

Fresh tarragon and a few thinly sliced radishes are set under an aspic glaze to garnish a whole salmon. The festive garland of pansies, radish roses and fronds of dill is another simple summery decoration for this quintessential party dish.

IMPROVISED FISH KETTLE

I do not have a fish kettle or even a pan large enough to hold a salmon – what can I do?

If you do not want to go to the expense of buying a fish kettle that will be used only rarely, you can hire fish kettles by the day from some fishmongers and large supermarkets for a special occasion. It is also possible to use a roasting tin as described in the box (right).

Alternatively, you can bake the fish on a baking tray in the oven. Preheat the oven to 160°C (325°F, gas mark 3). Brush a large piece of strong foil with oil or melted butter and put it on a baking tray. Put the gutted and cleaned fish in the centre (if it is too big the head and tail can be cut off), season it inside with salt, pepper, slices of lemon or herbs if you want to, and wrap it loosely in the foil, folding over the edges to seal the parcel.

If the salmon is to be served hot, cook it for 35 minutes per kg (15 minutes per lb). Remove the fish from the oven and leave it to set, still wrapped in the foil, for 5 minutes. If the fish is to be served cold, cook it for 22 minutes per kg (10 minutes per lb), then remove it from the oven. Keep the fish wrapped in the foil until it has cooled down completely.

IN A PICKLE

Can you suggest a variation on smoked salmon as a starter?

Raw salmon can be pickled with alcohol, such as vodka or tequila, and flavoured with herbs and spices, or marinated in lemon or lime juice. This has the same effect as cooking the fish because the acid in the alcohol or juice coagulates the protein, making it opaque.

In South America this marinated fish dish is known as ceviche and is flavoured with chillies, onions and garlic. The following recipe also uses lime or lemon juice but takes inspiration from Sweden's famous cured salmon dish gravad lax by flavouring the fish with dill.

IMPROVISING A FISH KETTLE

Fish kettles are convenient for cooking a large whole fish but if you do not have one, here are two ways to improvise. To cook a fish that is too large for a small roasting tin, cut off the head and tail, poach them separately, then reassemble after cooking, covering the joins with garnish. Or, curl the fish to fit in the tin.

IN A ROASTING TIN

Measure the length of the fish and choose a roasting tin that will hold it comfortably. (You could also measure your roasting tin and choose a fish that will fit in it.) Place an oiled rack in the tin, set the fish on the rack and pour in salted water, stock or court bouillon according to the recipe. Cover the whole of the tin loosely with foil and cook the fish on top of the stove or in the oven.

COOKING IN FOIL

Alternatively, cut and fold a double or triple thickness of strong foil slightly larger than the fish. Lay the fish on the foil and put it in the cold cooking liquid in a roasting tin. Cover the tin with foil and cook according to the recipe. When the fish is cooked, it can be lifted out easily by lifting the edges of the foil beneath it. Then transfer the fish to a serving platter for the final decorating and garnishing.

Pickled salmon and cucumber

SERVES: 4 - 6 as a starter
PREPARATION TIME: 15 minutes, plus several hours marinating
COOKING TIME: none

½ small cucumber
2 teaspoons salt
500 g (1 lb 2 oz) very fresh thick salmon fillet, skinned and chilled
4 tablespoons lime or lemon juice, or white wine vinegar
1 teaspoon caster sugar
Coarsely ground black pepper
1 tablespoon fresh dill
To garnish: sprigs of fresh dill and thin slices of lime or lemon

---

1 Score the skin of the cucumber lengthways all the way round, then slice it as thinly as possible. Place the slices in a plastic sieve and sprinkle them with the salt, shaking to distribute the salt evenly.
2 Place the sieve over a bowl and leave the cucumber to drain at room temperature for an hour, shaking it occasionally, until 4 tablespoons of juice has drained off. Rinse the salt from the cucumber in cold water and then drain well.
3 Slice the salmon fillet very thinly, as you would smoked salmon (see box, overleaf). The colder the fillet, the easier it is to slice.
4 Put the slices in a bowl. Pour over the lime or lemon juice or vinegar then add the sugar, pepper, dill and cucumber and mix gently by hand.
5 Cover and chill for 30 minutes, turning occasionally so that all the salmon is thoroughly coated with the marinade. The acid in the marinade will 'cook' the salmon, changing it from bright pink to a pale opaque colour, as it would be if heated.
6 When ready to serve, arrange the slices of salmon and cucumber neatly on individual plates and then garnish with sprigs of dill and slices of lime or lemon. Serve the pickled salmon with slices of brown or dark rye bread, plain or spread with butter.

SLICING SMOKED SALMON

If you need smoked salmon for a party, it is cheaper to buy a whole side and slice it yourself. First chill the salmon to make it firm and, using a long thin filleting knife, cut off any dry surface flesh and skin.

1 Pull out any small pin bones that are embedded in the length of the salmon, using a pair of tweezers.

2 With the sharp edge of the knife facing the tail of the fish, cut wafer-thin slices of smoked salmon, starting with small slices cut from the tail end and gradually working up to full-length slices. Keep the knife parallel to the fish and use a gentle sawing action. Interleave the slices as you go with nonstick paper.

RUNNING WILD

Wild salmon is very expensive. Is it worth the extra cost? And, if so, what are the best cuts to buy?

As the diet of wild and farmed salmon is now very similar, so is their taste, but the silvery early run salmon, fresh out of the sea, will have a finer flavour and texture.

The high price of wild salmon is due to the labour involved in its capture. Wild salmon spend most of their life in the sea and return to the rivers only to spawn. The fish gather in the estuaries, where they are usually caught in nets, or they swim on upstream, where they are caught by rod and line. The fishing season lasts from mid January to the end of October. The young fish are known as grilse after one winter at sea, and salmon after two or more winters, although they are all known as salmon in the shops regardless of their age.

Wild salmon is at its best poached or baked whole – grilse weigh up to 3 kg (6 lb 8 oz) and are the ones most often sold whole. Larger fish are sold in steaks and fillets. The tail end of wild salmon has moist flesh, while the larger middle-cut steaks can be a little dry, so do not overcook them.

SALT

EARTH AND OCEAN

What is the difference between ordinary salt and sea salt, and is one better for cooking?

Most ordinary salt is rock salt, the residue of ancient oceans mined from underground, which comes finely ground or in large crystals. Some cooks prefer to use coarse rock or sea salt (which has been evaporated from sea water, or from salt marshes), as these do not need the anti-caking additives used in many brands of finely ground salt. Sea salt is a good choice for both cooking and the table. One of the finest is Maldon salt from Essex, with large soft flakes that can be crushed by the fingers.

OVERSEASONED

What can I do if I have put too much salt in a dish?

It depends on the dish. In the case of a semi-liquid dish like a soup or stew, you can add a couple of peeled and sliced potatoes to soak up the salt: cook them until tender, then discard before serving. Alternatively, you may add a couple of spoonfuls of rice or pasta pieces, but these will have to stay in the dish after cooking. Other thick, bland foods, such as cream or yoghurt, can be added to help reduce the saltiness. The damage is harder to counteract in dishes which have a thicker consistency. The only solution is to cook a second batch of half the quantity of the recipe without salt, and then to combine it with the oversalted lot.

SALT REDUCTION

How much will it affect a recipe if I cut out all the salt?

You can cut the salt out altogether but it will affect the taste of the dish. People who need to go on salt-free diets soon learn to live without it, but for most of us, entirely salt-free food is unacceptable. One solution is to reduce the amount of salt you use in cooking, perhaps adding only half as much as formerly, and putting good sea salt on the table for diners to help themselves. (See also NUTRITION.)

SAMPHIRE

BEACH VEGETABLE

What is samphire?

A marsh plant, samphire is gathered in coastal regions and sold by fishmongers. Snap it up when you see it in early summer, or gather some yourself at the seaside, for it is delicious. Its salty, ozone tang goes well with fish and also makes a fine first course, served like asparagus with melted butter. It needs rigorous washing to get rid of any sand, but samphire should be cooked for only about 5 minutes. It is done when you can easily suck the flesh away from the fibre in the middle of the stem.

Samphire tastes equally good served hot, cold or raw and its unique salty taste of the sea makes it special.

SATAY

TENDER CUTS

What is satay, and how do I go about preparing it?

Satay is an Indonesian dish of pieces of marinated meat grilled on wooden skewers and served with a spicy peanut sauce. Traditionally, the meat used in satay is not cubed but minced and moulded around the satay sticks. However, delicious satay can also be made with tender cubes of meat: leg or rib of pork with a little fat; skinless breast or upper thigh of chicken; sirloin or rump steak (fillet is too dry); best end of lamb or lamb chops.

Marinating the meat for a few hours before cooking, as with the chicken in the recipe below, will tenderise as well as flavour it. Use bamboo satay sticks, which should be soaked in water for a few hours before using so they will not burn. They should be about 20 cm (8 in) long to allow the meat to be skewered along half the length, leaving a 'handle' to grasp during grilling.

Grilled chicken satay

MAKES: 20 – 30 sticks
PREPARATION TIME: 20 minutes, plus at least 2 hours marinating
COOKING TIME: 30 minutes

1 kg (2 lb 4 oz) chicken breast
2 tablespoons ground coriander
1 tablespoon ground cumin
2 teaspoons ground turmeric
1 tablespoon each finely minced ginger and garlic
1 large onion, finely chopped
2 tablespoons sugar
4 tablespoons vegetable oil
2 teaspoons salt
To use as basting brushes: 3 stalks lemongrass, bruised at the base
To serve: satay sauce (see recipe, overleaf)

1 Cut the chicken into 2 cm (¾ in) cubes and flatten them a little.
2 Combine all the other ingredients in a bowl then stir in the chicken,

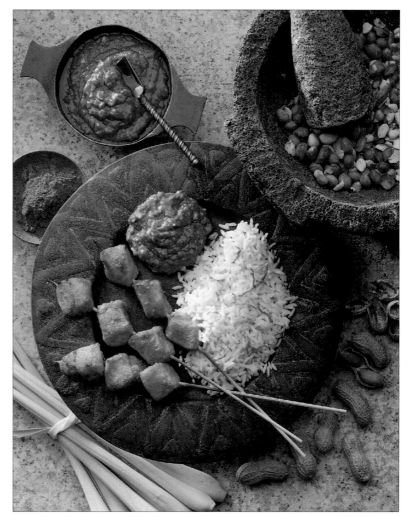

For an authentic Eastern taste, serve homemade satay with a sauce of freshly ground peanuts pungently flavoured with chilli, shrimp paste and galangal.

making sure all the pieces are well coated. Refrigerate the chicken for a few hours or leave overnight.
3 When you are ready to cook the chicken, preheat the barbecue or grill until red hot. Thread the cubes of meat onto the presoaked bamboo skewers and press as much of the marinade onto the meat as possible.
4 Grill the satay for 5 minutes per stick, turning once or twice during cooking and basting the meat often using the bruised lemongrass as a brush. Serve with satay sauce.

VARIATION

Whole, scored chicken breasts steeped in the same marinade can be grilled and served as a main course, with satay sauce alongside, plus rice and a salad or stir-fried vegetables.

PREPARING AHEAD

Can I make satay ahead of time and keep them warm?

Satay can be prepared up to several days ahead. Marinating for longer results in even more succulence and a richer flavour than meat not treated in this way. The satay can also be grilled or barbecued in the morning to serve in the evening, but should then be covered with cling film to prevent the meat drying out. To reheat, put the satay in a shallow roasting pan without crowding or overlapping them, and warm through in an oven that has been preheated to 150°C (300°F, gas mark 2). The satay is ready when the oil has taken on a sheen.

SEAFOOD FOR SATAY

Can I make fish or seafood satay?

Yes, but only a few fish stand up to being skewered in this way. Use fish with firm flesh, such as monkfish and conger eel. These can be cut up in the same way as meat and poultry, but the pieces should be slightly larger so that they do not fall apart when threaded onto the skewer. Prawns should be shelled and left whole. Thread one jumbo or two medium prawns onto each stick. To use scallops, cut them into pieces which will fit on the skewer. Lobster should be cut into medallions about 2 cm (¾ in) thick and then threaded onto the skewer.

SPICY PEANUT SAUCE

Do I have to buy the peanut sauce that is served with satay, or can I make my own?

The peanut sauce, also called satay sauce, is widely available but making your own is more satisfying and will taste more authentic. Most commercial brands of satay sauce leave out shrimp paste, a fundamental ingredient, because it does not have a long shelf life.

Ready-made satay sauce tends to be very thick as the ground nuts absorb some of the liquid over time. You can thin it by adding a little water or coconut milk, heating the sauce until lukewarm, and then stirring to make it smooth.

Leftovers

Leftover satay sauce should be used up within a day or two. It makes an excellent topping for grilled chicken, or a dressing for gado gado, the Indonesian cucumber, bean sprout and bean curd salad. It can also be used in vegetarian dishes, for instance mixed with rice, peas and carrots, or as a dip for crudités.

When making the following satay sauce, it is better to buy unsalted peanuts that have been shelled and roasted and then grind them yourself at home. The simplest way to crush peanuts is to put them into freezer bags, one inside the other, and pound them with a rolling pin until fine. Alternatively, you can use some thick chunky peanut butter, preferably unsweetened.

Satay sauce

MAKES: *about 1.2 litres (2 pints)*
PREPARATION TIME: *15 minutes*
COOKING TIME: *15 minutes*

2 stalks lemongrass
1 tablespoon chilli powder
1 cube, 2.5 cm (1 in), shrimp paste
2 large onions, chopped
6 candlenuts or macadamia nuts
2 cloves garlic
3 slices galangal or ginger
250 ml (9 fl oz) vegetable oil
75 ml (2½ fl oz) tamarind
   concentrate
2 tablespoons sugar
2 teaspoons salt
800 g (1 lb 12 oz) finely ground
   peanuts, or 500 g (1 lb 2 oz)
   crunchy peanut butter

1 To make the spice mixture, cut off the bulbous white root ends of the lemongrass stalks and discard their green shoots. Cut the root ends into thin slices. Put them, along with the chilli powder, shrimp paste, onions, nuts, garlic, and galangal or ginger into a mortar, or coffee grinder, and pound or grind them to a purée. If you use a blender or a food processor, you will not get the very smooth texture that is best for this sauce.
2 Heat the oil and fry the mixture over a moderate heat for 10 minutes, stirring all the time. When the spice mixture releases its aroma and the oil has become rich and red, add the tamarind and 750 ml (1 pint 7 fl oz) of water. Bring the mixture to the boil and simmer for 5 minutes.
3 Add the sugar and salt, adjusting them to taste, then add the ground peanuts or peanut butter, and stir well. Remove the sauce from the heat and allow to cool and thicken.

SAUCES

SMOOTH SAUCE

I'm familiar with the basic roux for making white sauces but mine are sometimes lumpy. How can I make a sauce with no lumps?

The first step when making a white sauce (see box, right) is to combine equal quantities of plain flour and melted butter, oil or another fat to form a pale golden roux – this is usually problem-free. The lumps come when the liquid is added, often to a roux that is too hot, so remove the pan from the heat and allow the roux to cool slightly before adding the liquid.

Lumps can be smoothed out by whisking the sauce briskly, or by liquidising or sieving it. However, if you leave too many lumps in the strainer, the sauce will be thinner than you intended.

TIME SAVER

What is an all-in-one sauce?

The all-in-one sauce is a useful timesaving method of making a white sauce in which all the ingredients are put into a saucepan and whisked continuously over a medium heat until the sauce is thick and very smooth.

Another option is to put all the ingredients into a liquidiser and blend them together for about 30 seconds, and then transfer the mixture to a saucepan and bring it to the boil, stirring continuously. The sauce should be simmered for about 25 minutes, a little longer than a traditionally made sauce, to ensure the flour is well cooked.

MORE BUTTER AND FLOUR

How do I make a binding sauce?

A binding sauce, such as that used in making croquettes or rissoles, is made in the same way as a white sauce (see panel, right) but with 50 g (1¾ oz) of butter and flour per 300 ml (10 fl oz) of liquid.

MAKING A BASIC WHITE SAUCE

The basic white sauce often used for savoury dishes is made with a liquid, such as stock or milk, and thickened with a cooked mixture of flour and butter. The finished sauce is often given an added flavouring such as cheese or parsley.

These flour-based sauces can be made either in a saucepan or a microwave. In many ways the microwave is easier to use as its exact timings and temperatures mean the sauce can be left for a while at any stage, if there is something else to attend to, without the risk of it overcooking or turning lumpy.

IN A SAUCEPAN

1 Melt 25 g (1 oz) of butter in a small saucepan then stir in 25 g (1 oz) of flour with a wooden spoon. Stir until the mixture forms a smooth ball in the base of the saucepan.

2 Cook the roux over a gentle heat, stirring occasionally, for 2 - 3 minutes until it has a sandy texture but has not changed colour. Allow to cool slightly before adding the liquid.

3 Gradually add 300 ml (10 fl oz) of hot milk to the cooked roux over a low heat, stirring until it is thick and smooth, then simmer gently, stirring occasionally, for 20 minutes.

IN THE MICROWAVE

1 Melt 25 g (1 oz) butter in a jug, on High for 20 - 40 seconds. Remove from the microwave and stir 25 g (1 oz) of flour into the butter to make the first stage of the sauce, the roux.

2 Add 300 ml (10 fl oz) of milk to the roux, and whisk it constantly until the mixture is well blended, most of the lumps have disappeared and the sauce is quite smooth and thick.

3 Return the sauce to the microwave and cook on High for about 1 - 3 minutes. Take it out every minute and whisk it well until the sauce is smooth and as thick as you want it to be.

JAZZ IT UP

What can I add to white sauces to make them more interesting?

There are several ways in which a basic white sauce can be altered to give a tastier result:

• CHEESE SAUCE: stir in 60 g (2¼ oz) of grated cheese (mature Cheddar, Gruyère or Parmesan) just before serving – the heat of the sauce will melt the cheese. If you are making the sauce to pour over cooked fish or vegetables, the cooking liquid may be used instead of some or all of the milk. Add a sprinkling of cayenne, mustard, nutmeg or hot paprika for a piquant flavour.

• MUSHROOM SAUCE: sauté 60 – 100 g (2¼ – 3½ oz) of thinly sliced fresh mushrooms in 20 – 30 g (¾ - 1 oz) of butter then stir them into the white sauce. Season with nutmeg and serve with fish or meat dishes.

• ONION SAUCE: sauté a medium to large onion in butter or oil before adding it to the white sauce.

• PARSLEY-SAUCE: stir in 2 - 3 heaped tablespoons of finely chopped parsley (or basil, chives, oregano, tarragon or watercress for other herb sauces) just before serving with fish, ham, or a selection of boiled or grilled vegetables.

LIQUID OPTIONS

What liquids can I use for sauces? Should they be added hot or cold?

The liquid you choose depends on the dish, but it should have a good flavour. A rich, homemade stock is good for many savoury sauces, but the water in which a particular vegetable has been cooked is the most appropriate liquid to use for a sauce that is to be served with, or poured over, that vegetable.

Milk is often used for white sauces and the classic Béchamel (overleaf), is given extra flavour by infusing the milk with onions, herbs and seasonings.

Whether you add hot or cold liquid to the roux should not affect the finished sauce, but if you use cold liquid the sauce will take longer to come to the boil. If hot liquid is added to the roux, the mixture must be stirred vigorously because it will thicken much faster.

Other liquids used for sauces include wine, a mixture of stock and white wine or cider, and dessert wines, which are often used in sauces to accompany puddings.

Béchamel sauce

MAKES: *300 ml (10 fl oz)*
PREPARATION TIME: *20 minutes, plus at least 10 minutes to infuse*
COOKING TIME: *20 minutes*

---

300 ml (10 fl oz) milk
1 small onion or shallot, peeled and studded with cloves
1 bay leaf
A few parsley stalks
6 peppercorns
25 g (1 oz) butter
25 g (1 oz) plain flour
Salt and black pepper

---

1 Pour the milk into a small pan and add the onion or shallot along with the herbs and spices. Slowly bring the milk to simmering point then remove it from the heat and stir.
2 Cover and leave to infuse for at least 10 minutes, but preferably 30 minutes or longer, then strain.
3 Melt the butter in a saucepan. Add the flour to make a roux and cook over a gentle heat for 1 - 2 minutes, stirring with a wooden spoon.
4 Gradually add the milk, stirring until the sauce is thick and smooth. Simmer for 20 minutes, stirring occasionally, then season to taste.
VARIATIONS
• MORNAY: stir in 60 g (2¼ oz) of grated Gruyère, Cheddar, or fresh Parmesan cheese, an egg yolk and a few tablespoons of single or double cream. This sauce goes well with egg dishes, chicken or white fish.
• SOUBISE: stir a purée of simmered onion into the béchamel. Serve it with meat or vegetables.
• VELOUTÉ: make in the same way as béchamel, but use stock instead of the infused milk, and cook the roux until it is a pale brown colour. Whisk a few tablespoons of cream in before serving to make a richer sauce. Serve it with poultry or fish.

FAT FREE

Is there any way to thicken a sauce without using a roux?

Yes, you can use cornflour to make a white sauce, using vegetable stock for a savoury sauce, or water and wine for a sweet sauce. It is a useful method for people on low-fat diets. A sweet cornflour sauce, such as the one in the following recipe, goes especially well with traditional steamed puddings.

Cornflour sauce

MAKES: *300 ml (10 fl oz)*
PREPARATION TIME: *5 minutes*
COOKING TIME: *10 minutes*

---

2 tablespoons cornflour
300 ml (10 fl oz) sweet white wine (or half wine and half water)
1 split vanilla pod

---

1 Put the cornflour in a medium-sized bowl and stir in 2 tablespoons of the wine to make a smooth paste.
2 Heat the remaining wine with the vanilla pod to just below boiling point, then strain onto the cornflour paste. Save the vanilla pod for use another time and stir the sauce well.
3 Return the sauce to the pan and bring it to a boil, stirring constantly, until it is smooth and thick. Simmer gently for 1 - 2 minutes, then serve.
VARIATIONS
Replace the vanilla with cinnamon, ginger, mace or nutmeg. To make a savoury sauce, use stock or stock and wine, sprigs of herbs plus a bay leaf and some peppercorns.

QUICK BUTTER SAUCE

I find roux-based sauces too heavy. Is there an alternative?

Many professional chefs now rarely make roux-based sauces, preferring to use reduced stocks and wine as the basis of well-flavoured sauces, sometimes with the addition of butter or cream. These sauces have a lighter texture than flour-based sauces and do not cloy the palate, although they are still rich. It is essential when making butter or cream sauces to balance

the flavour with a little lemon juice, vinegar or wine, to provide acidity, as in the recipe below.

Tomato butter sauce

MAKES: *about 300 ml (10 fl oz)*
PREPARATION TIME: *5 minutes*
COOKING TIME: *10 minutes*

---

1 large shallot, finely chopped
175 g (6 oz) unsalted butter, diced
2 large plum tomatoes, quartered
100 ml (3½ fl oz) white wine
A squeeze of lemon juice
Salt and black pepper
Chopped fresh herbs such as basil or chives, to taste

---

1 In a saucepan, sweat the shallots in a tablespoon of the butter, then add the tomatoes and wine, bring to the boil and simmer for 5 minutes.
2 When the tomatoes are cooked, beat the sauce vigorously until quite smooth then gradually whisk in the diced butter a piece at a time.
3 Pass the sauce through a fine strainer, pushing through as much of the tomato pulp as possible.
4 Whisk the sauce a final time, then taste it and adjust the acidity with a little lemon juice as necessary. Season with the salt, pepper and herbs.

KEEPING IT WARM

Can I make a sauce in advance and reheat it when I need it?

Most sauces can be made ahead and kept warm in a bain-marie for up to an hour. When you need the sauce, raise the heat, stir it until heated through and smooth, then simmer for a minute. Sauces can also be reheated in a microwave oven set on Medium-High; whisk the sauce every minute until well heated, thick and smooth.

Sauces can be chilled for several days, or frozen for one to two months, and then reheated. However, by the time you have thawed, reconstituted and stirred a frozen sauce back to the right texture, you could have made it from scratch. Egg-based sauces, such as custard, should not be frozen because they usually curdle after thawing.

VEGETABLE VARIETY

I'm a vegan. Are there any interesting sauces that don't use meat stock or dairy products?

Sauces made with vegetable stock can be made more lively by the addition of strong flavourings such as chilli, garlic, ginger, plenty of fresh herbs or a splash of wine, and thickened if you wish with puréed vegetables. The versatile vegan tomato sauce below is one of the most popular of all Neapolitan sauces. It is full of flavour, easy to make and delicious whether hot or cold. Serve it with rice, polenta or any grain dish, or with stuffed, grilled, or boiled vegetables.

Salsa pizzaiola

MAKES: 500 ml (18 fl oz)
PREPARATION TIME: 10 minutes
COOKING TIME: 30 - 45 minutes

1 tablespoon olive oil
1 medium onion, chopped
1 large clove garlic, crushed
700 g (1 lb 9 oz) fresh ripe tomatoes
    (preferably plum) skinned and
    chopped
2 teaspoons chopped fresh basil or
    oregano, or 1 teaspoon dried
1 teaspoon sugar
Salt and black pepper

1 Heat the olive oil in a medium saucepan and fry the onion gently for 5 minutes until lightly golden. Add the garlic and cook, stirring, for a further minute.
2 Add the chopped tomatoes with all their seeds and juice, then add the herbs, sugar, salt and pepper.
3 Bring the sauce to the boil, then cover the pan and simmer for 30 - 45 minutes, stirring occasionally until the sauce is thick and chunky. You can cook it longer if you want it to be thicker and less runny.

VARIATION

For a smoother sauce, the mixture can be liquidised or sieved. If you plan to do this, there is no need to skin the tomatoes first. You can also used canned tomatoes instead of fresh. Chopped fresh herbs can be stirred in or sprinkled on top.

SKINLESS

How can I stop a skin forming on a sauce after cooking?

Stir the sauce frequently while it is cooling, or cover the surface of the hot sauce with buttered greaseproof paper, buttered side touching the sauce, or some foil or cling film. A knob of butter added after cooking, or a few tablespoons of the liquid kept back and floated on the surface, can also prevent a skin forming, and can be stirred in when the sauce is reheated.

OLD FAVOURITE

My family want to try some bread sauce with their Christmas turkey. Is it difficult to make?

Not at all. Smooth, creamy and subtly spiced, it is one of the easiest sauces to make (see recipe, right). It is traditionally served in a sauce boat with roast chicken, turkey and game birds. Make it in a double boiler or a heavy-based saucepan but be sure to watch it carefully.

Bread sauce

SERVES: 4 - 6
PREPARATION TIME: 15 minutes, plus at least 15 minutes infusing
COOKING TIME: 15 minutes

4 cloves
1 small onion
300 ml (10 fl oz) milk
1 bay leaf
1 blade mace, optional
A pinch of salt
4 peppercorns
50 g (1 3/4 oz) fresh breadcrumbs
25 g (1 oz) butter
2 tablespoons cream, optional

1 Stick the cloves into the surface of the onion. Pour the milk into a small saucepan and add the onion, herbs and spices. Bring to the boil slowly, remove from the heat, then cover and leave to infuse for 15 minutes.
2 Strain the milk and return it to the saucepan. Add the breadcrumbs and butter and cook over a gentle heat for about 15 minutes, or until the breadcrumbs absorb the milk and the sauce is thick and creamy.

Pizzaiola is a chunky, vegetarian sauce full of the zesty flavour of fresh garlic, ripe plum tomatoes and basil. It can be used to liven up a variety of dishes.

SAUSAGES

HEALTHIER SAUSAGES

Are there some sausages that are more nutritious than others? How can I tell which they are?

Sausages with more meat and less fat are a better buy and better for you. Study the labels: a high price should reflect a high meat content. British pork sausages must, by law, contain at least 65 per cent meat, of which 80 per cent must be pork, but only half need be lean meat: the rest can be fat and offal. Beef, or pork and beef sausages need contain only 50 per cent meat, half of it lean. The non-meat part is made up of herbs, rusk, spices and water, with antioxidants, polyphosphates, and preservatives. Some Continental sausages are made of pure meat with just flavourings added.

WORLD OF CHOICE

Sausages make a good quick meal but my family get bored with the same ones. Are there some other types I could try?

Almost every region in England has its own variety of sausage. Some well-known regional specialities include sage-flavoured sausages from Lincolnshire and Kent and tomato-enriched ones from the Midlands, Oxford sausages made with veal, and the Cumberland variety which is not divided into links but coiled up in one long spiral. There are also sausages made with turkey, venison and wild boar.

Many other countries produce fresh sausages for frying or grilling. These tend to be more expensive, as they contain more meat than English sausages, and they are generally more highly seasoned.

One of the best-known frying sausages of France is the pure pork *saucisse de Toulouse,* a substantial, coarsely textured sausage, often not divided into links. The small *andouillette* has a stronger flavour as it is made of pig's tripe and offal

and is salted and then smoked. Another smoked sausage is the plump Polish boiling ring, which is now widely available.

Italian versions, called *salsiccie* (sausage), are often displayed tied up with twine; they are flavoured with herbs and sometimes whole peppercorns. A speciality from northern Italy is the long, unlinked *luganega,* which looks rather like Cumberland sausage.

German *bratwurst* are large, long and pale as they often contain veal or milk. If you like spicy sausages, try the ruby-red Spanish *chorizos,* Lebanese *m'anak* made of lamb and studded with pine nuts, or *merguez* from Algeria.

If you want to try a new way of cooking sausages, which is very good for most of the Continental sausages or British ones with a high meat content, try the recipe on the right for braising them in red wine with strong flavourings.

Choose an earthy red wine for this colourful supper dish of sausages with peppers, onions and mushrooms.

Wine-braised sausages

SERVES: 4
PREPARATION TIME: 20 minutes
COOKING TIME: 50 minutes

2 tablespoons olive oil
500 g (1 lb 2 oz) sausages
225 g (8 oz) baby onions, peeled
1 small red pepper, deseeded and
　coarsely chopped
100 g (3 ½ oz) pancetta or thick-cut
　streaky bacon, diced
1 clove garlic, crushed
2 teaspoons plain flour
150 ml (5 fl oz) red wine
100 g (3 ½ oz) mushrooms,
　thickly sliced

1 Heat the oil in a large, flameproof casserole. Add the sausages (do not prick them first) and when lightly browned all over, transfer to a plate.
2 Add the onions, red pepper, bacon and garlic to the pan and cook until all are lightly browned. Stir in the flour, then gradually add the wine.
3 Lay the sausages on top, cover and simmer as slowly as possible for 30 minutes. Stir in the mushrooms and cook for a further 10 minutes.

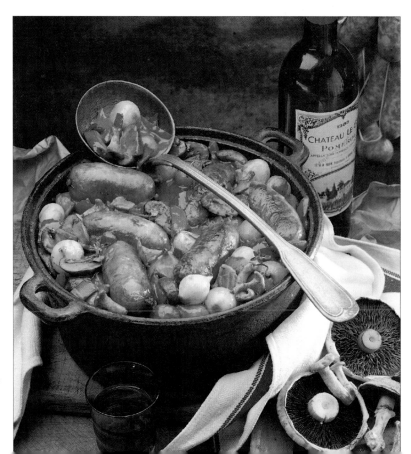

No bangs

I thought you were supposed to prick sausages before cooking them but have heard recently that you should not. Is this true?

After the Second World War, when meat was still scarce, sausages contained so much water that they exploded when cooked, which is why they were nicknamed bangers. Pricking was an attempt to prevent this, but now it should not be done as it just allows the juices to escape.

Sausages will burst if cooked at too high a temperature. Fry them gently for about 10 minutes, turning frequently until golden brown all over, or grill them not too close to the heat. One method that is guaranteed not to burst your sausages is toad-in-the-hole, where the sausages are oven baked and protected by Yorkshire pudding batter.

Sausage nicknames

Why do my American friends call frankfurters hot dogs or wieners?

The popular American smoked sausage in a roll (usually served with bright yellow mustard) has two nicknames because it is similar to two German sausages: the frankfurter, which was originally made in Frankfurt, and the wiener from Wien (Vienna). When a cartoonist drew a tail, legs and a head on the frankfurter to make it look like a dachshund, it was christened the hot dog and has remained so ever since. They can be made of beef, pork or poultry with added fat and need no cooking, just heating.

Smoked pork sausage

What exactly are saveloys?

The word saveloy is a corruption of the French term *cervelas*, which originally meant a sausage made with brains (*cervelles*). Now saveloy is a fat sausage made from smoked pork, frequently found in fish and chip shops. There it is heated up by plunging it into the hot fat, but it usually tastes better if poached in hot water like the French original.

Veggie versions

Are there any meat-free sausages suitable for vegetarians?

Vegetarian sausages, based on soya bean products, are widely available, and many speciality sausage shops sell innovative vegetarian sausages. Or you can try making your own Glamorgan sausages with a blend of grated hard cheese and breadcrumbs formed into sausage shapes, rolled in egg and fried.

Chinese bangers

Are there any oriental sausages?

Yes, Chinese food stores will stock *lap cheung* or *ap yeung cheung*, both suitable for grilling or frying (*cheung* is the Chinese word for intestine). They are small, knobbly looking pork sausages, flavoured with soy sauce and a small amount of alcohol. *Lap cheung* is fresh and is coloured bright red with paprika. *Ap yeung cheung* is air-dried and the Chinese usually steam it over a pan of boiling rice.

Custom made

I would like really lean, chunky sausages. Can I make my own?

Making your own sausages is easy and appealing because it allows you to use a high proportion of lean meat, and you can vary the texture and flavouring to suit your own taste by adding different herbs and spices. A butcher who makes his or her own sausages should be able to sell you sausage casings.

Many kitchen shops sell a mincer with plastic sausage nozzles or you can use a piece of plastic pipe about 15 cm (6 in) long, or a funnel with a large opening. Slide the end of the sausage casing onto one end of the funnel and push the meat mixture into it with a pestle or the handle of a wooden spoon. On the right is a recipe for hearty homemade sausages. They should be cooked and eaten within 24 hours of being made; unlike commercially made sausages, the only preservative these contain is salt.

Chunky homemade pork and herb sausages

Serves: 4
Preparation time: 15 minutes
Cooking time: 10 minutes

About 1 m (3 ft) of sausage skins, soaked in warm water for 10 minutes (or as per instructions)
1 tablespoon olive oil
1 small onion, finely chopped
500 g (1 lb 2 oz) lean pork, such as shoulder
1 ½ tablespoons chopped mixed fresh herbs, such as marjoram, oregano, parsley, rosemary, sage savory or thyme
1 tablespoon Dijon mustard
Salt and black pepper
Olive oil for basting

---

1 While you leave the sausage skins to soak, heat the olive oil in a small frying pan, add the onion and fry it gently until it has softened but not coloured. Transfer the onion to sheets of kitchen paper and leave it there to drain as it cools.

2 Pile the meat onto a chopping board. Chop it finely by holding two sharp knives loosely and parallel to each other. Lift each knife in turn up and down to chop in a smooth rhythmic movement (for details, see HAMBURGERS). Put the chopped meat into a bowl and stir in the onion and seasonings with a fork.

3 Drain and dry the sausage skins. Tie a secure knot in one end, then slide the loose end onto a handheld sausage maker or the sausage making attachment of a food mixer, gently ruffling up the skin so that the knotted end is at the opening of the attachment. Pack the meat mixture into the sausage maker and pipe it into the skins, smoothing it so that there are no air bubbles. Twist the skins at about 10 cm (4 in) intervals to make the sausage links. Tie the loose end securely.

4 Because they are moist, but do not contain any added cereal to soak up the juices, these sausages are better grilled than fried. Preheat the grill and then brush the sausages lightly with oil. When it is very hot, grill them for about 10 minutes.

SCALLOPS

CORAL DELICACY

Are there different kinds or sizes of scallops? Do you eat the corals?

Scallops are classified by their size, from the smallest queens, which are 7.5–10 cm (3–4 in), up to the great scallops, which can grow as large as 15 cm (6 in). The coral, or roe (eggs), inside the shell of females is prized for its sweet creamy taste and striking colour. It should not be discarded (as they do in the United States) but used as a garnish.

PREPARING SCALLOPS

Shelled raw scallops should be kept for no more than 24 hours; cooked, they can be kept for up to two days.

1 Since scallops don't have to be cooked live, they are usually sold ready-dressed with the white meat and the coral together on the half shell. Cut the small strip of muscle from the white part and discard it. Separate and set the coral aside.

2 The white meat can be halved through the middle or sliced if large. Scallops need only very brief cooking: 1 - 2 minutes deep-fried, grilled or poached; 2 - 3 minutes sautéed; 2 - 4 hours in a marinade to serve raw. Heat the coral for a few seconds at the end of the cooking.

DO NOT BUY WATER

Are fresh scallops really that much better than frozen? They are a lot more expensive.

Fresh seafood, if you can be sure it is absolutely fresh, is always preferable to frozen. With scallops it is particularly important to buy them on their shells: unscrupulous fishmongers sometimes offer shelled scallops that have been soaked in water overnight. This makes them swell to double their size, but they shrink back the instant they hit the pan. Cheap frozen scallops may also have been plumped up with water.

OFF-SEASON

Last summer I saw 'diver-caught' scallops on a menu. Can you tell me what this means?

Most scallops are trawled between November and March, from around the coasts of Scotland, Ireland, the Isle of Man and France, so their main season is winter. However, divers catch scallops throughout the year, and these are sometimes offered in restaurants, though they are unlikely to reach the shops.

SCONES

HIGH AND TIDY

What is the secret of well-shaped and beautifully risen scones?

Ideally, scones should double in size when cooked but they will not rise well and will be poorly shaped if the dough is rolled out thinly and unevenly.

Roll the dough 2 cm (¾ in) thick, using even pressure on the rolling pin. Dip the cutter in flour before cutting the scones out, and push straight down. If you twist, they will be ragged or slanted. Bake immediately in a hot oven as the raising agent starts to work the minute any liquid is added. Bicarbonate of soda and cream of tartar used with plain flour give a better lift than self-raising flour (see recipe, above right).

Plain tea scones

MAKES: 12 scones
PREPARATION TIME: 10 minutes
COOKING TIME: 8 - 10 minutes

---

225 g (8 oz) plain flour
1 teaspoon bicarbonate of soda
2 teaspoons cream of tartar
A pinch of salt
40 g (1½ oz) butter or block margarine, diced
40 g (1½ oz) caster sugar
150 ml (5 fl oz) milk

---

1 Preheat the oven to 220°C (425°F, gas mark 7). Grease a baking sheet, or two if you have a spare.
2 Sift the flour, bicarbonate of soda, cream of tartar and salt into a bowl. Rub in the butter or margarine with your fingertips until the mixture resembles fine breadcrumbs, then carefully stir in the sugar.
3 Make a well in the centre, pour in the milk and mix with a flat bladed knife to a soft, but not sticky, dough.
4 Turn the dough out onto a floured surface and knead lightly to smooth it. Using a floured rolling pin, roll it out to a thickness of 2 cm (¾ in). Then, using a 5 cm (2 in) cutter, cut out as many rounds as you can. Make a ball with the trimmings, reroll and cut more rounds.
5 Place the rounds on the baking sheet and dust the tops with flour. Bake immediately for 10 - 12 minutes until well risen and light brown. Cool on a wire rack for 15 minutes. Eat the scones fresh with butter and jam.

ADDING FLAVOUR

What ingredients can I add to a plain scone mix for a change?

To make fruit scones, add 50 g (1¾ oz) of mixed dried fruit to the recipe above, and ½ teaspoon of ground cinnamon; or 50 g (1¾ oz) chopped dates and the grated zest and juice of an orange. For cheese scones add 50 g (1¾ oz) of grated Cheddar cheese, ½ teaspoon of mustard and a pinch of cayenne pepper. Half a teaspoon of mixed dried herbs is better for making savoury scones than fresh herbs, which can produce green streaks.

SEAWEED

HIGH NUTRITION

Why does anyone eat seaweed?

Seaweed is quite delicious, with a pleasant fresh saltiness reminiscent of the sea. Vegetarians have always recognised the importance of sea vegetables, which are a valuable, and inexpensive, source of concentrated essential vitamins and minerals. They also rely on carrageen or agar-agar, seaweed used for thickening and gelling, instead of animal-derived gelatine.

Orientals have always been more ready to eat sea vegetables than Westerners, and seaweed is particularly popular in Japan with its long jagged coastline. The proliferation of Japanese restaurants in large European cities has spurred interest in sea vegetables, and there is a wide variety of dried marine vegetation now on sale in Oriental foodstores and healthfood shops.

Seaweeds are eaten as vegetables (they go particularly well with fish), are used as garnishes and in dressings, and add a distinctive salty flavour to soups and snacks such as crispy rice crackers.

Dulse is a seaweed, rich in minerals, which grows all along the British coast.

SEASIDE PROVENDER

Can you eat seaweed gathered straight from the beach?

In theory you can, but you must collect it from a shoreline free of pollution. Laver weed, also called red laver or tangle, is used to make laver bread in Britain. It is the same variety called *nori* in Japan and sold dried in sheets. But it can take 8 hours boiling to make it edible. Purple fronds of dulse can be cleaned, brushed with egg, coated with flour or oatmeal and fried until it is very crisp.

NAME THAT SEAWEED

What are the different sorts of seaweed, and how are they used?

• ARAME has a particularly high calcium content and can be bought already shredded in a dark-green tangle. Very strongly flavoured, it is used in Japanese miso soup and a small amount makes an exciting addition to mushroom or seafood risottos as well as Oriental rice dishes. It needs a 5 minute soak and then 30 minutes cooking.
• DULSE, which is available fresh and dried, is good in soups and in vegetable or grain dishes. You can eat it deep-fried or, after a brief soak to soften it, shred it into salads or their dressings, for example the Oriental salad dressing on the right. This can be poured over cooked fish or grilled prawns, or served as a dipping sauce: you can also use prawn crackers to scoop it up.
• KOMBU is valuable in vegetarian stocks. A strip of kombu cooked with dried beans both speeds up their cooking time and contributes flavour – even a strip that has been simmered for 20 minutes in stock.
• NORI is one of the most common seaweeds. It is sold in sheets which can be lightly toasted for additional flavour and then used in sushi (see JAPANESE COOKING) or crumbled over rice or vegetables. Nori also comes ready-flaked, in which form it can be either sprinkled, uncooked, over rice dishes, or added to pancake or tempura batters for extra flavour.

Dulse, ginger and spring onion dressing

SERVES: 4
PREPARATION TIME: 10 minutes
COOKING TIME: 1 - 2 minutes if using fresh dulse; none if using dried dulse

85 g (3 oz) fresh dulse or 25 g (1 oz) dried dulse
4 - 6 spring onions, chopped
5 cm (2 in) piece cucumber, finely diced
5 cm (2 in) piece ginger, peeled and grated
1 teaspoon Thai fish sauce, optional
1 tablespoon lemon juice
1 tablespoon soy sauce
1 teaspoon soft brown sugar
1 tablespoon peanut oil or sunflower oil
1 teaspoon sesame seed oil

1 If using dried dulse, soak it for a minute in cold water then drain. If using fresh dulse, rinse it, put it into a pan with boiling water to cover and cook for 30 seconds. Drain and set it aside it to cool.
2 Press the drained dulse with your hands to squeeze out all the liquid, compressing it into a ball. Put it on a board and shred it, then mix in the spring onions and cucumber.
3 Mix the ginger, fish sauce, lemon juice, soy sauce and sugar in a bowl and stir to dissolve the sugar. Whisk in the oils, then toss in the dulse mixture. Use as a dressing or dip for spring rolls or won ton dumplings.

SEEDS

EATEN NOT SOWN

In the shops, seeds are sometimes on the spice racks and sometimes, like sunflower seeds, they are with the nuts. Are they spices?

The difference between seeds and spices is a hazy one, as many spices are themselves seeds. The distinction seems to be made between those that impart their flavour to other foods (for example, caraway, celery and mustard), which are regarded as spices, and those that retain their own flavour (for example, poppy seeds). All seeds, especially pumpkin, sunflower and sesame, are rich in essential minerals and vitamins, and they are also exceedingly high in calories.

Black seeds, such as poppy seeds, come in useful for adding a colour contrast to pale dishes. Both black mustard seeds and black (unhulled) sesame seeds can be bought in Indian shops, as can small black seeds called *kalongi*, which have a pleasant, earthy flavour.

SEED GUIDE

How do I use all the different seeds I see on sale?

• CARAWAY SEEDS are favourites in Central Europe where they are used with pork and potatoes, and in sausages and breads such as rye and pumpernickel. Sprinkle them over pork chops before frying, then add a drop of kummel, the caraway-flavoured liqueur, and a tablespoon of soured cream to the pan juices to make a sauce. The most popular English use is seed cake spiced with caraway.

• CELERY SEEDS are good added to winter soups and stews. Celery salt is a traditional English seasoning for hard-boiled eggs. To make it, simply pound five parts of lightly roasted celery seed with one part sea salt. Put the mixture into a jar, then seal tightly to store.

• MUSTARD SEEDS (yellow and black) are widely used in India to thicken and flavour. The yellow seed is milder than the black. Both are usually fried quickly in hot oil at the start of cooking, or added as a garnish at the very end.

• POPPY SEEDS pounded into a paste and sweetened with honey, or sprinkled generously over bagels and dumplings, are a feature of Jewish cookery. Try tossing them, alone or with breadcrumbs, in butter to dress egg noodles.

• PUMPKIN AND SUNFLOWER SEEDS have little place in cooking, even though they are nutrient-rich, and are best served as a snack.

• SESAME SEEDS are the most widely used and many people enjoy their nutty flavour. They come in three different colours: beige (unhulled), black (found in Oriental shops) and pearly white. In the Middle East, sesame seeds are made into a paste called tahina, pounded with chickpeas to make hummous. They are also the basis of the Greek sweetmeat halva.

Like most seeds, sesame seeds benefit from being gently dry-fried for 2–3 minutes. Scatter them over boiled carrots or a salad of raw grated carrots, or make a nutritious open sandwich by topping buttered wholemeal bread with sprouted seeds and sprinkling it with some toasted sesame seeds.

Sesame seeds are ground into two forms of oil: a light, almost tasteless oil for frying, and a dark toasted oil used in small quantities as a flavouring condiment.

SEMOLINA

HARD HEARTED

What is semolina made from?

Semolina is a coarse flour, usually of wheat or maize, which is left behind when the finer flour has been sifted out. Durum wheat semolina is used in Italy to make commercial pasta. It is too hard to use on its own at home, where it needs to be used in conjunction with either pasta or bread flour, usually in a ratio of one part semolina to three parts pasta flour.

As well as making pasta with it, Italians also use semolina to make gnocchi or small dumplings, which can be made either with potatoes or ricotta cheese.

Another good way of using semolina is to substitute it for some of the flour in cakes and biscuits, where the slightly gritty grains add a crisp texture. In Britain, semolina is traditionally used to make a rather bland baked milk pudding, the kind of food that is regarded as suitable for invalids.

SHELLFISH

SEA SALTY

When recipes say to boil shellfish in salted water, how much salt do I need to use?

The aim is to emulate sea water: use 150 g (5½ oz) of salt for every 4 litres (7 pints) of water. Shellfish should always be cooked in a generous quantity of well-salted water.

HOME FREEZING

Do shellfish freeze well?

It is not a good idea to freeze shellfish at home. The freezing process damages shellfish more than many other foods, and even commercial freezing, which is much faster than anything that can be achieved in a domestic freezer, causes considerable deterioration in flavour and texture. While frozen shellfish may be preferable to none at all, they are always much better when eaten fresh and in season.

LAVISH PLATTER

Is it possible to assemble a dish of fruits de mer in this country like the one I had in France?

Of course it is: we fish in the same waters and there is no explaining the fact that on one side of the Channel every seafront restaurant serves dramatic elevated platters of mixed seafood, whereas just 35 km (22 miles) north on the other side we are content with whelk stalls.

Choose whatever seafood is best in the marketplace, including at least three, and preferably five different varieties in a mixed price range: winkles and whelks as well as crab, lobster, oyster and prawns. Prepare the shellfish according to the instructions given for each in this book. Crab and lobster are often halved to make sure there is enough to go around.

To go for the full French effect, put a lampshade frame on the table with a wide bowl beneath it for

The best way to eat fresh shellfish is in the French style from a lavish iced platter. Here the centrepiece is crab and lobster, surrounded by frilly Pacific oysters, pink king prawns, brown-shelled whelks and small dark-shelled winkles.

debris. Arrange the seafood on a wide plate or small round tray lined with washed seaweed and cracked ice and set this on top of the frame in the middle of the table. Surround the platter with plenty of halved lemons plus one whole lemon stuck with hatpins or skewers for picking out the tiny little winkles.

Serve the fruits de mer with plenty of French bread, crab crackers and lobster picks, the largest white cloth napkins you can find, and plenty of finger bowls. Chilled white wine is probably the best thing to drink with this fishy spectacular. Time, however, is the most essential element when eating a platter of fruits de mer – it is a treat not to be rushed through in an hour.

SHORTBREAD

BREAKING BREAD

Why does my shortbread break straight out of the oven?

It could be because the dough was worked too much, which can make it tough and brittle. When making shortbread, the dough should be handled as little as possible.

You can also ensure that it does not break up by marking it into wedges or fingers before baking. Once cooked, cool the shortbread briefly in the tin then transfer to a rack to cool a little more. While it is still warm, put the shortbread on a hard surface and cut along the lines you have marked, using a bread knife and a sawing action.

Shortbread almost always breaks if you cut it after it has cooled completely. It is also brittle when it is cooked for too long. When it has been properly baked, shortbread is a pale golden colour, never brown.

GROUND RICE FOR CRUNCH

Why do some shortbread recipes contain ground rice?

Ground rice, rice flour or semolina are frequently added to shortbread dough to give it a fine-grained yet crunchy texture. The recipe for Foolproof Shortbread, overleaf, includes ground rice or rice flour.

Foolproof shortbread

MAKES: 8 wedges
PREPARATION TIME: 30 minutes
COOKING TIME: 30 - 40 minutes

115 g (4 oz) salted butter, softened
50 g (1¾ oz) caster sugar
115 g (4 oz) plain flour
A pinch of salt
50 g (1¾ oz) ground rice
   or rice flour
Caster sugar for dredging, optional

1 Preheat the oven to 180°C (350°F, gas mark 4). Grease a baking sheet. Put the butter and sugar in a bowl and beat until pale and fluffy. Mix in the flour, salt and ground rice or rice flour and stir until the mixture has begun to bind together.
2 Knead the mixture lightly to form a smooth, pliable dough. Transfer the dough to the prepared baking sheet and shape it quickly and lightly into a round 1 cm (½ in) thick; do not overwork the dough. Alternatively, it may be pressed into a special wooden shortbread mould then turned out onto the baking sheet.
3 Prick all over the surface of the dough with a fork, mark into eight equal wedges and flute or crimp the edges decoratively. Bake for 30 - 40 minutes, until the shortbread has cooked to a pale golden colour.
4 Allow the shortbread to cool on the baking sheet for a few minutes, then transfer to a wire rack to cool a little. While it is still warm, put the shortbread on a hard surface and cut or break into the marked wedges, then leave it on the wire rack to cool down completely.
5 Dredge with caster sugar before serving. The shortbread can be stored for up to a week, wrapped in a layer of baking paper in a biscuit tin.

SHRIMPS: see PRAWNS
SLOES: see PLUMS and SPIRITS

Ground rice gives this heavenly shortbread body and texture without making it brittle, while dredging it with sugar adds sweetness and a delicate crunch.

SLOW COOKERS

REMOTE COOKING

I work all day; is there any way I can cook when I'm not at home?

Yes, with an electric slow cooker. They have been around since the 1970s, although the idea of slow cooking is not new. Stews and soups have been cooked gently all day in ovens alongside the kitchen range for many centuries.

Today's slow cooker usually consists of a glazed earthenware bowl and lid set into an outer casing, with an electric element between the two. The heat is extremely gentle with no 'hot spots', so you can leave the food for long periods without ever having to stir it.

WISE USE

Can you tell me what kind of foods cook best in a slow cooker?

Slow cookers are perfect for the tougher, cheaper cuts of meat which are tenderised by long slow cooking. The steam condenses on the lid and falls back into the pot to keep the food moist. But a slow cooker will not brown the meat, so brown it first in a pan to improve the appearance and flavour.

Because the temperature is so low in a slow cooker, the cooking liquid must be brought to the boil before adding it to the slow cooker, otherwise it would take far too long to reach the correct temperature for cooking meat. Resist the temptation to remove the lid during cooking. The food does not need stirring and you will be lowering the heat in the cooker.

Meat with a high fat content should be trimmed and browned first, and then the fat drained off because it does not 'bake off' as it does when cooked in a hot oven.

As well as making casseroles and stews, slow cookers can be used for cooking chutneys, curds, fruit, jams, overnight porridge and both milk and steamed puddings.

SMOKED FISH

GOOD LOOKS

How can I be sure a smoked fish is of a high quality?

Look for fish that are plump and shiny. Any which look dry and shrivelled, with the flesh pulling away from the bones, are past their prime. Smoking was originally a method used, together with salting and drying, to preserve fish for long periods. Today it is done mainly to add flavour and is not meant to preserve the fish for as long as traditional smoking.

Much smoked fish is artificially coloured to suggest that the fish has been smoked for longer than it has been. Natural dyes which do not affect the taste are used, but there is an increasing demand for naturally coloured smoked fish as some people are allergic to dyes.

HOT AND COLD

Why does some smoked fish need to be cooked and others not?

It depends on how it has been treated. There are two methods of smoking, hot and cold, and the appearance and texture of the finished product is different.

Hot-smoked fish and seafood such as buckling, eel, kippers, mackerel, mussels, oysters, swordfish, trout and tuna has dry, firm flesh and looks as though it has been cooked. It does not need further cooking because the high temperature of the hot-smoking process cooks the fish, though it is sometimes heated through for serving. It does not keep as well as cold-smoked fish and seafood.

Cold-smoked fish, for example Arbroath smokies, bloaters, cod, haddock and finnan haddock, has the velvety translucence of fresh seafood and almost always needs to be grilled, poached or steamed. But delicate cold-smoked halibut, salmon, sturgeon and cod's roe are eaten uncooked. (See also SALMON.)

GOOD COMPANIONS

What is a good accompaniment to smoked fish? It is so strongly flavoured I find it hard to choose the right partner.

Smoked foods are often eaten on their own – kippers or smoked haddock for breakfast, buckling or smoked salmon with brown bread to begin a meal. And their strong flavours make them ideal for mashing into pâtés and mousses, often with added horseradish, which are served on toast. Smoked fish go particularly well with bland carbohydrates such as rice, as in kedgeree. Combined with raw vegetables and eggs, they also make a very tasty salad (see below).

Smoked mackerel and fennel salad

SERVES: 4
PREPARATION TIME: 30 minutes
COOKING TIME: 8 minutes for the eggs, none if using leftovers

---

300 ml (10 fl oz) mayonnaise (see recipe page 233)
4 eggs, size 2, hard-boiled
25 g (1 oz) gherkins, thinly sliced
25 g (1 oz) capers, drained
2 tablespoons chopped parsley
500 g (1 lb 2 oz) new potatoes, cooked and sliced
1 medium fennel bulb, about 500 g (1 lb 2 oz), thinly sliced, and leaves reserved
1 small crisp lettuce
1 large bunch watercress
4 smoked mackerel fillets

---

1 Put the mayonnaise in a bowl. Cut the eggs into thin slices, reserving eight slices for the garnish, then stir them into the mayonnaise with the gherkins, capers, parsley, potatoes and the sliced fennel.
2 Arrange a generous bed of lettuce and watercress on four dinner plates. Spoon a quarter of the mayonnaise salad on one half of each plate and arrange a mackerel fillet beside it.
3 Garnish each salad with the reserved egg slices and fennel leaves. Serve with a warm bread such as focaccia, or one made with olives.

SMOKED COD'S EGGS

I see smoked cod's roe everywhere now: what can I do with it?

Smoked cod's roe may look like a strange lump, but it is simple to handle. Just scrape the delectable salty inner flesh from the tough outside membrane, then mash it or slice it thinly to serve on toast or water biscuits as a snack.

Alternatively, you can blend it with garlic, olive oil and lemon juice to make the Greek purée of cod's roe called *taramasalata*, which in Greece is more usually made from the roe of grey mullet. The taramasalata you make yourself will have a fresher, deeper flavour than the bright pink versions you can buy in the shops.

Taramasalata

SERVES: 6 - 8 as a starter
PREPARATION TIME: 15 minutes plus chilling time
COOKING TIME: none

---

60 g (2 ¼ oz) white crustless bread
4 tablespoons milk or water
250 g (9 oz) smoked cod's roe
1 clove garlic, crushed
200 ml (7 fl oz) olive oil
2 tablespoons lemon juice
1 tablespoon hot water
Black pepper

---

1 Put the bread in a bowl, pour on the milk or water and leave to soak while you prepare everything else.
2 Scoop the cod's roe out of its skin and put it in a mixing bowl. Squeeze the bread with your hands to press out all the water and add it to the roe with the garlic. Beat well with a wooden spoon or electric whisk.
3 Add the oil, drop by drop, as for a mayonnaise, beating all the time to make it into a thick, creamy paste.
4 Gradually beat in the lemon juice and hot water and season with black pepper. Taste the taramasalta and add more lemon juice if you like. Spoon the mixture into a dish and chill.
5 Serve with hot pitta bread, crispy toast or crudités. Taramasalata also makes a good sandwich filling or a perfect baked potato topping.

SNAILS

GARDENER'S REVENGE

Is the garden snail edible?

Yes, in theory you can prepare garden snails for eating, but they require a period of starvation first to rid them of impurities, which requires some expertise and makes their preparation time-consuming.

It is much better and easier to buy snails in cans already cooked, often with shells included in the pack, so that you can stuff them back inside with plenty of garlic and parsley butter, then heat them through and serve with good bread to mop up the buttery juices.

SOFT FRUIT

DELICATE WASH

Should soft fruits be washed before you eat them?

It depends on the type of fruit and where it came from. Wild blackberries should always be washed but those sold in the supermarket are cultivated and should not need it.

Do not wash raspberries, loganberries or tayberries as it will spoil their juicy texture. Strawberries, too, should not be washed, unless they are particularly dusty.

Blackcurrants, gooseberries, redcurrants and whitecurrants should be put into a colander and rinsed under a gently running tap.

ADDING FLAVOUR

What can I do if I find I have accidentally bought strawberries that are virtually tasteless?

If serving such strawberries with cream or ice cream, you can develop their flavour by dusting them with sugar and leaving them to stand for about an hour. Slice any large ones first. Sprinkling them with a little kirsch, Cointreau or Grand Marnier will also improve

the flavour. If the strawberries are to be put into a flan, or on top of a cake, they can be mixed with some hot, sieved strawberry jam, or glazed. This will compensate for the disappointing strawberries.

TRUE BLUE

What is the difference between a bilberry and a blueberry?

Bilberries and blueberries are actually members of the same family. The bilberry, which is also known as the blaeberry or whortleberry, is slightly smaller but more flavoursome and can be substituted for blueberries in recipes.

Wild bilberries grow on a low spreading shrub common to moorlands and mountains, and can be found growing anywhere there is heather. During July and August you can pick dark purple wild bilberries that are very tart, unlike the cultivated variety, which are larger, plumper, juicier and sweeter.

Wild blueberries are generally smaller than cultivated blueberries. Imported blueberries are available year-round, however, British cultivated blueberries are available only from April to October.

HULLING STRAWBERRIES

Soft fruits such as blackberries, loganberries, raspberries, strawberries and tayberries are each hulled in the same way.

Gently but firmly, pull the circle of green leaves away from the berry; the white central core, or the hull, of the fruit will come away at the same time. In some varieties, or if the fruit is not very ripe, it may be necessary to remove the core of the berry with the tip of a knife.

WILD HARVEST

There are so many blackberries around in the autumn, can you suggest some interesting ways of using them other than in jam?

Fresh blackberries have a wonderful affinity with autumn apples, sweet grapes and other hedgerow fruit such as sloes and wild plums. They are often cooked with these fruits in crumbles, pies and compotes or in suet pudding (see SUET).

Blackberries also go particularly well with game birds and are in season at the same time. The recipe below is for a domestic bird with a similar flavour to game, but if you cannot find guinea fowl, use small chickens instead. The blackberry stuffing makes them succulent.

Guinea fowl with blackberry stuffing and piquant blackberry sauce

SERVES: 4
PREPARATION TIME: 50 - 55 minutes
COOKING TIME: 65 - 70 minutes

---

60 g (2 1/4 oz) wild rice
Salt
85 g (3 oz) butter, softened
1 medium onion, finely chopped
2 dessert apples, peeled, cored and
    roughly chopped
2 guinea fowl, each about
    1 kg (2 lb 4 oz)
125 g (4 1/2 oz) blackberries, hulled
4 tablespoons chopped fresh parsley
Salt and black pepper
To garnish: washed blackberries
    and blackberry leaves, optional

FOR THE SAUCE
225 g (8 oz) blackberries, hulled
100 ml (3 1/2 fl oz) red wine
1 tablespoon plain flour
225 ml (8 fl oz) chicken stock
2 tablespoons demerara sugar
2 tablespoons blackberry or
    raspberry vinegar
Salt and black pepper

---

1 Cook the wild rice in some gently boiling salted water for about 45 - 50 minutes, or until it is cooked.
2 Meanwhile, heat 25 g (1 oz) of the softened butter in a frying pan, add

A colourful stuffing of wild rice, blackberries and parsley matches perfectly the gamy flavour of guinea fowl.

the chopped onion and cook over a gentle heat for 5 minutes, until it is softened but not browned.

3 Stir the apples into the onion and continue cooking for 5 - 10 minutes until the apples are just softened. Remove the pan from the heat and allow the mixture to cool.

4 Preheat the oven to 200°C (400°F, gas mark 6). Rinse inside the cavities of the guinea fowl and pat them dry with kitchen paper.

5 When the rice is cooked, tip it into a sieve, rinse under a cold tap and drain well. Add the rice, the blackberries and the parsley to the onion and apple mixture, season with salt and pepper and mix well.

6 Fill the cavity of each guinea fowl with the blackberry stuffing. Truss the birds neatly with string and put them in a roasting tin. Spread the remaining butter evenly over each bird, season with salt and pepper and roast in the centre of the oven

for 60 - 75 minutes, basting every 15 minutes or so until they are cooked; they are done when the juices run clear from a skewer piercing the thickest part of the thigh.

7 While the guinea fowl are in the oven roasting, put the blackberries for the sauce into a stainless-steel or enamel saucepan with half the wine. Cover and cook for 10 - 15 minutes or until they are very soft, then pass them through a nylon sieve to make a purée and set aside until needed.

8 Lift the cooked guinea fowl from the roasting tin and put them onto a heated serving plate. Cover loosely with foil and leave to rest.

9 To make the fruit sauce, skim all but 2 tablespoons of the fat from the surface of the juices in the roasting tin. Stir the flour into the juices, then add the remaining red wine and chicken stock. Bring to the boil, stirring and scraping any browned residue from the bottom of the tin.

10 Strain the gravy mixture into a saucepan then stir in the blackberry purée, the demerara sugar, and the blackberry or raspberry vinegar. Season it well and simmer gently, stirring frequently, for 10 minutes. Taste the sauce and add more sugar if necessary. Pour the finished sauce into a heated serving jug.

11 Remove the trussing string from the guinea fowl, then garnish with blackberry leaves and blackberries. Serve with the sauce. Baby carrots, runner beans, red cabbage and new potatoes are good accompaniments.

SWEET CROSSES

Which are the sweeter fruits, tayberries or loganberries?

Tayberries are marginally sweeter than loganberries, although both are crosses between blackberries and raspberries. As with any fruit, the sweetness can vary.

SUPERIOR GLAZE

I am always impressed by the fresh fruit tarts I see in patisserie shops – how do they make the fruit look so shiny?

By glazing the fruit. The easiest glaze is made from jam, ideally the same flavour as the fruit in the tart. This should be heated with 1–2 tablespoons of water, sieved to remove any seeds, stones and skin, then brought to the boil and brushed or spooned over the fruit.

Redcurrant jelly or apricot jam can be used as general-purpose glazes. Alternatively, fruit juice can be thickened with arrowroot to make a clear glaze (see also TARTS).

STOP IT COLLAPSING

Why does my summer pudding always collapse?

There are several reasons why this might happen. The bread may not have been dry enough or the syrup not heavy enough; there may have been gaps in the bread lining the basin; or perhaps the pudding was not weighted down properly or thoroughly chilled. The secrets to making a good summer pudding are relatively simple, and you can apply them to the party-sized Summer Pudding recipe below.

Use good quality uncut bread, and buy it two to three days beforehand so it can dry out. Dry bread will absorb the juice from the fruit better and will swell, rather than just become soggy and disintegrate. Cook the fruit just long enough for it to soften yet remain whole. This will ensure you have a lusciously heavy, syrupy juice. Most importantly, make sure that the pudding is really well-weighted down.

Summer pudding

SERVES: 12
PREPARATION TIME: 30 – 40 minutes, plus 24 hours chilling
COOKING TIME: 15 – 20 minutes

225 g (8 oz) redcurrants, removed from stalks, rinsed and drained
500 g (1 lb 2 oz) blackcurrants, removed from stalks, rinsed and drained
350 – 450 g (12 oz – 1 lb) sugar
Finely grated rind and juice of 1 large orange
225 g (8 oz) raspberries
225 g (8 oz) loganberries or tayberries
450 g (1 lb) blueberries, rinsed and drained
225 g (8 oz) strawberries, halved if large
14 – 16 thin slices stale white bread, crusts removed

FOR SERVING
425 ml (15 fl oz) double cream
1 level tablespoon caster sugar
2 – 3 tablespoons rosewater
1 – 2 tablespoons orange flower water

1 Put the red and blackcurrants, the sugar (adding to taste), orange rind and juice into a large stainless-steel saucepan. Stir well, then cover the pan and cook over a moderate heat, stirring frequently, until the sugar has dissolved and the juice begins to flow, about 10 – 15 minutes.
2 Add the remaining fruits to the pan, stir to mix, then cover and cook for 10 – 15 minutes until all the fruits are softened, but not broken up. Remove from the heat.
3 Cut a round from one of the slices of bread, making it large enough to fit the bottom of a 2 litre (3½ pint) pudding basin, and put it in the base of the basin. Then cut the remaining bread slices in half lengthways and line the sides, overlapping the slices and not leaving any gaps. Reserve the rest of the bread for the top.
4 Carefully spoon all the fruit and most of the fruit juice into the lined basin, reserving any leftover juice. Completely cover the surface with the remaining sliced bread, cutting extra slices if necessary.
5 Stand the bowl in a deep dish to catch any juice that may overflow. Cover the top closely with cling film and place a small flat plate on top with some heavy weights. Chill the pudding for at least 24 hours. Pour any remaining juice into a bowl, cover and chill until needed.
6 Just before serving the pudding, whip the cream lightly with the sugar, rosewater and orange flower water and pour into a serving bowl. Remove the weights and cling film from the pudding. Gently run a palette knife around the side of the pudding to loosen it from the basin, then turn out onto a serving dish.
7 Spoon some of the reserved juice over the pudding to make it glisten and also to colour any pale patches. Pour any remaining juice into a jug and serve with the pudding. Once it has been turned out, serve the pudding immediately, accompanied by the flavoured cream.

VARIATIONS
Substitute some of the berries in this recipe with cherries, sliced peaches or sliced apricots. To make a winter pudding, use tree fruits such as dessert apples, apricots, pears and plums flavoured with a little ground cinnamon or allspice, and use slices of wholemeal bread instead of white. Or, use reconstituted dried fruits flavoured with cinnamon to fill a wholemeal bread case. Serve with the flower water flavoured cream.

SORBET: see ICE CREAM

SOUFFLE

HIGH RISE

How do I bake the perfect soufflé?

Soufflés are relatively easy to make as long as a few basic rules are followed. To produce a hot soufflé, egg whites are stiffly whisked and folded into a thick, flavoured sauce then cooked in a straight-sided dish.

The consistency of the panade, the thick basic sauce, is crucial. It must be soft enough so that the whisked egg whites can be folded easily into it. If it is too thick, the soufflé will not rise properly. If it is too thin, it will knock air out of the whisked egg whites and the soufflé will not rise properly.

Under or overwhisking the egg whites will also result in a poorly risen soufflé. Follow the instructions below for a savoury soufflé.

This Cheddar-topped soufflé cooks to puffy, golden brown perfection. Add a little Dijon mustard to highlight the savoury cheese flavour of the basic sauce.

Cheese soufflé

SERVES: 4
PREPARATION TIME: 1 hour, plus 30 minutes infusing time for the milk
COOKING TIME: 30 minutes

225 ml (8 fl oz) whole milk
1 slice of onion
1 small carrot, sliced
½ celery stick, sliced
1 bay leaf
4 peppercorns
25 g (1 oz) salted butter, plus extra for greasing
1 tablespoon Parmesan cheese, finely grated
25 g (1 oz) plain flour
½ teaspoon Dijon mustard
4 eggs, size 3, separated, plus 2 extra egg whites
115 g (4 oz) Cheddar cheese, grated
Salt and black pepper

1 Put the milk, onion, carrot, celery, bay leaf and peppercorns in a small saucepan and bring them slowly to the boil. Remove from the heat, cover and set aside to infuse for around 30 minutes. Strain, reserving the milk.
2 Brush a 1.4 litre (2½ pint) soufflé dish all over with melted butter, taking it right up to the top, and sprinkle the Parmesan cheese over the base and sides of the dish.
3 Preheat the oven to 180°C (350°F, gas mark 4). Melt the butter in a saucepan, stir in the flour and cook gently for a minute or two, stirring continuously. Remove the pan from the heat and stir in the milk.
4 Return the pan to the heat and bring the sauce slowly to the boil, stirring continuously. Continue to cook the sauce for 5 minutes, until it thickens, then lower the heat, stir briefly and simmer the sauce gently for around 10 minutes.
5 Remove the pan from the heat and allow to cool slightly. Beat the mustard, egg yolks, Cheddar cheese and the seasoning into the sauce, reserving a tablespoon of the cheese.
6 In a large bowl, whisk the egg whites until they form stiff peaks. Fold 2 tablespoons of the whisked egg whites into the cheese sauce, then carefully fold in the remaining whisked egg whites, using a cutting and folding action. Be careful not to overmix, but make sure there are no visible flecks of egg white.

7 Gently pour the soufflé mixture into the prepared dish. Using a table or palette knife, pierce the surface of the soufflé 2.5 cm (1 in) in from the edge of the dish and carefully move the knife in a circle around the edge of the mixture to release any trapped air bubbles and ensure that the soufflé rises evenly.
8 Sprinkle the reserved cheese over the top of the soufflé and bake for about 30 minutes, until the soufflé is well risen, golden brown and just firm to the touch: the centre may be slightly soft. Do not open the oven door to check on the soufflé for at least 25 minutes. Serve immediately.

VARIATIONS

Add 1 - 2 tablespoons of chopped fresh mixed herbs with the cheese, or use Stilton instead of the Cheddar.

For a spinach soufflé, replace the cheese with 225 g (8 oz) of cooked, chopped and drained spinach then gently fold in 2 tablespoons of grated Parmesan and a pinch of nutmeg.

For a seafood soufflé, add 200 g (7 oz) of drained and flaked canned salmon or tuna and 1 - 2 tablespoons of chopped fresh tarragon.

FORWARD PLANNING

How far ahead can I make the base of a soufflé, and how many eggs should I use?

The panade, or basic sauce, of the soufflé can be made in advance and kept in the refrigerator for several hours before using. It should then be reheated gently before folding in the whisked egg whites.

If the whisked egg whites are folded into a cold base, the volume of the soufflé will be lost, as the sauce will be much stiffer and it will be difficult to fold the whites in lightly. It is essential that once the egg whites have been folded in, the soufflé is baked immediately.

To serve four people you need four whole eggs, size 3, plus an extra two egg whites. The amount of filling you need depends on the type of flavouring being added.

KEEP IT CLOSED

Is it an old wives' tale that you should not open the oven door when baking a soufflé?

Opening the oven door is unlikely to be a disaster unless your kitchen is very draughty, but you are much more likely to make a successful soufflé if you keep the oven door closed during cooking. The soufflé should increase in volume by at least half and sometimes as much as double and to do this it must cook at the correct temperature. Opening the oven door will cause a sudden drop in temperature.

BURNT OFFERINGS

My soufflés always burn on the outside - what should I do?

Baking in too hot an oven will result in a creamy-centred soufflé that is well risen but burnt on the outside. This type of soufflé will collapse very quickly. Check first with an oven thermometer if your oven settings are above normal; if so, choose a slightly lower setting.

To test how well a soufflé is cooked, open the door a little, put your hand through and give the dish a sharp nudge. If the soufflé is very steady, it will be dry in the centre; if it trembles a little, it will have a slightly set centre; in either case it is done. If it wobbles easily, the soufflé will still be liquid in the centre and you should leave it in the oven for a few minutes longer.

Put it on ice

You can make individual soufflés in advance and freeze uncooked until required. Preheat the oven to the temperature specified in the recipe and cook them from frozen, adding 5 minutes to the cooking time.

CLINGING TO THE SIDE

Should a soufflé dish always be buttered and lightly floured before the mixture is poured in?

Yes, because the combination of grease and dusting, with flour, caster sugar, finely grated cheese or very fine breadcrumbs, provides the right surface for the soufflé to cling to as it rises in the dish.

NECESSARY FRILLS

Do I really have to bother with a paper collar? My soufflés seem all right without them.

A hot soufflé may be baked without a collar, but as the mixture is delicate, it could rise unevenly or with a crown in the centre. This does not affect the taste.

Cold soufflés, which are not cooked but set, need a collar to support the mixture until it chills and sets, otherwise it will simply flow over the sides of the dish. The greaseproof paper collar should stand at least 2.5 cm (1 in) above the rim of the soufflé dish.

The 'collar' area of a cold soufflé is often decorated with ingredients such as chopped nuts or grated chocolate and the stunning visual effect of the chilled mixture rising above the dish after the collar has been removed is what distinguishes a cold soufflé from a mousse.

SOUP

TOO MUCH SALT

What can I do to rescue a soup that is too salty?

Add some unsalted stock, milk or cream, which will dilute the flavour as well as the saltiness, or add a large peeled and halved potato and simmer for 20 minutes: the potato will absorb some salt as it cooks. Remove the potato before serving.

Overseasoned soup is quite a common problem, especially if you use stock cubes, which are very highly seasoned. It can also be a problem with homemade stocks if they contain salt, as soups are often boiled until reduced, concentrating the seasoning. It is best to leave the seasoning of stocks and soups until the end, or if you are using a stock cube, use half a cube to the prescribed amount of water.

GIVE IT BODY

How can I rescue thin soup?

The easiest solution is to reduce the soup by simmering it without the lid to evaporate some of the liquid, but this can take some time and could concentrate the seasoning too much. Alternatively, thicken it with beurre manié, cornflour, or arrowroot (as you do for a sauce).

If the soup contains cooked vegetables, all or some of these can be puréed (by mashing, sieving or liquidising) and then stirred back into the soup to thicken it. Alternatively, add some finely chopped vegetables which will cook quickly in the soup and can also be puréed.

WHICH FAT?

Does it matter whether I use oil or butter to cook the vegetables for soup, and what do I do if the soup is very greasy?

Any oil or fat can be used to sauté the vegetables for soup. Butter, meat or poultry dripping, olive oil or vegetable oil, will all give their individual flavours to the soup. Margarine does not provide such a good flavour and low-fat spreads are not suitable for frying because many of them are almost half water.

After sautéeing the vegetables, a little flour can be stirred in to soak up any excess fat and form a roux, and the resulting soup should not be greasy. If you do end up with a greasy soup, pour or spoon off any oil that comes to the surface, or if you have time, chill the soup so that the fat solidifies on the surface and can be easily lifted off. For a fat-free version, the oil or fat can be eliminated and the vegetables just simmered in the stock.

The substantial spiced vegetable soup below is cooked with very little oil, and with the exception of a green pepper, can be made with ingredients in the store cupboard.

Chilli vegetable soup

SERVES: 4
PREPARATION TIME: 20 minutes plus soaking and cooking beans
COOKING TIME: 30 – 40 minutes

---

250 g (9 oz) mixed dried beans (such as black-eyed, butter, chickpea, haricot, kidney, pinto)
2 tablespoons sunflower or olive oil
1 large onion, chopped
1 large green pepper, deseeded and chopped
1 clove garlic, crushed
2 tablespoons flour
1/2 – 1 teaspoon chilli powder, to taste
400 g (14 oz) canned tomatoes with juice, roughly chopped
500 ml (18 fl oz) vegetable or chicken stock

FOR THE GARLIC TOAST
1 loaf French bread
25 g (1 oz) butter, softened
1 clove garlic, crushed

1 Prepare the beans you have chosen according to the chart in DRIED BEANS. When they are ready for their final low-boil, put those that require a longer cooking time into a saucepan with 1 litre (1 pint 15 fl oz) of fresh unsalted water. Bring it to the boil,

A colourful selection of beans and a buttery garlic toast topping make this chilli-flavoured vegetable soup a satisfying choice for winter evenings.

reduce the heat, then cover the pan and simmer, adding the other beans according to the bean cooking chart. When all the beans are just tender, drain and set aside.
2 Heat the oil in a medium-large saucepan and sauté the onion for a few minutes. Add the pepper and garlic and fry for 2 minutes. Stir in the flour and the chilli powder and then cook, stirring, for a minute.
3 Add the tomatoes and the stock, bring to the boil, and stir until lightly thickened. Add the cooked,

drained beans, then cover the pan and simmer for 30 minutes until the beans are very tender.
4 Preheat the grill. Cut the bread into 2 cm (3/4 in) slices, put them on a baking sheet and grill on one side until lightly toasted. Mash the butter and garlic together. Turn over the bread, spread the untoasted sides with garlic butter and grill until they are lightly browned.
5 Place the soup in bowls and top each with two pieces of the hot garlic toast. Serve immediately.

CLEVER GARNISHING

Can you suggest some interesting new garnishes for soups?

Garnishes should look attractive, be edible and complement the flavour of the soup. Some typical examples include a sprinkling of fresh herbs or spices on a thick, rich soup, or more robust croutons or cheese on a lighter soup. Here are some more ideas:
- Whole sprigs of herbs, such as basil, dill, marjoram, mint, parsley, or thyme, or chopped leaves.
- Shredded lettuce, cress, spring onion or watercress, or diced or sliced raw vegetables, such as cucumber, sweet pepper, tomato.
- Chopped, shredded or sliced vegetables, blanched or cooked, such as cabbage, carrot, courgette, leek, mushroom or peas.
- Whole edible perfumed flowers, such as borage, chive, heartsease, and thyme, or marigold petals.
- Croutons of fried bread or toast, slices of French bread, dumplings.
- Cream, soured cream, fromage frais or plain yoghurt, swirled on in an attractive pattern.
- Cooked and finely chopped or shredded meat, ham or poultry, or pieces of crispy bacon.
- Thinly shredded smoked salmon, smoked sturgeon or salmon roe.

EGG ENRICHED

I have heard you can thicken a soup with egg. How do you do it?

Adding egg to thicken a soup is a little tricky as it will curdle or scramble if overheated. Beat one or two egg yolks (or whole eggs) in a bowl and stir in a little of the hot soup. Then strain this into the pan and stir over a gentle heat until thickened; do not allow it to boil.

This method can be used for a hot soup or one to be served cold (which will thicken further on cooling). For an even richer soup, the eggs can be mixed with some cream. The Greek recipe (right) is for one of the most famous egg-thickened soups, based on chicken stock and flavoured with lemon.

Mixing egg yolks and cream with a little of the soup then gently pouring it back into the pan will give a delicious thick and velvety texture to this lemon flavoured chicken soup.

Avgolémono

SERVES: 4
PREPARATION TIME: 10 minutes
COOKING TIME: 20 minutes

---

1 litre (1 pint 15 fl oz) good chicken stock
Salt and black pepper
50 g (1 ¾ oz) long-grain rice
2 eggs, size 3
2 tablespoons lemon juice
To garnish: lemon slices and sprigs of thyme or parsley

---

1 Pour the stock into a saucepan, bring to the boil and season with salt and pepper to taste. Add the rice and simmer gently for 10 - 15 minutes or until the rice is tender.
2 Beat the eggs and lemon juice in a small bowl. Add 150 ml (5 fl oz) of the hot stock, beat well, then stir it into the soup. Reheat very gently, stirring constantly to give a thick, creamy soup (do not allow it to boil or the soup will curdle).
3 Pour the soup into serving bowls and garnish with lemon slices and sprigs of thyme or parsley.

NO STOCK

If I want to make a quick soup and have neither homemade stock nor cubes what can I use?

You do not have to have stock to make soup as long as the other ingredients provide flavour. You can also make a quick stock to use in a specific recipe. Chop a selection of vegetables such as carrots, celery, leeks, mushrooms, onions or potatoes. Sauté them in butter first, or just simmer them until tender in water with flavourings such as herbs, citrus peel, juice or wine. The resulting stock can be strained, or the vegetables may be puréed with the stock by liquidising or sieving to give a thick puréed soup.

If you want to use a stock base, good-quality stock is now available in jars or bottles which can be kept in the store cupboard with cans of consommé, which can also be diluted and used instead of stock. Chilled fresh stock is also sold in cartons in supermarkets; it can be kept in the refrigerator for two or three days, or frozen.

The following recipe for Gazpacho, the celebrated cold Spanish soup that needs no cooking, is a good example of a highly flavoured soup that is nevertheless made without stock. (See also STOCK.)

Gazpacho

SERVES: 4
PREPARATION TIME: 1 hour (or 15 minutes using a liquidiser) plus 30 minutes soaking
COOKING TIME: 5 minutes for the crouton garnish

---

1 thick slice white bread, crusts removed
2 large cloves garlic, crushed
2 tablespoons red wine vinegar
4 tablespoons olive oil
500 g (1 lb 2 oz) ripe tomatoes, skinned, deseeded and finely diced (reserve juice)
1 large red pepper, quartered, deseeded and finely diced
1 large green pepper, quartered, deseeded and finely diced
1 medium Spanish onion, grated
1 large cucumber, peeled and finely diced
½ teaspoon salt
Black pepper to taste
1 sprig fresh basil or marjoram
250 ml (9 fl oz) ice-cold water
To garnish: 50 g (1 ¾ oz) croutons

---

1 Cut the bread into small cubes and put them in a large mixing bowl. Add the garlic and vinegar and crush together with a fork. Gradually add the olive oil, mashing it all to a paste. Stir the tomato pulp and juice into the bread mixture.

2 Set aside a quarter of the diced peppers then put the rest of them, the grated onion and the cucumber into the bowl with the bread and tomato pulp mixture. Add the salt, the pepper to taste plus the basil or marjoram and stir well to combine. Cover and leave for 30 minutes, allowing the flavours to amalgamate and the juices to seep out.

3 Rub the soup through a sieve into another bowl, pushing down on the vegetables with a wooden spoon until you get about 600 ml (1 pint) of smooth, thick purée. Stir in the iced water and chill until required.

4 Alternatively, for a soup that is thicker and crunchier, the iced water can be liquidised with the vegetables remaining in the sieve, sieved again and then added to the soup.

5 To serve, pour into soup bowls and sprinkle the croutons and the reserved chopped peppers on top, or hand them round separately in small bowls. Crushed ice cubes can also be added just before serving.

VARIATION

For a quick but equally delicious version of gazpacho, put all the ingredients, roughly chopped, in a liquidiser (in batches if necessary), purée and then rub through a sieve and chill until required. There is no need for you to skin and deseed the tomatoes when using this method.

THICK AND RICH

How do you make cream soups?

By mashing, liquidising or sieving the soup to a 'cream'. Cream soups do not necessarily contain cream. They may be thickened by purée-ing vegetables (especially starchy ones such as potato or root vegetables) with stock and these can then be sieved for a smoother texture.

Soups are also often thickened with flour, in the form of a roux or beurre manié. Cream can be added to enrich the soup and should be stirred in at the end of cooking. The following soup recipe is thickened with flour and double cream.

Cream of mushroom soup

SERVES: 6 - 8
PREPARATION TIME: 15 minutes, plus 10 - 30 minutes standing time
COOKING TIME: 40 minutes

---

500 ml (18 fl oz) milk
1 small onion, sliced
1 small carrot, sliced
1 stick of celery, sliced
1 bay leaf
3 parsley stalks
1 blade of mace
6 black peppercorns
50 g (1 ¾ oz) butter
1 medium onion, chopped
250 g (9 oz) mushrooms, sliced
500 ml (18 fl oz) beef, chicken or vegetable stock
½ teaspoon salt
Black pepper
25 g (1 oz) plain flour
150 ml (5 fl oz) double cream
2 tablespoons chopped parsley

---

1 Pour the milk into a saucepan and add the sliced onion, carrot, celery, bay leaf, parsley stalks, mace and the peppercorns. Heat gently until just simmering, then remove from the heat, cover and leave to stand for at least 10 minutes, but preferably for around 30 minutes or longer.

2 Melt half of the butter in a large saucepan and sauté the chopped onion gently for 2 minutes. Add the mushrooms and sauté for 5 minutes, stirring occasionally. Add the stock, bring to the boil, cover and simmer for 10 minutes. Liquidise well to a smooth, thin purée and reserve.

3 Melt the rest of the butter in a large, clean saucepan, stir in the flour and cook gently to a sandy textured roux. Gradually add the strained, flavoured milk, stirring well until thickened and smooth, then simmer gently for 20 minutes.

4 Add the reserved mushroom purée and stir well over a gentle heat. Cook the soup at simmering point for another 2 minutes.

5 Stir the cream into the soup then reheat it gently, without boiling. Check the seasoning and then serve sprinkled with chopped parsley.

Smooth and warming, this mushroom soup is enriched with double cream and sprinkled with fresh parsley. Serve it with fresh bread for a light lunch or supper.

SOUTH-EAST ASIAN COOKING

DIFFERENT CURRIES

What is the difference between the curries of South-east Asian cooking and the curries of India?

The range of South-east Asian curries is wide. Some use dry ground spice mixtures similar to those used in Indian cooking, but just as many use only fresh ingredients, such as chillies, coriander roots, galangal, garlic, ginger, lemongrass, shallots and sweet basil.

Some of the best curries use a combination of dried and fresh ingredients, so a korma prepared with dried spices may be given an aromatic top note with fresh coriander, mint and sweet basil. A typical Thai curry that uses fresh spices is the green curry below. It can be made with chicken, pork or prawns instead of vegetables.

Thai vegetable curry

SERVES: 2
PREPARATION TIME: 20 minutes
COOKING TIME: 15 minutes

6 Thai baby aubergines or
  2 courgettes
1 carrot
1 teaspoon sugar
2 green chillies, deseeded and
  roughly chopped
1 small bunch fresh coriander with
  roots, thoroughly cleaned, or
  pound the whole stalk and leaves
1/2 large onion, roughly chopped
2 cloves garlic, chopped
1 teaspoon shrimp paste
1 stalk lemongrass
2 thin slices galangal
2 kaffir lime leaves
3 tablespoons vegetable oil
500 ml (18 fl oz) coconut milk
20 green or french beans, trimmed
2 tablespoons fish sauce

1 Peel and cut the aubergines diagonally into slices 2 cm (¾ in) thick; if using courgettes instead,

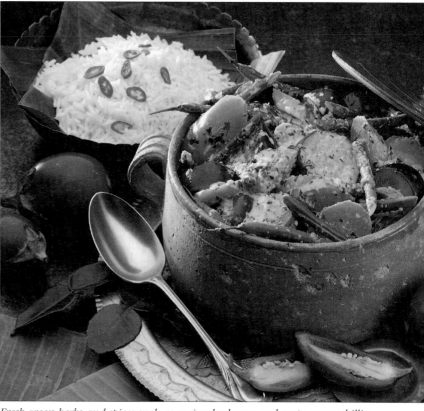

Fresh green herbs and spices such as coriander leaves and roots, green chillies and kaffir lime leaves add pungency to this Thai curry of vegetables.

peel and slice them. Peel and slice the carrot diagonally.
2 Finely grind the sugar with the chillies, coriander, onion, garlic, shrimp paste, lemongrass, galangal and kaffir lime leaves in a pestle and mortar, coffee grinder, or food processor (the mixture will be dry).
3 Heat the oil and fry the spice paste over a low heat for 5 minutes until it smells powerfully aromatic. Add the coconut milk and vegetables and bring the mixture to the boil.
4 Add the fish sauce, then lower the heat and simmer for 8 minutes. Adjust the seasoning and serve the curry hot with plain boiled rice.

JUICY FRUIT

What is tamarind used for in South-east Asian cooking?

The juice of the pulp around the seeds of the tamarind, sometimes called the Indian date, is used to give a fruity, sour flavour to many South-east Asian curries and spicy dishes. Those that do not contain tamarind juice tend to be cooked in coconut milk. Generally, tamarind is used with seafood while coconut accompanies meat and poultry dishes, but this is not a strict rule.

Tamarind is available in several forms, the most common being brown or black blocks of concentrated pulp, which must be soaked in hot water before using. When the liquid has reached the desired acidity, like very strong lime juice, it is strained and used for cooking.

Some Asian and Oriental shops sell bottled tamarind concentrate in a thick liquid form that needs no further straining. The concentrate is very tart and should be diluted in the proportion of one part tamarind concentrate to two parts water. If you cannot find any tamarind, you can substitute fresh lime juice instead. In the following recipe for cod or halibut with tamarind and Asian spices, choose whichever is most convenient.

Fish in tamarind

SERVES: 4
PREPARATION TIME: 15 minutes, plus
30 minutes salting time
COOKING TIME: 15 minutes

500 g (1 lb 2 oz) cod or halibut
2 teaspoons salt
1 teaspoon chilli powder
1 teaspoon ground turmeric
2 cloves garlic, finely chopped
1 large onion, finely chopped
2 tablespoons prepared tamarind
 pulp or concentrate, or
 2 tablespoons lime juice
1 stalk lemongrass, lower stem
 bruised

1 Clean the fish, cut it into large chunks, rub with salt and set aside for about 30 minutes.
2 Pound the chilli powder with the turmeric, garlic and onion in a pestle and mortar. Mix with the tamarind, lemongrass and 600 ml (1 pint) of water in a wok or small saucepan and bring to the boil.
3 Simmer for 10 minutes, add the fish then cook for another 3 minutes. Serve immediately with rice.

THAI-TASTING

I have bought some Thai stir-fry vegetables which come with a packet of Thai sauce - can I make this sauce at home myself?

There is no standard stir-fry sauce for Thai dishes as such. Thai cooking has adapted the basic Chinese stir-fry sauces by adding chillies to give the flavour a little kick.

The basic seasoning in Chinese stir-frying is soy sauce. Thai cooks will generally use fish sauce (also known as *nam pla*) instead, which is basically soy sauce infused with fermented fish extracts taken from various fish. *Nam pla* tastes salty, very much like strong anchovy sauce, and can be found in Asian shops and some supermarkets.

Like the Chinese, Thai cooks use sesame oil and garlic to season their stir-fries. The following recipe is for an all-purpose sauce that you can use to give your usual stir-fry dishes a Thai taste.

Thai stir-fry sauce

MAKES: enough to season 500 g
(1 lb 2 oz) of fish or meat
PREPARATION TIME: 5 minutes
COOKING TIME: none

1 tablespoon sesame oil
2 teaspoons chilli paste
1 teaspoon sugar
½ teaspoon black pepper
2 cloves garlic, very finely chopped
2 tablespoons fish sauce

1 Mix together the sesame oil, chilli paste, sugar, black pepper and garlic.
2 Add some cooking oil to the wok according to your usual recipe, then add the sesame oil mixture. When it comes to the boil, add the fish sauce, then your other stir-fry ingredients and cook in the usual way.

GREATER GINGER

What is galangal?

Galangal looks very like its relative the ginger root, but has a paler, pinkish colour. It cannot be eaten raw and is usually ground up with ingredients such as garlic, lemongrass and onions to make a paste.

There are two varieties of galangal, the greater and the lesser. Both are used in South-east Asian cooking but it is the lesser that is the most flavoursome. Galangal is not readily available in supermarkets but you can buy it in Asian stores.

PERFUMED LEAVES

What are kaffir lime leaves?

These are the leaves of a lime tree native to tropical Asia. The leaves are shaped like a figure eight, with two leaves held together from the tip to the base. The small fruit of the kaffir lime can also be purchased from Chinese supermarkets.

Imparting their full, fresh, citric flavour, both the aromatic leaves and the bitter rind are used in Thai cooking, primarily in chicken and fish dishes, but only the leaves are used in Indonesia. To use, slice the kaffir lime leaves finely, which will give a stronger flavour, or crush them as you would bay leaves.

THAI SWEETS

Are there any Thai puddings?

Generally most Asian meals do not end with puddings. Desserts tend to be eaten as snacks during the day and sweets, if served at all, are reserved for special occasions.

Thai puddings are usually based on grains such as rice, sago and sweetcorn, as well as coconut milk and tropical fruits such as bananas, jackfruit and oranges.

Many Thai puddings are sweetened with palm sugar, also known as jaggery, or coconut sugar. This comes in hard cylinders that have to be grated, cakes that can be broken up, or as a thick treacle in tubs. If palm sugar is unavailable, use some muscovado or demerara sugar melted with a little water for this popular Thai dessert instead.

Sticky rice and mango pudding

SERVES: 4
PREPARATION TIME: 25 minutes, plus
at least 4 hours soaking time
COOKING TIME: 20 minutes

250 g (9 oz) sticky rice
1 teaspoon salt
140 g (5 oz) palm sugar
500 ml (18 fl oz) coconut milk
2 large sweet Thai or Indian
 mangoes, peeled and sliced

1 Wash the rice and add water to just cover, about 1 cm (½ in) over the top of the rice. Soak overnight or for at least 4 hours.
2 Drain the rice and stir in the salt. Steam the rice for 20 minutes over a pan of boiling water, then set aside to keep warm until needed.
3 Melt the palm sugar with a little water in the microwave, or in a bain-marie, until completely dissolved: do not do this over direct heat as the palm sugar will burn easily.
4 Mix the melted sugar and coconut milk well together in a bowl.
5 To serve, place a few tablespoons of rice in each bowl, top the rice with the sliced mangoes and drizzle on 2 tablespoons of the coconut milk and palm sugar mixture.

SPAGHETTI

BEEFING UP BOLOGNESE

I find bottled Bolognese sauces taste quite bland. Is there an authentic recipe with more zip?

Many bottled sauces lean heavily on tomato purée and leave out ingredients with stronger flavours used by Italian cooks, such as chicken livers and fresh chilli. As the recipe below shows, these additions, along with fresh vegetables and herbs, combine to make a memorable sauce. This is a substantial dish and does not need anything more than a salad of mixed leaves dressed with a well-seasoned vinaigrette to follow it.

Spaghetti alla Bolognese

SERVES: 6
PREPARATION TIME: 30 minutes
COOKING TIME: 1 ¼ hours

1 tablespoon olive oil
25 g (1 oz) butter
50 g (1 ¾ oz) unsmoked streaky
   bacon, cut into 5 mm (¼ in)
   strips
1 medium onion, finely chopped
1 stick celery, finely chopped
1 small carrot, finely chopped
1 clove garlic, finely chopped
225 g (8 oz) lean minced beef
50 g (1 ¾ oz) chicken livers,
   roughly chopped
150 ml (5 fl oz) red or white wine
225 ml (8 fl oz) stock
2 tablespoons tomato purée
175 g (6 oz) tomatoes, skinned
   and chopped
1 chilli, deseeded and finely chopped
1 bay leaf
A pinch of dried oregano
Several stalks of parsley, chopped
Salt and black pepper
A pinch of grated nutmeg
600 g (1 lb 5 oz) spaghetti

1 Heat the oil and butter in a heavy saucepan and cook the bacon until it starts to brown. Add the vegetables and cook together, stirring, for a few minutes until they begin to soften.

2 Add the minced beef and lightly brown, breaking it up with a fork at the same time. Add the chicken livers and cook for a minute or two until they lose their raw look.
3 Add the wine and boil rapidly until it evaporates. Add the stock, tomato purée, chopped tomatoes, chilli, bay leaf, oregano, parsley and some salt and pepper to taste. Cook, covered, over a very low heat for at least an hour. For best results, the sauce should barely simmer.
4 Add some grated nutmeg, taste for seasoning and adjust if necessary, then remove the bay leaf and parsley.
5 Ten or fifteen minutes before the sauce has finished cooking, while it is still simmering, cook the spaghetti. When cooked, drain and toss with the sauce. Serve with some Parmesan cheese, passed around with a grater.

Two of the best-loved pasta sauces are meaty Bolognese, right, and creamy carbonara, left, with bacon and egg.

HOW MUCH SAUCE?

What is the correct proportion of sauce to spaghetti?

There are no hard and fast rules. Italians like their pasta with very little sauce, just enough to thinly coat it as the spaghetti itself has a good flavour. In Britain people like to add far more sauce. But if the sauce has a very strong, concentrated flavour you will need less of it. To feed four people who like a lot of sauce, allowing about 375 g (13 oz) of spaghetti, a sauce made with 500 g (1 lb 2 oz) of fresh tomatoes, or 200 g (7 oz) of sun-dried tomatoes, would be ample.

TOMATO-FREE ZONE

Do all Italian dishes include tomatoes? I'd like a change.

Italians do love their sun-ripened, richly flavoured tomatoes, but they do not use them in every recipe. One of the most popular dishes in northern Italy is spaghetti with bacon and egg, called *spaghetti alla carbonara*. This is fairly new, and it is said to have been invented when American servicemen arrived in Italy during the Second World War and handed over their breakfast rations of bacon and egg to bemused Italian cooks. The recipe below uses quick-cooking spaghettini, a thin version of spaghetti.

Spaghettini alla carbonara

SERVES: 4
PREPARATION TIME: 20 minutes
COOKING TIME: 15 minutes

---

2 tablespoons olive oil
175 g (6 oz) bacon, cut into
   5 mm (¼ in) strips
4 tablespoons white wine
1 whole egg plus 2 egg yolks, size 3
50 g (1¾ oz) butter, softened
4 tablespoons double cream
100 g (3½ oz) grated Parmesan
   cheese
Salt and black pepper
350 g (12 oz) spaghettini

---

1 Preheat the oven to 140°C (275°F, gas mark 1). Heat the oil in a frying pan, then add the bacon and sauté until crisp. Pour in the wine and let it bubble up then take the pan off the heat and set aside.
2 Warm a serving bowl which is large enough for the pasta and put in the egg and egg yolks, butter, cream, half the Parmesan and some salt and pepper. Mix well and put it in the oven for about 10 minutes to just warm through without cooking.
3 Meanwhile, cook the pasta. When it is cooked, drain it and mix it with the sauce. The heat from the pasta will just set the eggs.
4 Quickly reheat the bacon and wine and pour over the pasta. Pass the remaining Parmesan separately.

SPICES

HOME GROUND

Is it better to buy whole spices and grind your own?

Yes, because ground spices deteriorate rapidly, although some, like fenugreek, are so hard that they are almost impossible to grind at home. It is probably best to buy a selection, in small quantities, and grind them a little at a time. One advantage of buying whole spices is that you can roast them before you grind them (see below). You can grind spice in a stone mortar and pestle, or in an electric coffee mill. If using the latter, be sure to keep it for spices and have a separate one for grinding coffee beans.

DRY FRY

Indian recipes often call for spices to be fried lightly at the start of cooking. What does this do to the flavour of the spices?

This is dry-frying, and only applies to whole spices. They are heated gently for 2–3 minutes in a heavy frying pan without any oil, shaken now and then, until the seeds start to change colour. This has a beneficial effect, especially with certain spices such as cumin, for it draws out the flavour remarkably well. Most of the spices in commercial curry powders, and other mixtures such as garam masala, are treated in this way before being ground. In Indian cookery it is very important that the spices do not taste raw.

REPLACE OFTEN

How long do ground spices keep?

It depends on how fresh they were when you bought them. Those you grind yourself will almost certainly keep longer, as long as they are tightly sealed. All ground spices, even the home-ground ones, should be replaced with new ones after six months when they have lost their savour and begin to taste dusty.

NUTMEG COVERING

What is the difference between nutmeg and mace?

Not a great deal in terms of flavour, though mace is more powerful and, in Britain, has traditionally been used in savoury dishes. Nutmeg is used in sweet and savoury recipes. Both spices lie within the fruit of the nutmeg tree, as a peach's stone lies within its flesh; mace is the lacy covering that encloses the nutmeg.

ALL OR MIXED?

What is the difference between allspice and mixed spice, and are they interchangeable?

Although they are near enough in flavour to stand in for each other sometimes, allspice is in fact one single spice, the berry of an evergreen tree growing wild in South America and the West Indies. It got its name because it resembles a mixture of four spices: cinnamon, cloves, mace and pepper.

The term 'mixed spice' is a vague one which in Britain usually means a mixture of cinnamon, cloves, ginger, nutmeg and sometimes cumin.

PERSONAL BLEND

I had a homemade garam masala in India which was superb. Can you give me a recipe?

Garam masala is a mixture of aromatic spices which, unlike curry powder, does not need heating to mellow the flavour. It is usually added to dishes at the end of cooking or sprinkled on top just before serving to brighten the flavour.

To make 100 g (3½ oz) of garam masala, simply dry-fry in a small pan 2 tablespoons of coriander seeds, a tablespoon each of mace and black peppercorns, a teaspoon each of cloves and cardamom seeds and a 6 cm (2½ in) piece of cinnamon stick broken into pieces. When the spices smell rich and pungent, grind them together in a coffee grinder or pound finely in a mortar. Store in an airtight jar, away from heat and light.

SPICES: WHAT THEY LOOK LIKE AND HOW TO USE THEM

After more than a century of relative neglect, spices are back in favour in the West, boosted by the subtle ways of spicing | *for flavour and colour that we have learnt in recent years from the many Asian cuisines. Here are some of the best.*

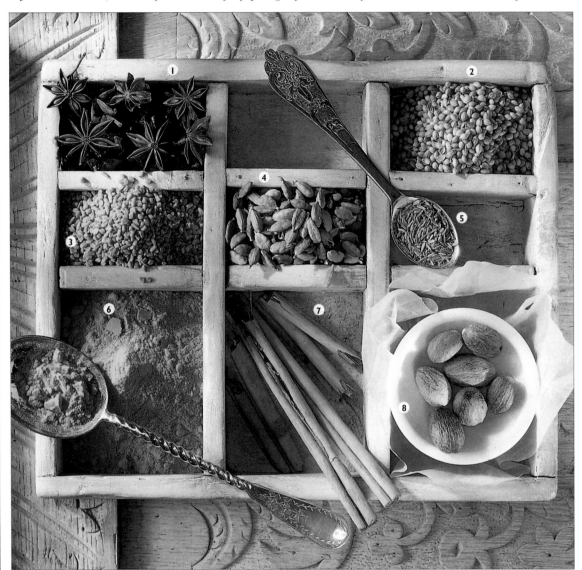

1 STAR ANISE has a flavour halfway between aniseed and liquorice. It is an ingredient of Chinese Five Spice powder.
2 CORIANDER SEED has a warm, citrus-like flavour. Use it alone or combined with other spices. It is always included in curry powder and garam masala.
3 FENUGREEK is an unusual spice, most identifiable as curry-like. It is not often used in the West, but is extremely popular in India. The squarish, hard seeds are crushed and roasted, then cooked with meat, fish and vegetables, and in curry powders. The leaves,

which have a strong, almost bitter taste, are used as a herb, both fresh and dried.
4 CARDAMOM has tiny, highly aromatic black seeds inside the loose pod. Green cardamom (pictured above) is best, but brown or white are also good. It is used in India in curries and in the Middle East to perfume coffee.
5 CUMIN is delicate and mild, and goes especially well with coriander. It is best bought as seeds and then gently toasted before use, whole or ground.
6 TURMERIC, usually sold ground, is perhaps the easiest spice to recognise,

because of its bright yellow hue. Often used for its colour as a cheap substitute for saffron, its flavour is actually fairly unremarkable and slightly bitter.
7 CINNAMON is the inner bark of an evergreen tree, sold either in papery rolls that resemble quills, or ground. Its fragrant sweetness can be used in both savoury and sweet dishes, such as rice pilafs, hot cross buns and apple tarts.
8 NUTMEG is best bought whole and grated when required. It is good used in cheese and vegetable dishes, milky sauces, junkets and rice puddings.

OUT OF THE LIGHT

Is it true that direct sunlight gradually destroys the essential oils in spices? Why are they sold in glass jars if light harms them?

Sunlight destroys chlorophyll, the plant's pigment, causing the structure of the spice (or the herb) to disintegrate. All herbs and spices should be stored in a cool dark place – the refrigerator is ideal – but attempts to package them in tinted glass have proved unsuccessful. It would seem that most people prefer to see what they are buying.

HOME GROWN

Which spices can be grown in Britain? Can you dry them?

Very few spices grow successfully in Britain as most of them are tropical plants. Even those that can be grown in a temperate climate, such as coriander, cumin and fenugreek, fail to reach their true potential in terms of flavour.

Curry plants (*Chalcas koenigii*) can be grown, if you can find them in a nursery. The small shrubby tree has aromatic leaves that are much used in Indian cookery. To dry the leaves, lay them on a rack, cover with muslin and leave in a warm dry place for a week to ten days until they are completely dry.

A juicy stem of fresh lemongrass may be potted up and grown under glass or as a house plant. The stalks are dried in the same way as curry leaves, but for a few days longer. Also easy to cultivate is the indigenous juniper shrub. The berries take two to three years to ripen, and must not be picked before they turn purple in the autumn. Dry them like curry leaves.

EASY-GOING PAPRIKA

If I'm adding paprika to a casserole or goulash, should it be fried first to release the aroma?

No, paprika is one of the most accessible of spices and can be treated like salt or pepper, and added without any treatment.

SPICY AND CRUNCHY

Using breadcrumbs for coatings is useful but so bland. Can I jazz them up with spices?

Ground spices may be mixed with breadcrumbs (or sifted flour) for coating fried foods, or with butter and flour as a crumble topping for fruit puddings. For instance, try using a pinch of saffron, turmeric or curry powder mixed with flour for coating fishcakes, croquettes or potato cakes, and ginger or cinnamon mixed with the topping for an apple crumble. Add a large pinch of ground nutmeg to a creamy cheese sauce or mashed potatoes. And mace will perk up bread sauce, spinach purée or creamed onions.

SPINACH

SALAD LEAF

Can I use spinach in salads?

Young, tender spinach leaves make splendid salads and mix particularly well with fruit; try them with grapefruit and orange segments or dried fruits. Spinach is good with dressings pungent with garlic or thickened with nuts and, since it can be cooked, is the perfect leaf for wilting with warm dressings. With added bacon, chicken liver and egg, poached or soft-boiled, these salads make lively substantial dishes to serve at brunch.

GREEN AND CRUNCHY

A local restaurant serves delicious crispy spinach which has been deep-fried, but is very light. Is it possible to do this at home?

Yes, it is, though it takes care. Spinach intended for deep-frying should be very fresh and very dry. After washing, pick it over carefully, removing any coarse stems and discoloured sections. Spin it in a salad dryer, then tip it onto a tea towel and toss it about gently until it is completely dry. Shred the spinach finely and fry a generous handful at a time in very hot oil over a medium to high heat for about a minute. Tip the spinach into a strainer set over a bowl, and while the oil reheats for the next batch, tip the cooked spinach onto a double layer of kitchen paper and shake with flaky sea salt.

This makes a dazzling garnish for fish or poached poultry, or in a tangle on top of a salad. However, the spinach should be used on the day it is cooked, and do not deceive yourself into thinking that crisp equals light and fat-free. Like all deep-fried foods, it will absorb a great deal of oil during cooking.

COOK FROM FROZEN

Can I use frozen spinach without thawing it first?

Frozen spinach is one of the most versatile and easy of all frozen vegetables to use, and is a very handy standby. Unlike many green vegetables, spinach stands up well to freezing and loses very little flavour and texture on thawing or cooking.

Chopped spinach can be added straight from the freezer to enrich hearty soups. With poached eggs and a creamy sauce it makes eggs Florentine, and it adds a colourful green layer to a fish pie. But it is best to thaw it slightly before blending it into a root vegetable purée, then heat the purée for a few minutes to warm through quickly.

SHOPPING LIST

How much raw spinach will be enough for four people?

Spinach loses about half its weight in cooking: to serve four people as a side vegetable, you need 1 kg (2 lb 4 oz) of washed fresh spinach to get 500 g (1 lb 2 oz) of cooked spinach. Freshly cooked spinach made into a roulade, such as the one on the next page, is a smart and colourful starter and is ideal for entertaining since most of the work can be done in advance. It will taste even better if you make your own taramasalata for the filling (see the recipe on page 345).

Fresh spinach and taramasalata roulade

SERVES: 6
PREPARATION TIME: 45 minutes
COOKING TIME: 20 minutes, plus
3 hours resting time

---

550 g (1 lb 4 oz) spinach, washed
25 g (1 oz) butter
Salt, black pepper and nutmeg
50 g (1 ¾ oz) Parmesan cheese,
   finely grated
5 eggs, size 1 - 2, separated
200 g (7 oz) cream cheese
2 - 3 tablespoons crème fraîche
   or Greek yoghurt
150 g (5 ½ oz) taramasalata

---

1 Removed the coarse stems and discoloured sections of the spinach leaves. Pack the spinach into a large pan with just the washing water clinging to the leaves, cover and cook for 4 minutes over a medium heat. Remove the lid, turn the spinach over and continue cooking for a further 2 - 3 minutes until the leaves have wilted thoroughly. Turn into a colander and leave to drain.

2 Line a 33 × 23 cm (13 × 9 in) swiss roll tin with some baking paper or buttered greaseproof paper.

3 When the spinach has cooled a bit, squeeze out the moisture with your hands and chop it finely. Return it to the pan and add the butter, salt, pepper, a good grinding of nutmeg and two-thirds of the Parmesan. Keep stirring gently until the butter melts and all is warmed through, then take the pan off the heat.

4 Preheat the oven to 180°C (350°F, gas mark 4). Whisk the egg whites to soft peaks. Beat the yolks briskly until creamy, then pour them into the spinach mixture and mix well. Gently fold in about 2 tablespoons of the whisked egg whites to loosen the mixture, then fold in the rest. Pour the mixture into the prepared tin, spreading it gently into the corners. Bake for 20 minutes until the top is just firm to the touch.

5 Leave the roulade to cool in the tin, then chill it for 2 hours. Remove from the refrigerator, cover with a just-damp tea towel and rest for at least an hour at room temperature.

6 Put a board or tray over the cloth-covered tin, then invert the tin to turn the roulade out onto the cloth. Peel off the paper.

7 Beat the cream cheese and crème fraîche or yoghurt together to a spreadable mixture. Spread it over the spinach base, then spread the taramasalata over the cheese. Add salt and pepper and roll up the roulade, lifting the cloth to help shape it.

8 Serve the roulade within an hour of rolling. To serve, transfer it to a serving dish and sprinkle with the remainder of the Parmesan.

A sophisticated combination of smoked cod's roe, fresh spinach and cream cheese makes a beautiful roulade that can be served with a decorative leafy garnish.

SPIRITS

PRESERVED FRUIT

Can any fruit be preserved in spirit, or do some produce better results than others?

Fruit preserved for a month or more in alcohol makes wonderful, easy-to-make winter desserts. Most fruits are suitable, with the exception of very watery ones such as melons as these dilute the alcohol, which may result in mould growth or fermentation.

For the best results, use ripe, unblemished fruit: berries should be hulled; currants, gooseberries and grapes stripped off their stalks; nectarines, peaches and plums should be halved and stoned; pineapples should be peeled, cored and sliced or cut into cubes; clementines and mandarins should be peeled and kept whole; and apples and pears should be peeled, cored and sliced. Firmer fruit such as peaches and pears are better if they are poached in a sugar syrup first.

Pack the prepared fruit into clean jars, layering it with sugar as you go, then cover with alcohol such as rum, brandy, kirsch, vodka or any flavoured liqueur, as in the recipe below. Cooked fruits are packed with their cooled sugar syrup plus an equal quantity of alcohol. With either raw or cooked fruit, spices such as cinnamon, ginger, star anise or vanilla can be added for extra flavour. Seal the jars tightly, and as long as the fruits are kept covered by the alcohol, they should keep for about a year.

Pineapple in kirsch

MAKES: 1 litre (1 pint 15 fl oz)
PREPARATION TIME: 20 minutes
MATURING TIME: at least a month

1 medium pineapple, ripe
225 g (8 oz) caster sugar
About 300 ml (10 fl oz) kirsch
1 cinnamon stick, broken into
*   three pieces*

1 Peel the pineapple and cut the flesh crossways into thick slices, then remove the central core from each slice. Cut the flesh into small chunks. Put alternating layers of pineapple pieces and sugar in a large clean jar, dropping in the pieces of cinnamon stick as you go.
2 Pour in enough kirsch to cover the pineapple completely. Seal the jar and leave in a cool, dark place for at least a month before using. Give the jar a shake occasionally to make sure all the sugar dissolves.
3 When ready, serve the fruit with a large spoonful of the steeping syrup. If you like, top with whipped cream, or some vanilla ice cream.

ALCOHOLIC FLAVOUR

When recipes include spirits, is it for the taste or the alcohol?

If the recipe is for preserving fresh fruit, both the flavour and the alcoholic content are absorbed by the fruit. But when spirits are added to cooked dishes or flambéed, they are used only for their flavour as the alcohol will evaporate during cooking or burn off when it is ignited. It is also usually for the flavour alone that alcohol is added to cold desserts, fruit salads, cakes

and cream fillings for pastries, as the quantity used is not large enough to have a significant alcoholic effect. If too much is added the dish will be too thin and watery and the taste overpowering.

FULLY COVERED

How do I stop the fruit from bobbing up out of the alcohol when I am trying to preserve it?

Fruit that is being steeped in alcohol needs to be totally immersed in order to save it from the damaging effects of air. Inevitably, however, the fruit will float to the top, exposing enough of the flesh to start the fermentation process.

To keep the fruit fully immersed, place a few balls of loosely crumpled greaseproof paper over them in the jar to weigh them down. Alternatively, if the opening of the jar is wide enough, cover the fruit with cling film and put a plate or saucer over that (see box, right).

FRUIT, GLORIOUS FRUIT

How long does it take to make a rumtopf from start to finish?

This fruity dessert (named after the German for rum pot), can be eaten after four to six weeks of steeping in alcohol, but if you have the patience, it is at its best if it is left in a cool dark place for at least three months to mellow and mature.

Rumtopf is made up of layers of stoned, stemmed and cut-up fruit steeped in spirit, and the time you actually spend on making it will depend on how many different types of fruit you put in it. Each addition takes about 30 minutes to prepare, plus an hour of standing time, before it is added to the jar. Traditional rumtopf jars are made of glazed ceramic (to keep out the light) but any large glass jar with a closely fitting lid will do.

Begin with the first fruits of the summer (usually strawberries) and keep on adding layers of other fruits as they come into season. Peaches, pears and plums are best. Because a rumtopf can be made

MAKING A RUMTOPF

For the first layer, use equal weights of fruit and sugar, and add about 700 ml (1 pint 5 fl oz) of rum or brandy to every 500 g (1 lb 2 oz) of fruit. For the subsequent layers, add 500 ml (18 fl oz) of spirit to every 500 g (1 lb 2 oz) of fruit and use only half the weight of sugar.

1 Put the fruit (strawberries are shown here) and the measured sugar into the rumtopf jar, mix gently and leave it to stand for an hour. Then pour in enough rum to cover the fruit by 2.5 cm (1 in).

2 It is essential that the fruit stays submerged, so cover it closely with cling film and put a small plate over that. Put more cling film over the jar then seal tightly with the lid.

3 Continue to layer in more fruit: prepare the next batch (peaches are shown here) by soaking it in sugar for an hour, then add it to the jar and pour on more rum to cover the fruit by 2.5 cm (1 in). Continue to add sugar-soaked fruit and rum until the jar is full. Cover it well and if necessary, weigh the fruit down with a ball of greaseproof paper.

with any amount of different types of fruit, there is no precise recipe (see box, previous page).

When you are choosing fruit, bear in mind that those with a high water content can cause fermentation so avoid apples, melon and oranges. Neither is it advisable to use sharply flavoured fruits such as blackberries, gooseberries and rhubarb as they will dominate the more delicate taste of the others.

SAY WHEN

If a recipe says to add 'a little' spirit, how much should I use?

Generally, it means anything from 1–4 tablespoons or until it tastes right to you. Check on the consistency as you add the spirit.

PURPLE GIN

How do you make sloe gin?

It is very easy. All you need is the patience and strength of will to leave it for at least three months, following the recipe on the right.

Sloes are hard and bitter but, when steeped with gin, will give it a unique aromatic flavour. Traditionally, sloes were picked only after the first frost, because after thawing they yield more juice. Today they can be picked as they ripen in late summer, and popped into the freezer for a short time.

Unlike a cool gin and tonic, which is often drunk as a summer apéritif, sloe gin is usually served as a warming winter drink. You can make it any time up to early October and the gin will be ready for Christmas, but the flavour will be even richer if you leave the sloes to steep for up to six months before straining and bottling, and then set the flavoured gin aside to mature until the following winter.

For a change, you can use the same quantity of damsons instead of sloes to make damson gin. They are too large to squeeze and should be pricked all over with a clean knitting needle or skewer, or a darning needle stuck into a cork. Then just follow the recipe.

Sloe gin

MAKES: 700 ml (1 pint 5 fl oz)
PREPARATION TIME: 30 minutes
MATURING TIME: 3 - 6 months

225 g (8 oz) sloes
175 g (6 oz) caster sugar
700 ml (1 pint 5 fl oz) gin

1 Bruise each sloe by pressing it between your thumb and forefinger; alternatively, put all the sloes into a strong polythene bag and crush them gently with a rolling pin.

Crushing sloes before adding them to the spirit will help to release their juice. Pinch them lightly to split the skins.

2 Put the fruit into a large, clean glass jar, add the sugar and pour in the gin. Cover the jar with a tightly fitting lid and shake well.
3 Store in a cool, dark place for three to six months, shaking it daily for the first week or until the sugar is completely dissolved.
4 When you are ready to bottle the gin, line a funnel with a double piece of muslin and strain the flavoured spirit through it into a large clean bottle. (You may find it easier to strain the gin into a clean jug first, and then pour it into the bottle.) Seal tightly with a cork or screw top and store in a cool airy cupboard.

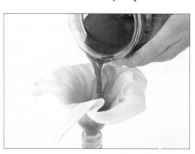

When the sloe gin is ready to drink, it is strained through a layer of muslin, bottled and tightly sealed for storing.

FRUIT FLAVOURS

I like sloe gin, but sloes are only available in autumn. Is there any other fruit I can use instead?

Yes, you can flavour a delightful summer gin with raspberries, redcurrants or strawberries (see recipe, below), and with soft fruits, it is ready to drink much sooner.

Strawberry gin

MAKES: about 700 ml (1 pint 5 fl oz)
PREPARATION TIME: 15 minutes
MATURING TIME: a week

About 225 g (8 oz) strawberries, hulled
700 ml (1 pint 5 fl oz) gin
About 115 g (4 oz) caster sugar

1 Lightly crush the strawberries with a fork. Place them in a clean jar, then pour in the gin to cover.
2 Seal tightly and leave to mature in a cool, dark place for at least a week, shaking the jar every now and again to disperse the fruit.
3 Strain the flavoured spirit through a funnel lined with a double layer of clean muslin into a clean jug. Stir in the sugar well to dissolve it. The gin is ready to drink when the sugar has dissolved. Pour it through a funnel into a clean bottle and seal with a new cork. Store in a cool place.

FINE FLAVOURED VODKAS

I like flavoured vodkas, but they are quite expensive to buy. Can I make some of my own?

Yes, not only is flavoured vodka easy to make, but the results can be more interesting than those you can buy. For example, a dried chilli makes a rose-coloured vodka in a very short time. Roast the chilli in a hot oven for 5 minutes, then stuff it down the neck of a bottle of vodka, or put it into a wide-mouthed jar with the vodka and seal tightly. The vodka takes on colour and flavour within a day but it will need at least a week to develop a strong flavour. Vodka flavoured with grapefruit, lemon, lime, or pomelo peel needs only two weeks to mature.

BLITHE SPIRITS

What spirits, other than gin and vodka, can I use to make my own special drinks, and what could I use to flavour them with?

Almost any clear spirit, such as inexpensive brandy, kirsch or rum can be infused with fruit to make drinks such as plum brandy or damson rum. Soak the fruit in sugar and the spirit and then strain off the alcohol. For best results,

allow the flavours to blend together for at least three months before straining. The flavoured spirits can then be drunk, although if stored unopened in a cool, dark place they will keep almost indefinitely.

You can also experiment with other flavourings such as herbs and spices. For example, a half-dozen crushed cumin seeds, a sprig of rosemary and a few cloves, steeped in a bottle of Greek or Spanish brandy, makes a delightful digestive

drink. Expansively flavoured spices such as cinnamon or star anise go well with heartier-flavoured fruit such as damsons, and vanilla will enhance the flavour of almost any fruit. Vanilla-scented fruits are best seeped in rum or brandy rather than gin or vodka.

The following recipe for Cherry Brandy produces a richly coloured spirit which is ideal for flavouring cream or creamy puddings as well as being drunk on its own. It looks most festive spooned over vanilla or pistachio ice cream and can also be mixed with fizzy water or lemonade to make a party drink or a refreshing sparkling cocktail.

Cherry brandy

MAKES: about 700 ml (1 pint 5 fl oz)
PREPARATION TIME: 15 – 20 minutes
MATURING TIME: 3 months

500 g (1 lb 2 oz) fresh dark cherries, such as morello
85 g (3 oz) caster sugar
600 ml (1 pint) brandy

1 Wash the cherries and pat them dry with kitchen paper. Remove the stalks but do not stone the fruit, then prick each cherry all over with a clean needle or skewer.
2 Put alternate layers of cherries and sugar in a large clean jar. Pour in the brandy to cover the cherries, weighing them down with balls of crumpled baking paper if necessary.
3 Seal the jar tightly and leave it in a cool, dark place for three months, shaking the jar occasionally until the brandy has taken on a deep rich colour from the cherries.
4 Strain the flavoured spirit through a funnel lined with a double layer of clean muslin into a clean bottle. Seal with a new cork, securing it into the neck of the bottle with a mallet. You can also use snap-on stoppers. The brandy can be drunk immediately. Store in a cool, dark place.

SQUASH: see PUMPKIN

Morello cherries and a little sugar give a bottle of brandy a dramatic colour and a delicate summery flavour.

SQUID

EASIER THAN YOU THINK

How should I prepare squid, and how do I cook it?

Squid is now often sold cleaned and prepared, fresh or frozen. It is available in a wide range of sizes, from 5–25 cm (2–10 in), although any that measure more than 18 cm (7 in) will be very rubbery. Squid is one of the easiest fish to tackle, as it has no readily identifiable innards (see box, below).

Medium-sized squid can be sliced for frying, either shaken in flour or in a light batter. Smaller ones can be incorporated into seafood salads and stews as they require scarcely more than blanching to cook, as in the recipe on the right. Larger ones, measuring 10–15 cm (4–6 in), are usually quite tough and chewy, but can be stuffed and baked.

Spicy squid salad

SERVES: 2 as a starter
PREPARATION TIME: 15 minutes
COOKING TIME: 5 minutes

2 tablespoons cooking oil
1 - 2 cloves garlic, finely chopped
2.5 cm (1 in) piece ginger, grated
1 fresh green chilli, deseeded
  and finely sliced
200 g (7 oz) small squid, prepared
2 teaspoons soy or fish sauce
1 tablespoon lime juice
2 teaspoons sesame oil
Salad leaves
6 leaves of mint or basil

1 Heat the oil in a pan, then fry the garlic and ginger over a high heat for about 30 seconds. Stir in the chilli, squid and soy or fish sauce and cook for a further 2 minutes, then remove the pan from the heat.
2 Stir in the lime juice and sesame oil. Divide the warm salad between two plates dressed with salad leaves, and scatter with mint or basil leaves.

CLEANING AND PREPARING SQUID

The pouch, fins and tentacles of a cleaned squid can be chopped, sliced into bite-sized pieces or left whole.

1 Pull the head of the squid and the soft innards that are attached to it, including the ink sac, gently out of the body. You can save the dark ink to use in the poaching liquid or cook it in a sauce to serve with cooked squid.

2 Cut off the tentacle cluster attached to the head and set it aside, then discard the rest of the head.

3 Pull out the clear central quill from inside the body of the squid and discard it. Cut off the wing-like flaps from either side of the body, but keep them. Peel away the thin, greyish membrane that covers the body - it should slip off easily - and discard.

4 The hollow body section can now be turned inside out and washed clean of any loose matter. Then turn it right side out. Use it whole for stuffing, or cut it into rings. The tentacles and the side flaps can be left whole or cut in half, depending on the recipe.

STARCH

POTATO AND RICE FLOURS

I have seen references in some cookery books (French ones in particular) to potato and rice flour as thickening agents. Could I use them instead of cornflour?

Potato flour, or *fécule de pomme de terre* as it is called in France, is the pure starch that is leached out by soaking potato gratings in water. The liquid is drained off, leaving behind the starch, which is then dried. Similar to cornflour and used in the same way, *fécule* needs only to be simmered gently for 1–2 minutes and should be added at the end of cooking; cook it any longer and the sauce will thin out again. It makes a good thickening agent and is better than cornflour for use in fruity or delicate sauces as it is both colourless and tasteless: cooks will find it worth bringing back some *fécule* from France.

Rice flour is finely ground rice and is used in Far Eastern countries to make thin rice noodles. In common with potato flour, it thickens sauces and stews without flavouring or adding colour to them.

FINE PEA FLOUR

What is besan flour? I have seen it mentioned in Indian recipes.

Besan flour, also known as gram flour, is used in Indian cooking and it is actually made from ground chickpeas (*chana dhal*). It is a very fine, soft flour, pale creamy yellow in colour, and is used to thicken soups and curries or made into a batter to coat vegetables or fish. But it must be stirred well or it will turn lumpy. This nutritious flour is also used in Provence and northern Italy to make crêpes, soups and special pastries. It is available from health food shops, Oriental or Continental food stores and the larger supermarkets. For flavour and also for texture, there is really nothing that is an adequate substitute.

STEAK AND KIDNEY PUDDING

FILLING PIE OR PUDDING

Is steak and kidney pudding very different from steak and kidney pie? Can I use the same dough and filling for both?

The fillings for both are similar; it is the way the filling is cooked that differs. Steak and kidney pudding is always made with a suet-crust pastry, and the uncooked mixture is spooned into the pastry before the pudding is steamed, as in the recipe below. For a steak and kidney pie, the meat filling is usually cooked before being put into a pastry case which is then baked to cook the pastry. Sometimes the meat is cooked in the pastry case and on these occasions, rump steak is generally used.

The traditional pastry used for a steak and kidney pie is suet-crust pastry but you can also use puff, flaky or shortcrust pastry with equally good results.

Steak and kidney pudding

SERVES: *4 – 6*
PREPARATION TIME: *50 minutes*
COOKING TIME: *5 hours*

FOR THE FILLING
500 g (1 lb 2 oz) stewing steak, trimmed and cut into 1 cm (½ in) cubes
225 g (8 oz) lamb or pig's kidney, trimmed and cut into1 cm (½ in) pieces
1 onion, sliced
100 g (3½ oz) mushrooms, sliced
3 tablespoons plain flour
½ – 1 teaspoon dried mixed herbs
Salt and black pepper
Dash of Worcestershire sauce, optional
125 – 150 ml (4 – 5 fl oz) beef stock

FOR THE PASTRY
300 g (10½ oz) self-raising flour
Salt and black pepper
150 g (5½ oz) shredded beef suet

1 Put the steak, kidney, onion and mushrooms in a bowl. Stir in the plain flour, herbs, seasoning and Worcestershire sauce, if using, and mix well, then set aside.

2 To make the dough, sift the self-raising flour into a bowl and add salt and black pepper. Stir in the suet and mix in about 200 ml (7 fl oz) of cold water to make a soft but not sticky dough. (Pour in the water gradually while mixing, and use all of it only if necessary.) Lightly grease a 1.7 litre (3 pint) pudding basin.

3 Set aside a quarter of the dough for the lid. Roll out the remainder on a lightly floured surface to one and a half times the diameter of the top of the basin. Line the basin with the dough (see box, right) and press it gently into position, flattening any creases and expelling any trapped air bubbles. The edge of the dough should overlap the rim of the basin by about 2.5 cm (1 in).

4 Spoon the meat mixture into the lined basin, spreading the meat out evenly. Add enough stock to come about two-thirds of the way up.

5 Roll out the remaining piece of pastry to a round 2.5 cm (1 in) larger than the top of the basin. Dampen the edge of the dough in the basin with water and cover the pie with its lid, pressing the edges together to seal firmly. Trim and seal the edges.

6 Cut a piece of greaseproof paper slightly bigger than the top of the pudding. Grease the paper lightly with oil and fold a 2 cm (¾ in) pleat in it. Cover the pudding with the pleated paper, top with a piece of similarly pleated foil, or cloth, and fold them down over the basin rim. Tie a piece of string tightly under the rim to hold the covering down securely. To make it easier to lift the basin in and out of the steamer, tie a string handle across the basin top, or tie the ends of the cloth together.

7 Put the basin in a steamer over a pan of boiling water. Cover the pan and steam for about 5 hours, topping up the water in the pan regularly to prevent it from boiling dry.

8 To serve, uncover the pudding and place the basin onto a warmed serving plate or platter.

PREPARING A STEAK AND KIDNEY PUDDING

Lining and sealing a steak and kidney pudding properly can be tricky, but it ensures that the filling stays rich and juicy as it cooks.

1 Loosely fold the rolled-out dough in half, and then in half again to form a triangle. Put the point of the triangle downwards into the basin and unfold it gently so that it does not tear, and line the base and sides.

2 Spoon the meat mixture into the lined basin, spreading the meat out evenly, then add the stock.

3 Place the lid on top of the filling and press to seal securely, then trim to neaten the edges, rolling the sealed edges so that they are facing inwards slightly around the top.

9 This robust family favourite needs no potato accompaniment. It is best served with just a simple, freshly cooked green or root vegetable such as broccoli, french beans or carrots and a large, strongly seasoned salad of various colourful leaves to temper the solidity of the pudding.

STEAMED PUDDING

LEAKS AND SPILLS

If water has accidentally leaked into my steamed pudding, is there anything I can do to save it?

It depends on the quantity of water. If a lot of water gets into a steamed pudding while it is cooking, it will be soggy. If only a small amount of water has leaked in, the pudding may be affected only in a small area and will still be palatable.

The best advice is to try to stop water getting into the pudding by covering it properly. Traditionally, steamed puddings are cooked in a deep bowl or basin that is covered with a piece of greased greaseproof or baking paper, pleated in the middle and topped with a cloth, or a piece of pleated foil tied securely with string. The pleats allow room for expansion when the pudding is cooked. The covering is needed to keep the pudding well protected from the boiling water beneath, so that it is cooked in the steam and is moist but not sodden.

When steaming puddings, do not let the water boil too furiously as this will make it lap over the top. Keep it at a gentle rolling boil, or boil the pudding in a slow cooker.

TIME SAVER

Can you cook steamed puddings in a microwave oven?

Yes, they can be made quickly and easily in a microwave oven and the result is a light, spongy texture, as the following recipe shows. Cooking your steamed pudding in the microwave not only means you save on time, you also avoid having a lot of steam in the kitchen.

A cup of hot water placed in the microwave next to the pudding will introduce some steam to the microwave oven and help to keep the pudding moist. This is also a good practice to follow when you are reheating precooked steamed and sponge puddings.

Take the fast lane to pleasing the family by cooking their favourite syrup sponge pudding in the microwave. It saves time and some of the washing-up.

Microwave syrup sponge pudding

SERVES: *4*
PREPARATION TIME: *20 minutes*
COOKING TIME: *5 - 7 minutes, plus 5 minutes standing time*

---

2 - 3 tablespoons golden syrup
50 g (1 ³/₄ oz) butter
50 g (1 ³/₄ oz) caster sugar
1 egg, size 3, beaten
115 g (4 oz) self-raising flour, sifted
A few drops of vanilla essence
3 - 4 tablespoons full-fat milk

---

1 Spoon the golden syrup into the bottom of a greased 600 ml (1 pint) microwave-safe pudding basin.
2 In a bowl, cream the butter and sugar together until light and fluffy, then gradually add the beaten egg.
3 Fold in the flour, using a metal spoon, until well mixed. Fold in the vanilla essence and enough milk to make the mixture a soft dropping consistency. Spoon the mixture over the golden syrup in the pudding basin and smooth over the surface.
4 Cook the pudding, uncovered, in the microwave on Medium power for 5 - 7 minutes until the top of the sponge remains only slightly moist.
5 Remove the cooked pudding from the oven and allow it to stand for 5 minutes. Turn it out onto a warmed serving plate and serve immediately with custard, or cream if you prefer.
VARIATIONS
Replace the golden syrup with the same quantity of jam or mincemeat.

Omit the golden syrup and add the finely grated zest and juice of a lemon or an orange to the mixture.

Make a chocolate sponge pudding, by replacing 25 g (1 oz) of the flour with sifted cocoa powder.

STEAMING

PRESERVING VITAMINS

In what way is steaming a better method of cooking than boiling, frying or roasting?

Steaming is the cooking of food in hot vapour rather than in liquid. As the food never touches the liquid, the loss of vitamins is significantly reduced. Furthermore, unlike frying or roasting, steamed food is cooked without fat, making it more digestible and highly suitable for invalids and those on low-fat diets.

You must, however, ensure that you always choose excellent ingredients for steaming – there is no help to be had from the flavour of butter or oil, nor does the food caramelise during cooking, so the raw materials must taste good without such assistance.

ESSENTIAL EQUIPMENT

I would like to steam more of my food for a healthy diet. Do I need any special equipment?

It is probably quite possible to improvise a steamer by using your existing kitchen equipment, but if you are intending to do a lot of steaming, it is worth investing in a dedicated steamer of some sort.

A variety of special equipment for steaming is available. Most common are oval or round steamers, which are rather similar to double saucepans, except that the top layer has holes in its base. Steam from the boiling water in the lower pan rises through the holes to cook the food, while the lid on the upper pan keeps in the steam.

Another popular steaming device is a stainless-steel, plastic or aluminium basket that opens and folds shut, rather like a fan. This can be used with an ordinary lidded saucepan. The basket stands on its own short legs to keep it clear of the boiling water; it fits inside most saucepans and is particularly suitable for foods that do not need

much cooking time as the water underneath the legs would otherwise have to be replaced often.

If you want to steam a large fish, a fish kettle is ideal: place the fish on the rack carefully and lower this onto upturned ramekin dishes to hold the rack out of the water.

Small pieces of fish can be plate-steamed: put the fish on a lightly buttered plate, season and set the plate in a pan of simmering water or on a trivet inside a frying pan half full of water. Cover the pan and cook the fish for 8–10 minutes.

Chinese cooking also employs steaming. Fish, shellfish and tender cuts of meat, often wrapped in thin pastry or vegetable leaves, and dumplings, are steamed in rattan baskets stacked over a wok of boiling water. (See also WOK.)

STEW

CRUCIAL FIRST STEPS

Are there any golden rules for making a perfect stew?

Good stews are made or lost in the early stages of their preparation. In many stews the meat is fried first (sometimes with carrots, leeks, whole or sliced mushrooms, peppers, onions or shallots), to give a rich flavour and to add colour to the sauce, which will be made with the browned sediment and dried juices that stick to the pan after frying the meat and vegetables.

If the sauce is not to look too pale and taste insipid, you must fry the meat until each piece is a good even brown colour. Fry the pieces a few at a time, so as not to crowd the pan, and keep the temperature high so that the meat browns and fries rather than sweats.

If the bottom of the pan begins to get too brown, you can deglaze it between batches of meat by pouring in a few tablespoons of stock, wine or water. Stir it vigorously to loosen the sediment, taste the liquid, and, if it is not burnt, reserve it to add to the stew. It will

not taste delicious at this point but as long as it has not burnt it will enrich and colour the stew.

The term stew is so widely used it can mean almost anything, but it is essentially food that has been slowly and gently cooked in plenty of liquid. In most stews the meat is cut into pieces before cooking on top of the stove, but the term is sometimes used for sliced, sautéed meat or poultry served in a sauce.

THE RIGHT TEMPERATURE

The meat in my stews is always stringy. What am I doing wrong?

Stews are a perfect way of using the tougher, cheaper cuts of meat. Long, slow cooking makes the meat tender and full of flavour. But tough, stringy meat can be the result of overcooking, especially if it is cooked at too high a temperature so that the liquid boils and breaks up the fibres of the meat.

The temperature at which the stew cooks should be no higher than 150°C (300°F), and this should be maintained for at least 2 hours. The aim is to achieve a very gentle simmering, with only the occasional bubble breaking the surface of the liquid. A heat diffuser made of wire mesh and placed between the hob and saucepan can prevent the stew cooking too quickly.

The pan should be heavy with a tight-fitting lid that keeps in the moisture. A pan that is too thin or buckled can cause the stew to burn at the bottom. Your pan should also be the appropriate size; small quantities of stew in a large pan will dry out very quickly, while too much food in a small pan might boil over.

Do not look under the lid of the pot too often as this will encourage evaporation, but when you do go to check on the stew, give it a stir.

VARIABLE QUANTITIES

How much meat should I allow per person in a stew?

As a general rule, allow 175–250 g (6–9 oz) of boned meat per person depending on the proportion of meat to other ingredients. If the stew includes lots of vegetables, for example, the smaller quantity of meat will be sufficient. When you are catering for a large group, use the smaller amount of meat as people tend to eat less at big functions.

A mainly meat stew will be rich and will need several side dishes in the form of carbohydrate (bread, pasta, potatoes or rice) and a green vegetable or salad. At the other extreme, the stewpot can contain everything for a complete meal, or indeed be a completely vegetarian stew. The traditional French recipe below, which features lamb, haricot beans and tomatoes, is a good example of a hearty stew.

Navarin of lamb with haricot beans

SERVES: 4 - 6
PREPARATION TIME: 20 minutes, plus 30 minutes soaking the beans
COOKING TIME: 3 hours

250 g (9 oz) dried haricot beans
3 tablespoons oil, olive or sunflower
1 kg (2 lb 4 oz) boned lamb
    (shoulder or fillet), cubed
500 g (1 lb 2 oz) onions, sliced
1 tablespoon sugar
25 g (1 oz) plain flour
500 ml (18 fl oz) meat or vegetable
    stock, or replace 125 ml (4 fl oz)
    of the stock with dry white wine
500 g (1 lb 2 oz) tomatoes, skinned,
    deseeded and roughly chopped
1 bouquet garni
1 teaspoon salt
1/2 teaspoon black pepper
1 large clove garlic, crushed
To garnish: sprigs of fresh thyme

1 Cover the dried beans with water and soak for 30 minutes. Drain them, put them in a pan of fresh water and boil the beans hard for 15 minutes. Drain, return the beans to the pan with fresh water to cover and simmer for 1½ hours. Drain and set aside.
2 While they are cooking, heat the oil in a large saucepan or flameproof casserole and fry the lamb over a moderate heat, turning it until it is browned all over. Remove the meat and drain any oil back into the pan.

A tender stew of lamb, haricot beans, sliced onions and tomatoes cooked with stock and herbs makes a warming meal for wintry evenings or weekend lunches.

3 Add the sliced onions and sauté over a medium heat for 5 minutes, stirring occasionally. Add the sugar and stir over a medium heat for a further 5 minutes until the onions are well browned, then stir in the flour and cook for another minute.
4 Add the stock and bring to the boil, stirring until thickened. Add the chopped tomatoes, the bouquet garni, salt and pepper, then the fried lamb with any juices, and return to the boil. Reduce the heat, cover and simmer very gently for 1 - 1½ hours.
5 Stir in the drained beans and the garlic and return to the boil. Cover the pan and simmer very gently for another hour until the meat and beans are tender but not mushy. Stir the stew occasionally so that it does not stick to the pan.
6 Remove the bouquet garni before serving the stew hot, garnished with sprigs of thyme and accompanied by a steamed green vegetable such as spinach and some rice or potatoes.

CAREFUL TRIMMING

Should I cut off all the fat and gristle from stewing steak before it goes into the pot?

Always remove any obvious gristle from stewing steak as this will not dissolve during cooking the way ordinary fat does. The fat may be left on to add moisture and flavour to the stew, or trimmed off.

A good compromise is to trim off any pieces of fat surrounding the meat but leave any marbled fat between the meat tissue as this will melt and add flavour to the dish. If you want to remove all the fat, make the stew a day ahead, chill and when cold, lift off any fat that has set on the surface. If you intend to trim off all the fat, remember to buy a larger quantity of meat.

Cooking your chosen meat on the bone, or adding the meat bones to the stewpot, will also give extra flavour and texture to the stew.

STOCK

PATIENCE IS A VIRTUE

Why does stock always take so long to make?

Meat or poultry stock needs long, slow cooking in order to extract as much flavour as possible from the bones. But vegetable stocks can be made quickly or slowly and fish stocks are always made quickly.

Cooked bones can be used for stock and do not need blanching, but will have lost some of their flavour and are not as good as raw bones. For poultry or game stock, use the carcass from a roasted bird. Avoid using lamb bones, which give an unpleasant flavour.

It is often better to place raw bones in a pan of cold water, bring them to the boil, then drain and refresh before using them to make stock. This will remove impurities that would give the stock a tainted taste and unpleasant grey colour.

Do not boil stock as this will make it cloudy. But after the bones and vegetables have been strained off, the stock may be returned to the pan and boiled to reduce it.

Raw beef bones can be used for an all-purpose Meat Stock like the one featured below.

Meat stock

MAKES: *1 litre (1 pint 15 fl oz)*
PREPARATION TIME: *5 minutes*
COOKING TIME: *3 - 4 hours*

750 g - 1 kg (1 lb 10 oz - 2 lb 4 oz)
   raw beef bones, chopped
1 onion, chopped
1 carrot, chopped
1 stick celery, roughly sliced
1 mushroom, sliced
1 bouquet garni
6 peppercorns

1 Put the bones in a large saucepan with 2.5 litres (4 pints 10 fl oz) of cold water. Bring to the boil, skim off thoroughly any scum that rises to the surface, then add the vegetables, bouquet garni and peppercorns.

2 Half cover the pan so the lid is tilted, reduce the heat and simmer gently for 3 - 4 hours until the liquid has reduced by more than half.
3 Remove the saucepan from the heat and strain the stock, discarding the bones and vegetables. Leave the stock to cool then skim off the fat that has risen to the surface. Use the stock immediately, or store in the refrigerator for up to four days.

VARIATIONS
For a brown stock, the dry bones and vegetables can first be roasted in a very hot oven for 30 - 40 minutes until browned at the edges, then transferred to the stockpot with the water. Alternatively, put the dry bones in a saucepan and cook over a gentle heat, turning occasionally, for 10 minutes until the fat runs. Add the vegetables and continue cooking over a medium heat for 15 minutes, turning regularly until they are well browned, then add the water.

Carefully skimming off all the scum that rises to the surface during boiling leaves a clear and tasty stock.

SIMPLY THE BEST

Can you suggest a good, fast recipe for chicken stock?

Chicken stock is one of the easiest and quickest stocks to make and it can be used whenever a well flavoured stock is required in a recipe. You will get the best flavour if you use a raw chicken carcass plus the giblets, but if you have cooked a roast chicken recently, you can use the leftover carcass from that instead. Include any uneaten pieces of chicken wing or drumstick in the stockpot; they will give the stock extra flavour.

Chicken stock

MAKES: *1 litre (1 pint 15 fl oz)*
PREPARATION TIME: *5 minutes*
COOKING TIME: *2 hours*

1 chicken carcass (raw or remains
   from a roasted chicken)
Chicken giblets, but not the liver,
   optional
1 onion, roughly chopped or sliced
1 carrot, roughly chopped or sliced
1 stick celery, roughly sliced,
   optional
1 leek, sliced, optional
1 mushroom or a few stalks,
   roughly chopped, optional
1 bouquet garni
6 peppercorns

1 Break up the carcass into several pieces and put it in a large saucepan. Add 2 litres (3 pints 10 fl oz) of cold water and bring it to the boil. With a slotted spoon, remove any scum that rises to the surface of the stock, then add the vegetables and flavourings.
2 Half cover the pan, reduce the heat and simmer gently for 2 hours until the stock has reduced by half.
3 Remove the saucepan from the heat and strain the stock, discarding the bones and vegetables. Reduce the strained stock if necessary then leave it to cool before skimming off any fat that rises to the surface. Use the stock immediately or store it, chilled, for up to four days.

COOL JELLY

My stock never seems to thicken even though I simmer it for hours. What am I doing wrong?

Stock is not supposed to thicken while it is still cooking, but a well concentrated meat stock should gel on cooling and any fat can then be scraped easily off the top.

When the collagen that is contained naturally in the meat bones dissolves during cooking, it forms the gelatine that later sets the stock. To make a really good jellied meat stock, try to get hold of a raw veal knuckle, calf's foot or beef marrow bone, and simmer it in plenty of water with vegetables and flavourings for about 4 hours before straining and cooling. If this stock is then reduced even further, it will form a syrupy glaze called a glace that is often used in classic French sauces. Glace can be frozen in ice cube trays for convenience.

STOCK FROM FISH

How does fish stock differ from a fumet or court bouillon, and how should they each be used?

Fish stock is made in the same way as meat stock in that the fish bones, heads and tails (and the shells of shellfish) are simmered in water with vegetables and flavourings. But fish stock is cooked for only 20–30 minutes as lengthy cooking will make it bitter. Once the stock has been strained it can be concentrated by further boiling. A glass of dry white wine added to the stock improves the flavour considerably.

After straining, the stock can be boiled slightly to reduce it to a more intensely flavoured fumet. Fumet can be used in fish sauces, soups and stews.

Court bouillon is the liquid used for poaching fresh fish such as salmon. It is made from water, white wine (or lemon juice or vinegar) and flavourings, but unlike fish stock, it does not contain any fish trimmings. Court bouillon is rarely featured in the finished dish.

A bouquet garni of bay leaf, celery, parsley and thyme adds a fresh note to meat, chicken and fish stocks.

Fish stock

MAKES: *1 litre (1 pint 15 fl oz)*
PREPARATION TIME: *5 minutes*
COOKING TIME: *30 minutes*

---

500 g (1 lb 2 oz) white fish
   trimmings (heads, bones, tails etc)
1 onion, roughly chopped or sliced
125 ml (4 fl oz) dry white wine
1 bouquet garni
1 tablespoon lemon juice

---

1 Put the fish trimmings in a large saucepan (breaking or folding over if necessary), add the onion and sweat them over a low heat for 10 minutes.
2 Pour on 1.25 litres (2 pints 2 fl oz) of cold water and the wine, then bring to the boil. Remove any scum that rises to the surface, then add the bouquet garni and lemon juice.
3 Half cover the pan so that the lid is tilted, reduce the heat, and then simmer for 30 minutes only.
4 Remove the saucepan from the heat and strain the stock, discarding the bones and other solids. Use it immediately or cool and chill.

MAKING IT LAST

How long will stock keep?

Stock should be cooled then kept, covered, in the refrigerator for four days (two days for fish stocks) or in the freezer for up to three months (two months for fish). It is best to reduce the stock by rapid boiling to get a concentrated stock for freezing. Frozen stock can be defrosted or reheated straight from frozen, but should be simmered for at least 10 minutes; it can also be diluted.

VEGETABLE VARIETY

I am vegetarian – can you suggest an all-purpose vegetable stock?

The following recipe can be used in cooking for vegetarians, as well as for anyone following a low-fat diet. Vegetarian stocks can be as bland or as strong as you like: the greater the variety of vegetables and herbs you use, the better the stock will taste. Because they do not contain any meat bones, vegetarian stocks do not set to a jelly.

Vegetable stock

MAKES: *1 litre (1 pint 15 fl oz)*
PREPARATION TIME: *5 minutes*
COOKING TIME: *1 - 1 1/2 hours*

---

750 g - 1 kg (1 lb 10 oz - 2 lb 4 oz)
   selection of vegetables: beans,
   broccoli, cauliflower, celery,
   fennel, leeks, mushrooms, onions
   and any root vegetables, cleaned,
   trimmed and roughly chopped
Selection of herbs such as bay leaf,
   dill, marjoram, parsley stalks,
   rosemary, tarragon, thyme
Large strip of lemon rind, optional
Blade of mace, optional
6 peppercorns

---

1 Put all the ingredients in a large saucepan, add 1.5 litres (2 3/4 pints) of cold water and bring the stock to the boil. Reduce the heat, half cover the saucepan so that the lid is tilted and simmer gently for 1 - 1 1/2 hours until reduced by nearly half.
2 Remove the saucepan from the heat, strain the stock and discard the vegetables. Leave to cool, then store in the refrigerator for up to four days.
VARIATION
A darker vegetable stock may be made by including aubergines in the vegetable mixture and adding clean onion skins or mushroom stalks.

STALKS FOR FLAVOUR

Why do stock recipes use parsley stalks? Is it considered a waste to use the florets or do they give the stock a bitter taste?

Recipes for stock often specify the use of parsley stalks because they have more flavour than the florets, which will turn bitter if cooked for several hours. This is also economical as the parsley leaves can then be used for garnishing.

Other herbs suitable for adding to stocks are the woody ones that will stand up to prolonged cooking: sprigs of marjoram, tarragon and thyme, as well as bay leaves. A slice of lemon or pared lemon rind is a good addition to chicken stock and onion or tomato skins can also be added to give a strong golden colour and extra flavour.

STORAGE

KEEP IT FRESH

What is the best way to store fresh food in the home?

The modern methods of chilling, freezing, wrapping and transporting food should mean that we buy produce at its very best: fruit and vegetables brought to perfect ripeness, meat and fish at the peak of freshness. Sometimes, however, the freshness is an illusion created by packing and refrigeration technology, and when you get the food home, spoilage will be rapid unless some of the professionals' techniques are employed.

Almost all vegetables store well in the refrigerator, where the low temperature prevents spoilage. If space cannot be found in the refrigerator for all the vegetables, use a cool, dark place instead as warmth and light will hasten their spoilage. Do not store them in polythene bags or airtight containers as the warmer temperature will make them sweat and rot. Keep potatoes in a dark place or they will go green and be inedible.

Never store bananas or unripe avocados in the refrigerator, as both develop black skins if refrigerated and their ability to ripen is impaired. Ripe avocados, however, can be stored for a few days in the salad compartment of the refrigerator. Keep strong-smelling fruit such as cut pineapple or melon well wrapped in the refrigerator, or their fragrance will affect the flavour and smell of dairy foods such as butter, cheese and milk.

In the refrigerator, cheese is best stored in waxed paper or foil which, unlike cling film, do not cause it to sweat. Very strong cheeses are best kept in a plastic box so that their aromas do not taint other foods.

Fish does not improve with storage. If it is to be kept for more than 12 hours, even in the refrigerator, scatter cracked ice over it, replacing the ice as necessary, and cover the container to prevent the smell of fish tainting other food. Shellfish perishes particularly quickly and for this reason, it is generally sold alive, frozen or precooked. If you are in any doubt about the length of time a quantity of shellfish has been stored, do not eat it.

All meat and poultry should be chilled; meat should be eaten within four days, poultry within three days. If you buy your meat from a high street butcher, store it loosely wrapped in greaseproof paper or foil as a plastic covering will cause the meat to sweat and then become slimy and decompose. However, most meat sold in supermarkets is wrapped in sealed packages containing an inert gas which avoids this effect, and these are best left unopened until the meat is needed.

THE BREAD LINE

Does keeping fresh bread in the refrigerator prevent it from going mouldy, or does this make it go stale more quickly?

The answer is yes on both counts. Using the refrigerator will prevent mould development, but as it is a very dry environment it also makes bread go stale very quickly. To store bread for long periods of time, slice it and keep it in the freezer. Slices can be toasted from frozen very successfully, and they can be defrosted in very little time if they are to be eaten untoasted.

KEEPING EGGS

How should fresh eggs be kept? I thought I should refrigerate them, but supermarkets never do.

Eggs can be stored perfectly safely in any cool spot, although they will keep for longer in a refrigerator. Many supermarkets now sell eggs individually stamped with a 'best by' date, so it is easy to keep track of their age. If you do store them in the refrigerator, take them out an hour or so before using: cold eggs will crack when you boil them and room-temperature eggs will whisk to a greater volume than cold ones.

STORAGE LIFE

How do I store dried foods such as beans, herbs, spices and coffee?

Dried pulses and beans should be bought from a shop with a rapid turnover to ensure fresh stocks. There is a great difference between beans dried last season and those from two or three years ago. Store dried pulses and beans in airtight containers·in a dark place and try not to buy more than two months' supply at a time. Although stored beans will be safe to eat, they do go stale and their skins will toughen.

Dried herbs and spices also have a relatively short storage life and although they look attractive in glass jars on a spice rack, this is the worst way to store them. To ensure complete freshness, store them in a cupboard or a dark airtight container and use within two months.

Coffee, both beans and ready-ground, will go stale in a cupboard within days. Store it in the refrigerator or freezer and use it from frozen for a perfectly fresh cup.

STRAWBERRY: see SOFT FRUIT

STUFFING

USED FOR CENTURIES

Are stuffings and forcemeats really the same thing?

These two words are often used interchangeably, and there is some confusion about their exact meanings, probably because forcemeat, which is finely chopped and usually made of spiced meat or poultry, is often an ingredient in stuffings. Both are used to fill meat, poultry and vegetables and have been used for centuries, especially to make roast meat go farther and to add flavour and moistness.

The staple ingredients for stuffings are breadcrumbs, which add bulk, and egg, which binds the stuffing mixture together. This can be confusing for cooks because it is natural to think that breadcrumbs will make stuffings stodgy, and that the egg will make it creamy because it visibly loosens the mixture when added to it. But, in fact, a high proportion of breadcrumbs will give a soft and tender stuffing, while using too much egg makes a stodgy stuffing once it has been cooked and the egg has set.

TAKE CARE WITH CAVITIES

I have heard that there is a risk of salmonella poisoning if I stuff the cavity of a bird. Is this true, and if so, is it safe to stuff it at all?

Meat and poultry are highly vulnerable to salmonella and the bacteria is only killed by thorough cooking (see FOOD POISONING).

With a large bird, such as a turkey, it is safer not to stuff the entire cavity, especially if you use a sausage meat stuffing. This is because there is a risk that by the time the rest of the bird is cooked and ready, the heat will not have penetrated to the centre of the substantial amount of stuffing used to fill a large bird, so it will not have cooked enough to kill off any bacteria. It is safe to stuff the neck end, which holds a lot of stuffing, as there is less meat between the source of the heat and the stuffing and there is a better opportunity for thorough cooking.

It is completely safe and also simpler to put an onion studded with cloves, a lemon, or a handful of peeled chestnuts into the body cavity of the bird to add flavour.

With a small game bird, such as pheasant or quail, you could stuff the entire bird as it takes less time for the heat to cook the smaller quantity of stuffing, providing you do not pack it too tightly.

There is some risk of salmonella in wild game birds as well as in domestic birds such as chicken and turkey. If you are going to stuff any bird, it is important that both the meat and the stuffing are thoroughly cooked to guarantee safety.

If you have any doubts at all and want to be completely assured that there is no risk of salmonella, cook the stuffing separately.

SUET

RICH, PURE FAT

Where does suet come from?

Suet is the hard, concentrated, white fat that surrounds beef and lamb's kidneys. It is now less often sold in solid form from butchers for grating at home – in supermarkets you will find suet sold already shredded and floured ready for use.

A rich, pure fat that contains a high percentage of saturated fatty acids, beef suet is traditionally used for cooking many dishes including dumplings, mincemeat, suet crust pastry and steamed puddings.

Lamb suet is not widely available although butchers will be able to order it for you; it has a stronger flavour than beef suet and is therefore less adaptable in cooking and a poor choice for sweet dishes such as steamed puddings or pastry.

LIGHTEN IT

Why is my suet pastry heavy?

There are several reasons why suet pastry may be heavy and stodgy. Check that you have measured your ingredients accurately and do not undercook or overcook the pastry. When you are steaming a suet pudding over a pan of water, ensure that water does not seep into the pudding as this too can cause the pastry to become heavier in texture. The following recipe for a Blackberry and Apple Suet Pudding combines suet and autumnal fruits for a sweet pudding with a delicious taste and texture.

Blackberries lend their rich colour to this luscious suet pudding. Combined with apples, they give moistness and flavour to the comforting pastry mixture.

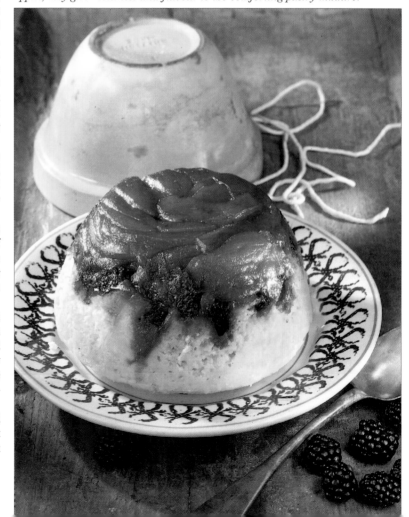

Blackberry and apple suet pudding

SERVES: 4
PREPARATION TIME: 20 minutes
COOKING TIME: 1 1/2 - 2 hours

115 g (4 oz) cooking apples, peeled, cored and sliced
25 g (1 oz) soft brown sugar
115 g (4 oz) blackberries, washed
175 g (6 oz) self-raising flour
A pinch of salt
85 g (3 oz) shredded suet
60 g (2 1/4 oz) caster sugar
About 150 ml (5 fl oz) full-fat milk

1 Put the apple slices in the base of a lightly greased 1.2 litre (2 pint) pudding basin, sprinkle with brown sugar and top with the blackberries.
2 Put the flour, salt, suet and caster sugar in a bowl and stir until mixed. Make a well in the centre and add just enough milk to produce a soft dropping consistency, mixing well.
3 Spoon this suet pastry mixture evenly over the fruit and level the surface of the pudding.
4 Cover the pudding with a double layer of pleated, greased, greaseproof paper or foil and tie securely with string. Make a string handle across the basin top to lift the pudding in and out of the steamer.
5 Place the pudding in a steamer over a pan of boiling water. Cover and steam for 1 1/2 - 2 hours, topping up the pan regularly to prevent it from boiling dry. Turn the pudding out onto a warmed serving plate and serve with custard or cream.

VARIATIONS
Use some other soft fruits, such as raspberries or loganberries, in place of the blackberries. You can sprinkle a teaspoon of ground cinnamon or mixed spice over the fruit before steaming. Add the finely grated zest of a lemon to the pudding mixture before spooning it over the fruit.

VEGETARIAN SUET

Is there a vegetarian alternative to using beef suet?

Vegetarian suet is widely available in supermarkets. It is made from hard or hydrogenated vegetable oils or solid white vegetable fat which is prepared in a similar way to traditional beef suet. It may be used as an alternative to and in the same way as beef suet and unlike beef suet, which is coated with wheat flour, vegetarian suet tends to be dusted with rice flour, making it appropriate for people who are allergic to wheat or those on gluten-free diets. Low-fat vegetarian suet has 25 per cent less fat.

Alternatively you can use the same quantity of finely ground Brazil nuts, a highly nutritious vegetarian substitute that can be used in all recipes containing suet. Brazil nuts melt in the same manner as suet and will provide a pleasing, rather grainy, texture. They contain 68.2 per cent fat with only 16.4 per cent of that being saturated fat – the rest is half monounsaturated and half polyunsaturated fat.

SUGAR

FINE LINE IN SUGARS

If a recipe calls for caster sugar and I've run out, can I substitute granulated sugar instead?

It depends on the recipe. In cakes made by the rubbing method, you can use the granulated sugar as it is. If you need a finer sugar, it is possible to grind granulated sugar in a liquidiser or coffee grinder: the result is more like icing sugar than caster sugar but it would be acceptable for making biscuits, pastry, icings and so on. Home-ground sugar is not, however, suitable for creamed cake mixtures as the volume of sugar will be reduced and result in a cake with a hard crust.

LOW-CALORIE SUBSTITUTE

Can low-calorie sugars be used in cooking in place of ordinary granulated sugars?

Generally, artificial sweeteners and sugar substitutes are much sweeter by volume than sugar and cannot be directly substituted for them in

---

MAKING FLOWER AND HERB SUGARS

Sugar flavoured with flowers or herbs gives a summery fragrance to cakes and desserts made with it. Suitable (insecticide-free) plants with lots of fragrance include bay, lavender, lemon balm, marigold, mint such as eau-de-cologne mint, rosemary, rose petals and violets.

1 Gently pull the petals from larger flowers such as roses, but keep smaller flowers such as lavender whole. Pull off the stamens and the green caps at the base. If you think they might have been sprayed, wash and dry the flower parts carefully.

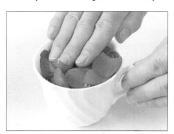

2 Measure the flowers in a cup, pressing them down gently. Use twice the amount of caster sugar as there are petals or leaves.

3 Layer the sugar and the flower petals in a lidded jar. Seal tightly and leave in a warm place for one to two weeks. Shake the jar every now and then. Smell the sugar and when it has absorbed the required amount of scent, sieve to remove the petals or leaves. Store it in a tightly sealed jar and use as required.

cooking. However, some brands of granulated sugar substitutes are specifically designed to be used in exactly the same quantities as ordinary sugar in cooking, so check the instructions given on the packet.

SYRUP RATIO

Does sugar syrup always require the same ratio of sugar to water?

No. Sugar syrup is simply a solution of sugar dissolved in water, and different concentrations are used for different recipes. A thin syrup is three parts water to one part sugar; a medium syrup is two parts water to one part sugar; and a heavy syrup is equal volumes of water and sugar. In simple, clear syrups, the sugar and water are stirred over a low heat until the sugar has dissolved, the mixture is boiled for a minute then removed from the heat (see box, right).

If any of these syrups are boiled for a longer time, more water evaporates, the temperature of the syrup increases and the sugar changes colour, deepening from pale yellow to dark brown and eventually turning into caramel. There are various stages to which the sugar syrup can be boiled (see list, right) and different recipes will require different stages of caramelisation.

TESTING TIME

What is the best way for me to test whether sugar syrup is ready?

It is best to use a sugar thermometer to test sugar syrup. First, put the thermometer in a bowl of hot water for a few minutes so it is warm before going into the syrup. Take it out of the water, dry it and place it into the pan containing the hot syrup. Make sure the bulb of the thermometer is covered by the syrup but not touching the base of the pan or you will get a false reading. If the quantity of syrup is small, tilt the pan to one side so that you can immerse the bulb.

When the syrup has reached the desired temperature (see the following list), remove the pan from the heat and place the thermometer back in the bowl of hot water to make cleaning the bulb easier.

Although a sugar thermometer is recommended for taking the temperature of your syrup mixture, do not worry if you do not have one. You can use the simple tests listed below to ascertain what stage your sugar syrup has reached.

• THREAD STAGE for thin syrups: 103°C (217°F). Thread test: dip two spoons into the syrup, back to back. Pull gently apart until a thin thread forms and then breaks almost immediately.

• PEARL STAGE for fondants and icings: 105°C (220°F). Pearl test: small pearl-like globules appear on the surface of the syrup, and if the thread test is repeated, the thread formed will be thicker.

• BLOW STAGE for ices: 110°C (230°F). Blow test: use a metal skewer with a small ring at one end. Dip the ring in the syrup then blow on it gently – a small bubble of syrup should appear.

• SOFT BALL STAGE for fondants and soft fudges: 115°C (240°F). HARD BALL STAGE for hard fudges: 120°C (250°F). Soft and hard ball test: drop a little syrup into a small bowl of cold water. Then gather it together with your fingers and it should form a soft or hard ball.

• CRACK STAGE for soft toffees: 136°C (280°F). HARD CRACK STAGE for hard toffees and spun sugar: 149°C (300°F). Crack and hard crack test: drop a little syrup into cold water and the pieces will become brittle and snap easily between your fingers. Crack is not quite so brittle as hard crack.

• CARAMEL STAGE for caramel coatings, decorations and praline: 170°C (340°F). Caramel test: the colour of the syrup will change from pale gold to dark brown.

STICKY BUSINESS

How do I avoid ruining my pan when making caramel?

As caramel is usually made in fairly small amounts, it is important to use a small pan as then it is easier

MAKING SUGAR SYRUP

Sugar syrup can be made to many densities, from the thinnest, used to sweeten fruit salads, to the thickest, used to glaze fruit. The best way to achieve the exact set you want is to use a sugar thermometer.

1 Put the sugar and water into a large heavy-based saucepan and heat it very slowly, stirring with a wooden spoon, until the sugar has dissolved. The syrup should not boil until the sugar has completely dissolved or the end result will be grainy. When the syrup is absolutely clear, turn up the heat and boil it briskly without any further stirring.

2 Use a dampened pastry brush to gently brush any sugar crystals that form back into the liquid. Keep a pan of hot water at one side to hold the pastry brush, the wooden spoon and the sugar thermometer.

3 Test the syrup using a proper sugar thermometer; when the setting point has been reached, stop the cooking process by standing the pan in a bowl of cold water.

to control the degree of heat and prevent the caramel from sticking. In a large pan there is the danger that the sugar will caramelise quickly, burn and stick to the pan.

The pan should also have a heavy base: a thin pan will buckle then heat will not be evenly distributed and, again, the caramel will burn. If the caramel does stick to the base of the pan, the easiest way to clean it is to add some cold water, return the pan to a low heat and stir gently; the hardened burnt caramel should gradually dissolve as the water increases in temperature. Repeat this process until the pan is thoroughly cleaned.

BROWN OR WHITE?

Is brown sugar any healthier to eat than white sugar?

Most brown sugar is refined sugar that has been treated with colour and flavour, and so there is no evidence to suggest that brown sugar is healthier than white.

Golden demerara sugar and the muscovados have traces of minerals and vitamins, so it could be claimed that they are marginally healthier than other sugars. However, to gain any benefit from these minerals and vitamins you would have to eat an enormous amount of sugar, which would not be healthy.

CRUNCHY MICE

I remember in my childhood being able to buy sugar mice at my local sweetshop. Can I make them at home myself?

Yes, very easily. Sugar mice only take a short while to make, keep for a long time, and are very popular with young children, who love to suck on the hardened shapes.

Sugar mice

MAKES: 8 mice
PREPARATION TIME: 30 minutes
COOKING TIME: none

500 g (1 lb 2 oz) icing sugar
1 egg white, size 2
3 tablespoons golden or corn syrup
Edible food colourings, optional
Silver balls
Shoelace liquorice or fine string

1 Sieve 375 g (13 oz) of the icing sugar into a bowl. Add the egg white and the golden or corn syrup and mix with a wooden spoon.

2 Gradually add more icing sugar until the sugar paste is of a similar consistency to pastry (you may not need to add all the sugar). If you want to make coloured mice, divide the sugar paste into separate bowls, one for each colour, and stir in a few drops of food colouring.

3 To shape the mice, divide the sugar paste into nine roughly equal portions and set one portion aside. Roll the other eight pieces into balls then pinch one end of each ball to make a teardrop shape.

4 Pull small bits of paste from the remaining portion, flatten them to make ears and, using a little water, attach them to the narrow end of the mice. Press in the silver balls to make some eyes, and add a string or liquorice tail to the rounded end.

5 Leave the mice to dry overnight on baking paper and store for up to a month in an airtight container.

With their liquorice tails and silver ball eyes, these candy-coloured Sugar Mice look as sweet as they taste.

SHADES OF BROWN

I get confused by all the different brown sugars – what are they used for and can they simply be substituted for white sugar?

It depends on the sugar. There are various types of brown sugar, with different levels of coarseness and colours that range from pale beige to deep dark brown – the darker the colour of the sugar, the richer its flavour will be.

Demerara has a crunchy texture and is good for making chutneys, for grilling as a topping on crème brûlée and for glazing baked ham. It should not be used when a quick-melting sugar is needed, or for jellies, as it will make them cloudy; for these, use white sugar instead.

Light and dark soft brown sugars can be used in fruit , cakes and other moist cakes, some biscuits, fudge and chocolate icings, toffee and fudge, chutneys and some sauces (barbecue, sweet and sour, chocolate and so on). As these sugars are moist they should not be used in light cakes which need creaming or whisking, or in light icings where the additional flavour and colour would not be desirable.

Light and dark brown muscovado sugars (also called Barbados or moist sugar) contain molasses; the darker the colour is, the more molasses and therefore the stronger the flavour. They are used in the same way as light and dark brown soft sugars. If you are substituting them for white sugar, take care that they do not mask delicate flavours.

To the rescue!

If your brown sugar has hardened in the store cupboard, wrap the pack in a damp tea towel and microwave it on Medium for a minute or two or until the sugar begins to soften. You can then use it as normal.

KEEP IT FLOWING

How can I ensure that sugar does not go hard in my cupboard?

Sugar should be kept in an airtight container in a cool dry place, and once opened, packets should be resealed between use.

Moist brown sugars such as muscovado are the ones that tend to go hard and lumpy, as exposure to air dries them out. Adding a slice of apple or bread to the container in which the pack is stored for a couple of days should restore moisture.

If you want to use the hardened sugar immediately, blend it in a food processor and then sieve it.

NUTTY LUXURY

How do I make sugared almonds?

They are very difficult for the home cook to make, as you need to achieve a very smooth, very hard fondant and it is difficult to set it properly. This delicacy is best treated as a shop-bought luxury.

SWEDE

ROOT CONFUSION

I have heard swede referred to as 'neeps'. Is it the same as turnip?

No, it is not. Swede is a larger, rounded winter root vegetable with coarse, pale orange flesh. 'Neeps', or Swedish turnip, is what swede is called in Scotland. In the United States swede is called rutabaga.

Although they are different from each other, swede can be substituted for turnip in recipes. Choose smaller swedes for cooking as large ones tend to be tough.

BUTTER AND SPICE

Is there a way to make the strong, coarse flavour of swede gentler and more sophisticated?

Swede, like the other winter roots, needs butter and loves spices. An excellent way of serving swede is to peel it thickly and cut it into

slices before being parboiled and grilled, then lightly spread with tapenade. Bacon is another tasty accompaniment. Parboil chunks of swede, drain them well then stir-fry in olive oil with chopped bacon and a teaspoon of cumin seeds.

Slow roasting brings sweetness and a soft texture to the vegetable and so pieces of swede are best roasted around a meat joint for 1–1½ hours. Alternatively, roast them on their own in a little olive oil and 10 minutes before the end of cooking, top them with slices of Cheddar, Gruyère or mozzarella cheese and return to the oven.

Swede is also good served as a purée, often mixed with other root vegetables (as in the recipe below), and this can soften its flavour.

Mashed swede and carrot with allspice

SERVES: 6
PREPARATION TIME: 25 minutes
COOKING TIME: 20 minutes

---

500 g (1 lb 2 oz) swede, cut into chunks
400 g (14 oz) large carrots, cut into chunks
75 g (2¾ oz) butter
4 tablespoons double cream or whipping cream
150 g (5½ oz) mashed potatoes
1 teaspoon ground allspice
Salt and black pepper

---

1 Put the swede into a large pan of water, bring to the boil and simmer for 10–15 minutes until soft.
2 Meanwhile, cook and drain the carrots, then put them into a food processor with the butter and cream.
3 Drain the swede, then return it to the dry pan, and shake over low heat to encourage evaporation.
4 Add the chunks of swede to the carrots in the food processor and purée them together.
5 In a large bowl, stir the mashed potato and the purée of swede and carrot together by hand. Season with allspice, salt and black pepper.
6 Spread the purée in an oven dish and serve immediately, or reheat in the oven when required.

SWEET AND SOUR SAUCE

KITCHEN PHILOSOPHY

Why do I find sweet and sour dishes on every Chinese menu?

Chinese culture is based on the yin-yang concept of universal balance and absolute harmony. Sweet and sour are only two of the many opposite elements which symbolise this philosophy, but they are the most commonly encountered.

The permutations of sweet and sour are endless as long as you stick to the fundamental principle, balancing honey and wine vinegar, honey and malt vinegar, even marmalade with balsamic vinegar or tomato sauce and pineapple juice. It is a matter of ingenuity and the ingredients you use are less important than achieving a sauce that is a harmonious blend.

Traditional Chinese sweet and sour dishes are made with plum sauce and rice wine, vinegar or lemon juice. The authentic sauce (right) is easy to reproduce. You can make a large batch, omitting the cucumber and the onion, and refrigerate it for up to a week. Add the vegetables just before cooking.

If you are using previously fried, battered pork or chicken, simply combine the sauce and coated meat in a wok or pan and stir to blend. Pork cubes are best floured and refrigerated for a few hours before being deep-fried for a sweet and sour dish as this makes them crisp.

Sweet and sour sauce

MAKES: 175 ml (6 fl oz)
PREPARATION TIME: 5 minutes plus 1 hour standing
COOKING TIME: 10 - 15 minutes

1/2 cucumber
1 teaspoon salt
3 tablespoons plum sauce
2 tablespoons malt vinegar
1 tablespoon tomato sauce
1 teaspoon sugar
1 tablespoon vegetable oil
1/2 large onion, sliced

1 Peel the cucumber, discarding the soft central seeds, then cut it into slices 1 cm (1/2 in) wide. Sprinkle it with salt and set aside for an hour. Squeeze the cucumber to remove as much moisture as you can, then set it aside for later use.

2 Place 150 ml (5 fl oz) of cold water in a saucepan with the plum sauce, vinegar, tomato sauce and sugar and bring the mixture to a simmer.

3 In a separate pan or wok, heat the oil and fry the sliced onion over a high heat until the edges begin to brown. Add the cucumber and stir rapidly for a minute or two.

4 Transfer the cucumber and onion to the simmering sauce and cook for a minute or two. The sauce can now be combined with other ingredients, such as chicken, pork or seafood, to make a superb sweet and sour dish.

VARIATIONS

To give a sharper taste to the sauce, use Chinese lemon sauce (a bottled sauce that can be found in Oriental supermarkets and some speciality food stores) instead of plum sauce.

Omit the tomato sauce but add a skinned and quartered tomato. Omit the cucumber and substitute a small can of drained pineapple chunks.

Use two stalks of spring onions, cut into 2.5 cm (1 in) lengths, in the sauce instead of the large onion.

This authentic Sweet and Sour Sauce is a harmonious blend of plum sauce and malt vinegar. Add vegetables and deep-fried cubes of meat for a complete dish.

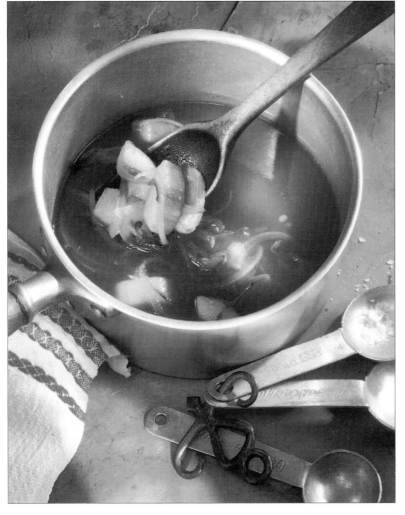

SWEET POTATO: see POTATO

SWISS ROLL

ROLL-UPS

What is the difference between a swiss roll and a roulade, and how should they be rolled up?

Swiss rolls are made from a light sponge mixture that contains flour. Roulades are based on a whisked egg mixture and contain very little or no flour, and are moister and softer than swiss rolls.

To prevent a swiss roll cracking when rolled, trim off its crusty edges then, while it is still warm, put it on greaseproof paper dusted with caster sugar. Roll it up loosely, rolling the paper with it, and leave it to cool in its wrapping. Then gently open up the roll slightly, remove the paper and spread the interior with jam, curd or cream.

Roulades are easier to roll, so can be filled before rolling up, as in the following recipe. They do usually crack when being rolled, but look attractive when dredged with icing sugar and decorated.

Chocolate and coffee roulade

SERVES: 8
PREPARATION TIME: 20 minutes, plus overnight cooling
COOKING TIME: 20 minutes

1 tablespoon instant coffee granules
100 g (3 ½ oz) plain chocolate
4 eggs, size 2, separated
100 g (3 ½ oz) sugar

FOR THE FILLING
300 ml (10 fl oz) double cream
1 tablespoon brandy or orange liqueur
To decorate: fresh berries or thin orange slices

1 Preheat the oven to 180°C (350°F, gas mark 4). Grease a swiss roll tin measuring 33 × 28 cm (13 × 11 in) and line it with baking paper. Dissolve the coffee granules in a tablespoon of boiling water and stir to a smooth paste.

2 Break up the chocolate and melt it in a heatproof bowl set over warm water, or in the microwave oven, then remove from the heat.

3 Whisk the egg yolks and sugar together in a large bowl until thick and pale, then stir in the cold coffee paste and melted chocolate.

4 Whisk the egg whites until stiff. Fold 2 tablespoons of the egg white into the chocolate mixture to loosen it, then fold in the rest.

5 Spread the mixture into the tin and bake for about 20 minutes or until it springs back when lightly pressed with a finger.

6 When the cake is cooked, remove it from the oven and put the tin on a wire rack. Cover the cake with a clean tea towel and leave it to cool for a few hours or overnight.

7 Sprinkle some caster sugar over a sheet of greaseproof paper, then turn the cake out onto this and trim off the crusty edges.

8 Whip the cream lightly, fold in the brandy or liqueur and spread it over the cake. Roll up the cake, using the paper to help you lift it. Dredge with icing sugar and decorate with fresh berries or thin slices of orange.

Cool whipped cream, delicately flavoured with a dash of liqueur, is enfolded in a light and moist chocolate roulade. A hint of coffee adds depth of flavour.

SYRUP

REFINED SWEETNESS

Are molasses, treacle and golden syrup the same thing?

No, they are not. Molasses is the syrup left over after sugar has been refined and crystallised from sugar cane. It is sold in several grades, from sweet and refined 'first' or light molasses, to thick, dark and slightly bitter blackstrap molasses. Treacle is a form of molasses, one that has been blended to produce a sweeter syrup which is less prone to becoming gritty. Golden syrup, which is sweeter than treacle, is made from refined white sugar.

Molasses has a dominating taste which gives a powerful flavour to sticky, moist cakes and puddings:

gingerbread and fruit cakes are probably the best known. It is also used for making toffee and fudge, and its slightly bitter taste can enhance savoury dishes such as pork and bean casseroles, gravies and barbecue sauces.

Lighter golden syrup is used as a sweetener in baking, or as a topping for ice cream or hot puddings.

SWEET LIQUID CORN

I have a recipe which calls for corn syrup - what is this, and can I use anything else instead?

Corn syrup is a clear, thick, sweet syrup with little taste, derived from corn kernels. It is very useful in cooking, as its moisture-absorbing qualities help to keep cakes and other baked items very moist.

There isn't really an exact substitute for corn syrup, which is widely used in the United States. There, it is available both in its clear form and with added colouring and flavouring to give it a flavour similar to molasses. In Britain, many of the larger supermarkets stock the clear version, but if you have trouble finding it you could try substituting golden syrup (although the flavour will be different) or glucose syrup.

TREE SUGAR

What is maple syrup, and how should I use it?

Maple syrup is produced from sap tapped from maple trees in early spring, when their sap is rising. The fresh sap is then boiled to reduce it to sugar or a reddish-brown, relatively thin and very sweet syrup with a positive flavour. Pure maple syrup is quite expensive; some brands are blended with cheaper corn or cane syrup, so check the ingredients on the label.

Most maple syrup is imported from Canada, whose national emblem is the maple leaf, and in North America it is typically served with pancakes and waffles. It may also be poured over thick plain yoghurt or vanilla ice cream, or over a pudding such as the one that follows.

Pilgrim pudding

SERVES: 8 - 10
PREPARATION TIME: 15 minutes
COOKING TIME: 1 1/2 hours

700 ml (1 pint 5 fl oz) milk
100 g (3 1/2 oz) fine cornmeal (polenta)
50 g (1 3/4 oz) unsalted butter, softened or diced
5 tablespoons black treacle or molasses
50 g (1 3/4 oz) granulated sugar
50 g (1 3/4 oz) dark muscovado sugar
2 eggs, size 2, beaten
1 teaspoon ground cinnamon
1/4 teaspoon ground allspice
85 g (3 oz) seedless raisins, optional
To serve: whipped cream or vanilla ice cream and maple syrup

1 Put 450 ml (16 fl oz) of the milk into a pan and bring to the boil. Sprinkle in the cornmeal, stirring continuously. Cook over a low heat, stirring continuously, for 15 minutes until the mixture is very thick and will hold its shape. Remove from the heat and stir in the butter. Mix well.
2 Preheat the oven to 160°C (325°F, gas mark 3) and butter a shallow ovenproof dish 25 × 23 cm (10 × 9 in).
3 Warm a metal spoon in very hot water and measure the black treacle or molasses into the cornmeal. Add all the remaining ingredients and mix thoroughly. Gradually stir in the remainder of the milk and mix well to blend it thoroughly.
4 Pour the cornmeal mixture into the prepared dish and spread it level with a knife. Bake for 1 - 1 1/4 hours until firm to the touch in the centre. Serve warm or cold, with whipped cream or ice cream and maple syrup.

SUGAR CRYSTALS

When I opened my tin of syrup I found that it had crystallised. Is it safe to use it like that?

Crystallisation, where syrup develops gritty particles, is a natural process which sometimes occurs after long storage at cool temperatures or even because of air bubbles in the syrup, but it is quite

---

MEASURING OUT SYRUP AND TREACLE

Measuring thick, sticky syrup can be problematic. To make the syrup pour more freely, warm it first by standing the open can or jar in a bowl of hot water for a few minutes.

1 To measure out a small amount, use a tablespoon, which holds about 25 g (1 oz) in weight. Dip the spoon in very hot water, dry it and then use it to measure the syrup.

2 To measure out a large quantity, put a small empty saucepan on kitchen scales and either note its weight or reset the scales. Then pour or spoon syrup into the pan until the right weight is indicated.

3 Some cake recipes call for the syrup to be added direct to dry ingredients, such as flour. Weigh the dry ingredient on the scales, then pour or spoon on the syrup until the right weight is indicated.

---

harmless. If you discover that your syrup has developed crystals that you think would spoil a dish, simply warm the can gently in a pan of hot water to dissolve them and then use it as specified in the recipe.

While it is not necessary to store opened cans of golden syrup in a cool place, as long as the container is sealed, it is best to keep black treacle where it will stay cool.

TAGLIATELLE

MULTICOLOURED PASTA

Can I make different colours and flavours of tagliatelle myself?

Yes, certainly. Tagliatelle is easy for the home cook to make, and is the pasta most commonly coloured and flavoured. A basic egg pasta dough is simply rolled out and cut into strips about 1 cm (½ in) wide and 25–30 cm (10–12 in) long. To add colour and flavouring, mix the appropriate ingredients with the egg before mixing it into the flour, as in the following recipe.

Spinach tagliatelle

SERVES: 4
PREPARATION TIME: 30 minutes
COOKING TIME: 5 minutes

50 g (1 ¾ oz) spinach
300 g (10½ oz) plain, strong or
   farina 00 flour
A pinch of salt
3 eggs, size 2

1 Wash and drain the spinach. Cook it gently for a few minutes in just the water that clings to the leaves. Drain, squeeze it very dry then chop finely.
2 Put the flour and salt in a bowl and make a well in the centre. Mix the eggs with the chopped spinach then pour the mixture into the well. Mix first with a fork, then use your hands until it just forms a solid mass. The dough should not be too moist - if it is, add a few more tablespoons of flour to the dough.
3 Take a portion of dough the size of a lemon and feed it through the pasta machine rollers, which should be set at the widest opening. Fold the strip in half, end to end, and feed it through the rollers again six or seven times until it is rectangular.
4 Lay out the pasta sheet on a clean cloth or a lightly floured surface and repeat with the remaining dough.
5 Reset the rollers to a narrower setting and crank the strips through the rollers once. Reset the machine to the next setting and repeat, then do this twice more, resetting the machine each time. The strips will become longer and will need to be cut in half to facilitate handling.

6 When the strips have reached the desired thinness, they are ready to be fed through the cutters and turned into thin tagliatelle strips.
7 In a large saucepan, heat some water to a rolling boil. Add the pasta, stir briefly and cook for 2 - 3 minutes or until al dente (cooked but firm).
VARIATIONS
• SAFFRON TAGLIATELLE: replace the chopped spinach with ½ teaspoon of powdered saffron.
• TOMATO TAGLIATELLE: replace the chopped spinach with 2 tablespoons of concentrated tomato purée.

Add flavour and colour to plain tagliatelle (bottom row) with saffron (top left), tomato (top right), cuttlefish ink (centre left) or spinach (centre right).

INKY BLACK

Will anything other than cuttlefish ink make pasta black?

No. Traditionally, cuttlefish ink has been used in Italy for colouring and flavouring risottos containing either squid or cuttlefish, rather than in pasta. Black pasta is a more recent innovation, and cuttlefish ink is the only satisfactory way of colouring it: add 2–3 teaspoons of ink to the eggs before mixing into the flour. Bear in mind that it will give the pasta a fishy taste so it is best served with a complementary fishy sauce. Cuttlefish ink is available from specialist fishmongers.

THE RIGHT SAUCE

What are the best types of sauces to serve with tagliatelle?

There are no hard and fast rules. Tagliatelle and most other egg pasta shapes are frequently served with tomato-based sauces (see PASTA), but in northern Italy, an area noted for its dairy and meat produce, tagliatelle is traditionally served with cream or meat sauces. Two common examples are mushroom and cream, with a little flour added to thicken the sauce, and the following chicken liver and ham recipe.

Chicken liver and ham sauce

SERVES: 4
PREPARATION TIME: 10 minutes
COOKING TIME: 10 - 15 minutes

225 g (8 oz) chicken livers
1 tablespoon olive oil
25 g (1 oz) butter
2 shallots, finely chopped
100 g (3 1/2 oz) cooked ham or
*   bacon, diced*
1 tablespoon fresh sage or
*   1/2 tablespoon dried sage*
75 ml (2 1/2 fl oz) chicken stock
3 tablespoons brandy
Salt and black pepper

1 Remove any discoloured pieces and fat from the chicken livers. Dry them thoroughly on kitchen paper and cut them into small morsels.

2 Heat the oil and butter in a frying pan and gently sauté the shallots for a few minutes until translucent. Stir in the ham or bacon and the sage, and cook for a further minute. Add the chicken livers and cook for a further 2 - 3 minutes, stirring from time to time, until they have lost their raw colour and become soft.
3 Add the stock to the pan, stir well and cook gently for a few minutes until the liquid has slightly reduced and thickened. Then add the brandy, season to taste and take off the heat.
4 Cook the pasta and drain. Place it in a warm bowl, reheat the sauce if necessary and toss with the pasta.
VARIATION
For a rich creamy sauce, add 150 ml (5 fl oz) of whipping or double cream to the livers with the brandy.

TAPIOCA

ROOT STARCH

What is tapioca, and what kind of dishes is it used in?

Tapioca is a starch extracted from the root of the tropical cassava plant, also known as manioc. The starch has to be detoxified before the tapioca can be sold commercially as some fresh manioc roots contain a toxic substance which is destroyed by a heat process. Tapioca is sold either as granules or flakes; both can be hard to find but most good health food stores and larger supermarkets stock either one or the other.

Tapioca is a useful, easily digestible starch. Flaked, it has similar thickening properties to cornflour and arrowroot, so is good for thickening sauces. The grains are best used like rice or barley to bulk out soups and stews.

Many people associate the grains with a rather bland milk pudding, but tapioca pudding is anything but bland when the milk is flavoured with cinnamon and enriched with cream or coconut milk, as in the following recipe for an unusual variation on crème brûlée.

Coconut tapioca brûlée

SERVES: 4 - 6
PREPARATION TIME: 10 minutes, plus 2 - 3 hours chilling time
COOKING TIME: 30 minutes

50 g (1 3/4 oz) granular tapioca
300 ml (10 fl oz) full-fat milk
300 ml (10 fl oz) canned
*   coconut milk*
1/2 teaspoon ground cinnamon
25 - 50 g (1 - 1 3/4 oz) caster sugar
300 ml (10 fl oz) double cream
2 - 3 tablespoons demerara sugar
To garnish: summer fruit or berries

1 Put the tapioca, milk, coconut milk and cinnamon in a saucepan. Bring to the boil then simmer over a low heat for 10 - 15 minutes until the grains are tender. Stir in caster sugar to taste and set aside to cool.
2 Preheat the grill and lightly butter a 1.2 litre (2 pint) heatproof dish. Whip the cream until it holds its shape, then fold it into the tapioca.
3 Spoon the tapioca mixture into the prepared dish. Sprinkle a layer of demerara sugar over the top to cover the surface. Put the dish under the hot grill until the sugar caramelises. Remove it from the heat, let it cool and then chill for several hours.
4 When ready to serve, crack the crispy layer of sugar with a spoon, and garnish with summer fruit or berries, such as raspberries.
VARIATION
For a plainer flavour, leave out the coconut milk and cinnamon. Cook the tapioca in 600 ml (1 pint) of milk with half a vanilla pod. Remove the vanilla then stir in the caster sugar and leave it to cool, then continue with the recipe as above.

PALM STARCH

Is there a difference between tapioca and sago?

They are indeed similar, but sago is extracted from the pith of the tropical sago palm. It is sold in granular form, and its pearl-like appearance explains why it is often called pearl sago. Sago is a particularly easily digestible starch and is often used in dishes for the sick and elderly.

TARTS

STICKY PROBLEM

Why do my tarts always stick to the bottom of the tin?

There are two possible explanations. First check the state of your flan or tartlet tins: the surface of cheaper ones, even those labelled nonstick, may become scratched or pitted after a time and this can cause sticking. Good quality tins are a worthwhile investment.

Second, don't allow tarts to cool in their tins for too long after removing them from the oven: they may stick if the pastry contains any sugar or fruit juice. Just leave the pastry case in the tin for a few minutes and when it is firm enough, slip it out carefully and leave it on a wire tray to finish cooling.

GLAZED OVER

How can I make a professional-looking glaze for a fruit tart?

Glazes add a sheen to the fruit which prevents the surface from becoming dry. Many people like to use jam or jelly made from the same fruit for the glaze, but a contrasting flavour and colour can enhance the taste and appearance of the tart. Apricot jam and redcurrant jelly both make attractive, general-purpose glazes.

For pale fruits such as apples and pears, an apricot glaze is best. To glaze a 23 cm (9 in) tart, put 100 ml (3½ fl oz) of apricot jam in a pan and stir in a tablespoon of water. Bring to the boil, stirring gently all the while, and boil for a minute. Pass the jam through a sieve, let it cool slightly then brush it over the tart and leave it to set.

A clear redcurrant glaze looks attractive on red soft fruits, as in the recipe for Strawberry Tartlets on the opposite page. The jelly should not be allowed to boil or it will discolour. It sets fairly rapidly as it cools in the pan, so you have to work quickly or reheat it gently.

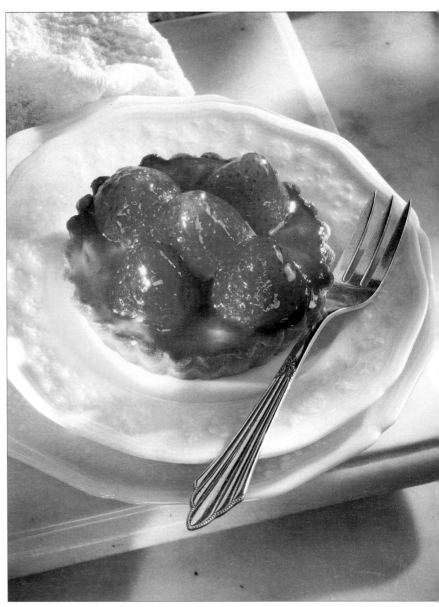

Turn simple strawberries into a bite-size luxury in a crispy glazed tartlet. For a professional touch, lay them on a cushion of luscious crème patissière.

PASTRY CUSTARD

What can I do if crème patissière does not thicken?

Crème patissière, or confectioner's custard, is thickened with both egg yolks and some starch, which is usually flour but sometimes a mixture of flour and cornflour. When making crème patissière, it is essential that the mixture does actually come to the boil, since it is only at boiling point that the starch grains will burst and thicken the custard.

CRUMBLY PASTRY

My fruit tartlets always end up crumbling when picked up. Could I use a firmer pastry?

You could try using pâte sucrée, a crisp, sweet pastry used in French patisserie. The flour is sifted onto a work surface, and the butter should be at room temperature so it will blend easily with the sugar and egg yolks, as in the following recipe. For easy rolling, chill the dough for an hour before use.

Strawberry tartlets

MAKES: 20 small tartlets
PREPARATION TIME: 45 minutes, plus
1 1/2 hours chilling time
COOKING TIME: 20 minutes

FOR THE PATE SUCREE
150 g (5 1/2 oz) plain flour
A pinch of salt
75 g (2 3/4 oz) butter at room
    temperature
75 g (2 3/4 oz) caster sugar
2 egg yolks, size 2

FOR THE CREME PATISSIERE
1 egg yolk, size 2
25 g (1 oz) caster sugar
1 1/2 tablespoons plain flour
125 ml (4 fl oz) milk
15 g (1/2 oz) unsalted butter
A few drops of vanilla essence or
    orange flower water, or
    1 teaspoon kirsch, rum or sherry

FOR THE TOPPING
500 g (1 lb 2 oz) small ripe
    strawberries or other fresh
    berries
150 g (5 1/2 oz) redcurrant jelly

1 To make the pâte sucrée, sift the flour and salt onto a clean work surface or pastry board.
2 Make a large well in the centre. Put in the butter, then the sugar and egg yolks. Using the fingertips of one hand, pinch and mix the butter, yolks and sugar together until well blended. Then draw in the flour, using a palette knife in one hand and fingertips of the other hand until the mixture forms a fairly soft dough.
3 Gently knead the dough, working it with the base of the hand a few times just until it becomes smooth. Wrap it in a polythene bag and leave to chill for an hour.
4 While the dough is chilling, make the crème pâtissière: put the egg yolk and sugar in a mixing bowl and beat well with a wooden spoon until smooth and creamy. Mix in the flour.
5 Heat the milk to just under boiling point, then add it to the egg mixture bit by bit, stirring until smooth.
6 Pour the crème pâtissière into a small, clean saucepan. Place it over a gentle heat, stirring continuously,

until the mixture comes to the boil and thickens. (If any lumps develop during cooking, take the pan off the heat and beat until smooth.)
7 When the crème patissière has thickened, remove it from the heat, beat in the butter and add the vanilla or other flavouring. Pour the mixture into a bowl. Wet some greaseproof paper, cover the crème patissière with it and set aside until cold.
8 To make the tartlets, roll out half the pastry thinly on a lightly floured surface. With a 7.5 cm (3 in) cutter, stamp out ten rounds and use them to line ungreased tartlet tins. Prick the bases well with a fork and chill for 30 minutes. Use the remaining pastry to line a further ten tins, and chill those. Meanwhile, preheat the oven to 190°C (375°F, gas mark 5).
9 Bake the chilled tartlets in their tins for about 10 minutes or until the pastry is pale golden. Leave them in their tins for 1 - 2 minutes to harden slightly, then slide them out carefully with a knife. Cool on a wire rack.
10 When the pastry cases are cold, spread a teaspoon of crème patissière in the bottom of each one, then top with a few strawberries.
11 To make the glaze, push the jelly through a sieve placed above a small pan. Heat gently, without stirring or boiling, for 1 - 2 minutes until clear.
12 Leave the jelly to cool slightly, then brush the fruit with it and leave it to set. The tartlets are best when eaten within 2 hours of filling.

AVOIDING SOGGINESS

How can I stop the pastry shell of a fruit tart from going soggy?

There are several easy preventive measures. As soon as the baked tart case comes out of the oven, brush the inside with some lightly beaten egg white: this will cook and harden on the hot pastry to form a seal. Also, use small to medium sized fruits and berries rather than big ones which need to be cut, as cut surfaces create more juice, and wipe soft fruit clean with kitchen paper rather than rinsing. Finally, don't fill the tart more than a few hours before serving it.

TEA

CHOOSE YOUR BREW

What is the difference between black and green tea?

Although there are many types of tea, they all come from the same plant, *Camellia sinensis*. The differences arise because of the area where they are grown and how they are processed.

Black teas, the most commonly known in the West, have a rich aroma and flavour and are in fact reddish to dark brown in colour. The leaves are picked and allowed to wither in the sun, then bruised and left to ferment, during which time their colour, flavour and astringency develop. The leaves are then dried to stop the fermentation process and preserve them.

Green teas have less aroma and flavour than black ones and are paler. The leaves are first steamed straight after harvesting to retain some of the colour and stop the fermentation process. They are then lightly rolled before drying.

Oolong tea is a cross between black and green tea as it is semifermented. Sometimes sold on its own, it is mostly used in blends.

TIME FOR TEA

Is there much difference between the various types of tea?

Different teas do have very different characteristics, and this can affect not only how they are drunk, but at what time of day.
● ASSAM tea, from north-east India, is strong and dark and, blended with a Ceylon and often an African tea, it makes up the 'breakfast' blends. Best drunk with milk.
● CEYLON tea is crisp and strong and distinguished by its amber colour. Best drunk with milk.
● DARJEELING tea varies in taste and price depending on when it has been harvested. Tea from the first 'flush', or harvest, is very delicate, the second flush is more mature

and the autumn harvest produces a thicker tea. You can buy all three from tea merchants, but Darjeeling bought in a supermarket will be a blend of second flush teas. Its delicate aroma and flavour make Darjeeling the perfect tea to have after lunch, and it is best drunk without milk or sugar.

• SCENTED TEAS such as jasmine, or Earl Grey which is flavoured with bergamot, a citrus fruit, are good in the afternoon and evening, drunk without milk or sugar.

• LAPSANG SOUCHONG, the smoked black China tea, is very refreshing as an afternoon drink. It is drunk without milk or sugar.

• GUNPOWDER, a Chinese green tea, and OOLONG, from Formosa or China, are very light and should be drunk without milk. They contain less tannin and caffeine than black teas, so are good after dinner.

SERVE IT CHILLED

How do I make iced tea?

Iced tea is extremely easy to make, but there are two things to bear in mind: always use good quality tea leaves and not tea bags or instant tea; and choose a tea that is suitable for drinking without milk, such as Earl Grey, as iced tea is served with slices of lemon or orange.

Make the tea in the normal way and when it is brewed to your taste, strain it into a jug, leave it to cool then chill it for an hour or so. Sweeten the chilled tea to taste and put some crushed ice in tall glasses. Pop in a slice or two of lemon or orange, add a few mint leaves, and pour the tea over the lot.

There's more to tea than a breakfast cuppa: a refreshing glass of iced tea is just the thing for summer afternoons.

COOKING WITH TEA

Are there any recipes in which I could use my favourite brew?

Tea can form the base of fruit and alcoholic punches, but it can also add flavour and colour to both savoury and sweet dishes. It can be surprisingly good in meat casseroles and pâtés, for instance, and scented teas can be used in ice creams. Use ordinary leftover tea for soaking dried fruits, especially prunes, for a compote, or for soaking mixed dried fruits for rich fruit loaves, as in the following recipe.

Fruit loaf with tea

MAKES: 1 × 900 g (2 lb) loaf, roughly 18 slices
PREPARATION TIME: 15 minutes, plus overnight soaking
COOKING TIME: 1 ½ – 1 ¾ hours

---

500 g (1 lb 2 oz) luxury mixed dried fruit (currants, sultanas, raisins, cherries, dried apricots, glacé pineapple and mixed peel)
250 ml (9 fl oz) strong tea, such as Assam or Ceylon, cooled and strained
225 g (8 oz) soft brown sugar
2 eggs, size 2, beaten
225 g (8 oz) self-raising flour
2 teaspoons mixed spice
1 – 2 tablespoons clear honey

---

1 Put the fruit and tea into a bowl, cover and leave to soak overnight.
2 Preheat the oven to 160°C (325°F, gas mark 3) and line a 900 g (2 lb) loaf tin with baking paper. Stir the sugar into the fruit and tea mixture and leave to dissolve for 5 minutes, stirring once or twice.
3 Stir in the beaten eggs. Sieve the flour and mixed spice over the bowl and mix well together till smooth.
4 Pour into the prepared tin and bake in the oven for 1 ½ – 1 ¾ hours or until a skewer inserted into the centre comes out clean. Cover with foil if the top browns too much.
5 Remove the cake from the oven. While it is still warm, trickle the honey all over it and spread with a pastry brush. Leave in the tin until cold. To store, wrap the loaf in foil.

TISANES

HERB AND FLOWER DRINKS

Can you use any type of flower or herb to make tisanes?

Any unsprayed, edible flower or herb can be used in tisanes, or herbal teas or infusions, but some are more flavourful than others. Herbs and flowers commonly used in this way include bergamot and camomile flowers; caraway leaves (caraway seeds give a stronger tea); dill leaves; elderflowers; fennel leaves, flowers and seeds; hawthorn and hibiscus flowers; lemon balm; lemongrass; lemon verbena; lime flower; mint (all varieties); rose petals or hips; and rosemary.

In addition, you can use angelica leaves (diabetics should be aware of their sugar content) and raspberry leaf (said to help with labour pains). Sage makes a refreshing tea, but it should not be drunk regularly for more than a week or two at a time, as the plant's antiseptic properties can cause potentially toxic effects. Thyme is also good as a tisane, but it is advised not to drink thyme tea during pregnancy.

Tisanes can be made with either a single herb or flower (as in the box on the right), or a mixture of several, with spices added, as in the recipe for Dill Tisane below. Whichever method you choose, they make a pleasant, caffeine-free alternative to tea and coffee. All tisanes should be drunk without milk and may be sweetened with honey or sugar if desired.

Dill tisane

SERVES: 3 - 4
PREPARATION TIME: 8 - 10 minutes
COOKING TIME: none

2 teaspoons fresh chopped dill
4 green cardamom pods, lightly crushed
1/4 teaspoon fresh chopped mint
1 thin slice fresh ginger
600 ml (1 pint) boiling water
To serve: thin slices of lemon

MAKING A TISANE

Either fresh or dried herbs and flowers can be infused to make a refreshing tisane. In the pictures below, dried camomile is shown.

1 Pour a little very hot water into a teapot, preferably made of glass and kept for making tisanes. When the pot is warm, discard the water.

2 Put a teaspoon or two of dried herbs, or 2 - 3 teaspoons of fresh ones, into the warmed pot and pour on 500 ml (18 fl oz) of freshly boiled water. (If your water contains a lot of chlorine, use boiled still mineral water instead.) Leave to infuse for 3 - 5 minutes, depending on how strong you like it – the deeper the colour, the stronger the flavour.

3 When the tisane is ready, pour some into a cup, using a strainer if the teapot has not got one built into it. Serve with a little honey and a slice of lemon if desired.

1 Warm the teapot by pouring in a little very hot water, then leave for a minute or two and discard the water.
2 Put the herbs and spices into the pot and pour on the boiling water. Leave to infuse for about 5 minutes.
3 Strain into cups and serve with a thin slice of lemon in each.
VARIATION
For a fruitier drink, add some grated zest of an unwaxed orange. To give a delicate hint, use 1/4 teaspoon, or 1/2 teaspoon for a stronger taste.

TOFU

PROTEIN-PACKED SOYA

I was recently given a recipe which calls for tofu; is this the same as bean curd?

Yes, it is. The word tofu is the phonetic translation of the Chinese 'dau foo', which means 'mash of bean curd'. It is also sometimes called soya cheese. Whatever it is called in recipes and on packets, tofu is a protein-packed, easily digestible product made from the extract of soya beans. In recent years in the West, it has become one of the basic ingredients for people on a vegetarian diet.

TYPES AND USES

What does tofu look like, and how do I use it?

Tofu comes in many guises: it is available fresh as large, rather soft, white cubes, or in harder, pale yellow pressed blocks; dried in cubes of about 2 cm (3/4 in) or in 7 cm (2 3/4 in) squares; and in UHT long-life packs. There is also brown, dried tofu skin, used for wrapping food into little parcels or for soaking in stews, usually sold in 60 cm (24 in) folded rounds. Many supermarkets now sell tofu in one form or another; large Chinese supermarkets will have the full range.

Tofu has little taste of its own but it absorbs the flavours of sauces, spices and other ingredients, especially if marinated before cooking. How you use it depends on the kind of tofu you have. Dried tofu is treated as a substitute for meat in stir-fries, curries and spring rolls, and can be stuffed much like pitta bread. Fresh tofu is used to bulk out minced meat and seafood, or as a substitute for them in vegetarian dishes. It is also often diced or shredded and added to soups like the Japanese miso soup, or mashed and mixed with chopped mixed vegetables, or made into deep-fried cutlets, as in the recipe overleaf.

Tofu cutlets

SERVES: *4 as a starter*
PREPARATION TIME: *25 minutes, plus optional 30 minutes chilling time*
COOKING TIME: *10 minutes*

---

300 g (10 ½ oz) soft, fresh white tofu cubes
1 large boiled potato, mashed
4 french beans, finely chopped
2 tablespoons finely grated carrot
1 stalk spring onion, finely chopped
2 tablespoons sesame oil
1 egg, size 3, lightly beaten
1 teaspoon salt
½ teaspoon black pepper
Cornflour, for dusting
Oil for deep-frying

---

1 Put the tofu in a mixing bowl and mash it finely with a fork. Mop off any liquid with kitchen paper.
2 Mix in all the other ingredients except the cornflour and frying oil. Blend well to a soft consistency, adding a tablespoon or two of water if the mixture is dry and crumbly.
3 Divide the mixture into four equal portions and press them to make lightly rounded, burger-like patties.

Dust the cutlets with cornflour. You can cook them immediately, but they will firm up a little if you chill them for 30 minutes beforehand.
4 Heat some oil in a deep-fryer or wok and fry the cutlets until they are golden brown and crisp. Drain on kitchen paper. Serve with sliced tomatoes and a chilli sauce dip.

SOFT, DELICATE SKINS

How do I use tofu skin?

Cut tofu skin up and cook it in soups and stews like meat, or soak it until soft to form the basis of many Chinese-style dishes. You can also use it to make delicate spring rolls quite unlike wheat-flour rolls, which were created by Chinese cooks in the West when tofu skins were hard to come by. The following recipe for Tofu Rolls uses fresh tofu in the filling as well. The rolls are mild in flavour but are usually dipped in a hot chilli sauce as you eat them. Tofu skins dry out and crack in time. Test whether they are still good by pressing gently; they should be soft and not brittle.

Tofu rolls

SERVES: *6; makes about 12 – 14 rolls*
PREPARATION TIME: *45 minutes*
COOKING TIME: *10 minutes*

---

500 g (1 lb 2 oz) minced pork
200 g (7 oz) fresh prawns, minced
100 g (3 ½ oz) fresh white tofu
1 small can crab meat, optional
2 cloves garlic, puréed
6 water chestnuts, chopped
2 stalks spring onion
1 egg, size 3, lightly beaten
2 tablespoons salt
½ teaspoon black pepper
2 tablespoons sesame oil
1 tablespoon cornflour
75 ml (2 ½ fl oz) water
2 large sheets of tofu skin
Corn oil for deep-frying
To serve: finely sliced cucumber and hot chilli sauce

---

1 In a mixing bowl, combine all the ingredients except the tofu skins and corn oil and blend well. To test for seasoning, cook a spoonful in boiling water for a minute. Taste and adjust the seasoning if necessary.
2 Unfold the tofu skins on a clean surface. Dampen a clean cloth and gently pat the skins all over with it to soften them. Cut the skins into strips about 25 cm (10 in) wide.
3 Put a large tablespoon of mixture on each tofu strip, 5 cm (2 in) from one of the shorter edges. With your fingertips, gently squeeze the mixture into a rough sausage shape running parallel to this edge, stopping about 2.5 cm (1 in) short of the long edges. Fold the end of the skin over the mixture, then roll over twice. Cut off the strip about 5 cm (2 in) away from the roll, then fold the sides over and roll once more to secure. Dampen the edge to seal and place the roll, seam side down, in a flat dish to sit for a few minutes. Make more rolls in the same way until all the filling has been used.
4 Heat some oil in a wok or deep-fryer and deep-fry two or three rolls at a time until golden brown. Lift and drain on kitchen paper. When cool, cut the rolls into 2 cm (¾ in) diagonal pieces and serve with sliced cucumber and a chilli sauce dip.

Mashed potato and crispy chopped vegetables add substance to these golden fried tofu cutlets, a protein-rich vegetarian starter for the whole family.

TOMATO

LET THE SUNSHINE IN

How can I choose a tomato with flavour? So many of them look good but taste bland.

Left to themselves, tomatoes are a seasonal vegetable (or more accurately, fruit), but they are now very widely grown indoors year-round, with no natural nutrients from the earth or ripening from the sun, so usually lack flavour.

It is best to keep recipes that are dependent on good, fresh tomatoes for summer, when they are in season and are outdoor-grown so have a better flavour. In early spring look out for Canary Island tomatoes, which are firm and have a refreshing, distinctive flavour. In winter, some smaller varieties have enough flavour to contribute to a sandwich; for cooked winter dishes it is often better and cheaper to use canned tomatoes, a purée or concentrate, or sun-dried tomatoes.

For stuffing, use the biggest ripe tomatoes you can find, such as Mediterranean Marmande, or beef tomatoes, as in the recipe below.

Stuffed beef tomatoes

SERVES: 4
PREPARATION TIME: 20 minutes
COOKING TIME: 1 ½ hours

8 large beef tomatoes
4 tablespoons olive oil
1 onion, chopped
1 teaspoon dried marjoram
2 cloves garlic, chopped
225 g (8 oz) minced beef
1 tablespoon thick tomato purée
75 g (2 ¾ oz) long-grain rice
Salt and black pepper
½ teaspoon ground allspice
3 tablespoons chopped fresh parsley

1 Slice the tops off the tomatoes and set them aside. Scoop the tomato pulp and seeds into a bowl, rub a bit of salt round the inside of the shell and leave upside down on plates to drain. Chop the tomato pulp finely.

2 Fry the onion and marjoram in half the oil over a low heat for some 8 - 10 minutes until the onion is soft and golden, adding the garlic for the last 2 minutes of cooking.
3 Add the minced beef and stir, mashing with a fork to break up the granules of meat. When the meat is browned, stir in half the tomato purée and half the pulp from the tomatoes, cover and simmer over a very low heat for 20 minutes.
4 Rinse the rice, drain it well and add it to the meat. Stir in 75 ml (2 ½ fl oz) of cold water. Season with salt, pepper and allspice, stir well and simmer for a further 10 minutes.
5 Preheat the oven to 190°C (375°F, gas mark 5). In a small mixing bowl, blend the remaining tomato purée with 4 tablespoons of cold water, then add the remaining tomato pulp and the juices that have run off from the upturned tomatoes. Season the mixture to taste and spread it in a baking dish large enough to hold all the tomatoes tightly in a single layer.
6 Stir the parsley into the meat and rice mixture and adjust the seasoning to taste. Spoon the still semi-liquid stuffing into the tomatoes, filling them about three-quarters full only to allow for swelling as the rice completes its cooking. (Any surplus can be stirred into the sauce at the bottom of the dish.)
7 Arrange the stuffed tomatoes in the dish, put their tops back on and trickle the remaining olive oil over them. Bake for 45 minutes or until the tomatoes are very soft and the stuffing has expanded to fill them. Check the sauce halfway through the cooking time and stir in a few tablespoons of water if it threatens to dry out. Serve immediately, giving two tomatoes to each diner.

CONCENTRATED FLAVOUR

What, if any, is the difference between tomato purée, passata and concassé?

In theory, purée and passata mean the same thing – that the flesh of the fruit or vegetable has been passed through a sieve to rid it of pips and make it smooth. In recipe

MAKING TOMATO CONCASSE

Freshly diced tomato flesh is useful in a variety of soups, stews and sauces. The tough skin is removed first, using boiling water.

1 Place the tomatoes, which should be very ripe, in a heatproof bowl and cover with boiling water. Stand for 1 - 2 minutes until the skin splits. Drain, refresh and pull off the skins.

2 Cut the skinned tomatoes in half horizontally and, cupping each half in your hand, squeeze out the seeds and surrounding liquid.

3 Put each half cut side down on a wood or marble board and cut the flesh up into small dice.

terms, what is usually meant by tomato purée is an intensely flavoured concentrate of tomato. It is sold mainly in cans and tubes, and is usually used to boost the flavour of cooked tomato dishes, to intensify flavour in casseroles, or to contribute tomato flavour to mayonnaise or cream-based sauces. Passata has become a supermarket term for pasteurised and sieved tomato sauce, and is sold by the jar or carton. It is usually imported from Italy and is an excellent convenience product for all kinds of tomato soups and sauces, both cooked and uncooked.

Concassé refers to the chopped flesh of tomato without seeds, pulp or skin. It is very popular with restaurant chefs and easy to make at home (see box on previous page). Use it as the basis of cooked sauces, salads and raw salsas, or stir it into warm seasoned cream to dress vegetables or pasta.

In addition, sun-dried tomato paste is now widely available. It is slightly more granular and a bit sweeter than plain tomato purée, but is used in the same way.

TASTY PARTNERS

What are the best flavourings and herbs to use with tomato?

Tomatoes respond well to liberal seasoning with pepper, or, in sandwiches and salads, to peppery cress and watercress. Add depth to cooked tomatoes with a splash of dry sherry or Tabasco, or some aniseed, cumin, fennel or paprika.

Tomatoes are commonly served with garlic and basil, but take well to a wide range of other herbs. Fresh mint and parsley are used in the following recipe for Fattoush, an Arabic puréed salad that is a relative of the Spanish cold soup, gazpacho. Fattoush can make a good starter or light lunch, or top it with a hard or soft-boiled egg to make a more substantial dish. It can be prepared an hour or two in advance, and served either chilled or at room temperature.

Fattoush

SERVES: 4 as a starter
PREPARATION TIME: 15 minutes
COOKING TIME: none

---

250 g (9 oz) firm, ripe tomatoes, skinned and roughly chopped
4 spring onions, roughly chopped
1 small green pepper, deseeded and roughly chopped
½ cucumber, roughly chopped
1 clove garlic, peeled and chopped
3 tablespoons chopped fresh parsley
1 tablespoon finely shredded fresh mint
Juice of ½ lemon
3 tablespoons olive oil
Salt and black pepper
1 pitta bread
To garnish: black olives and roughly torn parsley and mint leaves
To serve: lemon slices and hot pitta bread

---

1 Put all the ingredients except the salt, pepper and pitta bread into a food processor and process them to a chunky purée. Season to taste.
2 Lightly toast the pitta bread, break it up into a shallow bowl and spread the purée on top. The mixture can be served immediately, but can also be covered and set aside or chilled for an hour or two, during which time the flavours will develop.
3 Just before serving, stir the salad gently and garnish with the black olives, parsley and mint leaves. Serve with lemon slices and hot pitta bread.

DRYING TOMATOES

Can I dry my own tomatoes?

Tomatoes can be dried in the oven, left overnight at the lowest temperature. But this can never match the flavours that develop in the natural sun-drying process, and most British tomatoes lack the flavour that is the hallmark of shop-bought sundried Mediterranean varieties.

TONGUE: see OFFAL

Juicy tomatoes and softened pitta bread are the base of Arabic Fattoush, a fresh, chunky purée of salad vegetables which brings a touch of sunshine to the table.

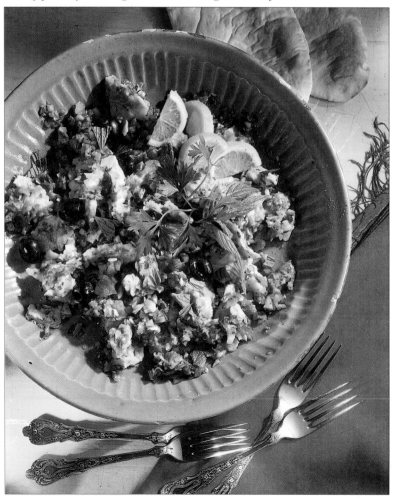

TRAYBAKES

LIGHTEN YOUR LOAD

I have been asked to run the cake stall at the school fair. What is the best way of going about it?

The first step is to round up as many other helpers as possible – the more of you there are, the less each person has to cook. The best way to approach it is to bake cakes in large trays and freeze them. Start a few weeks ahead, baking and freezing a few trays at a time, then thaw, decorate and slice the cakes a day or two before. It is best to offer a choice of flavours and textures, so make sure you do not all make only chocolate cakes.

The following cakes are all suited to being cooked in a large tray, and will keep in the freezer for up to three months.

Orange bread pudding

Makes: 20 squares
Preparation time: 45 minutes
Cooking time: 1 - 1 1/4 hours

700 g (1 lb 9 oz) stale white or
   brown bread, cut into cubes
Grated zest and juice of 1 orange
300 ml (10 fl oz) milk
350 g (12 oz) mixed dried fruit
175 g (6 oz) dark soft muscovado
   sugar
100 g (3 1/2 oz) soft tub margarine
4 teaspoons mixed spice
4 tablespoons marmalade
To decorate: 50 g (1 3/4 oz)
   granulated sugar

1 Preheat the oven to 190°C (375°F, gas mark 5) and grease a 30 × 23 cm (12 × 9 in) baking tin. Mix the bread, orange zest and juice and the milk in a bowl. Leave to soak for 15 minutes.
2 Mash the soaked bread with a fork. Add the dried fruit, muscovado sugar, margarine, spice and marmalade and mix well together, either by hand or in batches in a food processor.
3 Spread the mixture into the tin and level the surface with a knife. Bake for 1 - 1 1/4 hours until firm.

Feed a small army with a selection of traybakes: apricot sponge topped with a coconut meringue (left); bakewell tart (centre); and orangey bread pudding.

4 Remove the cake from the oven and leave it to cool in the tin for a few hours. When cold, cut it into four lengthways and five across to make 20 squares, and dredge it with the granulated sugar. Alternatively, wrap the uncut cake in foil and freeze. To serve, allow 2 - 3 hours thawing time, then cut into squares and dredge with granulated sugar.

Meringue-topped coconut and apricot squares

Makes: 20 squares
Preparation time: 20 minutes
Cooking time: 35 minutes

FOR THE CAKE MIX
225 g (8 oz) self-raising flour
225 g (8 oz) soft margarine
175 g (6 oz) caster sugar
4 eggs, size 2
Finely grated zest of 1 lemon
4 tablespoons apricot jam
100 g (3 1/2 oz) soft dried apricots,
   chopped

FOR THE MERINGUE TOPPING
3 egg whites, size 2
50 g (1 3/4 oz) desiccated coconut
100 g (3 1/2 oz) caster sugar

1 Preheat the oven to 160°C (325°F, gas mark 3). Grease a deep baking tin measuring 30 × 23 cm (12 × 9 in) and line its base with baking paper. Put all the cake ingredients in a large bowl and mix well together with a wooden spoon, then beat briskly until light and fluffy. Spread the mixture into the tin.
2 To make the meringue topping, whisk the egg whites until stiff, then fold in the coconut and sugar. Spread the topping over the cake mix and bake for 35 minutes until golden.
3 Let the cake cool thoroughly in the tin for a few hours then cut it into four lengthways and five across to make 20 squares. Alternatively, wrap the cold cake in foil and freeze. To serve, allow 2 - 3 hours thawing time, then cut into squares.

Bakewell traybake

MAKES: 16 slices
PREPARATION TIME: 35 minutes
COOKING TIME: 20 - 25 minutes

---

225 g (8 oz) shortcrust pastry
4 tablespoons raspberry jam
100 g (3 1/2 oz) soft tub margarine
100 g (3 1/2 oz) soft brown sugar
2 eggs, size 3, beaten
A few drops of almond essence
25 g (1 oz) ground almonds
75 g (2 3/4 oz) self-raising flour
2 tablespoons milk
25 g (1 oz) flaked almonds
To decorate: icing sugar

---

1 Preheat the oven to 200°C (400°F, gas mark 6) and place a baking sheet in it to heat. Grease a 28 × 18 cm (11 × 7 in) baking tin. Roll out the pastry, line the tin with it and prick it lightly all over with a fork. Spread the jam over the pastry and chill.
2 Put all the remaining ingredients except the flaked almonds in a large bowl and beat briskly with a wooden spoon for 2 - 3 minutes until smooth.
3 Spread the mixture over the jam-covered pastry and level the surface. Sprinkle on the flaked almonds. Put the tin on the heated baking sheet and bake for 20 - 25 minutes until golden and springy to the touch.
4 Let the cake cool in the tin. When cold, dredge the cake with icing sugar and cut into two lengthways and eight across to make 16 slices. Alternatively, put the uncut cake into the freezer unwrapped; once frozen wrap in foil. Allow 2 - 3 hours thawing time, then dust with icing sugar and cut into slices.

TREACLE: see SYRUP

TRIFLE

UPDATING A CLASSIC

Is there any way of making a trifle more sophisticated?

Yes, the traditional English dessert of sponge cake soaked in sherry or wine and topped with fruit or jam and custard, can be made more sophisticated by making simple changes to the basic recipe. For example, a Madeira cake, swiss roll or chocolate cake can be used instead of the fatless sponge cake. And instead of soaking the sponge in sherry, try using a liqueur such as Cointreau or kirsch, ginger wine or even a dessert wine.

The crushed macaroons which are often used in trifles can be combined with, or even replaced by, ground almonds or hazelnuts. Use a strong-flavoured jam such as morello cherry or ginger. Instead of using a vanilla-flavoured custard, make egg custard and add a few drops of almond essence or some grated chocolate. And the cream topping may be flavoured with sugar and a spirit such as brandy or a liqueur such as Cointreau.

In the recipe below, chocolate sponge cake, kirsch and canned black cherries are combined to make an unusual trifle.

Black forest trifle

SERVES: 6
PREPARATION TIME: 55 minutes, plus 5 - 6 hours cooling, softening and setting time
COOKING TIME: 10 - 15 minutes

---

600 ml (1 pint) whole milk
1 vanilla pod
2 eggs, size 3, plus 2 egg yolks
25 g (1 oz) caster sugar
300 g (10 1/2 oz) chocolate sponge cake
50 g (1 3/4 oz) macaroons, crushed
25 g (1 oz) ground almonds
425 g (15 oz) canned black cherries
100 ml (3 1/2 fl oz) kirsch
300 ml (10 fl oz) double cream
To decorate: toasted almond flakes and plain chocolate curls

---

1 Put the milk in a saucepan with the vanilla pod and bring to the boil. Remove from the heat, cover and leave to infuse for 20 minutes, then strain and discard the vanilla.
2 Put the eggs, egg yolks and sugar in a bowl and beat together until well mixed. Pour on the cooled milk, mix well and strain back into a clean pan. Cook gently, stirring continuously, for about 10 minutes or until the custard thickens slightly. Do not let it come to the boil. Pour it into a bowl and leave to cool.
3 Cut the chocolate sponge into small slices and arrange them over the base of a large glass bowl. Mix together the crushed macaroons and ground almonds and sprinkle over the chocolate cake.
4 Pour the cherry syrup into a bowl, reserving the fruit. Mix the kirsch into the syrup and spoon over the cake. Chop the cherries roughly and put them on top, then cover and set aside for 2 hours.
5 Stir the cold custard until smooth and pour it over the cherries. Cover and chill for 2 hours.
6 Whip the double cream lightly and spread or pipe it over the custard. The trifle can be served immediately, or covered and chilled overnight. When ready to serve, decorate with flaked almonds and chocolate curls.

TRIPE: see OFFAL

TROUT

FARMED AND WILD

What is the difference between rainbow trout, brown trout, sea trout and salmon trout?

Rainbow trout is a common fish, with silvery and multicoloured skin and delicate white flesh, sometimes tinged pink. Normally it will feed one person, although farmed trout can be larger. Farming trout has brought the price down considerably, but the flavour and texture of the fish have suffered.

Brown trout, with brown spotted skin, white flesh and a superior flavour, is the wild trout found in British rivers, and it tends to be available only to those who fish.

Sea trout is the same species as brown trout, but looks different as it goes out to sea and returns to rivers to spawn. Because it looks rather like a small salmon, with silvery skin and pink flesh, it is sometimes called salmon trout.

GOOD LOOKING

How can I identify a fresh trout?

As with all fish, look for firm flesh and shiny skin. The eyes should be clear and protruding, and the gills a bright red colour. And it should smell fresh and not look muddy.

Most experts agree that trout should not be washed but simply wiped with a cloth. Then remove the guts, gills and any weed from the mouth which might taste bitter.

FRESH CATCH

If I catch a trout, should it be frozen whole, or gutted first? And how do I cook it?

Gut it as soon as possible, by the waterside if you can manage it. It is a myth that keeping the guts in freshly caught fish helps to preserve them; if there is a delay before it will be frozen, it can affect the flavour. Then clean and dry the fish thoroughly before wrapping it well in freezer film. It can remain frozen for up to four months.

Trout can be fried, grilled or baked, but the best possible way to enjoy freshly caught fish is to cook it immediately, and as the recipe below shows, you don't need pots, pans, an oven or even cutlery.

Trout in newspaper

SERVES: 2
PREPARATION TIME: 5 minutes
COOKING TIME: 20 - 30 minutes

A few sheets of ordinary newspaper
2 fresh trout, gutted
A few fresh herbs, such as chives, dill, parsley or wild fennel
50 g (1 ¾ oz) butter, melted, mixed with 3 tablespoons chopped mixed fresh herbs, optional

1 Preheat a barbecue or light a small wood fire. When the embers have become very hot, sprinkle water on a few sheets of newspaper to get them damp, and put a fish in the middle of each sheet - if the sheets are small, use two per fish instead.
2 Tuck the herbs into the cavity of each fish and wrap the parcels up, folding in the ends. Put the fish on the barbecue or directly over the ashes of the wood fire. Leave to cook for about 20 - 30 minutes, turning once. When the paper parcel is well charred, the fish will be cooked.
3 Scrape off the charred newspaper and unwrap the rest. Brush the fish with herb-flavoured melted butter if you have made some and eat out of the paper with your fingers.
VARIATION
The fish can be cooked in an oven instead, preheated to 200°C (400°F, gas mark 6), for 20 minutes, however, it will lack the smoky flavour.

Yesterday's news and a small fire are all you need to turn trout into a feast. A riverside setting is optional.

TURKEY

TURKEYS WITH TASTE

Which breed of turkey is thought to have the best flavour?

Bronze turkeys, especially Norfolk Black and Cambridge Bronze, are the most flavourful and juicy. They are not intensively reared and are allowed to mature naturally and to develop a layer of fat under the skin which adds to their taste. Buy Bronze turkeys from good butchers, such as members of the 'Q Guild', or reputable poultry dealers. You may need to order in advance.

THE RIGHT HELPING

How do I calculate how much turkey to buy?

Allow 500 g (1 lb 2 oz) of dressed bird (that is, without its head, feet or giblets and before stuffing) on the bone per person, for a turkey that weighs up to 5.5 kg (12 lb). With a larger bird, allow 375 g (13 oz) per person. Remember to add a little extra if you enjoy leftovers.

STUFFING FACTS

How can I work out how much stuffing I will need - and is it safe to stuff the body cavity?

You will need around 225–280 g (8–10 oz) of stuffing for the neck cavity of a 4.5–5.5 kg (10–12 lb) bird. Do not stuff the body cavity as there could be a risk of salmonella poisoning (see STUFFING). If this amount of stuffing seems inadequate, make double the quantity and cook the rest separately.

SPOILED FOR CHOICE

What stuffings besides sage and onion go well with turkey?

There are many possibilities. For something different, try one of the recipes shown on the right. You can even use two different stuffings with one bird, one in the neck and the other cooked separately.

Sausage and bacon stuffing

MAKES: *enough to stuff and accompany a 5.5 kg (12 lb) turkey*
PREPARATION TIME: *10 minutes*
COOKING TIME: *5 minutes*

225 g (8 oz) streaky bacon, chopped
225 g (8 oz) premium sausage meat
225 g (8 oz) fresh brown
  breadcrumbs
1 tablespoon whole-grain mustard
1 tablespoon fresh or dried thyme
Salt and black pepper

1 Fry the bacon in a nonstick pan until it is brown and the fat starts to run. Drain, cool and crumble it with your fingers or chop finely.
2 Mix the sausage meat in a large bowl with the bacon, breadcrumbs, mustard, thyme, salt and pepper.
3 Cool the stuffing then use half to stuff the neck flap of the turkey (see page 393). Put the rest in a buttered dish, cover with foil and cook on the bottom of the oven for 30 minutes.

Lemon oatmeal stuffing

MAKES: *enough to stuff and accompany a 5.5 kg (12 lb) turkey*
PREPARATION TIME: *10 minutes*
COOKING TIME: *15 minutes*

225 g (8 oz) sausage meat
Grated zest and juice of 1 lemon
175 g (6 oz) fresh breadcrumbs
50 g (1 3/4 oz) chopped hazelnuts
50 g (1 3/4 oz) butter
115 g (4 oz) coarse oatmeal
50 g (1 3/4 oz) shredded suet
1 tablespoon dried marjoram
Salt and black pepper
2 eggs, size 4, beaten

1 Mix the sausage meat with the lemon zest, juice, breadcrumbs and chopped hazelnuts.
2 Melt the butter in a saucepan and add the oatmeal. Cook, stirring until golden and add to the sausage meat.
3 Cool the mixture slightly and mix in the suet, marjoram, salt, pepper and eggs to bind.
4 Cool before stuffing the neck flap of the bird. Put the rest in a buttered dish, cover with foil and cook on the bottom of the oven for 30 minutes.

COLD TURKEY

Can I defrost a whole frozen turkey in a microwave oven?

The most important question is, will it fit in the microwave? It is seldom feasible to defrost a turkey in a microwave unless it is a very small bird, or a turkey joint. If it does fit, follow the instructions for chicken in the oven's handbook.

COSY JOINT

Is there any way of cooking a turkey for just two people?

Yes, there are many small turkey joints available. Try breast joints or roasts, on or off the bone, as well as whole turkey legs and steaks. Some small turkeys are sold already stuffed or they can be cooked with one of the stuffings shown left. The smallest whole turkeys available usually weigh about 2.25 kg (5 lb).

OLD AND NEW

What are the traditional dishes to serve with turkey, and is there any way to ring the changes?

Traditionalists serve turkey with bread sauce (see SAUCES). Chipolatas wrapped in bacon are another favourite partner, as is cranberry sauce (see CRANBERRIES).

Brussels sprouts, with chestnuts or other nuts, are an expected vegetable accompaniment, but for a change try green beans mixed with toasted almonds. You could also add a dash of colour with a purée of parsnip and pumpkin, buttered well and seasoned with nutmeg.

Roast potatoes are good with roast turkey but Hasselback (fantail) potatoes are an attractive alternative. To make these, take whole, medium-sized peeled potatoes and make several fine cuts most of the way through the potatoes so that they are just held together at the bottom. Soak or rinse them in cold water, dry, then stand the potatoes in a roasting tin and cook in the usual way, basting regularly with butter. They are also delicious sprinkled with grated cheese.

SECOND TIME AROUND

What can I make with any pieces of leftover cooked turkey?

Once the turkey is completely cold, cut all the meat from the carcass, wrap or put it in a covered plastic box and refrigerate. If you do not want to keep eating turkey over the Christmas holiday, put the meat in a freezer container, pour over any leftover gravy, cover and freeze. Keep it for up to three months.

There are a variety of interesting dishes you can make with leftover turkey. Most take very little cooking, which may be a relief after the Christmas holiday marathon.

Make potted turkey by whizzing it up in a food processor with half its weight in softened butter, salt, pepper, nutmeg or mace, and some Madeira. Spoon the mixture into a pâté dish, press it down and cover with a layer of melted butter. Chill it for a couple of hours or until it is firm, then use it as a spread or sandwich filling. It will keep for about a week in the refrigerator.

Diced turkey can be mixed with a white sauce, or a velouté sauce made with turkey stock (see SAUCES and STOCK), plus lightly fried mushrooms and onions and turned into a casserole. Top this with cheese and mashed potato, or pastry, and bake until brown and bubbling. You can also make a turkey fricassée (see CASSEROLES) or layer the turkey and sauce with cooked pasta, then sprinkle it with cheese and breadcrumbs and bake.

For turkey with a Middle Eastern flavour, finely dice the meat, mix it with cooked wild or multigrain rice, nuts and raisins, season with a little ground cumin and coriander and use as a filling for filo pastry.

To make a refreshing salad, marinate turkey pieces in a generous amount of virgin olive oil, a dash of balsamic vinegar, a little crushed chilli, sultanas and some toasted pine nuts. Serve with salad greens.

You can cook the Traditional Roast Turkey (overleaf) confident that any remainders will be as delicious as the first round of bird.

HOW TO STUFF AND TRUSS A TURKEY

Rinse the bird under the cold tap and pat dry, then pull out any fat from inside the cavity. Cut out the wishbone from the neck end to make carving easier.

1 Lay the turkey breast side down, pull back the neck skin and heap the stuffing inside the pouch.

2 Pull the neck skin back over the cavity to cover the stuffing and secure it in place with a metal skewer.

3 Turn the bird breast side up and reshape the stuffing by patting it gently. Then prepare a piece of string which is long enough to encircle the whole turkey lengthways twice.

4 Push the legs down so the ends sit up very straight. Insert a trussing needle and string through the flesh of one knee, passing it right through the bird and out the opposite knee joint.

5 Turn the bird breast down and push the needle through both of the sections of one wing, through the skewered neck and then through both of the joints of the second wing.

6 Turn the bird on its side. Take hold of the end of the string where it entered the first leg joint and the end emerging from the second wing joint, pull firmly together and tie securely.

7 Turn the bird breast side up, tuck the tail into the cavity and fold the top skin over. Thread the needle right through, under the drumsticks.

8 Loop the string around one of the drumsticks and then the other. Tie both ends of the string together and sit the turkey in a roasting tin.

Succulent roast turkey with its crisp, buttered brown skin is served here with a choice of sausage meat stuffings, sharp cranberry sauce and rich giblet gravy.

Traditional roast turkey

SERVES: 8 - 10
PREPARATION TIME: 15 minutes (excluding making the stuffing and gravy)
COOKING TIME: 3 - 3½ hours

3.5 - 4.5 kg (8 - 10 lb) turkey
Sausage and Bacon or Lemon Oatmeal Stuffing (see page 392), or half-quantities of both
115 - 175 g (4 - 6 oz) butter, softened
Salt and black pepper

1 Preheat the oven to 180°C (350°F, gas mark 4).
2 Stuff and truss the turkey just before cooking it (see box, page 393), using half of your preferred stuffing mixture. Put the rest into a greased ovenproof dish and cover with foil.
3 Smear the surface of the turkey with butter. Line a large roasting tin with foil, bringing the edges up over the rim. Put the turkey in the centre, cover it loosely with another sheet of foil and tuck the edges inside the rim.
4 Roast for 3 - 3½ hours. Thirty minutes before the end of cooking, remove the top sheet of foil to allow the skin to brown and put the dish of stuffing in the oven to cook. To test if the turkey is ready, push a skewer into the deepest part of each thigh. If the juices run clear, it is cooked.
5 Allow the cooked bird to stand for 15 - 20 minutes as this will make carving easier (see CARVING). In the meantime, finish making the gravy.

GRAVY EXTRAS

How do I make giblet gravy?

Always ask for a turkey with giblets as these make a rich stock for a superior gravy (see recipe, right). Remove the liver as this would make the gravy taste bitter (if you like you can fry it then add it to the stuffing). If the turkey is frozen, look inside the cavity for the bag of giblets. Your turkey will be ruined if they and their plastic bag are cooked with the bird.

Giblet gravy

MAKES: 850 ml (1 pint 10 fl oz)
PREPARATION TIME: 10 minutes
COOKING TIME: 1 hour 5 minutes

Turkey giblets, without the liver
1 bay leaf
1 onion, peeled and stuck with 4 cloves
A few sprigs of parsley
6 peppercorns
1 teaspoon dried thyme
4 tablespoons plain flour
4 tablespoons port

1 Put the giblets (not the liver) in a saucepan with the bay leaf, onion, parsley, peppercorns and the thyme. Cover with 1 litre (1 pint 15 fl oz) of water and bring to the boil, then lower the heat and simmer for an hour. Strain and reserve the stock.
2 When the turkey is cooked and resting, pour off almost all the fat from the roasting pan. Add the flour to the pan and blend it into the fat with a wooden spoon, scraping up as much sediment from the bottom of the pan as possible.
3 Cook the roux for 1 - 2 minutes then gradually whisk in the reserved stock and the port and simmer for 15 minutes. Taste and season. Pour the gravy into a warmed sauce boat.

TURNIPS

PEPPERY FLAVOUR

Is it always necessary to peel turnips, and are there other ways of cooking them besides a purée?

Turnips do not always need to be peeled or puréed. In early summer, when tiny turnips with their leaves attached are available, just wash the tender skin and boil the turnips quickly to conserve their peppery taste. Try finishing the turnips in a flavoured butter, as in the following herb-scented recipe, and serve with duck, baked ham or lamb.

The pure white variety called Snowball, or those with their tops flushed with pinky mauve, are an excellent choice to use in a variety of summer stews and casseroles, such as those made with lamb. Large winter turnips are yellowish white, sometimes with flashes of green. They are at their best when no larger than a tennis ball but they do need to be peeled. They can be cubed and used in soups and stews.

You can cook and purée turnips with plenty of butter and pepper and combine them with potatoes or another root vegetable such as carrots. Alternatively, grate raw turnips and serve them with a dressing for winter salads, or slice large turnips, brush them with oil and grill until they are just tender.

Do not throw out the leaves of young turnips. They can be cooked in the same way as spinach and served as a vegetable in their own right, or incorporated into soup, or shredded and used as a garnish to vegetable dishes and salads.

Herb-buttered turnips

SERVES: 4
PREPARATION TIME: 5 minutes
COOKING TIME: 12 - 15 minutes

---

8 - 12 tiny young turnips, with
    leaves reserved and shredded,
    optional
Salt and black pepper
50 g (1 ¾ oz) butter
A sprig of rosemary
1 tablespoon snipped chives
1 tablespoon shredded mint
2 tablespoons chopped parsley

---

1 Wash the turnips gently and cut off the leaves, leaving 1 cm (½ in) green stalk attached. Put the turnips in a saucepan of salted water and bring them to the boil. Cook them for about 10 minutes until they are just tender, then drain thoroughly.
2 Heat the butter with the rosemary in a wide frying pan and turn the turnips in it for 2 - 3 minutes until they are shiny and just begining to show patches of colour.
3 Scoop out the rosemary, add the salt and pepper and then scatter on the chives, mint, parsley and turnip leaves, if using. Shake the pan to coat the turnips evenly then serve them in a warmed dish.

SCOTTISH STAPLE
What are bashed neeps?

Bashed neeps, which sound like turnips, are really puréed swede. The Scots call swedes turnips and the traditional bashed neeps and haggis are as essential to a Scottish Burns' night supper as whisky.

TVP

MEAT ALTERNATIVE
What exactly is TVP?

Textured Vegetable Protein (TVP) is made from soya beans ground into a flour after their oil has been extracted. The flour is mixed with water, then extruded to heat and expand the dough. Air is added, which helps to give the TVP a fibrous, spongy texture similar to meat. TVP can be bought as mince or in chunks, either plain or with an artificial 'meaty' flavour. When unflavoured, it tastes very bland.

Ever since TVP was introduced in the 1960s, it has been used as a meat extender by large caterers. TVP is also a common ingredient in many ready-made dishes such as meat-free sausages and burgers. The vegetable protein is a good source of fibre, is fortified with vitamin B_{12} and is very low in fat.

To cook TVP, soak it in water or vegetable stock according to the packet instructions. Use it in well-flavoured casseroles, pies, sauces or stews. Although it is similar to tofu, TVP is more processed.

Fresh chives, mint and parsley add contrasting colour and a summery flavour to these delicious young turnips which are bathed in rosemary-scented butter.

VANILLA

PURE FLAVOUR

What is the difference between vanilla extract and essence? Is it better to use a vanilla pod?

Vanilla is the pod of a climbing orchid and widely grown in the tropics, especially Madagascar and the West Indies. The bean pods are cured after picking and turn black.

The extract and essence are both made by soaking vanilla pods in alcohol to leech out the flavour, but vanilla essence, which often has syrup added, is more concentrated. Look for the word 'pure' on the label and avoid artificial vanilla, which is derived from clove oil.

Vanilla pods offer the best flavour of all, for they have subtlety; vanilla essence and extract can be rather overpowering when used with a heavy hand.

POTENT SEEDS

How do I use a vanilla pod?

The strongest flavour is in the tiny seeds and the pulp surrounding them, so the pod should be split open and the seeds scraped out for adding to custards or ice creams. Infusing a vanilla pod in hot liquid is an economical way to extract the flavour, as the pod can then be rinsed, dried and used again, usually as many as two or three times.

A good way to store vanilla pods after use, particularly when they have been recycled a few times, is in a jar of caster sugar. The sugar can then absorb the flavour of the pods and they will keep almost

indefinitely. Top up the sugar as you use it, for example in desserts, sprinkled over fruit such as fresh berries, or in the following recipe for a pleasantly sharp, lemon and vanilla scented sauce that is delicious served with fruit pies and steamed or baked puddings.

You can also store used vanilla pods in a bottle of brandy or dark rum. The alcohol can then be used as a flavouring agent in cooking, folded into whipped cream or simply splashed over fruit salads or ice cream. However, very fresh vanilla pods, which are moist and supple, are best kept wrapped in cellophane bags or foil; storing them in caster sugar will dry them out.

Vanilla and lemon sauce

SERVES: 4
PREPARATION TIME: 5 minutes
COOKING TIME: 10 minutes

50 g (1 ³/4 oz) vanilla sugar
1 tablespoon cornflour mixed with
 1 tablespoon water
300 ml (10 fl oz) boiling water
50 g (1 ³/4 oz) unsalted butter, diced
Juice and finely grated zest of
 1 lemon

1 Mix the sugar and cornflour paste in a bowl. Pour the boiling water onto the mixture gradually, stirring constantly with a wooden spoon.
2 Transfer to a saucepan and heat slowly for 5 minutes, then remove from the heat. Add the diced butter gradually, stirring until each piece has melted before adding the next.
3 Stir the lemon juice and grated zest into the sauce and serve hot.

PERFECT PARTNERS

Can you tell me why chocolate is usually flavoured with vanilla?

Though the Aztecs, who first made chocolate, mixed it with many different flavourings, including chilli, it was the combination of chocolate and vanilla that appealed when these two New World ingredients arrived in Europe. Chocolate and vanilla have been almost inseparable partners ever since.

VEAL

CARE FOR CALVES

How can I be sure that the veal I buy has been raised kindly?

The specific worry most people have when buying veal, or calf's meat, is that it might have been reared in very constrictive crates. Traditionally, veal calves have been crate-reared and fed a milk-based diet in order to produce a very tender, very pale flesh. Crate-rearing is banned in Austria, Britain, Denmark, Germany and Sweden, so only buy veal from these countries as the animal would have had room to roam as it grew, and look for a label indicating that it has been reared naturally. The veal meat of British calves is rosier than Continental veal but is still very tender.

KEEP IT SIMPLE

I find that breaded veal escalopes are rather heavy. Can you give me some ideas for lighter ways of cooking veal escalopes?

Veal escalopes taste tender and light without a coating and need only the simplest cooking methods. They should be pounded until they are about 5 mm (¼ in) thick, which ensures they cook quickly. If this has not been done when you buy them, place each escalope in turn between two sheets of cling film and beat it with a rolling pin; as the pin touches the escalope, let it slide from the centre to the side of the escalope to stretch the meat.

To cook the escalopes, heat a little olive oil in a frying pan. When it is hot, add the escalopes, allowing each one plenty of room, and fry over a fairly high heat for about 3 minutes, turning once. Remove the escalopes and keep them warm while you deglaze the pan with a few tablespoons of white wine, lemon juice or cream.

For a change from escalopes, you could try using veal chops. Marinate them for 1–2 hours, then fry over a moderate heat for 8 minutes or so, turning once. Veal chops can be partnered by more robust flavours such as aubergines, mushrooms, red peppers and tomatoes.

LEAN AND TENDER

Joints of veal seem too delicate to roast normally. What is the best way to cook one?

It is true that joints of veal are lean and fine-textured and, if they are not roasted carefully, tend to dry out. If you would like to serve roast veal, cook it at 160°C (325°F, gas mark 3) for 35–40 minutes per kg (15–17 minutes per lb) and baste the meat often during cooking.

Another useful way to keep a joint of veal moist is to marinate the meat first in a mixture of olive oil and lemon juice or white wine. Rosemary and garlic can be added for extra flavour. The meat should be basted often while cooking.

An easy alternative is to cook the veal joint gently in a heavy casserole dish by the moist, pot-roasting method, used in the recipe for Italian Veal Pot-roast, below. This will keep the joint tender and prevent the meat from drying out.

Italian veal pot-roast

SERVES: 6
PREPARATION TIME: 20 minutes
COOKING TIME: 3 hours

1.5 kg (3 lb 5 oz) boned shoulder of veal, plus the bones
A bunch of herbs comprising a large sprig of rosemary, several parsley stalks and a sprig of thyme, all tied together
2 - 3 slices of Parma ham
1 tablespoon chopped fresh sage
1 ½ tablespoons olive oil
1 onion, finely chopped
1 carrot, finely chopped
2 sticks celery, finely chopped
1 ½ tablespoons capers
3 slices of lemon, free of rind and white pith
Black pepper
1 bouquet garni
300 ml (10 fl oz) medium dry white wine

1 Put the bones and the bunch of herbs into a large saucepan and cover with water. Bring to the boil, skim the scum from the surface and then simmer, uncovered, for about an hour.
2 Preheat the oven to 160°C (325°F, gas mark 3). Lay the veal on a work surface, skin side down, and cover with the ham, cutting the slices to fit and overlapping as necessary.
3 Sprinkle over the sage and some black pepper (the ham is salty so there is no need for extra salt). Roll up the shoulder and tie it securely at intervals of 5 cm (2 in).
4 Heat the oil in a frying pan, add the veal joint, brown it all over, and transfer the meat to a plate.
5 Add the onion, carrot and celery to the frying pan and fry until the vegetables are softened and lightly coloured. Mix in the capers, lemon slices and seasoning.
6 Spoon half the vegetable mixture into a heavy casserole dish. Add the bouquet garni to the casserole and place the veal on top.
7 Add the wine to the frying pan and boil for a minute or so. Pour the wine over the veal and spoon the remaining vegetables onto the veal.
8 Strain the stock from the bones and boil it hard until it has reduced to about 350 ml (12 fl oz). Pour the liquid around the veal, cover tightly and cook in the oven for 1 hour 40 minutes, turning the veal over about halfway through the cooking time.
9 Remove the veal, carve it into slices and arrange them on a heated serving dish. Discard the bouquet garni from the casserole. Remove the vegetables with a slotted spoon and lay them on top of the veal, or, if you prefer, lift the veal slices, put the vegetables on the serving dish, and arrange the meat over them.
10 Check the sauce. If it is too thin, pour it into a frying pan and boil it for a minute or so to reduce, then pour it over the veal and vegetables. If you prefer, some of the sauce can be served separately in a sauceboat.

VARIATION
You can use turkey breast instead of veal: slice open the breast to form a large piece, cover with the ham and chopped sage and roll up.

VEGETABLES

ORGANIC AND FRESH

I want to buy organic vegetables but they are expensive and often look quite battered. Are they OK?

Organic vegetables can seem much more expensive than conventionally grown vegetables, and yes, they do often look sad and tired, because they tend not to sell quickly. One of the best ways to buy organic produce is to contact an organic cooperative and for a fixed price they will make regular home deliveries of seasonal vegetables and fruit. Alternatively, buy from a shop where you feel confident that the produce is fresh. Because it is not sprayed with fungicides, even organically grown produce deteriorates if it is left to sit around.

COVER UP

Should I put a lid on the pot when I'm cooking vegetables?

If you are cooking vegetables with minimal liquid, it is essential to keep them tightly covered to prevent them drying out and to allow the steam to build up in the pan and cook the vegetables.

Green vegetables such as shredded cabbage or runner beans can be cooked very quickly by plunging them into plenty of boiling water and leaving them uncovered so that the volatile acids which escape while they are cooking will not condense on the lid and fall back into the pan, as this can affect the flavour. This method conserves their colour, flavour and texture.

Roots and tubers such as potatoes, which are submerged in water and cooked for a longer time, are best partially covered. Covering these vegetables uses less fuel and prevents a lowering of the water level, which could leave some of them above the water. To partially cover a saucepan, set the lid askew or lay a wooden spoon across the pan and balance the lid on top.

PREPARING VEGETABLES FOR STUFFING

Fresh vegetables can be used to make attractive cases for stuffings. Make sure you leave the vegetable casing thick enough so that it does not collapse during cooking.

TOMATOES

Choose large tomatoes, then cut off their tops and gently scoop out the seeds and central pulp with a teaspoon. Rub a little salt around the insides of the tomatoes and turn them over to drain for 20 minutes or so. Prepare the stuffing, then fill the tomatoes and replace the tops.

PEPPERS

Halve the peppers lengthways or across and cut away the white pith with a small sharp knife. Shake or scape out the remaining seeds.

PUMPKIN

Cut the top quarter from the pumpkin and pull out the seeds and fibre with your hands. You can also cut out some of the flesh with a curved grapefruit knife. Leave a thick wall of pumpkin flesh if you are using the shell as a soup tureen or as a casserole for a stew.

CAREFUL SALTING

Is it always necessary to add salt to the cooking water when you are boiling vegetables?

Starchy vegetables and roots such as potatoes, carrots and parsnips are best cooked in salted water to allow the salt to permeate the flesh during cooking, to add flavour. For green vegetables, where the cooking time is brief, it is more efficient to add salt after cooking, and you will probably find you use less, which is a healthy option.

There is no point in salting vegetables that are to be mashed or otherwise made into a purée, since it is much easier to judge the right amount by salting the mash later.

CHOP AND FRY

What is a vegetable hash?

Hash is traditionally a dish made of leftovers in which the vegetables are fried and served hot. Bubble and squeak, made from leftover potatoes refried with cooked cabbage, is a typical hash.

Usually the mixture is stirred and turned in the frying pan to incorporate the crunchy browned bits, but vegetables can also be formed into cakes and fried until the outside is crisp and brown.

Potatoes are good used in hashes as they help to bind the vegetables together, however, other carbohydrate foods such as rice or fresh breadcrumbs, perhaps with an egg too, can be used instead.

The following recipe for hash made with freshly cooked sweet potatoes is sophisticated enough for a brunch party, served with bacon and spicy sausages or with poultry and pork. Unlike ordinary potatoes, cooked sweet potato can be quickly puréed in a food processor along with the seasonings and spices, but you must fork the cranberries into the mixture by hand to avoid breaking them up. The mixture can be prepared in advance and stored in the fridge but should be at room temperature when the cakes are shaped and fried.

Hashed sweet potato and cranberry cakes

SERVES: 4
PREPARATION TIME: 15 minutes
COOKING TIME: 35 minutes

900 g (2 lb) pink-skinned sweet potatoes, peeled and diced
2 teaspoons ground allspice
2 teaspoons celery salt
1 teaspoon ground coriander
Black pepper
85 g (3 oz) fresh or frozen cranberries, thawed
Flour for coating
Oil for shallow frying

1 Cover the sweet potatoes with water and bring to the boil. Cover and simmer for about 20 minutes, or until they are quite soft.
2 Drain the sweet potatoes, mash thoroughly and mix in the allspice, celery salt, coriander, a generous grinding of black pepper and then the cranberries.
3 Dust a work surface generously with flour, then shape the mixture into 12 cakes, turning them so that each one is well coated in flour.
4 Fry the sweet potato cakes in batches in hot oil and serve hot.

FRYING ORDER

How should I prepare vegetables for stir-frying, and in what order should I add them to the wok?

Vegetables to be stir-fried need to be cut so that as much of their surface area as possible is exposed to heat: that way they cook faster. The larger root vegetables should be cut into thin batons or sliced diagonally. Broccoli and cauliflower are best separated into small florets with the remaining thick stems sliced diagonally. Leafy vegetables should be finely shredded.

The most efficient order in which to add vegetables to the oil is: roots first, then florets, sliced pods, and beansprouts and leafy vegetables last, allowing a minute between each addition. Add any liquid such as soy sauce with the leaf vegetables, then cover the wok to allow the vegetables to steam slightly.

TOP GRILLING

What is a vegetable gratin and which vegetables are suitable?

A gratin is a dish with a crusty top, usually of cheese or breadcrumbs, baked in the oven and then finished by flashing it under a very hot grill, which gives it a gleaming brown topping. They make excellent winter vegetarian suppers.

Root vegetables, when combined with onions and cauliflower or broccoli florets, tomatoes, courgettes and sweetcorn, make fine gratins. Extra protein can be added in the form of cheese and nuts, within the gratin as well as on top.

In the gratin recipe below each vegetable is cooked separately and then combined for the final dish. Some of the preparation may be done ahead if this is more convenient. The vegetables could also be cooked sequentially in the same saucepan to save on washing up.

Gratin of vegetables and walnuts in a double cheese sauce

SERVES: 4 – 6
PREPARATION TIME: 20 minutes
COOKING TIME: 1 hour

400 g (14 oz) broccoli or
    cauliflower florets
500 g (1 lb 2 oz) potatoes, peeled
    and thickly sliced
500 g (1 lb 2 oz) parsnips, peeled
    and thickly sliced
Salt
2 medium leeks, sliced
85 g (3 oz) butter
40 g (1 ½ oz) plain flour
450 ml (16 fl oz) milk
2 bay leaves
125 g (4 ½ oz) mild Cheddar
    cheese, finely grated
50 g (1 ¾ oz) blue cheese, crumbled
Black pepper
2 tablespoons coarsely chopped
    walnuts

1 Preheat the oven to 200°C (400°F, gas mark 6).
2 Slice the broccoli or cauliflower florets and leave each with some of the stem attached. Slice the larger

Walnuts add crunch and protein to this vegetable gratin, smothered in a creamy sauce of Cheddar and blue cheese. A final grilling makes the top a toasty brown.

stems diagonally. Drop the florets and sliced stems into a large pan of boiling salted water and cook them until just tender, then drain.
3 Put the potatoes and parsnips separately into salted water, bring to the boil and cook for 5 - 7 minutes until only just tender, then drain.
4 Cook the leeks in half the butter in a saucepan until they wilt, then spread them in a large oven dish, smearing the butter in which they were cooked around the sides.
5 Melt the remaining butter in the saucepan, add the flour and stir for a minute over a low heat. Remove from the heat and add some of the milk, stirring it in a little at a time until the sauce becomes smooth.
6 Return the pan to a low heat and add the remaining milk and the bay leaves, stirring the sauce constantly until it reaches boiling point. Turn down the heat and leave to simmer, stirring occasionally, for 10 minutes.
7 Add half the Cheddar and all the blue cheese to the sauce and stir

until they have both melted. Season the sauce to taste, being generous with the black pepper.
8 Layer the potatoes on top of the leeks in the prepared dish, pouring a little sauce over each layer, then add the parsnips, and finish with a layer of the broccoli or cauliflower. Scatter the walnuts over the top. Pour the remaining sauce over the vegetables and then sprinkle the gratin with the remaining grated Cheddar.
9 Bake for 30 - 40 minutes until the dish is bubbling and golden brown on top. For a super-browned top you can finish the gratin under the grill if your dish is flameproof.

VARIATIONS
Add 50 - 85 g (1 ¾ - 3 oz) of chopped lean ham or drained canned tuna to the vegetables as you layer them in the gratin dish. Or, simply substitute carrots for the parsnips.

You could leave out the potatoes and parsnips, halve the quantities of milk and cheese and serve the gratin as a side dish to a meat course.

ROASTED SWEETNESS

I have only ever roasted potatoes and parsnips. Are there any other vegetables that roast well?

Roasting fresh vegetables intensifies their sweetness and gives them a lovely caramelised finish. Sweet vegetables such as onions, peppers and tomatoes respond particularly well to the treatment. Roast vegetables need not always be served hot. The salad of roast Mediterranean vegetables (below), served with an interesting bread, makes an excellent cook-ahead starter dish for a summer or autumn dinner.

Roast vegetable salad

SERVES: 6
PREPARATION TIME: 20 minutes
COOKING TIME: about 35 minutes

About 150 ml (5 fl oz) olive oil
3 medium onions, quartered
6 shallots, peeled
6 firm plum tomatoes, quartered
3 yellow, orange or red peppers, deseeded and quartered
2 large aubergines
1 tablespoon red wine vinegar
2 plump cloves garlic, chopped
Flaky sea salt and black pepper
6 - 8 basil leaves
To serve: 2 ciabatta loaves

1 Preheat the oven to 230°C (450°F, gas mark 8). Pour 5 - 6 tablespoons of olive oil into one or two roasting tins to cover the bottom and use your hands to turn the vegetables, including the whole aubergines, in it, smoothing the oil all over them.
2 Roast all the vegetables for 20 minutes, then remove all except the aubergines and set them aside.
3 Turn the aubergines in the oil and return them to the oven for 15 - 20 minutes. When their skins are quite wrinkled and the flesh is soft when pierced with a skewer, remove the aubergines from the oven, allow them to cool, then cut into chunks, each with some of the skin attached.
4 Arrange the vegetables on a large platter. In a small bowl, mix the remaining oil with the vinegar and chopped garlic to make a dressing

and sprinkle it over the vegetables. The salad can be served tepid or at room temperature.
5 At the last minute, grind the sea salt and pepper over the salad, and top it with torn basil leaves. Serve the salad with ciabatta bread.

VEGETARIAN

NO MEAT OR FISH

If I give up both meat and fish, how can I ensure that I am getting enough protein?

Since plant foods tend to contain less protein than meat, and in a form that the body finds harder to use, it is quite natural to wonder whether a vegetarian diet can meet your nutritional needs. However, a varied vegetarian or vegan diet should supply more than enough protein, provided enough food is being eaten to meet energy needs.

All of the amino acids humans require can be found somewhere in the plant kingdom, but you must choose foods from all the different plant groups – grains, pulses, roots, fresh green and yellow vegetables, nuts and seeds – so that the amino acids that are present only in small amounts in one group will be supplemented by those from another. The different sources of protein do not have to be eaten together but can be consumed at different times during the day. It is fascinating to see that long before the science of this was understood, many traditional cuisines combined pulses with grains, such as beans on toast, hummous and pitta bread, and lentil dhal with rice or naan.

HEALTHY SUBSTITUTES

I have just turned vegetarian. Can I adapt recipes which contain meat simply by replacing it with vegetarian protein substitutes?

You can. There are, for example, many soya products such as soya mince, which are not only rich in protein and calcium, but are made

Healthy option

Dairy products are an important source of protein and calcium for vegetarians, but because many contain high levels of saturated fat, it is important not to rely on them too heavily. Choose low-fat varieties where possible instead.

to look like meat and these can be substituted in some recipes. But remember that in removing meat from your diet, you are removing more than protein. Meat is also an important souce of iron, zinc and vitamin B_{12} and it is important to ensure your body gets enough of these nutrients as well.

Dried apricots, bread, fortified breakfast cereals, lentils and dark green vegetables contain iron, but the iron found in eggs, milk and plant foods is less well absorbed than the iron in meat, so you also need to eat foods rich in vitamin C (such as fruit and fruit juices, potatoes and vegetables) as this boosts the body's ability to absorb iron.

Rich plant sources of zinc are brazil nuts, peanuts, pine nuts and sesame and sunflower seeds. Vitamin B_{12} occurs naturally in foods of animal origin such as eggs, milk and dairy products. In addition, vitamin B_{12} is now added to many processed foods, including breakfast cereals, Marmite and bread.

YOUNG VEGETARIANS

My 12-year-old wants to become a vegetarian. How can I ensure that she gets all the nourishment her body requires?

Because of the growth spurt during adolescence, there is an increase in the nutritional needs of all young people and a well-planned vegetarian diet can meet these needs. Problems may arise, however, if the child does not follow a vegetarian diet sensibly, or if the switch to a vegetarian lifestyle is combined with erratic teenage eating habits. In addition, the high levels of fibre in a typical vegetarian diet can make it quite bulky and this may limit the amount a child can eat, resulting in reduced energy intake.

Children require less protein a day than adults, so a vegetarian diet is fine provided they eat a wide variety of foods. If a child is very young, it is best to combine cereals and pulses in a meal and include some soya products in the diet as these are high in protein.

The key is to plan the child's vegetarian diet carefully, and make sure he or she understands how to choose wisely. There is plenty of literature available on the vegetarian diet and you should make the effort to read through it together. Most schools now cater for students who do not eat meat or fish.

Extra care is needed if the child wants to switch to a vegan diet and cut out dairy foods. Milk and other dairy products provide most of the calcium children need, so the vegan child should eat soya products such as soya milk and tofu as well as fortified foods to provide adequate levels of calcium, or take calcium tablets. Supplements may also be required to boost the vegan child's intake of vitamins B_{12} and D.

FULL OF FIBRE

Vegetarian diets seem to include a lot more bread, pasta and rice than I am used to eating - isn't this very fattening?

Vegetarian diets do tend to be high in carbohydrate and fibre, but this is the balance that health experts are now recommending for everyone. Rather than being fattening, carbohydrate contains fewer calories per gram than fat, so you can eat more high-carbohydrate foods and still have a low calorie intake.

Carbohydrates are not as fattening as the sauces and toppings we like to eat with them. If weight gain is a particular concern, forgo butter and cream sauces and have low-fat accompaniments with your bread, pasta and baked potatoes.

VENISON

RED, ROE AND FALLOW

What kind of deer does venison come from: is it wild or farmed?

The venison most widely available comes from the red deer, which is the most commonly farmed deer, followed by fallow deer. If you are buying venison from a game dealer you may be able to choose wild roe deer shot by sportsmen. Limited quantities of wild venison are available in some supermarkets.

PINK AND JUICY

Sometimes when I cook venison it is very dry. What should I do?

As there is little or no fat marbled through venison or surrounding the flesh of young venison, it must be barded during roasting or braising to keep it moist. This means covering the joint with a thin piece of pork back fat, crackling or some strips of bacon to baste it as it cooks.

Allow venison to relax in a warm place for 10 minutes before serving, even with small cuts such as steaks and chops, which should be cooked quickly and served rare to medium. Resting allows the juices to settle back into the meat and become evenly distributed so that there is a rosiness throughout.

To add extra flavour to the venison for a casserole, marinate it first in an oil and wine mixture; the liquid it cooks in should keep it moist.

Healthy option

Even though venison is a red meat, it is lower in fat than chicken. Farmed venison is a good alternative to beef for people watching their fat intake. It is sold in steaks, minced, and made into sausages and burgers.

GIN AND JUNIPER

I know juniper berries go well with venison, but I can't get hold of any. Is there anything else that I can use in their place?

Nothing will really replace the taste of juniper berries, but try using a couple of tablespoons of gin in the recipe instead. Gin is flavoured with juniper and will give something of the right slightly bitter, pungent taste. In the recipe below, the meat is flavoured with redcurrants which, like juniper, have a special affinity with roast venison. Blackberries are also a good match.

Roast venison

SERVES: *6 - 8*
PREPARATION TIME: *5 minutes*
COOKING TIME: *1 - 1 3/4 hours*

A saddle, haunch or leg of venison
Large piece of crackling, pork back fat or 225 g (8 oz) streaky bacon
Black pepper and salt
1 tablespoon plain flour
600 ml (1 pint) game stock
2 tablespoons redcurrant jelly

1 Preheat the oven to 190°C (375°F, gas mark 5). Weigh the venison and allow 30 minutes per kg (13 minutes per lb) if the joint is large and 20 minutes per kg (9 minutes per lb) if the joint is under 1.8 kg (4 lb).
2 Lay the crackling or back fat over the top of the meat, or lay the strips of bacon, overlapping, on top of it. Season the joint with black pepper and roast for the calculated time, basting frequently. The meat should still be slightly pink when cooked.
3 Remove the barding and allow the venison joint to rest in a warm place for 15 minutes before carving.
4 Meanwhile, pour off most of the fat from the pan, sprinkle in the flour and cook for a minute. Whisk in the stock, redcurrant jelly, and the salt and pepper. Bring to the boil and simmer for 15 minutes. Taste and season the gravy again if necessary, then strain it into a gravy boat.
5 Carve the venison thinly and serve it with roast potatoes, cabbage, chestnuts, gravy and redcurrant jelly.

VINEGAR

MULTIPLE CHOICE

If a recipe just states vinegar, what kind should I use?

If the recipe simply states vinegar, look at the other ingredients in the dish before making your selection.

• BALSAMIC VINEGAR has a sweet-sour taste good with meat, salads or sprinkled on fresh strawberries.

• CIDER VINEGAR has a mild, slightly sweet flavour and can be used in fruit pickles and pork dishes.

• FRUIT-FLAVOURED VINEGARS, such as the recipe below which contains summer fruits, can be used on their own in fruit salads or mixed with oil to make a vinaigrette to serve with chicken, salad or vegetables such as asparagus.

• MALT VINEGAR, which is made from malted barley, is too strong to flavour salads but tastes good when served with fish and chips or used to make chutneys and pickles.

• SHERRY VINEGAR has a rich flavour that works well in meat casseroles, tomato soups such as gazpacho, and dressings for green salads.

• WHITE WINE VINEGAR is the best choice for mayonnaise and classic butter sauces. Both white and red wine vinegars are indispensable for salad dressings and marinades.

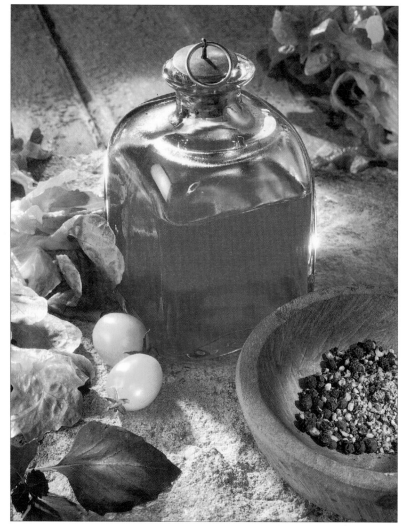

The attractive colour and sweet flavour of this fruit vinegar is easily created by macerating bright summer berries in cider or white wine vinegar for two weeks.

Summer fruit vinegar

MAKES: *about 700 ml (1 pint 3 fl oz)*
PREPARATION TIME: *15 minutes, plus 1 - 2 weeks infusing*
COOKING TIME: *10 minutes*

500 g (1 lb 2 oz) summer berries, such as raspberries, redcurrants and blackcurrants
600 ml (1 pint) cider vinegar or white wine vinegar
225 g (8 oz) caster sugar, or more

1 Pick over the berries then lightly crush them in a large bowl with the back of a wooden spoon to release some of their juices.
2 Pack the fruit into a sterilised jar (see CHUTNEY), then add the vinegar.

3 Seal the jar and shake well. Keep in a cool, dark place for 1 - 2 weeks, shaking the jar occasionally.
4 Strain the fruit-flavoured vinegar through muslin, or a paper coffee filter, into a small saucepan and add about 225 g (8 oz) of the sugar (more if you like) for each 600 ml (1 pint) of fruit vinegar. Simmer the vinegar for 10 minutes, then leave until cold.
5 Decant the flavoured vinegar into a sterilised bottle and seal it with a plastic or plastic-lined cork or a glass stopper (do not use a metal stopper as the vinegar will corrode it). The vinegar is now ready to use.

VARIATIONS

Use gooseberries, grapes or plums in place of the red summer fruits.

ENDLESS VARIATIONS

Can I make herb-flavoured vinegars at home?

Vinegars flavoured with herbs are easy to make at home and will add piquancy to casseroles, dressings, marinades, sauces and soups.

Choose a cider, sherry or wine vinegar, and marry it with either one herb or several. When combining flavours, consider the strength of each: tarragon, for example, might well be overpowered by chillies but can be enhanced with a few green peppercorns or some garlic.

The herbs must be fresh and picked before they flower. Leave them to macerate for two weeks then remove from the vinegar: they will deteriorate if left too long. Herb-flavoured vinegars can be stored for up to a year, providing they are kept in a cool, dark place. This will help to preserve the flavour and prevent fermentation.

The following recipe for chilli-flavoured sherry vinegar can be used with fried meat, sprinkled over roast vegetables or added to a salad of bacon or chicken livers.

Chilli sherry vinegar

MAKES: about 375 ml (13 fl oz)
PREPARATION TIME: 5 - 10 minutes, plus 2 weeks infusing
COOKING TIME: none

1 fresh green chilli, chopped
1 fresh red chilli, chopped
1/2 teaspoon mixed peppercorns
375 ml (13 fl oz) sherry vinegar

1 Put the chillies and peppercorns inside a sterilised jar. Pour in the vinegar. Seal the jar and shake well. Keep in a cool, dark place for two weeks, shaking the jar occasionally.
2 Strain the chilli-flavoured vinegar through muslin or a paper coffee filter into a sterilised bottle. Seal at once with a vinegarproof top.

VINE LEAVES

LEAFY WRAPPING

How do I prepare vine leaves?

Vine leaves that are preserved in brine need only be rinsed in cold water before being used. They are available from Cypriot and Middle Eastern food shops as well as some delicatessens and supermarkets.

If you have fresh vine leaves, cut the stems off close to each leaf, pack the leaves into a pan, pour boiling water over them and bring to the boil. Drain immediately into a colander and run them under the cold tap. This makes them pliable enough to wrap up a filling such as the rice and fish in the following recipe. These little parcels make ideal finger food for a party.

Lemon and olive oil dress these interesting parcels of filled dark green vine leaves. Inside is a well-flavoured kedgeree of smoked fish, eggs and white rice.

Kedgeree in vine leaves

MAKES: 32 parcels
PREPARATION TIME: 2 1/2 hours including cooling times
COOKING TIME: 1 hour

3 sprigs parsley
1 bay leaf
350 g (12 oz) smoked haddock
1 medium onion, chopped
90 ml (3 1/4 fl oz) olive oil
125 g (4 1/2 oz) long-grain white rice
2 eggs, hard-boiled, chopped
Salt and black pepper
About 40 prepared vine leaves
Juice of 1 large lemon
To garnish: lemon wedges

1 Chop the parsley leaves, reserving the stalks. Put the stalks into a wide saucepan with the bay leaf, then place the haddock on top of them and cover with boiling water. Bring the water back to the boil, then remove the saucepan from the heat, cover with a lid and leave until cool.
2 Drain the haddock, reserving the cooking water but discarding the herbs. Skin, bone and flake the fish.
3 In another saucepan, cook the onion gently in 2 tablespoons of the oil over a low heat, stirring until it is soft and pale golden in colour.

4 Measure the rice in a cup, noting how many cups it fills, then add it to the saucepan and stir until it is glossy. Using the same cup, measure out the reserved liquid the haddock was cooked in to equal one and a half times the volume of the rice. Add the liquid to the pan, bring to the boil, cover and simmer for 12 minutes.
5 Without removing the lid, turn off the heat and leave the rice to cook for a further 12 minutes.
6 Fork through the rice and gently mix in the flaked haddock, chopped eggs, parsley, salt and black pepper.
7 Reserve eight vine leaves, then spread out the other 32 in turn and place a tablespoon of kedgeree in the middle of each. Fold into parcels.
8 Arrange the parcels in a saucepan lined with the reserved vine leaves, separating each layer with leaves.
9 Mix the remaining olive oil with the lemon juice and 300 ml (10 fl oz) cold water. Sprinkle over the parcels and fit a plate inside the pan to keep them submerged. Bring to the boil, cover and simmer for 30 minutes.
10 Cool in the pan, then arrange the parcels on a serving dish. Brush over a little cooking liquor to give the parcels a gentle sheen and serve garnished with lemon wedges.

WELL-LAID TABLES

As our lives grow ever more rushed, entertaining usually has to be kept fairly low-key and relaxed. But there are occasions when a more formal setting is appropriate and it is then very reassuring to know how things ought to be done. Here is a problem-solving guide to setting and seating a well-organised dinner table.

PLACING THE CUTLERY

Laying the table follows a logical pattern. Cutlery is set out with the implements that are going to be used first on the outside, and works inwards course by course. Forks go on the left hand side, knives and spoons on the right. So if you are starting with soup, the soup spoon should be farthest away from the plate on the right, followed by the fish knife and fork if you are having a fish course. For a really professional look, line up the bottom edges of the cutlery an inch from the edge of the table with a ruler. If you do not have room to line the dessert fork and spoon up with the other cutlery, they can be put across the top of the diner's place; the spoon should go above the fork, with the handles pointing towards the hand that will pick them up.

GLASSES, NAPKINS AND SIDE PLATES

Glasses should be placed in a diagonal row just beyond the knife tip, beginning with the first to be used. This usually means that a medium-sized white wine glass for the first course is placed closest to the diner's plate, followed by a larger glass for red wine to accompany the meat course. A smaller dessert wine glass is laid at the end of the row, or kept back until the pudding is served. A tumbler for water should be placed in the centre, above the wine glasses, or to one side, but not lined up with the wine glasses.

If a bread or salad plate is used, it goes outside the forks on the diner's left, perhaps with a knife. Napkins can go on this plate or in the middle of the diner's place if the first course is not on the table.

FEEDING THE EYE

Flowers or candles will make a formal table look rich and warm, but you must take care to arrange them so that they do not make it difficult for the guests to see each other across the table. If you have a small dining table and want to make it look pretty, but still have enough room for the dishes, choose a light-coloured tablecloth as this will help to create the illusion of a larger table, and use tiny vases with only one or two delicate blooms in each rather than a large, elaborate flower centrepiece.

Create a glamorous yet welcoming ambiance by placing candles at intervals around the room, rather than on the dining table itself, if you are pushed for space. Chilling the candles in the fridge for at least 3 hours before lighting them will make them burn more slowly and help to prevent the wax from dripping. The more expensive candles, such as beeswax, are dripless, but even so it does help to keep them out of draughts, which will cause them to gutter and burn unevenly.

SEATING ARRANGEMENTS

The host should sit at the head of the table, the most important female guest on his right. The top male guest sits on the hostess's right, at the other short end of the table if there are four or eight diners, the hostess at the end if there are six. Usually men and women are seated alternately, but you can be flexible if you do not have equal numbers. Women are served first, starting with the chief female guest, then the men, starting with the chief male guest.

STYLISH SERVING

If the food is being served formally, the food is offered to the left of the diner and plates are cleared from the right. But if the table is cramped and this is awkward, serve whichever way is least disruptive.

If space is tight, do without side plates for bread or salad to keep the table as uncluttered as possible. It is quite acceptable for people to eat their bread off the tablecloth, and most people are happy to have their salad on the same plate as the main course and may even prefer it. Fill the water glasses rather than putting a jug of water on the table. Use a smaller size of dinner plate if you have a choice. And if you have a sideboard, arrange the food on it so your guests can serve themselves, leaving the table less crowded.

If you are worried that your servings are on the small side, use plates that are also modestly sized so the portions will look more generous. And a selection of small salad leaves or other garnishes can be added so that the dish looks more copious. In any case, you do not want to daunt your guests with extravagant helpings. Though nouvelle cuisine has passed its peak, the idea of enjoying smaller portions of food, beautifully presented, remains and has changed people's perception of how much they want to eat.

WHEN TO START

If you are perplexed by whether your guests should wait to begin eating until everyone is served, ask them to follow the French custom where hot food is eaten as soon as it is served, so it does not spoil. Cold food, which will keep happily, can wait until everyone is served.

WATERCRESS

GREEN GLORIOUS GREEN

How can I keep watercress bright green even when it is in soup?

By not overcooking it. The recipe (right) is for one of the most useful all-purpose soups because it is elegant enough for a dinner party but quick to prepare for a hungry family. It does not have to be served hot and does not require stock. The watercress is chopped and added to the warm potato soup base and therefore retains all of its brilliant colour and fresh taste.

Watercress soup

SERVES: 4 – 6
PREPARATION TIME: 10 minutes
COOKING TIME: 15 – 20 minutes
(plus several hours cooling and chilling time to serve cold)

700 g (1 lb 9 oz) floury maincrop potatoes, peeled
250 g (9 oz) small, well-flavoured waxy potatoes such as Jerseys, washed but not peeled
Salt and black pepper
2 cloves garlic
3 slim spring onions, finely chopped
150 g (5 ½ oz) watercress, chopped
To garnish: 2 sun-dried tomatoes, chopped (optional) and
4 tablespoons virgin olive oil

1 Slice the floury potatoes into evenly sized pieces slightly smaller than the waxy ones. In separate saucepans, bring the potatoes to the boil with 600 ml (1 pint) of water in each pan. Add a teaspoon of salt and the garlic to the floury potatoes. Cover and cook at a simmer.

2 When the waxy potatoes are just soft, drain their cooking water into the pan with the floury potatoes and set the waxy ones aside. When the floury potatoes are soft, mash them smoothly into the cooking water.

3 When the waxy potatoes are cool enough to handle, peel and chop them into fine dice and return them to the soup with the spring onions and watercress. Stir, taste and season with salt and pepper.

4 To serve, cool and chill the soup, or reheat it to just below boiling point. Serve the soup garnished with a scattering of chopped sun-dried tomatoes and a zigzag of olive oil.

Red sun-dried tomatoes contrast with bright green chopped watercress in this favourite soup, updated by a swirl of olive oil.

RICH SOURCE OF IRON

Is watercress really rich in iron?

It is. With 2.2 mg of iron per 100 g (3½ oz), raw watercress certainly makes it into the top league of healthy iron-rich vegetables. Only raw parsley, mint and lentils have more iron, and spinach has less.

Watercress is only really at its best when the leaves are absolutely fresh and vivid dark green, so avoid any with traces of yellowing. To keep watercress fresh, store it with the leaves submerged in a bowl of cold water – easier if you buy it in a bunch, not loose in bags.

DO NOT OVERCOOK

Can you cook watercress?

Yes, but only briefly. Watercress is often wilted into hot sauces and soups, to which it adds its lively green bite. Wilting occurs in an instant when watercress comes into contact with hot liquid. It does not need any more cooking than this.

Watercress is especially useful for combining with spinach or in potato-thickened soups, which are equally good served hot or chilled. Chopped watercress stirred into hot butter and seasoned with salt, pepper and lemon juice makes a refreshingly simple sauce for fish and looks equally beautiful with the white flesh of sea fish or the coral pink of salmon and trout. The sharpness of chopped watercress is also very welcome when stirred into purées of winter root vegetables, particularly swede. And it is excellent in soufflés, such as those flavoured with cheese.

STRONGER FLAVOUR

Is watercress the same as the cress you use for sandwiches?

No, several different plants with a peppery taste are called cress. The larger dark green leaves of watercress have a stronger flavour and are good for sandwiches but the tiny garden or pepper cress, sometimes combined with hot mustard seedlings, is more often used.

STRIKING COLOURS

I usually serve watercress in a bowl on its own. Can you suggest a more exciting way of using it?

Watercress and other ingredients with bite make good combinations; try walnuts, onions and strong cheese, particularly blue cheeses. In the following salad recipe dark green watercress makes a vibrant contrast against scarlet watermelon and salty white feta cheese.

Watercress, watermelon and feta cheese salad

SERVES: 4 - 6
PREPARATION TIME: 10 minutes
COOKING TIME: none

1 kg (2 lb 4 oz) watermelon
Black pepper
4 tablespoons olive oil
1 tablespoon lemon juice
75 g (2 ¾ oz) watercress, washed and trimmed
150 g (5 ½ oz) feta cheese, roughly chopped

1 Cut the watermelon into four or five slices, then cut the flesh from the rind and slice it into fairly thin pieces, removing as many seeds as you can and reserving any juice. Spread the watermelon slices on a flat serving dish, pour over the juice and season liberally with coarsely ground black pepper.
2 Beat the oil and the lemon juice together until they are creamy. Set aside 3 tablespoons of the mixture.
3 Lightly toss the watercress in the dressing until the leaves are shiny. Scatter the dressed watercress over the watermelon and top with the cheese. Grind on some more black pepper then trickle the reserved dressing over the finished salad.

VARIATIONS
For a winter salad, layer watercress on top of thinly sliced oranges and garnish with very thin rings of raw red onion and a few black olives. Dust the salad with coarse sea salt if the olives are not too salty. Or, make this salad with other types of ripe melon, such as cantaloupe, galia, honeydew or ogen.

WHEAT

HEART OF WHEAT

I hear that wheatgerm is very good for you. How can I use it?

Wheatgerm is the heart of a grain of wheat with all the nutrients of the grain intact. It is available natural or toasted, which gives it an even nuttier flavour. Its main use in the kitchen is as a breakfast cereal, adding a crunchy bite to muesli or sprinkled over fresh fruit and yoghurt. It can also be mixed into, or sprinkled over, bread dough.

HEAVY GOODNESS

Wholemeal breads tend to be heavy and wholemeal pastries are often stodgy. Why is this?

Wholemeal breads and pastries are made using 100 per cent wholemeal wheat flour, which is milled from the whole grain including the outer husks. This means that it contains more nutrients than the processed, dehusked white flours, but it also means that wholemeal flour needs to absorb more liquid than white flour to soften the ground husk. This often results in doughs or pastries that are heavier, though they are wholesome and nutritious with a good flavour. To avoid this heaviness, your recipe needs to be adjusted accordingly.

Wholemeal pastry is best used as a base for flan cases rather than a top crust, for it can become too heavy and does not have the light flaky texture of white flour pastry. To compensate for this, roll wholemeal pastry a little more thinly than pastry made with white flour, and always prebake or bake it blind if making a base or pastry case.

For lighter breads and pastries you can use half wholemeal and half white flour. This results in a less heavy-textured bread, like the one on the page overleaf, which has added crunch from wheat berries, which are whole husked grains of wheat also called wheat kernels.

Wholemeal loaf with wheat berries

MAKES: *2 small loaves*
PREPARATION TIME: *1 1/2 hours, plus overnight soaking*
COOKING TIME: *1 hour 20 minutes*

25 g (1 oz) wheat berries, soaked
    overnight in cold water
15 g (1/2 oz) fresh yeast, or
    2 teaspoons dried yeast plus
    1 teaspoon sugar, or 1 sachet
    easy-blend yeast
300 ml (10 fl oz) warm water
375 g (13 oz) wholemeal flour
175 g (6 oz) strong white flour, plus
    extra for dusting
2 teaspoons salt
Oil for greasing

1 Drain the soaked berries and rinse them well. Put them in a saucepan and cover with plenty of cold water. Bring to the boil, cover and simmer for 40 - 50 minutes until the berries are tender. Drain and immediately refresh under cold water. Dry them thoroughly in a clean tea towel.

Rinsing the hot, softened wheat berries in a sieve under cold running water immediately stops the cooking process.

2 Dissolve the fresh or dried yeast in half the water with the sugar, or add easy-blend yeast directly to the flour. Combine the two flours and salt in a large bowl, make a well in the middle and work in the yeast mixture and the remaining warm water to form a soft dough.
3 Turn out and knead on a lightly floured surface for 8 - 10 minutes until the dough is very smooth and elastic, then knead in the wheat berries. Transfer to a lightly oiled bowl, cover with cling film and set aside in a warm place for about 45 minutes or until doubled in size.

4 Preheat the oven to 230°C (450°F, gas mark 8). Grease two 450 g (1 lb) loaf tins with the oil.
5 Punch down the dough, knead it again briefly and divide it in half. Shape each half and put into each of the prepared tins. Loosely cover the tins with cling film and leave to rise until the dough almost reaches the tops of the tins, about 20 minutes.
6 Remove the cling film and bake the loaves for 15 minutes.
7 Lower the oven to 200°C (400°F, gas mark 6) and bake for 10 minutes more or until risen and golden. Take one of the loaves out of the tin and tap the base gently with your hand: it should sound hollow. If not, put it back in the tin and return the loaves to the oven for a few more minutes. Then cool them on a wire rack.

WHITECURRANT: see SOFT FRUIT

WINE

SAFE COOLING TIME

How long is it safe to leave white or sparkling wine in the freezer?

Not much longer than the 45 minutes it takes to chill it, without damaging the taste of the wine. Set a timer or you may end up with an exploded bottle (liquid expands as it freezes) and a large wine ice lolly.

White wines taste fresher at lower temperatures, and in the case of sparkling wines, chilling eases opening, prevents flying corks and reduces the chance of the wine frothing over. It is better to err on the cooler side when chilling white and sparkling wine, because once it is in the glass and held in the hand, it will warm up fairly rapidly.

WARMING RED

Is there a quick way to warm red wine to the temperature it needs to be for drinking?

The quickest method of raising the temperature of a bottle of red wine is to pour the contents into a glass jug and place it in a microwave on

Medium for 30-40 seconds. Alternatively, put the bottle in an ice bucket of warm water 20°C (68°F) for 20 minutes. Using radiators and fires are not a good idea, as they do not heat the wine evenly and you end up with hot spots. Wine served cooler than you like it needs only to be poured into the glass and cupped in the hands for a few minutes to warm it a few degrees.

Not all red wine needs to be at the temperature of a modern room, which is considerably warmer than the ambient temperature of rooms before the arrival of central heating. Anyone who has ever been in a large, draughty country house with stone floors has experienced room temperatures which are only a few degrees warmer than the cellar. In any case, warming is only really suitable for the more tannic and full-bodied styles, such as red wines from the New World and some older Italian wines. Wines from Bordeaux and Burgundy, and the majority of wines for everyday drinking, may be served cooler. And a light, fruity red wine, like those from Beaujolais or the Loire, may be served slightly chilled.

DO NOT RUN OUT

How much wine should I allow per person for a buffet lunch? And how much for a dinner party?

It is more relaxing to know that you have catered for all your guests to drink as much as they want than to run out of wine. But that need not mean that you waste money or your wine. Many retailers operate a sale or return policy on unopened bottles, and any unfinished open wine bottles can be restoppered and drunk within a couple of days.

In these health-conscious days, fewer glasses of wine will be consumed at a buffet luncheon than 20 years ago, but you should allow two to four glasses per person (a 75 cl bottle will fill six good-sized glasses). The nature of the menu generally served at a buffet lunch means that probably far more white wine will be consumed than red;

work on the ratio of 2:1. Lower to mid range priced wines served for parties do not need to breathe, so they can be opened as required.

Dinner party wine quantities are easier to predict as wines may be selected to match the courses. Allow four to six glasses for each guest.

WAKE UP THE PALATE

Can I serve wine as an apéritif?

Apéritifs are drunk to set the palate tingling, and this is best achieved by a cool glass of something bubbly. It need not be Champagne but could be one of the many less expensive sparkling wines. French Crémant de Bourgogne is made in exactly the same way from the same grapes as Champagne, but because the grapes are grown in a sunnier region of France the wine is softer and less acidic. Another interesting choice is Blanquette de Limoux from the south of France.

There are a number of softer, more exotically fruity sparkling wines from the New World, especially Australia. These and other sparkling wines make delicious apéritifs when mixed with fresh fruit juices such as mango, orange or peach, or with cordials such as blackcurrant, or liqueurs such as Cointreau and crème de cassis.

For those who prefer still wine, look for whites with a light fruitiness and fresh acidity. It is unwise to serve a heavily oaked wine as an apéritif. Choose instead one of the newer crisp, interesting wines from Eastern Europe; they are inexpensive and made in a light, fresh style from characterful grapes such as slightly spicy Pinot Gris or aromatic Gewürztraminer or Muscat.

Fine German wines make good apéritifs thanks to their outstanding fruitiness, fresh acidity, low alcohol content (around 8 per cent) and moderate sweetness. Look for those from the Mosel region made from the classic Riesling grape and labelled Kabinett or Spätlese.

Vermouth and similar herby fortified wines are somewhat out of fashion, but a glass of tangy Fino or Manzanilla sherry, or even a glass of chilled white port, whet the appetite and also go surprisingly well with first courses such as seafood or soup. For some elegant winter predinner warming, choose the drier versions of the darker, nuttier Amontillado and Oloroso sherries, which are a real treat. (See also FRUIT DRINKS and JUICERS.)

NEW TRADITION

What does it mean when a label says 'méthode traditionelle'?

This is one of the new terms being used to describe the best method of making sparkling wine, in which the wine undergoes a secondary fermentation in the bottle to create the bubbles. Until 1994 the term 'méthode champenoise' was widely used for this process, but this can now only be applied to Champagne. Good value alternatives to Champagne are labelled 'traditional method', 'classic method' and 'fermented in this bottle'.

SILVER STOPPER

Is it true that a silver teaspoon in the neck of an open champagne bottle will keep it from going flat?

There is no evidence to support this idea. Instead use a stopper specially designed for sparkling wine. They are widely available, inexpensive and much more effective than silver spoons. They also make good presents for champagne lovers.

ENTERTAINING WINES

I never know what wines to serve at a dinner party. Can you give me some easy rules of thumb?

There are some basic precepts: first, begin with the lighter styles of wine and move onto those with more body. This usually means a light white or red with the starter and a heavier white or red (possibly one that has been oak-aged) to accompany the main course. Dry wines should be drunk before sweet, so stay with drier wines with the cheese and before the pudding,

---

HOW TO OPEN A BOTTLE OF CHAMPAGNE

All sparkling wines are under a great deal of pressure in the bottle, so when opening them you should do it correctly and with great care.

1 Start by chilling the bottle. This not only makes the wine more refreshing but also eases opening and prevents it from frothing over.

The most elegant method is to immerse the bottle in a silver bucket of ice and water for 20 minutes or so. Alternatively, chill it for 45 minutes, but no longer, in the freezer or for up to 2 hours in the refrigerator.

2 Remove the foil at the mouth of the bottle. Untwist and loosen the attachment of the wire muzzle and slip the muzzle off, all the time covering the end of the cork with your thumb to guard against the possibility of it suddenly flying out.

3 Hold the bottle securely at an angle, pointing it away from yourself and others, and from any fragile objects nearby. Grip the cork firmly, hold it still and then twist the bottle. Ease out the cork, allowing a controlled release of pressure.

Do not fight a sudden release of the pressure. As long as you have a firm grip of the cork, the bottle can be opened safely. By holding the bottle at an angle, with a dry cloth for a better grip, any frothing over should be limited. If it froths, dip a finger down the neck of the bottle and the bubbles will subside.

unless you intend to open a bottle of port with the cheese, in which case it should follow the pudding. But many people prefer cheese after the pudding even when they are not going to drink port with it.

A final pudding course can be accompanied by a sweet dessert wine, even a relatively inexpensive sweet Muscatel from Spain. Always aim for a wine that is sweeter than the pudding, otherwise the wine will appear thin and tart. This may appear an extravagance, but many sweet wines are available in half bottles. Many New World late harvest Muscats and Rieslings are rich enough to be dessert wines.

WHAT IS ON THE LABEL

What do wine labels mean? How does an AOC wine differ from one labelled vin de pays, for example?

The label gives authenticity and, for wines made within the European Community, provides certain information. EC wines must state, for example, whether they are quality wines. In France this means wines are labelled AOC or Appellation d'Origine Contrôlée, or table wine, or one of the newer levels in between, such as vin de pays.

The wine label must also contain information on the region or country of production; the name and

address of the bottler or producer, as well as the volume of wine in the bottle and its alcoholic content. Non-mandatory information may be given to help the consumer choose and this could include the grape variety used, the vintage, or the method of production, for example, if the wine has been fermented in the barrel, or aged in oak barels to give a certain flavour.

SHOP ASSISTANCE

The selection of wines on sale is bewildering. Where do I start?

First decide on your budget and ask the advice of a wine merchant or shop assistant, telling him or her the occasion for which you want the wine and the food that you will be eating with it. Many are trained and have an extensive knowledge of wine. Alternatively, read the wine labels and any shelf-edge ticketing: wine merchants devote a great deal of time to putting helpful information across to the wine consumer.

The wine columns of newspapers and magazines are also a good source of suggestions, so read and experiment. When you find a wine that you particularly enjoy, make a note at the time. It is all too easy to forget the name a week later on your next visit to the off-licence.

A wine's character is derived principally from the grape variety or varieties from which it is made. New World winemakers have made choosing wine easier by labelling their wines according to the grape variety, such as Cabernet Sauvignon, Chardonnay, Shiraz, and so on. This practice has now been adopted in some of the more traditional wine making regions. If you discover that you like the taste of a Bulgarian wine made with the Merlot grape, you will probably also enjoy a Chilean Merlot.

Supermarket white wines are numbered to indicate the level of sweetness: 1 denotes the driest, so that a wine with a rating of 9 is an exceptionally sweet wine. If you like one wine ranked at 2, you may well like those similarly numbered.

WINES NAMED BY GEOGRAPHY

Traditional wines are labelled after the region they come from. The climate, soil and the regional grape varieties will all affect the character of the wine.

1 GRAND VIN DE BORDEAUX

2 Château Segonzac

4 PREMIÈRES CÔTES DE BLAYE
5 APPELLATION PREMIÈRES CÔTES DE BLAYE CONTRÔLÉE

6 12,5% VOL.   7 1993   750 ml

8 J. & C. MARMET-CHAMPION PROPRIETAIRES
CHATEAU SEGONZAC SCEA - ST GENES DE BLAYE (GIRONDE) - FRANCE
9 PRODUCE OF FRANCE

10 Médaille d'or
RECOLTE 1993

NR № 48255
Concours Général Agricole
PARIS 1995

1 This shows the wine is French, from Bordeaux. Grand Vin means that this is the château's main wine.
2 The wine is from a single property.
3 It was bottled at the château.
4 The place where it was made, a less well-known region of Bordeaux.
5 Denotes a quality wine level.

6 The alcoholic strength, shown as a percentage of the total contents.
7 The year the wine was made.
8 The name and the address of the proprietor of the château and vineyard.
9 The country the wine was made in.
10 Gold medal winner, 1993 vintage, in Paris in 1995; each bottle is numbered.

ANIMAL FREE

Are there special wines that are suitable for vegetarians?

It is a little known fact that some animal-derived products (such as egg whites and gelatine) may be used in the fining or clean-and-polish of the wine prior to bottling. Now some wines are being made with a non-animal-derived product for the fining operation, and supermarkets have begun to stock these and label them vegetarian wines.

DEEP BREATHING

Is it really necessary to open wine and let it breathe?

Not all wines need time to breathe: older red wines will deteriorate rapidly once they are exposed to the air, while prolonged exposure to air causes all wine to decline.

But allowing the wine to breathe can help to release the bouquet and taste of the wine in readiness for drinking: young tannic reds will become softer and fruitier if they are given some aeration.

Wine begins to breathe as soon as you pull the cork, although this has only a little effect because the surface area of wine exposed to the air is so small. The best method of aerating the wine is to pour it from the bottle into a decanter.

But most soft, fruity red wines require little time to breathe. And it is not usually necessary to allow bottles of white wine to breathe because their bouquet opens out quite quickly once the wine has been poured into the glass.

WINE AND FISH

People say that you can't drink red wine with fish. Is this true?

It depends on both the fish and the wine. Few people would consider a full-bodied Châteauneuf-du-Pape the ideal partner for a delicate dish of plaice. In fact, for most of us the tannin in the red wine reacts with the fish on the palate to create a metallic taste. But some red wines, such as those that have been made from the Gamay or Pinot Noir grapes, are lower in tannin and these are a much more pleasing match for fish. Red wine would also be the obvious choice for fish cooked in a red wine sauce.

In broad terms, it is safest to stick to the old maxim of red wines with red meats and white wines with white meat and fish, but pay careful attention to the weight and intensity of the flavours of the food to be served, as well as to the levels of acidity and sweetness in the sauces. Big flavoured dishes need hearty, robust white wines such as a hefty Crozes-Hermitage from the Rhône. Those with a high level of acidity or any degree of sweetness, need a wine with a slightly sweet edge, for example a German Kabinett, if the wine is not to appear thin and weak in contrast.

VEGETARIAN PARTNERS

Are there any wines which go well with vegetarian meals?

In partnering wine with vegetarian food, try to match the strength and taste of the wine to the flavour of the dish, paying attention to the sweetness and acidity. Many vegetables, such as carrots, have a degree of sweetness, and could be matched with slightly off-dry styles such as Chenin Blanc from South Africa. Tomatoes have a high level of acidity and so could take a cool-climate white such as wine from the Loire valley or an English wine.

For meals with a Mediterranean flavour, red wines from the South of France or Italy, such as Chianti are an appropriate choice. A rich Gewürztraminer or deep-flavoured Shiraz go well with spicy food.

WINES NAMED BY GRAPE VARIETY

New World wines are often called by the grape variety they are made from. If you like one, you will probably enjoy other wines made from the same grape.

1 CALITERRA

2 1995

3 Chardonnay

4 CURICO

6 13.5% vol

5 PRODUCED AND BOTTLED BY VIÑA CALITERRA LTDA.

7 PRODUCT OF CHILE

75 cl e

1 The name of the producer; here, one of the leading Chilean brands is shown.
2 The year the wine was made.
3 Chardonnay is the grape variety used to make this wine. It is used in New World and traditional wine making.
4 The region where the grapes were grown and the wine was made.
5 The company that bottled the wine.
6 The alcoholic strength, shown as a percentage of the total contents.
7 The country of origin; here, Chile.

CALCULATING COST

I know that much of the cost of a cheap bottle of wine is tax - can they offer good value?

The fixed costs of any bottle of wine, which include duty, VAT, packaging, production and transport, account, at the lowest end of the market, for more than half the price. The balance is the profit for both the supplier and retailer and the cost of the grapes. Leaving the profit aside, the more you pay for a bottle, the better the quality of the wine. However, wine making practices have taken such strides in the last decade that even among the cheapest wines are some that are very well made. Wines with excellent fruity character are available from Eastern Europe, the South of France, Italy and Germany, South Africa, South America and Spain.

SORTING OUT STORAGE

How should I store my wines if I don't have a cellar?

If you have invested seriously in the very grandest claret, for example, you should rent cellar space, or invest in a temperature-controlled cabinet. But for those of us with a case or two of everyday wines and a few special bottles, it is necessary to find somewhere at home.

The two greatest enemies of wine are heat and light. The ideal temperature range for a cellar is 10–15°C (50–59°F) with no wild fluctuations. The best option is usually a dark cupboard under the stairs, or a north-facing wall with a blanket over the wine to keep out the light. Bottles with corks should be stored horizontally because this keeps the corks moist. Dry corks shrink and let air into the bottles, which is detrimental to the wine.

FINE COOKING WINE

How much does the quality of wine matter when I cook with it?

The quality of the wine used in cooking matters more in dishes such as fruit salad, where the wine is not heated, than in dishes that require reducing or simmering. But do not be tempted to use any wine that is faulty or has any off-flavours as cooking will not eradicate them.

When wine is used in cooking, the alcohol evaporates as the wine is heated but the flavour intensifies, so choose enjoyable wines for cooking. In most cases you will need a wine that is fairly robust but not too expensive – a well-priced bottle from Eastern Europe or the New World would be a good choice. Using a wine from a particular region, such as for boeuf bourguignon, may give the dish a degree of authenticity, but red Burgundy is not an inexpensive cooking wine.

SAFE KEEPING

How long will a bottle of wine keep once it has been opened?

Mature wines decline rapidly once their corks have been drawn and it is best to drink and enjoy them immediately. But with most leftover wine, there is no harm in just replacing the cork as long as at least half the wine remains – any less and there will be too much air in the bottle, which will spoil the flavour. The more air in the bottle, the faster the wine will deteriorate.

Keep the recorked bottle in the refrigerator: heavy red wines will keep for three or four days; lighter reds and white wine will keep for one or two days, but they should be removed from the refrigerator an hour before you drink what is left.

There are gadgets on the market that can extend the life of an opened bottle up to a week. Some work by sucking out the air and creating a partial vacuum in the bottle; others by blanketing the wine from the air with a squirt of inert gas on the surface of the wine. Wine preserved by any method (including just replacing the cork in the bottle) is perfectly acceptable for use in cooking. However, if the wine smells like vinegar, throw it away. If you would not want to drink it, then you should not cook with it either.

ALCOHOLIC ICES

I've been told you can't make ice creams and sorbets with alcohol. Is this always true?

No, it is not, but do not add any more than is necessary to give a good flavour. Alcohol affects the way food freezes because it freezes at a lower temperature than water, so ice creams and sorbets containing alcohol freeze more softly than those without. Add just 90–125 ml (3¼–4 fl oz) of spirit or liqueurs to 600 ml (1 pint) of cream for ice cream, or to syrup for a sorbet. Wine is less of a problem because it has a much lower alcohol content.

USING SHERRY AND PORT

Can I use our half-empty bottles of sherry and port in cooking?

Sherry and port can be used to pep up casseroles, gravies, sauces and soups, and to marinate meats and fish. Sherry is a good substitute for Chinese wine in Oriental cooking, and you can add it to fruit cakes, custards and sweet sauces, flavour cream with it or use it to make trifle. Port can replace the water when making a syrup for fruit salad or to poach fresh fruit.

THE BEST CHOICES

How can I tell which sort of wine is best to use in recipes?

You will get a better result if you match the wine to the ingredients in the dish – this is particularly true when combining red wines and delicately flavoured foods such as fish or poultry. To avoid a coarse flavour, choose lighter red wines that are not too oaky in character. For coq au vin a simple vin de pays such as Bergerac or a Cabernet Sauvignon from the New World is preferable to a heavy Bordeaux. Choose a light Gamay for red wine sauces to serve with salmon.

Be selective, too, when matching fish with white wines. Delicate fish such as plaice and trout need white wines with lower acidity, such as a white Bordeaux or New World

Chardonnay. Oily and sweeter fish such as bass, mackerel and Dover sole are better with acidic wines such as Grosplant and Muscadet.

When you are cooking with fortified wines such as port and sherry, do not reduce the wines early during cooking because the taste will be too concentrated. Instead, add the wine at the end of cooking, heating it just enough to burn off the alcohol; you will use less and the flavour will not be too strong.

In the case of enclosed dishes such as pies, the alcohol should be evaporated while making the filling – do not expect that it will burn off while the dish is in the oven – or the aromas will be overpowering when the pastry is cut open.

If you are using gelatine, for example to make a Sauternes jelly, heat the wine to burn off the alcohol before you add the gelatine to the liquid as alcohol will reduce the gelatine's setting power.

For the Cheese Fondue (below) choose a dry white wine such as Bourgogne Aligoté or a Sauvignon Blanc. Do not try to make it quickly or the cheese will form a lump and will not blend with the wine.

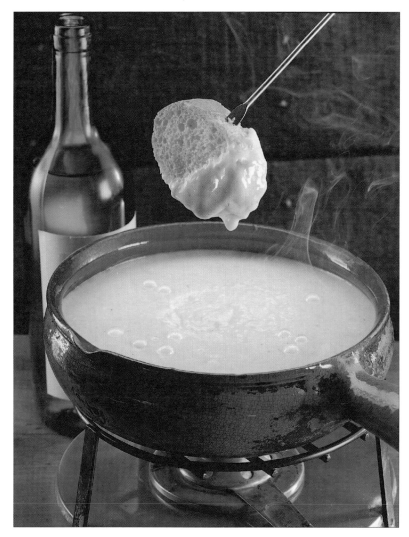

Cheese fondue

SERVES: 6 - 8
PREPARATION TIME: 30 minutes
COOKING TIME: 20 minutes

---

2 cloves garlic, halved
425 ml (15 fl oz) dry white wine
Freshly grated nutmeg
Black pepper
200 g (7 oz) each Cheddar,
    Emmental and Gruyère cheese,
    coarsely grated
4 level teaspoons cornflour
3 tablespoons extra white wine or
    water
3 tablespoons kirsch, optional
To serve: 2 French loaves, cut into
    2.5 cm (1 in) cubes

---

1 Rub the garlic around the inside of the cooking dish then place them inside. Pour in the wine and heat until it is warm but not hot. Discard the garlic, then season the wine to taste with nutmeg and black pepper.

2 Add the cheese to the pan and stir over a moderate heat until it melts. Increase the heat and keep stirring until the mixture begins to bubble slightly: the cheese and wine will not be completely amalgamated.
3 Mix the cornflour with the extra wine or water then stir it into the cheese mixture and keep stirring until it is smooth, well blended and bubbling, but still has a thin milky layer of liquid on the top. Stir in the kirsch and serve the fondue straight-away, placing the dish over a spirit or candle burner to keep it hot.
4 Serve the fondue with the cubes of fresh bread. To eat fondue, each diner spears a cube of fresh bread (or a boiled potato) onto their fork then dips it into the fondue dish to coat it with the thick, hot mixture.

Eating fondue is a cold-weather sport. At least half the fun is that it requires the guests to take an active part by spearing and swirling cubes of bread into the rich melted cheese well laced with wine and cherry-scented kirsch.

Healthy option

In Switzerland, drinking anything cold with fondue, such as chilled wine or beer, is regarded by the locals as folly. A glass of kirsch or a cup of tea are recommended as it is firmly believed that very cold drinks react with the cheese and make it indigestible.

WOK

QUALITY COUNTS

Is one kind of wok better than another? Do different types of stove require different woks?

Cast-iron woks are generally the best as they conduct heat more evenly and quickly than any other material, but they do need more careful treatment and seasoning with oil and salt (see FRYING).

Traditional woks are round-bottomed and need to sit properly over the heat without wobbling. As most gas rings are set with metal prongs, these provide a steadier base than electric rings set flush with the surface. But you can now buy slightly flat-bottomed woks that can be used on any stove, and also round metal wok-stands which hold woks steady above the rings of both gas and electric stoves.

MASTERING THE ACTION

Is there a knack to using a wok?

Yes, what is most important is the stirring action: you should use your wrist to scoop, flip and push the food continuously. A wok ladle has a curved end that is designed to get right to the bottom of the wok so that it is easy to flip the food over when stir-frying. Whether you use a wok ladle or a wooden spatula, every bit of food in the wok must be moved about constantly, over the entire surface of the wok. Most foods need no more than 5 minutes cooking, less with intense heat.

Using a wok ladle to stir-fry makes it easier to scoop and move the food continuously – an essential technique.

STIR-FRY SAUCES

Stir-fry vegetables sometimes come with ready-prepared sauces. Can I make one myself?

Yes, very easily. The basic sauce for stir-frying is simply a blend of seasonings: salt or soy sauce, pepper and a little sesame oil. You can also add oyster sauce, sherry, Chinese wine or any of the Chinese bottled sauces such as black or yellow bean, and a selection of fresh flavouring ingredients such as galangal, ginger, lemongrass and fish sauce, as in the recipe below for stir-fried vegetables. Soy and fish sauces are used in Oriental cooking instead of salt so if you use them, do not add any extra salt.

Mushroom, mangetout and baby corn stir-fry

SERVES: 4
PREPARATION TIME: 10 minutes
COOKING TIME: 8 minutes

6 large field mushrooms, sliced
12 mangetout, topped and tailed
12 baby corn cobs, left whole or
  sliced in two if large
2 tablespoons vegetable oil
1 clove garlic, crushed
1 tablespoon sesame oil
1 tablespoon fish sauce
100 ml (3 ½ fl oz) water
2 teaspoons cornflour, dissolved in
  1 tablespoon of water
2 tablespoons sherry or Chinese
  rice wine (Shao Hsing)

1 Bring a small pot of water to the boil and blanch the mushrooms, mangetout and corn cobs separately for a minute each. Drain and rinse them under the cold tap.
2 Heat the vegetable oil in the wok and fry the garlic for about a minute until it is brown. Add the blanched vegetables and stir-fry for a minute.
3 Add the sesame oil, the fish sauce and the water and stir vigorously as the liquid comes to the boil.
4 Add the dissolved cornflour and the sherry or wine to the wok and continue stirring for a minute. When the sauce has thickened, transfer the vegetables to a plate and serve.

KEEPING COLOURS FRESH

Is there a way of stir-frying bright green vegetables without them turning a dingy olive colour?

Yes, by first blanching green vegetables in boiling water for a few seconds and immediately running them under a cold tap. This will retain the green and as the vegetables have been slightly cooked, it will also speed up the stir-frying time, which is another excellent method of keeping green vegetables fresh and bright in colour.

NEVER BURNING

How do you stop the oil burning in a wok when you need to cook at a high temperature?

As soon as the oil begins to smoke, the prepared food should be put in and stirred rapidly. Nothing will burn if your stir-frying action is so vigorous and continuous that no morsel of food is in contact with the hot wok base and the hot oil for more than a few seconds at a time.

VERSATILE WOK

Can I use my wok for anything other than stir-frying?

The wok is an extremely versatile cooking utensil. It can be used for braising, boiling and steaming as well as for stir-frying.

With a domed lid (available from Chinese supermarkets), it can be used to braise a whole chicken, duck, or a large joint of meat, with the condensation inside the wok helping to keep the meat moist.

The wok is also especially effective for steaming. Put a pair of bamboo chopsticks across the bottom of the wok. Put the food in a deep plate and rest the plate on top of the chopsticks. Add water up to a level just above the chopsticks. Cover with a lid which fits over the wok without pressing down on the food to allow the steam to circulate and cook the food gently. In the recipe for Steamed Salmon Steaks on the right, cabbage leaves cover the fish to prevent it drying out.

A protective covering of green cabbage leaves keeps these wok-steamed salmon steaks beautifully moist and tender.

Steamed salmon steaks

SERVES: 2
PREPARATION TIME: 8 minutes
COOKING TIME: 20 - 25 minutes

2 salmon steaks, 200 g (7 oz) each
1 tablespoon finely shredded ginger
1 tablespoon light soy sauce
1 tablespoon sesame oil
½ teaspoon black pepper
1 tomato, quartered
2 large cabbage leaves

1 Place the salmon steaks well apart on a deep plate. Top with the ginger, soy sauce, sesame oil and the pepper and place the tomatoes on the side.
2 Loosely cover the salmon and its topping with the cabbage leaves.
3 Place a set of chopsticks in the wok then lay the plate on top. Add water to the wok to a level no higher than the base of the plate then cover and steam the fish over a high heat for 20 - 25 minutes, or until cooked.

WOODCOCK AND SNIPE

HUNG BUT NOT DRAWN

Are recipes for woodcock and snipe interchangeable?

These two game birds are related to each other and are quite similar in taste, but the snipe lives in marshes and can often have a slightly fishy flavour. They are both hung and cooked in the same manner; the main difference is their size.

A woodcock will feed one as a main course but snipe are very tiny, as small as 70 g (2½ oz), and will really only feed one person as a starter or savoury. Two snipe will make a more generous serving. Both birds are traditionally cooked with the head still on and the beak tucked back along the body. It can also be speared through the body as though it was a skewer.

It is also traditional for both snipe and woodcock to be left ungutted. They are usually served on croûtes, or with the entrails removed after cooking, mashed with salt, pepper and lemon juice and spread on the croûte. The entrails of the birds taste very strong and liverish.

Both birds should be roasted at 220°C (425°F, gas mark 7) with the breast spread with butter and then covered with a slice of bacon so that they will not dry out, as they have almost no lubricating fat of their own. Woodcock will cook in about 10-15 minutes and snipe only 6-15 minutes, depending on their size and how rare you want them. Woodcock and snipe are best cooked slightly on the pink side.

See also: **GAME**

YOGHURT

ALIVE AND ACTIVE

What does 'live' yoghurt mean?

With the exception of long-life yoghurt, all yoghurts contain active but friendly bacteria and are therefore 'live'. Yoghurt is a cultured product, produced by fermenting milk with bacteria. Several kinds can be used, but two of the most common are *Lactobacillus bulgaricus* and *Streptococcus thermophilus*.

To make yoghurt, the milk is first heated to destroy any unwanted micro-organisms, then a yoghurt starter containing the chosen bacteria is added to set and sour the milk. This produces a refreshing, slightly acidic flavour. The bacteria remain active even while the yoghurt is refrigerated, so the level of acidity gradually increases. This limits the storage life of yoghurt, which will eventually come to taste unpleasantly tart.

DIFFERENT CULTURE

What are bio yoghurts? Is it possible to make them at home, and are they specially nutritious?

Bio or BA yoghurt is made with different live cultures, called *bifidus* and *acidophilus*. It is often claimed that these particular bacteria aid digestion by supplementing the body's natural flora. When these bacteria are used as the starter for your own yoghurt they will reproduce and make bio yoghurt. Bio yoghurt is not as sharp as ordinary yoghurt, and has a milder, creamier flavour. All yoghurts are easier to digest than plain milk, because of the action of the bacteria, and they are a good source of calcium and phosphorus, which are essential for strong teeth and bones. Yoghurt is also said to be good for maintaining the general health of the skin and the digestive system, and yoghurts that have soluble fibre added to them may help to lower the level of cholesterol in the blood.

EASY ECONOMY

I spend a lot of money on fresh yoghurt; can I make my own?

It is easy and economical to make yoghurt at home. The exact flavour and texture will depend on the type of yoghurt used as the starter, the fat content of the milk (the higher the fat content, the thicker the yoghurt) and the time the yoghurt takes to thicken.

Practically any kind of milk can be used to make yoghurt: whole, semi-skimmed, pasteurised, UHT, sterilised, dried or evaporated. But fresh commercial yoghurt must be used as the starter for each new batch. Homemade yoghurt should not be used as it may have become contaminated with micro-organisms that would interfere with the setting of the new batch. Long-life yoghurts, which have been heat-treated to give them a long shelf life, are not suitable as a starter either, because this additional heating kills the yoghurt culture.

YOGHURT MAKERS

Do I need any special equipment to make yoghurt at home?

Yoghurt can be made in a vacuum flask or an electric yoghurt maker. The latter maintains a constant temperature providing ideal conditions for making yoghurt, which also tends to be more consistent in texture. A yoghurt thermometer, to test the temperature of the milk as it is heated, is also useful. But the recipe above right shows how easy it is to make delicious, economical yoghurt at home using only an ordinary vacuum flask.

Homemade natural yoghurt

MAKES: 600 ml (1 pint)
PREPARATION TIME: 5 minutes, plus 24 hours standing time and 6 hours chilling time
COOKING TIME: 5 minutes

---

600 ml (1 pint) whole milk
1 tablespoon plain yoghurt

---

1 Pour boiling water into a vacuum flask to sterilise and warm it.
2 Blend 2 tablespoons of the milk with the yoghurt and set it aside.
3 Pour the remaining milk into a saucepan and heat it until it is just about to boil. Remove the saucepan from the heat and set it aside until the milk has cooled to 45°C (113°F). Alternatively, to test it without using a yoghurt thermometer, the milk is ready for the next step when you can hold your finger in it comfortably while you count up to ten.
4 When the milk is ready, stir in the blended yoghurt starter and whisk them together lightly.
5 Empty the water out of the flask, pour in the milk mixture, seal and leave to stand for 24 hours in a warm place such as an airing cupboard. Do not be tempted to move the flask during this period of incubation as the yoghurt will separate and be inedible if it is disturbed.
6 Pour the yoghurt into a bowl and whisk until smooth. Cover and chill for at least 6 hours until thickened.
VARIATION
If you are using sterilised, UHT, dried or evaporated milk instead of whole milk, simply heat the milk to 45°C (113°F) and then stir in the fresh starter before proceeding as above.

FREEZE IT FOR LATER

Can I freeze yoghurt?

Full-fat yoghurts generally freeze better than lower-fat ones, although they will separate when thawed. All yoghurt should be defrosted slowly and given a good whisk before being used. Plain yoghurt can be kept frozen for up to two months. Yoghurt with added fruit, honey or flavouring freezes slightly better than the plain variety, and can be kept frozen for up to three months in the sealed carton it came in. Homemade flavoured yoghurt should be frozen in sturdy plastic containers with tightly fitting lids.

STAND IN FOR CREAM

If a recipe calls for cream, could I use yoghurt instead?

Yes, yoghurt can be used instead of double cream in many dessert recipes, such as cheesecakes, fools, ice cream, mousses and cold soufflés. The flavour of the finished dessert will be sharper when made with yoghurt rather than cream, but it will be just as satisfying.

Yoghurt is also an excellent substitute for soured cream in savoury dips, marinades and salad dressings. And in the Middle East it is strained overnight through a sieve lined with muslin to produce a soft yoghurt cheese, called *labne*. This is served plain, or flavoured with herbs such as thyme.

There are many types of yoghurt available, ranging from those with a very low fat content to creamy and thick Greek-style yoghurts, which can contain up to 7.5 per cent butterfat. But even the thickest yoghurt contains less fat and calories than fresh single cream, so it makes for healthier dishes.

YOGHURT BRULEE

Can you suggest a yoghurt dessert that isn't too complicated?

Rich, full-fat yoghurt makes a delicious dessert simply mixed with a strongly flavoured honey or topped with sliced or puréed fruit. Or try this quick yoghurt brûlée: put some fresh fruit, such as stoned cherries, or raspberries, in the base of individual ramekins. Cover it with thick Greek yoghurt and sprinkle a thin layer of soft brown or demerara sugar all over the top. Put the ramekins under a preheated hot grill until the sugar darkens and starts to bubble, then chill for 2–3 hours until the topping sets hard.

KEEP IT STABLE

Is there any danger of yoghurt curdling if I add it to a hot dish?

Yoghurt may safely be added to hot dishes such as casseroles, curries, sauces, soups and stews, provided it is done off the heat, at the end of the cooking time, just before serving, and as long as the mixture is not brought to the boil again after the yoghurt has been added.

But yoghurt will curdle when it is boiled, unless it has been stabilised (see below). Yoghurt must also be stabilised if it is to be added to a dish which is going to be reheated to boiling point, or if it is going to be used to marinate food, such as chicken or lamb, where some of the marinade will remain on the meat during cooking.

To stabilise yoghurt, blend a tablespoon each of cornflour and water and stir this mixture into 600 ml (1 pint) of yoghurt. Bring the mixture to just under boiling point, simmer gently for 10 minutes and then use in the recipe.

Even though Greek yoghurt has a higher fat content than ordinary yoghurt, it will nevertheless curdle when boiled so it, too, needs to be stabilised if it is going to be heated, as in the recipe for Mixed Vegetable Curry on the right. Stabilising the yoghurt is a precaution rather than a necessity here, as it is all too easy to overcook the yoghurt and make it curdle. This will not affect the flavour but the curry will not look as smooth and attractive as it should. With the yoghurt stabilised, the curry can also be made ahead of time and reheated.

Mixed vegetable curry

SERVES: 4 – 6
PREPARATION TIME: 20 minutes
COOKING TIME: 50 – 55 minutes

1 tablespoon olive or sunflower oil
1 onion, sliced
1 fresh green chilli, deseeded and
  finely chopped
2 cloves garlic, crushed
1 teaspoon each ground cumin,
  ground coriander, and chilli
  powder (hot or medium)
1 parsnip, diced
225 g (8 oz) carrots, sliced
1 sweet potato, diced
225 g (8 oz) closed cup mushrooms,
  wiped and halved
225 g (8 oz) cauliflower florets
2 tablespoons plain flour
60 g (2 1/4 oz) sultanas
225 g (8 oz) chopped tomatoes
150 ml (5 fl oz) vegetable stock
150 ml (5 fl oz) dry white wine
Salt and black pepper
1 teaspoon cornflour
150 ml (5 fl oz) natural yoghurt
100 g (3 1/2 oz) frozen peas
1 teaspoon garam masala
To garnish: fresh coriander leaves

1 Heat the oil in a large saucepan, add the onion, chilli and garlic and stir-fry for 3 minutes. Add the spices, stir and cook for a further 3 minutes.
2 Mix in the parsnip, carrots, sweet potato, mushrooms and cauliflower, and cook gently for 3 minutes more. Sprinkle the flour on, stir it in well, and cook for a further 3 minutes.
3 Add the sultanas, tomatoes, stock and wine and season generously. Stir gently but thoroughly. Bring the dish to the boil, cover and simmer gently, stirring occasionally, for 25 minutes until the vegetables are just cooked.
4 Meanwhile, blend the cornflour with a tablespoon of water and stir it into the yoghurt. Heat the mixture in a saucepan until almost boiling, then simmer for 10 minutes.
5 When the vegetables are only just cooked, add the frozen peas and cook for a further 5 minutes. Finally, stir in the stabilised yoghurt and garam masala and heat through.
6 Serve the curry garnished with sprigs of fresh coriander leaves.

YORKSHIRE PUDDING

THE RIGHT MIX

Is there any way I can be sure that my Yorkshire pudding will rise to the occasion every time?

Yes: by following the recipe on the right, your puddings will rise beautifully without fail, every time. The traditional Yorkshire pudding was made with half milk and half water, which produces a lighter, crisper batter than the soft batter you get by using whole milk only. Fat also affects the flavour of a Yorkshire pudding, and batter that is made with skimmed milk, though crisp, does not taste as nice. The following mixture is the one that will still produce the best pudding.

Foolproof Yorkshire pudding

SERVES: 4 - 6
PREPARATION TIME: 20 minutes, plus 30 minutes resting time
COOKING TIME: 40 - 55 minutes

---

100 g (3 ½ oz) plain flour
A pinch of salt
2 eggs, size 3, beaten
150 ml (5 fl oz) whole milk and 150 ml (5 fl oz) water, mixed
25 g (1 oz) lard or dripping, or 2 tablespoons vegetable oil

---

1 Mix the flour and salt in a bowl, make a well in the centre and add the eggs. Pour in half the milk and water mixture and gradually work in the flour with a wooden spoon. Then beat the batter with a balloon whisk, electric beater or wooden spoon until smooth. Add the rest of the liquid and beat the batter again until it is well mixed and the surface is covered with tiny bubbles, then leave it to rest for at least 30 minutes. While it is resting, preheat the oven to 220°C (425°F, gas mark 7).

2 Put your chosen fat in a roasting tin or ovenproof dish and heat it in the hot oven for 5 - 10 minutes, until the fat begins to show a haze.

3 Whisk the rested batter briefly. Remove the tin or dish from the oven and immediately pour in the batter. Cook for 35 - 45 minutes until well risen, golden brown and crisp. Serve the pudding cut in squares or slices.

VARIATION

To make individual puddings, use Yorkshire pudding tins, deep patty tins, or muffin tins. Make the batter as in the recipe, heat some fat in each tin until it begins to haze and pour in the batter. Cook for 15 - 20 minutes until the puddings have puffed up and are golden brown and crisp on the top. Serve them immediately, before they cool down and collapse.

Crisp, light, but rich in flavour, enticingly brown and perfectly risen, this Yorkshire Pudding never fails to satisfy.

HEAT AND BEAT

Why does my Yorkshire pudding go all soggy in the middle?

There are several possible causes. The first consideration is that Yorkshire pudding needs a lot of heat. An oven that is not hot enough will spoil a pudding, as will too little cooking. In addition, the batter must be beaten until it is well mixed and the entire surface is covered with tiny bubbles. The batter can be made up to an hour in advance, covered and left in a cool place to stand, but you must whisk it again before cooking it.

Hot fat or oil in the baking tin is one of the elements which makes the batter rise dramatically as it cooks, resulting in a crisp, light pudding. Before cooking, heat the fat in a hot oven for 5–10 minutes until it begins to haze. When you are ready to cook the batter, it should be poured quickly into the hot fat and immediately put in the oven to cook on the highest shelf.

If you cook a pudding in too small a dish, it makes the pudding mixture more dense so that it cannot rise properly; a small roasting tin is an ideal size. When all of the conditions are right, the batter rises and becomes crisp and browns evenly as it cooks, but Yorkshire pudding quickly loses its crispness after it has been taken out of the oven and it is for this reason that it should be served immediately.

Yorkshire pudding was once cooked directly underneath the beef roasting on the oven shelf or on a rotisserie, so that it 'caught' and soaked up some of the meat juices as it cooked. This pudding was full of flavour when cooked, and used to be served, with some gravy, as a first course before the roast, to take the edge off hungry appetites where there was not much meat to go round. But it was heavier than one cooked separately in its own fat, which is the way it is most often cooked today.

The modern Yorkshire pudding is baked at a high temperature. If your oven cooks slightly cooler than the setting indicates, turn it all the way up; what you are aiming for is 220°C (425°F, gas mark 7). Do this after the beef has been moved away to be rested.

NO HOT AIR

Is it possible to cook Yorkshire pudding in the microwave oven?

No, because a Yorkshire pudding needs hot air to make it rise and the air inside a microwave does not get hot. For the same reason it is not possible either to brown and crisp the skin of a joint or poultry in a microwave or to cook puff pastry.

VERSATILE BATTER

Can Yorkshire pudding batter be used to make any other dishes?

Yes, several. The best-known dish is toad-in-the-hole, made with partly cooked sausages put in a roasting tin. Yorkshire pudding batter is poured over them and they are then baked in a hot oven. Ingredients such as prawns, chopped ham or bacon may be substituted to make individual savoury batter puddings. For extra flavouring, add some chopped herbs such as parsley, sage or thyme, or ground spices such as chilli and garlic.

Yorkshire pudding batter can also be sweetened and used for making warm desserts. Clafoutis, for example, is a homely traditional French dish made with black or red cherries. The cherries and sweetened batter are baked until the batter is soft and golden brown, then sprinkled with sugar and served warm with cream. Other fresh fruits such as sliced apples, apricots, peaches, pears or plums, or dried fruits such as raisins and sultanas, can be baked in batter to make excellent puddings. Ground spices such as cinnamon or mixed spice added to the batter before baking give extra flavour.

The following recipe shows how simple it is to combine sweetened Yorkshire pudding batter, apples and cinnamon into a delightful and appealing warm dessert.

Apple and cinnamon batter pudding

SERVES: 4–6
PREPARATION TIME: 30 minutes
COOKING TIME: 35–50 minutes

100 g (3 ½ oz) plain flour
1 teaspoon ground cinnamon
A pinch of salt
2 eggs, size 3, beaten
300 ml (10 fl oz) whole milk or milk and water mixed
50 g (1 ¾ oz) caster sugar
2 tablespoons sunflower or other vegetable oil
350 g (12 oz) cooking apples (peeled and cored weight), sliced

1 Preheat the oven to 220°C (425°F, gas mark 7).
2 To make the batter, mix the flour, cinnamon and salt in a large bowl. Make a well in the centre and add the eggs and half the milk (or milk and water mixture).
3 Gradually work in the flour, using a wooden spoon. Beat the mixture with a whisk or wooden spoon until it is smooth, then add the remaining liquid. Add the sugar and beat the mixture until well mixed.
4 Put the oil in a roasting tin and heat in the oven for 5 - 10 minutes, until it shows a haze.
5 Remove from the oven, quickly arrange the apple slices in the oil at the bottom of the dish and pour the batter over the top. Return to the oven and cook for 30 - 40 minutes until well risen, golden brown and crisp. Cut the pudding into squares or slices and serve it with cream, crème fraîche or custard flavoured with a little rum or brandy.

VARIATIONS

This pudding can also be made into individual puddings, as in the recipe for Yorkshire pudding. You can also replace the apple with other fruits, such as bananas, mangoes, pears or rhubarb, and flavour the batter with spices other than cinnamon. For instance, try crushed cardamom or coriander seeds with mango; ginger, fresh, candied or dried, with pears; and vanilla and a whole clove with the rhubarb. Finally, add a tablespoon of Grand Marnier to the cream.

ZABAGLIONE

NO WAITING

Can zabaglione be made ahead of time and kept for a while?

No. The sweet confection called zabaglione should be made at the last minute. If it is left to stand for more than 5–10 minutes, it will start to separate. It will also separate if it is cooked for too long, or if the mixture gets too hot while it is being whisked. Once made, the zabaglione should immediately be poured into stemmed glasses or dessert dishes, and served while it is still warm and frothy.

Zabaglione

SERVES: **4**
PREPARATION TIME: **5 minutes**
COOKING TIME: **10 - 15 minutes**

4 egg yolks, size 3
60 g (2¼ oz) caster sugar
75 ml (2½ fl oz) Marsala wine
To garnish: toasted flaked almonds

1 Put the egg yolks into a mixing bowl, add the sugar and whisk them together quite briskly for a minute. Gradually mix in the Marsala wine, whisking a little more gently.
2 Put the bowl on top of a pan of gently simmering water. Whisk the mixture briskly for 10 - 15 minutes until it becomes thick and creamy and stands in soft peaks.
3 Immediately pour it into serving glasses, or dishes, and decorate with the flaked almonds. Serve the warm zabaglione immediately, with or without sponge fingers or delicate biscuits on the dish underneath it.

A warm frothy mixture of Marsala wine, egg yolks and sugar makes a last-minute dessert. Top zabaglione with flaked almonds and serve it with almond biscuits.

SWEET FROTHY SABAYON

What is sabayon? Is it just another name for zabaglione?

Yes, it is the French corruption of the word zabaglione. Both are made by whisking egg yolks and sugar with alcohol (usually white wine in the case of sabayon, but sometimes sherry or Madeira), but they are served in different ways. Whereas zabaglione is served as a warm dessert, sabayon is usually cooled as soon as it is frothy by plunging the pan into cold water while continuing to whisk it and then used as a dessert sauce. Whipped cream or flavourings such as vanilla and citrus peel are sometimes added.

ZEST

ZESTY FLAVOUR

What is zest and how do I use it?

Zest is the outermost part of the rind of oranges, lemons, limes and other citrus fruit. This part of the rind is full of tiny capsules containing a very highly flavoured volatile oil, and it is this oil that gives an intense flavour to many savoury dishes, sauces, cakes and desserts such as the elaborate Lemon Curd Ice Cream Gâteau shown on the right. For the purest flavour, the zest must be removed from the fruit without even the smallest trace of the bitter white pith underneath it. The easiest way to do this is to use a zester or a stainless-steel potato peeler, or you can rub it carefully against the finest cutter on a grater.

Waxed fruit should be washed first, very gently with a soft brush and in warm, not hot, water. Scrubbing the fruit hard with a stiff brush can damage the skin which will release the oil, and it will be washed away with the water.

Lemon curd ice cream gâteau

SERVES: 8 - 10
PREPARATION TIME: 30 minutes, plus several hours freezing
COOKING TIME: 10 minutes

4 large lemons, washed
175 g (6 oz) icing sugar, sieved
300 ml (10 fl oz) thick soured cream
600 ml (1 pint) thick double cream
225 g (8 oz) lemon curd
40 g (1 1/2 oz) caster sugar
A few drops of vanilla extract or
  vanilla essence

1 Line a 1.7 litre (3 pint) loaf tin with baking paper. Finely grate the zest from three of the lemons and put it into a mixing bowl with the icing sugar. Squeeze the juice from one of the grated lemons, strain it into the bowl and stir until the icing sugar is completely dissolved.
2 Pour the soured cream and 425 ml (15 fl oz) of the double cream into the sugar and lemon mixture. Whisk until it forms soft peaks.
3 Spoon a third of the lemon curd into the lined loaf tin, dropping

To produce fine, even strands of zest, hold the fruit firmly with one hand and pull the zester down the side.

This spectacular frozen gâteau is made with a rich mixture of sweet and soured creams marbled with lemon curd, and decorated with shreds of lemon zest.

heaped teaspoons at random, leaving space around each one. Gently pour a third of the flavoured cream over the lemon curd. Spoon on another third of the lemon curd at random, then pour another third of the cream over that. Repeat the layering with the remaining curd and cream.
4 Gently push a fork through the dessert and pull it from side to side along the whole length of the loaf tin to create a marbled pattern with the lemon curd. Cover the tin with foil and store it in the freezer for several hours, preferably overnight. It can be stored in the freezer for up to a month at this stage.
5 About 2 - 3 hours before serving, thinly pare the zest from the last lemon with a stainless-steel potato peeler and cut it into fine shreds. Put the shreds into a small saucepan with 25 g (1 oz) of the caster sugar. Pour in 150 ml (5 fl oz) of water and stir over a moderate heat until the sugar dissolves. Bring the syrup to the boil, then reduce the heat and

simmer gently for about 5 minutes until the shreds are tender. Take off the heat and leave to cool.
6 Put the remaining double cream and caster sugar in a mixing bowl, add the vanilla and whisk until the mixture will hold soft peaks. Spoon the cream into a piping bag fitted with a large star nozzle.
7 Remove the ice cream from the freezer and turn it out of the tin onto a serving plate. Gently peel off the baking paper. Decorate the top with the cream mixture, piping it in shells or rosettes, in spaced diagonal lines. Any remaining cream can be used to decorate the bottom edge. Return the decorated gâteau to the freezer until you are ready to serve it, but do not store it for longer than a day or two at this stage.
8 Thirty minutes before you want to serve the ice cream, take it out of the freezer and leave it to soften at room temperature. Drain the lemon shreds and arrange them on top. Cut the gâteau into slices to serve.

GLOSSARY

ACIDULATE To add lemon juice or vinegar to cooking or soaking water to prevent certain vegetables and fruit from discolouring.

AMUSE BOUCHE/GUEULE French term meaning 'mouth amuser', this is a miniature appetiser designed to titillate the palate before dinner.

ANTIPASTO The Italian hors d'oeuvres; it can be a single item but is usually a plate of six to eight different foods.

BAKE BLIND To bake an empty pastry case with the base weighted down with greaseproof paper and dried beans or rice to prevent the case rising during cooking.

BALLOTINE A leg of chicken, or a whole small bird, boned and stuffed before cooking.

BASTE To spoon liquid or melted fat over food during cooking to prevent it drying out and add extra flavour.

BEIGNETS Fritters; beignets soufflés are made from choux pastry and deep-fried.

BLANQUETTE A white stew, usually of veal or chicken, made without frying the meat first and thickened with an egg yolk and cream liaison.

BLINI A thin pancake made with buckwheat flour, using yeast as a raising agent.

BRINE A strong solution of salt and water that is used for pickling or preserving.

CEVICHE Fish or shellfish marinated in lime juice until the fish is 'cooked' by the action of the acid, and served with a sharp dressing.

CHANTILLY CREAM Double cream whipped until it holds its shape, with icing sugar and vanilla essence folded in to taste. It is often piped over puddings and cakes.

CHARLOTTE A pudding made in a mould lined with slices of buttered bread, filled with fruit and cooked.

CHASSEUR A dish or a sauce that is made with white wine, mushrooms, shallots, tomatoes and tarragon.

CHINE To remove the backbone from a rib roast or rack of meat before cooking, to make carving easier.

COCOTTE/RAMEKIN A small fireproof dish in which individual portions of food are both cooked and served.

CONFIT A dish of duck or goose cooked in its fat, packed into jars and covered with more fat to preserve it.

CONSOMME A clarified soup, usually made with meat.

COULIS A sauce made from vegetable or fruit purée.

CREOLE French-influenced tropical cuisine, also found in Louisiana in the United States of America, flavoured with chilli, peppers and tomatoes.

DEGLAZE/DEGLACER To dissolve the brown sediment left on the bottom of a pan after roasting or frying by adding liquid and stirring.

DEVILLED Food that has been seasoned with a spicy sauce, usually containing pepper, chilli and mustard.

DISGORGE To extract bitter juices from vegetables by salting, soaking or washing.

DRAWING (*of poultry*) To pull out the entrails, leaving a clean carcass.

DROPPING CONSISTENCY Term used to describe the correct consistency of a cake mixture before baking: it should drop off the spoon with gentle persuasion.

EGG WASH Beaten egg, sometimes mixed with a little water, brushed over pastry and bread before cooking, to give a shiny golden finish.

EMULSION A smooth, stable mixture of oil or melted fat and egg yolks, plus vinegar or citrus juice, such as hollandaise or mayonnaise.

FLORENTINE A savoury dish that contains spinach and Mornay sauce, usually with eggs or fish.

FLUMMERY A pudding made from eggs and milk, rather like blancmange, flavoured with ground almonds.

FOLD IN To incorporate a light airy mixture, such as whisked egg whites, into a heavier one by using a gentle lifting motion.

FRANGIPANE A filling for pastry tartlets or flans made with butter, eggs and ground almonds and flavoured with almond essence, kirsch or orange flower water.

FRAPPE Iced, or set in a bed of crushed ice.

FRITTATA A substantial flat omelette which includes a variety of vegetables and cheese, eaten hot or cold.

GALANTINE A type of terrine, usually made with poultry, which is cooked and set in its own jelly, served cold.

GAMBAS The French term for several large prawns, also known as crevettes.

GANACHE Chocolate and double cream mixed together over heat to form a very rich filling used in truffles, or for coating or filling cakes.

JULIENNE Vegetables, or citrus rind, that have been cut into very fine strips.

KNOCK DOWN/KNOCK BACK To punch or knead risen dough to push out air that may have formed large, unevenly shaped holes.

LIAISON The ingredients for thickening and enriching a sauce, soup or stew, such as egg yolk, cream or blood.

MACEDOINE Small, diced mixed vegetables, usually including root vegetables.

MACERATE To soak food, usually fruit, in a syrup or liquid such as alcohol, to allow the flavours to mix.

MIREPOIX A bed of roughly diced vegetables, usually carrot, celery and onion, used in stocks and braising.

MOUSSELINE A raw meat or fish purée mixed with double cream, used as a stuffing or to make quenelles or cooked in small moulds and served warm with a sauce.

REDUCE/REDUCTION To thicken and concentrate the flavour of gravy, sauces, soups and stocks by boiling.

RICE PAPER A lightweight, edible paper made from the pith of a tropical tree, used as a base for macaroons and other sweetmeats.

RUB IN To use the fingertips to combine fat with flour and other dry ingredients until the mixture looks like fine breadcrumbs.

SALMIS Game birds or duck that are first lightly roasted or browned in fat, then jointed and stewed in a wine sauce.

SCALD To heat milk until on the point of boiling.

SCORE To cut through the skin of joints, particularly pork, before cooking to make carving easier.

SEAR/SEAL To brown meat rapidly all over in fat, to give it flavour and colour.

SLAKE To dissolve thickening agents, such as cornflour, in a little cold liquid before they are added to the hot liquid which is to be thickened.

SOUSE To marinate and cook strips of oily fish in a pickling mixture containing vinegar, spices and flavourings.

SPATCHCOCK A squab or small chicken split open by removing the backbone, then cleaned, flattened and grilled.

STEEP To soak a food for several hours, so it absorbs flavour from the solution (as in marinating), releases the flavours present in food, or reduces the salt content.

SWEAT To gently stew food, usually vegetables, in butter, oil or a little stock until very soft but not coloured.

WELL A hollow or dip made in a pile of flour into which other ingredients are placed prior to mixing.

A

ℐNDEX

Bold numbers indicate headlist entries
and *bold italic text* indicates recipe entries.